PROKIDS, INC.
The Message and The Movement
A Guide for Parents and Professionals

Dr. David L. Roberts Ph.D.

Copyright © 2011 Dr. David L. Roberts Ph.D.
All rights reserved.

ISBN: 0615428908
ISBN-13: 9780615428901
Library of Congress Control Number: 2010942946

Introduction to this Five Volume Edition

At the Mercy of Externals: Righting Wrongs and Protecting Kids, was first published in 2003. This book was revised and republished in 2007 as a second edition, and in conjunction with my second book, Psyche-Soulology: An Inspirational Approach to Appreciating and Understanding Troubled Kids. Now, and under the title of ProKids, Inc., The Message and the Movement: A Guide for Parents and Professionals, both books are being combined into one printed work. In addition to the books I have also included my antiviolence program under the title of "K.I.T. Cadets: Kids In Touch Against Violence". I have also included both my thesis and dissertation research relative to my Roberts Grief and Loss Analysis Scale (RGLAS) to encourage others to help me continue the research relative to this instrument as well. The purpose for this compilation is to offer all five works to students, parents and professionals under one title for the sake of both completeness and continuity.

ProKids, Inc., The Message and The Movement is also offered in conjunction with an interview series under the same name, with David L. Roberts, Ph.D. being interviewed relative to his own professional and personal perspectives regarding the subject matter of all three texts. During these comprehensive interviews Dr. Roberts is able to go into greater detail about his philosophies and experiences associated with high risk kids. The series of six interviews offers even more insight into the Spiritual beliefs which serve as the foundation of every aspect of Dr. Roberts' life and work relative to the populations he serves compassionately and professionally. The recorded interviews help to make the messages and approaches even more personal than simply reading printed text. During the interviews Dr. Roberts expresses his views and concerns in such a way as to give the readers an opportunity to literally hear Dr. Roberts' voice as they read and study his written texts.

Dr. David L. Roberts Ph.D.

Dr. Roberts has a great deal of both personal and professional experience to support every aspect of his work with high risk kids and families. He grew up in the Mobile, Alabama area from 1954 through the turmoil of the Vietnam Era, the Civil Rights Movement, and all the related civil unrest, not to mention the so-called Cold War and the constant threat of nuclear annihilation. His educational background includes:

- a Bachelor of Arts degree in Literature, with a minor in music from the University of South Alabama, Mobile, Alabama - 1976;
- two Master of Science degrees - one in Administration – 1986; and one in General Psychology – 1989; both from Georgia College and State University in Milledgeville, Georgia;
- and a Doctor of Philosophy degree in Clinical Psychology from the California School of Professional Psychology, Los Angeles, California Campus (now a division of Alliant International University) – 1993.

All of his degrees and varied experiences acquired in different parts of the so-called "deep south", and in California, give Dr. Roberts a very unique perspective on people and cultures. Dr. Roberts interacted with people from all over the globe given the extensive international mix in the state of California where he lived for nearly 16 years. During that time Dr. Roberts even learned to speak enough Spanish to be able to work and teach in that language. His willingness to learn Spanish endeared him to the Hispanic people he served, especially when he moved from Los Angeles to Riverside County. The era during which he grew up while living in Alabama continues to have a very significant impact on how he views people of all races, cultures, and socioeconomic standing.

The single most important factor is Dr. Roberts' ability and awareness of the need to understand every aspect of the populations he serves before he can ever begin to offer interventions and solutions relative to people's lives and circumstances. More frequently than at any other time people are preparing for jobs within the job category commonly referred to as the "helping professions". However, many of these people, who truly in most cases have the best of intentions, are clueless when providing services especially to traditionally underserved populations throughout this country and even beyond the borders of the United States of America. Good intentions <u>*do not*</u> equate with competence. More and more people with the best of intentions are actually doing the most harm, and then blaming those they serve for being ungrateful or "unresponsive to treatment".

Dr. Roberts takes pride in his ability and willingness to learn before he leaps into any previously uncharted situation. When specific religious views and dogma are introduced into the mix things get even worse. However, when professionals decide to understand and utilize simple non-religious Spiritual approaches, doors open in every aspect of treatment, even if the word "God", or any other reference to a higher power are never uttered. The most effective intervention programs are those which seek to serve people of all faiths and cultures, without any agendas to change their minds relative to religious views which no one can prove or disprove anyway. Dr. Roberts adheres to the idea that the Energy that is us is God within us – pure and simple. God is all there is and all there is *is* God. This suggests that people do not have to change who they are; they simply need to change their focus and the way they use their Energy. People readily agree with this approach given the fact it is the same Energy whether we use it rightly or wrongly. Dr. Roberts views this as either the right use, or the misuse of God. This approach appeals to virtually every kid Dr. Roberts has ever served, given the fact it focuses on choices rather than on sin and shame, and good versus evil philosophies.

The single most unifying global factor is that human nature and emotions are basically and even genetically consistent regardless of culture. This means that while our "nature" component is the same, the environmental/contextual factors are quite different from culture to culture. Usually when people are having problems relative to behavior and emotions it is because they are experiencing complicating factors which in many cases are actually beyond their abilities to control or even influence. If professionals do not understand and identify these complicating factors specific to every culture and circumstance, no intervention in the world will be effective relative to effecting change.

These kinds of awarenesses are what make Dr. Roberts unique from many other psychologists and master's level therapists and caseworkers – not to mention other professionals outside the so-called helping professions. People who have not worked out their own issues and complicating factors CANNOT be good therapists and should never have contact with people in need of psychological interventions and assistance. Furthermore, people who are not parents CANNOT work as effectively with children as people who fully understand their role of parenting through firsthand experiences. If we are not effective with our own children, we CANNOT be effective with other families and their children. There are many things in life that we cannot understand without experiencing them directly, and one of those (out of many categories) is parenting. If you are not a parent then do not even try to address parenting issues and problems without extensive education and supervised training. Other examples of issues to stay away from professionally include: rape/incest; sex and sexuality issues; trauma, such as that experienced in wartime; third world countries where groups of people are targeted solely based on gender, ethnicity, or sexual orientation; and people living in poverty. These are just a few of the many examples available.

The theories and content of both of Dr. Roberts' books, combined within this five volume edition, are invaluable relative to understanding all of these issues and topics. His models, topics, theories, lists, research, and approaches will prove to be practical and useful to anyone who either has children and/or works with kids and families. It is imperative for all professionals – especially those who are not parents themselves and are working with children in any capacity - to fully recognize and understand their limitations with this population. At the very least it is imperative to follow all of the Ethical Principles and Standards put forth by the American Psychological Association, and other professional oversight groups.

One of the biggest and most important ethical issues is that of competence. The best gauge of competence is that of whether or not people keep coming back to you for further assistance and follow up visits. Or, whether or not other professionals are more successful with their kids and parents as clients than you appear to be when comparisons are made. If these observations are made then refer people to others who *are* more competent in specific areas rather than run the risk of damaging those who are frequently the most vulnerable. The information shared within this current five volume edition will make the difference between effectiveness and disaster for all of those we serve either as parents or as professionals within any occupation which puts people in direct contact with and supervision over kids and their families. Failure to grasp and embrace this perspective of competence will only result in people being more damaged than they already are in many cases. We should all adhere to the oath "to at least do no harm".

As you read through these texts please keep in mind that all of our lives are lived out and through various contexts, some of which are tangible, and others which are more philosophical in nature. The contexts I have identified in At the Mercy of Externals are: home/family, community, school, politics, religion, and society. Within any and all of these contests lies the opportunity for both abuse and victimization. I strongly urge every reader to take a very active role in understanding the issues and conflicts at this moment in our lives and circumstances. I watch a lot of news commentary in order to stay as fully informed as possible relative to all of the complicating factors we face everyday of our lives. If we do not make and take the time to be fully informed and aware of external factors which threaten our very existence, then how can we possibly be of service to people in need. More and more people are willing to compromise both their morals and values by focusing more on not getting caught versus doing what is right. I see this reality at all levels of our culture and society, both nationally and internationally. This kind of thinking is clearly evident in the lives of both kids and adults alike.

It is my sincere hope that through the words contained within these pages we can all learn to be better and stronger adults for children everywhere. Our failure to achieve this goal will lead to a very bleak outlook for current and future generations. We must see this kind of mission as an urgent matter relative to improving every system within which kids learn and grow in order to insure their future successes. It is imperative that we provide a better world for our children and grandchildren than we are currently seeing play out around the globe. Divisions must be replaced with acceptance and unity. Discord must be replaced with peace and harmony. Injustice must be replaced with love and compassion. Arrogance must be replaced with humility and service to others. And, greed must be replaced with giving and sharing. I know that within the pages of these texts each reader will find a sense of renewal and recommitment to both Divine Right

Dr. David L. Roberts Ph.D.

Action and Divine Right Thought. Allow yourself as parents and/or professionals to be inspired both by the printed text and by the interviews. Anyone working with children clearly needs to see their respective job as a sense of calling, and in some cases, even a ministry of outreach to society's underdogs. Please put all of these ideas, philosophies, research, and theories into action within your own communities and workplaces. Dr. Roberts' challenge to each and every reader is for all adults to make this world a better place for kids who will be our adults of tomorrow.

www.ProKidsInc.org

www.DavidLRobertsPhD.org

AT THE MERCY OF EXTERNALS

❖ ❖ ❖

Righting Wrongs and Protecting Kids

✫

2nd Edition

DAVID L. ROBERTS, Ph.D.

Copyright 2011
All Rights Reserved

No part of this book may be reproduced, stored in a retrieval system, or transmitted by any means - electronic, mechanical, photocopying, recording, or otherwise - without written permission from the author.

Dedication

THIS BOOK IS DEDICATED TO
GRANNY, MELISSA, ADAN, SUSAN,
and to all of the kids I serve or have served,
especially remembering those who have died.

Table of contents

Foreword		5
Chapter I	Foundations of Beliefs	9
Chapter II	Roberts FLAGS Model	25
Chapter III	Adult Roles and Responsibilities	47
Chapter IV	Insult and Injury	61
Chapter V	Contexts of Abuse and Victimization	75
Chapter VI	Results and Losses Associated With Abuse and Victimization	105
Chapter VII	Kids	121
Chapter VIII	Balancing the Scales	137
Chapter IX	In Defense of the Underdogs: Those truly at the Mercy Of Externals	159
Chapter X	Pairing and Parenting: The Basics	179
Chapter XI	Breaking the Cycles	197
Chapter XII	Myth and the Need for Critical Thinking	211
Appendices		229

Foreword

The ideas contained within this book have been developing, at least experientially, since the day I was born. Now it is finally time to sit down and begin putting them on paper as a way of sharing with others what I have learned along the way. My original questions as to how to proceed with this project stemmed from both the dilemma of how to make the presentation, and from my concerns about being honest and open relative to my own personal life and history. Finally I recognized these as two separate yet connected perspectives. The sections dealing with my personal history are very different from the intended theme of this book and will be designated as "The Past that Lived in My Present", separating this information from information related specifically to the purpose of the material presented. I have decided to "listen to [and follow] the teachings my blood whispers to me" as indicated by Hermann Hesse in his prologue to <u>Demian</u>, a powerful book first introduced to me in college, at the age of 17. At that time I realized life is indeed a journey - or a process as I now think of it. So, it is my desire to share with you, the reader, some of the insights I have gained along my own personal path. I believe this book will touch the lives of those who are intended to read it. Therefore, I am going to trust this process as well.

I am very proud to have reached a point where a work in progress has culminated in the writing of <u>At the Mercy of Externals: Righting Wrongs and Protecting Kids</u> – now a 2nd Edition. Most of the readers will be able to benefit from their own personal journey of assessment and discovery/recovery relative to histories of abuse and victimization. Each of you will then have an opportunity to pass this book and it concepts on to others as a way of sharing with them the benefits you have gained from the experience of reading and applying the concepts found herein to your own life and family.

For those readers who have an interest in teaching and are searching for materials to use for various self-help/therapy groups, the subject matter of this book offers countless opportunities to customize and present the concepts under several different headings. The beauty of my Roberts FLAGS Model and its related concepts is that it adapts well to any number of different group settings in need of educational materials. As you read the following pages you will be able to see how the entire process adapts very well to groups regardless of culture and ethnicity, educational level, or background. This is true because the very nature of the model allows individuals to apply the lists and diagrams to their own unique needs and circumstances, using the book itself as a textbook and training guide for each group member and leader.

For instance, if someone is leading a group for those dealing with chemical dependency issues, the title "A.D.U.L.T. Education: Acceptance, Determination, Understanding, Love, and Trust" serves as a very strong description of the focus of the group. A leader of such a group simply needs to apply the RFLAGS Model and related concepts to the goals of any program transforming it into a psychoeducational class that can be spread out over a four to six week period.

Another example would be that of using the RFLAGS Model to address specific issues and objectives within educational settings to address teacher and administrative effectiveness in the classroom and on the school campus. An appropriate program title would be "U.S.E.R. Friendly: Understanding Student Emotional Reactivity". The RFLAGS Model would be a great format to use in increasing awareness of why kids in school settings are not progressing and advancing in spite of maximum efforts by school personnel. A good example of this is related to the need for educators to understand that quite often the lack of success on the part of students goes beyond the context of school and is impacted by factors within other contexts especially within the home/family context described in this book. One of the most valuable aspects of <u>At the Mercy of Externals: Righting wrongs and Protecting Kids, 2nd Edition</u>, is that the model and related theories offer a clear explanation of the external factors often impeding a student's ability, and even their willingness and desire to learn. The chapters addressing other points of consideration within the scope of this text lend themselves well to open discussion and critical thinking in applying the concepts to any particular setting.

Other examples would include a group for parenting called "H.O.M.E. Improvements: Honoring, Opening, Mending, and Empowering". A class addressing domestic violence and victimization could use the title "B.E.A.T.E.N. Down: Battered, Emotionally Abused, Threatened, Endangered, and Neglected". For at risk youth a great program name would be "K.I.D.S. With Hope: Kindness, Individuality, Determination, and Success". Finally a program title for those being trained to work with kids in such roles as volunteers, daycare workers, counselors or mentors would be "R.O.L.E. Models: Respect, Optimism, Love, and Encouragement". I am sure you will be able to come up with other program titles to meet the needs of any psychoeducational group, seminar, or workshop that you have the responsibility for and opportunity to lead.

When using this book and the RFLAGS Model and related concepts, encourage group members to participate fully in the discussions. This process would include identifying and applying various topics specific to the goals of your group. As a group leader you can be creative in your presentation of the materials and can trust the process if you are well prepared and fully understand the concepts found within these pages. If you begin the process with your own efforts to conduct an open and honest evaluation of yourself and your history it will be easy to encourage others to do the same. Always keep in mind that nothing about the model and related materials create any of the negative emotions associated with histories of abuse and victimization. These emotional scars are simply brought into conscious awareness where they can be faced and dealt with, sometimes through professional help and guidance if the realities seem to be too overwhelming and frightening. Remember that if we are not careful the past will live in our present as it did in mine (much less so now). It is only by addressing this reality and the realities creating the underlying negative emotions that we can move forward and right the wrongs and protect the kids in our care regardless of the role we play in their lives. After all, every adult is at least indirectly responsible for the world as it exists today relative to the kids who will be the adults of tomorrow. I truly hope <u>At the Mercy of Externals: Righting Wrongs and Protecting Kids, 2nd Edition</u>, will serve as a guide for adults and adolescents everywhere, and in all walks of life, to begin the process of both healing wounds and preventing all abuse and victimization of kids in the future. My greatest dream is that this book will serve as such a starting point.

Chapter I

Foundations of Beliefs

My desire to become a psychologist stemmed from my fascination with human nature and what makes people "tick" so to speak. Part of that desire included a need to understand myself, as well as the people who played significant roles in my life. Of particular interest were the members of my immediate family and my relationships with them. Because of my belief that the complicating factors from my childhood also complicated my adult years, I became determined to leave the past where it belonged and create more productive patterns of thinking and behaving to help me fulfill the roles I would assume as I matured. By using a metaphorical microscope to carefully examine my 'self' and various factors from my past, I have discovered some amazing ways of understanding what makes people tick which have nothing to do with blaming or scapegoating. The alternative is to understand people for whom they are rather than for whom we might like them to be. This approach allows us to move forward without all of the hatred and resentment resulting from harmful experiences during childhood.

Another significant discovery was the understanding I gained of the importance of effectively fulfilling our adult roles and responsibilities as they pertain to children of all ages. My work as a psychologist has made me painfully aware of the damage done to kids when these roles are neglected and not taken seriously. In today's world of being so busy and self-absorbed it is easy to forget that the kids in our lives still deserve our complete commitment to be the best we can be for them and for ourselves. One of the most rewarding outcomes from my interaction with kids is watching them learn and grow — even in my roles as father and grandfather. As you read this book you will learn how to facilitate the same process for kids more effectively and appropriately than ever before. In other words you will be able to optimize your effectiveness to match your intentions and hope of making a difference relative to the roles you choose. You will also have the opportunity in some cases to be that one adult who makes a positive difference in the lives of kids under your care. If you successfully apply these approaches to your role as a parent then you won't need to place so much hope on interventions from "outsiders". This level of effectiveness will occur only after each of us completes a thorough and honest process of self-assessment and evaluation, seeking professional guidance when the task appears to be too daunting and painful to complete alone.

    I feel as though I have been given this process as an inspired task, one that I accept wholeheartedly, by sharing with the world the things I have learned over the last several years and especially intensifying about 1986. It was at that time that I began to pursue what ultimately became my career as a licensed clinical psychologist. While this book is not *about* me, it comes from *within* me relative to almost unbelievable life-altering experiences I have had both on a personal and a professional level. Within the pages of this text I will share only a few very personal accounts associated with my journey through childhood and early adulthood as they relate to an understanding of how I know what I know. As I look back to 1986 and the years between then and now, I am amazed at how carefully and clearly my ideas have evolved. I firmly believe the process of writing this book originates from a Source much greater than myself alone, and actually is a gift from that Source through me to the world.

    My younger brother recently asked me, as we discussed some sensitive historical family matters, why I get so emotional about such things. At that moment I didn't know how to respond and I simply indicated that my emotions are probably associated with my perception that I have been through a lot. In the months since that conversation I have come to realize how my training, education, and profession have made me intensely aware of and more sensitive to incredible hardship in the lives of people around the world. These experiences made it necessary early on that I participate earnestly in my own personal therapy as a continuation and amplification of an ongoing process of honest and open self-evaluation. I know this is one of the main reasons, as an important first step, for my successes and reputation as a licensed clinical psychologist. My decision to start my own therapy resulted directly from my desire to work continuously toward becoming the best person I can become; always trying to be the best I can be at any given moment and yet still striving for more knowledge and wisdom as my process continues.

In spite of barriers often associated with race and culture, I have been able to go into geographical areas and interact with people of amazing diversity, and be accepted. For me this has been and is a very humbling experience making me extremely conscious of the never outdated concept of "man's inhumanity to man". I see more and more how this lack of consideration and regard appears to be based in both arrogance and ignorance which often results in abuse/victimization of others within the contexts of home/family, school, community, society, politics, and religion.

While this book will focus primarily on the first three contexts of home/family, school, and community, I will also attempt to address the last three more lofty and philosophical contexts of society, politics, and religion. The effort will be to propose ways my model, and its various components, are rather universally applicable. Within this text I hope to gain the attention of adults within all readily identifiable roles, as well as the attention of people in more global positions of power and influence over others. This list of adult groups will start with parents, relatives, and other individuals from the first three contexts who are directly responsible for children and for others who are in some ways vulnerable.

From there I will attempt to expand the list to include people and groups dominating the contexts of societal, political, and religious influences, and who are always at least ethically responsible for children and others who truly are at the mercy of numerous external factors. This second list will include: individuals, groups, and world leaders who set societal standards; politicians and political factions serving as policy and law makers; and religious leaders at all levels who in many cases unsuccessfully attempt to address spirituality and moral values. We will attempt to discover realities existing within the respective ideologies espoused by leading nations as they try to find a middle ground between the poles of extremism relative to an almost complete breakdown of antiquated traditional conservatism toward destructive and reckless forms of liberalism. This represents a shift from too much control and domination to a growing lack of regard and consideration for self and others. I will propose roles of leading nations to make efforts toward righting the wrongs in countries currently exhibiting overt examples of abuse and victimization resulting in horrific acts of terrorism. Frequently religion, gender-based violence, and race/ethnicity are the bases of both disagreement and justification in developing nations.

I do not intend to come across as someone who has all of the answers, or as one who whines about today's corruption and immorality, longing for a return to the "good ol' days". With my Roberts FLAGS Model I simply intend to propose ways of examining and understanding our current conditions to first recognize the urgent need for change and balancing. It is then possible to begin identifying, developing, and implementing opportunities somewhat systematically and formally, as a process of healing and repairing centuries of abuse and victimization present throughout history and currently within all contexts and around the world. This book, with the model and related materials, will give all adults, especially those serving in professional roles, a means to understand and teach the concepts offered within these pages.

Therefore, the purpose within these pages is to initiate the changing of this world toward the creation of a better world for us and for those generations to come. It is time to correct the errors in the ways adults and leaders view our responsibilities individually and collectively as compared to the relative context or contexts in which we act, or in some cases, act out our hopelessness and helplessness. This approach is better than blindly and foolishly denying the unfulfilled obligations we hold, especially to children. As we correct we also prepare a much more desirable existence for ourselves and for those yet to exist. We must identify both the abusers and those "underdogs" who are the victims, or who see themselves as the victims of abuse. This book is all about honest self-examination by adults and leaders who, by the very nature of these roles, are put in positions of power and influence whereby they either build up or break down.

It is time to teach to every man, woman, and adolescent the responsibility and obligation for ourselves, each other, and especially for the children who are constantly brought into our care, either directly or indirectly. This must be done regardless of whether we ignorantly and arrogantly deny, rather than acknowledge and accept, our unquestionable calling. Each generation prepares the way for the next. To stop the existing destructive cycles we must begin now to understand and correct ourselves on all levels and in all quadrants.

In both theory and reality the concepts of parents and leaders are the same and are, therefore, somewhat interchangeable. So true is this that the very leaders of nations and the world have a significant necessity to nurture all under their care, not to dominate, but to teach in the sense of guiding each "underdog" group to shake off its stigma of victimization and stand up to the abusers. I define "underdogs" as those who are vulnerable to people in any position of power and influence as determined by a number of both biological and environmental factors. Abusers are not leaders, nor effective parents. They are the destroyers of all that is good and pure within the innocence of those truly vulnerable enough to be abused.

This is the true representation of an "underdog" – the very real, rather than accepted and worn, vulnerability associated with Fear, Loneliness, Anger, Guilt, and Shame (FLAGS). An "underdog" is simply any child, adult, group, new idea, or new ideal which must be nurtured into reaching its full potential. Those who are truly vulnerable in life have few, if any choices and are indeed easy targets. Those who are not helpless, and yet claim to be victims, are merely buying into the one-down position resulting from a history of victimization, and yet ironically coupled with a future of new opportunities. Traditional thoughts that bind and limit our motivation to learn and grow are no longer acceptable. Such traditions are often defended from a basis of Fear, Loneliness, Anger, Guilt, and Shame (FLAGS) based in unresolved issues rather than from actual ongoing abuse/victimization. This thinking insists that we keep acting out our emotion-based anxieties and frustrations, rather than deal with and correct a destructive past living within our present. To break such cycles requires nothing less than identifying, understanding, and facing the emotions fueling our frustrations and causing us to not care.

Most of my approaches to psychology, including the development of these concepts, are grounded in the Existential and Humanistic philosophies as applied to psychology from literature by the well known psychologists, Dr. Rollo May and Dr. Carl Rogers. These are the same philosophies beautifully implied within the pages of many of today's books dealing with spiritual approaches to viewing and reviewing life and existence. I was particularly inspired by the recent writings of James Redfield and his <u>Celestine Prophecy</u> collection; and by <u>The Third Millennium</u>, written by Ken Carey. My most recent inspirations come form Mick Quinn and <u>The Uncommon Path</u>; and Ken Wilber's 20+ works regarding Integral Spirituality and Psychology. These writers are true visionaries who, at the turn of the new millennium and beyond, both confirmed and expanded my own beliefs about the latent potential beginning to awaken within the universe and the souls of people.

In addition to a great deal of reading about philosophy, psychology, and spirituality, I have had many wonderful, and often times difficult experiences which have brought me to my present understanding of purpose in my own life. I feel I have an obligation, as we all do, to share with others those insights which have helped advance me through my process of living and growing. The title of this book, <u>At the Mercy of Externals</u>, is extracted from <u>The Book of Runes</u>, by Ralph Blum. It suggests that many of us spend our lives looking outside of ourselves for answers which can only be found within and in relation to ourselves and others. Furthermore, it indicates that those factors which are the most detrimental to our growth and development come from external sources and are often associated with abuse/victimization. Also taken from <u>The Book of Runes</u> is a powerful prayer, one which has advanced me rapidly forward in my process. When spoken with true commitment it opens one's life to all possibilities for learning and growth. The prayer is: "I will to will Thy will." At first read it may seem simple. However, I think it requires a great deal of exploration, and even translation into one's own words. For me the best translation is something to the effect that with all of my being, and from my heart, I desire to desire what You desire; or I want to want what You want, as the only spiritually based philosophy which makes any sense. True Spiritual growth and maturity is indicated by the revision of the prayer to simply "I will Thy Will." "I want what You Want." "I desire what You Desire." If there truly is some overriding universal process, then why not tap into its Source and maximize its progression. I firmly believe that the Energy that is us is God or the Source within us.

The Past that Lived in My Present

Allow me to share with you a little of the educational and technical history of how some of my theories and continuing queries have evolved. None of my life had any sense of identifiable purpose until I began taking control of my life and destiny in my late 20's. My earlier experiences did not have any real conscious intention. I let go and began to follow my intuition, but my intention became directed only as I consciously and earnestly sought spiritual guidance from God as the Source (not the religious concepts of god) and stepped aside as much as I had learned to do. The point is that even though I was not consciously aware of how to proceed, I proceeded and trusted the urges coming from deep within my soul.

With an undergraduate degree in English Literature and a minor in music, and after many years of an unsatisfying career in the field of both retail and wholesale credit, I decided to return to school to work on a Master of Science degree in Administration at Georgia College. Close to the end of this endeavor, I realized I was only getting deeper into the credit field. After deciding I was too close to finishing this degree to quit, I completed the courses and graduated in June 1986.

Toward the end of this program, I decided to follow my heart and pursue a degree in Psychology as I had wanted to do for many years. So, in June 1986 I began taking two prerequisite courses which were required before I could qualify for the Master of Science degree in General Psychology, also at Georgia College. Needing a project for a research design class, I decided to study grief - not in the traditional sense of death and dying; but relative to unresolved losses and bereavement associated with and resulting from dysfunctional backgrounds of abuse and victimization. With this research project I began the development of the Roberts Grief and Loss Analysis Scale (RGLAS), an instrument designed to detect unresolved grief which impairs and complicates current adult functioning. I gained recognition for this initial effort at the University of Georgia PSI CHI Conference in April 1987, when I made my first research presentation. It was a graduate level competition, and I knew I would be disqualified because my initial research was conducted for an undergraduate class. However, I was told by the judges that I would have won "hands down" because my ideas were original and innovative, which are the bases of good research. This was the "go ahead" I needed.

From my initial efforts, I worked with the RGLAS questionnaire as the focus of my master's thesis, at which time I constructed and analyzed the current form of the RGLAS. I completed my MS in Psychology in June 1989, and then took a giant leap of faith. Using all the courage I could find at the age of 35 I quit my job, sold most of everything I owned, and left the southeast to attend the California School of Professional Psychology in Los Angeles (CSPP-LA), now associated with Alliant International University. I started this program in August 1989 only two months after completing my second master's degree. For the next four years I worked and sacrificed to earn my Ph.D. in Clinical Psychology, graduating from CSPP-LA in June 1993. CSPP accepted my master's thesis as Study I, and allowed me to continue my research with the RGLAS by conducting validity and reliability studies to further substantiate the RGLAS as a useful tool in the detection of unresolved grief resulting from dysfunctional family backgrounds. In other words, this research served to indicate whether or not the RGLAS works as a measurement of unresolved grief. Fortunately both my thesis and dissertation research yielded very successful results supporting the usefulness of the RGLAS.

My ideas for this particular research came from my own experience of growing up in a very conflicted, restrictive, and abusive family environment. Both of my parents were raised during the difficult time surrounding "The Great Depression", by very abusive fathers. Both were middle children in the sibling line up, my dad growing up in rural Mississippi, and my mother growing up in a city in Alabama. My parents were not bad people, and none of this is intended to serve some type of need to blame or find fault. I am simply talking about reality and the kinds of complicating factors which made their adult lives difficult both as a married couple and as parents. As we go through my model the terms reality, truth, and honesty will be major components in the self-examination required if this presentation is to be understood as applicable to people in general.

My beliefs are that adults have a responsibility to make sure we are stable emotionally, mentally, psychologically, and spiritually as the only hope for children to have a secure base from which to experience the world. Because my parents never resolved the losses and unresolved issues from their own abusive backgrounds, my younger siblings and I have had many problems trying to deal with life during childhood and adulthood. Each of us as siblings had a different experience with our parents because of the differences in our ages. I am the oldest, preceding my brother by four years and my sister by fourteen years. My memories of the problems and tragedies early in my parents' marriage are very different from the memories of my siblings, indicating that each respective experience in our family was different and very subjective. When thrown in with differences in personalities and factors of time and other life events, it is possible to see how each family member has a different perspective on what happened, and how the family dynamics changed and evolved over time.

The important factor to remember is that while some aspects of the environment changed, the basic personalities of our parents changed very little during the times in which we lived as children and adolescents under their roof. Through the end of my parents' lives there was a great deal of denial and an insistence there was "a lot of love in our home" during those years. The reality is that while our parents perhaps "meant well", and were truly using what they convinced themselves to be the right approaches, they were in actuality taking their anxiety out on us, rather than resolving it for and between each other. As you will see in the chapters to follow I have developed the Roberts FLAGS (RFLAGS) Model as a way to understand these patterns of dysfunction and how everyone tends to act out emotion-based anxiety. As we go through the model and the various components, you will see how this process evolves and continues, setting people up for a great deal of negative Karma, in the sense that whatever we set into motion is what comes back to us. Virtually every culture has some form of this concept as a part of its overall cultural philosophy. You will also be able to see how this negative and ineffective process can be broken and changed into something which works rather than something which destroys. The goal is to change negative patterns and perceptions into actions which will generate a positive future and heal relationships from within, between our "self" and our higher "Self", and between us and other people when and where there is an opportunity or a desire to do so.

Because of the experiences in my own life, along with my own set of complicating factors, I have spent most of my adult life trying to recover from my past. I can honestly say that while my recovery continues, I have made considerable progress and now I am ready to share my discoveries with you as I have with others during and after the years of my education and training in the field of psychology. My required formalized training has ended; however, I see all of my future as an opportunity and obligation to myself to continue learning and growing. Even the revision and republishing of this book will certainly prove to be a valuable personal "training" experience now and into the future. I believe it will open many new doors as I continue seeking fulfillment of a process in life toward ultimately maximizing my spiritual growth, development, and maturity.

Of particular importance to the development of the RFLAGS Model and the writing of this book were the experiences I had while I was in my Ph.D. program and in the years since. Beginning in September 1990, my first two years of practicum and internship experience were within two different community-based, non-profit clinics. It was at this time I began to realize my future in psychology would be spent primarily in the provision of services to underserved populations. This approach made it difficult to pay back student loans, but for me it is the most satisfying and challenging.

For my third and final year of pre-doctoral training, I decided I wanted to work with "high risk youth", the only population with which I had not had any experience. I applied for and was accepted into an internship program with an emphasis in gang prevention. Services were provided to low income families through The Family Service Center within an elementary school located in East Los Angeles. Though quite nervous about what to expect and whether or not the community would accept me, I went in with an intense desire to learn, without an attitude of knowing it all or having all the answers. I had begun to study Spanish a few years earlier and found that the people in East LA, with whom I had the privilege of working, appreciated my efforts to learn and speak their language. My internship at this site continued for two years, at both the pre-doctoral and post-doctoral levels. As confirmation of my acceptance by the community I was even given the honor of speaking at the commencement exercises at the end of my second year of service. The invitation to speak was extended to me by the parents of the children at the school and was one of the greatest honors I could have ever received.

The staff and families associated with this school made me feel welcome. In an effort to address the needs of the children in East LA relative to the excessive violence they faced on a daily basis, I developed an anti-violence program, called "KIT Cadets: Kids In Touch Against Violence" (available upon request from the author). Each time a group of kids completed the six-week program we had a public assembly at school to award the certificates and invited the parents to the program. Because, at the time, this school was part of the Healthy Start Program within the state of California, the funding for the provision of services was made possible through a state grant.

During the first year of service at the site, I became fascinated with the gang culture given the fact I was working right in the middle of it on a daily basis. I began to understand the dynamics of gang involvement and decided I wanted to work specifically with this population as well. Six months prior to my assignment in East LA I had been jumped and robbed by three gang members close to where I was living. In spite of this I knew I wanted to understand how dysfunction and circumstance played a part in the lives of these kids, not only in their homes, but within the other contexts as well. Soon I was given another opportunity to obtain a part time job working under supervision and through a gang prevention grant at an additional school site just east of East Los Angeles. This school was an alternative community school established specifically for middle school kids with serious behavior problems, most of whom were gang kids. I had this job for almost three years, which gave me an incredible opportunity to work under supervision with gang kids and their families and the dysfunctional environments that provided the impetus for kids to act out by joining gangs.

One other factor relative to job opportunities came through employment at a private psychiatric hospital where I worked as a psychoeducational instructor with substance abusers diagnosed with other psychiatric conditions such as depression and anxiety. I was asked to co-facilitate groups with other therapists and was given the opportunity to develop my own group formats. The group topics included: abuse recovery, anger management, loss and grief, and family dysfunction. It was during this time I developed the earliest forms of my RFLAGS Model, as I tried to come up with a focus for each of these groups. The patients in the program were actually participants in my own initial program development.

One additional element that prepared me for the work I do currently was involvement for an extended period of time in my own therapy. I started therapy in my first year at CSPP-LA as a requirement for graduation, and as a way to help me deal with the stress of a Ph.D. program and the culture shock of moving from "the Deep South" to California. This, along with some other significant complicating factors in my personal life, kept me in therapy for several years. Therapy was the best investment I could have ever made in my "self" and my future. My therapist was an excellent guide, who helped me explore the answers I needed relative to my own history, and relative to my desire to be the best therapist I could possibly be. I firmly believe every therapist needs a solid background in having been "on the couch", so to speak, if they are to be effective. For it is in finding answers and insight into our own "dysfunction" that we are able to help others with the same process. How can we possibly help people solve their problems if we have not identified and resolved our own issues first?

Sometimes people with the best of intentions actually do the most harm simply because, quite often, people assume they need no personal assistance, or they have no personal issues or problems. In my opinion, virtually everyone can benefit from some degree of ongoing self-examination, simply because no one comes from the perfect family, a concept existing only as an ideal. Therapy is primarily an educational experience in which a *competent* licensed therapist shares with a client their wisdom gained through experience and education, representing my belief in each of us within the therapeutic context being both learner and teacher. Hopefully the therapist has more to offer than to gain from experiences and interactions with clients.

This last thought of the teacher continuing to learn is what kept me in therapy for so long. As I began to work with extremely dysfunctional families associated with gang kids and juvenile offenders, I found myself being faced with reflections of my own past relative to abuse/victimization and emotional neglect. I began to experience unresolved grief reactions as I listened to kids talk about the essential elements of childhood of which they were deprived for various reasons. Deprivation resulted not always because parents didn't care, but because the parents' unresolved issues interfered with their ability and responsibility to provide for the children in their care on every level. Parenting is a full time job and a lifelong commitment regardless of whether or not parents stay together in a successful relationship. It requires sacrifice as needed to provide effectively for children; not sacrifice of the self, but sacrifice in the sense that even after survival issues are satisfied, kids have to be the first priority until they reach the age when they can effectively care for themselves and live independently.

As I was confronted with these unresolved issues, I found my own anxiety level going up at times. I learned to use this as a gauge indicating a need to look at my own emotional state before I could help people find their respective answers. If a parent does their job right, they successfully raise their children to leave them - to become independent, responsible, "functional" members of society. Though my family provided me with the material factors such as food, clothing and shelter which I needed as a child, I never had the nurturing or guidance needed to teach me self-discipline, self-confidence, self-esteem, critical/creative thinking, or good problem-solving/decision-making skills. All of my decisions were made for me until I reached the age of 16 and to some extent until I got married at the age of 20 primarily as a means of escaping the very restrictive environment in which I was raised.

By continuing in therapy, I was able to take all of my concerns and questions back to my therapist who guided me through the often difficult and painful exploration of what I believe to have been the reality of my past. As I found my own answers, I was able to take my insights into therapy with others and try them out in appropriate and professional ways on my clients. This served as a means of fine tuning them for me personally, and as a way of learning to generalize my experience and insight into situations which were at least similar to my own on an emotional level. I became, and still am, both teacher and learner. Once I resolved my issues I was able to terminate my personal therapy, but not my learning process.

The reality is there are some issues we cannot handle without professional guidance. It was as though my therapist gave me the parenting I needed, which went beyond basic physical necessities, to give me a solid basis from which to grow and learn on my own. At the same time, my therapist helped me find the ability to effectively work with one of the most difficult populations in psychology - "at risk or high risk youth". Other than a few very basic useful components, I have discarded most of the past that interfered with my ability to effectively deal with life as an adult. In other words I feel I have resolved much of the dysfunction I experienced as a child. Again, none of this is about blaming. It is only about reality, truth, and honesty, which are the same elements I introduce my clients to whether they are adults or kids. My model is rooted in these factors, with resolution of dysfunction being based in simple universally accepted and acknowledged spiritual concepts. Again, the object of my work is to help others heal one's relationship to "self" and then between self and others regardless of the context, or the nature of the relationship. This is why I consider my methods to fall under the heading of Spiritual Psychology.

In the chapters to follow I intend to share with you the RFLAGS Model which is the center of my understanding of how adults and kids tend to act out emotion-based anxiety, rather than face the negative emotions and their origins which create the anxiety. I will attempt to connect all concepts to this model; therefore it is important for each reader to have a clear understanding of how it works. Many of my insights come from the experiences I have had presenting my theories to others both as a psychologist and as a college instructor, and in addition to understanding my own personal experiences. Because the entire presentation has grown and continues to grow,

I will also propose ideas for further consideration during this presentation. It is my hope that the RFLAGS Model will be expanded to fully achieve the status of being "my gift from the Source to the world" through input and reciprocation from the readers.

Because the RFLAGS Model actually comes toward the end of the conceptual sequence, after the presentation of the model in the next chapter, I will back up to the beginning so we can explore the actual adult roles and responsibilities we are suppose to adopt. We will look at how some key words have different meanings to different people, especially looking at labels and often times unconscious prejudices/biases adults possess and convey to kids. In the process I will refer directly to the model as a means of tying everything together at all levels of the presentation.

Conceptually the sequence flows from Adult Roles and Responsibilities; Abuse/Victimization; Contexts of Abuse/Victimization; Complicating Factors; Losses and Grief; Personality Traits; the RFLAGS Model; to Breaking the Cycle. Within these pages we will: start with what we hopefully are doing right and the good things we have experienced; move into what we actually may be doing or have experienced; and look at the environments in which victimization occurs. From there we will identify adult patterns of dysfunction; see how all of these components create the need to act out emotion-based anxiety; and finally move into changing perspectives and resolving the negative influences from the past. The final chapters will be more along the lines of a where-do-we-go-from-here approach, in which I will suggest some possible expansions of the presentation to more universal perspectives and applications.

As I guide you through this process of self-examination, problem identification, and ultimate resolution, I hope you will find the faith and courage to be both open-minded and honest. I also hope you will continue to see in my writings the courage I have discovered and used to get beyond fear, even as I present several different personal aspects of my history and process. As I said earlier, this book is not *about* me. It is from *within* me relative to insights I have gained to date in my own life process. I believe my ideas are valid and have been successfully developed and shared since 1986 within various settings and with extremely diverse audiences from many walks of life. Based of my successes as a psychologist I know these methods and theories have been tried and proven many times over. Countless numbers of kids and families have benefited from my outreach to those who appear to be hopeless and helpless relative to their life perspective and circumstances.

Now, with courage as our banner, LET'S GO!

Chapter II

Roberts FLAGS Model

Different theorists have many different ways of attempting to explain how human behavior develops. By now people in general readily accept the influences of both genetics and the environment upon the ultimate result of who we become as adults. No one denies the significant interactions between the personality traits and other genetic factors we are born with, and the factors outside of ourselves which help determine how these traits ultimately manifest themselves behaviorally as we grow up and mature. I personally believe the interaction between us and the external environmental factors continues until the day we die. However, I also believe the most critical interactions relative to shaping personality characteristics occur when we are children, especially during the early years. While I believe it is possible to overcome and compensate for deficiencies during those significant early years, I believe even more strongly in giving kids what they need so ideally there is nothing, or at least very little, to mend.

The main developmental theorist I want to focus on relative to understanding my model and the development of maladaptive behavior is Erik Erikson. He was one of the first psychologists to view personality development as a process occurring across the entire lifespan. His first five stages, which cover infancy through adolescence, are the most relevant to this text. Without successful mastery and completion of these early stages, the adult stages of development will likely be quite complicated, with very few productive accomplishments possible throughout the remaining lifespan.

Erikson's "eight stages of man" are:
   trust vs. mistrust (infancy);
   autonomy vs. shame and doubt (ages 1-3);

initiative vs. guilt (ages 3-5 or 6);
industry vs. inferiority (ages 5 or 6-12);
identity vs. role confusion (ages 12-18);
intimacy vs. isolation (ages 18-35);
generativity vs. stagnation (ages 35-60);
integrity vs. despair (age 60-death).

As you look over the above list, think about a couple of factors. First of all, each of us is born with the unspoken assumption the world will be a safe and friendly place. Secondly, we innately assume we will be loved and nurtured, with all of our needs hopefully being met as they were prior to birth. Finally, we assume our parents will be the ones who make all of this happen. Unfortunately, depending on many different possibilities, *none* of the above may turn out to be reality. As children we cannot control either our environment or the people in it, much less the conditions of the environment into which we are introduced.

Take a little time to think about the quality of the people and the environment as they existed at the time you were born. Really spend some time looking honestly at what was happening, and at the personalities of those within your birth reality. Hopefully, for many of you this awareness is a positive one, as it was for me initially. On the other hand, there are likely a number of readers for whom this reality is rather disappointing and even shocking and traumatic. For others like me, the first few years may have been relatively safe and stable. However, this environment may have taken on a rather tragic twist as life began to throw some very difficult realities into the mix which then changed everything in the future. Even if we are not abused by people we can feel abused by life's events.

The Past that Lived in My Present

By all accounts my birth reality on Friday, May 7, 1954, at 2:12 P.M. must have been quite stable and hopeful, with the exception of having been born breech. Rather than being delivered normally, I was reportedly pulled into the world with a pair of forceps. Perhaps my reluctance to be born was prophetic, possibly even setting me up for some of the distance between my mother and myself which lasted throughout her life. Maybe she never forgave me for the 36 hours of painful and difficult labor she reportedly endured.

When I was born my parents had been married for nearly two years, with both of them working and enjoying the post World War II boom. At the time of my birth we were living in a small apartment close to the downtown area. After about two years my parents built a small house outside of the city and in an incorporated area advertising itself as "The All White City", as printed on the welcome signs until the Civil Rights Movement in the 1960's. My dad was apparently proud to have a son for his first child. Even though he worked as a mortician at the time of my birth, he took a job two years later in December 1956 at a newly opened textile mill, where he worked until he retired. This kind of stability is an important factor relative to his philosophies of security and his priorities which resulted for many people who were products of "The Great Depression".

My dad's jobs as a mortician, and later as a worker at the factory, required him to work rotating shifts. Because both of my parents worked, most of my time was spent with my maternal grandmother; with my dad on his days off; and later with Bell, our housekeeper my parents hired after they moved from the main city and into the suburban community. I have only a few memories of my mother prior to the time when my brother was born in June 1958. Unfortunately, they are not pleasant ones. I can only wonder if mom was ever happy. However, all of my memories prior to June 1958 of my maternal grandparents, my dad, and Bell are very positive. I believe they gave me a reasonably stable basis upon which to begin my life. According to Erikson's stages of development, I gained trust, autonomy and initiative given their love and support.

All of this changed drastically, beginning with the birth of my brother on June 3, 1958. My mother quit her job just prior to his birth, apparently with some resentment and probably at the insistence of my dad who reportedly wanted her home "to raise his children". Shortly after these events, my parents sold their first house and started construction on another one in the same area. Because the first house sold so quickly, we moved into a government housing project to wait for the new house to be completed. Very soon after this move, I have the first really vivid memory of hearing my mother scream upon receiving the news by phone that her father, brother, and brother-in-law had all drowned while fishing at a reservoir in or near Paducah, Kentucky. All of the families were visiting my mother's brother who lived there with his wife and two children. Suddenly our family was faced with an unpredictable tragedy that left three women widows and four children fatherless. My dad would likely have died as well if not for the fact he was unable to get the time off for vacation.

This tragedy was especially difficult for my mother to face because of her own unresolved issues from the past relative to her father, issues that I would not understand until a few years after her death (that is another book!). While I never knew him as such, my grandfather reportedly had been a very abusive, violent alcoholic who would disappear for extended periods of time, leaving my grandmother to provide for her three children as best she could during and after the Great Depression and through World War II. My grandmother remarked once with tears in her eyes, "there are some things far worse than divorce", indicating the zeitgeist of the times when women were powerless over such abuse and victimization.

As you can imagine, with all of these family tragedies my life also took a traumatic turn for the worse. In June 1958 I found myself with a mother I hardly knew. I could no longer spend the same amount of time with my dad, maternal grandparents, or Bell because of the changes initiated by my brother's birth, which included the fact I was no longer an only child. We then moved from the only home I had known for two years, and my grandfather and two uncles tragically died.

All I remember from the years during childhood after that horrible summer are the constant fights between my parents, and my attempts to take care of and console this unpredictably vicious, depressed, anxious, angry woman I called "Mama". My dad, whom I had loved and trusted, suddenly became this angry, sadistically cruel, frightening man who started abusing me both physically and emotionally because of the tension between him and my mom. All of my time was spent trying to please them in an effort to protect myself from their attacks which were impossible for me to understand as a child. My love for my dad turned to hatred and what he called respect became nothing more than fear, resentment, and compliance. My dad was, and continued to be a control freak throughout virtually all of his life. His love turned to total emotional neglect as my world, as I had known it, fell apart. My mother continued to be vicious, angry, unpredictable, and manipulative throughout her life until just before she died in April 2000. The two of them managed to keep the family divided to meet their own needs for control and revenge. As for many people, my anger toward them lies in the fact they got away with this, with many outsiders thinking we had the perfect family. How can I forgive my parents for things they wouldn't even acknowledge much less apologize for doing?

The only good thing for me that came out of the tragedy is that my maternal grandmother moved into a basement apartment my parents offered to her in the new house. This meant my grandmother moved into my environment and lived there all of my years while growing up from 1958 forward. My initial separation from her lasted only about six months. She was clearly the saving grace that kept me from becoming a total emotional wreck. Even at the age of 100, my grandmother's love for me never changed, except to grow stronger. Interestingly enough, in many settings I have found the love of a maternal grandmother to have been a stabilizing factor in the lives of others who have also endured very dysfunctional backgrounds. During all of the years following the tragic deaths, Granny continued to give me the love and support I needed. She sensed my vulnerability from all of the conflict and abuse that I endured in the house just above her basement apartment.

The important point here is that even a relatively solid basis was subject to being torn apart at a crucial point in my emotional development. This resulted in part from a series of unavoidable and unpredictable events, and also by the unresolved issues from childhood present in the lives of both of my parents; factors brought to the surface by the tragedy. Also illustrated is the fact that early on the emotional void with my mom was filled by two "mother" figures in my life – my grandmother and Bell, whom I loved as much as I loved my grandmother. Without these first few good years I cannot begin to imagine how many more emotional scars I would have had to deal with as an adult. So many people lack even the relatively solid basis I had at the beginning of my life. I don't know how I would have survived without this factor.

Dr. David L. Roberts Ph.D.

Following the deaths my trust turned to mistrust as I tried to carry on in the ways I had known previously as my reality. At age four it was hard to comprehend how any environment can change so quickly, and so permanently. The very people I had trusted were not available to me because of their own processes of bereavement and adjustment. The woman I should have been able to trust as my mother turned out to be emotionally unstable and unpredictable during all of my remaining years at home. My dad became unavailable emotionally, with the only remaining experiences with him being very negative and extremely unpleasant. As my home/family environment or context fell apart, the stage was set for me to develop many maladaptive ways of dealing with emotions and life. Into this already negative mix, abuse was introduced in the forms of extreme conflict between my parents, exposure to very fundamentalist and extreme religious views, and actual physical and emotional abuse from both of my parents. My dad even took on the same apparent characteristics of both of my grandfathers who were often gone, certainly unavailable emotionally, and very abusive when in the home. Without intentionally doing so, my parents recreated much the same kind of environment each of them endured as children, though possibly not quite as extreme in the present as in their respective pasts. My dad's father was apparently very similar to my mother's father, especially relative to the physical and emotional abuse and neglect.

Referring back to Erikson's model, take note as well of how these events also turned my trust into mistrust, my sense of confidence and autonomy into shame and doubt; and turned my sense of initiative into guilt. Along with all of this came a real sense of being totally confused about every facet of life. At this time religion became the only model presented to me as a way of making sense out of chaos. However, the Baptist religion into which I was introduced taught me I was a worthless sinner whom God would punish harshly for wrongdoing. Even "God" was abusive and I thought all of this was my fault. After all, the adults in my environment told me they were the ultimate authorities next to God. Questioning of their authority resulted in seriously abusive consequences. Fear and intimidation told me they were "right" on all counts and that to doubt them or God would result in more bad things happening. You can only imagine how all of these factors set me up to fail miserably at the next stage of development – industry vs. inferiority. What a way to start out in my experiences with school and the world outside of the home/family context!

Hopefully, I have successfully set the stage for you to understand the concept of emotion-based anxiety, and then to begin seeing how we tend to act this out behaviorally, rather than deal with it, explore it, and learn from it. It is important to explain that the details I have presented about my past are a presentation of my own reality. While I am sure most of it is true, I am not actually sure of the accuracy of some of the details or the perspective of some of what I consider to be facts. Remember, these are the memories of a young child recalled with no ability to discuss them for clarification with any of the characters involved. I am absolutely sure, however, of the emotional scars resulting from the behaviors I clearly remember from my parents. The only things I may have some confusion about are details, not the overall experiences.

However, this doesn't matter because, regardless of the facts, this was and <u>is</u> my reality. Of utmost importance is the awareness that my emotions connected to this reality are factual and are the result of the past as I recall having experienced it, even though I may be a little confused about details of some of the circumstances. In other words no one can dispute how I feel in the present about and because of the past. Furthermore, any distortion of the past I may have is not my fault. As children we will fill in the blanks on anything which does not make sense, certainly when there is no opportunity for questioning and correction. The unfortunate reality is that a child tends to internalize these past emotions, even to the point of denial and unawareness, coupled with the tendency to blame themselves for all of the negative experiences.

As in many families, no one in my family is willing to talk about any of this at a level where we could understand each perspective and correct any misperceptions. These subjects are taboo in the sense they are the past and the past is better left alone – "let sleeping dogs lie". The other factor is that the realties of everyone involved are subjective, and after so many years who can say with any certainty what is factual any more for anyone, other than a few "newspaper-like" details. Reality is subjective and each of us has to deal with our own subjective reality as best we can. Keep in mind, too, that everyone involved in these dramas now have their own likely subjective distortions of what actually happened and why. I have also found many times the perpetrators of abuse tend to suppress the memories of what they did to others who were the unfortunate targets of their victimization.

"The past" is a scary subject for a significant number of people. Even many of my clients and friends say they see no point in living in, or re-living the past. I actually agree with the notion of not living in the past. However, because the past often lives in our present on an unconscious level, I believe it is necessary to at least review the past as honestly and openly as we can in an effort to understand our historic reality and deal with the effects which often complicate our current lives. This needs to be done both by adults and adolescents, and usually with professional guidance. An unhealthy past results in later years being filled with doubt, insecurity, deprivation, and unpredictability, all generating a complicated emotional repertoire which we then act out behaviorally and emotionally. The "scary past" is the very one which seriously needs to be exposed, not necessarily in great detail, but in whatever detail is necessary to define it. Also, whenever and if ever possible, the details of the past should be checked out and either verified or corrected. However, this is possible only if those involved are open to communicating about the past. Certainly this is not a requirement, but can be beneficial if the option is available and desirable.

As we go through the RFLAGS Model and the other concepts associated with it, please understand that none of the process I present is about blaming, judging, or scapegoating. Rather than being seen as accusatory, I hope you will see the process simply as the expression of reality-based awarenesses and observations; in other words, an expression of our own subjective "Truth", and in many instances when sharing with you my past, *my* own subjective "Truth".

Over the years I have come to understand the difference between judging another person or situation, as opposed to simply stating a reality-based perception or observation. Sometimes people really are superficial and abusive, and to say so is simply to state a non-judgmental observation. To go any further and put a value of good or bad, right or wrong on it then makes it judgmental. The observed characteristic just is, and is part of the other person's subjective process, and is open to change and reevaluation on the part of the observer if improvements are made by the one being observed. The trick is to learn the difference between the two ideas and to also check our motivation for the expression of such awarenesses. Sometimes these kinds of observations should be kept to ourselves and filed away for our own information and at times for our own protection, being careful not to turn these observations into judgmental ways of dealing with or categorizing someone. In spite of the awareness, I believe we need to look behind and beyond what we see in an effort to see the person we are actually observing, thereby learning to *separate what people do from who they actually are*. This, however, is much easier to do with kids than with adults, because behaviors become more permanent indicators of who we are if they are not checked and corrected at least during late adolescence. People can change, but the more permanent a behavior becomes, in the sense of being automatic and unconscious, the less likely people are to make those changes.

The RFLAGS Model serves as a visual and intellectual way to understand the development of maladaptive behavior. It is a means of helping us to understand that behavior is not necessarily representative of who we are as a person. It certainly is not representative of who we could be with the opportunity and willingness to resolve the emotions fueling the anxiety and the need to act out rather than feel bad or deal with the emotional basis. *Separating who we are from what we do is a key part of this concept!*

I do not believe in or support the use of labels, especially for children, because we tend to treat people according to the label(s) we impose upon them. For instance, I believe there are no such categories as "bad kids", "incorrigibles", or "a problem child". There are simply kids who do bad things or make bad choices, and kids who have problems. Though fairly subtle, this rather minor change in wording greatly affects the implications and perceptions. It amazes me how children are often referred to as bad kids, incorrigibles, and problem children even in professional circles and research literature. Check out research presented in the various psychological and psychiatric journals dealing with the subject of "The Problem

Child" and other such stigmatizing terminology. To me this is extremely offensive and serves as a means of perpetuating the focus on behavior as being a true representation or manifestation of the actual character of the person behind the acts. Much of this goes back to the psychoanalytic notion of "characterological disorders" and is clearly associated with outdated religious philosophies focusing on sinners and condemnation.

Even though Sigmund Freud, often referred to as "the father of modern Psychology", set the stage for the investigation into human nature, many of its originators and subsequent followers have done a great deal of damage. They did so by labeling people as the problems or symptoms they exhibit, even labeling some lifestyles and personal identities as problematic when indeed they are not. We have come to accept as fact that if we make mistakes we are flawed in some way, especially if we tend to repeat the same mistakes, or appear to continuously make new mistakes. This thinking allows us to trap ourselves into believing "this is just the way I am. What I do wrong is an innate part of who I am and it cannot be changed." As we start with the RFLAGS Model and move into the other topics, hopefully each of you - who can see the need to do so - will be able to find the courage and the willingness to change your perspective relative to yourself and others. Clearly this is where the concept and implementation of honest self-assessment/evaluation/examination comes into the process.

Visually the Roberts FLAGS (RFLAGS) Model contains four segments: Negative Emotions, Anxiety/Depression, Hopelessness/Helplessness (giving up), and Acting-Out Behaviors (see diagram below and Appendix A). This serves as a very useful graphic of the process evolving from negative emotions into the maladaptive acting-out behaviors which generally result from the unresolved issues and emotions.

ROBERTS FLAGS MODEL

| Negative Emotions | Anxiety/ Depression | Hopelessness/ Helplessness | Acting Out Behaviors |

FEAR

LONELINESS

ANGER

GUILT

SHAME

Between Anxiety and Acting Out is the element of hopelessness/helplessness derived from the perception and choice of giving up or not caring, and/or feeling like no one else cares either. Conceptually the RFLAGS Model works in a cyclical fashion, always moving in a clockwise direction. The process is to identify each individual's respective terminology, patterns and elements under each of the segments of Anxiety/Depression, Helplessness/Hopelessness, and Acting-Out Behaviors to bring these into conscious awareness, and ultimately into conscious control. The goal then becomes that of understanding the emotion-based state of anxiety which is generally acted out rather than dealt with and resolved.

Starting with the emotions, note that the "F" is "Fear"; the "L" is "Loneliness"; the "A" is "Anger"; the "G" is "Guilt"; and the "S" is "Shame" - FLAGS. These are all negative emotions and certainly are not the only emotions which can be experienced. They are, however, the emotions which I believe, from both personal and professional experience, to be the most problematic, especially when they occur simultaneously and were created within and from a history of abuse and victimization. The result is a state of anxiety and possibly depression, which can be overwhelming and debilitating. Depression alone tends to be experienced in a passive manner, while depression associated with emotion-based anxiety tends to be acted out behaviorally, and often to extremes with extreme consequences resulting either immediately or ultimately.

The idea with the model is that the "FLAGS" are *waving* as an indication something is happening and going wrong. You can think of someone's life as being "stormy". However, the problem is most people are cut off from awareness of their emotions and, therefore, never identify them or deal with them. The focus tends to be on the resulting emotional state of anxiety/depression which is undesirable and something to be eliminated or avoided by whatever means available - often times in a maladaptive manner which only complicates and intensifies the emotional basis existing beyond conscious awareness. Elimination and avoidance of the unpleasant emotional state becomes the focus and eventually becomes second nature and unconscious as well in the sense of becoming an automatic reactive choice. The resulting problematic behaviors have the potential to become so habitual as to become permanent maladaptive coping styles.

I also believe depression generally accompanies anxiety, possibly even at times resulting from it as people realize their lives (rather than acknowledging their emotions) are out of control. On the other hand, I do not believe anxiety always accompanies depression, which when experienced as the only emotional state tends to be very passive and non-motivational. However, as I indicated above, a state of anxiety and/or anxious depression tends to be acted out rather than resolved. All of this is by degree in the sense that the stronger the negative emotional basis is, the more intense the resulting negative emotional state will be.

The acting-out behaviors then become an external means of trying to soothe, control, and/or eliminate the unpleasant internal negative emotional state. Even though the behaviors may originate from an internal impetus, they manifest themselves as something which can be seen as an external factor. Therefore, rather than looking inside for the source of control, we look outside of ourselves for tangible and/or conceptually solid means of feeling better and trying to cope. This then leaves us *"at the mercy of externals"* as the book title indicates. Rather than serving as solutions, these external elements also become part of the problem and a further source of fuel for the negative emotions already creating the emotional state we seek to escape or eliminate. Having been at the mercy of environmental factors as children, it is easy to accept also being at the mercy of all external factors as we grow older.

Let's examine each of the emotions. Fear is an emotion experienced by everyone at various times and in various contexts. Unfortunately it is difficult for people to admit fear, feeling that doing so indicates they are in some ways cowardly and vulnerable. Sometimes there is even a sense of shame associated with fear, especially for men who are taught culturally that any degree of fear is a shameful sign of weakness often associated with women. I see this quite often in the gang kids and juvenile offenders I work with as clients. People don't always see fear as being subject to degree, ranging from simple nervousness to sheer panic; nor do they see fear as normal and necessary to survival. Sometimes fear can be experienced without the other emotions being present. But think about how complicated fear becomes when it is accompanied by a feeling of loneliness and the "fear" this loneliness will continue. Fear can even be seen as a basis for the other emotions in this model. Perhaps these first two emotions are accompanied by anger related to the feelings of being lonely and afraid. Couple these three negative, unpleasant emotions with the feeling of guilt that I should be able to be strong or brave, and the shame of feeling flawed, weak, and out of control.

Clearly this combination of FLAGS has the potential to lead to an emotional state which will possibly include both anxiety and depression. Now assume the individual with this emotional combination is cut off from and unaware of the emotions fueling the resulting physical/behavioral manifestation of the emotion-based condition. Both anxiety and depression are experienced as physical conditions, as well as emotional states. Anxiety seems to reside in the chest or in "the pit of the stomach". This person has only the awareness of feeling bad, often accompanied with the intense desire to eliminate and/or escape this reality. Rather than use the emotional state as an indication of the need to examine and deal with the emotions causing this state, let's assume the individual becomes so overwhelmed they give up out of a sense of helplessness/hopelessness. This individual will then move into some means of acting out and reacting to the emotional state in a maladaptive, problematic manner.

The entire process of acting out emotion-based anxiety originates in the general condition of being cut off from emotions, which I believe is learned in childhood from adults who, in one extreme, stifle the honest, appropriate expression of emotions. In the opposite extreme another possibility is that children learn inappropriate expression of emotions, believing it is okay to act out rather than face emotions because emotional needs are neglected or appropriate behaviors are not modeled and encouraged. Either way children often become adults with no idea of how to deal with frustration, loss, anger, and/or disappointment; and with little or no ability to cope or to soothe themselves appropriately. Beginning in childhood and continuing into adulthood, these children seek outside sources of relief to guard against simply feeling bad, making them even more vulnerable to external factors. This results in a population of adults and kids who take their frustrations out on themselves individually, and on others by targeting people either in isolation or within groups or contexts. This process has led to what I call "moral bankruptcy", present within people of all ages in our societies and cultures globally.

It is important to also see that the emotions do not necessarily occur together. Sometimes we are just afraid, lonely or angry. Even when emotions occur in isolation, we still need to be in control of them to avoid acting out toward ourselves and/or others. I tell my kids and adult clients all the time: "just because you can, doesn't mean you should". Many times people will use an emotion as an excuse to act out in some manner. For instance some people will say "I hit the wall because I have a bad temper." My response is that it is necessary to control the temper rather than use it as a reason to proceed with the maladaptive behavior. By blaming the "temper" as the culprit, thereby using it as an excuse, we never have to take responsibility for our actions and willingness to follow through.

Think about guilt and shame for a moment. Infants are not born with a sense of either guilt or shame. Of the three FLAGS, these are the only ones which I believe are exclusively learned emotions, often being taught to us at early ages by adults. However, fear, loneliness and anger can easily be identified in infants as survival skills which get them the attention they need for their care and inclusion. My favorite example is the parent(s) at the mall with a small child. The child begins to act out the fact they are tired, bored, frustrated, etc. I am not talking about the child who throws a temper tantrum because they can't have the toy they want, but the screaming child who really is tired. The parent usually starts telling the child to "stop that! Everyone is looking at you". What is the truth in this situation? Who is everyone actually looking at?

The answer is everyone is looking at the parent and thinking: "why can't you see your child is tired and either needs a nap or at least an opportunity to have some fun?" The parent, on the other hand, is telling the child how ashamed they should feel for what is a natural reaction for the kid under those kinds of circumstances. This inaccurately teaches them the whole world is looking at *you* and misjudging what *you* are doing as being a bad child who embarrasses mommy or daddy, and who has no consideration for the feelings of others. Oh the guilt of feeling responsible at the age of four for having screwed up your parent's day simply by being tired and bored, and having the nerve to express these feelings in a manner which causes your parents to come under scrutiny. How dare you bring attention to the inappropriateness of your parents' lack of consideration for your feelings and needs?

With time (and therapy) it is possible to get rid of most of the guilt and shame instilled in us as children. Some of it seems to last forever, especially if the people who instilled these emotions continue to make the same attempts in our adult lives. Always remember that if you are doing nothing wrong to yourself or to others, there is no need to feel either guilt or shame. Remember, people in the world who are supposedly watching us spend too much time worrying about what everyone else is thinking about them to ever spend much time thinking about the rest of us.

People have no right to impose their beliefs upon others. There are things about my own life and nature that many people might disagree with and object to. However, I don't care what they think as long as I know my heart is pure and my intentions are good. I have learned that most people will not express their opinion to your face unless they are given the opportunity to do so. I simply never ask what people think unless I truly want to know. Certainly there are times when the impression we make upon others is important, but those times are generally by our own choice such as job interviews and following rules at work to get a good performance appraisal or a promotion. These situations are different from the unnecessary negativity imposed on us by others.

As we talk about abuse and victimization later you will see how people often feel entitled to pass judgment, quite often based on some closed-minded set of religious, political, and/or social beliefs. The very act of passing judgment is often an act of victimization and therefore a way of acting out an individual's own anxiety present in their life and history. If we have something in our life which brings feelings of guilt and shame upon ourselves from within rather than simply from standards placed upon us from others, then these behaviors need to be looked at and dealt with. Otherwise throw away all unnecessary feelings of guilt and shame, and learn to protect yourself from them. After all, why not get rid of as much unhealthy emotional baggage as possible?

Let's examine a little more closely the segment in the RFLAGS Model entitled "Anxiety", and look at other words people use to describe the emotional state of anxiety, and how it manifests itself physically. As I indicated earlier anxiety is experienced on a physical level as well. Anxiety is even hard to distinguish from its opposite physical state of excitement. Both are accompanied by muscle tension, increased heart rate, fatigue, headaches, agitation, faster breathing rate, sleep disturbance, changes in eating habits, and changes in other bodily functions. I know when I am excited about something, and if the excitement is intense and continues for a long period of time, I experience these physical changes. I am not talking about sexual excitement (even though I guess an extended state of sexual excitement could also qualify). I am talking about a state of anticipation based in positive emotions such as joy, confidence, love, pleasure, etc., rather than anticipation based in the negative FLAGS. The difference between anxiety and excitement lies in the emotions creating the state.

Even without guilt and shame, the other three, fear, loneliness and anger are quite enough to still create anxiety. Moving from only one emotion to acting out is not the same as acting out anxiety. Emotion-based anxiety is created by a combination of emotions which may grow from just one to others. The very act of acting out an emotion can create the conditions to bring on the other FLAGS as well. As we act out we tend to complicate our lives and the emotions associated with our condition, rather than find solutions to the problems that created the emotions in the first place.

To further understand the state of anxiety or anxious depression, consider some terms and phrases we tend to use to describe this state. Study the list in Appendix B to see how we identify and experience anxiety. This list is the first of several throughout the book, all of which are extremely important in the understanding of and application of the model. It is, therefore, critical that you take the time as each list is mentioned to study it and understand how it applies to the concept being illustrated. This current list is by no means complete, so feel free to add your own descriptive terms to it. It comes from my own perspective and from the classes I teach when I present the RFLAGS Model to various groups.

From the list in Appendix B you can see how some of the terms used may seem redundant. However, keep in mind that sometimes when people say "I'm angry", or "I'm anxious", they are expressing a more complicated condition than they realize by virtue of the fact they may be cut off from the awareness of a combination of emotions which actually might be involved. Many times kids are taught they are to be seen and not heard. They are also taught their feelings either don't matter or are unimportant and irrelevant. It's no wonder people don't know how to identify emotions when many of us were taught at an early age to suppress them, or were taught in some way not to trust our perceptions of emotions. Children learn this from phrases such as: "You can't possibly feel that way;" or "How dare you feel that way;" or "If you do that or express that again, I'll...." There is also the assumption children don't really have feelings or the ability to understand life events prior to the onset of puberty. Any emotions prior to then which don't correspond to adult perceptions of what is appropriate are frequently squelched. Oh the confusion from being treated as something less than human when we were children.

Finally, let's look at the last phase of the cycle, the Acting-Out phase. For a reactive choice to be considered as an 'acting-out behavior', it must be preceded with a degree of hopelessness/helplessness, giving up, and/or not caring. This is usually expressed in some form of thought or statement like: "Screw it! No one else cares, so why should I?" At this point the individual will likely give up on the hope of feeling better and will then make a maladaptive choice in an effort to eliminate, avoid, or escape the emotion-based state of anxiety. This state of anxiety is also similar to anxiety associated with physical feelings of withdrawal and detox from any maladaptive behaviors such as drinking, using drugs, or smoking. Remember, the person is about to act out emotion-based anxiety rather than use the physical feeling of anxiety as a gauge to identify the emotions needed to be faced and dealt with appropriately. In order to avoid relapse relative to substance abuse a person needs to also remind herself or himself the anxiety associated with physical withdrawal is temporary and will pass. However, the state of anxiety remaining once the feeling of actual physical withdrawal subsides will be based in the emotions originally fueling the need to escape the emotion-based anxiety in the first place.

Take a few minutes and look carefully at the next list (Appendix C) of possible acting-out behaviors and impulsive reactions from which people can choose. While this list is rather long, it is not necessarily all-inclusive. Chances are many of you will be able to identify with some of the possibilities. Some of you may even come up with a few more of your own which I have not thought about yet. As you look over the list, remember this model is usually presented to an audience of people seated in front of me. The presentation is very interactive, with participants providing their own list of items at any given part of the seminar. If you find others that I missed I would like to hear from you so I can add your items to my list – www.DavidLRobertsPhD.org.

As you reviewed the list you may have even been a little shocked at how many of the items pertain to your own coping style. Please do not be overly alarmed by this, as this is not uncommon. Remember that many of the items are problematic only when they are out of balance or out of control. For instance, we all have needs for eating, sleeping and sex. Exercising, reading, watching TV, and withdrawing all can be positive things to do unless they are excessive. The key factor for some of the possible choices is control and balance. As you can clearly see, however, some of the remaining possible choices should never be made, or should be eliminated if they are already part of your coping patterns and personality. Any extreme distress you may experience now or in the future relative to any of the lists and issues included in this book will hopefully signal your need to explore these issues with a mental health professional who can guide you through them safely and successfully.

One other list (Appendix D) I want to include in this chapter is a list of the problems/issues we seek to escape from by acting out our emotion-based anxiety. As with the previous list, this list is not necessarily all inclusive, so feel free to come up with some other items and pass them along to me so I can update my records. Generally the problems and issues underlying our negative emotions of Fear, Loneliness, Anger, Guilt, and Shame (FLAGS) are numerous and depend upon the degree of dysfunction we experienced in childhood. So, do not be alarmed or surprised if you find quite a few in the list that again pertain to your own life and history. Remember, too, none of this is intended to make anyone feel they have a lot wrong with them. There is nothing *wrong* with any of us who have been abused or victimized in the sense of being inherently and permanently flawed relative to personality characteristics. The purpose is to help people recognize the dysfunction in the present, which is based in the past, and which will impede progress in the future. View these lists with both hope and courage, and then find the determination and commitment to make changes which will uncomplicate your existence from this point forward.

Much of the elimination of this maladaptive process lies in the need and ability to face unpleasant feelings rather than seek to avoid them. Instead of moving forward into the acting-out phase, one should back up and sit with the emotional state until something can be learned from it. The only exception would be with any psychological state which is out of control and/or debilitating (as with major depression, bipolar disorders, or more serious mental disorders which are primarily chemically/physiologically based), or is potentially life threatening. It is important to recognize one's limits relative to dealing with emotions which may in reality be overwhelming, and which may require professional guidance and assistance.

If an individual lacks the ability to deal with the emotional state of anxiety and the feeling of physical discomfort, they will then make one or more reactive choices. These choices will represent either an act of victimization of self, victimization of other, or some combination of both. Any choice made at this point has the potential to become reinforced as a way to feel better by escaping or avoiding, without the realization that the behavior chosen is only an escape or avoidance and not a solution. The probability of the behavior becoming part of the complicating factors creating the emotional basis of the anxiety increases substantially as the psychological connection between the behavior and false feeling of relief becomes stronger. The maladaptive behavior then further complicates the person's life by increasing the negative emotions already present. This is a process whereby an individual learns to unconsciously abuse self and/or others as a way of perpetuating the history of victimization. Certainly if these types of coping choices start early enough in life, they will likely become part of someone's adult personality, thereby creating and recreating the same kind of chaos the individual experienced in childhood and adolescence.

Clearly there is a connection to this process and any process of addiction. However, while I believe in a possible genetic predisposition for addiction to alcohol and other substances, I believe addiction comes in many forms. Furthermore, I believe every maladaptive behavior is based in, and/or perpetuated by anxiety and the need to act out anxiety rather than learn to face it. After all, the existence of a genetic predisposition alone does not account for the initial choice to drink or use. For example, my parents did not drink; but, they acted out in some very maladaptive, habitual ways which only served to complicate their own lives and the lives of those around them.

I am not saying everyone who feels anxiety will act out in a maladaptive way. Much of the choice to act out depends on history; the degree of emotion-based anxiety; and on an individual's ability to cope effectively and soothe herself or himself appropriately. Perhaps the genetic predisposition is not to addictive tendencies, but rather to an inability to effectively deal with anxiety. The more likely someone is to be wired for extreme anxiety relative to genetic and environmental factors, possibly the more likely it is they will choose to act out rather than learn to face negative emotions and cope with them. Even though addiction becomes physical relative to substance use, I believe the strongest form of addiction is the psychological addiction to a euphoric escape experience derived from external acting-out factors, rather than generated internally through appropriate coping skills consciously, willfully developed and applied from within.

For instance, I suspect there is likely a genetic predisposition toward anxiety on my mother's side of the family. The other possible explanation could be that a complicated environment could somehow wire the brain to always be on the alert for incoming negativity and other unpredictable factors. Either way I can see a pattern of anxious personality styles with my mother's maternal aunt, my mother, myself and my sister, and my daughter. All of us would be described by my dad as being "high strung and overly sensitive, and nervous". This seems to come back to the basic assumption of an interaction between environment and genetically based personality factors.

The only way for me to achieve zero anxiety is through meditation and self-hypnosis. Otherwise, I seem to experience some degree of "feeling" anxious much of the time. My therapist helped me to identify this factor in my personality. Once it was brought into my conscious awareness I vowed to work on it and change it. To accomplish this I am learning more and more to use any state of anxiety as a gauge and as a motivator for change; and I am learning to reduce the degree of anxiety I feel by identifying and understanding the emotions underlying and fueling it. I do this during meditation by telling myself I am actually "rewiring" my brain to function from a level of calm rather than from a level of anxiety. This is an especially useful tool for visualization during both meditation and self-hypnosis. The effort is a very conscious one, and one which takes a great deal of practice. But with time I find this process of working to calm myself down is becoming more second nature, like the anxiety has been in the past.

I am also learning to allow myself time to process feelings and review negative experiences from the past as a way of understanding them and learning from them. In other words I allow myself to stress out a little at a time without stressing out about the fact I am stressing out. This comes after the awareness that my state of anxiety is telling me there is more to learn. I no longer see anxious depression as something to be acted out. I see it as an opportunity to find increased understanding for the purpose of re-parenting myself and simplifying my emotional nature. It is nothing more than a process of undoing the damage which was done to me unintentionally by my parents and undoing damage which also resulted from the events in my life which I could not control or avoid.

This chapter is one of the most important in the book simply because the RFLAGS Model is the core to understanding all of the material. You will likely want to refer back to this chapter from time to time for further clarification as we move through the other parts of the overall concept. We will now move backwards to see how the negative emotions develop and where they come from. So, hold onto your hats. For some of us this will be a bumpy, yet exciting and enlightening ride!

Chapter III

Adult Roles and Responsibilities

Now that we have looked at and understood the RFLAGS Model it is time to back up and see how the negative emotions (FLAGS) develop. In this chapter we will explore what we as adults should be doing compared to the reality of what we actually are doing in many cases. All of us should take our role as adults in the lives of children very seriously. This is true regardless of whether the role is that of a parent, grandparent, aunt, uncle, teacher, administrator, law enforcement official, counselor, therapist, social worker, lawyer, judge, clergy, volunteer/mentor, or any other type of authority figure or role model. Children will model what they see as their only way of acquiring new behaviors and coping styles. As adults it is important to remember we are modeling something at all times. My hope is we will all work to make sure we are modeling positive characteristics rather than negative ones.

During my years of training and work experience in the field of psychology I have had many occasions to study and learn about human behavior. As I mentioned earlier everyone is a product of both their genetic predisposition's and of the environmental factors present in our lives. With regard to environmental factors, I think everyone agrees the years since World War II have been filled with many rapidly changing aspects. Of particular importance are the emphases on human rights in all regards, and the advances in technology. In my lifetime I have seen societal values swing from the extreme right to the extreme left and back to the right, with both extremes being dangerous and destructive relative to emotional/psychological well being. I believe we are currently witnessing and participating in a balancing act whereby we are seeking a somewhat middle ground which can facilitate the most beneficial stance for healthy growth and development for people of all ages.

The changes I am most concerned with are those changes which have affected, and continue to affect, "the family", even as the traditional definition of "family" continues to evolve and change. Over the last few decades we have watched as families changed from working father and mom at home, to both parents having to work for families to survive economically. From there we went to an unprecedented decline in family stability as evidenced by rapidly rising rates of separation and divorce. The statistics we see today relative to such factors as violence, youth "at risk", and teen pregnancy all result from the world which we as adults have created for "our" children. I use the word "our" to emphasize the global responsibility each of us has to create a safe and hopeful environment in which "our" children can live and grow. As adults we have not done a very good job in recent years of creating such a world.

On the other hand I do not believe our adult predecessors did such a good job either. If you were born and raised prior to the 1970's there were few laws to protect children or women from abuse. People turned their heads away from all forms of domestic victimization believing these issues to be a "private family matter". This was a time in the United States of America when white men ruled supreme and control over kids was intended to break wills and bring them into submission and into compliance with the rules. Religion even found ways to justify abuse and victimization toward women, children, and people of "color". This was a time of boom rather than bust for some, and a time of increasing educational opportunities for young people, opening their eyes to many of the world's injustices.

During this time and since, attempts have been and are being made to redefine respect, fairness and acceptance as significant, but almost unconscious issues. We talk about these issues as they pertain to conscious human and civil rights outside of the home. However, I believe there was, and is, a struggle for equality going on inside the home as well. This is especially true with children who have gained enough sophistication in recent years to understand that respect toward anyone, even toward adults, must be won rather than demanded or expected as some kind of entitlement which somehow comes with adult status. Kids are way ahead of adults in this regard. This is evident as adults struggle within all contexts to retain positions and powers of unquestionable authority and control. For instance,

I was taught to respect all adults without questioning their respectability. Failure to do so resulted in rather severe consequences within any setting or context. These kinds of one-up approaches toward kids no longer work. This fact needs to be accepted and dealt with as an obvious factor within today's reality.

During the decades since the 1960's adults in many roles taught us by example to be materialistic, hedonistic, self-absorbed, selfish, and uninvolved or under involved relative to our responsibilities to one another. People wanted to give children everything they never had, and in so doing took away some of the very principles needed to survive and grow. Such principles include: a work ethic; delayed gratification; regard for human life; and common sense fear which in the past kept many of us from experimenting with risky choices which could have proven to be self destructive. Sure we can place responsibility for much of this on the media, movies, music, toy manufacturers, and technology, but who are the profit seeking beings behind these institutions? Adults!

It is my goal in this book to get each of us to examine where we are relative to our roles and responsibilities to and for children. I want each of us to realize that the very problems existing for and with children were created and facilitated by proceeding generations. It is time to stop blaming children for their problems and begin to see our parts in creating those behaviors. It is time to stop expanding juvenile justice lock-down programs and start working as adults to discover the very elements which are missing for ourselves so we can then help teach these values to the children we have neglected and continue to neglect.

The only way to teach such values is to connect children of all ages with positive role models inside and outside the home. Too many of us are detached from our own very real responsibility for the chaos and violence we see in the lives of children today. This is something I see very clearly being modeled and reflected in the lives of children who take no responsibility for their actions either. Rather than seek to "fix" ourselves as adults, we seek opportunities to "fix" the children in ways where we as adults do not have to be involved, generally because we are too busy and too detached to see the truth. There is also the factor in many instances where adults are uninvolved simply because they are so self absorbed and choose to listen to the messages of punish, conquer, and control; rather than assist, guide, respect, and redirect.

As indicated previously, I believe many adults seem to have a feeling of arrogance and entitlement relative to respect from kids. The old "just because I said so" attitude doesn't work anymore. Kids are too sophisticated for that. Even kids know they have the right to be treated with respect. After all, they are simply adults in the making. The old ways of beating, yelling, threatening, and intimidating required very little time. With the right combination of these destructive approaches any child could be brought under "control", or, rather, into compliance and submission. With the exception of my maternal grandmother, my parents and other adults involved in my childhood were unbelievably adept in convincing themselves that their negative approaches to child rearing were right. They were also adept in their denial that children have emotional needs which must be recognized and attended to with care. Failure to fulfill our roles and responsibilities results in permanent scarring which will impact a child negatively on into adulthood, thereby creating the FLAGS.

I believe many adults use kids as a punching bag, both literally and figuratively, upon which to act out their own emotion-based anxiety resulting from various unresolved issues. Rather than take the time to learn new approaches to interaction and communication between kids and adults, many adults still resort to the outmoded standards that didn't really work in the past. After all, 'who are children anyway, that I should take time out of my materialistic pursuits of pleasure and satisfaction to fulfill my unspoken obligation to be an effective role model?' I see this quite often in schools where some teachers seem to be more interested in control than they are in teaching. For some educators, as with others in positions of authority over children, respect is demanded and expected, rather than earned. Think about the arrogance of many law enforcement officials as well who feel because they enforce the law they are entitled to also be above the law within their codes of silence and "good ol' boy/girl" networks. I see this quite often within juvenile justice systems as I follow the progression of kids from arrest to juvenile hall, through the court process, and on to sentencing. Control by adults within these settings needs to be monitored carefully and regularly. Those in any position of power and authority/control which can be used abusively should be reprimanded and removed when necessary if they are unwilling to comply with reasonable, ethical principles and standards. Overloaded systems are no justification for preying upon the vulnerability of minors, regardless of their patterns of acting out emotion-based anxiety, simply for the sake oftentimes of money, numbers, job security, and politics.

Respect is never a given in any situation. I cannot respect anyone whom I fear or hate for trying to bring me into submission before they are willing to interact with me in a positive and respectful manner. This seems to represent some kind of need to first establish a one-up position which is beyond challenge. No adult is ever better than any kid or other adult. It is only necessary to impose control onto a situation that is out of control. Once control is appropriately gained, the next step is to establish an atmosphere where an attempt at reasoning and understanding can be made as quickly as possible. This requires mutual consideration and respect which must be initiated and modeled by the adults involved, not demanded from kids first. To demand it from kids sets up the competition, leaving kids with no way to back down with dignity. As adults we often arrogantly demand things we could never expect or even hope to receive from other adults. Simply being an adult doesn't entitle *anyone* to respect!

Those who are jaded beyond any willingness to learn different approaches need to step aside. Educators are important, but only if they are effective in educating students on all levels. From my own experiences of working in the schools in different areas around Southern California and now in the deep south, I have seen many teachers who feel so victimized and unappreciated they hide behind union structures and contracts at the expense of educating children. They often do this rather than deal with the problems in an effective or considerate manner. They often focus so much on themselves as the victim that they fail to see how they in turn victimize the students through a blatant neglect of their responsibilities as teachers. Sometimes those who protest the most are the least effective in their roles as educators. Certainly no one should be victimized; but no one is any more special than any other person. The feeling of being important and essential has in many cases led to arrogance and a sense of entitlement. Many adults cannot stand the fact that respect is no longer a given because of their relative position of authority over kids, or because of their positions in life relative to other adults. Respect is necessary; but it must be earned not demanded. Above all else respect must be reciprocal under the new paradigm of human rights for all children and adults alike.

In my seminars and brochures I use the concept of: "in the competition between ADULTS vs. KIDS, no matter what the score, everyone looses." Really think about what this sentence is saying. In spite of this truth I see on an almost daily basis the struggle by adults to maintain control over kids just for the sake of control. In this kind of battle generally the adult will win, but what have they really gained by proving that in a position of authority I can control a kid? I understand in many settings some degree of control must be established and maintained. However, once that control is achieved the focus needs to then shift to that of modeling and teaching self control through some degree of positive interaction which, again, includes mutual respect and consideration. Systems need to allow for both the training and the time necessary for adults to learn and model such values if kids are to have the opportunity to change their behaviors and learn the values they are otherwise being forced without success to adopt. Being an effective role model is time consuming.

Again, as the title of my book indicates, control simply for the sake of control doesn't work except to gain some degree of compliance or submission which clearly represents the breaking of someone's will. Because the "one-up" position exists in many situations, in my work as a therapist with kids I teach them how to deal with this reality in a manner which will not further complicate their lives. Without the realization by a kid that self-control is a necessary and desirable characteristic in most situations, compliance is nothing more than a one-down position of being at the mercy of an external force which, without submission and obedience, can bring about some negative consequence or punishment. This kind of compliance feels to any individual like they are kissing someone's rear end. While I would never do this myself, in reality I do see the need on occasion to back down from the competition established by another person when it is in my best interest to do so until I can find another solution to the problem. This, however, is much easier for adults than it is for kids. I no longer fight defective systems directly. Instead, I do so through the communities affected and victimized. After all, most systems intruding upon the lives of kids are closed and protected by their own internal codes of silence, cover-up, corruption, and secrecy.

If nothing more is learned by the individual in compliance than external control imposed simply for the sake of control then, once the external force is removed, the source of control is also removed and the individual, whether child or adult, will resume some undesirable, possibly destructive, behavior. Look at how adults are often out of control in their unbridled pursuit of "happiness", consumerism, materialism, and success. For example, this is evident by the number of adults who recklessly and carelessly spend money and are overextended relative to indebtedness. I believe this lack of self control results from either the lack of internal control possibly taught to us when we were the kids, or from the imposition of excessive external control which when removed can lead to a destructive inability to establish appropriate self-control. On a more global scale this is also a risk when world powers intervene in abusive situations in other countries, with the only intent of bringing them into submission. Arrogant nations and world leaders, like individual adults, may be good at problem identification; but are themselves oftentimes still struggling with problem resolution within their own countries. This is as true in America as in any other country in the world.

Experience continues to teach me that any kind of acting out behavior results from the lack of intrinsic self-control which was not successfully taught to us by adults from previous generations. They tried to "scare" us into compliance with the rules through physical and emotional abuse, rather than helping us as young children learn to do things simply for our own best interest and the best interest of others. Or they neglected to teach any form of control at all. Many of the adults today try unsuccessfully to control adolescents for the sake of control. The mistake in this approach is in the lack of ability to enforce such approaches through fear and intimidation available to our predecessors. Thank God children can no longer be beaten, neglected, and ignored without consequences; and thank God people outside the home are no longer given permission to paddle or spank children in school and other settings, with the exception of some religious (faith-based) private schools in this country. These are commonly some of the groups seeking vouchers to support private education.

One additional mistake in this approach of control for the sake of control is the tendency for adults to wait until it is almost too late, during those adolescent years when the need for self-control is so critical. If a child has not learned self-control at an early age there is no point in establishing competition between adults and kids during adolescence in an effort to force control. The only way to deal with adolescents who are out of control is to help them see how being out of control is complicating *their* lives. It is necessary to give kids the opportunity to see how their actions are not getting them any of the considerations they are demanding. To accomplish this goal the adults must resolve their issues and be in control of their behaviors in order to model and explain appropriate means of gaining consideration and cooperation. Kids need to see that making demands doesn't work for them any more effectively than it does for adults. Please don't misunderstand me. Kids need rules and responsibilities with clear consequences for not following through on reasonable expectations. But, kids also need to have reasonable opportunities to gain rewards for positive behaviors.

Don't use guilt and shame by asking kids to feel sorry for adults in the sense of owing adults some consideration, especially when the child feels the consideration given to them previously in the form of unchecked, unsupervised freedom is being withdrawn. At this point parents and other adults must take the time to learn to communicate with and reason with any kid who is out of control, rather than panic and try to enforce control which never existed previously, or existed only on a limited basis. If given the opportunity to do so, many kids will eventually calm down and listen if they are approached from a position of respect relative to the fact kids are nothing less than future adults and human beings who deserve to be treated fairly. Realistically, kids need to see the advantages to *them* of behaving in an appropriate manner both in the present and into the future. Furthermore, kids and adults must learn to deal with boredom and frustration in an effective, rather than destructive manner, sometimes by simply learning to tolerate and learn from these aspects of life. Both can serve to motivate in positive ways if looked at in a different light.

My fear is that adults do not want to take the time out of their already busy schedules to learn new approaches to deal effectively with kids regardless of the role the adult plays in a kid's life. By writing this book I truly hope to give everyone an opportunity to understand that child-rearing principles are actually quite simple, though not necessarily easy. No one is exempt from responsibility for the well being of kids, even if only in some indirect manner, if there is such a thing. The complex task is that of unlearning negative patterns of interaction from the past and replacing those with the simple concepts found within these pages. The initial investment of time will be the most significant, because with time the ability to improve interactions between adults and kids will drastically reduce the wasted time and energy spent in conflict and open competition between adults and kids. Kids don't like chaos in their lives anymore than adults and will readily admit this when asked.

The most basic task is to make the new concepts as automatic and unconscious as the dysfunctional approaches already are; i.e. replace the old with the new on a conscious level until the new becomes second nature. My basic philosophy in working with adults and kids is: "if it hasn't worked so far, it probably will not work in the future. Therefore, rather than continue wasting energy by doing the same things, why not try something new?" I find most adults and kids to be very open to the possibility of making life simpler. This is what my work and writings are all about.

As we think about what adults should be doing as opposed to the reality of what we are actually doing in many cases, remember the use of labels we addressed in a previous chapter. I firmly believe the labels we use with kids and the categories into which we try to stick them reflects our general view of kids and our corresponding awareness of the kinds of responsibilities we believe we have toward them. If we think of kids only as "bad kids", "incorrigibles", or the "problem child", we will focus our attention and efforts only on the behaviors a kid exhibits. Our first goal should be that of looking beyond the negative behaviors to actually see the kid and the potential within every child for good.

In therapy with kids I always look to find at least a tiny piece of heart which I can then identify as the true, innate identity of who a child is meant to be or become with appropriate guidance. Also, I work very hard to be aware of the likelihood a child's behaviors may reflect or mask something or some set of factors which are not readily apparent. The phrase "for no apparent reason" doesn't imply there is no reason, only there is no reason that is easily identifiable. Bottom line is, I separate what a kid is doing from who they really are if the behaviors are negative. Every kid deserves that kind of respect and consideration. Kids know, at least on an unconscious level, what unfairness and disregard feels like. No kid will ever be able to interact with an adult in a positive manner if the odds are against the kid in the sense of the kid not having a chance to avoid being misjudged and misunderstood.

Adults in positions of authority generally talk about opposition and defiance from kids without seeing that sometimes this is simply active resistance to a no-win, unfair situation from which the kid cannot escape. So, as a kid why not fight the "opponent" rather than give in? Law enforcement officials frequently resort to this tactic as a means of getting kids to commit crimes so they can then be arrested, rather than helped, and removed from the streets and neighborhoods. Adults need to understand there really is no way to establish limits and boundaries with adolescents who are out of control unless the kid can see there is some benefit to their well being to accept such restrictions. Any victories won during open competition and conflict between adults and kids are only temporary and are of no substance. However, if measures are taken during the earlier childhood years to instill intrinsic morals and values, then competition generally will remain at a lower level than if such groundwork is not laid, simply because one can appeal to the higher nature already established within the kid's psyche. On the other hand, if a positive foundation is not established early on, then adults must work very hard with kids to help them tear down the maladaptive bases and start over from the standpoint of what is in their best interest for now and into the future. The best interest of others will have to come later!

Our first responsibility as adults toward kids is that of questioning and understanding our commitment to kids and our motivation to work with them, regardless of our role(s) in their lives. No matter how indirect our role may be, we still impact the world in which kids are raised. I once heard a therapist refer to kids as "trolls". In another instance someone told me a teacher had referred to a student as an "undesirable element" in the classroom. There is no way anyone with these kinds of prejudices can go into any encounter with a kid and be successful. Labels always reflect prejudices and biases.

Child rearing, a responsibility shared by every individual involved in a child's life, requires an almost selfless approach to giving each child what they need individually in the effort to recognize and nurture both their uniqueness and potential. To do anything less is unjust and immoral. If we cannot be fully committed to giving children the very best care possible to insure healthy spiritual, emotional, intellectual, and psychological development, then we should limit our direct connections with kids. Individuals should not begin to take on the role of becoming parents until they have worked on their own issues and understand the commitment they are (or should be) making to the little ones they will create. This kind of thinking and commitment to individual well being should be taught even during the middle school and early high school years, given the fact that sexual activity often begins now in early adolescence.

Sadly, however, because of so many divisive groups within the political, social and religious contexts in this country, the real tragedy would be in the difficulty of developing a consensus of what the concept and definition of personal well being would actually be. The difficulty would exist within the many hidden and overt agendas which adults in differing factions espouse. This is especially true when considering extreme religious and political biases rather than focusing on common spiritual principles underlying all religions. These principles include: giving unconditional love and acceptance; being non-judgmental; practicing altruism; having an awareness of interconnectedness; and living the concept of Karma which is nothing more than the concepts of "The Golden Rule", or "what goes around comes around". As you can see in this example, the competition between groups exists within other settings and contexts, just as it exists between kids and adults. Part of my purpose in exploring these issues is to increase awareness about the victimization of many individuals and groups taking place within many different arenas. These concepts of victimization within contexts outside of the home will be explored further in a later chapter. Big powerful nations also can be viewed as "adults" with certain roles and responsibilities. Arrogance and ignorance have the same negative results on a much larger scale between countries/societies, and religious and political extremism.

Now that I have explored with you some of the negative factors relative to what adults are often times doing, let's take some time at this point to review the listing of actual Adult Roles and Responsibilities I have included as Appendix E. This list includes as many of the positive things adults should be doing as I have been able to identify to date. As with other lists please understand this list consists only of items identified by me and through the seminars I teach. The list can be amended to include other items that may be identified. Please review this list now.

After reading the first part of this chapter and then considering the list of things we should be doing, some of you may have been shocked at the contrast. In all references I make to the human condition, again please understand I am not judging or blaming. I am simply sharing my perceptions on what I have observed to be reality and truth relative to my own life and what I see exhibited in the lives of others through my personal and professional interactions. Rather than looking to find fault, I am seeking to do problem identification and then problem resolution. I am always open to amending and adapting my perspectives to new realities and truths. Furthermore, I am aware that my own truth is continuously evolving and growing. My goals within this writing are: to teach what I have learned to date; learn from the experience of writing down my own observations and thoughts; and provoke and encourage critical thinking in others. This process begins with individuals and moves out to groups and, in some cases, factions within the contexts identified previously that will be addressed in more detail as we go.

As you carefully look over the list, try to pick out any words or phrases which possibly could be interpreted in different ways by different people or groups. Such words and phrases would include discipline, control, punish, and limit. Each of these concepts has within it an opportunity for abuse/victimization if defined in a negative and inappropriate manner.

Think about the concept of *discipline* and the different contexts and settings in which the word is used. When teaching this segment in my seminars, I always pull these words out and ask people to give me the first words they associate with each of them. Generally, the first word associated with discipline is some form of corporal punishment such as spanking. According to Webster's Dictionary the word "corporal" is defined as: "of, relating to, or affecting the body." Therefore, corporal punishment means bodily or physical punishment usually in some form of hitting, or at least in some form which could either hurt in the sense of abuse and victimization, or lead to death in the sense of corporal punishment as in a death sentence. Don't forget about military discipline that exists for the sole purpose of breaking wills and assuring compliance with orders from superiors during combat situations. This is necessary only in the military and not in other settings, especially involving kids.

Even today in some of the extreme conservative factions, people speak of the need to return to corporal punishment as a way of dealing with problematic behavior. Hopefully each of you will begin to see how this kind of approach or "remedy", if you will, simply involves only the time and effort necessary to hit, yell, and conquer. Nothing is gained and very little time is involved compared to the time it will take for each of us to unlearn inappropriate measures and learn new ones. With these old measures there is no investment of time into the well being of children, who are simply frightened, shamed, outraged, and broken down into compliance and submission. By these means adults can then remain in their positions of authority, arrogance and entitlement, keeping kids in their places of being seen and not heard. It is interesting to me how generally the older adults, people from within male dominated cultures and societies, and those within the contexts of abusive extremist religions who espouse the victimization of those who are different from themselves, are the only ones who adamantly support such notions. Reflected in this as well are varying degrees of education and cultural influences. Hopefully society will eventually progress beyond these puritanical efforts to control others so certain groups can simply maintain their positions of power. This concept can readily be applied on an international basis as well.

Think about figuratively how "corporal punishment" is dealt out within political, social, and religious contexts relative to issues such as race, ethnicity and other forms of diversity such as homosexuality. The goals in many settings of victimizing others is for groups in positions of perceived power to maintain their position by "bodily" or physically keeping others in their "places". Think about it! Was this country founded upon religious freedom as the impetus to leave Europe; or was it founded upon the religious victimization of others with white Anglo Saxon Protestants as religious extremists establishing themselves and their religious beliefs as the ideals? Look at how this kind of thinking continues to be carried out around the world today in the form of terrorism and terrorist acts.

As I near the end of this chapter about Adult Roles and Responsibilities, let me give you two more lists. In the first we can identify factors that constitute the "ideal family" (Appendix F), and in the second explore the mistakes adults are often times making (Appendix G) to varying degrees depending on each respective individual. As you review this second list remember that children have to live with the choices and mistakes made by adults. Children have little or no ability to shield themselves from any chaos created by adults. Therefore, one of the single most important characteristics to be modeled by adults is that of forethought, or the ability to consider the consequences to self and others of any decision to be made. Be sure to compare these lists to the list of things we should be modeling (Appendix E). The contrast is quite extreme between adult roles and responsibilities and the list of mistakes. However, the factors describing and defining the "ideal family", almost parallel the list of adult roles and responsibilities.

I believe these lists speak for themselves and tie very well into the next chapter where we will look at abuse and victimization. The mistakes made by adults generally set the stage for mistreatment, and for inappropriate and ineffective patterns of interactions with kids. Again, keep in mind we are exploring factors which create, establish and perpetuate the negative emotions (FLAGS) which lead to anxiety we then tend to act out in maladaptive and often self-destructive ways. Please see this as nothing more or less than an identification process of the negative factors impacting many of us everyday either as the target/victim, or as the "victimizer". As we learn to live out our appropriate roles and responsibilities we will begin to right the wrongs and move closer to the principles contained within any set of ideals.

Chapter IV

Insult and Injury

After looking at the adult roles and responsibilities, what constitutes the "ideal family", and then at the mistakes often made by adults, we will now look more specifically at abuse and victimization. Remember we are moving from the ideal to the factors existing as reality in many cases. I will use the terms abuse and victimization somewhat interchangeably with more emphasis on the term victimization. I believe most people associate the word abuse with children more than they do with the victimization of adults. Generally the concept of abuse is associated more with child abuse and possibly with spousal abuse or elder abuse, but the term victimization applies to people on all levels, within all contexts and quadrants, and at all ages. Someone or some system victimizes most everyone at some time in their lives. Because I will try in later chapters to connect all of these concepts to larger contexts other than the context of home/family, it is important to use a term to which anyone can relate; and a term that is universally applicable regardless of culture. None of my ideas or theories is intended to be exclusively representative of North American culture as many of the wrongs I am addressing exist within numerous other countries and cultures around the world.

Hopefully, as you read the previous chapters you were able to find connections between the material presented and your own subjective past. Remember there is no such thing as "the perfect family", which exists only as an ideal. Therefore everyone comes from some degree of dysfunction in the sense there is always room for improvement. For some of you this experience may have been somewhat difficult. Again, if this is true I hope you will be aware of any limitations relative to your ability to deal with the intensity of your feelings on your own and that you will seek professional help if necessary. Some of you may already be recognizing the negative feelings of Fear, Loneliness, Anger, Guilt, and Shame (FLAGS). If this is true for you then I would ask you to be careful about how you proceed through this chapter.

Every reader is likely to discover some degree of abuse and victimization not only in her or his past, but possibly in the present as well. Some readers may also discover ways in which you are victimizing others, possibly even on an unconscious level. You may find this to be true within the context of current interactions and situations in the present with spouses, family members (extended or immediate), work associates, classmates, or various social, political, and religious contexts. As you come to not only understand abuse and victimization, but to see it in the things people say and do, you may become stressed beyond your ability to deal with these feelings on your own. If you experience such occurrences of intense anxiety and/or depression, please find a licensed mental health professional that can help you deal with whatever surfaces. Above all, find the courage to face whatever you discover rather than close this book and decide it is all too painful. Remember that courage does not mean facing a situation without fear. Courage means finding the ability to move forward and do what is best *in spite of* the fear which is there. If you are not afraid who needs courage?

Keep in mind that my book will not create any new feelings. My writings and public presentations regarding the RFLAGS Model will only bring into conscious awareness those emotions and memories which already exist. The process presented in the model cannot create histories of abuse/victimization and the resulting FLAGS; however, the recollection of them can be revived. Research to date with the Roberts Grief and Loss Analysis Scale indicates that in a situation where the RGLAS is given prior to and subsequent to the formal presentation of the entire RFLAGS Model, some scores may actually decline (worsen) at posttest. This possibly indicates that one's history of abuse and victimization may have been ignored as something either too painful or irrelevant, with the significance being realized by participation in the seminar. Don't be afraid to proceed; just be cautious. Be especially careful not to feel guilty or ashamed of feelings and thoughts that emerge. Remember we are only identifying your subjective experiences and emotions relative to the past. We are looking only to see if, how, and to what extent the past continues to live in our present often times without our conscious awareness of it. We are not looking for opportunities to blame or judge, only for opportunities to identify and understand.

Allow me to state again that many people, including adolescents, tell me they do not want to relive the past. As I stated earlier I agree with this sentiment. However, I believe it is critical to identify at least enough of the past to understand the dynamics and the sources of current distress. This is necessary even if that distress exists only on an unconscious basis fueling our current anxiety and motivating our acting out behaviors and feelings of hopelessness without our conscious control or understanding. This is the concept of being at the mercy of factors outside of ourselves (externals). The fear of looking at the past is what keeps many of us locked into current patterns of repeating the same mistakes over and over again. It also keeps us believing we are trapped and cannot make desired changes. This fear also keeps us from exploring, nurturing, and reaching the full potential within ourselves and in the children for whom we bear the responsibility of being positive role models regardless of our connection.

Remember, too, that none of this is about bashing or hating. By identifying the reality of the past and possibly the present, you will likely learn about characteristics of significant people from the past that you may not like. As stated previously I believe it is always necessary to try and separate what people do from who they are. As you try to do this keep in mind you may find this to be much more difficult with adults because behaviors of adults tend to be more permanent, and tend to also more accurately represent the personalities of the individuals. The point I am trying to make is that the possibility exists of loving someone such as parents, siblings, spouses, and other significant individuals, but not being able to like who they are, what they do, or have done. Often times the rage associated with all of this results from the feeling these individuals got away with what they did or are still doing, with no accountability for their actions or the results of their victimization of others. Within this rage you can see the resentment toward the arrogance and feelings of entitlement with which adults do their misdeeds toward children, and misdeeds toward other adults whom they treat like children. This rage and resentment represents the abuse and victimization addressed within this chapter.

Dr. David L. Roberts Ph.D.

Allow me to address a little further the personalities of abusive individuals who feel the need to victimize and control others. Within the field of psychology, therapists currently use the Diagnostic and Statistical Manual, Fourth Edition (DSM-IV-TR) - which gets revised periodically - as a guide for diagnosing all forms of psychiatric and psychological disorders such as mental, emotional, intellectual, developmental, personality, and those related to substance use and dependence. Prior to the release of the current edition efforts were made to reevaluate symptoms and categories of disorders. During this process many revisions were made and several new disorders were proposed, especially related to disorders of personality which are diagnosed only for adults. Anyone who reads the DSM-IV-TR (and I am not suggesting you do so) will find some aspects of their own personalities within its pages. This means nothing more than identifying unhealthy aspects of human nature. Symptoms have to be pervasive and prove to be interfering with healthy functioning to be considered as diagnoses. The fact that personality disorders are assigned only to adults further substantiates my belief in the opportunities we have to help improve the ways kids live their lives. We can do this before their behaviors become more permanent parts of the adult psyche and develop into symptoms of more permanent forms of maladaptive adult functioning and coping styles which constitute personality disorders.

Since I began my studies in psychology I have learned to identify the problematic personality traits exhibited by families presenting with extreme symptoms of dysfunction. The main negative characteristics or traits exhibited by many moms within these families include:

intense changes in mood ranging from relative calm to intense rage;
a limited perception of people as either all good or all bad, with no gray areas;
histories of unstable relationships;
various forms of manipulation and divisiveness which serve to protect a position of power and control over people and keep them loyal;
creating chaos in her life and in the lives of others;
being openly hostile and cruel; experiencing only shallow emotions which change rapidly;
displaying dramatic and over exaggerated emotions when provoked or threatened;

having little or no capacity for enjoyment of life;
expressing a very negative outlook for present and future situations prior to death;
easily influenced by others;
being confrontational;
blaming others for her problems;
denying responsibility for her actions;
and preoccupied with being scrutinized and judged by others.

Deep within their souls many mothers possess the capacity to love and have fun. I am not questioning their love, only the capacity to deal effectively with life and those around them. There is generally no conscious ill intent. However, they often hurt themselves and those closest to them by an unwillingness to learn from mistakes and to resolve issues from early childhood on into adulthood. Often they believe the pain and unresolved issues from the past are too frightening to face and then work through effectively and successfully. Many also believe there is no need for improvement and everyone else has problems, but "not me". It is easy for people with maladaptive characteristics and coping styles to switch quickly from being the victim to being the victimizer.

When religion is involved in the mix it is easier to hide behind religion as the only defense against the onslaught of emotions which loom just below the surface. With this influence people sometimes live to die in the sense of believing there is nothing good in this life, only in the next, which can be descriptively visualized from the symbolic teachings of many religious texts and institutions. Because these moms make few efforts to change, children have to deal with many unresolved issues and emotions on into adulthood which could have been eliminated through simple changes in communication, coping styles, and changes in perspective. I believe this to be a very serious and tragic reality within many families. Everyone should be able to look into the faces of deceased parents without regret and resentment, but this is often not the case.

Dads directly involved in families often display some of the same characteristics as the moms within extremely dysfunctional family environments. However, their overall personality and ways of dealing with life can be quite different in the manner in which they are manifested. These characteristics or traits include:

feelings of self importance;
preoccupation with status in the community relative to what others think;
having a sense of entitlement;
feeling special and superior;
displaying arrogance relative to race, women and children;
using fear and intimidation to control;
publicly humiliating others;
being unpredictable with regards to when (not if) extreme rage will be expressed;
being unnecessarily defensive;
being intentionally cruel in order to dominate and force others into submission;
remaining emotionally unavailable and uninvolved;
taking no responsibility for the pain caused to others;
possessing no interest in opinions of others which differ from his;
exhibiting no expression of any emotion which could be interpreted as weakness;
being physically and emotionally abusive;
remaining aloof and uninvolved as a way of avoiding conflict;
seeing himself as the peacemaker with his ability to control by fear;
demanding respect without regard to respectability;
and sometimes believing that his role of father includes only responsibilities for
providing discipline and material needs.

    I share all of this information about personalities and parenting styles not only in an effort to understand it better myself, but to help each of you realize that I have come to understand what I teach through all of my personal and professional experiences. I write also with the hope every reader will make efforts to heal relationships in this life before it is too late. Even more importantly, I write to help others recognize and avoid these kinds of mistakes and injustices and be able to create very positive relationships from the beginning, with only minimal need to correct things in the future.

ProKids, Inc.; The Message and The Movement

The Past that Lived in my Present

Unfortunately, the personalities described above represent many of the characteristics of people I knew when I was growing up in the South during the mid 1950's, 60's, and early 70's. My memories especially from age four on are anything but positive, with continuing efforts from my parents to hurt and isolate me. Most prominent are the memories of abuse, which only changed as I got older to be less and less physical, but always and increasingly emotional. Until I was 14 years old, my dad would whip my brother and me with the same belt and in the same manner as he would whip his hunting dogs. He beat them to break their wills and to bring them into submission and control. As with us, when he whipped the dogs for barking or otherwise disobeying, he would yell at them stating how sorry they would be if they ever disobeyed him again. I saw this and heard this on many occasions even though I tried to hide or block the noise while I cried. Even now, just recalling these memories my hands tremble, I feel sick at my stomach, and I have tears to my eyes.

My mother's abuse of us, while oftentimes physical couldn't compare to the abuse from my dad. Mom's abuse was more often emotional, especially in the use of my dad as a way to scare us and to make sure we "got it" when he got home, oftentimes after she had already slapped us around and whipped us herself. She would make us wait and worry anywhere from a few hours to a few days, seeming to enjoy torturing us and watching us try to appease her with the hope she wouldn't tell. The physical abuse toward me stopped at age 14 when I physically challenged both of them. My dad always reminded me after that point not to think I would ever be too big for him to take me down. I believe that the abuse toward me and my brother was their way of physically acting out the conflict between them and within their marriage, and because of their own histories of abuse and victimization.

Can you see how this required relatively little time on their parts, and yet had a very devastating and lasting effect on my brother and me? Their failure to work out their feelings from having been abused as children and their marital conflicts makes this all the more infuriating. Just because they could treat us this way doesn't mean they should have done so. There are no excuses for this, only ways to identify it and try to understand it in an effort of trying to move beyond it. My parents generally did not admit remembering most of what they did, with my mom excusing it as having said and done things when she was angry which she "really didn't mean". Can you feel how insulting that is? My dad on the other hand did acknowledge his part of this a few years ago when I confronted him, but offered no apology. He actually had the nerve to say "we had a lot of love in this house." Ironically, people in our community thought we had the perfect family and that my brother and I were very well behaved. They didn't understand the severe consequences we faced for getting out of line.

The result of the kinds of problems created for me by my parents' dysfunction showed up in the form of intense anxiety and self-doubt. The personality characteristics of this "underdog" position took hold and required a lot of work initially to undo and repair the damage. I had no self-confidence and actually came to believe as truth almost all of the negative things said and done to me when I was growing up. For most of my life I have lived with a sense of impending doom, believing nothing would ever work out for me. My life during childhood was based in deprivation and an intense fear of unpredictable situations and people. These factors continued to haunt me as an adult. The one thing I take a great deal of credit for is the fact I have never let fear stop me. I have always found the courage to move forward in spite of fear.

I know what I know by experience and by the effort I have put into understanding and resolving my dysfunctional past through my own personal therapy, and through education and job experience within the field of psychology. None of this has come easy for me, and I hope my sharing of these personal details will help others move forward more quickly in their own process of self examination and resolution. This is extremely important both for the sake of individuals and for the sake of children who will be impacted by our adult lives. As we move through the remaining sections of this chapter each of you will see how the negative emotions (FLAGS) develop, and how unfair it is to subject children to our unresolved grief and losses from the past.

Before we move into an open discussion of abuse and victimization, take a few minutes to study another of my many, yet important lists (Appendix H). This one is about Kids Roles and Responsibilities, in the sense of what children are suppose to be able to do. As you read it think about how a perfect world for children would look, compared to the reality of the environments in which many children are raised. It isn't enough for adults to say: "We didn't mean to." There is no justification for not giving children what they need. There are, however, many reasons why children act out their emotion-based anxiety which results from not having the necessary nurturing and modeling to give them a good start in life. One of my main goals is to move people away from their sense of arrogance and entitlement which allows them to seek opportunities to deny responsibility for the problems kids have and to blame kids for everything they, as kids, are doing wrong. As you look over the list think about your childhood relative to your opportunities just to be a kid. Also be aware of how simple the lives of kids are supposed to be from infancy into young adulthood.

Now let's move carefully into the very unpleasant realities of abuse and victimization. There are actually four types of abuse: sexual, physical, emotional, and neglect. My distinction between the first three and the last is that sexual abuse, physical abuse, and emotional abuse are all very active forms of abuse. They constitute an almost unlimited number of bad things done or said to others. Neglect, on the other hand, is very passive in that good things which should be done, said, or provided to others are withheld, either intentionally or unconsciously.

I am not going to spend a great deal of time on sexual and physical abuse. Everyone knows what these are about, and I see no need to relate disturbing details from cases I have had over the years of working with kids and families in the field of psychology. There are, however, a few important observations I would like to share about these two forms of abuse and victimization.

First of all, sexual abuse is by far the most traumatic because it includes all four forms of abuse. It is, of course, always sexual. It also always includes a physical assault and invasion. And, it is always emotionally abusive considering the threats which usually follow, along with the message, whether spoken or unspoken, that the victim is nothing more than an object to which anything can be done. This indicates there really is no sense of you and me, only a sense of you as what I want with no regard to you as an individual thereby neglecting many childhood needs. Adults who sexually abuse children are simply attracted to children as sexual objects regardless of how they may attempt to rationalize this in their minds. Any consideration of sexual orientation is secondary to the child being the stimulus for sexual arousal. Men and women molest children as sexual objects regardless of whether they are gay, straight, or bisexual. In my opinion, adults attracted to children as sexual objects constitute a different categorization without any regard to sexual orientation and more along the lines of children as objects of sexual attraction similar to fetishes. Appropriate labels would be heterosexual, bisexual, or and homosexual predators.

The second category, physical victimization, is, of course, always physical, and is always emotionally abusive as well and, thereby, neglectful. No one who physically abuses others, regardless of age, does so without the result of emotionally scarring the victim. Along with the physical abuse comes a long list of messages that generally are expressed verbally as the physical abuse is being administered. After all, a rational, calm individual never conducts physical abuse. The abuser or victimizer is generally angry or enraged, and out of control, or sometimes mentally or emotionally disturbed. No history of the abuser having been abused excuses an abuser from their deeds, regardless of the form the abuse takes. Clearly, abuse, even in the form of emotional abuse is inexcusable.

Emotional abuse or victimization is the literal act of adding *insult to injury*. Included in my definition of emotional abuse are the other commonly used terms of "mental" and "verbal" abuse. While emotional abuse is only emotional abuse, it is what cuts into the core of who we come to believe we are relative to issues of self-esteem, self-worth, and self-confidence. When coupled with the other forms of abuse, including neglect, the damage is only intensified on all levels. People, especially those in positions of power and authority, often use emotional abuse as a way of trying to shame others into doing the right things. This of course, never works. It only serves to establish the FLAGS that lead to anxiety/depression, hopelessness/helplessness, and the development of various acting-out behaviors.

Even if the active forms of sexual and physical abuse never occur, the abuse and victimization from being neglected is emotionally damaging as well. Clearly, as a child, my parents provided everything I needed materially with respect to clothes, food and shelter. However, after age four they rarely ever provided any form of emotional support and nurturing I needed to become a psychologically healthy, high-functioning adult. Neglect can also include the failure to provide even the basic emotional/psychological necessities. This is where the element of investing time comes into play, because neglect sends the emotional message that an individual is not worth the time and effort it would take to provide for them relative to all aspects of physical and psychological well being. Neglect, is therefore, emotionally abusive as well, and can be physically abusive if basic physical needs are not being met. Neglect results from individuals who are too self-absorbed or too emotionally or mentally impaired to care for others for whom they are responsible. One of my basic premises in this book is that adults are neglecting the needs of children and often times the needs of other adults with whom they may be connected.

Having addressed all four forms of abuse, I want to really concentrate on emotional abuse (Appendix I) because of the capability emotional victimization has to put the nails in the coffin, so to speak, in the sense of sealing one's fate. For this segment I want you to go back carefully and courageously in time to your childhood and recall the abusive things said to you by other people who played significant roles in your life, and in your subjective history. I want you to see how emotional abuse really reinforces all other negative experiences you have had or may experience in the future. I want you to be aware that we never forget the hurtful things done and said in the past. And I want you to be painfully aware of any emotional abuse you may inflict upon others. Even when people are not resorting to sexual or physical abuse, emotional abuse is now the first effort made in many cases and contexts to bring someone into submission. I see this quite often between adults and kids within all contexts. Again, keep in mind how any form of abuse/victimization fuels the FLAGS, and how little time is involved or invested in such abusive efforts. There is, however, a great deal of wasted energy which could be used more effectively to learn new approaches and deal with unresolved issues. Unfortunately, few people see this as a desirable or even necessary alternative, and continue the attempt to make a process work which is doomed for continued failure and frustration.

Even though there are laws against sexual and physical abuse, and physical neglect, there are no easily enforceable laws against emotional abuse or neglect. Because of this we need to assume and establish some moral and ethical "laws" which will dictate the need to stop the emotional victimization of others as well. Emotional victimization serves no purpose other than to inflict mental or psychological pain upon others. It is used as a means of trying to intimidate and control, and to "challenge" others to do well. Emotional abuse tends to be handed down from one generation to another, often times with us as adults using the same words and phrases upon others we heard as kids from significant adults in our lives.

As you review the next list (Appendix I) think about the three types of abusers/victimizers I have been able to identify. First, there are those who abuse from positions of power and an arrogant sense of entitlement. Then, there are those who are acting out their own FLAGS which exist in the present because they remain unresolved. When drugs and alcohol are added to the mix for this abuser (male or female) the victimization is generally more intense and violent. The third abuser is the one who acts out a history of abuse toward others modeled for them by others and sometimes culturally sanctioned. Included for the victim(s) of this person could be a need to act out their FLAGS resulting from current abuse by victimizing others who are vulnerable to them. This is especially true in situations of domestic violence, and on a more global scale of victimization perpetrated on groups by people in social, political, and religious positions of power and domination.

I have included another list (Appendix J) of just such terms and phrases which are designed to serve any number of negative purposes. Keep in mind that any form of abuse usually occurs during times of intense emotion and is a form of acting out emotion-based anxiety within the abuser. Therefore, the more intense the emotional basis, the more intense the abuse or victimization is likely to be. This can be said of any form of acting out or maladaptive behavior. Again, look for familiar items in the list, and add any items to the list which have not been included to date. Sadly enough this list is the longest one in the entire book.

Generally, there is one question that precedes any abusive statement. That question is: "What's wrong with you?" For me this question was always coupled with the word "boy". As soon as the question is asked, a whole barrage of answers to that question (as indicated in Appendix I) is then thrown at the intended victim. My experience was for these abusive statements to be made to me during the act of physical abuse as well as at other times. It is important to remember that anything said to you abusively is intended only to cause shame and guilt, and should not be looked at as being the truth under those circumstances. The truth is there is *nothing* wrong with you, in the sense of being permanently scarred, which can't be fixed. It is also important to remember that the question in adulthood becomes "what's wrong with <u>me</u>" if you buy into the abuse.

As you looked over the list you may have seen some phrases which didn't sound especially abusive. There are times when some of these statements may actually be a true observation of someone's behavior. Remember the statements are abusive only if they are negative in connotation and context, and/or based in negative emotions. Statements, which are simply expressed as observations based in fact, are not necessarily abusive. However, there is always a fine line within situations that tend to be abusive. Even if someone experiences only emotional abuse the damage to one's self image, self-confidence, and self-esteem can still be extreme.

Emotional abuse is now used as a replacement for physical punishment in many cases. Many adults in varying roles resort to emotional victimization as a means of trying to motivate changes in behavior. Think about the level of disrespect and disregard conveyed to the intended victim of such tactics. Also think of how impossible it would be to respect anyone who is putting you down, especially when the abuse is directed at a child from an adult. Generally, adults will not take abuse from other adults, and children will not take abuse from other children. Why, then, would we expect children to take abuse from adults?

It is important to see the desperation represented by the use of emotional victimization. When adults have failed to give young children the proper guidelines, limits and structure prior to adolescence, many adults engage in open conflict and competition with children and teenagers in an effort to bring them under control. Because kids are too sophisticated to fall for the "old ways", everyone loses in this type of interaction. This endeavor is futile and will only lead to further rifts between adults and kids. Kids may comply, but will likely do so with resentment and hatred toward the adult or even toward any abusive system. After all, please do not limit your application of any of these writings to problems between parents and their children. Open your understanding to include all contexts or settings where abuse and victimization can occur. Also include interactions between many different age groups and levels. The concept of differing contexts will be covered more fully in the next chapter and later chapters as well.

One last consideration in this chapter is that of the purposes of abuse and victimization (Appendix J). If there were no purposes served then abuse and victimization would be pointless. While I have already addressed such purposes in general terms, please take a few minutes to look over the last list for this chapter which specifically names many of these purposes. As with other lists you may be able to identify a few purposes not listed.

With these ideas in mind of possible purposes served by abuse and victimization, let's now move into the area of contexts where abuse and victimization can occur. I will attempt to connect all of this to the various settings in which people of all ages and considerations are targeted and mistreated. Hopefully, my writings will open up new perspectives and will motivate discussion about how to identify and change current patterns evident within all contexts where human nature and the FLAGS are acted out.

Chapter V

Contexts of Abuse and Victimization

In previous chapters I have referred several times to the notion of contexts in which abuse and victimization can occur. In this chapter I want to continue with this idea in an effort to expand on my application of the RFLAGS Model to settings outside of the home/family context which is the first of the six contexts I have identified. Such expansion is a relatively new endeavor in this project, though it has been one of my intentions all along. I have only begun exploring the concept of such applicability during lectures and seminars in recent years. Therefore, at this point in time, my efforts to some extent may be rather tenuous and certainly exploratory in nature. Hopefully I can stir up enough controversy to provoke discussion and further exploration and application of my proposals within all of these other contexts. Nothing within these chapters is intended to offend or single out any specific groups or individuals. My intentions are to identify and resolve misuses of power and authority at all levels and in all settings. Believe me I like a bit of a challenge in life, and I see the taking of certain risks as both exciting and necessary in order to promote growth and stop the abuse and victimization of all those who are vulnerable.

Much of the credibility for some of the statements made in this book is a direct result of the awarenesses I gain through my work with kids and families as they try to navigate successfully through various agencies, institutions, and organizations. This is particularly true from this point on through the end of the text. Because some of my suspicions are difficult to prove I bring them into this writing because if they are accurate, then people, especially in low-income families, are in many cases being unjustly and more frequently targeted. Anytime adults with abusive tendencies are in charge there is always the possibility of victimization rather than assistance. Reflected within this statement is the true nature of such individuals to control and dominate rather than to assist and guide. While suspicions are by nature difficult to prove, they are often worthy of investigation. Children are easy targets for abuse within the contexts outside the home/family. This is not only possible, but is very likely because children are minors and their records in any setting, especially educational and justice related, are protected in many cases more than the kids are protected. What a great way to avoid objective and unbiased outside oversight and scrutiny.

The six contexts I have identified relative to my RFLAGS Model in which abuse and victimization can occur are: home/family, school, community, society, politics, and religion. I believe these contexts to be rather universal, and to be inclusive of all possible considerations relative to abuse and victimization. As I attempt to identify their composition remember they are listed in an order of movement away from and outside of the home/family context relative to growth and chronological development. The contexts are also listed ranging from subsystems to larger and more universal systems which have their own sets of subsystems. They move away from the subjective and limited exposure during childhood to a more adult perspective of exposure and later involvement in more complex arenas. "School" refers to the formal educational process that usually ends in late adolescence or early adulthood, and pertains generally to chronological considerations prior to or associated with those ages. It is the only category that is somewhat restricted experientially. The other contexts remain constant categories throughout life, and are to be seen as dynamic and ever changing.

The home/family context is just what it sounds like. It is constant in the sense one generally always has a home/family context in which to live. Certainly, one is always affected by this context even in adulthood by any remnants from the childhood home/family context. As people advance into adulthood and old age, the exact nature or composition of this context changes. It generally expands into our own adult home/family context which we create, then to the expansion of this context into the additional home/family contexts and constellations created by any future generations. One important realization is how the definition of home/family constantly evolves and changes to include previously non-traditional factors relative to composition and newer traditions. Reorganization and redefinition of the home/family context reflects the spiritual evolution of our existence away from arrogance and entitlement to more inclusive viewpoints relative to the diversity found within all aspects of human nature. Such a process moves us away from restriction and closed mindedness into an atmosphere of fewer prejudices and greater opportunities for more rapid spiritual growth by allowing for greater expression of human differences in perspective and lifestyle. The ideal home/family context should be the model for the other contexts with regard to basic well being and positive human interaction.

Clearly the home/family context is the most important context relative to emotional, psychological, and spiritual well being. Relative to size and number, this context is much smaller in scope than the others, but not in its impact on individuals, compared to the other contexts. With regard to impact on individuals, it is extremely important to understand the role of the home/family on preparing people to face the complications present within the other contexts. If the home/family context is not safe and nurturing, then the individuals living within this context will be unprepared to successfully face the larger contexts. After all, it is likely everyone will face some degree of abuse and victimization in the outside world. This fact alone further substantiates the need for adults in the home/family to be effective role models, and the need for the home/family environment to be a safe haven to which we can return when the outside world attacks.

For children, the next context outside of the home/family to which they are forcefully exposed is that of school. With exposure to school comes the rapid exposure to and influences from the other contexts. Generally speaking, prior to starting school, exposure to the other contexts has been somewhat limited and certainly biased and often controlled by the adults immediately present in children's lives. Hopefully, as children venture out into the world they have been given a secure basis within the home/family to give them the ability, confidence, and courage with which to explore the other contexts. Hopefully, too, the home/family context will be a stable environment which models appropriate standards, patterns of interaction and coping strategies for children and for society at large. The ideal of a nurturing, loving, accepting family should be the model for how we treat each other in the world as well. Like the Pointer Sisters sang years ago, "we are family", especially in the sense we are all related on a spiritual level.

Dr. David L. Roberts Ph.D.

Prior to an introduction into the school context, it is likely children will have had some exposure to: societal expectations and realities; adult religious and political beliefs; and to the context of community through general adventures into various community settings, as well as through the media. Some associations relative to the outside world already will have been revealed to children through the experiences of significant adults as children witness, with limited ability to understand, the adult attempts to successfully navigate through the other contexts. This is a major part of the whole concept of being role models. Children learn from our experiences as we display those experiences to them through our actions and attitudes; our biases and prejudices; and certainly through our reactions to and interactions with children in the home/family environment.

One concern I have for school systems in general is possible abuse/victimization in the form of denial of rights to children of low-income families who are viewed and labeled as troublemakers, bad kids, and lost causes. The current trend seems to be that of suspending or expelling these kids from districts for any reason imaginable. I am sure that in all cases these so-labeled kids and their families are not even fully informed about due process. Low-income families, especially from cultures which blindly accept rather than question authority, would be easy targets for this type of victimization when it is occurring. School systems, especially during times of conservative political influence, need to be monitored by independent parties/boards who could objectively scrutinize the implementation of educational policies. This is necessary if kids are to be protected from any misuse of power and authority. If money was reallocated at all levels to intervene in the lives of kids who are troubled, then schools could set up programs to help these kids succeed rather than make efforts to get rid of them. Simply questioning families whose kids get suspended frequently and expelled would likely reveal the misuse of power in a significant number of cases. Closed systems are always dangerous and injurious!

Now let's consider the context of community and the various elements it contains. My definition of community includes the geographic area in which we live, work, play, attend school, and socialize. Communities are composed of various businesses and organizations which help to determine the overall attitude predominant within that area relative to societal, religious, and political views. Many of us even choose our community relative to various factors which we feel will best serve our interests and perceived sense of well being and safety. Generally our community reflects our personal values and our biases; or they reflect our socioeconomic level or social class as the other extreme. Choosing a community for many people is a luxury, and is assumed to be a right to which everyone is entitled. Even within the context of community it is possible to see how the issues and elements of the other contexts impact and define the environment of any given community.

Of extreme concern to me is the existence of separatist kinds of communities which are either chosen by middle and upper classes, or are dealt with as inescapable by those who do not have the luxury of choosing their community and are forced to live in less than desirable areas. The desert region of Southern California in which I lived for nine years was a good example of this kind of dichotomy. There was a clear division between the east and west sides of the valley. Lines were drawn both relative to ethnicity and culture, and to socioeconomic status. The valley was littered in the western half with walled communities, which were ever increasing in number. "Locals" and "snow birds" alike inhabited these walled communities. The snow birds were those who "fly" in for the winter months mostly from Canada and the Northwestern and Midwestern states. They were generally retired white couples who usually bring with them all of the prejudices and restrictions from their conservative communities which they sought to recreate there in the desert. Their power was based in their mere numbers and in the very significant part they played in the economic and political considerations in the area.

The eastern half of the valley was primarily composed of people from various Spanish-speaking countries and cultures who generally worked the agricultural and service oriented jobs available to keep the communities in the western region clean and beautiful, and to keep those people comfortable and happy. The west was rapidly creeping into the east as we witnessed a siege of land needed to accommodate the fun-loving and wealthy retirees and tourists. The walled communities within the larger community of the valley only served to separate "us from them". The conservative and frequently bigoted Caucasian people would occasionally come out to enjoy the festivals and cultural events provided by the "others", and then return to their closed-in and sheltered communities.

Even more striking were the differences between groups and communities within the larger cities such as the Los Angeles area. While living there I was shocked to realize that many of the kids I worked with in East Los Angeles had never even been to the Pacific Ocean, no more than 10 to 15 miles away. Community issues are so much harsher in areas where people who are below the poverty level live in overcrowded conditions with very limited options and opportunities. Even transportation can be a serious obstacle for people who want a job, a better job, or more education and job training.

Because obstacles are oftentimes so huge, it is difficult to motivate kids and adults in these low income areas to seek out available opportunities designed to raise their standards of living. Furthermore, because of a number of different fears it is virtually impossible to get a kid to leave the only familiar environment to become a resident at programs such as Job Corps. For kids and adults within impoverished areas these communities often serve as the only reality or sense of worldview they have. These kinds of factors clearly increase the FLAGS for people who are abused and victimized within all six contexts. So many times in areas of limited opportunities survival needs are quite different and the home/family context is generally dysfunctional allowing for no secure basis to face the other contexts. Also, abuse and victimization simply from life circumstances is significant enough to create an almost endless cycle of abuse and victimization within all arenas because limited options increase, perpetuate, and exacerbate vulnerability.

Regardless of race and ethnicity, these considerations are important from a more universal perspective as I look for correlations and connections between abuse and victimization identified in the home/family context and in those contexts beyond this initial environment. I personally believe the arrogance and sense of entitlement exhibited from the privileged toward the underprivileged and disadvantaged in any geographical area is shameful. These factors resemble the same kind of ignorant arrogance and entitlement exhibited by many adults in general relative to children regardless of ethnicity and culture. I also believe the perceived rewards often associated with being an older Caucasian person – and increasingly by people of other races as well - in the United States have perpetuated the arrogance and sense of entitlement we see being defended so desperately by aging Caucasian groups and other conservatives today. This is evident in struggles to end affirmative action programs, and in attempts to deny basic rights to groups of people through proposals such as Proposition 187, an anti-immigration act in California during the mid 1990's. The big issue for the moment is immigration reform and social classes divided according solely to socioeconomic status.

People no longer want to use the terminology used previously to identify "whites" as the "European Americans" we are. Think about the arrogance with which history has been distorted to imply that Anglos discovered America as though it didn't exist until the Europeans arrived. Those throughout history who have fought for "religious freedom" have been much more savage and barbaric than many of the cultures which they have attempted to dominate and destroy in the name of God or some religion. This distortion is one way I see the dynamics of control and arrogance displayed by many adults on more personal levels being played out in the more universal context of society.

Society, the fourth context, is nothing more than a collection of communities and cultures, or subsystems. Each community represents a certain zeitgeist developing from both internal and external factors which help set certain specific community and social values and mores. Societal values of the identified "majority" are not always accepted by everyone; and, conflicts tend to be acted out within the political and religious contexts when such values are challenged or defended by either of the sides involved. Communities often oppose or ignore certain cultural values and norms that may exist as sub-communities or sub-cultures when compared to the larger context of society which generally sets the tone for what is considered both desirable and acceptable. Often times the values and norms of subcultures are not bad or wrong when compared to what are considered to be the "norm". They are just different, and these sub-communities often exist because the majority culture refuses to acknowledge and incorporate their existence. I am also addressing the fact we are still a very classist society, even in most parts of the world. Please don't think I am promoting a return to communism or a redistribution of wealth. I am simply identifying what I perceive to be divisive factors defining our current reality. Today the term "majority" deceptively refers primarily to people in positions of power and authority who set standards, create policy, and make laws, and yet have little to do with actual numbers of people within any given population. Majority is still tied more to race than to other factors. These are the groups with both the wealth and political power needed to sustain their existence and position.

As is true today with kids being too sophisticated to accept previously assumed practices based in arrogance and entitlement, communities and subcultures are fighting against what has been accepted for a long time as the norm. I believe these are the battles currently being fought within the political and religious contexts as those in perceived control seek to retain control - "those" often being various older Caucasian groups. I also believe these battles by the subcultures in this country began in the 1960's during the various human and civil rights movements. No one can argue with the concept of basic human rights. However, people often feel threatened when rights are sought for specifically named groups such as women's rights or gay rights, which are then perceived as asking for some kind of "special rights", rather than basic human and civil rights.

Much of the discussion and controversy I seek to inspire relative to the different contexts lies in the idea of moving away from power struggles based on "color" issues, or based in outdated puritanical dogma which leads to witch hunts and scapegoating all in the name of some form of God. The movement is toward a consideration and appreciation for diversity associated more with cultural implications and differences. Webster's Dictionary defines the adjective "ethnic" as: "of or relating to races or large groups of people classed according to common traits and customs". As an adjective the word "ethnic" is defined as "being a member of an ethnic group who retains the customs, language, and social views of the group". The prefix "ethno-", as in "ethnocentric", is from the Greek "ethnos" referring to "nation or people", and to "neither Christian nor Jewish, [rather] heathen nor gentile". "Ethno-" is defined as "race, people or cultural group". Even the origins of the word 'ethnicity' seem to be based in an us-or-them kind of categorization of people as being outside of the majority group.

My point is that even though ethnicity is often associated with race, it allows room for an even greater emphasis upon group membership in all of the contexts which is identified by customs, culture, and even language. The shift away from the association of ethnicity and color allows for a better opportunity to appreciate differences based on culture, allowing for the fact many groups are often composed of people from many races anyway. Therefore, I see no need for division along the lines of color which comes in many shades and can so easily be blended into other hues as people seek to further divide and/or connect. Realistically I believe the greatest differences between people in this country today have more to do with class and socioeconomic status than with other factors attributed to historical injustices to which many people still cling. Please note that I do not equate class with standards of living. In other words, people living at a "lower class" level can still have a high standard of living.

For a society to be successful there can be no tolerance for arrogance and entitlement, as there can be no tolerance for people playing the victim role and using their oppression as an excuse to give up and act out emotion-based anxiety. Power based in arrogance and entitlement is gained and maintained at the expense and victimization of others. I believe my approach, along with approaches currently being explored by other people in addressing diversity, will help to dissolve some of the competition for recognition; and, can lead to an open identification of and appreciation for diversity which in most cases has little or nothing to do with color. I also think "European Americans" need to look at their own ignorance and their lofty pursuits at the expense of others, and acknowledge and make amends for mistakes from the past.

Furthermore, I think other groups need to work to clean up their acts and images as well relative to seeking opportunities to better themselves rather than continue blaming others for their plight. One of the best indications of where people are relative to controversial issues of diversity can be found in the comedy shows presented on the various cable channels. Watching such shows is a great way to discover where the different cultural groups are in the process of acceptance and appreciation of the diversity within all of us. If given the freedom to be cruel and abusive, even comedy can be used to victimize others. It can also serve to perpetuate many of the stereotypes and myths born of ignorance and separation. Anglos used this approach for many, many years. People of all ethnicities need to realize that many opportunities in life are lost through bad choices and irresponsible behaviors such as: substance use; promiscuity; poor management of finances and consumer credit; not taking advantage of available opportunities for education and job training; and having a lower standard of living. A standard of living is determined by more factors than just poverty, opportunities and locale. It has to do with pride and self-concept in spite of major obstacles.

Now let's move into the political and fifth context with all of its absurdities, abuses, and lack of ethics and professionalism. The political context has become nothing more than an arena in which to act out special interests relative to power struggles driven by money and the desire to be in control. The single biggest promoter and proponent of this reality is the media which I personally believe share spaces in both the community and societal contexts as they report local, state, national, and international stories. At times the media is as equally without ethical standards as are those within much of the political context. Those in the media are also responsible for the feeding frenzy relative to invasions into personal issues which often times have nothing, or at least very little to do with someone's professional abilities. As fewer numbers of people and groups control corporations, including the media, the special interest groups have the means through which to promote their causes and biases. More and more information is becoming known publicly relative to the kinds of people and groups who head the very sources of information made available to the public. This kind of ownership allows control over the content of what we are told is "truth". Corporate executives give the directives that can facilitate the continuation of biases, misperceptions and erroneous interpretations of relevant issues thereby reducing the degree of objectivity.

As I watch journalists comment on and report events of "interest", I see how they actually represent many of the ways in which the rest of society acts out emotion-based anxiety. I watch them with their seeming sense of being above and beyond accountability and respectability, which again reflects the same kind of arrogance and sense of entitlement I have witnessed in the competition between adults versus kids. Media personnel are often driven strictly by ratings and a need to be on top and the first to report something no matter how damaging or erroneous the details may be either to individuals or to groups they target. Think about the lives of different public figures identified as fair game. Also think about the power struggles between the political "left" and "right", and the stereotyped images perpetuated for many people from various diverse groups which do not fit into the agendas of those perceived, though deceptively so, as being in the majority. In my opinion, many of those in the media as a group personify that which is so blatantly wrong in society - an outright willingness to abuse and victimize to fulfill some self righteous need to act out their own emotion-based anxiety and dissatisfaction with life. In this sense it is possible to identify the competition set up to be "on top", and to be the best for no other reason than to meet some self-serving desire cloaked in the form of rhetoric used to justify injustice. Such people truly represent the emptiness many seek to fill at the expense of others, even if the targets happen to be children, depending upon the need, agenda, availability, and context. All parts of the U.S. Constitution guaranteeing and protecting human rights should be backed by an equally sound set of ethical standards and principles which are practiced and upheld by those who use the Constitution as a justification for and defense of offensive actions.

Consider for a while "Corporate America" which affects us in every context. Corporate America bombards us in our home/family context primarily through the media, especially through television and various technological advances. As I stated earlier much of any community composition is defined and impacted by the businesses within it. Schools often times have certain additional educational and recreational programs funded from grant money supplied through various businesses and corporations to supplement education (this can be a good thing). Even the tobacco companies have supported good causes. Big business certainly plays a huge role in society at large and in politics because money talks, influences, and controls. So many aspects of society seem to come down to a money and numbers game with greed overriding any regard for ethics and the concepts of responsibility and accountability.

Also consider all special interest groups who buy influence in politics simply to give them ever-greater opportunities to make money even when making money leads to the destruction of people's lives and our environment. Think about the lobbying which happens all the time to keep standards of pollution control to low limits regardless of the effect on the environment. Think about how the tobacco companies bought influence in Congress for many years in order to sell a product that is both addictive and deadly. I believe those who represent the states where tobacco is a major cash crop should also be held more accountable for any part they continue to play in perpetuating the fallacy that smoking is not harmful enough to be addressed, controlled, and ultimately eliminated.

Economies based in vulnerability to dependency on oil and the production of or participation in acts that can have detrimental effects on people and the environment can be and need to be redirected. For example, money wasted by government agencies fighting the import and distribution of drugs, along with money spent protecting access to oil could be diverted into programs to assist these economies in setting up industries to develop and utilize alternative energy sources, and to stop environmental destruction. I find it hard to believe there aren't people waiting for funding who are already available with ideas and inventions to change and strengthen unstable economies acting out the FLAGS relative to their own survival and complicating factors. Of considerable interest would be investments in alternative fuel sources. Oil dependent economies, including our own, need inspiration and assistance in making changes. Those economies based in illegal drug trade where terrorism abounds would be forced to seek other economic means of survival if the value of drugs dropped to a level where they are no longer a profitable commodity. In the long run the decriminalization of drugs would not create any more problems than we already have simply because of the reality that drug use is detrimental in a number of ways. Eventually the problem would balance itself out and dealers wouldn't be recruiting new users since the profitability would be gone, especially if monies were diverted toward improving impoverished areas. Based on my professional experiences I would have to say the so-called "war on drugs" is not working anyway.

Having lived years ago in a tobacco producing state where I listened to various media reports and word-of-mouth accounts, I believe the tobacco companies have been (and still are) spreading their lies around the world, especially to developing nations viewed as major international markets. American cigarettes sell very well overseas, especially when coupled with the myth of idealism associated with the American way of life as being the best way of life. They are actually exporting death everywhere. I believe the United States and other industrialized nations should take a very serious position relative to our need to be effective role models to developing nations. This is another opportunity for us to see on a larger scale the role of "parents", or simply as adults and leaders in positions of power and influence within different contexts, providing a healthy example of the most appropriate ways to live and treat others. This cannot be done at the expense of others or to further some cause or hidden agenda. And it should not be done from the arrogant stance of the American way being the only way other than as a consideration and possible example for basic issues of freedom and human rights, and not for the sake of domination or control.

One of the biggest travesties in recent corporate history at several contextual levels is the excessive profit of a few at the expense of many, accomplished through outright lies and deceptions, with many of the culprits having never been criminally prosecuted. It is frightening to think that corporate leaders and government officials, for their own gain, readily finagle business practices through loopholes either created politically within bills signed into laws, or simply without regard for laws and ethics. For example: energy "crises"; insignificant changes in drug formulas allowing for extension of patent rights and market control; the possibility that some diseases are more profitable to maintain than to cure; special interest groups; dirty politics; and the underhanded inclusion of provisions within bills signed into law that serve as political extortion. These are only a few of the obvious misuses of power and influence especially prevalent within the United States of America.

Based on statements I have heard from public officials and researched on line, a prime example of deceptive legislation is that of "Homeland Security" and the US Patriot Act. Apparently different law enforcement agencies are bragging about their ability since "9/11" to invade people's privacy more than ever. This is apparently aimed at fighting street crime and gangs, and made possible because of a loophole in the law allowing gangs to be identified as domestic terrorist groups. The general population believes money allocated for "Homeland Security" is being spent on the kinds of terrorist acts associated with the attacks of 9/11/01. Gangs only terrorize each other and not the general population. They are in no way even similar to the concept of global terrorism. Because this is true then an investigation into the deceptive misuse of federal tax dollars needs to be conducted relative to the legislation and legislators who made this possible. This would even include the Bush White House and the office of the US Attorney General under George W Bush. This is a tremendous misuse of power and a source of significant abuse and victimization of the American public, and especially of kids in low-income areas. Full disclosure of legislation in a simple easily understood format should be made available to the general public every time a law/bill is proposed at any level of government.

Think about how big business creates a great deal of torment for those at the lower ends of the socioeconomic spectrum. Through all forms of advertising we are told what is best for us in terms of looking good, feeling good, and attaining the highest standard of living. Advertising seems to perpetuate the disparity between those with and those without the things "needed" to make life better. Think about how advertising causes problems between parents and kids when families cannot afford to buy the things kids are told they need in order to fit in with others. Think about how advertisers promote drug use by suggesting there is some pill or potion for anything from which we suffer, including being a few pounds overweight. These kinds of influences in the USA, along with a failed welfare system, have served to perpetuate the societal myth there is always an easy way out. Kids and many adults believe it is possible to get something for nothing, and that people and other systems owe us something. Kids often times have: little or no ability to tolerate frustration; a very poorly defined or nonexistent work ethic; an unrealistic desire to have a good job without doing anything to make that happen; very little willingness to work their way up the ladder of success; and a limited ability and willingness to delay gratification of some desire. In other words people and contexts perpetuate an unrealistic view of the world and life in which people are victimized and exploited.

Many systems operate without a sense of conscience or a sense of responsibility for their actions. This is true of any system not operating or functioning at an optimal ethical level, and without any form of outside scrutiny and accountability. This is clearly a day and age of "buyers beware" because profits are being made through deception disguised as assistance or relief from troubles and pain. Advertisers and promoters are covered by the fine print on paper, on the TV screen, and by disclaimers provided at the end of radio commercials which they know generally go unheeded. Many people and systems seem to have forgotten the concept of "what goes around comes around". My gang kids use this expression frequently and, as I explained in an earlier chapter, can understand what this means relative to flirting with danger and destruction, even if the destruction is of the self. This concept holds true for any system, just as it does for any individual. Everyone and every system creates its own hell so to speak by not being careful of what is set into motion. For every action there is a clear consequence, and those who gamble eventually lose. Think back and become painfully aware of how quickly companies turned 9/11 into a way to make money at the expense of a very vulnerable audience. All of these issues represent a general and unspoken awareness of and abhorrence for problems and deceptions we believe to be real and cannot effectively prove. Many people share with me the same feelings and justifiable paranoia that there is much we suspect and cannot control or influence because of numerous areas of secrecy and privilege. This alone is my justification for many of the statements I make. I watch and listen just like others and wonder where those in positions of power and authority will actually take us next. I am not sure who to trust anymore in any of the contexts outside the home/family environment.

Politics - not much more needs to be said relative to this context. The two dominant political parties in this country have drawn a line between them and each childishly dares the other to cross the line. Everyone on both sides seeks to expose and destroy the other to the point that controversy related to unimportant matters when compared to the common good of the nation takes the forefront in all arenas. People in the conservative arenas have made tremendous efforts to impose their hidden financial and religious agendas, and their need to control and manipulate in an effort to maintain power and position. Beware of the current term "faith-based" as another ploy to retain recognition since the term "religious right" didn't work out so well. The right wing factions are comprised primarily of wealthy European Americans who arrogantly seek to protect their positions of unquestionable authority to which they feel entitled. At the other end of the conservative spectrum are those who often proudly hold conservative religious beliefs based in blind ignorance and allegiance. Fortunately their fundamentalism and prejudices are deceiving fewer and fewer people. Their stance is held without regard to the common good of all other diverse groups. The attempt is to impose the beliefs of a prominent and divisive minority on the rest of society and the world as a way of remaining in positions of power and influence. The improvements of some of these factors within the political context following 9/11 quickly dissolved back into partisan politics as the world began to take it all in stride and move on.

Think about how Washington, DC is used by politicians to maintain the greatest level of influence. It is no longer important for the differing parties to work together for the well being of all. Campaigns and candidates should represent different issues and concerns as related to the well being of this nation and the world without dividing matters along "party lines". Separation of church and state is critical to our survival. The conservative groups are trying to use politics to impose their out-dated morality and values upon those who seek to move ahead and find new approaches to problem solving which need to include some of the basic truths of humanity and spirituality. Such approaches should not be too narrowly defined or dictated by any minority as being what is best for all. These kinds of struggles also tie in very directly to how people and groups within all contexts seek opportunities to act out emotion-based anxiety, rather than face and deal with the emotions which fuel these acts of hopelessness and desperation. So many people today seem to be fighting demons (FLAGS) within themselves by flailing their arms aimlessly at objects and issues outside of themselves. This kind of thinking is the fuel for many acts of terrorism around the world as people react to their own respective internalized FLAGS.

Think about how religion has also become big business with televised evangelism and exploitation. Just like with comedy and diversity I would encourage everyone to tune into the different religious channels, which apparently includes the FOX news channel, as a way of recognizing the ignorance filtering through the conservative religious groups. It is often very hard to find any remnant of spirituality within the messages they present to the listeners. Religion often seeks only to promote its own causes and dogma. Those within any extreme form of religion, in the sense of being defined as self-righteous and arrogant, seek to recruit people to their side and their limited view of the world. People have the right to believe whatever works for them. In my opinion they also have a responsibility to insure that their beliefs are not destructive to themselves or to others.

As you watch the broadcasts on the religious channels, look objectively at the desperation, regardless of religious affiliation, followers use to convince themselves and others that their way is the only way. Look at the limited amount of education audience members and followers often have as exhibited by the ways of expressing themselves, often only parroting what they are told to say and believe. Even those who are educated in other fields are also often heavily educated from within a religious bias that discourages questioning and exploration of alternative ways of seeking and knowing God. People are taught to be afraid of such exploration as being sinful and blasphemous. However, no one in these groups is willing to entertain the possibility such tactics could be interpreted as mind control. Consider those in other countries who kill themselves and others in the name of their God.

These conservative religious groups, here and around the world, seek only to further their various causes and their idea of helping or controlling others only serves to promote their agendas. They truly believe in what they are attempting to do, having successfully deluded themselves as to both the basis and unspoken purposes represented by their actions. However, their beliefs often reflect a desperate need to hold onto something they perceive as being meaningful and necessary. Many of their followers in my opinion also have an unconscious and unhealthy need to be controlled and are easily influenced. Once you are in it is difficult to get out because of the fears of going to hell, not receiving the seventy-two virgins, provoking the wrath of God, and the fear of losing the love from God. Sounds an awful lot like emotional abuse described in chapter four doesn't it? Help comes only in the form of becoming part of "the flock", or accepting some form of domination in many cases. Only those "within the flock" are helped in times of need (to use their terminology).

Outreach to others outside of any particular religious faction is often for the sole purpose of recruiting them into that particular religion, even if this has to be done in some form of deathbed guilt trip, or by teaching their extreme beliefs to children. They are real opportunists looking for any point of vulnerability which can be used to fuel guilt, shame and fear. Even Catholics reserve communion only for those who have been converted officially into "the church", which is also defined as the family of God. This implies that all of those outside of the "church" regardless of the denomination are also outside the family of God. How much more arrogant can anyone get, especially in light of recent "revelations" of sexual abuse and victimization perpetrated against parishioners by clergy and nuns, all of which was covered up for years under the ever popular "code of silence" existing within other contexts as well. The "church" even set itself up as being above the law when it comes to reporting abuse and victimization. As the "Church Lady" from older episodes of Saturday Night Live would say: "Isn't that conveeenient?" What goes around comes round!

Within their struggles it is possible to see how these religious groups are trying to fight against people such as myself who now practice what they refer to as blasphemy and an abomination against God. True spirituality focused on the spiritual evolution of humanity is nothing more than a return to the basics of Spirituality, excluding all of the hidden agendas present in today's religions. I see my work in the field of psychology as a non-religious ministry of outreach, with the difference of not trying to convert anyone to any particular way of thinking. My only goal is to encourage others to seek God in their own way and from within. To look for God outside of oneself is another form of being at the mercy of externals. Spirituality is a way of promoting the development of healthy morals and values, not for the sake of avoiding judgment, damnation and hell; but, simply because pure unadulterated spirituality is the only thing that makes sense. How arrogant it is for religions to teach that their "group" is the only select few who are worthy of God and certain perceived rewards.

Before leaving this segment take some time to examine abusive beliefs and statements associated with people in positions of power and authority outside the home/family context. This list (Appendix K) is similar to the list of abusive statements made by adults to kids generally in one-on-one scenarios. However, this list addresses the arrogance and destructive nature of people encountered on a larger scale in all of the other contexts outside the home/family context. You will be able to recognize how these items apply to the contexts we just covered. Following this list is a list (Appendix L) representing the faulty thinking of victims of larger scale abuse/victimization beyond the home/family context. Understanding the relevance of these lists is critical in understanding how people can be made to feel vulnerability and weakness associated with the FLAGS. Review the list from Chapter 4 (Appendix J) of the purposes of abuse and victimization and apply those items to the next list of abusive statements and beliefs. When you study the list of faulty thinking also compare these items to those in the list in Chapter VI of the results of abuse and victimization. Refer to any of the lists in the appendices at any point throughout your reading for clarification and relevance. Failure to utilize and understand these lists/appendices will reduce your understanding of the applicability of this content within this book.

A model similar to my RFLAGS Model that explains the process of abusive people in positions of power and influence abusing others would probably look something like the model shown below. This model applies more specifically to larger scale abuse and victimization rather than simply day to day kinds of negative interactions any of us are likely to experience. Larger scale abuse and victimization isn't always apparent initially, especially within the societal, political, and religious contexts. Even the ways of acting out I have listed below are different from those associated with more direct and personal experiences identified in the RFLAGS Model (Appendix C). Let's call this model the Roberts Abuse by People in Positions of Power and Authority Model, or RAPPPA. Just kidding! That was the best I could do! Remember the models are cyclical with one stage leading to another, and with the acting-out behaviors only making the FLAGS worse, thereby perpetuating the entire futile process.

ABUSE BY PEOPLE IN POSITIONS OF POWER AND INFLUENCE MODEL

| Negative Emotions | Conquest & Conquer | Complete Selfishness & Disregard | Acting-out Behaviors |

ACTING OUT BEHAVIORS

Lying	Deceiving	Cheating
Embezzling	Stealing	Black Mailing
Threatening	Gesturing	Posturing
Grand standing	Molesting	Raping
Pillaging	Plundering	Destroying
Forging	Misrepresenting	Breaking promises
Making false promises	Indulging	Hiding
Running	Ruling	Dominating
Covering up	Creating fear	Intimidating
Physical violence	Abusing/victimizing	Paying/bribing
Seeking like-minded others	Corrupting	Defeating
Competing	Defying	Denying
Defending	Accusing	Offending
Expecting	Fantasizing	Planning/Scheming
Engaging	Recruiting	Soliciting
Befriending	Winning/gaining	Obsessing

Having explored the six contexts in which victimization and abuse can occur, let's now consider another element necessary in the understanding of my concepts. I have noticed in my dealings with people that there are certain factors, which I refer to as complicating factors or risk factors, which will increase the likelihood of someone being victimized both within the home/family context and in the other contexts as well. A complicating factor is any aspect of being human which makes one vulnerable and sets them apart as different from "the rest". These factors are both personal and environmental.

To give you a better understanding of what complicating factors are, I have included a list of items (Appendix M) which have been identified to date. This list is *extremely* important since many people in the so-called "helping professions", educators, and law enforcement fail to take these factors into account. It is impossible to work effectively with low income, disadvantaged kids and families if people do not understand all of the realities present in their lives. For anyone to work with any population and not understand the realities in their lives is the highest form of incompetence, and a major violation of established professional ethics. As you review this list I again encourage you to try and identify other elements which have not yet been identified. Also look very carefully at identifying any complicating factors present in your life currently or historically.

The Past that Lived in My Present

Having included the list of complicating factors, I come to another one of those parts of this book where I feel I should reveal to you more of my own history. In other words I want to give each of you an opportunity to understand how my set of complicating factors increased my likelihood of being victimized within all six of the contexts. This is intended to be a forum only for sharing and understanding so each reader can understand how I know what I know. Again this book is not about me, but it does come from within me based on both my subjective personal and professional experiences. Hopefully my words will challenge everyone to examine their prejudices and to open their minds to learning about the factors present in everyone's lives which make each of us unique. Each person has their own very personalized set of issues and complicating factors which shape us, and which influence the way we view others and the world. Remember this book is all about honesty, reality, and self-examination for the purpose of changing human interaction and lifting it to a higher spiritual level.

My set of complicating factors can be summed up rather simply and quickly, and even though you have already read about some of them, I will recap them briefly in this segment and then add to them at the same time. It goes like this.

I was born in 1954 during the post World War II era, to middle class parents, each of whom came from very dysfunctional backgrounds. Neither of them ever worked through their own sets of complicating factors which then impacted my life in a very negative way, especially after the tragic deaths of my mother's family members in 1958. I was born in Alabama, and began the first grade in September 1960 at an elementary school in the suburban city which billed itself as "the all white city" until at least the late 1960's. This is an important factor for later as we consider the impact of the civil rights movement.

School was a very frightening environment for me, primarily because my home/family context was so unstable. I was sent into the world with no self-confidence and with very low self-esteem. Because my home/family context became so abusive, it is easy to understand my fear of the world. I started school filled primarily with fear, loneliness, anger (which was buried very deep within), guilt, and shame. The FLAGS were waving and I had no resources from which I could seek help and understanding. Furthermore, people in general didn't give much credence to emotional/psychological issues at that time in history, especially relative to a child's perspective.

The FLAGS became my internal guides of how to respond to the other contexts. Because the FLAGS are negative rather than positive, every experience I had was faced with dread. I hated to get up in the mornings because of my fear of what the day would hold relative to its unpredictability and my perceived lack of control over probable events. All of this was based in being deprived of the emotional strength and stability I should have been armed with prior to starting school. This is a clear example of the emotional neglect I described in a previous chapter. The only "tool" I was given was an extremely distorted image of God who was to be feared rather than viewed as a source of comfort and aid. Thanks to my parents and the local

Southern Baptist Church and its minister at that time, even God served as a source for the FLAGS. I had the wrath from God and from my parents to worry about, along with the belief taught to me by those who "loved" me that if you had a problem, you simply had to pray about it and it would go away if your faith was strong. That never worked. It actually made me feel like an even bigger failure given the fact even my "faith" was faulty!

The only early memories I had of attending church are those of my dad taking me outside to whip me with his belt on the sidewalk for not sitting still during church services. After the whipping I was given no time to regain my composure, being told to "dry it up or I'll give it to you again". I was then brought back into the church sniffling, fighting hard not to cry, and feeling like everyone in the church was looking at me. After all, I had been told they were and that I was a shame and a disgrace to my parents for embarrassing them like I had done. I was no more than three or four years old, possibly younger because my parents started taking me into the church building rather than leaving me in the nursery. This was another one of my dad's control freak tactics he used to teach me a lesson.

I was never allowed to dance because dancing was sinful, even for first graders. My mother caught me dancing at a birthday party once with my first grade friends. When she arrived to pick me up she saw me dancing, and ordered me to the car after I was met with a slap across my face in front of all of my friends. I guess I was a little slow in understanding the concept of sin. However, I learned the concept of the FLAGS very early on. Needless to say, I was never invited back to this friend's house. This experience and others served as major complicating factors which impeded any opportunity to learn effective social skills as a child. To further complicate socialization I was allowed to visit only one friend a week for one hour. My parents told me they did not want me to be a "nuisance" in the neighborhood. Most of the rest of my time was spent at home alone and working in the yard which I had to maintain, along with help from my brother, from a very early age. Keeping up the yard allowed Daddy to "piddle around" and work on his projects, and also allowed him to spend more time away from home hunting and fishing. I always felt like an unpaid hired hand as a kid.

I was always made to look different because of my parents' conservative ways of dressing me and cutting my hair. My dad cut my hair until I turned

16 and could afford to pay for my own hair cuts after I began working my first real job. Even at age 16 my haircut, this simple act of asserting my independence, was taken as an act of defiance. The standard retort when I complained about looking different was: "if everyone else jumped off the bridge I guess you would jump too." In addition to limiting my socialization, all of these tactics proved to be complicating factors as well because they were intended to squelch my individuality and to impose strict external control for no other reason than to break my will.

To make matters even worse relative to school my vision was so bad I couldn't see well at all and didn't realize it until the fifth grade. My grades were bad and my parents were forever punishing me for this because teachers told them I was intelligent, but that I was not living up to my potential due to laziness and not applying myself. When I say I didn't realize I couldn't see, I guess I mean I didn't make the connection between not being able to read the eye chart and my low grades. I already felt so much like a nerd I didn't want the added injury of having to wear glasses; so, I memorized the first five lines of the eye chart. In the fourth grade I tried to tell my parents I needed glasses, but they accused me of lying and wanting attention. They went to the school and the teacher told them I had read the chart successfully. Because of my fear of getting in trouble for having memorized the eye chart, I took the punishment they doled out with their belief I had lied and had also embarrassed them yet again. In the fifth grade I broke down and cried when the teacher tested my eyes, telling her I could not even see the big letter "E" at the top of the chart. I begged her to call my parents for me so they would know I wasn't lying and would take me to the eye doctor. After I got my glasses my grades improved to the level of A's and B's, and in the sixth grade I received an achievement award. However the damage to my self-esteem had already been done. It took me until my mid thirties to finally get to the point where I could wholeheartedly believe in myself.

Things got worse when my younger brother started school making all A's and was able to skip the second grade. I was always compared to him both academically and relative to his athletic ability. Comparing me to him further set me up to hate him and to seek out any opportunity I could find to fight with him. Only in recent years have we been able to get completely beyond feeling distant from each other because of the dynamics our parents set up between us. Even as Dr. Roberts I have received very little respect from my family members due to other complicating factors primarily related to major differences in religious, political and social beliefs.

Much of the distance between my family and me was always justified using religious reasons. However, this was not the true reason as the real reasons were based in a fear of what others think relative to what my parents perceived as a life of sin primarily because I am outside of the church and their way of thinking and believing. Because I came out to them when I was 29, I was completely disowned for nearly 15 years. This act of being orphaned as an adult through no fault of my own set the stage for me to finally embrace and accept every aspect of my total identity. Believe me, I gained much more that I ever lost. I have a letter from my mother I received while in graduate school in 1991 telling me I am from the devil, and telling me she and my dad didn't know why I was ever born. It took me getting a BA degree, two master's degrees, and a Ph.D. to finally convince myself I am not what they told me I was. Believe me, my RFLAGS Model comes to you from my heart and from my own difficult life experiences. And, we are not finished yet. Obviously I grew up knowing that I was "different" from the other boys.

Rather than being given a natural athletic ability (and good vision) like my brother, I was given the complicating factor of musical ability. I was such a disgrace. I couldn't play sports and I wasn't interested in hunting, so the distance between my father and me continued to grow, as did my jealousy toward my brother. Because of looking like a nerd and because of my lack of athletic ability I was the target of much abuse and ridicule by other kids at school.

These factors continued to plague me throughout my entire school experience even into college. Fortunately, my college experience was somewhat less traumatic simply because people tend to become a little less cruel as they get older. If someone had taken the time to teach me I really believe I could have played some sports. I was a very good swimmer and learned to water ski, both of which I enjoyed tremendously. In an adult education program I attended during my junior and senior years of high school I actually ran a touchdown while playing football. No one in this program knew my history of being "sports-less", so I had a chance to try some new things. I can also see how my lack of self-esteem and self-confidence served as complicating factors for me as well. Believe me all of these factors are connected and interrelated.

My sense of shame in my abilities was amplified by my dad's reluctance to attend any of my recitals or other musical performances. He very readily and eagerly attended all of my brother's sports events. My mother even had to insist my dad attend my first college graduation. No one in my family has ever attended any of my graduation ceremonies for the different graduate programs. I am their oldest son and one of the few people in the family to have ever graduated from college, and the only one in the family, both immediate and extended, with a Ph.D. All of these experiences caused a great deal of emotional, mental, and spiritual damage that took me years to identify and then overcome. This is true in varying degrees for virtually anyone if you will only be honest about your past. While my story isn't as bad as some, it was bad enough. I can't imagine how I would have survived if additional external complicating factors had been thrown into the mix.

Let me summarize by reminding you I grew up in a strict Southern Baptist environment in the "Deep South" just prior to and during the civil rights movement. I can remember all of the factors of discrimination such as the white and colored water fountains and bathrooms, as well as dining areas and waiting rooms. Not only did I watch the news accounts of then Governor George Wallace and the problems in Birmingham, I lived through some of the horror created by "white people" and supported by my own parents in response to integration and change. This was a disgraceful time to be white and I am amazed at how recently it all happened.

I became a high school dropout in the eleventh grade because of the violence in the county school district where I lived. I completed my junior and senior years in an adult education program rather than stay in the middle of the chaos and violence where no one was learning anything productive. I made this choice rather than attend one of the little private "Christian" schools which popped up all over the area. My high school was on national news during the 1969-70 school year, my tenth grade year, because of riots and bomb threats resulting from the forced integration and rezoning of schools. The Southern Baptist Church I attended even had men stationed outside to keep African Americans from trying to attend the church services on Sundays, all in the name of God and based on arrogance and entitlement. In addition there was the hippie movement and all the drugs and music which went along with that culture. It was a time of drastic changes.

Fortunately I never bought into any of the bigotry and prejudice I was exposed to during my childhood. I remember watching on TV all of the disgraceful acts committed by whites (who, more often than not, also claimed to be Christian) against blacks. At the same time I had to listen to my parents' commentary on and justification of the horrible and shameful acts of abuse and victimization. With the utmost respect and sincerity I look up to Rosa Parks as one of my role models because of her one act of defiance that changed history forever. As I grew into an age when I could question all of this I had to do so secretly and internally. When I challenged my parents' beliefs and use of racial and ethnic slurs I was met with insults and an occasional slap across my face for being a defiant, disrespectful, and uppity "n----r lover". Imagine what would have happened to me if they had known that I was secretly harboring the reality that I was gay - at least by my early to mid teens. This reality almost ended with me committing suicide if not for the intervention of a college professor when I was 18. My attempt to change my sexual orientation by marrying proved to be a major disaster, with the exception of having fathered a wonderful daughter who has given me six beautiful grandchildren over the years. If anyone could have changed this complicating factor it would have been me. I am amazed that I survived my childhood, especially in light of this major secretive life I had to hide and try to bury, almost literally. No child should ever have to live like this.

The other big issues at that time, especially in the Deep South, were the Beetles; men with long hair; the "shameful and defiant acts of those hippies"; and men identified as "fags, queers, and perverts". Any human behaviors and ideas that didn't meet the standards and approval of "Christian white folk" were fair game for ridicule and scorn. Only as an adult did I finally have the opportunities to really gain contact with groups outside of the closed, conservative, religious and ignorant white culture. My home/family history of abuse and victimization coupled with chaos and turmoil in the world and within <u>all</u> of the other contexts made growing up very difficult. Also important to the time were the constant threats of a nuclear war; being drafted into the war in Vietnam; and all of the religious extremists predicting the sure and eminent end of the world. Thank God for my maternal grandmother; for the relatives and neighbors who occasionally addressed how mean my dad was; and for the misfit professor at a private Baptist college who opened my heart and mind to unimaginable realities and potential. Other than these factors, along with some degree of intelligence and a desire to rise above all of this and learn from these experiences, I have no other explanation for my qualities of resilience, transcendence, and determination. Keep in mind that I had only an extremely distorted version of God as any source of spiritual guidance. Obviously that has changed as I moved forward and away from all of this negativity and falsehoods.

Many people have complicating factors and secrets they drag with them from childhood into adulthood. Secrets of any kind further complicate other complicating factors. Remember, too, I had help along the way as I entered adulthood, so I didn't have to face my past realities alone. I sought professional help as an adult and always looked for opportunities to learn how to deal with the remnants from the past more effectively. Furthermore, I continuously seek out new people and resources that help me to grow and learn. I see my life as an ongoing process rather than as a means to an end, and I look forward to whatever lies ahead simply because I will always be able to learn something which will both advance the growth of my soul and will be worth sharing with others.

Also remember this account of my past is my reality. As I said before I am not completely sure of the accuracy of the details of some of the early instances. However I am painfully certain of the emotions connected to these events, and of the scars, some of which may never heal completely. Even though taking control of my life cost me my family for many of my adult years, this loss is nothing compared to all I have gained. The chances are I would never have done most of what I have pursued simply because I would have still been under their control, foolishly and pointlessly living my life to please others at my own expense. I allow no one to impose unreasonable limits on my life and am a stronger and more spiritual man for having tried and succeeded. Ironically, abuse and victimization can make people stronger if they learn to recover from the damage. Remember from Chapter I there is no opportunity to fail, only opportunities to learn and grow.

I am often amazed that as a "white" man I am able to work with gang kids and juvenile offenders without them having any idea of the ways I can relate to and understand them as underdogs. I tell them that I know how bad it feels to feel bad, and I encourage them to never do that to another human being. Because they too know how bad it feels to feel bad, they are able to connect with me without a need to know how I can look beyond what they do and be able to see their souls. These kids represent my heart and soul, and couldn't even begin to understand how working with them has helped me to get through my own issues and insecurities. I tell them all the time (without being able to explain why) that I never ask them to do anything I haven't had to do in some form in my own life. Somehow they just know on a professional level that I am for real and that I care.

Chapter VI

Results and Losses Associated With Abuse and Victimization

Having looked at abuse and victimization, and at the contexts and complicating factors, let's turn now to the results and losses associated with victimization. In this chapter we will identify and describe possible factors of unresolved grief associated with losses. We will see how losses arise from the results of being victimized, with loss being one of the results. We will also look at how loss and grief are acted out in the varying contexts as well as on an individual level. In addition we will look at how these unresolved losses get passed down from generation to generation through different personality types and patterns of negative interaction and perception.

Abuse and victimization leave a lasting imprint upon the psyche of the victim. The duration of the victimization and its intensity determine the depth of the imprint or wound. Quite often these wounds go unhealed for an entire lifetime. As with all significant wounds, even though healing may occur, there will be a scar to serve as a reminder of the past, with the prominence of the scar equal to the severity of the injury. Open wounds are those which cannot heal due to infection and inattention.

If an individual had a very healthy home/family context as a child, the chances are that individual will be able to face any form of victimization experienced in adulthood in a much more appropriate and healthy manner. Even life can seem to be a source of victimization as we face uncertainty and loss throughout our entire lifespan. Given a solid psychological foundation from which to face negative situations we will not only survive, but also gain strength to prepare for any other negative event which is almost inevitable in the ever-revolving cycles of life. No one stays on top or at the bottom forever.

This book and especially the material covered in this chapter are directed at those of us who did not have a solid basis from which to grow as a child. It is also written for those of us who had to deal with various complicating factors that made the world outside of our home/family (and sometimes inside our home/family) an unsafe and frightening place as well. Our ability to cope generally depends upon the dysfunction and trauma from the past - the open wounds and the prominent scars. Hopefully by now each of you is beginning to see how the Fear, Loneliness, Anger, Guilt, and Shame (FLAGS) originate from the deprivation and unpredictability we experienced as children.

As you have seen from my own life, even a good start can go horribly wrong if traumatic events occur prior to the development of a strong ability to cope with such events. This is intensified even more when the adults involved in our childhood did nothing to resolve the issues related to their own dysfunctional backgrounds. The ability to function in adulthood is even more chaotic and problematic when, from the very beginning of life, an individual was abused and victimized, and forced to experience other complicating factors with little or no period of positive influences and opportunities. Abuse and victimization are inexcusable. Negative life events and experiences we are sure to face are not the problems. The problems lie within our ability to cope with these elements as determined by our upbringing and the emotional states of the adults within all contexts who were responsible for teaching us and giving us the things we needed in order to grow and function at optimal levels. In other words, the problems arise from the numerous negative results and losses associated with abuse and victimization, remembering that abuse also includes neglect, perhaps better described as deprivation.

In my professional and personal experiences I have become aware of the concept of unresolved grief which can either be active and chronic, or can lie dormant on an unconscious level until triggered in adulthood by some negative life event. This is what I believe is meant by complicated bereavement, meaning grief extending beyond some reasonable time period or healthy emotional reaction. From my observations and experiences I also believe unresolved grief is particularly likely in the midst of multiple losses whether these are obvious losses as with death and dying, or are more abstract and subtle as in losses of childhood, innocence, and hope associated with victimization and various complicating factors.

The Past that Lived in My Present

I believe this concept of unresolved grief is what happened in my own family for both of my parents. Their lives were likely somewhat dysfunctional even in early adulthood prior to their meeting and getting married. It is also likely the first six years of their marriage were relatively okay, with less significantly damaging conflicts occurring than those that would come later. My mother's marriage to, and subsequent divorce from, a very abusive older man also served as a major source of distress and guilt. She got married at 18 because of a pregnancy which resulted in a miscarriage due to extensive domestic violence, no details of which came out until after her death in 2000. This was a major missing piece in all of my past as well. So it is fair to say the unresolved grief and emotions from the past were probably simmering on an unconscious level in both of them. My dad demanded that my mother keep her previous marriage a secret which she was to have taken to her grave.

As the years progressed and my parents tried to deal with the differences between them relative to characteristics of individual differences, the unresolved factors continued to heat up. The final trigger for them probably started with all of the changes I delineated earlier just after I reached my fourth birthday, culminating in the tragic deaths of my grandfather and my uncles. Unfortunately none of the unresolved issues were allowed to become conscious. However, both of my parents began vigorously acting out the emotion-based anxiety that was already present from the past and never dealt with. My dad even tried to murder my mother when I was seven or eight years old due to the fact her previous marriage had to be revealed. He had been nominated to become a deacon in the Baptist church I mentioned previously. Because he was married to a divorced woman he had to disqualify himself and explain why to the board of deacons. The conflict over this event led to months of tension which culminated into him strangling her over the kitchen sink in front of me and my younger brother. If my grandmother had not heard the commotion and rescued my mother, she would clearly have died right in front of me. Talk about reinforcing my fear of my dad. None of the reasons for this were revealed to me until after my mom's death and my dad was never held accountable for attempted murder. This will become a topic of family secrets at a later point in this book.

The main reason I still have so much trouble respecting my parents is because their discipline toward me was hypocritical, and was only intended to impose external control simply for the sake of control and compliance to their way of thinking. Their approaches to "mold my character" allowed for no recognition of or respect for my own individuality. Their abuse toward me gave them an opportunity to act out their own frustrations and conflicts. These abusive actions also facilitated their need to break my will and force me into compliance through fear and intimidation. I also believe they sensed my resilience, which they interpreted as being hateful, strong willed, and defiant, when I was still quite young. As a result they felt the need to mold me in such a way as to protect their needs for control and compliance. All of these factors created for me the many negative personal and emotional results and losses I have had to face and deal with in adulthood. This was true for me in all of the contexts I have identified in a previous chapter. My parents needed to blame outside sources for all of the mistakes they made. This approach allowed them to rationalize their actions according to their religious beliefs in the external influences of Satan and evil. In their minds they were fighting what they saw as sin and as defined by the context of religion to which they desperately ascribed until the end.

It is obvious to me that, while much of what I am saying is purely speculation relative to dynamics within the members of my family, my interpretation of their emotional states makes sense. Clearly life events can further complicate and exacerbate unresolved grief and emotions from the past by adding to them. Experts on grief indicate an individual can only grieve one loss at a time. However, that is not to say the collective unresolved grief from previous losses doesn't complicate and extend the current grief reaction. My mother could not stand to talk about the deaths of her relatives ever in her lifetime. Neither their deaths nor the collective emotions from the past were ever identified and resolved. For her, as well as for my dad, the FLAGS existed in extremely intense forms which may be a good way of understanding the intensity of factors or symptoms associated with the various personality and psychiatric disorders identified in the DSM-IV-TR, including alcohol and drug abuse/dependence.

As I mentioned earlier, the process of dysfunction tends to be handed down from one generation to another. Even though neither of my parents had alcohol or drug problems, they perpetuated the dysfunction from their respective pasts to my siblings and me through their intense physical and emotional abuse. Murray Bowen, a well-known family systems therapist, identified this "multigenerational process" and used "genograms" as a means of tracking such trends and behaviors. A genogram is basically a family tree display used to identify significant people and events from the past which served as exacerbating factors and/or triggers, intensifying the dysfunction and insuring the likelihood of it continuing and being passed on to the next generation. Anyone reared in a dysfunctional environment, even relative to complicating factors and victimization in other dysfunctional contexts outside of the home/family context, will pass the dysfunction along unless they identify it and work to stop it. Even as a child I told myself I would never do the same things which were done to me by my parents to my own child or children. I believe my ability to see the problems during my childhood resulted from the unconditional love given to me by my maternal grandmother. I also had the opportunities to observe the contrasts between my family and other families in the neighborhood to see those like my own or worse, against those which seemed to function on a more appropriate level. I am certain that much of my resilience and defiance were fueled by these environmental influences.

The determining factor in whether or not dysfunction gets passed along to future generations lies in the conscious awareness of the abuse, victimization, and neglect/deprivation from the past. As in my life, I had the opportunity to consciously compare my family to others, and I knew how genuine love felt and sounded from "Granny". She was a wonderful woman - not perfect, but wonderful – who lived to be 100 years old. For others the process of problem identification can begin simply through positive interaction with an effective, non-arrogant role model; someone who looks beyond the behaviors of a kid and sees the kid behind those behaviors. As a psychologist

I always look for a little piece of heart in the kids I serve, which I then seek to nurture by creating a safe and mutually respectful atmosphere in which we can explore the soul and psyche of each kid and family. I lightheartedly refer to this approach as the philosophy of 'Psyche-Soul-ology', a term I coined myself. It is amazing how much difference, even in my own life, one person can make when they appear at just the right time and with just the right skills. The only way to avoid the continuation of the multigenerational process is for each individual to identify and work through her or his own unresolved issues always resulting from victimization and neglect/deprivation.

Please allow me to share a little about my research with any mental health professionals and other interested parties in my reading audience. For both my Master's thesis and my dissertation I conducted research to develop the Roberts Grief and Loss Analysis Scale (RGLAS), an instrument designed to detect such unresolved grief and related issues in adults and as addressed in this chapter. I believe with further research the RGLAS could also be used to detect the same factors in adolescents from about age 12 and up. The intent is to measure grief associated with losses from dysfunctional backgrounds rather than from grief relative to traditional associations with death and dying. Test scores reveal indications of current levels of dysfunction and coping skills. While additional research needs to be done to further establish its reliability and validity, the results to date indicate the RGLAS is measuring something more than just depression and anxiety. No other professional involved in the supervision or review of my research has ever questioned its face validity, a further indication of the correctness of my perception of adult dysfunction being based in unresolved grief and emotions from the past. At the risk of sounding too technical, the RGLAS is intended for use within therapeutic settings as an assessment tool in conjunction with other assessment instruments and techniques, to include assessment/intake interviews.

Based upon my experience and upon my research and education, I also believe much of what is diagnosed as depression among people in general is simply unresolved grief which results from deprivation and unpredictability associated with abuse and victimization, including neglect, in childhood. Unresolved grief will always include elements of depression and/or anxiety, which are based in negative (in the sense of being unpleasant) and yet appropriate emotions - the FLAGS. (Parenthetically and relative to the FLAGS, let me say that when I refer to the FLAGS as negative, I do not intend to imply they are inappropriate. I wish only to convey the necessity of correctly identifying the negative emotions in an effort to control them rather than be controlled by them in the sense of learning from the resulting anxiety and depression.) Deprivation is easily understood as neglect regardless of the form it takes. At the beginning of my graduate training as I began to think about the nature of emotional states, I thought of them being based less in thought and perception, and more in the FLAGS. Rather than emotional or psychological states being created by irrational thoughts as suggested by researchers such as Aaron Beck, I believe the psychological states of depression and anxiety create the irrational thoughts which then serve to establish hopelessness and lead to the destructive acting out behaviors we have already discussed.

Furthermore, I believe the states of depression and anxiety, especially anxious depression, unless physiologically generated, are better described as emotional states rather than as psychological states because of the negative emotional bases from which they are generated. I believe even depression associated with grief is purely emotion-based, with hopelessness resulting from the negative or irrational thoughts generated from the emotional state, not vice versa. Negative and irrational thoughts will not result and take hold if the individual is able to successfully identify and face the emotions associated with any negative event. Even with positive emotions such as joy and contentment, emotional states of over zealousness and reckless abandonment will not result if these emotions are also identified and dealt with in the sense of keeping things in perspective.

This distinction is necessary in order to give people the accurate perception of being able to face and resolve their grief from the past. To say depression and anxiety are based in irrational thinking ignores the more logical sequence of: events or experiences creating emotions which then lead to an emotional state resulting in hopelessness and the need to act out emotion-based anxiety to avoid bringing the emotions to, or experiencing them at, a conscious level. If the events and emotions are positive, the emotional state will be that of some degree of happiness, contentment, or even temporary euphoria. However, if the events and emotions are negative, the resulting emotional state will be that of depression and/or anxiety. If depression is emotionally based rather than physiologically based as with chemical imbalances in the brain associated with major depression and bipolar disorders, I believe it will likely be mixed with anxiety. This mix makes it a more active emotional state, in the sense it is likely to be acted out if it is not faced and dealt with from an emotional perspective. Depression alone, as with physiological depression, tends to be more passive and can be quite debilitating. One could even argue that the act of giving up and withdrawing is a way of acting out depression. However this kind of withdrawing tends to be without intention or purpose, and often originates in the debilitating effects of the chemical imbalances in the brain associated with depression.

Both depression and anxious depression result in hopelessness as one tries unsuccessfully to act out the emotional state as a way of avoiding the physical state they create. When people experience an emotionally based state of anxious depression, they talk about the way they feel. I believe the feelings they are referring to are physical rather than psychological in nature relative to their manifestation and conscious awareness. People will often think of depression and anxiety as feelings that should be listed on a chart. To successfully identify the associated emotions, an individual must first check their physical sensations, or remember how they felt physically at the time the emotions were experienced. This is my way of distinguishing between a feeling and an emotional state. For instance a feeling of love can result in an emotional state of joyous abandonment and excitement which are experienced as physical sensations. Actually, and as mentioned in Chapter II, there is very little difference in the physical manifestation of anxiety and the physical manifestation of excitement. For example, I can feel both excited and anxious at the same time about a public presentation of my workshop materials. I can only make the distinction through conscious effort. Both sensations are emotional states manifested in physiological arousal based in emotions. The difference lies in the perception of one state as positive and pleasant, and the other as negative and unpleasant. However, both are based in the autonomic nervous system which creates the fight or flight sensations.

In order to keep people from becoming confused I need to distinguish in more detail the difference between emotions and physical manifestations of those emotions. When we ask someone to identify a feeling - as with the use of a "feelings" chart - we are actually asking them to check their physical state as an indicator of their emotional state in the sense of using the physical state as a spring board for free association. The person is actually identifying the first word(s) which come to mind as associated with and manifested by the physical state. I teach kids and families to use their physical bodies and sensations as indicators of their current emotional state. I encourage people to learn to identify the physical signs of emotions and use these as a gauge to literally regulate the emotional pressure building up inside. Because adults and kids are generally cut off from the awareness of emotions this process requires a great deal of conscious effort at first. Many individuals will move rapidly into a stage of acting out before they even realize they are being controlled by their emotions. I am not referring to control in the sense of stifling emotions; rather, in the sense of learning to identify and deal with emotions before they take over and serve as the controlling factor which then determines an individual's behavior. This inability to recognize and deal with emotions is taught to us during childhood within many of the six contexts relative to the denial of and suppression of emotions as actual reactions and experiences of children. Children are often taught to deny their emotions rather than being taught to develop appropriate coping mechanisms and appropriate expression of emotions.

Many of my kids (clients) will tell me they hit walls and throw things as a means of releasing their anger. My response is to encourage them to identify their anger before it reaches a point where it needs to be acted out. As stated previously I often tell kids and adults: "just because you can ..., doesn't mean you should." In other words just because you can hit a wall, drink or use, beat your spouse or partner, victimize a child or adult, or act out some form of prejudice, etc., doesn't mean you should. If children are not allowed as early as possible to learn the proper expression of and identification of emotions, they will learn to either turn their anger inward and upon themselves, and/or throw it outward toward others. By teaching children and adults to see their bodies as a tank with a pressure gauge attached, people can literally learn to regulate emotions before the emotions progress to a point of dominating the individual's thoughts and actions. This is accomplished by becoming aware of one's breathing patterns; level of arousal; heart rate; blood pressure; body posture; body language, including gesturing; energy level; degree of agitation; tone and volume of voice; sweating; dry mouth; tears; difficulty speaking; rate of speech; etc.

When I mention the issues associated with unresolved grief, I am basically referring to two different categories - the results or outcome of victimization (Appendix N), and the losses associated with victimization (Appendix O). This of course means it is time for two more of my crucial lists. I make the distinction between results and losses associated with victimization as losses being one of the results requiring further delineation. My goal is to help each of you recognize the connections between the Fear, Loneliness, Anger, Guilt, and Shame, and the results and losses associated with abuse and victimization. As you look at the respective appendices which follow you will be able to see how these two categories of results and losses differ. You will also be able to see how losses need to be identified, acknowledged, and resolved through an appropriate grief process. This way adults can be effective role models and can avoid creating unhealthy environments and contexts for children we are given charge of in different capacities throughout our lives. At this point in the book we are only exploring and identifying issues and elements related to ineffective adult behaviors negatively impacting children. Efforts will be made in a later chapter to identify solutions and alternative ways of dealing with these components. Keep this in mind especially as you review the lists and find some of the results and losses to be difficult to face. In other words, keep reading and remember there is nothing wrong with you. There are simply things which may be wrong in your life, and these can be corrected.

After studying these lists, and identifying those factors which apply to your own life, give some thought to how these factors can result from victimization and neglect within contexts outside of the home/family as well. Also think about the reality of how difficult life is without the safety provided within a healthy home/family environment. Furthermore, try and connect results and losses to the development of the FLAGS. Keep in mind that many of the problems we experience in adulthood relative to the appropriate expression of emotions result from the inability to properly identify and express these emotions in childhood. If someone is raised in an unhealthy home/family environment the expression of emotions is stifled either through emotional victimization, or through the denial from adults that kids even have emotions other than anger, which should be repressed and controlled rather than expressed.

As emotions are stifled children basically learn their emotions are not real or are insignificant when compared to those of adults. We are often taught unintentionally (in the sense of there being no other recognized alternatives) by the adults from our past to act out emotions rather than identify and resolve them. This is the reason we move into hopelessness and develop irrational thoughts, and resort to acting out rather than backing up to deal with the origins of the emotion-based anxiety and/or depression. As this process of acting out continues we further complicate our lives and the lives of those around us always asking the question: "What's wrong with me?" The more accurate questions should be: "What's wrong with where I came from and what I've been through; and how can I resolve the FLAGS from the past?"

This is probably a good point at which to explore personality types and parenting styles which set up the abuse and victimization and resulting complications. I believe the single most important element relative to victimization, next to the unresolved issues and grief from the past, is arrogance. I cannot express this strongly enough. Arrogance is defined in Webster's as an expression of an exaggerated sense of one's own worth or importance in an overbearing manner. It is further defined as a feeling of superiority, and as presumptuousness. Along with arrogance comes the sense of entitlement I have mentioned in a previous chapter. In both my personal and professional experiences I encounter arrogance exhibited by adults on a regular basis in the community, in the workplace, in the schools, in different religious settings, in the justice and law enforcement systems, in government and politics, etc. Nothing makes me angrier than to see anyone defend their position of arrogance and entitlement toward any other human being, especially toward children and adolescents.

People who are arrogant are often control freaks and are generally very defensive (as well as offensive) and insecure. They choose from a number of tactics which include: playing games; being passive/aggressive; competing to be right or on top; playing the victim and/or victimizer according to their needs and purpose; retaliating; back stabbing; judging; being territorial; being vicious and cruel; being sarcastic; being deceptive and blatantly dishonest; etc. Arrogant people generally are very threatened if their positions of superiority and power are not acknowledged, or if they are challenged. Religious leaders, politicians, people who espouse bigotry and prejudices, parents, teachers and other school staff, and people in the law enforcement and justice fields present prime examples of people with such characteristics when working with kids of all ages. Many times arrogant people are acting out their own FLAGS and emotion-based anxiety in an effort to compensate for their lack of positive self image and self perception which never developed in childhood. Quite often they are acting out all of the FLAGS in ways modeled for them by improper role models when they were growing up. For others the sense of arrogance and entitlement comes from a position of perceived status and importance which may have originated in childhood as well by growing up within a home/family environment of privilege. These are people who as kids were taught that they were more special than everyone else – the prince and princess complexes.

A major problem relative to arrogance lies within the concept of strength in numbers. A few good examples are religious leaders, teachers, politicians, and law enforcement – so-called "peace officers", all of which often exist within closed groups in which membership status is perceived as being above and beyond that of the ordinary citizens. This is not true for all people within these groups, and while I am not sure what the actual percentages would be of effective to ineffective, I believe the percentage in the negative group would be rather alarming if kids and adults impacted by these groups were polled. Adults within all of these roles need to realize they are no better than, or more important than any other groups involved in the lives of kids. The scary fact is people in these groups can do considerable damage if they function from an arrogant stance and sense of entitlement, both based in power struggles (competition), and a need to control others and situations. Many in these groups want their jobs to be respected, and to be respected personally and professionally regardless of their respectability. I am talking about respectability relative to how they interact with and feel toward others, especially toward children.

For example, I have had the experiences of teaching these very principles to teachers and school staff. Afterwards I was able to observe them in their respective jobs creating all of the FLAGS within children through emotional abuse by using the same abusive verbal statements we had just covered in a workshop and as identified in a previous chapter in this book. This represents an intense form of denial of, and resistance to the possibility these adults may have some issues to resolve, or have some need to do their own honest self examination/assessment. This is the kind of arrogance, coupled with ignorance which sets up children to fail and then get blamed for their own failures. The really sad fact is that many of these adults actually mean well. They are just not willing to examine and change their approaches to kids in order to have a positive impact on the kids' lives and futures. Shame and guilt only lead to very poor self-images and are very prominent components of the fear, loneliness and anger identified in the RFLAGS Model. As we begin to understand the results from abuse and victimization, we also begin to resolve and eliminate guilt and shame from the FLAGS mix by recognizing all of the hurtful messages we were given as kids as the lies they really were. These ineffective and inappropriate approaches will continue to exist until the multigenerational cycles of abuse and victimization are acknowledged and broken by everyone. I have been able to break these cycles in my life, and so can you!

It is important to know that the very adults who often make the negative headlines in the news are likely living out and acting out their emotion-based anxiety which resulted from emotionally unhealthy experiences within the home/family context. My proposals are presented only as realistic explanations of destructive patterns, not as excuses for or justifications of them. Also important are the influences from the other contexts in which abuse and victimization occur against kids by adults who do not make the headlines or get the negative publicity they deserve. These adults include: abusive, ineffective teachers or school staff; self-serving politicians; an abusive police officer, who along with a partner beats up a kid who runs, and/or plants evidence or exaggerates and creates information to make sure that charges will stick; or religious leaders who are just as human as everyone else yet preaching that others are worthless, evil beings; etc. All of these people perpetuate the victimization that any given kid may be experiencing within the home/family context. This is what I mean when I talk about complicating factors which open anyone to further abuse because of the fact kids generally cannot control what is done to them in any context. This is what I mean by arrogance relative to kids being the targets of many injustices based on an adult's need to be right and in control.

The kids we are raising today will be the very ones in the headlines tomorrow if we do not deal with our own issues and then dedicate ourselves to raising healthy kids; or deal with our unresolved issues before we ever bring kids into our lives. Anyone who becomes a parent or works directly with kids, regardless of their role, needs to take an oath and recognize the seriousness of such associations. Any formal connection between an adult and a kid should be thought of as a marriage in the sense of a matching or union for the sake of establishing a nurturing, spiritual bond, the length of which is defined by the circumstances and situation surrounding the association. The oath for each union between adult and child, as parent, guardian, or professional, should take the form of some solemn vow such as this:

<u>An Oath To Children</u>

At this moment I choose to take you into my life. I do so either by creating you as a parent would; or by willingly accepting the fact our paths have crossed through no design of your own. I have chosen this role as part of my own journey through life, and the crossing of our paths is the direct result of my own destiny. Because of this I will take very seriously the responsibility of providing for you in every way. My responsibilities will be limited only by the role I will now play in your life. Therefore, I promise to know myself at the deepest level possible. While striving to be the most positively effective role model I can possibly be for you, I will seek to resolve every negative element from my past. I will give you the acceptance and respect you deserve, and I will correct very quickly any mistakes I *will* make along the way. I am here to meet your needs, and ask only that you apply yourself to the fullest level of your potential. I seek not to make you, but only to nurture you into the exciting discovery of your true nature relative to who you can become. I want only to set the potential into motion, and then applaud as you learn to create the motion for yourself, as your Self. This is my solemn and heartfelt commitment to you in recognition of the wonder of your uniqueness.

This kind of oath, even taught to adolescents before they choose to become sexually active and risk becoming parents, should be posted on the walls, notebooks, refrigerators, and bulletin boards in every adolescent and adult environment as a constant reminder of our spiritual obligation as caregivers for children. The continuous reminder of this obligation would help to establish full awareness for everyone from an early age on relative to the development of personal morals and values. Adults provide the building blocks for the future relative to the world of possibilities and hazards we create for the generations of kids to follow. Each successive generation should work very diligently to advance the spiritual evolution of the world and mankind relative to our position in the universe, moving ever closer to existing as the image of God according to original intention. The Source that is God is the ultimate example of the perfect adult/leader who gives us everything we need to grow into eventual perfection. All we have to do is listen to the "whisperings of our souls" and seek guidance from effective role models who will guide us and then let go as we learn and grow, creating the motion for ourselves. I firmly believe that the energy that *is* us is God *within* us. Please see your role as parent and/or professional a higher Sense of calling.

Chapter VII

KIDS

I have decided to call this chapter simply "KIDS" – not good kids, bad kids, at-risk kids, problem kids, or gang kids – just "KIDS". In an earlier chapter I addressed the issue of our tendency to label kids and place them in certain categories. As you will remember, one of my main points was to emphasize how our use of labels and categories directs our thinking toward and interaction with kids. The labels also clearly reflect our biases and prejudices, and allow us to fall into the pit of ineffectiveness, no matter how honorable and altruistic our intentions may be. While to this point my focus has been on adults and the mistakes we make, the most important element in writing this book is for each reader to understand how what we do as adults affects the kids for whom we are directly and indirectly responsible.

My role as father to my now adult daughter Melissa is the best role I have ever played in this drama we call life. As she was growing up I always managed to separate what she was doing from who she was at any given moment. As her father I marveled at her imagination as I watched her play. I spent time with her lying on the floor and listening to music. Outside we would sit and feel the wind on our faces and we would watch the clouds as they formed and changed. I tried to give her at least a good start in life. In later years all of the groundwork paid off as I have watched her struggle with many obstacles and heartaches in her life. Melissa is an incredible poet and I hope each of you will have the opportunity in the future to hear her story chronicled through her own creativity. Her life also confirms my belief in the importance of at least having a good beginning, especially relative to the development of resiliency and the ability to transcend negative experiences.

Even though Melissa's mother and I were divorced since Melissa was three years of age I remained a very active and consistent part of her life in spite of the fact Melissa and I were separated by distance. I always paid my child support and I always made arrangements for her to spend summers and Christmas vacation with me. Divorce is certainly not ideal, but it doesn't have to be totally devastating for the kids involved. Melissa always knew beyond the shadow of a doubt that I continued to love her with all of my heart. She has never had to question this fact in spite of the regrets common for kids whose parents are divorced or separated. Giving up my day to day physical presence in her life was one of the hardest things I have ever done. Rather than seeing the divorce as an end to my role as Melissa's father, I was able to see my role as having only changed. I grieved the loss of my direct presence in her life and worked very hard to create something new by making my somewhat indirect presence in her life work for both of us regardless of many obstacles and much opposition.

From a very early age I always taught Melissa to separate who she is from what she did. Once, in an attempt to insult me, my mother said: "That child doesn't know the difference between you as her father and you as her friend." For me this was quite a compliment and my reply was simply: "She knows the difference." With my daughter I could be both, but always making sure my role as her father remained the more predominant role of the two. Kids need to know through adolescence that their parents will be consistent in the parental role if they are to feel safe. They count on our consistency to nurture and guide them in the right manner and in the right directions. When we fail to play our part effectively by trying to be their friends kids get lost in the confusion of being kids and in the confusion of needing, and not having the proper role models to successfully lead them into becoming high functioning, independent adults.

In the example above of my mother's commentary on my parenting skills, she was actually making a reflective statement on her definition of the parental role. In her mind, kids are to only recognize the authority of parents as she and my dad had so clearly demanded from me. What she was commenting on was the fact Melissa and I could have fun together. What my mother failed to see prior to her statement was the proper balance I always maintained between the two different aspects of my roles, with the greatest emphasis always on my role as father. When Melissa was growing up my role included all of the factors I identified in the chapter about adult roles and responsibilities. In that list I identified many different hats we need to wear relative to our connections with kids. The point I failed to emphasize is how much more responsibility we have as parents. In comparison to other adult role models, parents _must_ make sure all of these required obligations are carried out, balanced with the need to also enjoy being a parent, and to enjoy being an observer and active participant in the wonder of each kid's uniqueness.

Let me clarify my definition of the role of parents as friends to kids. A friend for any of us is someone we see as an ally and an equal. Friends are loyal, trustworthy, and can be counted on to provide support and guidance in times of need. However, the relationships between friends tend to be somewhat fragile, and are subject to being dissolved due to any number of factors including differences of opinion, betrayal, and separation by distance. It is possible to bring in new friends to either replace the old ones or to simply add to the list. Friends also tend to see each other as equals in the sense of choosing to be friends, and in the sense of having things in common relative to similarities and common interests. Unlike friends, it is not possible to replace family – believe me, I know. The significant difference is the connection by "blood" which exists within families and not with friends. This connection clearly implies an unspoken obligation to be loyal and to stay together in appropriate ways. Parents who seek primarily to be friends with their child or children are likely acting out unresolved issues from their respective pasts. This will result in at least some degree of ineffectiveness which will deprive their children of opportunities to learn from adults who are adults – not from adults who still need to see themselves as kids.

Parents, on the other hand, bring children into this world either by choice or by accident. It is very important to recognize the fact that in families there are many different personalities involved. I believe reality suggests that in some cases we would not necessarily choose to associate with the people in our families if not for the simple fact we are together as family. Look at how people within families do not always get along or even like each other in some cases. Before parents create a child some thought should be given to the lifelong commitment needed to love, accept, and nurture any child regardless of whether or not they meet our own expectations. As parents our goal should be to simply raise a child to be the best they can be, making sure they have the resiliency and ability to transcend any losses; also making sure as parents we are not the ones creating such losses.

Kids born into families have no say in the matter. Always remember that no child ever asks to be conceived or born! An infant is created and a soul fills that body. As parents we do not get to choose from a list of desirable characteristics we want a child to possess, and in that sense we, too, are the victims of chance. It is simply a happenstance union of egg and sperm which determines the outcome relative to genetic possibilities. While males have millions of sperm present to fertilize the available egg, there is a tremendous factor of chance in the particular egg present at the moment of conception given the number of eggs available in the female's body. Children can be wanted and intended, wanted (after the fact) and unintended, or are completely unwanted. There simply are no other possible combinations associated with bringing kids into this world. Sometimes kids can be "wanted" for the wrong reasons. These include the ideas of having something to love, saving or keeping a relationship, or receiving a government check. Once the reality sets in that the child did not solve the problems, quite often the child then becomes an unwanted nuisance and hindrance.

In addition to the factor of chance relative to genetic possibilities, there are numerous random factors coming into play relative to the physical development of the fetus, and also of the child once they are born. The result of all random factors is the uniqueness of each child – those parts of each of us which serve to identify who we are physically, as well as the potential for personality development, and personal growth and achievement. Who we become as an individual relative to the physical and genetic characteristics is impacted and determined significantly by the environments in which we are raised. Other factors include the people in those environments who are responsible for our care, along with our own resiliency and ability to transcend heartache and hardship if our external components and contexts are not favorable.

As you can see, the home/family context is crucial. This is the only context we as parents can directly and willfully control. It is the one factor in the lives of kids which determines how they will experience and survive the contexts outside of the home/family environment. Because of the randomicity of so many chance factors, it is also possible to see how easily complicating factors for kids can develop. Randomicity sometimes results in extremes. Without an opportunity to balance out the extremes created through no intention of our own as individuals relative to the creation of our physical identity, factors which complicate our lives tend to dominate our lives and serve as the fuel which feeds our emotion-based anxiety.

I see these elements among my friends and among the kids and families with whom I work. For example, Susan, one of my closest and dearest friends was born with spina bifida. This left her with numerous complicating factors relative to her physical abilities and appearance, and relative to how her family and the world reacted to and interacted with her. Susan was old enough to have been born prior to the recognition of the rights of those with handicaps and disabilities. There were also a number of environmental factors which served to further complicate her life even into adulthood. She was not able to go to college, and was denied many of the opportunities for personal growth and development most of us take for granted. However, in spite of her complicating factors both inside and outside of her home/family context, Susan used her resilient spirit to transcend many of the obstacles which potentially could have impeded and further handicapped her. Though her body was deformed, she was blessed with physical beauty, and an incredible mind and spirit which allowed her to fight against and beat many of the odds she had to face.

Think carefully about how this one physical factor complicated Susan's life in all of the contexts I have identified. The context in which she found the most comfort was that of religion, which for her focused more on spirituality than on outdated edicts and dogma. She was lucky someone didn't decide at birth that she shouldn't be allowed to live. Her contributions to my life and to this world would never have happened, and her uniqueness would never have been celebrated. Susan was who she was by conscious intent, determination, and purpose, allowing her to take control of the external factors which sought to destroy her and keep her down within virtually every context of her existence. Fortunately, laws have been enacted within the other contexts which ultimately gave her the protection and some of the acceptance she deserved. Susan lived to be 63 and was truly an inspiration to all who knew and loved her.

Another example of resiliency and the ability to transcend is that of Charlie, my childhood friend I have known since first grade. Charlie always had to struggle with learning difficulties concerning math and reading. Looking back it is clear to me that he had, and still has ADHD. He was given a very creative mind and a loving and supportive family. His mother made sure he had whatever help he needed in order to be successful. Fortunately his parents never put him down through emotional or physical abuse. Instead they always encouraged him, steering him in the direction of college and the career of his choice. This is a good example of how the home/family context helped him to overcome the obstacles and to face the outside contexts which had the potential to disable him. He is now a very successful architect working overseas under contract with a major American-based company. Even as a child I envied the loving environment relative to Charlie's family, and I respect so much his determination to succeed, even if he has had to learn a few lessons in humility and caring for and about others along the way.

Having given you some examples from the lives of my daughter and two friends who have had to deal with complicating factors, let me now turn to the kids I encounter within the context of my profession as a psychologist and as a psychoeducational instructor. With wholehearted enthusiasm I dedicate my entire focus professionally toward the kids who are labeled by the rest of society as troubled, bad, undesirable, delinquent, incorrigible, 'the problem', deviant, dangerous, etc. Also within this focus I am able to work with the adults, including parents and family members, who directly impact the lives of these kids. It is important for each of you to know that the kids I work with come from all walks of life, and come in all sizes and cultures imaginable. These kids are generally victimized within all of the contexts because of arrogant and ignorant adults who perpetuate their sense of exaggerated self importance and sense of separation, thereby not taking any direct responsibility for helping to create the environments in which these kids are raised. This is true both from within families and outside the home/family context.

In this chapter and throughout other parts of this book I want to share with you my perspective relative to working with any population of kids who have problems, make bad choices, and do bad things. As I stated in an earlier chapter, I know my role as a psychologist is very different with kids compared to the roles of people in settings where more control over situations and environments is necessary. However, as I also stated earlier, once control is established relative to providing a safe environment, optimum benefits and opportunities to the kids within any setting, the issue of control and domination needs to take a leap backwards and out of the way. Adults in any role need only enough authority and respect necessary to effectively perform their roles for the kids they have vowed to serve.

My first step in dealing with kids referred to me from various settings within the community including community based agencies, schools, social service programs, and justice related organizations, is to establish rapport and an environment of mutual regard and respect. My primary goal is to create an environment which will facilitate the opportunity to know and understand any kid in order to better identify and meet their needs. My first statements to kids serve as indications that I am likely different from many of the adults they have encountered in the past. I assure them I have no need to control them, which would be a pointless intention anyway. The last thing I want is for a kid to feel any expectation from me of needing to bow down to my authority. I make sure to never convey any sense of arrogance or sense of being entitled to receive respect from them. After all, we have just met and they do not know if I deserve their respect. I clearly recognize the need to earn their respect, and I avoid any form of competition relative to power struggles or perceptions. I am not offended by language and I do not make the use of words an issue as my goal is for kids to speak freely and not be on guard. My only limitation relative to language is that words not be thrown at me as weapons and out of disrespect. Because I am respectful I ask for and get this consideration in return. Only one kid has ever threatened me and did so on two different occasions. Both times I literally stood up and told him not to continue any further with his threats, indicating that I didn't deserve to be treated like this. Both times he sat back down and later told me the only reason he trusted and respected me was due to the fact that I was not afraid of him. This kid was one of the most out of control clients I have ever had. Once I proved myself to him by standing up to him our professional association improved completely.

My first interview with a kid is conducted with the kid alone. The only exception is if they are below the age of 7 or 8, or if they are somehow unable to adequately speak for and represent themselves. This will usually limit the time a younger kid is willing to spend with me, making the encounter somewhat brief, and will then include more parent/guardian participation than I have with older kids. The initial goal is to get a clear picture of the kid's perspective and sense of reality as to why he is seeing me professionally. Many kids don't always know the facts associated with their lives, but can always tell you what they think are the facts when asked in the absence of adults. In fact, in many cases I never work with or meet the parents or guardians as oftentimes the kid is referred to me as a requirement of probation. This was especially true when I worked in California. Because I worked in a community-based clinic the financial paperwork needed to set up a case was handled prior to my first actual appointment. Quite frequently the parents of the kids I generally work with couldn't care less about family therapy and only want me to "fix" the kid without involving them in the process. In some cases the insistence on including family therapy is actually absurd and can be detrimental to the goals of helping the kid. This is especially true if the family is extremely dysfunctional and/or the kid is at least sixteen or older.

Ironically, and contrary to many professionally recognized theories or interventions, success with a kid and without family involvement is not only possible, but at times in the kid's best interest. Virtually all of the kids I see appreciate the opportunity to meet alone with me because historically meetings about the kid with adults outside the family have been unfair and upsetting to the kid. In these kinds of meetings the kid sits there being talked about as if they weren't even in the room. More often than not, the kid listens to a long list of "what's wrong" with them, with the adults not being honest about their own flaws and inappropriate behaviors which increase the kid's motivation to act out. I have learned that adults only tell a fraction of the truth relative to the ways they act out inappropriately with their kids and in their homes. Generally adults are quite surprised when I ask them in front of the kid "what do you do that contributes to the chaos in your lives?" I assure them that while I do not know the truth, I am aware that both of them do and I can only hope they are giving me an accurate account of the problems they experience. Even then I know I am only seeing or hearing a relatively small part of the total reality.

When I have the opportunity to do so, I explain my therapeutic approaches to the family member(s). I stress that my main focus will be on the well being of the kid, with an effort to uncomplicate the kid's life, which in turn will benefit everyone involved. Furthermore, I stress the parents' or guardians' need to respect the kid's right to a reasonable amount of privacy, having already explained to the kid the limits on confidentially prior to this exchange with the adults. Other than issues required by law, I only report things I think put the kid at serious risk of unusual or extreme harm to themselves based on risky behaviors or faulty thinking. Even then I always give the kid the chance to talk to the adults first or allow me to do it for them and hopefully in the presence of the kid. A kid will not talk to anyone they can't trust, and I believe in most situations it is better that they talk to someone rather than to no one.

In many cases families are accustomed to being blamed and judged for the problems existing within their lives. I very quickly address this by establishing that my job is to make observations and then be honest about what I see, not out of a need to be right, and with a willingness to make adjustments as we go along. If they have a history of what I call "therapist jumping" I suggest they jump before we even get started given the fact they won't always like what I have to say. I also set limits by telling them I won't allow them at any point to turn on me and blame me for problems existing before they ever walked into my office. I have had no more than 5 families get angry with me since I began providing therapy in 1990. Even then, with the exception of one case, I was able to work with the kid in spite of the unwillingness of family members to cooperate and participate in the process. Also in those cases the family members continued to keep me up to date on the issues they felt still needed to be addressed. One case in particular was successfully closed when the kid finished high school, an accomplishment that no one in his family ever expected to see.

From the start I stress to the kid my desire to try and help by getting to know them, treating them with respect and fairness, and acknowledging my inability to assist without their permission and cooperation. I always validate their perceptions and observations of people in their lives once I believe their perceptions to be accurate, even if this means agreeing that a person(s) or situation(s) is extremely difficult to deal with or face. From there I help them identify ways of facing and dealing with the realities of people and situations in such a way as to avoid further complications for themselves. I stress that unfortunately in many cases I have to teach them to survive and grow in spite of people and factors which are frequently unchangeable. By giving any kid the opportunity to objectively identify reality it is possible to get them to learn to respond rather than react to situations where they simply cannot win, even if they are justified in wanting to do so. They can clearly see that taking care of themselves is not the same thing as giving in and letting an adult win. It is only a matter of protecting *their* butts without kissing the butts of others. It is possible to get this point across by giving them examples of situations in which I, as an adult, still have to use this approach, also acknowledging that it is much more difficult for them than it is for me given the fact that kids are automatically at a disadvantage. Kids appreciate my style and candor.

As much as possible, and as it is appropriate, I try to make the encounters with kids relaxed, and occasionally fun and comical. When I feel resistance to an issue I leave it for awhile as there are usually many other things to address. Once mutual respect and regard are established effectively it is possible to laugh with kids at their own absurdities and extremes. From the moment I take on a case I assure the kid they are now "one of my kids". I then pledge to do all I can reasonably do professionally to help, guide, and back them up as long as I know I can trust them to be honest with me. Regardless of challenges to the contrary by other professionals and adults, I believe that most kids are very honest and open with me, especially after I explain to them that I am required by law to protect their privacy, given certain fully explained limits relative to confidentiality.

Every once in a while I get fooled and I don't hold back my own sense of disappointment, betrayal, and anger, especially when the dishonesty led me to defend them against adults in positions of authority over them. I have also learned not to stick my neck out too far until I am as sure as I can possibly be that it is the right thing to do. This kind of betrayal has happened to an extreme in only two situations out of literally hundreds of cases. Both times I made the kid very aware of how I felt, pointed out their need to feel shame and guilt, asked for and received an apology, as well as a promise not to be deceptive with me again. I believe it is important to be real with kids when their words and behaviors affect you either negatively or positively. Through these approaches kids learn it is possible to trust, respect and regard another person to such an extent that the kids feel badly when they feel they may have jeopardized a connection with someone who genuinely cares for and about them. Don't get me wrong, I am never punitive with a kid, only real. Anything more would make it personal and unprofessional, a fine line which must always be regarded and never crossed.

My main focus with kids is on the reality of how their choices are complicating their lives. In this sense my only goal is to help them figure out how to uncomplicate things for their sake alone. There is no threat in this. I do not pretend to have all the answers, nor do I pretend to know everything that would be best for them. Also, I try to understand the reality of their lives and the perceptions they have of their respective reality before I try to proceed with problem resolution. Always, I attempt to undo any damage I perceive to have been done by others through the process of labeling created within the contexts outside of my office. I simply model for the kids the way adults in all roles are suppose to treat them, with the balance of influence directly related to the role and experience of each adult involved.

As stated previously my role as a father to my daughter has been the best and most rewarding role and identity I have ever assumed. Within the parameters of reasonable professional limits, I play this same kind of role in the lives of the kids with whom I work. I have even found that many single moms will bring their kids to me as a male therapist for this very reason. The role of being a single mom is a very difficult one, especially with regard to raising sons. I do not mean in any way to sound chauvinistic in this position. Most of the single moms and their kids would agree with my statement as well. I have even had kids jokingly refer to me as "Dad", and even though they laugh it off I acknowledge their perception and put it into perspective for them. Keep in mind that many of the kids I work with have no dad immediately present in their lives. Even the ones who do have fathers or father figures present in their lives use me as a measure of what a good father should be. This is very useful when working with the entire family in therapy. I use my role as therapist to model the proper interactions which should take place between parents and their kids, always working not to get caught in the middle of parent/child conflicts.

I believe the single most significant factor missing in the lives of kids is balance. I am not sure kids have ever had much balance in their lives at any time throughout history. Hopefully as a result of the spiritual, not religious, evolution of the world this concept is beginning to surface as a major item of focus needing to be addressed to better the lives and futures of children. In relationships between adults and kids, regardless of the role of the adult, the scales should always be incredibly out of balance, and always tipped in favor of the kids. As adults we have an obligation to meet the needs of kids, even if we have to do so at the expense of our own needs at times. I am not saying we have to sacrifice ourselves 100% of the time. After all, we need to give to ourselves first if we are to be effective for others. However, our needs should never take precedence over the urgent and essential needs of kids, especially within professional interactions. Sometimes the needs of kids can be put on hold if they are not urgent and significant enough to be taken care of immediately. The reverse cannot be true of our needs being met at the expense of kids. No matter how urgent our needs are we still have an obligation to see that the needs of kids are met at least temporarily through some other source until we can return our focus to them. Parenting is a full-time job until kids become self sufficient and independent. Other adult roles are more confined relative to time and situation.

What does balance in the life of a child look like? To me balance does not come in the form of compromise in terms of this *or* that, rather, in the form of this *and* that. Love and regard for any kid cannot be measured in terms of balance. These elements should always be to the fullest level possible and free of conditions. Balance looks like proper amounts and degrees of: freedom and limits; responsibility and leisure; self exploration and guidance; creativity and structure; individuality and connectedness; praise and constructive observation (rather than criticism which is judgmental);

self expression and respect for others; spirituality/intuition and freedom to think; morals/values and rights of others; self focus and other focus; expression of emotion and self control; self support and support from others; and ability to soothe oneself and the need to be soothed by others. These are only a few aspects of what likely could be another of my long lists.

The kids I work with have very little balance in their lives, which means most of their lives are lived out in the extremes, and at the mercy of external factors. In many instances single parents will cling to their children in times when their own emotional needs are out of balance, only to discard the kids when life gets better or they meet someone new who replaces the kids relative to their role as provider of care and emotional support. It is quite common for many adults to see kids relative to the benefit kids can provide to them. Even more frightening is the fact that some people have children and/or assume other roles to interact with kids without any forethought to the needs of kids who will be left in their charge. This means that in many cases kids are brought into the lives of adults for the primary purpose of meeting needs and filling emotional deficits of the adults. The only goal for creating children and for working with children should be the expressed desire to experience the enrichment of life associated with nurturing and guiding children into adulthood. Children should never be accidental and unwanted. Nor should anyone enter into any association with children with their own agendas and needs at the forefront of their motivation. Sometimes motivation and needs fulfillment can be dominant and unconscious, especially when there are issues of loss and unresolved grief present in the adult. This is why honest self-examination is so crucial for all adults.

Effectiveness is much more important than intention relative to associations with children. As I have said, people with the very best of intentions can sometimes do the most harm. After all, kids are judged according to the behaviors they display. These behaviors often indicate how effective adults have been in giving kids the balance they need, not how bad, undesirable, or problematic a child is. Balance means a kid is in control intrinsically rather than extrinsically through fear and intimidation which lead to compliance and broken wills. External controls also result in emotions which are way out of balance and which have been created for kids by adults. Extreme examples of personality characteristics can cover a wide range. The opposite ends of the spectrum go from being spoiled and arrogant relative to feeling more special than they really are, to being out of control and acting out in undesirable and unacceptable ways. In many cases kids know what they are doing is wrong, but do not know how, or at times even want to control their actions. The balance between these extremes manifests as a child who becomes a high functioning adult with incredible regard for self and others relative to conscious awareness of the interconnectedness between and among all elements of the universe.

Now let's focus on balance and what this involves for adults. Remember my belief is in the responsibility all adults have for the world we create for ourselves and for children both in the present and in the future. As I indicated earlier I believe the world has been and is going through a balancing act relative to all of the changes in perspective that have occurred since the end of World War II. From much of what I hear and read I believe people are focusing more on our respective selves and our place in the universe relative to spirituality and relative to our spiritual obligations to be effective role models for kids. The focus turns more and more to the need for loving, nurturing families and support for both adults and kids if balance is to be achieved.

Balance has quite a different meaning today than it did during the times of ancient societies and civilizations. I believe my writings reflect the zeitgeist of the current day and age as did the writings from the past. Even though the contextual factors may change relative to the need for balancing, the basic spiritual truths in my writings and the writings of others will remain constant. It is the evolving Truth which is literal relative to inspiration, not the transitory historical details. We must seek only to present and promote a universal Truth of unconditional love and acceptance, with no room for judgment, discrimination, or inequality within any of the contexts addressed herein. We must seek only to celebrate diversity among kids and adults and focus on the spiritual evolution happening in the world today as a means of balancing relationships between adults and kids. It is the Truth heard in our hearts, from within any truly inspired writings, upon which we are to focus. This is the kind of balance adults need to be seeking and passing along to children.

Factors in the lives of adults which need to be in balance include: professional and personal roles; time for self and others; work and "recreation"; aspirations and reality; secularism and spirituality; focus on self and altruism; loving and being loved; learning and teaching; liberalism and conservatism; individuality and connectedness; emotionality and rationality. Again, these are but a few of the endless combinations of opposing issues and extremes in our lives. However, this should establish a good basis for each of you to generate more subjective examples.

With regard to some issues and extremes there is no room for balancing, only for eliminating the negative extremes in any pair. For instance, there can be no balancing between: love and hatred; acceptance and intolerance; knowledge and ignorance; understanding and bigotry; peace and violence; spirituality and prejudice; love for children and victimization or neglect; reciprocity and selfishness; positive regard and disregard. This list, too, is virtually endless, with the point being there are simply some things that need to be eliminated rather than balanced.

Imbalances and misunderstandings always result from arrogance, ignorance, separation, feelings of threat relative to position and status, and a lack of willingness to open oneself to other possibilities and perspectives. I believe the unwillingness to be open is based in fear. Furthermore, I believe the unwillingness to remain separated out is based in loneliness and anger. Shame and guilt exist on both sides of any separated groups where one group is perceived to be dominant or in control. On the "up" side, guilt and shame are often conscious processes based in the repressed awareness that to dominate is wrong. From the perspective of the "down" side, guilt and shame also exist on an unconscious level. This is from the perspective of being made to feel inferior, when in fact the very actions establishing and perpetuating the perception of domination are nothing but lies based in arrogance, ignorance, and victimization. As I stated earlier, guilt and shame are acquired emotions and can be eliminated as long as there is nothing upon which to base these emotions. On the "up" side, guilt and shame sometimes result from things done to and withheld from others; whereas, on the "down" side the feelings of those targeted are based in what has been done to and withheld from them. Through a process of eliminating the negatives and balancing the other factors, it is possible for both sides to move toward positions of acceptance and understanding.

In the next chapter I will begin to connect more closely how each of us fits into the RFLAGS Model. Hopefully, each of you already has a better understanding of the ways we act out emotion-based anxiety upon ourselves and upon others. We will look at how and why kids make the choices they make relative to our own responsibility as adults for creating the opportunity and need to make such choices.

Chapter VIII

Balancing the Scales

I want to focus again on the concept of arrogance. This time the focus will concentrate more on how some segments of society have fought actively against arrogance since the 1960's with the whole Civil Rights Movement, the hippie generation, and with the efforts of every equal rights group, even through today, joining in the fight for change. Everyone was basically fighting against those identified as part of the "establishment" who held onto and forced their perceived positions of authority and power as the norm since the so-called "discovery of America". European American males dominated within every context based upon the biblical and religious precept of a male godhead ruling the universe and having the church as the obedient, submissive bride of Christ within the Christian religions. Men, and especially white men, saw themselves as the "great providers" for their families and for everyone else in the world. European American women and children submitted to this notion based on traditional values and morals from the past, partly for status, and partly because this was accepted as the norm. Other groups were held at bay by the negative emotions (FLAGS) associated with abuse and victimization.

Even the government of this country was founded upon the notion of religious freedom for the benefit of European immigrants, and was modeled after the governmental structure of the Church of England. (Remember the "P" in WASP stands for 'protest-ants'.) Many of the early settlers from Europe saw this as an opportunity to promote and preserve their own limited views of the world relative to religious beliefs and doctrine. What actually resulted from much of this was the beginning of a tremendous experiment of various religious groups attempting to peacefully coexist with each other at the expense of the people already living on this continent.

The land, people, and cultures were conquered on the pretense of saving the souls of its inhabitants, using the name of God to mask greed for both materialism and power. I believe the establishment of a democratic society was somehow part of the overall plan for the spiritual evolution of the world. However it got thrown off track by ego-based flaws of the originators of "justice".

Don't get me wrong. I do support the freedom associated with living in a democratic society. However, I think the decades since the 1950's have sought to balance out the flaws which have remained in effect almost from the beginning. Many of those flaws are directly related to the imbalance of power established by and for European American males. In this day and age where so many people are fighting to keep out the illegal immigrants, we have allowed arrogance to blind us to the reality that unless people in this country are Native American we were all immigrants here at some point in our respective ancestral histories. No one is better than anyone else! Better *off* doesn't mean better *than*.

As an optimist I personally believe (hope?) the pendulum is currently seeking to settle more into a moderate position where the recognition of equality for all people ultimately becomes the norm. The realist in me recognizes we have a long way to go to accomplish this balance. A position of moderation and acceptance of all undeniable forms of diversity will keep a limit upon the possibility of our society becoming a decadent and immoral one. This will be achieved through a sense of balance within each individual in any society as each of us recognizes our responsibility and need for self-examination and self-rectification; and also by a general shift in focus from differences to commonalities.

Furthermore, a true recognition and acceptance of unchangeable diversity will also be necessary for this balance to be achieved. Diversity has much more to do with who we are than with what we do relative to observable behaviors. It is necessary for each individual to temper their behaviors relative to their own personal balance and to some degree to the balance of society. This is not to take away the right for some to fight conformity. It simply comes back to my belief in an individual's right to be and do as long as these things do not hurt other people. I am not referring to people being hurt in the sense of being offended from an arrogant perspective of judging others as wrong according to their own rigid sets of standards. I simply believe the ways we define morality and values are also becoming more balanced, moving away from a puritanical, Victorian era viewpoint, toward a more realistic recognition of and appreciation for diversity. It is only within these kinds of parameters that it will be possible for people to each possess their own beliefs with a more prominent focus on spirituality rather than upon the self deceptive notions of control and a limited view of God and God's purpose.

Arrogance, a sense of entitlement, and a misinterpretation and misuse of the word respect are all associated with people who perceive themselves as being in positions of authority and dominance over others. Experience and common sense teach me that arrogance, coupled with ignorance, is the great offender and destroyer of justice and balance. Any position of authority should be seen as a position of leadership rather than one of rule. People can only be ruled through compliance and submission. Therefore, anyone in a position as a ruler is actually in a position of power, which should not be confused with respect.

For example, I will respect a leader who truly represents the people being lead, as in developing nations where people need a credible teacher to lead them out of deprivation. However I will not respect a person in a position of power who seeks only to rule and dominate. Haven't we learned anything from history, including recent and current historical injustices and outright bad decisions and policies? In a situation of being ruled, there may be no choice immediately available for me to do anything but submit, with submission being mixed with resentment and anger. The only times I would submit to a ruler is when I am afraid not to, or when there is some advantage in it for me relative to job and advancement in any personal and professional areas of my life. However, my submission will only be temporary, as I will seek to remove myself from this position of being dominated and controlled as quickly as possible once the benefit to me no longer exists, or when I can find some reasonable means of escape. As an adult I can play this game only when it is necessary in order to advance my causes, and only because I know I have the ability and freedom to make choices. I also have the ability to make decisions and learn from my mistakes. In addition I have the determination never to be dominated or controlled by anyone or by any abusive situation.

Dr. David L. Roberts Ph.D.

On the other hand, I will follow a leader when the leader is worthy of my consideration, and I will gladly be a team player as long as the goals of the team match my own goals which I seek to balance between my welfare and the welfare of others. While by nature I am now much more of a leader than a follower, I recognize my need to learn by example in many situations in life where I can respectfully submit to someone who knows more than I do. Or I can submit to someone from whom I wish to learn as a result of the respect I feel toward them. Furthermore, I want to be appreciated for who I am and for what I already know in the sense of what I have to contribute, believing the relationship between leaders and followers, or rather between teachers and students, is reciprocal. Each of us has something to teach and at the same time something to learn from the experience. Depending upon the circumstances of the situation, hopefully the teacher has more knowledge to impart. If not, the teacher is in a serious state of denial and position of arrogance, and should therefore step down and assume the role of student. A ruler can either talk to a captured audience, or switch roles to that of a leader/teacher and experience the reciprocity of such an exchange of information and the generation of new ideas and different perspectives. In life we all need to assume different roles ranging from student to equal participant to teacher.

In this sense a leader is basically a teacher, which means the role of teacher is temporary and transitory. In other words the role of leader should exist only when it is necessary to reach a common goal and the common good, and only until those being lead or taught have also learned how to lead or teach. In reality and ideally, shouldn't all of us be able to change roles from teacher to student at the drop of a hat relative to our own personal and spiritual growth and that of others? In light of these concepts, is it any wonder why Anglos, and particularly European American males, have fought so hard in the last four or five decades to retain their positions of power? Is it any wonder why the various conservative religious groups have also fought within all contexts, especially within the social and political contexts, to remain in control relative to the rigid, self serving moral standards they seek to force upon society? Because they believe in a punitive, arrogant God many religious people live their lives in fear and submission, rather than serving a God who loves and teaches us by example to accept all diversity without evaluative judgment which seeks only to divide people into groups of us versus them. Think about how the Bible has been used to justify white supremacy, even to this day. Look at how those who participate in hate group activities carry banners proclaiming their "Christianity", and verbally proclaim many of the extreme views and beliefs of fundamental religious groups. As a student of psychology I believe there is serious impairment for anyone or any group afraid of new ideas and perspectives. This is especially true when thinking outside the boxes can lead each of us more rapidly through the process of Spiritual evolution, and toward the resolution of issues which only fuel the FLAGS and our need to act out.

Much of this country was founded upon the need to escape from persecution and domination, only to re-establish much the same principles and experiences against others for centuries in this country. In my opinion many people have lost sight of spirituality which cannot be limited within the confines of outdated religious dogma and doctrines. Spirituality is progressive and dynamic, rather than traditional and static. I believe very much in the spiritual evolution of the world and its inhabitants which includes all living things, each with its own position of importance and relativity. I believe we will see the death of arrogance and the birth of balance within a reasonable period of time as the older generations die out and take with them many of their biases and prejudices which they hold onto as an acceptable way of living and thinking. After all, when something ends, something new always begins,

Balance will only be achieved when each of us is willing to give up our selfish needs to be on top, so to speak; and only when each of us is willing to be teacher and student, lover and beloved. Jesus of Nazareth and many other historical spiritual leaders – all of whom are sons and daughters of God – acknowledged themselves as teachers and as messengers from God. None of them meant or asked to be worshipped; they only meant to be copied. As teachers each of them came to teach us as students to see ourselves as the sons and daughters of God. From there human nature and our ego-based needs to dominate and control (which are based in the Fear, Loneliness, Anger, Guilt, and Shame in my RFLAGS Model) have sought to turn spiritual teachings into divisive religious sects. By doing so, people have bastardized the original intention, relative to the messages from God of unconditional love and acceptance. Coupled with this is the need for balance between our explicit responsibility to self and others.

Many people seem to have their heads buried in the sand relative to righting wrongs and protecting kids. Not long ago I saw a news report that attributed the increasing number of deaths of law enforcement officials in the late 1990's to a decline in respect for these individuals. Immediately I recognized the arrogance and absurdity of such an explanation. It is like I have stated earlier, kids and adults are too sophisticated to give respect to those in positions of power without considering the respectability of these individuals. When people speak of defiance of authority, which I hear all the time relative to kids, I believe they are actually referring to a defiance of arrogance which can finally be acknowledged and addressed in recent years due to changes in perception and perspective sparked in recent decades. No one will continually disrespect someone or some reality that is respectable. Many law enforcement officials may in reality be dying in the line of duty as a direct result of the actions of those who still seek to abuse and victimize others relative to law enforcement's demand for unchallenged respect and submission. This possibility is especially true relative to the injustices and secrecy established and perpetrated under the guise of Homeland Security and the U.S. Patriot Act.

Think about the last time you may have been stopped by a law enforcement official for suspicion of some violation such as speeding, failing to yield, or jay walking. Initially my reaction, and the reaction of many others in such circumstances, is one of fear. My voice sounds shaky, and my hands are trembling as I try to find my driver's license and automobile registration. This reaction is based in my fear of what the officer may do to me relative to some kind of power play, expecting me to humble myself and submit to his or her perceived position of domination over me. For me this feels too much like the past that lived in my present for many years. I deeply resent this feeling in spite of the fact I may actually have broken the law. Even though I may get angry for having gotten caught, I will be able to accept that fact and face my consequences more readily if the officer treats me with respect. What kinds of needs are met for officers who need to victimize the offender who is not out of control, oppositional, or threatening?

I am not seeking to diminish the role law enforcement officials play in any society; however, and as everyone knows, a few bad apples can spoil the image of the whole bunch. Think about the kinds of atrocious acts peace officers have to commit to even draw attention beyond their own "Internal Affairs" departments. The point I am trying to make is that respect has to be earned. It cannot be demanded or legislated. Because some positions of authority are necessary for the public welfare, it is important for people in those positions to resolve and balance any aspects of their personalities creating a need to abuse and victimize. If anyone complies with the expectations of an abusive individual, it is out of fear, not out of respect. Many people in society today have these two concepts very confused! Every profession needs to create, publicize and enforce a rigid set of ethical principles and standards. I would bet that such ethics actually exist in theory within the groups I am addressing, but are simply ignored rather than upheld and enforced.

My constant focus on religion, politics, community leaders, public servants, and society are reinforced by all of the chaos and terrorism (abuse/victimization) present and predominant around the world. 9/11 only brought home to the United States the harsh realities many people in other countries have lived with currently and throughout long periods of history. Everyone in positions of power and authority should be as altruistic and honorable as those public servants and private citizens who died while engaged in heroic efforts to save and assist others during the aftermath of 9/11.

American arrogance is a good example of how foolish it is to believe we can't be vulnerable, or to expect that everyone will like and respect us because of our prosperity and grandstanding. It is time to look back historically to see how and why other great nations and civilizations have crumbled throughout time. I think about the people in the United States who suddenly displayed flags in many public places to heighten visibility. Where were these symbols of patriotism before 9/11, and what criteria will people use to determine the time when it is appropriate to take down the flags and put them away?

Flag waving only in the face of a crisis is nothing more than a divisive and arrogant act to prove that "might makes right", all cloaked in a deceptive cover of patriotism and unification. Think about how many of those flags after 9/11 were also flown along with the confederate flag, clearly supporting my suspicions. Flag waving occurs all of the time in other countries as a way of separating themselves from us and showing disrespect, disregard, and hatred toward the arrogance of both American leaders and for the American people. Patriotism based in any stance of us against them, with "us" seeing ourselves as better than "them", can only serve to cause further division between the us/them groups rather than serving to unite people.

A prime example exists in our efforts immediately following 9/11 to solicit support from other nations. Most of the world leaders outside of the United States were at first reluctant to join what appeared to be "our cause" rather than join what should have been promoted even prior to 9/11 as a united "worldwide cause" against terrorism. Even the rhetoric initially used by political figures following 9/11 literally paralleled the very thinking and jargon we attack and punish in kids who promote and commit acts of violence as a way of acting out the same FLAGS created for them due to forms of social injustice. Because of my job as a psychologist I was shocked at the extent of hypocrisy and ignorance exhibited by such reactions from political leaders. Only when these reactions became more thought-out responses were we able to begin effectively addressing terrorism and join as a team member with other nations in a unified effort to identify, stop, punish, and block perpetrators of abuse and victimization. Then along came the whole issue of Iraq and the need to make a show of force to let the world know not to mess with the USA. This again left us standing alone with looks of shock and despair (not "shock and awe") on our faces when this didn't work out as promised. Notice I didn't say as planned. And we wonder where kids learn to think and act the way they do!

By focusing on these issues, I am attempting to establish some credence for the perspective of how each of us should recognize our respective roles as opportunities to be teacher and student, giver and receiver, even antagonist or promoter. I want us to now turn our attention to our adult roles and responsibilities relative to the children directly and indirectly in our charge.

In this section I want us to redefine the home/family context relative to the concept of balancing and the roles we play at any given point.

Let's start with what a family would look like where the lives of the adults are balanced. Remember, one of my biggest points relative to the contexts in which abuse and victimization can occur is the importance of a healthy home/family environment as far as establishing a strong foundation for kids before venturing out to face the other contexts. For adults to have balance in their own lives adults would have already started a process of honest self-examination and self-rectification. Notice I used the word process, indicating self-examination as a life long effort, with the intensity of the effort ideally declining in the future through an increase in insight, wisdom, and self-awareness. Hopefully this process started before the adults became parents. However, it is better late than never. I genuinely believe if adolescents were taught these concepts concerning adult roles and responsibilities, and the need for self examination even during the middle school and high school years, then parenting could be taken on more effectively and hopefully not until adulthood.

In order to understand adult roles and responsibilities adults first need to identify the goals of raising children. One of the primary reasons for having children should be to enrich the lives of the parents. Their enrichment should come in the form of an intense desire to successfully raise kids to be healthy adults. In this sense parents should not take on the role of ruler. Instead, the role of leader and teacher is the only effective stance to take. Remember, the imbalance of parent to child should always be to the benefit of the child. In other words the scale should only be tipped for the parents to assume the dominant position of role model for the purpose of then nurturing a kid's own ability and need to balance both internal and external processes. The scales should never be tipped in favor of a parent's need to dominate and control simply for the sake of ruling. How many of you have ever heard the expression "I rule the roost around here"? This should never come out of the mouths of parents and adults in any roles or settings. It is necessary for kids to follow rules, but not from the perspective of being ruled. Think back about the statement made to me by my mother about my daughter not knowing the difference between me as her friend, or me as her father. What my mother was actually commenting on was the sense of balance I had with respect to my relationship to my daughter. The relationship was balanced, even though at times I had to assume my role as father/teacher for her to understand her need to learn appropriate behaviors relative to herself and others. Balance, as it pertains to the roles we play in kids' lives, is always between love, acceptance, and nurturing, and the elements of teaching and guiding. Anything less is not in the best interest of kids.

The balanced home/family context would also include an adult's ability to balance personal and professional considerations, as well as a balance between personal goals and objectives and the goals and objectives of being a parent. As long as kids are under our care we owe them the consideration they deserve. No decisions directly or indirectly affecting the lives of children should ever be made without the full consideration of the impact our decisions will have on their lives. Failure to give such consideration is based in the arrogant position that kids will adjust and simply get over it. Like it or not we as adults have a major responsibility to serve kids, not the other way around. Until adults are ready to accept this reality, no significant roles and associations with kids should be established. Adolescents need the opportunity to fully understand the seriousness of becoming parents before they engage in any sexual activity that could produce a child. They also need to identify what is missing in their own home/family context and seek to either correct it or establish the determination they will not continue the dysfunction from their childhood into the lives of the next generation.

Also, the balanced family would focus on respect for individuality and the good of the child relative to what each kid wants and needs out of life. I believe if kids are given a solid basis in the first 4 to 6 years, parents can relax a little as children reach adolescence. If kids are taught balance and self control from the beginning of life as intrinsic qualities and characteristics, the chances are they will be able to utilize these values as they venture out on their own in an effort to explore and establish their own sense of self. After all, by the time a kid reaches adolescence we as parents can only hope we have given them the skills needed to navigate and negotiate their way through the many issues they will face. Trying to impose control externally simply for the sake of control during adolescence is pointless. Control placed upon kids who are out of control must be tempered with the appeal for kids to uncomplicate their own existence for their sake alone by learning internal self control which they were never taught. I have seen this approach work time after time with the kids who are referred to me for therapy. To impose control for the sake only of compliance and control results in anger and resentment, thereby teaching kids that control is only necessary when someone is watching. This seems to be a very viable explanation of impulsive behavior, especially in the cases of families rooted in extreme religious beliefs; and families that include people from the military and law enforcement arenas. Kids from these families often revolt and get into as much trouble as other groups of "at risk youth". To me the term "at risk" applies to kids who come from home/family environments at both ends of the spectrum where there is either neglect, or the atmosphere of extreme control and domination.

As I work with kids and their families in my role as psychologist, I see many parents from various backgrounds and environments coming in with the attitude of simply "fix my kid". They will openly lie and minimize the part they often play in creating the problematic behaviors they are asking me to fix. They will even become very defensive when I turn to them and suggest, strictly as an observation, that the choices they have made in their own lives have helped to create the problems their kids are now experiencing for themselves. Parents often times like to play the victim, asking "why me?" followed by the statement, "I/we did the best we could." Parents sometimes have a strong sense of guilt and awareness of the responsibility they bear for the downfall of their kids. However, they seldom admit their mistakes and push this awareness to the back of their minds. The other adults involved directly and indirectly in the lives of any kids also need to own up to the responsibility they share as well. No one is without responsibility for the world we have created which makes it possible for kids to take guns to school to kill others for the wrongs existing in their own lives. I am not seeking to blame anyone in this case in the sense of pointing a finger. I seek only to reveal what I consider to be the truth about mistakes we have made for many years. Even in the Old Testament we are warned about "the sins of the fathers". Arrogance keeps us as adults from claiming our part for the trauma kids experience and then create for others as a way of acting out their own emotion-based anxiety.

When it comes to the consideration of blame, I know this serves no purpose. I am constantly amazed how people are so accustomed to being abused and victimized (which is what I believe blaming and criticizing to be) they are almost always on the defensive. One of the most difficult parts of my job is to get people to actually listen and hear what I am trying to say. At the same time, the most rewarding aspect of my job is when parents and adults can actually hear and understand my words for the help and support they offer. I have no need to victimize anyone by making them feel worse than they already do. I must try to help them deal with their own sense of shame and guilt, as well as with the other FLAGS of fear, loneliness, and anger. I know when a parent tells me they have done the best they knew how to do, they are actually telling the truth. People often do not know what to do and seldom ever think about the need for self examination and rectification in order to successfully transcend their respective pasts and provide the elements needed by children to grow up healthy in all respects. After all, very few people recognize their need for professional help much less actually ask for it.

A parent's feeling of shame generally comes from the fear of what others are thinking about their effectiveness as a parent. I have already addressed this issue earlier of how we are taught at very early ages to falsely believe the whole world is watching us and cares about what we are doing. For instance, the issues within my family really are no one else's business unless I choose to share them as a means of teaching my concepts. No one has the right to judge my family or me for any of the mistakes that have been made. I dare anyone to sit in judgment of my family or me for all we have been through. We are all good people who have simply made mistakes and bad choices. In this sense we are no different than anyone else. This kind of thinking allows me to hold my head up high and encourage others to look beyond their own arrogant need to judge rather than face these same and other problems within their own families. I can only hope those of us in my family, along with other people and their families, can work out our differences before it is too late in this lifetime for ourselves and for future generations.

It is also very easy for others involved in a child's life to avoid facing their failures by blaming kids for their ineffectiveness. Some teachers are very good at this in many situations. Oftentimes teachers allow their arrogance to keep them from seeing the need to approach some children differently, recognizing their own personal limits and tendencies to victimize in some cases which impede their ability to help. As I have said with families, if something is not working relative to problem solving efforts, it probably never will. Therefore, why not try something different? No one is above this kind of scrutiny. I acknowledge that the challenges for teachers and other professionals to work effectively with youth at risk are often enormous. However, these challenges require well thought-out responses toward the goal of meeting the needs of these kids. There isn't a single profession associated with kids which doesn't require extra effort, skills, and a higher level of commitment and ethics.

I am glad to hear through the media of people wanting to hold teachers and other school personnel accountable for their performance and abilities. I will be glad someday to see the same standards applied to those who work within the juvenile justice systems, including district attorneys, public defenders, judges, probation officers, and all staff who work in youth placement facilities and juvenile detention centers. It is a known fact that certain kinds of jobs attract people with specific abusive personality profiles, with an intense need to control, belittle, and dominate. People with such tendencies should be screened out rather than hired in positions of authority over kids. The approach of judging kids solely based on what is recorded on pieces of paper or computer records is wrong. Every kid deserves the opportunity to spend time with someone neutral like myself and other effective caring professionals who can get to know who a kid really is on the inside and make recommendations relative to their future. It is wrong to depend solely on the often inaccurate accounts which are used as evidence to convict kids of crimes. Judges, attorneys and staff in various settings often discount the opinions of professionals such as me as representing the ideals and philosophies of "bleeding heart liberals" who are out of touch with reality. Years ago I actually had a probation officer tell me this to my face. People like this should be encouraged to listen to those of us who are trying to redirect the lives of kids rather than to simply punish and control them.

I even find some within my own profession who take such an uninformed and unintelligent approach to dealing with kids at risk. Locking kids up without making sure each kid gets the help they need and deserve is again an arrogant and ignorant position of dominance and submission for the sole purpose of control. When people are saying there aren't enough resources, those in positions of power and authority should be less politically motivated and less concerned with their popularity and ability to maintain their positions, and more motivated to serve the good of kids involved. It is too easy for others to sit and judge from the sidelines about what causes kids to act out and what needs to be done about it. For some reason at this point in history the tendency is to get rid of kids as though they are the problem. This is obviously much easier than expecting changes from those who arrogantly believe they have played no part in kids' lives relative to having contributed to the negative choices made by kids. Even corporate America is willing to do anything it takes to make a buck off of kids, no matter what the potential consequences may be. It is time to hold everyone accountable for the mistakes we are making, not in the sense of blaming, rather in the sense of finding solutions which we all must generate and participate in if things are to be better for future generations. The only way such solutions will be found is for everyone to undergo some process of self-examination and rectification.

Now let's consider how unbalanced families look relative to some very basic formulas or profiles. Keep in mind my RFLAGS Model and how people of all ages tend to act out emotion-based anxiety. Always look for connections between the past and the present relative to the emotions fueling the anxiety and the tendency to act out. We will look first at a family where both parents are together. Next we will examine blended families where parents are separated/divorced and remarried. Finally we will look at single parent families. Much of this will be familiar to many of you, so we will not spend a great deal of time on these topics. I simply want to help make the connections between the past and who we are in the present.

Generally, when families are together with the biological parents and all of their offspring living under the same roof, there are fewer problems for the kids. However, there is often at least one kid who exhibits problematic behaviors and is considered to be the one acting out the emotion-based anxiety of the family as a system if the family structure and patterns of interaction are out of balance. These kinds of families can range from being overly involved to being significantly under involved. Also remember there is no such thing as the perfect family, and that all families fall somewhere short of this ideal. Family compositions can range from totally dysfunctional to nearly perfect, with all families falling somewhere within the range. However, when thinking about families and balance the range is more of a curve, with balanced families falling exactly in the middle of the range from extremely under involved to extremely over involved. My personal belief is that many of today's families are more toward the tails of the curve rather than in the middle, making the curve inverted rather than bell-shaped. The more balanced families become the more positive the curve becomes, with families shifting away from the extremes toward the mid-range of a pendulum which is well-balanced and keeping perfect time.

Families who are overly involved can range from families where one or both parents are control freaks, to families where there are no real boundaries relative to where I end and you begin. The control freaks are the parents who rule rather than lead and teach, and they do so through fear, intimidation, and humiliation. Families with no real boundaries are also into control and are those who are over protective, and who have no respect for privacy and individuality. According to my education and experiences the strange result from both of these extremes is they produce dependent children who clearly exhibit all of the FLAGS, along with many unresolved grief issues on into adulthood. The children in these families are victimized and abused at least emotionally by never being given the opportunity to learn to be self sufficient with a strong awareness of who they are and what they are capable of accomplishing.

Those kids whose parents are overly involved grow up confused, resentful, and unsure of themselves. These kids tend to make many mistakes during adolescence and in adulthood through defiance of arrogance because they were never given the opportunities to learn appropriate skills which would help them function at optimal levels as adults. Anytime families fail to give kids what they need in order to be healthy in all respects are guilty of neglect and deprivation, which we identified earlier as passive forms of abuse and victimization. Arrogance and ignorance come into the picture relative to parents' beliefs there is nothing wrong with their parenting skills, and therefore, convince themselves there is no need for self-examination and rectification. Parents need to look at the issues fueling their own needs to act out their unresolved emotions and anxiety from the past upon each other and upon their children.

Keep in mind also how each of these patterns of parental ineffectiveness creates complicating factors which make the world outside of the home/family context even more threatening, and more of an opportunity to act out when kids think no one is looking. Some kids will act out as a result of peer pressure. However, I think it is important to look at the extent of acting out and the kinds of acting-out behaviors chosen. Plain and simple, if a kid takes a gun to school and kills his classmates, even if this is the first offense, either this kid has serious mental problems which should have been identified and attended to by family members and professionals, or he is acting out all of the FLAGS which have built up as a result of various forms of abuse and neglect. Neglect can also include a lack of much needed monitoring and supervision of kids, their friends, and their activities. Kids who kill frequently come from homes where there is either serious over involvement or serious under involvement. In either case, parents of these kids must be in a serious state of denial, and are the very parents you see in the media playing the victims. I base this observation in the simple reality that kids do not just wake up one morning and decide to kill without some prior history of evidence indicating this potential for extreme violence. Adults are not as innocent as they want us to believe they are. Furthermore, adults are not as innocent as they need to believe they are either.

Now let's shift focus to the idea of blended families where parents are separated/divorced and have remarried. Often times these adults bring other children into the picture from previous marriages, and they then have one or more children together. In my opinion there are two very big mistakes made by adults who become romantically involved following separation/divorce. First, many adults tend to jump into rebound relationships because they are unable to deal with the emotion-based anxiety which probably created the first bad marriage, and served as the motivation to marry again without working on the unresolved issues.

Secondly, adults fail to consider how the presence of someone else will effect the kids involved, especially when the motivation is for "all of us to be a family again". This is actually an adult fantasy need imposed upon the kids as a way of trying to make kids embrace advantages, existing primarily for the adults involved. Divorce and separation only reinforce the reality that intimate relationships are fragile as opposed to the parental connection which is permanent even when ignored and abandoned. Parents are entitled to happiness and they need adult companionship; however, an adult's *first* responsibility is to their children and their well being until the kids are old enough to live on their own. Many adults expect kids to love the new partner as though they were their biological father or mother. This is too great a demand to make of kids. Adults should be satisfied if the new spouse and the kids can simply agree to peacefully coexist. If more than this is possible, then great. However, this should not be an expectation as expectations limit the range of possible responses.

It is extremely important for all adults to remember that kids generally have no say in decisions adults make, even though the decisions will greatly impact the lives of kids as well. Adults expect kids to accept changes without any complaining and with total acceptance and compliance. This is adult arrogance and ignorance at its best. As long as we are happy, kids should be happy too. As far as I am concerned, parents forfeit their right to make any rash decisions which can potentially have an adverse impact on the lives of kids simply by virtue of being parents. I am not saying adults should allow kids to dictate and rule the lives of the parents; rather, that adults need to take their time to communicate effectively with all involved before moving forward. This approach keeps kids from acting out their emotion-based anxiety which will surely develop from separation/divorce situations.

Adults who are separating or divorcing have a responsibility to work out their issues appropriately and not at the expense of the children who are often used as pawns, with kids feeling they have to choose between parents relative to love and loyalty. This is almost criminal and certainly immoral. I am glad to see some communities now requiring counseling and negotiation with respect to settling marital issues of property and custody. Kids of separated/divorced parents are scarred for life; whereas, the lives of the adults tend to mend and move forward, except in those cases where people continue repeating the same mistakes by not recognizing the need for honest self examination and rectification.

Again, the defiance of kids in blended families is a defiance of arrogance resulting in the lack of consideration given kids relative to their feelings, desires, and needs. Kids resent being treated with less respect than is demanded from them, and they will act this out by openly challenging the role of the stepparent. Rather than seek to mend the wounds which have resulted from the lack of consideration and regard, parents and parental figures usually set up the competition of you will do as I say, rather than admit the mistakes, apologize, and seek forgiveness. This represents true respect for kids. I am amazed at how healing the words "I'm sorry" can be when spoken from the heart by a parent or other adults. After all why should a kid forgive us if we cannot or will not admit the wrongs we have done to them? To have a parent look you in the face and tell you "there was a lot of love in this home", when you know in your heart and soul that this is a lie, is a very insulting experience.

While parents may mean well, there is no greater hurt than the denial of how what adults do effects kids. When love is expressed properly it doesn't hurt or leave open wounds which sometimes never heal. This is especially true when kids are dealing with complicating factors such as sexual orientation, or some form of handicap/disability, which makes them feel less than others anyway relative to self esteem issues. Homosexuality can be a form of handicap, not in the same sense of some type of physical impairment, but in the sense of the resulting discrimination and bigotry. This is forced upon those who are gay from families and society which often times arrogantly holds onto its need to believe that people (especially males) who are anything less than heterosexual are deviant and evil. Some of you reading this book at this very moment have a homosexual or bisexual child living in your home. Hopefully, you will seek the information necessary from such organizations as Parents and Friends of Lesbians and Gays (PFLAG) (not to be confused with my RFLAGS) with many local chapters nationwide, before it is too late. There are increasing indications that many unexplained adolescent suicides are due to FLAGS related to sexual orientation. Homosexual and bisexual individuals are truly at the mercy of external factors, as they are handicapped not because of themselves, but because of the limits society, politics, and religion tries to place on them.

In my experience I have found single-parent families to be the most problematic and chaotic, especially when a single mom is the head of the household. Like it or not, there are basic differences between men and women, even if these are perceived rather than actual differences relative to parental roles. I have made this statement to many single moms, all of whom agree with me. Kids miss the presence of a father or at least the presence of a positive father figure. I also believe boys have a much more difficult time dealing with this than the girls do. Quite often boys feel they become the "man of the house", and believe mom cannot tell them what to do. This is made even worse when moms look to their oldest son to take on the adult role, as what is referred to as the parentified child. Many moms make the mistake of becoming dependent upon their children, especially their sons, for emotional support following separation/divorce. This mistake becomes very problematic as the kids get older and feel like no one can set limits with them. This results when parents allow the roles to become reversed – a mistake that should be avoided at all costs. Parents need to always be firmly in the role of parents no matter what the circumstances are. When they feel unable to fulfill their roles as parents, it is extremely important for them to seek adult, if not professional support to help them through whatever transition is occurring. Both males and females should carefully choose who will be the stepparent of their kids for the sake of all involved.

The roles between parents and kids should never become reversed or confused. When this occurs the scales are way out of balance, and adults are expecting more from kids than they have a right to expect. In times of trouble families need to pull together and support each other; however, the roles cannot be reversed without dire consequences in the future. When a child is given the role of an adult, they feel they are in control of the situation. Because kids have no idea how to be an adult, especially if there are no effective role models in their lives, kids will fail miserably and jeopardize their own futures. This will result because they were never taught self-control, effective decision-making skills, anger management, responsibility for actions, respect for self or others, or the ability to tolerate frustration. These skills which are lacking result from the fact kids have had to take on adult roles and responsibilities without any period of training relative to successfully acquiring and executing these traits. These deficits also result from ineffective and inappropriate role models both within the home/family context and outside in the other contexts as well. Boys always agree with the observation that many times they are cheated out of an opportunity just to be a kid because of the need they feel to protect moms who still present themselves as victims in many divorce/separations situations.

When the scales are out of balance in single parent families, kids pay a high price for the imbalance. This kind of profile sets kids up to be fully at risk for failure and the need to act out. The problem for parents at this point is the lack of effectiveness at attempts to impose control. Kids who have never been taught control from within are simply not going to accept control from the outside in the sense of being able to take it in. They will bitterly fight against such attempts with open defiance of arrogance, even if the arrogance exists on an unconscious level within the lives of both adults and kids. This is where I see many battles raging in many settings between adults and adolescents who are in competition with each other for positions of power and domination. Kids will actually fight arrogance with arrogance. That should come as no surprise, since this is what they have encountered throughout much of their lives. In this kind of competition of wills, everyone loses, especially the kids who will grow up to have lives equally as complicated and chaotic as the lives of the adults who were responsible for their care.

The only approach with adolescents at this point is to appeal to their own sense of self preservation and get them to see how their decisions and actions are complicating their lives more than the lives of the adults involved. It is only fair for adults to hope an adolescent can do something for their own survival rather than for the survival of others in their lives. This is also the time to provide kids with effective role models outside of the family who can then guide and nurture kids in the right direction as a neutral party with no hidden agendas; i.e. no need to control or dominate, compete or win. As any kid learns self control and survival skills the adults in their lives will also benefit from the changes. Unfortunately many adults will very arrogantly have the need to take credit for any positive changes kids make. While on the other hand, they readily blame kids for anything the kids do wrong. Arrogance! Arrogance! Arrogance!

Chapter IX

In Defense of the Underdogs: Those Truly at the Mercy of Externals

This chapter is dedicated to the nearly 2500 kids I have worked with since 1990, as well as to the kids I will work with in the future. The kids I am referring to as underdogs are the outcasts and throwaways from society, who by their own often unconscious choices for survival have set themselves up to be hated and rejected by most everyone they meet. These are the kids who are the by-products of the world we as adults have created, and they are the ones we seek to scapegoat as the dregs of society who should all be locked up and forgotten. These are the kids who frequently are motivated from an unconscious level to consciously choose to become criminals, drug addicts, alcoholics, gang members, punks, runaways, taggers, freaks, devil worshippers, goths, head bangers, etc. These are the kids who frighten us as we walk down the streets and inside the malls of most any city; the ones whom we fear will rob us or kill us if they need or want something we have. These are the kids in our communities who, motivated by rage fantasies and revenge, walk into school settings and kill classmates and school staff, after having killed their parents at home. They represent kids who futilely cried out for help many times before they got to the point of being so obviously impaired relative to emotional, intellectual, and psychological functioning. As children they have grown up under the most adverse conditions of abuse, deprivation, and numerous complicating factors from within all of the possible contexts. These are the very kids I work with in different settings, trying to reach out to them when others write them off as lost causes. They reflect what is wrong in our society and in our world. We are the ones who have created the world making all of this possible, and we are responsible initially for the choices they make.

More and more adults among us are beginning to wake up and see our responsibility for these lives in peril. Some among us are finally coming to realize the answers are not found in building more detention centers, or in strengthening the laws to treat these kids as though they are adults or urban terrorists under the U.S. Patriot Act and Homeland Security. Rather the answers are to begin assisting kids at risk much earlier in their lives before they begin entering the juvenile justice systems, or become runaways living on the streets of impoverished communities and larger cities. Somehow the world has never offered them the hope of success or even of life beyond a certain very young age. When these kids say "I don't care", they really mean "Why should I care? No one else does!" This is the true hallmark of feeling both helpless and hopeless.

From my heart I believe these kids are in part and in some cases the result of many years of debilitating public assistance programs which have taught adults and kids it is possible to get something for nothing. They are also the result of the numerous societal changes, including a breakdown in previously acceptable family systems, which have taken place over the last 3 to 4 decades. The welfare system, which is finally under some degree of reform, has taken away a sense of pride for many people who receive rather than work for material possessions and personal gains. This along with disability programs failing to properly monitor true need for such assistance only allow for more abuse and victimization by fostering dependency and limited awareness of opportunities, many of which still need to be developed. People of all ages and cultural groups, regardless of race, have been given the sense of easy come easy go, allowing kids to believe there will always be something or someone to bail them out of any kind of trouble. Some parents of kids growing up below the poverty level have forsaken their kids and have shown them the world is not a reliable or safe place in which to live. Many of these parents have taught their kids it is okay to break the law, and that you only get in trouble because you were dumb enough to get caught, not because you did something wrong. While some families truly need help, there are many others who fraudulently milk the systems for all they can get, even seeing their kids as sources of income.

Kids and many adults, regardless of socioeconomic status, have little or no sense of delayed gratification. Some kids and adults living in extreme poverty situations will take what belongs to others out of a sense of entitlement, with no regard for the value of human life and the rights of others. Adults and kids alike in these situations often do not care, or sometimes do not see the criminal nature of their actions. This is currently referred to as "pro-criminality" or "pro-criminal thinking". These are kids who, in many cases, have been dumped on since the day they were born, and who exhibit behaviors which have been modeled for them by adults within the contexts and environments in which they were raised. Sometimes even adults outside of the home/family context model and spark negative behavior because of our tendencies to approach these kids with prejudices and extreme misperceptions. How arrogant and ignorant of us to expect them to consider and accept better ways of thinking and living if we fail to approach them with the respect they deserve as human beings first and foremost. Then and only then can we begin to address the behaviors which make these kids so threatening, even to themselves and to society.

I am basing these observations about families, who are considered to be of lower socioeconomic status, upon my experiences of working primarily with families who fall into this category. Please keep in mind that in this chapter I am using examples of kids who comprise a very small percentage out of all the kids in this country. Understand, too, I blame the systems providing the opportunities for dependency and fraud for some of the problems I am identifying, and not the people participating in the programs. Therefore, within the population of kids and families I work with I have seen many more extreme instances of abuse/victimization and neglect. There are much higher percentages within this relatively small percentage of the total population of all forms of dysfunction, including people who have kids just to receive more assistance from government and community agencies. It is much more likely kids in this category will have been born as a result of carelessness, and quite often are unwanted or at least unwelcomed. More adults in the lives of kids in this group are likely to have criminal histories and extensive histories of drug addiction and alcoholism, often times coupled with serious mental and emotional problems. It is also probable that kids born into this level of poverty and hardship may not have received good health care and nutrition either during pregnancy or after birth. Furthermore, more females in this category are likely to have used alcohol, drugs, and tobacco during pregnancy, and are more likely not to receive adequate prenatal care and guidance. Please understand I am not saying everyone who has received assistance from welfare and other programs has failed to provide loving and safe environments for their kids. The above factors, however, unfortunately play significant roles in the lives of many of the kids I work with professionally. Keep in mind that the kids from "functional" home/family environments generally don't end up in mental health clinics or the juvenile justice systems. Living below the poverty level and within low-income areas doesn't guarantee broken lives and unproductive futures. However, these conditions do considerably increase the probability of such outcomes.

If you will notice, European American kids committed many of the recent acts of extreme violence reported in recent years through the media. My experience tells me more acts of violence committed by European American kids would be reported if the media weren't so quick to point the finger at other ethnic and cultural groups. As I pass through the waiting area outside of any juvenile courtroom, I generally see kids from every cultural and ethnic group except European Americans. My own speculation as to the explanation for this is related to prejudice on the parts of law enforcement officials and systems, and to the fact parents of European American kids are often better able to afford attorneys who keep kids out of court and detention. It is also possible that not as many European American kids get into trouble on a higher percentage basis because of their positions of perceived privilege and opportunity, never being as fully exposed to all of the complicating factors of being below the poverty level and being "non-white". I believe European American kids resort more to hate crimes and forms of physical violence associated with membership in extremist white supremacy groups, hard rock cultures, and satanic cults. I also believe that a significant number of European American kids who commit crimes are spoiled, arrogant brats who have little or no regard for the rights of others or any greater sensitivity to the value of human life than kids from other cultural groups. Nowadays more European kids are drawn into groups, including gangs, which previously were associated with different minority groups. While there are many factors to consider in determining possible outcomes, they do not foretell with certainty any results.

Again, I believe society is also responsible for this reality as evidenced by a higher percentage of people from groups other than European Americans being below the poverty level, with higher concentrations of lower SES groups in inner cities where they receive more negative publicity. I also believe in areas where criminal acts are committed by European Americans living below the poverty level, other European Americans are in such a majority - as in parts of the Southeast and Midwest - these acts do not get much attention and are probably under reported. These are the areas where white men still reign supreme and the "good ol' boy networks" are still alive and well. After all, who pays any real attention relative to crime and lower SES issues in Midwestern states and backwoods Alabama, Mississippi, Tennessee, Arkansas, Georgia, Kentucky, North and South Carolina, Virginia, and West Virginia? Some militia and white supremacy groups in these areas may be watched and monitored by government officials. However, they don't get much media coverage unless they are ranting and raving in the streets and on the Internet about white power, the desire to overthrow the government, or bombing federal buildings, churches, and abortion clinics. Perhaps war should have been declared on the terrorist groups and individuals that are comprised of European Americans and other American citizens after the Oklahoma City bombing of the federal building, an act based in hatred and extremism. This was no different than the attacks of 9/11, with virtually all acts of terrorism in this country prior to 9/11 being perpetrated by "whites" for centuries.

Another major area of concern to me that tremendously impacts the lives of the "underdogs" is the actions of politicians with opportunities to circumvent the democratic process. They often pass legislation that was either voted down by the people or blocked in the courts when presented on ballots in the form of initiatives, referendums, and propositions. One of the best examples of this was the famous California Proposition 187 in the mid 1990's that sought to drastically change immigration laws and procedures generally as they applied only to people from different Spanish-speaking countries. This proposition has not really been heard of since it got blocked in the courts until the California recall election in 2003. While

Proposition 187 was voted in by the public, it was successfully blocked in the courts. However, many of the laws and rights relative to immigrants have been affected by legislation quietly and deceptively shuffled through state and federal systems disguised by such movements as Welfare Reform, Healthcare Reform, and changes in immigration policies which had nothing to do with protection against terrorism.

I personally believe we need to limit the flow of people into this country, a practice common in many countries around the world. However, I also believe we need to help those who are already here regardless of legal status, who have established themselves in this country, working the jobs most American citizens do not want to work. Furthermore, I believe we need to continue working with the governments of Mexico and Central and South America to improve their economic situations, thereby making it less attractive for people from these countries to migrate to North America. Most of these people who live in this country do so under extremely deplorable conditions just to survive. It is sad to realize how bad things must be in their own countries that make hardship in this country look like the fulfillment of a dream.

It is also time to stop focusing exclusively on people from Spanish-speaking countries as though they are the only ones living in this country illegally. There are many others from around the world doing the same thing without gaining much media focus, at least prior to 9/11. Probably the U.S. sees the political ties with countries in other parts of the world as being more important than the political ties to the developing nations south of our border. It is also probable that we see the countries south of our border as being less of a threat relative to our economic well being, with the only exception being illegal immigration. Hopefully the people in the southern half of this hemisphere are not regarded as less desirable relative to their usefulness to further our selfish North American pursuits of prosperity and materialism often at the expense of others. After all these people existed historically within the Americas before our European ancestors left Europe to come to North America.

All of these elements from the community, social, and political contexts are experienced inside the home/family context and beyond as factors which give kids cause to act out their emotion-based anxiety. The families and kids I work with are often the victims of many of the reforms currently taking place. Non-Hispanic/Latino people I spoke with in Los Angeles actually voted for Prop. 187 foolishly believing we would be able to end gang violence by sending all of the people primarily from Spanish-speaking countries back to Mexico. Political rhetoric attached to such measures is usually inflammatory and misleading. These actions and beliefs still continue through present day views and sentiments. After all, many ethnic groups in the western states believe anyone who speaks Spanish or has a Spanish accent is automatically from Mexico. In my work with gang kids, I have found the greatest majority of them to be U.S. citizens who are entitled to the same rights afforded to all other Americans. Furthermore, Spanish-speaking people come from a number of different countries other than Mexico. Some of the most dangerous are from El Salvador.

I use these examples to point out the arrogance and ignorance of people in power who are making decisions and laws which then become complicating factors for others. In many cases this is often done without a real sense of reality or responsibility. Politicians and voters are sometimes too far removed from the truth to be able to make unbiased decisions without creating undue hardship for those groups targeted as threats to position and power. Politicians are so interested in being elected and re-elected they will cower to the demands of any group they believe will get them into "office" which is nothing more than a deceptive term for a position of power. The George W. Bush administration and conservative present day politicians are prime examples of this.

I believe it is a huge mistake for any of us to think that government officials will always represent the people when it comes to sensitive issues such as human rights and other considerations related to social injustices. Politicians are so interested in promoting the causes of special interest groups which got them elected they lose sight of the overriding principles of spirituality upon which this nation was founded – principles such as life, liberty, the pursuit of happiness, equality under the law, and justice for all. God forbid anyone should fall into a category of being undesirable and outside the protection of these principles simply because of unchangeable differences which are perceived as threatening to groups of people (such as ultra conservatives) who are actually in minority status, and yet hold positions of power. Everyone needs to wake up and join forces against any groups of extremists who seek to keep the scales out of balance in this and other parts of the world. Remember with balance there are no extreme positions which result in gains for some at the expense of others. Arrogance and ignorance exist in all contexts and must be identified and eliminated by replacing it with acceptance and appreciation for diversity and the parts all of us play in creating a better way of life. This represents idealism and moderation at their best, huh? If you really think critically about the ideas I present they reflect a moderate position of fairness and equality for all which should be considered by every politician. This might even help end bipartisan political views as we know them today.

Obviously I am by nature a thinker. I am also an observer, a teacher, and a healer. And, you are right I am using this book as an opportunity to scream out some of my views. Even though I am "white" I have experienced numerous forms of heartache and challenge in my own life. Through all of this I have gained the strength and courage I need in order to face whatever lies ahead. I have also learned to appreciate and defend those who are in positions of being the underdog, this through an acquired ability to learn about and appreciate their struggles. Most important of all, I have learned from all of those whose paths have crossed my own regardless of their ethnic/cultural origins or other forms of diversity. For all of my challenges and experiences I am a better person and I am more spiritually grounded than I have ever been. I am grateful for all I have gained and most of all for the opportunity to work with targeted underdogs who need guidance and support. In every experience there is an opportunity to learn something. Hopefully, each of you will see my ideas and experiences in this book as an opportunity for you to learn something as well. Nothing shared within these pages is done with malice or ill intent, only with the hope of sparking enough controversy to initiate productive discussions leading to changes in perspectives, and changes in myths disguised as reality and truth.

With the preceding paragraphs as an introduction, allow me to share with you my experiences of working with society's underdog kids. Within each of my kids it is possible to find a piece of heart I can then work with to help them find themselves in spite of the heartache and hardship in their own lives. By occasionally sharing limited and appropriate parts of my own personal issues with my kids, I allow them to become aware of my ability to recognize many of their struggles by giving them the respect they deserve and need from others. By example I show them the kind of respect I want in return, and I have never had a kid completely turn on me. I have had kids who get angry, but not with me. After establishing rapport and trust, and because I treat them with respect I can say virtually anything I want to them relative to my observations of and perspective of truth and reality in their lives. For many of these kids this is the first time any adult has treated them in this manner.

Success is hard to judge in this population of kids so labeled as "bad kids", "problem children", "troubled youth", "at risk youth", "undesirable elements", "incorrigibles", etc. This makes it especially difficult for anyone to work with these kids if they need to see instant and measurable results. The results can only be measured with time in the span of years, for much of what I do is to plant seeds for future growth when the conditions are right. I never enter into a competition with these kids, nor do I have any need to be right, although at times I do insist that I know what I am talking about even if they choose to dismiss it for the time being. I trust my instincts and intuition, as well as the ability of each kid to take things in regardless of occasional outward protest and resistance.

My days at work are always challenging and sometimes frustrating, especially when I get bogged down in the same caseload for extended periods of time. This happens as kids and families keep getting into trouble and don't seem to be making as much progress as I would like to see. I have to recognize their right to make mistakes and be very careful not to take things personally. Furthermore, I have to recognize that these kids continue to struggle for survival within the very contexts which have given them cause to act out their FLAGS and resulting emotion-based anxiety. I care about these kids and they know that, but sometimes I have to let them go if they are not ready to work on their issues. Amazingly, many of them come looking for me as they get older and need further guidance or assistance. I can let them go because I trust my ability to have planted seeds which will likely begin to grow someday, even if I am not there to see this happen.

The greatest joy for me is to be the very first person to effectively connect with a kid who is believed to be particularly difficult. This is what keeps me going as afar as rewards from my job. To watch a kid relax and let go of that tough exterior as they realize I am not a threat is truly exciting and humbling. To then experience the establishment of mutual trust and respect is even better. All of my kids will tell me their gang moniker, and I use this as an indication of the level of trust we have established, occasionally reminding and reassuring them of confidentiality. This also indicates they have allowed me to enter their world as a friendly observer, with some kids even referring to me as "homie", "homes", or "dog" which are the names they use to refer to their fellow gang members and friends. These terms represent an acceptance rather than an insult as many people tend to think. All of this is proof to me that it is impossible to inspire others if we, ourselves, are not inspired. Our professional associations with this population of kids must be met with a high degree of both passion and compassion.

The biggest threats to their success in treatment are the extent of their substance abuse and the extreme negative conditions of their families and communities. Drugs, alcohol, and dysfunctional environments are very difficult factors with which to compete. Many of the kids are drug addicts and alcoholics by the time they are referred to me. Most of the families are too uninvolved in the lives of their kids to be aware of the extent to which their kids drink and use, with most families seeing the gang as being the biggest and only competitor against them. The families are not usually aware to what extent they are also competing with drugs and alcohol. Sometimes this is also true because of the family's lack of knowledge relative to substance abuse, and because of the fact some kids are really good at deception. The other reality is the extent of drug and alcohol use in many of the homes and in the communities. Parents often allow kids to drink and use drugs at home convincing themselves it is better than kids being under the influence out in the streets. Wow, does this ever send the wrong message!

Remember joining a gang is simply another way kids act out their emotion-based anxiety. As they become more involved in the gang lifestyle, which is truly a choice, they get caught up more and more in the negative elements associated with this identity. Realistically gangs exist for the sole purpose of establishing and protecting a territory in which to conduct illegal activity to include the selling of illegal drugs and weapons. The larger a gang is the more organized it will be and will likely be involved in more criminal activities in addition to weapons and drugs, and with more extensive national and international networks. The older gang members, even from within the prison systems, will often use the younger kids referred to as "youngsters" to do the "dirty work" so they can avoid the likelihood of facing three strikes and life in prison. This kind of attention appeals to the younger kids who feel they need to prove themselves to someone, especially to receive the acceptance, attention and praise from positive adult role models they so desperately lack and yet crave in their lives. The answer to this is not to establish laws to increase already harsh consequences applicable to kids. The best alternative is to put money into prevention and early intervention, not into incarceration which serves only to ease the minds of those who are uninformed and sitting judgingly, arrogantly, and ignorantly on the sidelines pretending to have all the solutions. However, it all comes down to politics, biased and incorrect societal views, and to money and numbers games for existing law enforcement agencies and organizations, all of which are very difficult factors to change or even impact.

Gangs, hate groups, satanic cults, hard rock cultures, and white power/supremacy groups, which arguably are gangs as well, serve to unite kids for a common cause which can only be achieved through loyalty, mutual trust, respect, and support. This also sounds a little like churches and various civic and political organizations doesn't it? People within these groups unite for the same reasons, but generally with less detrimental consequences. Keep in mind there are many different kinds of gangs to which many of us belong, sometimes for the same reasons as the "gang members". Take a little time to review the following lists of what the families of these kids have to offer compared to what the gangs have to offer. Picture a kid standing in the middle of these two lists and try to understand how easy it is for many kids to turn to gangs as the only alternative and hope for what limited future they believe they can count on anyway. Pay particular attention to the numerous factors in the "family" list (Appendix P) which are based outside of the home/family context. Then pay attention to the appeal of a gang subculture (Appendix Q) relative to the open defiance of arrogance and ignorance, not authority, and see how drastically the scales are tipped against the kids from these kinds of environments and with these kinds of complicating factors.

Within these lists I have tried to include factors which are relative to kids from any level of socioeconomic status. I think at times people arrogantly and ignorantly believe many of the factors on the "family" side of the list only apply to those from the lower socioeconomic levels of society. Furthermore, I think kids act out differently relative to their class status, if for no other reason than the simple fact that money plays an important part in the choices they make. Kids from all levels/classes drink and use drugs, while kids from higher income levels are less likely to steal in order to drink and use, unless they do so just for the "rush". Also kids with more money available to them are likely to have cars and better clothes, as well as better living conditions all the way around. Therefore, the issues for middle to upper class kids relative to acting out are more likely to be from a self-indulgent stance of privilege and reckless abandon, especially when the adults in a kid's immediate environment are not very involved in the life of the kid.

Two of the most significant factors for kids who act out are the lack of parental supervision, and the lack of various positive things to do. This again, is especially true for kids from lower socioeconomic levels. Families in higher socioeconomic levels can provide a greater variety of activities, but may not provide any better supervision or involvement in the lives of kids than families at other levels. In other words, money and privilege are very significant factors in determining both the ways kids act out, and the motivation to act out.

Ironically, one of the most positive aspects of my childhood years was the role the church played in providing activities. While I do not agree with the religious beliefs I was taught along with the activities, I am very grateful for the fact I had something to do as a kid. The church we went to had numerous music programs, recreational and social activities, and weekend retreats. Because the church was so far removed from reality and so afraid of losing control over its members, especially the younger ones, by them being exposed to the temptations from the devil/world (interchangeable terms), that as I grew older I found no value in many of the lessons I was taught and left the church because of its very narrow minded perspective. However, as a child I am grateful for the opportunity to have been privy to the privileges associated with group membership. In my job I am reluctant to refer kids to churches because of my fear of the damage which can be done in the name of God to an already abused kid. This is the reason for my appeal to churches and religious organizations to focus more on common Spirituality than on particular religious dogma arrogantly and deceptively based in a need to control the minds and lives of members.

One other positive experience for me was my membership in Boy Scouts of America. I was very active in a scout troop, reaching the rank of Eagle Scout and becoming a member of the Order of the Arrow. This organization also provided me with many opportunities to participate in activities which would not have been available to me otherwise. God knows my family didn't do much together constituting anything fun or pleasant. I looked forward each year to summer camp and to the weekend camping trips we would take to various sites. Actually I have many fond memories of my years as a Boy Scout. It is too bad kids nowadays think of such associations as being for nerds and schoolboys.

Another tremendous factor for me during my childhood was the fact my siblings and I always had adult supervision. My mother didn't work and my maternal grandmother lived with us and was usually around to cover when our parents were unavailable. Often times the supervision by my parents was too strict and amounted to control simply for the sake of control. However, it limited our opportunities to get into trouble. I know I would have acted out more than I did if I had not been so closely monitored. The same was true for other kids in my neighborhood who had the same or similar types of supervision. The ones who didn't have this factor were known as the troublemakers in the area.

Probably the only other valuable life lesson I learned as a child was the sense of a work ethic, along with an appreciation and respect for the things I worked to obtain with regards to both material gains and to other kinds of goals and aspirations. My dad always made it very clear that no one owes us anything, and that anything worth having is worth working for and waiting for with respect to short term vs. long term gains. Looking back I can see how my dad believed a family works together and shares the responsibility for making things work out. After all, he grew up in a fairly large family, with everyone working together to run a small farm and fight against poverty and hardship due to the times and to irresponsibility on the part of their father. I only wish my dad could have tempered and balanced these principles with a sense of fairness and gentleness which he lacked. Perhaps I could have appreciated him more as my father if he had worked through, rather than acted out, his unresolved issues from the past.

I am emphasizing here the important elements from an era which has passed – along with a few positive elements such as opportunity, togetherness, and values. I see these factors missing for all of the kids with whom I work as a result of the changes occurring during the past fifty plus years. Many of these changes have been very positive, and I would never even suggest a return to the past. I am simply waiting and hoping for people to find a way to incorporate the good elements from the past with the reality of today's world and people. I sometimes wonder where we would be today if the focus in the past had not been so out of balance relative to perspectives on power and domination. If the focus continues to shift more to equality and appreciation for diversity, we will likely begin to incorporate more of the positive aspects from the past without actually returning to or holding onto the past as many conservative groups would have us do as a society. This would only be a repetition of the previous mistakes, and would serve to indicate very clearly our inability to learn from our historical errors.

I firmly believe the kids who fall into the underdog category act out in reaction to emotion-based anxiety created by the FLAGS. At the other extreme of the spectrum from privileged to "privilege-less", I believe those kids who fall into the former category act out based in arrogance and ignorance. The higher each of us moves up on the scale, the more difficulty we have relating to the struggles of those behind us. We tend to forget what it feels like to feel bad; at least until we begin to recognize the empty existence we created with our exclusive pursuit of material happiness. At that point we as adults often begin to act out our own emotion-based anxiety which results from the FLAGS created by our own greed and failure to accomplish those things which are truly important. At the other extreme are those adults who never really try to accomplish anything positive, dragging the past with them every step of the way. These are the ones who seek to bring everyone around them down to the same level of misery and hopelessness. These are the ones who play the role of victim or victimizer, or some combination of both. If nothing else, I hope this book will help each of us pinpoint where we are within these lists and spectrums. I hope each of us will then seek the solutions we need to resolve the unfinished business from the past, and work to heal the relationships to ourselves and to others which have suffered and/or have been destroyed as a result.

One of the most significant aspects in the lives of kids who are actually underdogs is the concept of survival. When kids lack appropriate role models they are left to their own devices relative to figuring out how to negotiate their journey through life. Because these kids are also acting out their emotion-based anxiety created by and within all of the contexts in which abuse and victimization can occur, they are going to make many seriously negative unconscious choices — unconscious in the sense they are unaware of the motivation (FLAGS) fueling these choices. For those sitting on the sidelines who do not know or understand the need simply to survive on a day to day basis, we have no right to judge or even make decisions or suggestions relative to what should be done with these kids. Talk with and listen to people like me who work in the trenches so to speak and have a good read on realities as they exist in the lives of many.

Let's go back for a moment to my belief in the transient opportunity to help kids turn their lives around. Remember my explanation of the behaviors of kids being more temporary compared to the behaviors of adults which tend to be more permanent and more truly a representation of whom they are. It is much more difficult to separate what adults do from who they are as people relative to personality characteristics. Even the kids I work with are able to recognize the differences between themselves and the adults they see. I agree with the need for strict penalties for adults who are serious repeat offenders of violent crimes relative to issues of parole and early release programs. Again I base this position in my belief it is much more difficult for adults to change habitual behaviors than it is for kids. Ironically two of my kids who are serving lengthy prison sentences write to me about their desire to learn and grow in prison. This clearly reflects the work we did together with them telling me they wish they had really taken my efforts and words to heart. Both of these guys are studying to become psychologists in prison and plan to make a difference within institutional settings in the lives of fellow inmates. My influence is even passed on and into higher levels of confinement. This is why it is so important for us to pour all of our efforts into giving young offenders the opportunities which will help them to avoid creating permanent ways of acting out. If kids must be confined they must also receive very positive and effective attention and interventions from adults who understand, and who lack hidden agendas, and who will give them the insight they need into the principles I am writing about in this book. Too many adults within juvenile justice agencies follow the "might-makes-right" approach of control, domination, and the breaking of wills and spirits.

Survival refers to our ability to exist on the planet and to fend for ourselves. For most of us as children we took for granted there would be those around us to provide for our survival needs. Kids who grow up in contexts where neglect, deprivation, and unpredictability are commonplace will not be able to take such things for granted. One of the saddest things for me is to hear a kid locked up in juvenile hall talk about how much better he or she feels compared to living in a destructive home/family environment, and/or out on the streets. For many kids confinement is a reprieve from the daily hassles and uncertainties of trying to survive in an unsafe and unfriendly world. They talk of the fact that while being confined everything, including structure, is provided for them.

I know that in many cases it is necessary to confine kids who break laws and are dangerous to themselves and to others from a criminal perspective. However, I do not see the merit in using this strictly as an opportunity to punish without also seizing the opportunity to teach and divert or redirect energy and effort. This can only be accomplished by fully incorporating effective and appropriate mental health services and interventions into the mix delivered only by well-trained professionals knowledgeable and successful in working with this population. For now the lack of properly screened and trained staff are the biggest tragedies and travesties within juvenile detention facilities, placement facilities, and departments of juvenile probation and parole. When my kids get locked up, for many of them it is the first time in a long time they have felt reasonably safe. It also may be the first time they have been able to get clean and sober from all substances. All of these factors together create an incredible opportunity to do some very intensive work to resolve the FLAGS, and to teach kids self control by modeling and teaching appropriate means of coping with and facing life.

Unfortunately the kids in these settings encounter more of the same kinds of ignorant arrogance and need to control from staff members and various legal system staff which they experienced at the hands of family members and adults in other contexts. Therefore, the opportunity to help many of these kids is lost because of the lack of awareness of the real needs and issues of these kids. As I visit with the kids in juvenile hall who are referred to me prior to being locked up, I have other kids who will ask who I am and why they are not allowed to talk with me as well. It is hard for me to explain to them the reality that the "system" is not set up to accommodate them and meet that need. I believe there is not a single juvenile offender who doesn't need and wouldn't benefit from an opportunity to speak with a qualified, well-trained mental health professional, unless of course a kid is severely impaired either mentally or developmentally. Kids are starved for positive interaction with caring adults.

Unfortunately, those in positions of political and social power and authority are more concerned about pleasing their constituents than with the real need of helping kids turn their lives around. People on the outside see kids according to the labels they use to define and identify them. This is clearly another example of arrogance and imbalance at the expense of the kids who need our help and attention. These people tend to be older, arrogant European Americans who have money and who also hold onto the outdated views of kids simply needing to be controlled and taught a lesson. When will people learn that to teach a lesson requires compassion and unconditional regard not further abuse and victimization? When will adults, especially older adults, take responsibility for the selfish and destructive choices they have made which have created the environments leading to such destruction? When will adults realize the need for honest self-examination and rectification relative to improving the dynamics and levels of dysfunction existing at all levels and in all contexts? Until these changes are made and the ignorance, arrogance and selfishness are acknowledged and eliminated none of the needed changes will take place quickly enough to stop the loss of kids to ever increasing apathy and misunderstanding.

I even agree to some extent with proposals being presented to decriminalize drugs, consensual sex, gambling, and any other currently identified criminal act which causes little or no harm to others. I believe we need laws that protect others, especially kids, from being victimized by irresponsible acts committed against them. However, I do not agree at all with the attempts to legislate morality. Again, these are issues based in politics and money. Think about how much money is wasted on investigating, prosecuting, and punishing offenders of victimless crimes. These are issues which get politicians elected and provide jobs for people who feel the need to control and dictate how others should live their lives. The monies in the budgets of agencies fighting victimless crimes could be spent more effectively and less wastefully through prevention and diversion programs other than confinement and incarceration. Redirection and support services should be critical components of any programs related to juvenile and young adult offenders. Programs could be developed even using my RFLAGS Model and related concepts to teach the need for internal control based in self-respect, mutual regard, and higher standards of living for both juvenile and adult offenders.

While we are in the process of trying to balance the scales with personal responsibility, open and honest self-examination, and rectification, why not throw everything possible into the pot that needs to be balanced. Laws do not stop people who engage in behaviors where there are no victims. If anything, the laws create many more opportunities to break other laws and increase criminal activity where there are victims as in illegal drug trade and its associated violence. It would be better in my opinion to use the money spent fighting victimless crimes to teach people the art of balancing their choices in connection with the lives of everyone else.

I am surprised how many of my former beliefs and opinions have changed having now witnessed firsthand the problems facing people who fall into the categories of kids with whom I work professionally. Gangs and other criminal factions will only be diminished when the scales in all contexts are finally balanced and tempered with mutual respect, unconditional regard and a true awareness of the interconnectedness of each of us relative to our places in the world. By coming to understand the survival needs of most of the kids I identify as underdogs I have been able to open my heart and mind to alternative ways of viewing and interpreting the world and the people in it. I no longer feel contempt for others except as it relates to ignorant arrogance people take pride in, and any mistreatment of people and especially of kids. Hopefully the day is coming where others like me will take a stand against the so-called norms and fight to correct the wrongs being perpetuated. The only victims of many behaviors are the persons acting out the FLAGS - those who truly learn to perpetuate their history of victimization acted out upon them from external sources and turning it inward and against themselves rather than resolving the issues from the past.

Chapter X

Pairing and Parenting: The Basics

I want to spend a little more time in this chapter focusing on the changes which have taken place in the last 50+ years. Beginning with World War II lets consider how the "family" has changed from the two parents - working dad and homemaker mom - model, to an almost total lack of definition and clarity at this point in time. Remember to think of societal changes as represented by a swinging pendulum that only keeps perfect time when it swings in balance — not too far to the left or to the right. The significance of these changes is extremely important relative to the concepts of pairing and parenting.

You can also picture this idea of a pendulum in what is referred to in statistics as the bell-shaped curve which is exactly what it sounds like. This concept was also identified previously. When graphing statistical data the middle 64% represents whatever is considered to be "normal" for the population or group being studied. From there and out to both the right and the left are areas referred to as the tails of the curve. This simply means that the more people move out from the middle and toward the curves representing the extremes, the more they deviate or stray from the norm. Some degree of deviation is always expected, and even hoped for and useful, depending on the population being studied. The mid range is considered to be the mean or the average, with the lower end of the curve generally representing the less favorable range; and the higher end the most favorable. A good example would be graphed indications of intelligence or IQ.

When thinking in terms of societal standards and conditions it is better to think of the tails or the full range of motion for the pendulum as simply being extremes, with any extremes generally being negative and a clear indication of a lack of adequate balance relative to change. For a clock to run accurately the pendulum must swing to both the right and the left and cannot stay simply in the middle. However if the range of motion is too wide the timing will be off. The same is true in thinking about change on any level regarding the six contexts of home/family, school, community, society, politics, and religion.

Through most of my life I have heard that during World War II women for the first time were literally pulled out of their homes and put to work in factories to support the war effort. Because so many of the men were involved in different military roles, the labor force in this country apparently was reduced to such a low level that women were the only solution. At the end of the war many of these women were sent back into the homes as the men returned to take over the jobs in the factories. In my opinion this exposure to the workplace set the stage for the ultimate struggle by women for equality and recognition which occurred in the 1960's and 1970's. Women were given a chance to see themselves as more than just wives and mothers and I believe many of them returned to their previous roles reluctantly and with a degree of resentment.

With all of the social unrest in the 60's and 70's people realized that the those traditions previously established and taken for granted as reality not only needed to be challenged, but needed to be changed. This was a time of extremes when the pendulum was swinging away from conservative thinking toward much more liberal thinking initially resulting in chaos and confusion often accompanying times of tremendous change. While there have been other times of extreme change throughout history, I believe recent decades to be the most pertinent in the United States to the issues we are still struggling with today. At the same time that many good things came out of the uproar, there were many issues of adjustment, redefining, and acceptance which are still occurring today in the sense of still looking for balance and something representing an agreeable composition of factors.

Along with tremendous improvements in the recognition of basic human rights for all came the fight from conservatives to maintain the status quo. After all, what man wants to give up his position in what was previously a male dominated existence, with all of the privileges associated with being on top as a figure of speech? Suddenly women were burning their bras in public and demanding that they were not only equal to men, they were exactly the same as men. Even some women fought this kind of thinking which today seems to have settled into the range of equality relative to ability and competence, rather than to the idea that men have to stop being men and women have to stop being women. There are differences, associated with gender, which I think are recognized as reality. However, these are limited to more obvious physical characteristics than to any other aspects. Men fought against the ideas of having to become part of all aspects of family life, including sharing roles previously defined as being female. There was an even bigger adjustment to the ideas of having to share the workplace and jobs of leadership and management with what was literally referred to as the "weaker sex".

Having lived in the South during these times of change even into my early adult years, I watched and had to adjust as well to the breakdown of assumed male roles, particularly that of white male privilege. My first job outside of the business world which I left in 1988 was as the only male member of a 16-member crisis evaluation team at a private psychiatric hospital in Georgia. I found out very quickly that these women, including the female supervisor, really weren't interested in giving me my previously assumed birthright of being listened to just by virtue of being white and male. With some time I was able to adjust not only to being a team member rather than the boss, but also to the fact that women generally have different and effective ways of accomplishing established goals. This job also gave me my first opportunity to work closely with African Americans who shared the 11 to 7 night shift with me. Because we worked the night shifts we had a lot of time to sit around and talk when things were quiet on the units. I quickly learned how ignorant I was relative to historical issues for black people, many of which both shocked and shamed me as a white male.

What an incredible time to be alive and become part of a struggle to right the historical wrongs existing in this country for centuries. All of this means that if a poll was conducted today to determine what are considered to be the standards representing the "norms" of today, the issues included in the 64% mid range would be quite different than those of the 1940's and 1950's. All of the wrongs in this country until the current changes were based completely in white European (WASP) arrogance and extremism. It is possible to see how the dominant segment of society during those years did a very poor job of nurturing the healthy development of a new civilization, much the same as parents and other adults are responsible for nurturing the healthy development of children. This again ties into my RFLAGS Model which can also be used to identify how the FLAGS were created for the "underdogs" of the times – and believe me there have been many different "underdog" groups throughout the founding and development of what became the United States of America. The RFLAGS Model also helps to identify and explain how these groups who were abused and victimized for so long developed the FLAGS which created the emotion-based anxiety still being acted out today as the pendulum continues to search for the balanced range of motion.

One of the most serious results of the social unrest of the 60's and 70's was the breakdown of a traditional family structure, but with nothing to replace it that could insure the stability of families for the sake of kids and adults alike. For the first time, however, there were laws enacted which made child abuse illegal, giving kids the first opportunity to even speak out and seek protection for themselves. Also, in recent years there have been new laws enacted against domestic violence and elder/dependent abuse. However, nationally there are no consistently enforced laws to guard against domestic violence, with the only known deterrent to on going abuse seemingly being the incarceration of the abuser, which can be both male and female.

Many times I have had male/female couples in my office talking about issues of domestic violence. There is still a desire on the part of some women to be seen as victims in order to gain sympathy and control, especially in circumstances of divorce/separation, and domestic violence. However, more and more I am seeing trends where the females are the perpetrators of the violence and the cause of the breakdown of relationships, and yet only focus on how they are still being victimized by playing the "weaker sex" card.

In one particular case a woman came into my office with a bruise on her face. Her tearful telling of the story of her victimization stopped when her 13-year-old son told her to tell me how she was the one who always attacked his dad first. The kid went on to tell me of mom's history of hitting, kicking, biting, ripping dad's clothing, insulting his masculinity, pushing, and cussing toward dad with this being the only time dad ever got mad and hit her. Mom got really angry with her son and with me as I confronted her on her behaviors. I assured her it is equally as wrong for women to become violent as it is for men. It is often more dangerous for women given the fact men in general are physically stronger than most women; but it is also wrong for women to provoke rage in others. I told her I was surprised this was the first time in their 20 year marriage he ever got physical with her given her history of assaulting him repeatedly and regularly. She was rather insulted and indignant about all of this, trying hard to hold onto the fact I should see her as a victim. I simply told her that in her case of domestic violence the process would likely stop if she would stop provoking her husband's rage.

I met with her husband the next week and listened to him cry about how bad he felt about hitting her. While I let him know that I do not condone his act of violence, I assured him that I hold everyone to that standard regardless of gender or age. He told me his wife had refused to come with him that week and he thought it was funny when I told him how I had confronted her on her history of assaulting him. He felt like he got support and could see that his self-restraint had actually lasted longer than it might have for most. Both parents reported later that the violence had stopped, with mom able to see how she had actually provoked it over the years. They clearly understood that I was against the actions of both of them. If her son hadn't been sitting there to speak up in defense of his dad, I would likely have never known the truth as the dad admitted being embarrassed about being attacked by his wife and probably would not have told me.

The chances are that many of the cases of domestic violence against men and perpetrated by women go unreported or are under reported. I know of times when both parties were equally responsible for the situation of domestic violence and only the man was arrested in spite of his obvious injuries. Women and men both need to press charges against abusive partners and stick by their right to do so, especially if they have no intention of ending the relationship. Domestic violence is one of the most frustrating issues to deal with professionally as women generally won't leave abusive relationships, sometimes for a number of valid reasons. However, even with tremendous sources of support they still refuse to see the reality that such abuse is likely going to continue. Perhaps laws should change so that any parties involved in domestic violence are arrested and prosecuted equally, with incarceration seeming to be the only deterrent to continued violence. When I left the state of California at the end of 2004, efforts were being made to make domestic violence reportable if there are kids in the home. Soon this is likely to be added nationwide to the list of mandated reports already dealing with other forms of abuse and victimization.

It is important to tie all of these issues to the reality that probably all of these adults are acting out emotion-based anxiety created by the FLAGS. With a history of previous abuse/victimization the current levels of violence are likely as bad as or worse than in the past. This is where it is possible to see how someone who has been abused can continue to be a victim or become a victimizer as well, if not toward the one abusing them, then toward others including children in their care. Sometimes abusive experiences can create FLAGS which never existed from the past. However, people who were not abused during childhood are much less likely to take abuse, or allow it to continue with someone in adulthood.

With the tremendous rise in the divorce rate since the 1970's came a huge number of other issues way beyond the scope and intent of this book. So at this point I only want to address the changes in relationships and in our reasons for trying to pair up with another. A huge motivator for pairing is the reality of loneliness no one wants to feel. However, the reasons for getting and staying married have changed from historical survival issues to really trying to pair up based on romantic love and some sense of mutual purpose in life.

I am not sure where the term TLC (Tender Loving Care) originated, but I find it useful in trying to identify factors which could at least increase the probability of successful pairings between consenting adults. In my search for meaningful and useful ways to teach different concepts I have come up with what I call the "TLC's" representing at least some of the minimum requirements before anyone should even consider a relationship as long-term. Obviously in my use of these letters the two most important elements are Trust and Love. From there I am amazed at how many of the other elements all start with the letter "C". My list includes:

Compatibility	Consideration	Communication
Commitment	Compromise	Competence
Compassion	Concern	Comfort
Connection	Caressing	Caring
Coping	Control (self)	Commonalities
Continuity	Companionship	Comradery
Change	Choices	Consistency
Contingency	Character	Charm

    While there are others, such as respect, which start with different letters of the alphabet, these are a good place to begin, especially with the concept of compatibility. One of the biggest mistakes I think many people make today is to start out a new relationship sexually, before the two people have a chance to really know about other equally important aspects. Oftentimes, when the sex is good people quickly assume this means we must be in love. It is all too easy to use the "L" word when people are sexually aroused, only to regret it after the lustful passion has again subsided. Love must develop, even if it appears to be a love-at-first-sight experience. While I do believe love-at-first-sight is possible, it doesn't guarantee any hint of success or longevity until the two people have a chance to really get to know each other on all levels.

    Perhaps one of the most important indicators of compatibility is the ability to communicate effectively and comfortably. Frequently in the early stages of relationship development couples are able to talk about non-emotional issues presented more as factual and historical information, giving each person a chance to learn personal data and details one about the other. This is a very good time to look for personality characteristics, one of the "C's" I failed to list. The kinds of things you look for through communication, both verbal and non-verbal are issues of reciprocity and goodness of fit relative to the pairing. Look for things like: attentiveness, interest, understanding, appreciation, respect, courtesy (another "C"), comfort level, openness, quirks, emotionality, degree and depth of mutual exchange, intimacy, passion, and all of the other "C's" listed above.

If the communication patterns aren't compatible then nothing else is worth pursuing if looking for intimacy and longevity. One critical factor is the opportunity for each person to be open and honest about thoughts, feelings, desires, and observations. With each of these timing is everything, especially avoiding situations already emotionally charged. Expression of deeper levels of personal aspects should be attempted in such a way as to encourage reciprocal communication and not used as a game to set someone up or try to trap them. If games are the only way you can try to communicate then you really should look at the need to review dynamics from the past and to become aware of the presence of the FLAGS you might be ignoring.

When expressing thoughts, feelings, desires, or observations the use of "I" statements is critical. If the word "you" comes out of your mouth as a primary part of any sentence then you, as the speaker, have set up an offensive situation in which your partner will feel the need to be defensive. This is the pattern most people in all situations use and expect to encounter, so the use of proper communication skills will take some time to adjust to, but should be practiced and maintained. As long as you are only saying what "I" think, feel, want, or see then any defensiveness from the other person will clearly be their problem and a by-product of their own baggage since your intentions are only to communicate and not play games or offend.

I would urge each reader to find a good book about communication and really study it with a partner. This is a major stumbling block for most people. Intention behind all communication is important and should be conscious and well thought out. Always make certain you honestly know what your intentions are before you attempt to say anything important. Then choose the right approach; wait for, rather than try to create "the right moment", and then trust yourself and breathe as you speak. Stay relaxed and non-aggressive even if your partner reacts negatively. The inability of your partner to deal with reasonable, open, honest, non-threatening communications is a huge sign of incompatibility if it happens with any even slight hint of regularity.

It isn't possible to be satisfied or grow within the context of any kind of relationship where communication is not possible and constructive. This is true of couples and for couples who are or may become parents. Open, constructive communication about parenting issues is the only way to ever hope to be effective in raising kids. Appropriate and effective communication is equally important in all of the contexts outside of the home/family context. Listen to how offensive many approaches are toward communication, oftentimes setting up cycles of competition, and of defense and offense even between parents and kids, or just between adults and kids in other contexts. Competition should be limited to sports and real games. Just listen to world leaders, politicians, and corporate executives who get nowhere in their efforts to communicate especially when each participant is pissing in the other's ears and calling it rain water – a Southern colloquialism. Everyone could really benefit from studying and practicing the "art" of communication.

One last important factor is to express intimate and/or sensitive subject matter without the expectation of what a response, rather than a reaction, will be. It is okay to have the hope of what a response will be. However, in all situations and contexts expectations limit the range of possible responses the other party or parties are free to make. If the hoped for response isn't received then it is possible your feelings, observations, and statements were unreasonable, unrealistic, or simply incorrect. The only other possible explanation is the indication of serious incompatibility issues. If your efforts to communicate are positive, reasonable, and correct then you could consider factors such as insensitivity, rigidity, and uncompromising as possible personality characteristics of your partner. If whatever you expressed was critically important to you and unchangeable then the relationship is doomed. Remember relationships end simply because partners are incompatible, not because one or the other is good or bad; right or wrong. It just means both of you made the wrong choices in trying to establish a relationship. If ending it is necessary try to do so amicably. Also, make sure your study of communication includes a segment of effective and appropriate patterns of communication between adults and kids. Basically, don't do anything different with kids than you should do in communicating with other adults. The only difference is that with kids, sometimes "no" just means "no".

For a sense of familiarity and comfort to develop and evolve, the two people must be willing to risk being emotionally intimate and vulnerable in addition to the vulnerability associated with sex. This requires both people be fully dressed, unaroused sexually, and even around friends or family members as a test of sincerity. At that time if they can still look each other in the eye and say not only do I love you, I also like who you are, there is an indication of something real and more than just lust. If the idea ever comes to mind that the other person "would be really nice if...," then it is time to run like hell, as this is an indication you don't really like who the person is currently. At that moment you are literally thinking they would be really nice if they were someone other than who you sense them to be. This process is frequently unconscious, but should not be overlooked, as it is clearly a red flag that you and this individual are probably not compatible. Many times people who have FLAGS from abusive backgrounds are motivated to join in a relationship to either change or otherwise rescue an individual. This is not a reason to become involved romantically with anyone.

For many of the years prior to my study and work in the field of psychology and the "helping professions", I had a clear unconscious tendency to look for people who needed to be rescued, believing that if I just loved them enough they would change just for me. How foolish! However, with my role during childhood and within my family as caretaker and rescuer of my mom, I was simply following the only means I had ever learned relative to trying and having my emotional needs met. At times my actions would unfortunately result in favorable outcomes, not enough to make it worth the effort, but enough to make it seem so and, thereby, reinforce the approach.

As I took my first job at the psychiatric hospital I mentioned earlier, I realized I could get paid to take care of others. Please don't misunderstand me. There is nothing wrong with taking of care others *unless* that is your only way of trying to get your own unfulfilled needs met. If this characteristic is as strong a part of your personality as it was for me, then consider finding a job which will allow you to fulfill this important need. You can then look for people in your personal life who can meet you on balanced and equal ground in their ability to provide the same service to you as needed. A failure to recognize this aspect of your personality will result in a lifetime of disappointment and wasted efforts toward establishing and maintaining any healthy and satisfying adult relationships. However, before you join one of the so-called helping professions, make sure all of your personal issues related to limits and boundaries have been completely identified and addressed. A failure to do so will result in a tendency to take responsibility for your clients and even to become inappropriately involved in their lives. Work on yourself first before, or at least while you are training relative to assisting and guiding others professionally.

All too often I see this need to be a caregiver as a motivating factor for people to pair up. This coupled with the mistaken notion that because the sex is good we must be in love, sets up both parties for misery and failure. Remember, seeking out unhealthy and unproductive relationships is one way I have identified through which people tend to act out the emotion-based anxiety created by the FLAGS. This doesn't mean there is something wrong with you. It simply means there is something wrong with where you have come from, not having had the opportunity historically to experience what love and healthy relationships involve. With this in mind it is easy to see that since there is nothing wrong with you, the matter simply becomes that of undoing the past misperceptions. It is then important to seek out and learn new approaches and patterns which can lead to successful outcomes in relationships and in other areas of your life as well. All too often I see people unknowingly wasting precious energy trying to make something work which is doomed before the effort ever begins, given the reality of there being no chance of succeeding at something inevitably impossible. Rather than continue making the same mistakes, seek help in finding ways to channel the energy into something which can hopefully yield a favorable result.

I am always amazed at the rationalizations adolescents use in deciding to pair and/or become parents. Ironically, their reasons are often no more futile or absurd than the reasons and justifications of their adult counterparts. When I talk with kids about sexual activity between males and females, I ask both genders to make sure the person they are having sexual intercourse with is the person they would want to be the parent of their child if something goes wrong and pregnancy results. Most of the time both kids and adults admit they aren't even thinking about that possibility, and would generally answer the questions with a "no". And yet many of these individuals continue to take this risk and are then surprised when the female of the pair gets pregnant.

It is time for everyone to get their heads out of the sand and address obstacles interfering with the opportunities of educators to teach all of these aspects and concepts of sex and sexuality to teenagers. This should be done at least by the 8th grade, and then again during high school as kids gain a higher level of emotional maturity and development. For instance, I am no longer invited to go into high school classrooms and talk only about mental health issues in a required health class because the process required by schools to approve the presentation and then get permission from the parents for their kids to participate is too complicated. The religious issues and other sources of ignorance and stupidity need to be identified and challenged in an effort to be realistic about human nature. Discussions about sexuality do not encourage sexual behavior. In fact health professionals tell me that honest, open discussions and presentations generally make kids hold off longer before they become sexually active. I know this is one of my treatment goals with kids on a one-to-one basis.

With pairing and parenting as such significant issues, it is totally irresponsible on the parts of adults not to allow their kids to make fully informed decisions about issues in their lives, including any form of sexuality, which they have to face anyway. This denial and resistance only leads to kids gaining a lot of misinformation and therefore, making serious mistakes affecting them in many cases for the rest of their lives. Recently I learned that kids believed for a while that a popular soft drink killed sperm either by boys drinking it or by girls douching with it after sex. Another serious yet common misperception is that smoking even a small amount of marijuana reduces a male's sperm count to zero. Kids fail to see the absurdity in these beliefs. Furthermore, by refusing to provide complete educational information regarding sexual issues no one is really thinking about the children born into situations where the parents aren't even able to care for themselves yet, much less for a child. This is no less true for adults than for the kids I work with constantly.

Because parents often fail to address sexuality and other sexual issues at home I do so as part of my professional role as a psychologist when it is appropriate to do so. While I approach sexual topics differently with boys than I do with girls, I still make sure the same information is conveyed. The only time I ever gave a condom to a young female who asked me for one, her mom discovered it. When mom was told that I had given the condom to her daughter, rather than address this issue she reported me to the principal and I almost lost my job at a training sight as a result. When the mother called me I told her my policy was to simply make kids aware that I had condoms available if they were either sexually active or even considering it as an option. Kids had to ask me for a condom to even get one. I suggested the mom go and ask her daughter why she wanted the condom and have a responsible discussion as a parent with her daughter, rather than try to blame me for a decision I had tried to talk her daughter out of making. That was my first and last time to give condoms to girls. Ironically, when parents find their sons with condoms, even if there is some concern, there is generally no big uproar, and the parents readily accept my reasoning and suggestion that it is time to have a responsible parental conversation with their sons. I never ask a kid to lie to a parent, even if it means I may get confronted. I do, however, limit my risk of confrontation by making sure it will be worth whatever issue I will ultimately have to defend. I tell all kids that, like it or not, girls can get pregnant and boys can't.

Take a few moments to go back and reread the vow I presented and proposed at the end of Chapter VI. Really take it to heart as you think about what an awesome and even overwhelming role it is to become a parent. Not enough people put a great deal of thought into what parenting means, given the fact that the role is a lifetime biological commitment, even if the parent role is abandoned on an emotional level. All too often the decision to become parents is made solely for the sake of the individuals about to become pregnant, and not for the sake of the child who will be the result. Such thoughts prior to conception should include a strong emphasis on the preparedness of the individuals to even consider taking on the responsibility, especially when you remember that much of the outcome for that child depends on their qualifications for the job as parents.

This is why it is so critical for people everywhere in other adult roles and with other adult responsibilities for the well being and welfare of kids in addition to parenting, to review the respective lists of unquestionable obligations. I am addressing those responsible for educating and training the very ones who will likely someday make the choice to become parents. A major part of the purpose for writing this book is to offer materials which will be useful in sharing and teaching these concepts to adolescents in middle and high school settings, as well as for adults, even those who are already parents, regardless of age. Something has to be done now to address the responsibility many adults and adults as leaders ignore relative to the world conditions being created in the present for future generations. Adults in all settings need to be held accountable for any failure to honor their obligation to assist children in all arenas and aspects of life. Within contexts outside the home/family a thorough assessment of possible short term and long term outcomes should be conducted before decisions are ever made and implemented. This kind of approach should at least make adults in positions of power and authority stop and think about the impact their actions will have on future generations. Even indirectly we are all paired up with kids regardless of our roles.

Some of this will actually take a great deal of courage and determination if educators and other professionals are to stand up to threats and intimidation blocking their ability to do their jobs of preparing kids to face life as productive adults. People have become too easily scared off by litigation every time someone doesn't like the way things are done given that issues being challenged are being handled appropriately. Obvious publicized mistakes associated with many forms of religious extremism suggest it is time to limit the ability of organized religion to influence and direct the lives of people "paired" professionally with kids and given the responsibility of guiding them into and through life. This is especially true for people who need to be trained in some cases to think for themselves, rather than simply accept and believe everything they are told as long as the word "God" is attached to it.

When any society reaches a point where people are afraid to face realities of everyday living because of domination and misinformation provided by leaders, it is time for some of us to be brave enough to challenge the apathy and passivity facilitating these injustices. Perhaps it is time to get lawmakers at all levels to stop or at least limit the lawsuits clearly blocking progress in the fields of education. Reasonable guidelines are needed, but because education and even the legal systems have become so political, no one knows where to turn or how to act because of a fear of offending even one small group. This is especially true if the term "faith-based" is connected to any group.

When the complaints and opposition of a few block effective and appropriate pairing of adults and kids, I say "SCREW 'EM"! Let those few who cause the greatest amount of opposition retreat to the islands of fantasy created by the groups who dominate their minds and lives for the restricted and biased forms of education they seek. It is obvious that many of these small, yet vocal groups are holding everyone sway in our efforts to move forward. These groups should be forced to be as self-sufficient as they are self-serving, and made to get out of the way for the rest of us who want more than their narrow minded ways. The problem is that many adults are still afraid the "wrath of God" might be real and that we all run the risk of hell if the conservative groups are right. It is time to step up to the plate and establish a means of educating everyone which addresses the real issues of today including a need to understand true adult roles and responsibilities.

With regard to pairing and parenting it is time to address the foolishness with which people in many parts of the world fight for the right to occupy lands, and thereby, people. A piece of land designated in some former time as "sacred" for various groups of people who were each supposedly and reportedly chosen by God to possess the land at all costs does not justify killing each other in order to occupy any territory. Who are we kidding? Where are their gods in all of this? It is so true that many of the atrocities being carried out around the world appear to be based in centuries of hatred and prejudice created, justified, and perpetuated by organized religions. Let it go! Give the lands back to God and share them equally, educating our children about man's inhumanity to man. What good is a concept of divinity that is used to justify murder and other horrific acts of abuse and victimization? We need to identify those issues, such as oil, holding captive different parts of the world and use the technologies already available to free ourselves from such entrapments. People always tend to focus on the more obvious surface behaviors, mistakenly identified as issues, as being the real problems, when in reality the issues fueling the observable behaviors go much deeper and are based in FLAGS and outrageous histories of abuse and victimization. Children are always the most vulnerable in these situations and need to be protected through the healthy pairing with adults acting as parental figures and leaders who care and understand the results of abuse and victimization. This kind of aggression mentioned above is as futile as the gangs fighting over turf in local communities they don't even own.

Pairing and parenting are so much more global than to be seen only as traditional and limiting concepts relative to and restricted to certain contexts and regions. Sometimes leaders as parental figures need to pair properly with others who share the same goals for the common good of everyone, and especially for children who cannot protect and defend themselves. This would result in an effort to unite victims, including the United States and other nations vulnerable to oil-based economies against those trying to abuse and victimize us by keeping us dependent. How foolish is it for us to allow any world leader to try scaring and punishing others by cutting off supplies to anything when we have the means to make ourselves independent. For countries truly dependent on outside support such sanctions can be effective in bringing about compliance. But, how stupid is it for leading nations to allow for such vulnerability when we have the capabilities to avoid it by ending the competition and decreasing exposure to dependency.

These are clearly some of the same tactics used within societal, political, and religious contexts as well. Until all adults are held accountable for our own allowance for entrapment and restrictions on many aspects of our lives, then how can we effectively teach proper adult roles and responsibilities to successive generations? We must at the same time make every effort to protect children around the world and in every context, including home/family, from continuing to be, or becoming victims as a result of vulnerability created by adults. This is where the innocence of children is so obvious. All you need to do is turn on the television to see the suffering of children everywhere who cannot escape vulnerable situations created by adults. This is true even in countries not so blatantly torn apart by war, street violence, and other acts of terrorism. Imagine again how much worse all of this is in the contexts outside of the home/family context if things aren't even stable and psychologically/emotionally healthy in the home and with family members.

Basically we will need three approaches to correcting the wrongs at all levels. The first is that of interventions aimed at recognizing and changing errors currently being made by adults, to include the concepts of leaders within all contexts as having this kind of inclusion as well. Secondly, interventions must be aimed at helping kids and adults from all walks of life heal from the wounds of abuse and victimization caused by the pendulums swinging out of control in numerous contexts and relative to numerous issues around the world. Finally, given the fact that all of these issues are world issues, and the indications that the RFLAGS Model and related concepts are internationally applicable, we must begin to implement and teach as prevention the appropriate and effective utilization and practice of adult/leader roles and responsibilities as a way of protecting future generations from abuse and victimization. In other words it is time to identify, rectify, and learn from enormous errors which keep being repeated throughout history. What is the point in history if not to learn from previous mistakes from every level including personal/individual to more global and philosophical applications on much larger scales?

Pairing and parenting apply to the proper match between leaders and others in positions of power and influence with the people under their domains. As with laws and efforts to protect children in the United States from abuse, effective world leaders have an obligation to work together to stop acts of terrorism which abuse and victimize countless numbers of innocent people. Sometimes, as with consequences for child abuse, abusive leaders in any capacity must be held accountable for the acts of victimization and be punished. This also applies to leaders within the corporate systems. The process of then helping the victims of abuse and horrific acts of violence and injustice becomes a humbling experience of assuming roles as effective leaders who can guide and teach in an effort to heal and rectify. This cannot be done out of arrogance and must be done relative to the realities of the people being assisted, and must be done altruistically. The concept of teaching people to fish rather than giving them a fish clearly applies. Much chaos and conflict is likely to erupt initially, but with the right planning, preparation, methods and efforts eventually pendulums can swing in perfect balance.

Chapter XI

Breaking the Cycles

So far we have looked at a number of issues and different segments of the RFLAGS Model and its components. One of the things we identified is the concept of loss associated with dysfunctional backgrounds relative to abuse and victimization. I have referred to a process of unresolved grief associated with these losses and the resulting FLAGS. Because grief is so often only connected with issues of death and dying, I want to help each reader identify grief as it applies to more non-traditional losses. You might want to refer back to Chapter VI and to the list of losses associated with dysfunctional backgrounds. Also keep in mind the complicating factors making people vulnerable, with the higher number of complicating factors correlating directly to the degree of unresolved grief.

As I indicated earlier some of these unresolved issues can go relatively unnoticed until some traumatic or otherwise significant event triggers an overreaction to a given life situation, or even to some phase of development associated with change. I sat in a seminar a few years ago in which the presenter was talking about some of the same topics I am addressing, specifically applicable to adolescents. He kept using the phrase "for no apparent reason", repeatedly implying that sometimes kids do things without obvious cause or motivation. I was surprised that he never attempted to even suggest what some of these non-apparent reasons might be, so I want to address this issue here.

In both my personal and professional experiences I have come to believe that all behavior is purposeful, even if the purposes are unconscious in nature. The only exception might be relative to those behaviors associated with severe forms of mental or physical illness which are not only unconscious, but also often beyond the control of the individual so impaired. All too frequently people simply observe behavior and accept it as not only the problem, but also as the only issue requiring attention and remedy. This is so far from the truth and so widespread that I find such thinking to be alarming. Sure, in a crisis situation where problematic behaviors are life threatening then the behaviors have to be the sole focus until the person is restored to some reasonable degree of emotional stability. Once this is accomplished then the most difficult part of the process is to identify and resolve the underlying emotions which create emotion-based anxiety/depression resulting in feelings of hopelessness/helplessness and the need to act out the physical state which feels so bad. This is where the idea originates of knowing how bad it feels to feel bad.

The first step in the process of working through underlying issues is to help people break the automatic cycle of acting out rather than facing the FLAGS. For adults, the need to act out will usually be so completely habitual and automatic as to be beyond the conscious awareness of the individual. With older kids it is generally possible to take them back in conscious memory to a time when the acting out behaviors started and to a point where they can begin to relate specific events and emotions to the resulting changes in behavior. Like I said it is much easier to work with kids before they actually develop personality disorders in early adulthood. These disorders are defined and identified as well established, unconscious patterns of maladaptive behavior intended to ease the unresolved grief and stop the bad feelings, if only temporarily and/or in an effort to escape them. The fact there is nothing wrong with us is grounded in the fact that these maladaptive behaviors develop in childhood in an effort to cope with abuse and victimization. In most cases the number of and degree of ineffective coping behaviors observable in adulthood correlate directly to the degree of abuse and victimization experienced in childhood.

One of the best ways to help people identify maladaptive behaviors is to help them identify the ways in which their lives are out of control and the degree to which their lives are complicated. From there it is possible to identify specific actions they are taking which only serve to keep the vicious cycles of complicating factors in motion and even at times increasing. As people begin to see how their lives are out of control and are able to see that nothing they are currently trying to use as remedies or solutions are working, they can then begin to realize that the same effort being wasted in futile attempts to resolve issues can be put to better use. The way to help people realize they are not to blame is to help them recognize the underlying desire to make their lives better and more balanced. It is then possible to help those people begin looking at the FLAGS and to begin seeing how these are connected to the past. The best indication of the existence of a history of abuse and victimization is to have a person try and imagine what would be a reasonable reaction or response by others to the life circumstances they are facing. If the reactions they are having are more extreme than would normally be reasonable then the chances are unresolved issues from the past are fueling their overreactions.

At this point it is time to begin helping people make real, not imagined connections, relative to how the past is living in their present. It isn't necessary to go back and relive the past as I indicated previously. However, it is necessary to identify enough of the details to give the person a clear picture of the enormity of what they may be ignoring. Of utmost importance at this point is to help the individual realize they have been and are doing the best they know how to do; not that it is necessarily the best thing to do, it is simply all they know. By emphasizing this option it is possible to face all of these factors and resolve all of the issues to such a point as to begin the process of healing and uncomplicating their lives now and on into the future. This process is intended to help those who recognize that their need for professional help is based on two primary reasons: first, because their past is too painful to face alone; and, second, to see that it isn't about them as much as it truly is about where they have come from and what they have been through. This allows the individual to lighten up on themselves and begin to make changes which will lead to a higher standard of living and the resolution of unresolved grief associated with very real losses they have experienced and dismissed as just part of life.

The statement "that's just the way I am" is really a cop out simply because it is sometimes believed to be easier to live miserably than it is to face the past as the source of many of the current ineffective attempts to cope and move forward. The other self-defeating belief is that there is nothing which can be done to change things. While there may be some truth in that statement relative to a few factors such as missed opportunities and other losses which cannot be retrieved, just the awareness that change is possible makes it easier to accept the things which cannot be changed, or at least cannot be changed immediately. Most everyone, and certainly people with extremely intense FLAGS, really should seek out help from a well-trained and highly recommended therapist. Remember, any therapist is being hired by you to help according to your set of actual needs. If you are not simply being resistant to treatment, and the match with a therapist doesn't fit, look for another therapist with whom you feel comfortable and from whom you feel a high level of positive regard. Don't allow fear or denial to stop you from seeking the assistance you need! Also, please don't be afraid to insist they read my book.

As people begin to literally identify all of the things they lost during childhood because of abuse and victimization, even if these only included emotional abuse and emotional neglect, there is a very clear grief response to this reality. The easiest model I have found for understanding grief as a process of recovery is the model presented years ago by Elizabeth Kubler-Ross. The stages of her model are: denial, anger, bargaining, depression, and acceptance. Sometimes people think of the process as being linear. However, anyone who has applied this model to their own process of grief understands that while all of the elements are included, they tend to repeat themselves toward acceptance as the goal. Depending on the significance of the loss and the intensity of the FLAGS, some of these stages can be expected to repeat at different times throughout a lifetime, hopefully less often and less severely with varying degrees of resolution and growth. Acceptance is more along the lines of learning to incorporate the losses in a healthy manner into your history of significant events from which you have learned and grown.

As a side comment, it is a good experience to take the time to sit down and make a chronological list of every significant event that has occurred in your lifetime. Start out by writing down every event, both positive and negative, as quickly as you can remember them. Then go back and put them in order chronologically. This will help you in your therapy and in your life in general. Keep the list and add to it from time to time as you remember or even learn about events and experiences, to include your future experiences and events as well.

It is interesting to me that people often think accepting something means it is also necessary to like whatever it is that is to be accepted. Most things which are grieved are not okay in the sense of being accepted *and* liked. The reality is to simply accept the fact that whatever has happened has happened and needs to be faced and dealt with. Remember as I paraphrased earlier from The Book of Runes, by Ralph Blum: you may not always win in every situation, but you can never lose, because there is always an opportunity to learn something valuable. Many of life's greatest lessons are learned by suffering through, in the sense of going through experiences which are really hard to accept. The successful incorporation of these events and what can be learned from them are immeasurable and build amazing strength and character.

It is critical to help people understand the recovery process from issues associated with a history of abuse and victimization is oftentimes a lifelong process. Realistically, the complicating factors which led to the maladaptive coping styles and influenced the development of the FLAGS and the emotion-based anxiety all occurred during the critical period of childhood. It is unrealistic to think that everything can be resolved overnight. I believe the process of recovery is not the one traditionally used in referring to the process of breaking the cycles of addiction, except as it relates to the physical recovery from damage resulting from such acting out behaviors. Recovery, in my view, is from the underlying factors and FLAGS fueling the desire to drink and use. A failure on the part of many so called recovery programs is the denial that there is an emotional basis to virtually everything we do, even if those things we do are positive and motivated by underlying positive emotions as well. In spite of any possible biological predisposition to drink and use, the choice to start is a conscious one and will likely only lead to addiction if the individual sees substance use as a means of escaping emotional pain. Perhaps the biological basis is not that for addiction, but toward personality traits interfering with someone's ability to effectively cope with and control anxiety and the FLAGS. There may be biological/genetic factors, coupled with environmental factors, inhibiting someone's resilience and the ability to transcend loss and hardship.

As people begin to move into the process of true recovery, it is possible to then give them some skills to reinforce their belief and confidence in their ability to move forward. Most important of all is the need to keep them grounded in the reality that the process of growth and development is truly a lifelong process and should not be seen as a means to an end. Unfortunately organized religions have taught us that "salvation" is simply a single act of acceptance followed by repentance and a promise to never sin again. That approach doesn't work in that context any more effectively than it does in real life. This narrow-minded way of magical thinking sets people up for failure, which is a flaw of many "conversion" experiences. Even true spirituality is a process of growth and development and there is no promise that just because you choose to believe something, life after that choice won't sometimes be difficult. When people are told all you have to do is believe in order to achieve or attain something, they feel they have failed when things don't work out as promised. Imagine how Dorothy would have felt in the land of OZ if she hadn't returned to Kansas when she clicked her ruby slippers together. Such experiences leave people feeling they are inadequate even when it comes to salvation; or they feel they don't deserve even the salvation they sought. This fosters a belief I really believe to be flawed and perpetuates the perception of being unworthy, vulnerable, and weak.

For these reasons I believe people need to be steered away from organized religions, especially those which are punitive and judgmental, preaching hell-fire and brimstone kinds of philosophies. I am shocked at the conservative groups which are allowed to go into juvenile halls and tell the kids they are worthless pieces of crap without God. They already feel bad enough without being further victimized and abused. The messages should be along the lines of hope and the reality that everything you need can be found within the soul of any individual. It is just a matter of finding the right guidance to bring into awareness the insights which can then be put into practice. As I indicated earlier, my job as a psychologist allows me to "minister" to people without the need to recruit them or convince them of any particular way of thinking. I can encourage them to discover their own sense of God and Truth.

In the past I have given some of the juvenile offenders I work with copies of <u>The Celestine Prophecy</u>, by James Redfield. The intention is to introduce them to a healthy concept indicating there is a force bigger than we are which has a purpose for each of us which we and only we can fulfill. I can then tell them that things they have done so far in their lives aren't part of that plan, but can be used as a way to learn and grow even from the negative experiences they have had and the negative things they have done. Even if their level of reading skills isn't high enough for the book, many of them will benefit from the concepts taught to us as professionals from within the pages of <u>The Celestine Prophecy</u> and of many other books sometimes incorrectly dubbed as "New Age Spirituality". This is such a misnomer in the sense it perpetuates the views of organized religion that all ancient concepts of spirituality not sanctioned and ordained as acceptable are somehow evil and dangerous. People, it is time to wake up and smell the coffee so to speak, and begin to openly fight the dependency, ignorance, and arrogance fostered and espoused by many religions! Even though <u>The Celestine Prophecy</u> is fictional the main point of spiritual insights being a threat to organized religion is well taken.

The very first insight in <u>The Celestine Prophecy</u> is the idea many things happening in our lives are the result of Coincidence with a capitol "C". The kids I work with are always intrigued by this concept, especially when I point out all of the events which had to transpire for us to be sitting in the same room together. I focus on all of the negative experiences they have had with other adults in the home/family environment, and at least to some extent in all of the other contexts as well. My kids treasure the opportunity to work with someone like me who really is interested in getting to know them as who they really are, rather than judge them by their behaviors and lack of skills in a number of areas, including education. Perhaps no connections with kids are accidents. However, connections frequently become missed opportunities for both kids and adults to learn from each other and grow, especially when adults fail to fulfill their roles effectively and appropriately as outlined within these pages.

So many of the kids I work with either have significant learning disorders and difficulties which have gone undetected, or they are really behind in their skills in reading, writing and math. Any combination of these factors leaves them feeling dumb and stupid. When you add special education to the list of other complicating factors then the mixture of issues only gets worse. Even though special education doesn't have the same connotations as it did in the past, it still carries the stigma in the minds of kids, especially since other kids and even relatives can be quite abusive about it. For these reasons when I interview a new client I always ask for their perception of how intelligent they are. Generally they will tell me something negative, until I ask them what they could do if they really pushed themselves and could get caught up on their skills. Then their answers are much more positive and I can always mark them on the intake form as average to above average, using a letter grade of "C" as average. Most of them can identify at least one area in which they feel they could excel, and all of them agree they could make C's with a few A's and B's thrown in if they really pushed and were supported. Therefore, there is nothing phony about marking them as average to above average since this is their own perception. I really believe in the notion kids and adults will perform better if the expectations of educators and trainers are high enough to challenge them without setting them up for failure.

As strange as it may sound, be careful not to overlook the skills kids acquire even from their criminal activity, street life, and gang involvement. By helping them identify skills learned from these very real kinds of experiences, it is possible to capitalize on things they already know and simply need to redirect. Such skills include: marketing, planning, goal setting, follow through, sales, recruiting, procuring, purchasing, importing/exporting, investment, returns, profits, bargaining, bartering, supply and demand, team building, team spirit, artistic ability/creativity, critical thinking, setting ideals and standards, etc. As you can see, and probably have never previously considered, kids often have many acquired skills which would prove very useful in life if used in positive ventures and directions. Never underestimate the opportunities you have to creatively find ways to connect with kids within the context of professional roles. No one taught me what I know while I was sitting in a classroom. I have learned it through some degree of trial and error from the kids with whom I love to work. I will use whatever ethical and legal means I can discover to help me relate to them and to protect them as their advocate whenever necessary.

Let's look at issues relative to breaking the cycles of acting out emotion-based anxiety relative to abuse and victimization in the loftier contexts outside of the home/family. First of all abuse and victimization outside of the home/family context tends to target groups of people and prey upon their perceived vulnerabilities. Furthermore, some of the complicating factors alone result in abuse and victimization just by virtue of their very existence. While many situations are created by choices, even if they are unconscious, simply making and working toward different choices can change many situations. Frequently the perception of being trapped is a misperception based in the limited ability to even believe there could be other options. Also, the excuse of being trapped can be an act of denying the availability of other alternatives. This is where courage and determination are needed in order to make different choices and move forward.

The point is when complicating factors are either unchangeable, or are perceived as being unchangeable, these factors are experienced as abusive and victimizing. Look again at the list of complicating factors to see those which may be either realistically outside of someone's conscious control, or are perceived as being. Remember one of the ways to act out is to buy into the victim role, which means that sometimes things can be fought and changed with a simple change in perspective and perception. This is what happened during the times of social unrest and change in the United States during the 1950's, 60's, and 70's. People in many different categories and groups who had previously bought into the hopelessness/helplessness position realized they were living in houses without real walls. During these decades of unrest some people had to reach in and pull some of the people out, while others just went with the flow and waited until the imaginary walls were torn down. These are probably some of the people in these different groups who still want to see themselves as victims rather than seize the opportunities to make changes, even if those changes may be difficult to create and maintain.

One of the main things I focus on with clients is the concept of a standard of living. As I said before, even people living below the poverty level can have a relatively high standard of living as exhibited by the pride they feel within themselves and for the material things they have. As one's standard of living improves generally people become more motivated to make additional changes which will continue to improve their situations. I see this in many families who use what they have available to create a good standard of living and at the same time encourage their children to make even better choices than they made or were able to make. Kids accepting this encouragement and way of thinking are the ones who break the cycles of vulnerability and continue to make positive changes in their lives. This again is an example of the importance of the right kinds of conditions within the home/family context if the other contexts are to be navigated and conquered successfully.

One of the biggest mistakes I still see people making is the failure to learn from previous mistakes and from the mistakes of others. I have very little respect for people who irresponsibly create children they are not ready to provide for, or even capable of providing for on all levels. One mistake may be excusable, but repeated mistakes and bad choices without any regard for the impact on kids is unforgivable without some sincere efforts on the parts of both parents to correct things and at least work toward fulfilling their obligations and responsibilities. Laws cannot regulate irresponsible sexual activity between consenting sexual partners. Therefore, I say again it is important to really begin teaching accountability, responsibility, and appropriate values to adults and to kids. Adults in all arenas need to recognize and accept our need to model the right kinds of standards to the kids observing us in all settings. We are responsible and it is time to stop ignoring this reality.

The time has come for adults to address and change all of the faulty perceptions we have established and perpetuate. The time has also come to stand up to any adults who are supposed to be leaders and hold them accountable for their lack of honesty, their deception, and the lack of general concern for all people. This level of accountability goes beyond that represented by such leaders utilizing divisive sets of unethical standards and group membership accepted as "just the way things are". It is time for all of us to stop accepting the hypocrisy and misinformation we are being fed on a daily basis especially in all of the contexts outside of the home/family. People in positions of power and influence are not promoting fairness and sound ethical standards. It seems that so many of the choices and decisions made in the contexts outside of the home/family are motivated by greed and self serving interests, and not for the common good of this country and of the world.

In the 1950's through the 1980's people stood up to things accepted as norms and truth and began to set limits on opportunities for abuse and victimization. This kind of momentum needs to continue by searching out and identifying all areas where deception and secrecy reign. Even in this country people in leadership positions within all of the contexts outside of the home/family get greedy and begin to think they are above ethics and decency if their power isn't open to full review and monitoring. I believe this is true at all of the top levels especially within the corporate, religious and political domains.

Accountability is a must when it comes to answering to the public in general who have reached a point of trusting foolishly that everything is under control, that what we are being told is accurate, and that the best interests of everyone are safe. During the early phases of the "War on Terrorism" I watched helplessly as I our president and others in positions of power and influence made threatening statements only provoking more hatred toward us from the rest of the world. I think if more of us were bold enough to say so we would find few people really trust all of what we are being told is the truth, or that what we are being told is all we need to know. I feel much of what I hear and read from the media is suspect, even if the media personnel believe in what they are saying. In reality, who knows what the truth is anymore? In our desperate struggles to reach the top I am afraid the vast majority of people in this country are at the mercy of external factors we aren't even challenging, and in many cases are actually ignoring. We have grown lazy and complacent in the monitoring of the systems upon which we depend for our very survival.

All of these considerations are logical given the severity of situations around the world and the need to break cycles of ineffective and inappropriate beliefs and actions. I think the Republicans in the U.S. got into the White House and Congress for a period of time so we can finally get to see their true colors and see how ineffective and dangerous their thinking really is. Who in their right mind would stand in the way of reasonably controlled scientific research using dormant human embryos to affect cures for untold numbers of diseases and conditions around the world? While I am pro choice I am not a proponent of abortion as birth control. However I do not see the harm in using nothing more than cells created in a laboratory to make such incredible progress, probably even sanctioned by God, just because of protests made by a few relatively small, yet powerful and vocal groups of conservative extremists. The politicians who need votes are afraid to stand up to these groups even if this stance jeopardizes the welfare of countless others. The midterm election of 2006 sent a clear message that the American majority no longer want this climate of deception and division to continue. The 2008 elections screamed out even louder against lies and abuses of power and authority. Hopefully we will see even more progress in the years ahead.

When anyone gets to the point of crossing ethical boundaries whereby actual human beings are being either destroyed or duplicated within laboratory settings, then there will be cause for concern. Until then get out of the way and let the common good of the vast majority of people who do not buy into narrow-minded conservative views benefit from God-given medical and other technological advances. We need leaders who are more focused on reality than on re-election. I am tired of seeing everything get thrown into chaos and conflict simply because there are political elections coming up soon. The lines were already being drawn for the 2012 presidential election and each of us will pay a price for this, even around the world, until politicians figure out that the political arena doesn't have to be a shooting gallery. They also need to see that religion should not be allowed to influence elections and national/international interests and concerns. This is clearly spelled out in the U.S. Constitution relative to separation of church and state. Thank God for the victory in Alabama when the monument of the Ten Commandments had to be removed from a government building.

If clergy focused on spiritual maters rather than on legislating morality the world would be a better place for all and everywhere. Have you ever tried to imagine how elections would look if lines weren't drawn according to divisive party politics? What would we actually debate if people could begin to identify and agree upon a common good by which everyone could win? Wouldn't this help break the cycles of dysfunction within this country and represent a true moderate stance politicians are supposedly seeking? Again, I think it is time to stand up and demand accountability and ethics in all areas of life. There is no right time to become indifferent and unconcerned.

By recognizing life as the process it is rather than trying to see it as a means to an end, we can begin to see that efforts made toward breaking cycles, and reducing and eliminating abuse and victimization are only stages in a process of evolution – spiritual evolution. Interventions at all levels should be viewed as nothing more than the first steps toward taking our spiritual evolution seriously and beginning to see that each of us must accept our respective roles and responsibilities as part of this process. If we begin to recognize not only our abilities to destroy ourselves individually and collectively, but also the underdeveloped abilities to construct and grow, then our interconnectedness will become more apparent.

We are not separate groups of people segregated and defined by arbitrary barriers, borders, and boundaries as we believe. We are the human race, a rather large group of spiritual beings having, to date, a somewhat negative and disappointing human experience. The extreme advances in recent decades continuing to explode almost exponentially are not accidents. They are Coincidence and Opportunity over which we fight for ownership and recognition. All advancements with the potential to improve the well being and raise standards of living for everyone are to be shared, not owned. Ours is not a process of uniting as one; it is a process of recognizing that we *are* one. With this change in thinking we can seriously begin to break the destructive cycles and promote the process of healthy cycles of living – universal cycles of living - where every ending always mark the beginning of something new.

Chapter XII

Myth and the Need for Critical Thinking

After giving much thought to the content of this the last chapter in my book I have decided to focus on myth and the need for critical thinking. The acceptance of myths as Truth is one of the problems we face, along with the lack of critical thinking in the world representing two major obstacles in our process of spiritual evolution. In my opinion I believe that myths fall into two categories. First, there is the concept of myth as an attempt to explain things which cannot be proven, or are at least not readily understood. Secondly, myth represents the collective group of unchallenged and oftentimes unspoken rules accepted as Truth which determine the flow of life and the zeitgeist of any particular moment in time. In the first application myths are those early attempts within ancient cultures and civilizations to explain natural phenomena, and early perceptions of spirituality and the existence of factors and forces greater than ourselves. The second consideration addresses how early myths get revised to some extent throughout time and get passed along as Truth and traditions which somehow have to be honored and adhered to blindly.

On the other hand we have the concept of critical and creative thinking which to me represents the means by which we can challenge myths accepted as Truth and tradition. By challenging myth we are able to make determinations as to what is no longer applicable and useful, as opposed to other elements which can continue to serve as foundations for growth and exploration. As we look back in time it is possible to identify myths which have existed and only partially evolved within all of the 6 contexts I have identified.

First let's look at the home/family and myths associated historically with this context. Very early myths included barbaric notions of survival needs which were real at the time. These included the concepts of males as hunters and gatherers, and females as caretakers of the cave and children. The grunts of males were taken to be law and the females, while playing important roles relative to survival of the group, were given specific jobs within very confined areas where the groups dwelled. These were clearly male dominated societies, with male behaviors viewed equivalent to the basic instincts of animals, so that the men generally had all of the privileges and freedoms, even sexually, and the females were very subservient. Children and virginal females also made very good sacrifices to the gods whom were believed to control natural phenomena, especially natural disasters such as severe weather conditions, seasonal changes, volcanoes and earthquakes.

Without trying to make this a detailed historical account I will assume everyone reading this book has at least some awareness of mythical roles and responsibilities within the home/family context which had not changed much since the Stone Age until the last half of the Twentieth Century. Clearly there were vast improvements in living conditions and in all areas of agriculture, industry and technology throughout this time frame. However, the notion of traditional male and female roles remained rather unchallenged until the 1950's. During the early years of the Twentieth Century the lives of children improved in this country to some extent with the advent of child labor laws which represented the first identification of a period of adolescence and the need for secondary education beyond the basic "3 R's" of reading, 'riting, and 'rithmetic. These initial changes were partly because of a move away from primarily agricultural-based societies and economies to a more industrialized/mechanized existence. As these changes occurred people were finally able to move around the country and ultimately the world through the advent of automobiles and communication devices, and eventually through extreme advances in transportation and technology. Many professionals of today focus research on how all of these changes have impacted the lives of adults. All too often we fail to recognize the even more tremendous impact of change on kids who have to put up with adults whose lives are in states of almost constant turmoil and transition.

It is possible to see the progress we have made as our needs for survival changed more into opportunities for growth and development. However, it is equally easy to see how the myths of the past are still being clung to and fought for in many arenas all around the world. In the more advanced cultures of the world it is possible to see some critical thinking taking place, challenges being made, and some changes occurring. While these more advanced cultures and societies are beginning to move forward, the "War on Terrorism" since 9/11 and the wars in Iraq and Afghanistan have made all of us aware of the barbaric conditions continuing to exist in geographical regions still dominated and controlled by males and religious extremism even in the United States. The 2008 election of the first African America president caused a whole new uprising based in fear and discrimination, primarily within the ranks of older white Americans.

It is important to recognize many of the myths of the past are still accepted as Truth even in the more advanced societies. Even within the United States and in the home/family context there are still struggles being made to discover and stabilize new male/female roles, and to redefine the adult roles and responsibilities toward children. As I stated previously, any initial periods of radical change seem to be fraught with chaos and confusion. This is clearly represented by the on going lack of stability in any sense relative to appropriate family structure and definition. When people immigrate into this country from primarily male dominated societies, one of the biggest acculturation issues is that of men trying to retain their positions of unquestionable power and authority over women and children. Also, I see a lot of opposition to myths associated with religious extremism from within the country of origin as well. Hopefully as we continue to search for balance we will be able to find a set of standards which work for home/family issues in this and other societies. Because the United States is such a blending of cultures this is likely a good testing ground. So far when my RFLAGS Model is presented in public seminars, workshops and classrooms it is well received and appears to be effective in challenging myths associated with family issues regardless of cultural or ethnic differences.

A few years ago I had an older man from a Spanish-speaking country refer to me as being from "Gringo Landia" or the white man's culture. This occurred during a workshop for Spanish-speaking people and this gentleman was challenging my views on abuse and victimization as they apply to the concept of discipline. He clearly recognized he was alone in his views after I confronted him in front of a group composed entirely of

Spanish-speaking people, telling him literally "it takes a lot more time and energy to learn how to be a good parent than it does to hit and yell." The entire audience agreed with and supported me, indicating a clear acceptance of my model and related concepts in spite of the fact I am indeed a gringo, at least on the outside. As the evening progressed my opponent became an ally and was able to see the Truth in my beliefs regardless of our cultural differences.

Now let's consider myths existing within the school context. One of the most obvious is the elitist attitude of educators being part of a closed system and clearly seeing non-members of the educational field as "outsiders". I have experienced this first hand as a representative of kids who are referred to various mental health settings to address psychological needs often accompanying learning difficulties. Many agencies, within all of the contexts frequently have their little song and dance routines they use when no outsiders are around to hold them accountable for misdeeds committed against those who are the most vulnerable.

This is especially true when the parents and kids present are thought to be ignorant (in the sense of being uninformed) and vulnerable relative to a full understanding of rights, policies and procedures, and due process. Because of my reputation of being seen as an advocate for kids and families, as well as supportive of school-based efforts to offer the best options available, I am respected and am not seen as being oppositional. However, there is a fine line I am not allowed to cross. Doing so results in efforts to exclude me from future meetings. My tactics are to empower kids and families by making them fully aware of their rights and by encouraging them not to accept the myth that those in charge always have their best interests in mind. Believe me, many times people in all arenas will only seek to serve and protect their own best interests, especially when the best interests of other parties are likely to cost money over and beyond usual financial considerations. My best efforts are focused on informing people of their rights out in their communities and in my office, rather than during meetings where I might be viewed as adversarial.

The next biggest myth within the school context is that many teachers are victims and therefore, are not able to do their jobs, much less be effective. As with other professions including psychology, most people enter these fields with hopes, ideals and dreams of the changes they want to make in the lives of kids and adults. Unfortunately, the realities of actually trying to make a difference are quite often a stark contrast to the fantasies which motivated us to make the efforts in the first place. Rather than take this as defeat, see it as challenge and opportunity.

There are people within the educational systems who are very effective in spite of some very real odds. Because of the breakdown in the home/family environments kids seem to be more difficult to reach at times, partly because of legitimate trust issues they have with adults in general. Unfortunately with the role of teacher or educator oftentimes comes the myth "I am an authority figure who deserves unquestionable and unchallenged respect. Furthermore, my only job as a teacher is to teach you textbook information and not have to deal with you on a behavioral or relational level."

The reality is that kids today are too sophisticated to fall for this kind of thinking from any adult. This is why I think we have so much defiance and so much poor taste in kids relative to what they consider as funny and appropriate. Kids seem to feel a desire for revenge against adults who continue in many cases to take them for granted and try to push them around. These are not even conscious awarenesses on the part of most kids. Because public school staff members are no longer allowed to use corporal punishment to force compliance, it is almost necessary for all educators to have a back up degree in psychology and human relations in order to be successful. As times change, every system impacted either directly or indirectly by the changes is obligated to shift and adjust to changes as they occur. This is extremely necessary within educational settings which must adapt and grow to adequately keep up with and even try to anticipate and predict changes in the real world outside of the classrooms. It is only through such efforts to adapt and adjust within all contexts that the chaos and confusion can begin to subside and true progress can begin. The myth of a classroom easily and readily conducive to learning no longer applies, so face it and deal with the reality of changes which are occurring. Quite often any successful approaches in dealing with the most troubled kids and problematic behaviors require very different and creative efforts involving communication and shared problem solving processes.

The community context contains numerous myths as well. First of all the myth of communities being equal now that civil rights laws are in effect really needs to be addressed. In the South it is almost comical to watch as white people in different locales and neighborhoods run from blacks who are seemingly believed by whites to be chasing them around simply to destroy their European American existence. Unfortunately and regardless of ethnicity and cultural backgrounds, a few people in any neighborhood who have a lower standard of living than the others can bring down every aspect of that neighborhood. Because of concerns over property values and general pride in any area where people live, the reasonable standards relative to an agreed upon standard of living set by residents in a particular area should be acknowledged, enforced, and accepted by new residents. As I mentioned previously, a standard of living is not determined by socioeconomic status as much as it is established by a sense of pride in oneself and in one's possessions and environment.

I have very little respect for people who have a low standard of living and seemingly have little or no pride in themselves unless conditions exist which are somehow completely beyond their control. I attribute this in part to systems and circumstances helping to remove the concept of a work ethic whereby people work and have an opportunity to feel good about themselves and about what they have gained materially. With community-based programs to facilitate opportunities for education, jobs, and appropriate housing, more people have opportunities to raise their standards of living. Failure to do so or even see the need to change is generally based on faulty value systems and myths people have bought into from the stance of continuing to be victims of various historical factors which no longer exist as the insurmountable obstacles they once were.

Communities are in reality divided into classes whether we want to see that or not. Hurricane Katrina in the summer of 2005 hit all of us in the face with this reality in this country. However, there are many people in neighborhoods who have raised their standards of living and have improved the environments in which they live, allowing them to now take pride in what they have. While it may be difficult for some adults to get additional job training and education, by raising standards of living and teaching kids the importance of dreaming and pursuing their dreams through education and determination, more and more people will be able to give kids a chance to raise their standards of living even higher than those of their parents.

It is only fair that people with higher standards of living than others have a right to protect themselves from being subjected to those with lower, yet changeable standards. Many people even within "inner city ghettos" take pride in their neighborhoods and protect them from decline once the areas are transformed, improved and become free from domination by criminal factions. The acceptance of different groups by others, including groups referred to as "low lifes" or "trailer trash", depends on the acceptance of their responsibility to clean up their acts if they want to stop being looked down upon. While I do not agree with labeling and judging, I do feel an obligation to protect myself and what I have accomplished from anyone or anything that threatens the standard of living I have worked hard to achieve. Believe me, there is a big difference between thinking I am better than others, compared to realizing I am better off than some because of the ways I have pushed myself to gain education, experience and respect. Believe me none of these personal gains were handed to me by virtue of simply being white.

I went to college and graduate school with people recognized as being from different minority groups who had their education paid for at least partially if not fully in some cases. In order to have reached my goals relative to education and profession I found myself heavily in debt, owing almost as much as I paid for the house I was finally able to buy at age 45. If I continue to push myself I hope to pay off my student loans before I turn 77 as the repayment schedule now stands over a 30-year period. Remember, I do not associate myself much with stereotypical European American groups, so I am not obsessing about how to get rich. I am basically hoping to be able to pay myself out of debt before I die. I believe if I could do it without any support from anyone including my family, anyone can do it. None of my efforts were any easier for me than they would be for any others given the opportunities and standards existing in today's society. This is especially true in states like California where there is more financial assistance in advanced educational programs for non-European Americans than for European Americans. These factors help in at least challenging the myth of privilege.

One of the best community-based and federally funded programs available to low-income kids today is Job Corps. The closest one to the desert where I lived and worked in California was located about seventy-five miles away from my base office. Everything, including room and board, education (high school diploma or GED, and college), job training, transportation, basic medical/dental/vision, and clothing is provided without any financial obligation to anyone who at 18 is unemployed, low income, and sleeping in their parents' home. The age ranges for admission are 16 to 24. At the end of their training the trainees, as they are called, are guaranteed a good paying job, and are given a check for a significant amount as starter money.

The job training opportunities offered are very usable skills in today's job markets, with starting salaries higher than for those without the Job Corps training. If you have Job Corps facilities in your area that are not up to the highest standards then start a campaign to make them accountable for a failure to provide the services they are expected to provide. If there isn't a Job Corps facility relatively close to you then check into establishing one. The reality is that in more than nine years of taking a total of probably two hundred kids to see this program only three actually went into the program. This was in spite of my efforts to take them to orientations, for interviews, and for eventual residence once there was a spot for them at the facility, thereby eliminating virtually all external obstacles I could address.

The biggest obstacles for most of the low income kids I work with are the lack of courage to take a favorable risk, and the fact there are rules and structure which are enforced during the time kids are in training at Job Corps. The zero tolerance rules kids hate the most are about the need to stay clean and sober. It is appalling to see how blind kids and adults are to the destructive effects of drugs and alcohol, including marijuana. I can get kids to stop gang banging easier than I can get them to stop using and drinking. Substance abuse and dependence quite often represent the kinds of obstacles people with lower values and standards of living, regardless of socioeconomic status, are not only ignoring, but are able to convince themselves aren't really a problem. These are some of the present day community myths kids and adults need to face and resolve.

How foolish it is to let reasonable rules stand in the way of an absolutely free opportunity to get a good start in life. Job Corps eliminates all of the obstacles and excuses if kids will just make the commitment to attend and accept the rules and structure. The length of stay depends on the individual's abilities and level of dedication which determine the time needed to complete educational and job training needs. This program alone eliminates any excuses on the part of low-income kids who complain about a lack of opportunities. What they are really complaining about is the lack of easy opportunities which never will exist anyway. Even get-rich-quick criminal schemes and ventures come with a price. There is nothing to be lost by making a legitimate investment of time and effort into your future. Any legitimate future created by an individual can never be taken away. In addition to training at Job Corps all trainees are given access to support staff who are there all along the way to help them be successful and to even help them stay clean and sober.

Keep in mind myths are only as strong as the degree to which we accept them as unchangeable and unquestionable truth. Societal myths include such things as: strength in numbers; might makes right; entitlement; some groups being better than others; us versus them kind of thinking; money and materialism will lead to happiness; my well being and profit at the expense of others; lack of responsibility and accountability; it's only wrong if I get caught; interconnectedness and universality don't exist; the environment will protect itself; natural resources are limitless; something for nothing; etc. As you can see there are numerous myths lived out as truth by many adults and kids in all arenas at the societal level. It will take others like myself to begin speaking out about the injustices and erroneous assumptions and acceptance of myths as Truth if we are to finally see progress being made as these myths evolve into more current day realities and applicability.

Many of these societal myths also apply to the contexts of politics and religion as well. I have already addressed these contexts rather extensively. Again, one of the most significant myths to be challenged in the political context is the assumption those in power really have the best interests of society at large in mind. I believe because of the perceived importance of some conservative groups relative to a politician's reelection, these groups are often treated as if they are majorities. If the facts were known, I also believe we would realize that more and more people are actually against the self-serving interests of most conservative groups and issues within this country and in countries around the world.

Unfortunately many of the hippies in the 1960's and 70's became the yuppies in the 80's and 90's by buying into some of the same myths they were fighting against at an earlier time. These are the ones of us labeled as "the baby boomers", and are the ones moving into the retirement age range. Hopefully not all of the baby boomers have forgotten their spirit of radicalism and desire for changes and improvements in the world at large. Having been born in 1954, I am kind of on the tail end of the boomer generation. It may have helped that I got to watch and learn from their efforts before I finally made the choices of how to start my own progressive campaigns against arrogance and ignorance. I take pride in the fact I have learned to recognize and challenge ways of thinking which were never really appropriate anyway. I am fortunate enough to have found the courage to step outside of the boxes I was exposed to as a kid and as a young adult. Hopefully my efforts to write and publish this book and others will inspire people to do the same relative to their own sense of calling and uniqueness.

The last context I want to spend a little more time with is that of religion. In one of the psychology classes I taught at the local community college in California, we talked about myth and how myth applies to issues of sexuality. I always, of course, took an antagonistic approach to challenge what the students accepted as Truth, which included the reality of how extensively the myths associated with organized religion impact and influence virtually every level of our existence.

One of the most obvious and yet infrequently thought about indicators was the influence religion has had on the establishment of Latin-based languages initially within countries and cultures ultimately if not initially dominated by Catholicism. While I am not an expert in linguistics, I have noticed while learning and speaking Spanish how very sexist the nouns are in this and in other Latin-based languages. It cannot be an accident that things associated with the idea of women as being subservient to men are associated with conventional religious thinking. The languages reflect concepts of God being male and the church being female in the sense of being the bride of Christ. Feminine and masculine roles and responsibilities are given either feminine or masculine forms. One of the women in my class who was fluent in Spanish had never thought about this was rather astounded, commenting that I "must have too much time on my hands" to have been able to make that observation. I laughed and pointed out the fact that I don't take anything at face value anymore, and have found the study of Spanish to be an enlightening revelation of cultural nuances and myths within the "Latin" cultures. Remember until recently religious services in the Catholic Church were conducted strictly in Latin. Latin-based languages in Mexico, Central, and South America were introduced by Europeans who spoke languages based to some degree in Latin. Clearly the Catholic Church superimposed its sexism on the cultures they invaded and destroyed throughout the centuries and around the world.

She and a few other class members were intrigued by this reality, and could not refute it as fact. I pointed out the English language has some forms of words that identify gender, but that because of the challenges of myths in the last half of the Twentieth Century, many efforts have been made to correct these. For instance, many words ending with "man" have been modified to "person" or to "woman", such as chairperson or congresswoman. Some words such as salesman have been modified to such an extent as to now be genderless as in referring to someone as a sales associate. In the Latin languages everything related to God is masculine, and to the church is feminine. This is one of the most blatant examples I have found of an ever-present reminder of the myths of gender roles and religion. Words associated with emotions attributed to stereotyped feminine characteristics are also feminine, with harsh emotions being considered as masculine. It is amazing how the Latin languages reflect so many of the cultural dynamics within these countries. Talk about constant "subliminal" reminders for women of position in life relative to men and to religion. Men are constantly reminded of their need to be intense and nasty, with such words for anger, dirty, and bathroom being masculine in form.

I say all of this to point out that it is time to challenge all components of organized religions which try to keep people down, dependent and trapped in their abilities to think and to live. The biggest myth associated with any religion is that of infallibility, along with the myth that religion is to be found in a building or through someone ordained or otherwise blessed, or through some act indicating faith, confession, commitment, and dedication. I am very free as a spiritual being because of breaking away from the teachings of organized religion. It took a lot of courage initially to simply look over the edges of the boxes, much less to actually step outside of and away from what I had been taught as my only salvation and hope of heaven.

Think of how horrible it is for people to believe in any god that would want them to kill themselves and others in that god's name and then be rewarded for doing so in the afterlife. How tragic are the circumstances of vulnerability and abuse/victimization giving people the need to buy into such foolishness, myth and fallacy. The very religious texts believed to be the infallible and literal words of many gods are in many cases the very same books which, when written, allowed for the killing of people (especially women) for what are now considered to be basic human rights. These are the same writings whose authors justified slavery and attended public executions as entertainment and sport when people, usually women were caught in the act of something considered by religion to be sinful. These are the very same writings that promote the abuse and victimization of women and children by insisting on subservience and the concept of "spare the rod and spoil the child". They also promote the concepts of God as being vengeful and judging – something to be feared. One of the abusive statements my Dad used against me as he beat me with a belt was to threaten "to put the fear of God" in me, likening himself at that moment to the image of God.

I am amazed at how ignorantly and arrogantly many religious people, regardless of religious affiliation, claim to believe in religious writings as literal truth and yet pick and choose as it suits their needs what to believe and actually implement in their daily lives. For instance, it is my understanding of Christianity that Jesus came to replace the Law with Love. However, there are only four books dealing with the life and teachings of Jesus. All other books in the New Testament appear to be the creation of new laws for the establishment of "the Church". It is ironic how these new laws lost sight of the spiritual nature of what Jesus was trying to teach, thereby losing sight of the Love. My spiritual beliefs are something I strive to live out in every aspect of who I am and what I do. In recent years I have come to believe so strongly in the concept of Karma and that what goes around comes around, I really seek to limit my exposure to negativity as much as I have learned to do so to date. I have also come to believe very strongly in the concept that I have some purpose in life I and only I can fulfill, and that the only thing making any sense in this existence is to want what God wants at every level of my being.

True spirituality is genderless and yet virtually all of the larger traditional religions are still male dominated. It is about time people are beginning to challenge the myths of celibacy and heterosexual male dominated clergy. These myths are nothing more than laws expressed in ancient Jewish texts and established by early Christian leaders to set standards of the day for the religious institutions they were trying to form. This is likely also true in the Muslim traditions as well. People who are truly spiritual are equal in all regards. Those focused on universal spiritual concepts of One Source, unconditional love and acceptance, being non-judgmental and truly altruistic, and not self absorbed, self serving, or materialistic. Spiritual people are both self and other focused; truly altruistic; see ourselves as connected to everyone and to everything; and are constantly seeking guidance and wisdom through numerous sources including both spiritually strong people and spiritually sane written materials. Unconditional love and acceptance have little to do with literally embracing everyone, and everything to do with recognizing and respecting individual processes.

Think about how the extremists within the three prominent feuding religions – Muslims, Jews, and Christians – all seek to dominate, conquer and control geographic locations basically because of land considered to be sacred to each group. Again, where is God in that? Also consider the reckless use of ancient religious texts in these pursuits to command place and privilege, with the possible end result being that of total annihilation. Who would be on top then? What a horrible way to end struggles needing to end in peace through compromise and recognition that we are all created equally by God. No religious text taken literally in today's times should be used as a basis for anything less than the sense of Spirituality and Soul within each of us. No one knows what the Truth is anyway, so why not take a leap of faith forward and toward a common ground of acceptance of and appreciation for the diversity among all people in all regions of the world.

Each individual based in pure spirituality approaches people only when it is appropriate to do so, and at the same time models the spiritual concepts listed above. People are not recruited into spirituality. Rather, people become spiritually aware as their focus shifts from self to Self in relation to others. Spirituality must be lived and modeled rather than institutionalized, and can only be perpetuated by people who speak out loudly against the injustices everywhere by identifying and challenging all forms of abuse and victimization within all of the six contexts as they exist around the world. None of this can be accomplished through self-serving societies, partisan political factions, or divisive religions. Effective challenging of injustices must be done through the power of the Originator of the Universe — the Creator and Voice of "one-song" (uni-verse) as taught by Dr. Wayne Dyer, a man deeply grounded in non-religious Spirituality.

Even publishers and distributors of printed materials have a responsibility to market materials promoting healthy spiritual and psychological growth. Writers and other professionals who are truly spiritually based must take the lead in teaching spiritual concepts which can be grasped by individuals at all levels according to their own needs and abilities relative to each respective process. Basic spiritual concepts can be easily understood and are universally acceptable. Every human being, including children and adolescents, responds favorably to unprejudiced love, acceptance, and altruistic assistance intended to strengthen and nurture, rather than dominate and control. Predators are those individuals, groups, organizations, institutions, and governments who prey upon the innocence and vulnerabilities of others. Those of us who are focused on spiritual growth and development must become the promoters of universally applicable spiritual concepts.

Retrospectively I have learned that once I broke free from misleading and dangerous myths accepted by many as truth I have been able to move forward and grow at a phenomenal rate. Not that life has been easy or always fun, but that my life now has a feeling of purpose and direction I never had in the past. I want to optimize this existence as much as I can on a spiritual level so I can follow the process to become the best I can become, whatever that involves.

When I was a child growing up in an abusive and chaotic home/family environment in the Deep South, also being victimized by religion, I couldn't have ever imagined I would be where I am now in terms of my life experiences and philosophies. As a child I always said I wanted to be a doctor when I grew up so I could help people who "felt bad". I thought the only kinds of doctors were MD's, so I gave up on that notion until in 1993 when I walked across the stage during my graduation ceremony and was announced and hooded as Dr. David L. Roberts. I started crying from sheer joy, wishing that my family had cared enough to attend my graduation, but realizing that in spite of all of the hardships and disappointments in my life I had beaten the odds. I had actually achieved the professional status my soul whispered to me even as a young child and all because I jumped out of the boxes and sought my own TRUTH which then became my freedom.

I live, work, write, and teach from somewhere very deep within my Soul. This is also the place where I process information in an effort to turn the good stuff into wisdom and insight which I can then share with others. At the beginning of each semester as a professor I began my college classes by telling the students that "if I do nothing more than teach you to think critically, then I will have done you a great service." I believe that I have gained a tremendous amount of wisdom through the experiences life has offered me, and even more importantly from the experiences which I have searched for as I changed my belief systems, values, and perception of Spirituality. For the first time in my late 20's I gained sight of the person I really could become, realizing that all of the lies I was told as a kid through the abusive statements and actions of my parents were simply just lies. I am so glad I found the courage to act in spite of fear, and the determination not to allow my feelings to interfere with my goals.

One final litany about the kids I serve. My job and work with kids at risk are my passion. I consider myself to be a very fortunate man and am always awed and humbled by the opportunities to connect professionally with kids often thought of by others as unreachable. At times I wish I was a man "of color". But, the amazing thing is that I get to reach out to all cultures and ethnicities as a European American male who doesn't fit any of the stereotypes currently associated with those within my own culture/ethnicity. I know many people in various settings look at me as just "another f-----g white guy", oftentimes assuming, because of my shaved head appearance and without knowing me, I represent some branch of law enforcement. There is no greater satisfaction in the world for me than to be able to connect with and reach out to kids who have no real reason to trust me in the first place. It is heartbreaking to me when I learn I am the first person in a long lineup of adults with whom a kid has been able to talk and not feel judged or labeled. There is no excuse for this reality, and as for adults who have any regular contact with kids, we need to feel shame for any ineffectiveness. This sense of shame should serve as a motivator to make the necessary changes which would facilitate our opportunities to make positive differences in the lives of kids who are so much in need of support and understanding.

Within twelve months spanning 2002 to 2003 three of my kids have been murdered as the result of gang related violence. These were the first out of hundreds I have met and served since starting my training in 1990. I was deeply saddened by their deaths and at the same time harshly reminded of the fallacies residing in the myths associated with the streets and so-called street justice. I watched as the brother and friends of the first kid polished the black casket with their blue "rags", ignoring the reality that the kid in the casket died for no other reason than that of foolish and desperate choices he had made along the way. With the second kid I looked into his dead face and recalled the promise and potential which was buried with him and all for nothing. The third death occurred in August 2003 and I was given the awesome and extremely difficult responsibility of giving this news to a group of twenty minors court ordered to a lock-in placement where I had the privilege of being their psychologist. All but two of these kids knew the kid who died and were frightened and horrified by the gruesome manner in which he died and manner in which his killers disposed of his body. The kids and staff all referred to me as "the Doc" and each of us shed tears together over the loss of one who tried so hard and yet faced unimaginable odds. As a unit of staff and kids we celebrated the life of this kid through a moving and memorable flag ceremony whereby the flag was lowered to half-staff, a ceremony repeated for several days. Until just six weeks prior to his death, and for a period of eight months we gave this kid something he had never had in his entire life – an environment of unconditional love, support and safety in which he clearly knew people cared for and about him. What a sad tribute to say that this kid had been in virtually every system available since birth and yet never encountered anything positive until he reached our unit.

In all three of these cases I was able to remind myself I had given these kids everything I had to offer professionally and to some extent on a personal level. One of my closest colleagues told me she respects me most for my willingness to give my heart to my kids. These kids – my kids - would have told you the same thing. While I cannot mention these guys by name I dedicate this book partly in memory of their lives and the connections we shared. I was also reminded by their deaths that I can only do so much, and that the effort is worth every moment of frustration and even sorrow I may experience along the way. I thank God often for the chance I have been given to make a difference in the lives of kids basically thrown away by most of society and in some cases even by their own families. Because of the extreme nature of the populations I generally serve the indications of progress are sometimes hard to find. But every time I see a kid in the streets who is glad to see me, or have a kid return to me in later years for additional guidance and support, I am reminded it is all worthwhile. I was favorably known within all of the gangs in the areas where I worked and I am proud of that fact. The respect I receive from these kids is immeasurable as is the satisfaction I receive simply from doing a job I truly love. There is no doubt in my mind I am fulfilling the purpose for which I was called to serve.

The completion of this book is another of many significant milestones in my life. The only thing I take credit for is my discovery of and willingness to live out my Spiritual beliefs. It is amazing me to realize this venture is the culmination of a process which began in 1986 as the idea for an undergraduate research project I mentioned earlier in this book. I am awed by everything this manuscript represents. I am also humbled by the many experiences included within and stand behind the insights I have gained throughout my entire professional training and work experience as a psychologist. I thank the Source clearly at work in my life and through me as I believe this and all I have to offer is truly a gift to the world from God and through me. I cannot begin to imagine how or why I was given this assignment, but I am very grateful for the opportunity and the privilege, and I am proud of my willingness to commit myself to this calling.

Believe me the feelings I often experienced of <u>F</u>ear, <u>L</u>oneliness, <u>A</u>nger, <u>G</u>uilt, <u>S</u>hame, frustration, doubt, uncertainty, and insecurity could easily have destroyed my determination. As I said earlier I never ask anyone to do anything I haven't done in one form or another relative to taking risks which ultimately will result in growth and accomplishment. I challenge each of you to find the same place deep within your Soul where you can begin to search for and process new and productive ways of living. Remember, one of the biggest factors is the ability to think critically. I truly wish you the best as you discover and facilitate your own process toward a clear awareness of purpose and direction. Hopefully you have discovered that one of the main themes of this entire project is to never forget how bad it feels to feel bad, and to never make another living creature, human or otherwise, feel that way. Furthermore, when you see people hurting in a way with which you can identify, if it is appropriate to do so, and after you have successfully addressed your own issues, help them. Memorize both this concept and the vow from adults to kids found toward the end of Chapter VI. These factors alone will give you a solid basis from which to right the wrongs in your life and in the lives of kids who are directly and indirectly in your care.

APPENDICES

Appendix A

ROBERTS FLAGS MODEL

Negative Emotions	Anxiety/ Depression	Hopelessness/ Helplessness	Acting Out Behaviors

<u>F</u>EAR

<u>L</u>ONELINESS

<u>A</u>NGER

<u>G</u>UILT

<u>S</u>HAME

Dr. David L. Roberts Ph.D.

Appendix B

DESCRIPTIVE TERMS AND PHRASES USED TO DESCRIBE ANXIETY AND ANXIOUS DEPRESSION

Bored
Angry/mad
Annoyed
Burned out
Overwhelmed
Stressed out
Anxious
Tired/exhausted
Down
Confused
Can't cope
Uptight
About to lose control
Need to get away
Falling apart
Anguish

Depressed
Frustrated
Pissed off
I've had enough
Ready to explode
Nervous
Apprehensive
I'm in a bad mood
Trapped
Can't take it anymore
Losing my mind
Tense
I'm backed into a corner
Desperate
Disappointed
Irritated

Appendix C

ACTING OUT BEHAVIORS AND IMPULSIVE REACTIONS

Drinking/using
Using tobacco products
Sex
Eating too much/little
Sleeping too much/little
Self-mutilation
Suicide
Taking risky chances
Head-banging
Biting fingernails
Self reproach/loathing
Withdrawing
Isolating
Somaticizing
Playing the victim
Shopping/spending money
Gambling
Exercising
Reading
Watching TV
Working
Running away
Pretending
Manipulating
Blaming
Scapegoating
Subverting
Gossiping
Fantasizing

Avoiding
Being overly materialistic
Hoarding
Excessive cleaning
Organizing
Obsessing
Exhibitionism
Being arrogant
Feeling superior
Shunning/rejecting
Violence (all forms)
Criminal acts
Discrimination
Judging
Victimizing others
Yelling
Hitting
Destroying things
Rape
Molesting
Being self righteous/pious
Denying reality
Arguing
Becoming divisive
Hating
Making drastic changes
Undermining
Searching
Day dreaming

Thrill-seeking	Partying
Always going out	Dating recklessly
Being unfaithful	Controlling
Divorce	Greed
Intimidation	Bullying
Living irresponsibly	Living an unethical life
Being unjust/unfair	Demanding/ordering
Being cruel	Being hurtful
Playing games	Thinking irrationally
Joining negative groups	Getting pregnant
Being needy	Disregarding rights of others
Being rude/crude	Being inconsiderate
Procrastinating	Acting without thinking
Mislead/deceive	Adopting extreme beliefs
Unyielding	Uncooperative
Living as a slob	Vicious and mean spirited
Disorganization	Rigid and uncompromising

Appendix D

PROBLEMS/ISSUES WE SEEK TO ESCAPE OR ACT OUT

Emotional pain
Abuse/victimization
Hatred
Anxiety/Depression
Perceived Reality/Truth
Sexual orientation
Abandonment
Neglect
Self loathing
Underachievement
Financial problems
Lack of moral values
Poor coping skills
Mistakes
Lack of a support system
Dysfunctional childhood
Poor family relations
Societal taboos
Being judged by others
Environmental factors
Lack of perspective
Lack of opportunities
Lack of understanding
No sense of belonging
Ignorance
Lack of forgiveness
Limited view of the world
No sense of purpose
Personality problems

FLAGS
Trauma/Loss
Hopelessness/helplessness
Sadness
Poor self image
Identity issues
Failure
Denial/Repression
Rejection
Overachievement
Being or feeling trapped
Low self esteem
Bad decisions
Negative consequences
Conflict
Loss and grief
Prejudice, racism, bigotry
Poor judgment
No future dreams or plans
Biological factors
Lack of alternatives
Employment problems
Lack of acceptance
Appearance
Persecution
Lack of self-control
No sense of spirituality
No sense of direction
Mental/Emotional problems

Fear of losing control
Unfulfilled needs
Fear of success
Boredom
Lack of motivation
Lack of creativity
Doing nothing
Lack of involvement
Isolation
Deprivation
Lack of pride
Lack of courage
Fear of taking risks
No desire to learn/explore
Disappointment
Negative beliefs
Divorce/breakup

Sexual issues
Lack of patience
Illness
Lack of challenge
Lack of inspiration
Lack of critical thinking
Lack of interests/hobbies
Fear of the unknown
Unpredictability
Lack of trust
Lack of accomplishments
Lack of strength
Comfort in stagnation
The need to be desired/loved
Frustration
Negative perceptions
Infidelity

Appendix E

ADULT ROLES AND RESPONSIBILITIES

Love	Nurture
Care for/about	Provide for
Encourage	Empower
Support	Teach limits
Teach self control	Teach respect for self/other
Teach morals/ethics	Teach appropriate behaviors
Teach values/work ethic	Teach priorities
Model appropriate behaviors	Guide
Assist	Believe in kids
Increase self esteem	Increase self confidence
Support individuality	Maximize potential
Instill hopes/dreams	Teach courage
Listen	Accept
Avoid judging/labeling	Discourage abuse
Avoid being abusive	Protect
Give attention/time	Create a safe environment
Answer questions honestly	Communicate with kids
Encourage openness	Encourage honesty
Encourage trust	Defend kids
Challenge appropriately	Respect
Control	Discipline
Punish/give consequences	Reward
Watch/observe	Supervise
Accept responsibility	Allow appropriate emotions
Apologize	Reward only extra effort
Compromise	Forgive
Comfort/soothe	Teach effective coping skills
Respect privacy	Teach spirituality, not religion
Encourage responsibility	Teach decision-making skills

Teach conflict resolution	Teach problem solving
Teach planning skills	Learn from mistakes
Always consider kids	Model appropriate choices
Correct/improve conditions	Alter maladaptive patterns
Teach humility	Avoid creating FLAGS
Provide traditions	Encourage fun/play
Share activities	Develop talents and abilities
Validate feelings	Be reasonable
Be fair	Encourage independence
Encourage education	Encourage achievement
Be realistic	Seek guidance and education
Encourage respect for natural environment	Discourage negativity
See kids as human beings	Be psychologically healthy
Avoid labels	Promote inclusion
Promote acceptance of self and others	Teach appropriate use of time
Encourage healthy exploration	Be real/genuine
Encourage social responsibility	Support uniqueness
Don't be arrogant	Avoid the need to be right
Avoid the need to dominate	Don't always need to be liked
Praise kids	Respect/love yourself
Appreciate kids	Don't spoil kids
Don't push extreme conformity	Teach balancing and centering

Appendix F

FACTORS CONSTITUTING THE 'IDEAL FAMILY'

Loving parents	Stability
Consistency	Predictability
Mutual respect	Nurturing
Consideration	Communication
Connection	Peaceful environment
Unconditional love	Trust
Self control	Spirituality
Work ethic	Quality of life
Higher standard of living	Moral values
Ability to learn	Sharing
Ability to teach	Mutual concern/regard
Reciprocity	Balance
Appropriate role modeling	Individuality
Encouragement	Empowerment
Acceptance	Recognition
Reward	Reasonable limits/boundaries
Healthy degree of privacy	Age-appropriate expectations
Assistance	Mutual caring
Fun	Excitement
Traditions	Planning
Goal setting	Forethought
Foresight	Appropriate structure
Responsibility	Protection
Safety	Non-threatening environment
Non-judgmental	Humility
Belongingness	Assurance
Continuity	Reality
Honesty	Freedom of expression
Togetherness	Compatibility

Cooperation	Support
Aesthetics	Education
Appreciation	Willingness
Well being	Adaptability
Flexibility	Dependability
Resilience	Compromise
Healthy involvement	Sense of roots/ancestry

Appendix G

MISTAKES OFTEN MADE BY ADULTS

Lack of unconditional love
Bad choice of partners
Dependence on welfare
Domestic violence and chaos
Promiscuity
Family secrets
Non-acceptance of individuality
No future goals or plans
Self-loathing
No sense of a work ethic
Little or no self pride
No pride in possessions
Questionable moral values
Abandonment
Poor eating habits
No limits or self control
View children as nuisances
Resent and blame your kids
Poor parenting style
Not encouraging kids
Poor judgment
Place too much responsibility on kids
No desire to improve things
Unresolved issues from the past
Adults who act like kids
No sense of responsibility
Treating kids like adults
Unpredictability
Obsessed with what others think

Becoming a teenage parent
Families with multiple parents
Drugs and alcohol abuse
Frequent relocations
Lying/deceit
Abuse/neglect
Broken promises
No self respect
No self confidence
Low standard of living
No pride in living situation
Lack of cleanliness
Poor communication skills
Poor hygiene
Substandard living conditions
Inconsiderate of children
View kids as income potential
Focus mainly on self
No nurturing or bonding
Negative outlook/worldview
Mood swings
Instability
Self-defeating attitude
Displacing emotions onto kids
Lack of emotional maturity
Blaming others for problems
Inconsistent parenting
Deprivation/neglect
Pettiness/jealousy/envy

Poor impulse control
Playing the odds
Denial of reality/truth
No respect for kids
Judgmental
Kids not viewed as priorities
Not teaching kids to dream
Teaching shame
Using kids as pawns
Failure to protect kids
Making kids feel obligated
Competition of wills
Stubbornness
Won't admit mistakes
Not emphasizing education
Whining
Refusing help
Do as I say, not as I do
Disregard a kid's need to know
Not caring
Strong need to control
Threatening to remove love
Not separating actions from identity
Teaching prejudice/hatred
Living life through your kids
Giving up
Keeping kids dependent
Ignoring spiritual needs

Poor coping skills
Self destructive lifestyle
Unresolved grief
Poor problem-solving skills
Holding grudges
Poor role models
Failure to instill hope
Jealousy toward kids
Using kids as weapons
Viewing kids as property
Double standards between sexes
Cultural clashes
Unable to forgive
Unable to apologize
Playing the victim role
Not seeking help
No honest self-assessment
Unfair to kids
Poor listening skills
Strong need to be right
Strong need to be liked
Labeling
Extreme religious beliefs
False sense of pride
Setting unrealistic goals
Breaking kids down
Creating FLAGS
Not being true to self

Appendix H

KIDS ROLES AND RESPONSIBILITIES

- Grow
- Mature
- Play
- Bond
- Avoid stress
- Have fun
- Love
- Listen
- Observe
- Be honest
- Be loved
- Feel confident
- Follow reasonable rules
- Develop positive self-concept
- Be considerate
- Learn good social skills
- Appreciate nature
- Avoid being selfish
- Avoid becoming materialistic
- Learn morals and values
- Value personal property
- Stay out of trouble
- Think before acting
- Accept responsibility
- Avoid drugs and alcohol
- Report problems created by adults
- Be themselves
- Recognize appropriate behavior
- Express emotions appropriately
- Learn
- Achieve
- Explore
- Do not worry
- Feel safe/secure
- Do chores
- Respect human rights
- Trust
- Copy/mimic good behaviors
- Be open
- Feel proud
- Understand limits
- Respect themselves
- Care for and about others
- Learn to cope
- Appreciate things and people
- Tolerate frustration
- Avoid being self-centered
- Learn to be spiritual
- Value life – self and other
- Avoid violence
- Learn from mistakes
- Accept reality
- Learn limits and self-control
- Choose friends wisely
- Report abuse/victimization
- Understand sex and sexuality
- Understand love
- Express their individuality

Become independent
Seek answers
Avoid expecting too much/little
Dream
Develop talents and skills
Make friends
Use good judgment
Respect reasonable authority
Avoid/resolve conflict
Ask for help/guidance
Develop their bodies and minds
Learn to be independent
Take responsibility for actions
Separate sense of self from actions

Question
Plan ahead
Find hope
Allow room for mistakes
Study
Make good decisions
Appreciate diversity
Recognize unfairness
Talk about problems
Help others
Learn to be self-sufficient
Learn about adult issues
Accept consequences

Appendix I

NEGATIVE/HURTFUL STATEMENTS OR THE ANSWERS TO THE QUESTION: "WHAT"S WRONG WITH YOU?"

You are lazy, fat, ugly, dark, stupid, etc.
You will never amount to anything
I am ashamed of you
Why can't you be more like…?
God is watching you
God will punish you

You act just like a girl
You act just like a baby
I'll beat the hell out of you

Because I said so that's why
You should be ashamed of yourself
You are so hateful
You are not worth my time or energy

No one else will ever want or love you
I am going to tell everyone what you did
You cause all of my problems

No one will ever believe you
Don't you talk to me that way

Don't give me that look

You are good for nothing
I wish you were never born
Everyone is looking at you
You are just like….
God knows everything
I wanted a boy/girl instead of you

You act just like a boy
I'll slap the crap out of you
This hurts me more than it hurts you
Don't argue with me
Your face will freeze like that
You are nothing but trouble
Get out of here, I am tired of looking at you
You'd feel bad if I died
You are killing me
You are more trouble than you are worth
You little liar
Don't use that tone of voice with me
You will respect me or I'll show you

Dr. David L. Roberts Ph.D.

You will do what I say or else

If you don't like my rules there's the door
You think everything is so easy
My mom/dad would have killed me
You better make me proud

I'll box your ears
What, are you dumb/retarded?

Wait until I get you home
You thought I forgot didn't you
If you…, I will….
Dry it up or I'll let you have it again

Do you want a diaper and a bottle?
You were adopted

You are not welcome in this house/family

I am going to teach you a lesson

I'll show you who's boss

You have no right to be angry with me
My life is none of your business

That's not normal
That's nasty
Sissy
You're no son/daughter of mine
I don't care what you think

You are my child, not theirs

You don't appreciate anything
You don't appreciate me
When I was your age….
Don't ever think I'm stupid
I'll give you something to be afraid of/cry about
I'll knock you into tomorrow
Boy, don't think I can't take you down
Wait until your ….gets home
The boogeyman will get you
Don't get smart with me
I'll beat you until you can't sit down
You are no longer my child
If you do that I won't love you anymore
Get a good education because you will never…
You have to break down a boy's will
I'll take you down a notch or two
Don't ask any questions
You wouldn't understand anyway
You're too young
Cry baby
Fag/Queer
Have you lost your mind?
I don't care what other people think
No one will tell me how to raise my child

You are never satisfied
I am glad your…isn't here to see this
You better ask God to forgive you
All you do is whine
Don't tell me how to run my life

Shut up

I am going to leave you

I have no life because of you

I'm going to give you away

If you tell anyone, I'll…

I taught him/her better than that

You owe me

You are not really my child

You are going to be just like your…
Your mom/dad was….

Look at you
I'll show you
Children are to be seen and not heard
Just pray about it
When I get through with you…
You have to earn my love
I know you are doing something bad
Don't come crying to me
You are mine and I can do what I want
I don't know why you were ever born

Want. Want. Want.
Nobody likes you
You bother everyone
Do as I say, not as I do
You better learn to keep your mouth shut
Shut your mouth or I'll shut it for you
Get out of my sight and don't ever come back
If I didn't have kids I could meet somebody
You can't leave; I need the money
He/she gets that from his/her….
If I want your opinion I'll ask for it
If you go out that door don't ever come back
Your mom/dad never loved you, as much as I do
Shut up or I'll do it again
You are a disgrace to the family and me
How could I love you?
Don't speak until spoken to
Don't embarrass me
You are going to pay for that
You don't deserve anything
You are always sick
You have no common sense
You are nothing unless I say so
You are from the devil
I wish you were never born

Dr. David L. Roberts Ph.D.

It's going to get worse before it gets better   Your daddy/mama is a….
You better listen to me   I told you so didn't I?
If we were back in…, things would be different
You think you have problems now? You just wait
You don't know your ass from a hole in the ground
You are nothing but a troublemaker and a loser

Appendix J

PURPOSES SERVED BY ABUSE/VICTIMIZATION

Control
Sexual gratification
Create fear
Displaced anger/aggression
Break someone's will
Act out anxiety/tension
Punish/hurt someone close to the victim
Express non-acceptance
Enforce rule compliance
Instill guilt
Enforce silence/secrecy
Force conformity
Enforce religious beliefs
Force dependency
Force obedience
Rule over
Force submission
Continue the abuse
Direct attention away from self
Blame
Fulfill selfish needs/desires
Feel better than another
Squelch emotional expression
Squelch self-expression
Enforce any belief system
For pleasure
Keep someone from leaving
Prevent abandonment
Reminds the abuser of someone else

Dominate
Intimidate
Exploitation
Demand respect
Force change
Revenge/getting even
Express hatred
Express dislike/disapproval
Shame/humiliate
Secure a bond
Squelch individuality
Squelch intelligence
Keep someone down
Brain wash
Force loyalty
Enslave
Meet a need for power
Protect one's position
Scapegoat
Reduce boredom
Feel important
Establish separation
Eliminate/annihilate
Squelch creativity
Cruel and sadistic
Prove a point
Prevent rejection
Reduce personal fear
Self-loathing

Destroy self concept
Reduce fear of exclusion
Act out regret
Act out the FLAGS
Punish oneself (self abuse)
Control other compulsions

Deny a right to privacy
Act out resentment
Act out jealousy
Guard against loneliness
Control other impulses
Dictate

Appendix K

ABUSIVE BELIEFS AND STATEMENTS FROM PEOPLE IN POSITIONS OF POWER AND INFLUENCE

They are dumb/stupid
We know your weaknesses
They need to believe us
You can trust us
Don't think or ask questions
We are better than you are
We are above accountability
We are wiser than you are
We are above scrutiny
No that's not what you really see
We wouldn't do you wrong
We did "it" for them
You didn't ask the right questions

What we really meant was ___.
Money and numbers are all that matter
You don't need to know everything
We are sorry. No, *really*, we are sorry
They will never know

This is good enough
This will teach them a lesson
It is always the luck of the draw
No one tells us what to do
What they don't know won't hurt them
We don't need to be team players
It's not any of your business

They will believe anything
We know your vulnerabilities
We wouldn't mislead you
We know what is best for you
Accept what we say as truth
You are all fools anyway
You can't touch us
We are above the law
You can't outsmart us
That's not what we really meant
What do they know anyway?
It was in the small print
We didn't really do anything wrong
We are too smart to get caught
It was only a few little white lies
It is only wrong if we get caught
Might makes right
It is better to cover up than own up
This is all they deserve
We didn't mean to
We have legitimate power
We must get them before they get us
Why should we answer to them?
Our way is the only way
Strength in numbers

Dr. David L. Roberts Ph.D.

Who are they to tell us what to do?   Let's just change the rules/laws
We will handle this our way   Oh well!
We serve the best interests of everyone Follow us
If it is in the Holy Writings it must be truth
Let's see how many ways we can interpret that
What do you think they would believe?
Rules/laws don't necessarily apply to everyone
Deny guilt and hope for reasonable doubt!
You should be ashamed for suspecting and doubting
You put us in power; how could you have been wrong?
How can I say this so it at least sounds legal or ethical?
You have only the rights we are willing to give you
It is their fault because they gave us the power

Appendix L

FAULTY THINKING BY VICTIMS OF LARGE SCALE ABUSE/VICTIMIZATION

(In all of these statements "I" and "we" are interchangeable)

There is nothing we can do

This is just the way things are
They are important people who wouldn't lie to us
They are supposed to respect the law
People in positions of power are honorable
They are stronger/bigger than we are
No one will listen to us
Our voices/votes don't count
It has been this way for a long time
This is what was prophesied
Pray and everything will be fine
This is good enough
They said they were sorry
Things will only get worse if we oppose them
It is better to be nice/polite
It doesn't really matter anyway
I don't have the time or the energy to fight

Time will tell, so let's just wait and see

If it is in the Holy Writings it must be true

We have always been persecuted
We are at their mercy
It is okay as long as they apologize
They are smarter than us
We are powerless
No one will believe us
No one will help us
Nothing ever changes
Might does make right
This is God's will
They are scholars
This is all we deserve
This is just our luck
It is best to suffer in silence
They are too powerful
Let someone else handle it
That doesn't really affect me anyway
They wouldn't really do that
Some things are better left alone

It is not worth the hassle
Let's see how many other ways we can interpret that
They are religious leaders and would never do anything wrong
We can only hope they have our best interests at heart
Things have to get worse before they can get better
Profit and personal gain can't possibly be more important than the common good
Powerful organizations are okay as long as they provide financial support to our cause

Appendix M

COMPLICATING FACTORS/RISK FACTORS

Low socioeconomic status
Religious affiliation
Gender
Low or high intelligence
Poor impulse control
Appearance
Being unwanted
Dysfunctional family
Unpopular beliefs
Mental/emotional problems
Negative personality traits
Being spoiled
Lack of education
Lack of planning skills
Lack of personal choices
Speech problems
Acculturation issues
Unrealistic expectations
Limited support/encouragement
Limited coping skills
Low tolerance of frustration
Need for instant gratification
Poor decision-making skills
Unemployment
Unpredictability
Abandonment
Isolation
FLAGS
Inability to care
No sense of life purpose

Ethnicity
Sexual orientation
Cultural differences
Non-conformity
Unattractive/very attractive
Medical conditions
Being unloved
Extreme beliefs
Perceived as being different
Being abused/victimized
Negative outlook
Where someone lives
Lack of hopes and dreams
Lack of internal control
Physical impairment
Language differences
Unmet needs
Limited opportunities
Sexual acting out
Poor management of anger
Lack of patience
Low self-concept
Peer pressure
Deprivation
Loss/death
Rejection
Self-doubt
Lack of motivation
Hopelessness/helplessness
No future goals

Dr. David L. Roberts Ph.D.

Appendix N

RESULTS OF ABUSE/VICTIMIZATION

Negative self-concept
Confusion
Need to protect oneself
Criminality
Adjustment disorders
Depression/anxiety
Victimization of others
Sense of impending doom
Poor sense of internal control
No awareness of choices
Poor communication skills
Suspicious/paranoid
Violent/aggressive fantasies
Rebellion
Boredom
Lowered expectations
Inappropriate morals/values
Lack of joy/passion
Lack of dreams/goals
Not learning from mistakes
No universal perspective
Feeling at the mercy of…
Inability to forgive
Inability to trust or love
Distorted sense of reality
Fear of emotions
Denial
Continued deprivation
No sense of purpose/direction

Helplessness/hopelessness
Becoming deceitful/deceptive
Need to separate/isolate
Personality disorders
Psychotic disorders
FLAGS
Maintaining a victim role
Self-defeating attitude
Inability to make changes
Problematic relationships
Blame self and others
Lack of assertiveness
Numerous ways of acting out
Frustration
Desperation
Needing instant gratification
Poor coping skills
Lack of contentment
Searching for "the answer"
Repeating mistakes
Absence of spirituality
Poor physical health
Inability to move forward
Inability to attach/bond
No self assessment
Fear of the past/future
Lack of courage
Fear of unpredictability
Limited life satisfaction

Constant search for meaning
Ongoing vulnerability
Inability to question/discern
Limited creativity
Difficulty prioritizing
Uncommitted and unmotivated
Obsessive
Easily traumatized
Inability to take criticism
Judgmental
Jealous/envious
Procrastination
Become a poor role model
Seductive
Provocative
Limited sense of right/wrong
Fear of losing
Emptiness

Easily mislead/deceived
Easily controlled
Difficulty saying "NO"
Inability to plan
Limited initiative
Driven
Compulsive/impulsive
Extreme self criticism
Taking everything personally
Petty
Poor use of time
Inability to relax and enjoy
Easily riled
Overly emotional
Cold/insensitive/uncaring
Unresolved grief
Fear of losing control
Negative relationships

Dr. David L. Roberts Ph.D.

Appendix O

LOSSES ASSOCIATED WITH ABUSE/VICTIMIZATION

Childhood	Innocence
Security/Safety	Love
Peace	Self
Hopes/dreams	Ideal family
Assurance	Assistance
Healthy development on all levels	Self confidence
Healthy self concept	Sense of future
Identity/individuality	Respect for self/others
Positive regard	Control
Consideration	Communication
Trust of self/others	Opportunity
Pride	Fun/play
Excitement	Imagination/creativity
Positive role models	Personal growth
Broken will/character/spirit	Acceptance/fitting in
Positive outlook/attitude	Morals/values
Spirituality	Belief in others
Happiness/joy	Healthy perspective
Knowledge/learning	Curiosity/wonder
Friends	Sanity/emotional stability
Understanding (Why me?)	Home
Privacy/boundaries	Possessions
Nurturing	Caring about self/others
Healthy desire	Motivation
Commitment	Predictability
Ability to cope/soothe	Ability to control/influence
Ability to concentrate	Achievement/success
Ability to leave/escape	Social interaction
Support system	Openness (many secrets)

Good judgment
Ability to help
Ability to reach out for help
Positive self concept
Praise/reward
Ability/desire to look forward
Sense of importance/significance
Encouragement
Value for life
Friendliness/kindness
Honesty/trustworthiness
Belief in goodness
Accurate sense of responsibility
Satisfaction
Positive fantasies
Quality of life

Decision-making skills
Ability to stop the abuse
Ability to question/discern
Positive recognition
Healthy daily habits/routines
Confirmation/validation
Reason to live
Courage
Remorse
Getting needs met
Clarity of thought/perception
Positive worldview
Feeling wanted
Healthy reality
Healthy sexual development
Higher standard of living

Dr. David L. Roberts Ph.D.

Appendix P

FAMILY FACTORS

Violence
Neglect
Public assistance/disability
Few limits/boundaries
FLAGS
Divorce/separation
Alcohol/drugs
Role reversal
Feeling trapped
No work ethic
No sense of ethics
Lack of mutual respect
Money/affluence
No regard for children
Safety issues
Kids taking care of kids
Multiple fathers/mothers of siblings
Personality disorders
Emotional distress
Bad neighborhood conditions
Outcasts
Uneducated
Foster home placement
Teenage/immature parents
Family secrets
Multigenerational problems
Dishonesty/deception

Abuse/victimization
Conflict
Fraud
Total control/rigidity
Absent parent(s)
Poverty/low SES
Criminal activity/history
Hopelessness/helplessness
Lack of future plans/goals
Low morals/values
Discipline
Low standard of living
Sexism
Acculturation issues
Single parent
Pregnancy
Negative role models
Mental illness
Chaos
Targeted by society
Low class/classist society
Poor self concept
Lack of security
Unsanitary conditions
Family history of dysfunction
Prejudice
Trust issues

Stunted emotional development   Deceased parent(s)
Lack of adequate supervision   Privilege
Materialism   No sense of balance
Lack of regard for others   Lack of value for life
Exposure to weapons   No interaction/togetherness

Dr. David L. Roberts Ph.D.

Appendix Q

GANG/GROUP FACTORS

Criminality as a badge of honor
No limits
Death as honorable
Parties/socialization
Physical injury
Girls/sex
Money
Sense of family
Loyalty/solidarity
Respect
Goals/plans
Acceptance/belonging
Cars, clothes, etc.
Identity
Prejudice/hatred
Lack of remorse
Structure
Addiction to risk and the rush
Heroism
Praise/recognition/reward
No respect for outsiders
Chance to prove oneself
No work ethic
Occasional in-fighting
Accountability
Comradery
Hierarchy
Heroes
Awed/feared by others

Freedom
Drugs/alcohol
No responsibility
Violence
Popularity
Back up
No school
Trust
Courage
Hope/help
Love
Excitement
Status/importance
Self-focused
Disregard for enemies
Strength in numbers
Attitude/defiance
Antisocial behavior
Elitist existence
Instant gratification
Secrecy
Fearlessness/courage
Victimization of self/other
Discipline/consequences
Code of ethics
Mission statement
Leadership
Success/accomplishment
Copied by others

No sense of future	Peer pressure
Personality disorders	Mental/emotional disorders
Chance to become an "adult"	Safety and security
Mediation	Abandonment of family
Pro-criminal thinking	Competition
Planning	Organizing
Defending	Offending
Defiance	Regrets

Psyche-Soul-ology:

✢ ✢ ✢

An Inspirational Approach
to Appreciating
And Understanding Troubled Kids

Psyche-Soul-ology:
An Inspirational Approach to Appreciating And Understanding Troubled Kids

2nd Edition

All Rights Reserved © 2011 by David L. Roberts, Ph.D.

No part of this book may be reproduced or transmitted in any form or by any means, graphics, electronic, or mechanical, including photocopying, recording, taping, or by any information storage retrieval system, without the written permission of the author.

This book is dedicated to those who are currently serving troubled kids, and to those who plan to work with troubled kids in the future. Our dedication to be the best we can be in the respective roles we play in the lives of these kids must be based in a sense of Calling; and carried out with respect, understanding, appreciation, inspiration, and compassion.

Contents

Foreword		271
Chapter I	Myths and Misperceptions	275
Chapter II	Nature vs. Nurture: Developmental issues	305
Chapter III	Abuse and Victimization of Kids	323
Chapter IV	Criminality	347
Chapter V	Substance Use and Addiction	361
Chapter VI	Sexual Issues and Concerns	373
Chapter VII	Intelligence, Talent and Potential	393
Chapter VIII	Psychological Issues and Concerns	409
Chapter IX	Be part of the Solution and Not Just Another Problem	427
Chapter X	Interview Techniques and First Impressions	441
Chapter XI	Funding and Focus Needs	461
Chapter XII	Psyche-Soul-ology	481

Foreword

Every day when I go to work I am reminded all over again of the awesome responsibility I have to be the best I can be for myself and for the kids I serve. My work is my passion and I take very seriously the role I play in the lives of my clients. This current text contains many ideas and examples of how to work effectively with troubled, high-risk or at-risk youth with the intention of helping adults, in all roles pertaining to kids, match their efforts with their desired outcomes and goals. As I continue my career I am always amazed at how biased and ineffective many adults are relative to the parts we all play in the lives of kids. With this book I hope to give people the tools needed to actually produce favorable outcomes through appropriate interactions, relationships and associations we have with the kids in our charge either personally or professionally.

My first book, <u>At the Mercy of Externals: Righting Wrongs and Protecting Kids, 2nd Edition</u>, raises and addresses many issues faced by adults and kids in various situations and contexts. It has been revised and is now offered as a companion text to this book. The title suggests a two-step approach to the problems families, kids and professionals face relative to successfully guiding kids into adulthood. The concept of "righting wrongs" suggests the need to intervene with adults in an effort to improve effectiveness through an ongoing process of open and honest self evaluation and assessment. "Protecting kids" suggests that when adults conquer our own unresolved issues from the past, the kids in our care can be protected to a large extent from abuse and victimization which comes in many forms and occurs within different contexts. Awareness of unresolved issues comes through understanding the Roberts FLAGS (RFLAGS) Model which graphically explains how we tend to act out emotion-based anxiety rather than face the issues from the past often fueling our negative emotions of <u>F</u>ear, <u>L</u>oneliness, <u>A</u>nger, <u>G</u>uilt and <u>S</u>hame. The intensity and severity of the negative emotions is directly related to the degree of abuse and victimization we experience during childhood. These ineffective and damaging patterns of interaction are then passed down to the kids with whom we have contact and for whom we have responsibility.

At the Mercy of Externals: Righting Wrongs and Protecting Kids, 2nd Edition, clearly goes hand-in-hand as a companion text with the current work Psyche-Soul-ology: An Inspirational Approach to Appreciating and Understanding Troubled Kids. I recently entered a contest for self-published writers and received a critique of my first book. The critic liked the overall concepts and the material's content and quality. Commentary from numerous readers, including college students, parents, and professionals, supports my belief in its effectiveness relative to providing insight into issues faced and seldom understood by people outside the real life situations of troubled kids. Through my second book I intend to step up to the challenge and offer the means for identifying, correcting, and resolving the issues and concerns I raise. What makes my approaches different from those of other professionals is my foundation of a purely spiritual, non-religious perspective which supersedes many views and beliefs of organized religions. I see my career as both my calling and passion in life and consider my role as a licensed clinical psychologist to also be a ministry - without any religious affiliation - which reaches out to society's throwaway kids and their families. As a very important part of my job and my thinking I constantly seek out spiritual guidance as I work and continue my own process of open and honest self evaluation and assessment relative to personal and professional growth and development.

Through the current text I will reintroduce some of the topics and perspectives from At the Mercy of Externals: Righting Wrongs and Protecting Kids, 2nd Edition, as they apply to the issues and subjects introduced within this material. Because I am a practicing psychologist who specializes in the population of troubled, at-risk, and high-risk kids I will be able to offer appropriate and specific case examples to help validate some of the points I will raise. All names and other specific details of each case example have been changed to protect personal privacy and confidentiality. As you read you will encounter everything from myths to misperceptions relative to issues of psychological development, sexuality, addiction, criminality, and intelligence, all mixed with tried and proven approaches which maximize efforts to reach and guide kids successfully into their respective and subjective futures. The RFLAGS Model will be revisited and connected to all of this as a very important frame of reference. As you read you will be able to see how this book takes kids and adults out of the bondage to external factors and gives them the internal perspective needed to successfully move forward in life. Of utmost importance is the willingness on the part of the reader to look openly and honestly at your own beliefs and techniques used in interacting with kids. From there it will be equally as important to make internal and external changes and adjustments as needed which will ultimately lead to effectiveness and successful outcomes regardless of the roles we play in kid's lives.

New to this text will be the introduction of codes of ethics, codes of conduct, and the concept of moral development and responsibilities which need to shape our value systems and the way we prioritize things in our lives. Be sure to look again at the Oath I proposed at the end of chapter six in my first book and keep in mind the significance of this as a place to start for all adults. I will also introduce and share the basic spiritual beliefs I use as a constant guide in my work with kids and even in my interactions with my own daughter and my grandchildren. I believe that through this book we can begin to agree upon some basic standards and building blocks which will improve the overall conditions of people within all of the contexts of home/family, school, community, society, politics, and religion. You will have the opportunity to see troubled kids through my eyes and will learn to see them for whom they really are rather than judge them for and by what they do and say. These are critically important changes in perspective and reference which need to occur within each of us and within all settings and contexts in which kids live and learn.

Chapter I

Myths and Misperceptions

Many people today talk a lot about "those kids", using various labels and phrases which do nothing to identify and assist the kids behind the labels they attach. However, very few people talk about "those adults" who are ineffective in their attempts to reach this misunderstood and mistreated group of kids. I am always amazed at the inappropriate and damaging techniques often used during interactions with kids in general, not only within the home/family context, but in various settings outside this context and by professionals who have supposedly been trained to teach, guide, or otherwise supervise kids. Some kids are actually more traumatized by adults outside their home/family environment than they are within it. I believe one of the main reasons for these mistakes is based in the unwillingness of many professionals to learn about other people, cultures and realities as part of their professional training. One of the most arrogant, ignorant, and damaging attitudes held by many adults, often referred to as "do-gooders", is the belief that: *'I already know enough, based on my own life experiences, to know how to assist every other group.'* Or, even worse, are those adults who think everyone should see things their way and through their often biased and subjective ways of looking at life and the world. Furthermore, I am certain one of the main reasons for my effectiveness with troubled, high-risk kids is based in the fact I did everything I could to learn both from my past and from the realities many families face daily by literally going into those environments. I did so with the desire to learn about the people I wanted to serve before I ever tried to imagine how I could be of assistance to them on any level. This is part of what makes my professional life so rewarding and satisfying.

There isn't a work day that goes by when I think I really don't want to go to work today. Sure there are times when I think about getting a few extra hours of sleep, but that's never enough to make me call in sick or dread my day. I consider myself to be one of the luckiest people anywhere simply because I love my job – literally everything about my job, except of course some of the paperwork. My work as a licensed clinical psychologist is truly my calling in life and that aspect about which I am the most passionate. All of this is due to the fact I get to work with some of the most wonderful and incredible kids in the world. The kids I am referring to are those at risk of having the greatest number of problems and getting into the most trouble because of numerous complicating factors, poor judgment, and lack of self control. Webster's defines passion as an "intense, driving or overmastering feeling". It is associated with "ardent affection" and "a strong liking for or devotion to some activity, object, or concept." The affection I feel for my kids is that of simply pouring my heart into my work with them. When they succeed, fail, get injured, or die I am easily moved to tears because I have an emotional investment in them which exceeds my professional requirements. One of my co-workers said this is because "you give them your heart." My satisfaction comes through their success and the awareness I had at least some part in helping that happen.

In my first book <u>At the Mercy of Externals: Righting Wrongs and Protecting Kids, 2nd Edition,</u> I give some of the history of how I found my niche in the field of psychology. Because I'm sure you have already read that text I won't go into the historical aspects of my decision. However, I will go into the reasons I chose this population as the major focus of my professional efforts. Keep in mind that I grew up in the so-called "Deep South" and moved to Los Angeles in 1989 to begin my Ph.D. program in clinical psychology. As a European American I grew up surrounded by religious extremism and hatred based in the rawest forms of bigotry and prejudice. My introduction into the culture which is California was a bit of a shock at first, but I quickly learned to appreciate my surroundings and the people and diversity I encountered. In spite of having grown up in Alabama during the entire Civil Rights Movement of the 1950's, 60's and 70's I never bought into any of the racism. However, I didn't fully understand the horrors of discrimination and prejudice until I moved to Los Angeles. I am so grateful for the awakening I experienced through my graduate training, especially the experiences I had in and around East Los Angeles and Upper South Central Los Angeles.

My training with this population of kids labeled as at-risk, high-risk or troubled youth began in September 1992 as a predoctoral psychological intern in a gang prevention task force program literally located behind the Los Angeles County, University of Southern California (LACUSC) Medical Center. This is the hospital featured at the opening credits of "General Hospital", an old, but popular daytime soap opera. I was working in Murchison Street Elementary School and the area of Ramona Gardens Housing Project, home of the Hazard Gang named for Hazard Park in the same area. The movie "American Me", filmed in the early 1990's, was filmed in this area of East Los Angeles. I was working in a Family Service Center at the school with families and children primarily living in and around Ramona Gardens. I went into this area knowing I knew nothing about the culture of East LA, rather than thinking I knew everything I needed to know because of my graduate training toward my Ph.D. and previous degrees and life experiences and perspectives. Thank goodness I had already learned of the arrogance most European Americans exhibit in various respective fields when working with so-called minority populations. My ignorance and the awareness of my ignorance allowed me to be fully accepted by the people who lived within this community.

I remember the first few weeks of driving into an area most people were afraid to enter. In the mornings the gang members were still sleeping, but in the afternoons they would be hanging out on the street corners and would 'dog' me (stare at me) when I drove by. There was a four-way stop at the bottom of the hill where I would have to come to a complete stop. I could feel them staring at me and was always uncomfortable, but knew they had to be wondering who I was and what I was doing in the neighborhood. This continued until one afternoon when I stopped at a convenience store at one of the two entrances into the area. As I got out of my car I was approached by two obvious gang members who asked me for money. I told them I didn't give out money and walked into the store.

While inside the store I thought about the possibility of this being an opportunity to introduce myself to them and tell them who I am. It made sense and, while I didn't have the money to spare as a graduate student, I decided to give both of them $5.00 each. I called them over to me in the parking lot and offered them my hand in friendship after giving them the money, telling them my name and describing my training as a graduate student in psychology working at the school site as part of an internship. After assuring them I was not involved in law enforcement or any kind of undercover work with immigration (as was often their assumption), I explained the nature of my training as that of providing assistance to kids in the area, some of whom were probably even related to these two guys. I asked them to remember my face and my car, asking them to also tell their friends who I am. They agreed and assured me I would have no problems in the area because of the way I had talked to them. This was my first experience of gaining respect from a group hated by most people and judged as worthless throwaways because of their behaviors. I understand this perspective of outsiders and have learned not to make the same mistake, realizing that these guys are human beings too and deserve respect as such even if I can't respect the criminal activity in which they involve themselves. From that day on I never had anyone stare at me as I drove in or out of the area. I learned about the communication network within the gangs and the importance of understanding and learning how to use that to my advantage so I could work with them more effectively and without being viewed with suspicion.

My decision to accept this internship in East Los Angeles was made in February 1992 for the beginning of the next school year which would start in September. This would be my last predoctoral training program before I completed the requirements for my Ph.D. in clinical psychology. There was a list of other possible training sites, but no one in my school was signing up for this one. Realizing that the group of kids known as troubled youth was about the only population I had not worked with during any of my previous trainings, I decided to give it a shot. So, I applied for the opportunity and was hired by the school staff after an interview. The program at the elementary school was funded through a Healthy Start Grant offered at that time by the state of California. Murchison Street Elementary School was one of the first schools in the state to receive the so-called "seed money". The Family Service Center would have to be self-supporting by the end of the third year. My internship was called a Gang Prevention Task Force which ultimately became a force of only one from my graduate program, with other students choosing trainings in different areas of the city.

Just two weeks after accepting the September 1992 internship position for the 1992-93 school year, I got mugged in February 1992 by three gang members only two blocks from my apartment. I had decided to get out of my apartment and go for a walk to a local park one afternoon at about 4:00 PM. The walk to the park took me through the gang territory of "Avenues", but along a major street which I had walked many times before and only during the daytime hours. In the past I had a habit of walking and looking down, usually deep in thought about any number of things running intensely through my head. Therefore, I didn't hear or see these kids running up to me. Suddenly I was startled as they grabbed me, with one on each side holding weapons against my ribs - one had a knife and the other was holding a sharpened screw driver. I couldn't tell if the one behind me was armed as he was the one who immediately started going into my pockets.

I had tried to imagine such a scene several times in the past, trying also to imagine how I might actually react to such an event. To my surprise, rather than being frightened, I was enraged. From my mouth came a whole string of obscenities clearly reflecting my extreme displeasure at what was happening. It was obvious to me these kids realized they had probably grabbed the wrong guy. I had sense enough not to overreact in a way that would get me stabbed or cut. However, I reacted enough to let them know I wasn't going down lightly. Because I was watching the weapons, constantly waiting for either of them to draw back to stab me, not even once did I see their faces. My thoughts told me I would fight back rather than get stabbed, but not carry this to the point of them thinking that stabbing me was their only choice for their own protection. They kept telling me to "shut the fuck up" and I kept yelling that back to them wanting to know why they were doing this to me and repeating many of their own words back to them. In hindsight I believe they were thinking I must be crazy not to be afraid and finally pushed me forward telling me to walk ahead, pick up my wallet, and not look back. As they ran away they yelled out "we know where you live". I yelled back "fuck you – you don't know where I live".

In the process of all of this I lost $35.00 cash which I needed for gas and food for the week, along with two gold rings which couldn't be replaced. My keys were thrown into a very large patch of ivy. I never found those primarily because I was too afraid of the rats known to live in that stuff to even venture very far into it. I walked back to my apartment still fuming about all of this. As I got to my building I had to ask the manager to let me into my apartment, explaining to him what had happened in case he needed to re-key the outside doors. Fortunately I had duplicate keys for my apartment and my car, but lost several other keys which had to be replaced.

As I thought about all of this I began to realize how lucky I was not to have been hurt or killed. I was also upset that no one on this busy street stopped to help me. As time passed over the next few days I became quite paranoid for about two months, jumping whenever I heard noises as I walked from my car into the building. It took a while for me to get over blaming myself and simply accept the fact I had been a victim of a crime. I never called the police because I couldn't give them a description of anything but the clothing of the kids. This is how I came to understand the importance of all gang members dressing and looking exactly alike in order to make it more difficult to identify them. I told all of this to my neighbor across the hall in my apartment building who was a member of this gang. Despite my protests he insisted this would be taken care of because I was his friend. I have no idea what happened to these kids after that encounter with my neighbor who I knew and trusted. In a remarkable manner my neighbor always looked out for me. He was older than the kids who robbed me and always told me he respected the work I was doing with gang kids.

As I'm sorting through all aspects of having been mugged, a feeling of dread begins to seep in as I think about the internship in East LA I had just accepted two weeks earlier. It was absolutely too late to change it and I looked toward September with a sense of uncertainty relative to what I was getting myself into within what could turn out to be a completely hostile environment. The only good thing about the mugging experience is that I still use it today to let kids know how bad it feels to be a victim of what they do. Kids always tell me "I would never do that to you Dr. Roberts". I tell them "of course not, you know me. But if you saw me walking down your street wouldn't it go through your mind that I might be an easy victim with money if you didn't know me?" They readily agree, giving me a chance to tell them how messed up it is for them to think that kind of behavior is okay under any circumstances. I can use it to try and get them to imagine the life situations of any victim and what impact such a robbery might have on that person and their family. They always discuss this with me and learn something from the discussion. Fortunately this was the only time anything even close to this has ever happened to me. The lesson I learned is to always pay attention to things going on around me, especially in a large city like LA. Growing up in the South this kind of thinking wasn't necessary. What a hell of a way to learn this lesson. I am glad now that I had something for them to steal because kids usually agree with me these guys would likely have stabbed me out of anger for not getting anything of value from me.

One of the most amazing things for me about my journey to Los Angeles and graduate school at the California School of Professional Psychology, now part of Alliant International University, was my exposure to cultural diversity even within the student body which included students literally from around the world. Through these kinds of experiences I began to see that differences between people are based more in socioeconomic and cultural differences than in racial differences. The so-called "races" aren't as clearly divided today as in the past and people of the very same race are often quite diverse when they have different cultural backgrounds. This awareness is the basis for my beliefs in the need to move away from race as a dominant distinction and focus more on cultural aspects and poverty as the true differences and indications of diversity. Even for me, the cultural differences in the South were mild when compared to the cultural differences found in California. Imagine the level of culture shock I experienced. I had even considered myself to be rather advanced in my thinking and beliefs compared to others in the South, but soon found I had a lot more to learn.

The people who taught me the most about possible differences between race as a perspective and culture as a perspective were the people from different Spanish-speaking countries and from African Americans I encountered through several different settings. Most associations with African

Americans were within professional contexts in California, and more as friends while still living previously in the South. However my personal connections outside of my school environment to those from different Spanish-speaking countries and cultures were more on a friendship basis. At first I couldn't figure out why my level of comfort was so high, especially with people from different parts of Mexico, Cuba and El Salvador until I began to see the similarities between these cultures and the culture in the South. One evening, while visiting the family of one of my Salvadorian friends, it occurred to me that gatherings within these cultures as in the South, center on family, food, and special occasions. Even though at that time I couldn't speak a work of Spanish, I felt like I knew these people and could relate to the familiarity I associated between them and my own cultural background. The other most prominent (though unfavorable) factors were that both cultures were generally male dominated, with a huge significance placed on extreme conservative religious views. Through close friends I had many such experiences and opportunities to learn about different aspects of the respective heritages, traditions and lifestyles.

I also had an opportunity to see Hispanic people as some of the most genuine people I had ever met, especially if they were immigrants from their countries of origin. Very few of those I met were taking advantage of the American welfare system or disability, with probably 99% being gainfully employed in jobs most Americans wouldn't want because of the feeling that as Americans we are above many of the menial jobs requiring hard labor or tasks considered to be boring and meaningless. Even if I didn't like or agree with some of their customs I always knew where they were coming from with regards to our interactions. They didn't try to hide or pretend like a lot of Americans do in order to look better than we really are. I also had the opportunity to understand how hard their lives had been in their countries of origin. It always amazed me to see how some of these immigrants lived, finding it hard to believe that things in this country could actually be better for them than what they left behind. It wasn't until December 1993 when I had a chance to visit with a friend of mine deep into Mexico in the state of Nayarit that I had a chance to see true hardship for myself on a scale which would have been impossible for me to imagine. I have never seen such poverty in my life and, after a two week stay, came back to the US with a different perspective of the realities many Hispanic immigrants try to escape by coming to America.

The single most amazing experience I had in Los Angeles was with a very close friend of mine who lived in the same apartment building with me. His name was Adan Lopez (Adam in English) and he was included in the dedication of my first book along with my grandmother, my daughter, and Susan. Adan became a tremendously important part of my life and experiences in California. Much of my perspective and many of my beliefs are based on the things I learned through and with him. He was an undocumented immigrant who was diagnosed with a terminal illness at the age of twenty-seven. He had lived and worked in this country for about seven years paying income taxes and money into our social security system which he couldn't recover or claim. He died at the age of twenty-eight, only eighteen months after his diagnosis. I became a significant and important person in his life as well, taking it upon myself to help hem get the healthcare and other assistance he so desperately needed. His decision to stay in this country was based on the reality that medical care was better here than it would have been in his hometown in Mexico. Even though he had one sister in the area and a number of friends from his "little town" none of them knew how to access the services he would need in an effort to fight his illness, or for the additional help he needed as he reached the end of his life.

As Adan neared his death he began to use me somewhat like his confessor, telling me that I was the only one who knew "both of his faces" – not in the sense of being two-faced, but in the sense of having two very separate and distinct lives and personalities. He revealed many things to me about his past as a child which included an extreme history of abuse and neglect in Mexico. Domestic violence and alcoholism were the only relationship dynamics he had ever known and he found himself in the streets at the age of eight trying to support himself and his family any way he could. As a result he became involved in a great deal of illegal activity in Mexico which continued through his adolescence until, with the help of his friends, he had the opportunity at twenty years of age to come to Los Angeles and begin working in a factory. This allowed him to support himself and even send money to his mom and siblings back in Mexico. It is easy to see in Mexico the families who have relatives sending them money from the US compared to those who have to exist on what they can earn in Mexico alone. The contrast is shocking and extremely sad.

Adan had a really difficult time trying to work out the issues related to his past, believing, according to religious doctrine, that he was destined to spend an eternity in hell because of his involvement in criminal activity during his childhood years. Together we explored different spiritual perspectives which gave him the peace he needed before his death in February 1992. Through our efforts to make some sense out of his life we were able to learn a lot from each other, all of which served both of us well. There is no doubt in my mind we met so I could help him die with dignity, and so that through his death I could learn to live and to be of service to people in ways I could never have imagined. Eventually I was able to give Adan's mother the peace she needed as well. I had the privilege of meeting her and his siblings with a friend I knew through Adan during our trip to Mexico nearly two years after Adan's death. His mother was so grateful that I and others could send her son home for burial with the generous donations from friends and coworkers who knew him and loved him. He was a good person with a beautiful soul. That had nothing to do with many of the choices he had to make in his life just to survive as a child. Unfortunately Adan's need to survive overshadowed the goodness in him for many years. Two of my most prized possessions were given to me by his mom and oldest sister during my visit and in appreciation for my efforts to help their son and brother. While in Mexico my final gift to Adan and his family was providing a beautiful monument for his grave. These very wonderful people, and especially Adan, touched my life in ways I could have never imagined. I will be forever indebted to Adan and his family for this. Not only did they accept me as a "gabacho" (white American outsider), they saw me as a friend and brother, welcoming me into their lives and into their family. These are the kinds of experiences I had while in Los Angeles and in Mexico that literally changed me forever and clearly influence and impact the way I still see and interpret things today.

The single most important bit of wisdom I gained from all of this is the reality that people will do things as a result of lives based in hardship and chaos which they would never do under other circumstances and conditions. It became very obvious to me how wrong we are, especially here in the

United States, and especially as European Americans, when we arrogantly judge and label those individuals and groups we don't know much about or understand. Not only do European Americans judge and misjudge, so do those from the different cultures and backgrounds who become successful in this country and turn their noses up to those who haven't yet "conformed" and who seemingly cause them to be ashamed of their own heritages and roots.

Because of these aforementioned experiences, I have been given the opportunity to know with certainty that behaviors, especially of kids, do not necessarily represent the true character or souls of people. There is a very big difference between making an observation and being judgmental. Judgments literally become personal because we tend to assign labels and descriptions to a person's character. Observations are nothing more than an acknowledgement of what is visible and obvious on the outside relative to behaviors, characteristics, and words. Ignorance simply means that someone doesn't know. Arrogance is when the individual knows they don't know and are actually proud of it, with no desire to change their frame of reference or learn something which could change their minds and increase their understanding. The *arrogantly ignorant* are the ones who do the most harm especially when they put themselves in positions of power and authority over those judged as being less than they are. These are all too often the people who take on roles and responsibilities relative to kids and others easily identified as underdogs and throwaways; and these individuals are without any doubt the most dangerous. Those considered as underdogs and throwaways in society are those who are the most vulnerable and those with the least abilities and means to defend themselves from abuse and victimization.

In my work as a psychologist I have to deal with the aftermath of injustices which can be caused by life circumstances, uncontrollable situations and factors, and by people who are directly responsible for the development and well-being of children. This is what is meant by the phrase "at the mercy of externals" – those factors over which we have very little if any real or perceived ability to effect or change. Because there can be so many things beyond our control, everyone should be extra careful to control those things which we are able to direct and influence. This is extremely important for adults who are in control of the lives and outcomes of kids of all ages. I am constantly shocked with the reality of how ineffective people are in actually directing and redirecting the lives of kids, and even more so when the kids in question are the troubled kids referred to in the title of this book.

As I began my second predoctoral internship in September 1992 at Murchison Street Elementary School I started asking all kinds of questions about the area, the kids, their families and the overall environments in which they lived. I was appalled to learn that each family had a basic plan of what to do to protect themselves when gunfire erupted at any given moment and on a daily basis in the housing project and in the neighborhood around the school. In getting to know each one of the kids and their families I was assigned to serve I would always ask about this and would ask what this experience was like for them. Needless to say the artwork drawn by these K through 6th grade kids was very dark and depicted a lot of violence and death. Generally speaking, I was dealing with single mom's whose kids were the offspring of active members of the Hazard Gang. Even if families weren't directly associated with the gang activity they were all affected tremendously by the violence and criminal activity associated with it.

I spent so much of my time just trying to help these kids and families deal with their emotional distress and daily realities of horrific experiences and events. Every kid I met had either seen someone dead on the streets or had witnessed a shooting of a friend or family member. They had to deal with extreme family problems which included domestic violence and serious alcohol and drug use within their homes and in the area, not to mention all of the gang and criminal activity. It was very common for kids to find used syringes on the sidewalks and in the shrubbery, especially in the housing project. These kids literally lived within a war zone with no way to make peace for themselves, and in many cases with no way to escape from the area by moving. Where could they go but to other areas that were equally as dangerous! A trip to a store was a major outing and many of these kids had never even seen the Pacific Ocean which was no more than about 10 miles from where they lived. Their entertainment consisted primarily of video games and movie rentals, with many parents afraid to let them play outside for obvious reasons including trying to protect them from being recruited into the local gang.

I was given most of my cases either directly from teachers and other school staff or by simply sitting in the front office and getting to know the kids who were seemingly always in trouble. These were usually boys. As a result of the extreme violence in the area and even on the school campus I developed a program called "K.I.T. Cadets: Kids In Touch against Violence" (available by request from the author). Each group lasted for six weeks, consisted of eight to ten kids from the third or fourth grade and up, and included group discussions and skits. During each weekly group the kids could participate in safety as they discussed and acted out roles and experiences very real in their lives outside the school. It was a very effective program. At the end of each six week group each kid was given a certificate and was graduated as a "K.I.T. Cadet" and charged with the responsibility of trying to make and keep the peace at school as Ambassadors of Peace. Every Monday morning at this school site the principal held a general assembly for the entire student body and staff. He and other staff made announcements and took care of school related business. It was during these assemblies that my K.I.T. Cadets were graduated and presented with their certificates. Each time I explained the purpose of the program to all of the students, telling the other kids to watch and see if these "cadets" were living up to their assigned mission. The program was so popular some kids were actually offended when I told them I had to limit it to the kids who got into the most trouble. One kid even told me he would start getting into trouble if that was the only way to get into my group. As a result I gave him the "special privilege" of working with me on a one-to-one basis for a relatively short period of time.

I liked the experience at Murchison Elementary School so much I volunteered to do one of my postdoctoral internships at this site for the second year – 1993-1994. The biggest success story I had during my two year internship was a kid by the name of Ricardo who I met when he was in the fifth grade, about half way through the school year. He was always in the office and was disliked by virtually every teacher and staff person in the school. He fortunately came from a stable two-parent family, and in spite of his parents' efforts Ricardo just wouldn't calm down. He was extremely intelligent and had a strong desire to be gang involved someday, always acting tough on and off campus. I recruited him into my group and into private therapy. He very reluctantly agreed and found my role as his therapist to be very different from his experiences with adults in other roles in his life. We had fun together and he looked forward to the time we spent during the sessions at school. I got to know his family really well and they were amazed at the changes in their son which became apparent very quickly both at home and at school. When he graduated as a "K.I.T. Cadet" he was very proud of his accomplishment and took his roles as a peacekeeper and a peacemaker very seriously and very appropriately. Everyone was thrilled at the progress and the changes in every aspect of his life, including his academic performance. At the beginning of Ricardo's sixth grade year he was elected as president of the student council and served in that role all year. At the end of the year and during his graduation he was given an award for excellence and achievement. Everyone in the audience cheered and his parents and I welled up with tears of joy. I asked Ricardo once what made him change his direction and behavior. He replied, "All I could see when I wanted to fight was your face, and I just couldn't do it. I knew you would be disappointed in me."

During this graduation I was given the opportunity to be the guest speaker, unanimously voted on by the parents who regularly attended and supported activities and events in the Parent Center which was part of the Family Services Center on campus. This was one of my proudest moments ever and yet one of the most humbling experiences in my life both before and since. Their invitation represented a great deal of acceptance and appreciation for my two year involvement in their lives and in their community. I had started learning Spanish and wanted to give my commencement address in both English and Spanish. At the last minute I chickened out and asked Arturo, the center director, to translate my speech and then read it with me paragraph after paragraph, side by side. I thanked the people in the audience for everything they had taught me and for the level of trust they developed for me in spite of the fact I was so clearly an outsider to their world and experiences. I urged them to take a good look at themselves with the purpose of continuing to try and improve their lives and life conditions and situations. As I spoke I could see some of the women elbowing their husbands and boyfriends to get them to listen to what I had to say. I assured them I would never forget the experiences and opportunities they had given me to know them and to learn from them. I specifically thanked all of the kids, and especially Ricardo for giving me the most incredible memories and moments anyone could ever hope to have, assuring them I would never forget any of them either. From these experiences I gained a very solid basis from which to begin what became my career of working almost exclusively with troubled kids who live in and through some of the most horrendous hardships and conditions imaginable.

My training in and around the Los Angeles area also included: three years at Lincoln Alternative Education Community School in San Gabriel just outside of LA; nine months through the Los Angeles Learning Centers/Los Angeles Educational Partnership at Elizabeth Street Learning Center in Cudahy, and at Foshay Learning Center in Upper South Central Los Angeles; and at Orange County Community Hospital in the City of Orange. All four of my training experiences overlapped at different times giving me a great deal of exposure to different communities and populations within Los Angeles and within the LA unified School District and the San Gabriel Unified School District. There was no better training ground than Los Angeles for the work I continued to do in the California desert around Palm Springs, known as the Coachella Valley, until December 2004.

Lincoln Alternative Ed. was a sixteen week program provided through LA County Department of Education to middle school kids who were identified as high risk kids for gang involvement and criminal activity. These kids were given an opportunity to work informally with a probation officer and also catch up on their academic skills. Each school-based internship program I trained in, including this one, were model programs in the area and in the state of California. It was during my training at this site that I had the opportunity to develop my own interview format (summarized at the end of Chapter 10) which I still use to this day when interviewing kids for the first time. This was also my first exposure to the population of middle school kids who were acting out in their respective school environments. In all of these settings I had opportunities to work with kids from very large and very well known Hispanic, African American and Asian gangs. This was also the first setting in which I worked almost exclusively with kids and not their entire families. I found this to be equally effective with this population, believing in the Murray Bowen approach to Family Therapy of self-differentiation whereby changes in one family member can effectively change the entire family system. Many times I would have parents contact me to ask exactly what I was doing with their kid that was helping them to make desired changes in their lives.

One client who really stands out in my mind was a girl by the name of Monique. I would call her "Sneaky Moniquey" because she was always finding ways to get into trouble without getting caught. However, some of her activities put her at a high risk of getting into serious trouble. Initially she hated the name I gave her, but in time would actually joke with me about it. I have a plaque in my kitchen that has a very nice "thank you" message on the front given to me by Sneaky and her mom when I ended my work with her. My success with kids at this school and at Murchison Street Elementary School earned me a great deal of recognition and positive feedback to my supervisors. This eventually landed me an invitation to present my "K.I.T. Cadets Program" at the International Congress of Applied Psychology in Madrid, Spain in the summer of 1994. It was also during these years that I began to receive other opportunities to talk about the work I was doing and still do with this population.

My job as Change Facilitator through the Los Angeles Learning Centers/Los Angeles Educational Partnership allowed me to work at school sites in and around the LA area at learning centers. These centers provided non-traditional services to kids and their families actually on site at each school for kids in grades K through 12. This was a project, rather than an internship, privately funded through the Wellness Foundation and based on a model developed by Howard Edelman, Ph.D., a well known professor from UCLA. As a change facilitator I had the responsibility of assisting teachers and administrative staff in changing their approaches to addressing students' needs on all levels. This was a very big project with the ultimate goal of increasing academic performance and excellence by meeting all needs of the kids and their families in a non-threatening environment. This setting eliminated the stigma often associated with going to county agency buildings for assistance. Each agency usually involved in the lives of low income families would provide services to families at the school site, actually increasing the likelihood of families seeking out and utilizing the services they so desperately needed. This approach "enabled" (a term used by Dr. Edelman as one of the components of his model) the family in order to increase their stability and success in different areas of their lives.

The Learning Centers offered me opportunities to get to know even more professionals and people from different walks of life and to understand the problems and obstacles people often face through no fault of their own. It is easy to see within these settings how difficult life can be for many people - circumstances often beyond their control and beyond their abilities to influence and affect without assistance. The model worked, but I was amazed at how much resistance we got from teachers and other school staff primarily because of union and contract issues. It was shocking to see how many educators were unwilling to go the extra mile to assist families who were in the greatest need of help and guidance. It was also frustrating to see how many of those who resisted and protested the most were European American and working in schools with student populations composed almost entirely of different ethnic minorities.

My last training experience was at the Orange County Community Hospital in the City of Orange. This was a private psychiatric hospital where I worked as a psycho-educational instructor and group facilitator. The population with which I worked at this hospital was a group of dual diagnosis patients who had serious addiction problems along with other psychological disorders. My job on the unit at this hospital was extremely beneficial to me because this is the setting where I originated my RFLAGS Model. I was given the responsibility of leading psycho-educational groups related to abuse, grief and loss, anger management, and dysfunctional family histories. Having never led groups like this I had to come up with program formats for each of these groups. It was through these efforts that everything from my graduate research (beginning in 1986) relative to grief and loss associated with losses from dysfunctional backgrounds really gelled. By using these patients as test groups for my model I was able to put together a program format for each of these groups that eventually became the formats I use in my workshops, classes and in my first book <u>At the Mercy of Externals: Righting Wrongs and Protecting Kids, 2nd Edition</u>.

    The only other training experiences I had in the Los Angeles area were a nine month practicum at Hollywood Sunset Community Clinic and a nine month internship at Glendale Family Service Association. These were significant experiences, but were less directly responsible for the work I now do as my specialty with the population of troubled kids. Probably the single most important factor on a personal level was my involvement in therapy for over 5 years as a client with a wonderful therapist in North Hollywood. My therapy began as a requirement for my graduate program and continued during most of my training experiences and education. It is impossible to be an effective professional, especially a therapist, if we haven't been on the couch, so to speak, to understand the perspective of a client and to work out all of our own issues and problems. Too many people are good at problem identification and no good at problem resolution simply because they have never figured out how to face and deal with their own problems. These are the people who do the most harm in spite of their intentions, especially if they hold positions of power and authority over kids.

    When I said I used patients and clients as test groups or even as individual test subjects, what I mean is that I practiced on these people as a group facilitator with the intention of learning everything I could about my craft as a psychologist. As I worked very intensely through my own therapy to understand myself and my past, I took what I was learning back to my clients as offerings which might help them as well. Also, as I encountered issues and experiences from clients I didn't know how to address, I took these back to my therapist. Together we figured out how to address these issues and experiences for the clients and oftentimes for myself. The most difficult issues for me to address with clients were the ones that hit a little too close to home relative to my own personal life experiences. All of these efforts together helped me to work on and work out many of my issues and insecurities in order to be the best therapist I could possibly be for my clients. At the same time I was able to begin and facilitate my own personal and spiritual growth which I will talk about throughout this book.

I have to admit that from all of my experiences and training I have developed a serious lack of patience and regard for arrogant adults who work with kids and families regardless of their role. It's bad enough when parents are unprepared and ineffective, but for professionals who *choose* their careers there are no excuses. This factor is especially evident within my field of psychology and with therapists of all levels and professional degrees; within all academic settings and institutions; and within all areas of law enforcement, to include juvenile halls and placement programs. The thing I hate the most is the labeling of kids relative to their behaviors and other outward signs of acting out. Included in the list of labels are terms and phrases such as: incorrigibles, bad kids, trolls, little demons, problem children, losers, lost causes, unreachables, undesirable elements, evil, delinquents, deviants, worthless beings, menaces to society, dregs of society, brats, nuisances, etc. All of these terms are quite damaging to the kids to whom they are applied, clearly reflecting an outward bias against each so-labeled kid.

Labeling, in my opinion, reflects a tremendous amount of ignorance and insensitivity, and clearly reflects serious issues and problems within the person who applies these labels to kids. I also think adults who have no children of their own are at greater risk for judging and misjudging kids because of their lack of any direct parental perspective. There are many things in life which cannot be understand unless they are experienced personally and subjectively, and I think the experience of being a parent is one of those experiences. That is not to say that people who have no children of their own can't learn to be effective. It simply means they have to try harder to understand and realize their lack of personal perspective as a potential obstacle to their intentions and outcome goals. This would be the same as me saying I know how it feels to be a juvenile offender or a gang member. My lack of direct awareness means I have had to work very hard to learn what their perspective is even though I can't tell them I know exactly how it feels to be one of them. My lack of direct awareness doesn't mean I can't try to find other ways of attempting to understand their subjective experiences. For instance because of my history of abuse described in my first book, I do know how bad it feels to feel bad as a kid. From there it is possible for me to *imagine* what they might be experiencing; generally acknowledging that their sense of feeling bad is likely much worse than anything I could ever know. But at least they can see I have something personal to which I can compare their experiences of life and the world. I can also assure them I have been working with this population long enough to have a very good idea at least about what life is probably like for them without insulting them by saying "I know exactly how you feel." What an incredibly arrogant, ignorant, and insulting thing to say to virtually anyone if we haven't walked in their shoes.

Labeling is the same as categorizing and stereotyping and as such ignores and diminishes the uniqueness of each and every individual. That is why it is important to label only the *behaviors* of both kids and adults rather than use the behaviors as ways of defining every aspect of a person's character and personality. For example think of the kid who *does* bad things, the child *with* problems, or the kid who *exhibits* deviant behaviors. It is also important to understand that arrogant, ignorant adults say things to kids they would never say to another adult, or allow another adult to say to them. Kids today are too sophisticated to accept that level of disrespect and disregard without reacting negatively and defiantly to it. As adults we have no respect for other adults who aren't respectable, so why should we expect any different perspective from kids.

Arrogant people who are in positions of power and authority are especially dangerous and threatening to kids. It is alarming for me to see how many teachers, social workers, probation officers, juvenile hall staff, youth placement staff, and officers within the different law enforcement divisions think they have the right to label and thereby discard kids whose actions and lives don't meet with their approval. In my own experiences of observing and overhearing adults in positions of power and authority over kids, I am appalled at how little effort is put into helping these kids redirect their lives, as opposed to simply making their lives a living hell. There is no doubt kids have to be held accountable for their actions. However, such accountability should not be in the form of abuse, victimization, or disregard for the kid behind the labels and the behaviors. Kids are reachable and can be redirected with the right guidance by helping them see what is in their own best interest. Those kids who don't take advantage of the opportunities to learn from people who are effective in their efforts to reach and assist will simply pay a price for their refusal or inability to learn from their mistakes and bad behaviors. However, they will at least know the difference between what is appropriate and what is not.

In addition to labeling, another big concern I have is related to adults who lie and exaggerate events in order to make things worse for kids. I have heard several cops make the statement that "I won't write up any offense I can't make stick." There are incidents where probation officers and teachers will write false reports to insure that kids "will get what's coming to them". Some police officers often seem to feel they don't care if a kid is dead or incarcerated simply because either way the kid is "off my streets". One cop a few years ago was openly talking in juvenile hall and in front of me about one of my kids. However, he did not who I was or about my association with the kid he was trashing. He made the statement to juvenile hall staff that "this kid's a lifer. It's just a matter of time before I will be able to get him through the juvenile justice system and on to prison for good. Even if he gets killed before then, he's still of my streets." The juvenile hall staff interrupted the cop and introduced him to me identifying me as the kid's psychologist. The cop was shocked and I assured him I would make my client aware of everything I heard the cop say about him.

Fortunately (and I believe as an act of Karma) that cop was later relieved of his duties because of alleged sexual misconduct with underage girls at a local high school. Rather than do prison time he was allowed to simply vanish into the woodwork so to speak. He was the resource officer actually assigned to that particular high school campus at the time of the incidents. This conversation about my kid is just one of many examples I can't back up with actual proof, but only because I don't have access to the juvenile records. I spend a great deal of my time with kids and their families trying to empower them to stand up and defend themselves from these abusers. The kids and families targeted the most by law enforcement agencies and educational systems are generally those with the least abilities, means, and opportunities to defend themselves. I am amazed these kinds of injustices go undetected by the so-called monitoring systems supposedly in place to keep people in these positions of power and authority in check.

I wish I didn't need to write a book of this nature, but I feel I have an obligation to be open and honest about what I see, hear, and know even if I can't prove it with hard evidence. The mentality of many adults today is that of only getting upset when they get caught doing something wrong. Until then everything is okay as along as no one finds out. This very message is given to kids in juvenile justice settings, including placements, every time an official falsifies documents and records; turns their back to a situation after encouraging one minor to "take care of" another minor for them; covering up incidents to protect themselves and their jobs even at the expense of some kid getting serious consequences for something actually sanctioned by staff as okay; or simply breaking the rules and then telling kids to keep quiet about it or "don't tell Dr. Roberts". All of these kinds of behaviors and attitudes only reinforce the same behaviors and thinking in the kids. It is no wonder to me kids do the things they do since many around them are doing the same kinds of things in all arenas and contexts of society.

Even within school settings kids and families are told certain kinds of educational support services aren't available to them simply because school districts don't want to pay for such services. This happens quite often and throughout this country. There are other instances when parents are told that school staff members are acting in the best interest of their kid when it is clear to everyone else the decision only benefits the school. A good example of this is what some schools call an "opportunity transfer". This occurs when a school decides it can no longer deal with the behaviors of a kid and decides to literally dump him or her on another school. On more than one occasion I have been in school-based meetings where this is the decision, only to shoot them down by openly revealing the true intent behind their deception. The really bad thing about all of these kinds of examples is that quite often supervisors and administrators know about and are in on the deceptions in a number of different settings. This is no less true for corporate officials and politicians who line their own pockets at the expense of others, or religious officials and institutions who cover up the misconduct of their clergy. It is shocking to see how far reaching these conditions are within all arenas of society. Is it any wonder why kids act and think the way they do? There are far too many angry adults who have little or no compassion working with kids, often acting like kids themselves complete with defiance, temper tantrums, and breaking rules while hoping not to get caught.

Before I leave this chapter I want to propose a set of ethical principles and standards which need to be adopted, implemented and applied to adults in all positions of power and authority over kids. As a psychologist I am required by law, by the American Psychological Association, and by the California and Alabama Boards of Psychology to comply with a set of very specific and rigid ethical principles and standards in order to do my job and keep my license. My opportunity even to become licensed depended upon my clear and specific understanding and acceptance of these mandates before I could even get through the licensing process. In my opinion no one working with kids should be held to any standards lower than these exact kinds of conditions if they are to be employed to work within any context, and with children of any ages. Furthermore, systems supposedly in place to monitor people and contexts should be very active and vigilant in enforcing the acceptance and utilization of these conditions on an ongoing basis. Such monitoring should occur for people to even be hired and to keep their jobs related to working with kids if they are in violation of these guidelines. The frightening thing is many of these monitoring boards and groups look the other way rather than enforce the rules needed to protect kids and their families, often using the excuse of being overloaded with cases and paperwork. If everyone was forced to understand and sign a statement of acceptance of such principles and standards, and was monitored accordingly by neutral independent parties, kids would be much safer and professionally assisted rather than victimized. My proposed principles and standards follow. I have formulated these guidelines and suggested mandates based on those established by the American Psychological Association for practicing and licensed psychologists as my model of reference.

Ethics Regarding People Employed or Volunteering in Positions of Power and Authority over Children Through Late Adolescence and Into Early Adulthood

Principles

I. Competence

    A. Achieve an appropriate level of training and education to understand the psychological, developmental and emotional needs of children through late adolescence and into early adulthood.

    B. Be aware of limits and boundaries pertaining to professional roles relative to teaching, guiding, and directing. Never blur limits and boundaries through inappropriate social relationships.

    C. Understand all aspects of diversity, being aware of and in control of any personal prejudices and biases you may have.

    D. Participate in continuous education and training to insure compliance with these guidelines.

    E. Be fully aware of complicating factors which contribute to the likelihood of kids or young adults engaging in negative and destructive behaviors, always separating what they do from who they are meant to be and meant to become.

II. Integrity

    A. Integrity is defined as a strong set of professional and personal values based in honesty, fairness and respect.

    B. Never engage in false, misleading, or deceptive practices which would create a dishonest or deceptive interaction or association.

C. Be aware of your own belief systems and never allow these factors to harm others in any way.
D. Be completely specific and honest with children and young adults about your professional role and responsibilities in their lives within all contexts.
E. Avoid dual relationships such as social interaction or trying to be a friend when such associations are not part of you professional role or in the best interest of the child or young adult.

III. Professional Responsibilities

A. Do not attempt to provide services for which you are not fully trained to provide.
B. Recognize limitations on your abilities to help, console, teach, or assist, and seek assistance from other professionals as needed and appropriate.
C. Work closely with professionals from other fields and disciplines as this applies to the best interest of the child or young adult.
D. Be aware of and concerned about the ethical compliance of others. Never allow misconduct to go unreported.
E. Do not use your professional role as a means of meeting your own personal unmet needs beyond a simple and reasonable amount of job satisfaction, especially the needs to be liked, needed, accepted, and especially the needs to control, dominate, punish, shame, or humiliate.

IV. Respect for Rights and Dignity

A. Recognize and honor the value within every child and young adult regardless of your personal belief systems and biases.
B. Never engage in harassment, discrimination, or coercion of any kind.
C. Appropriate peer pressure can be effective in compliance with rules as long as illegal measures, shame, and humiliation are never used.

D. Disciplinary instruction and actions as sanctioned by program, institutional, and organizational guidelines should be given and applied fairly, consistently and on a one-to-one basis away from other staff (when possible), children and young adults.

E. Always teach and guide by example through consistent right actions, behaviors, and choices. Always maintain self control and self restraint, never interacting with a child or young adult when you as the adult are emotionally charged or out of control.

V. Concern for the Welfare of Others

A. Determine what is in the best interest of a child or young adult and utilize appropriate and effective techniques to address the individual's needs and issues.

B. Always avoid and minimize harm to others. As dictated by the context or setting, efforts to control and maintain control should be minimal and efficient. Once control is established or restored, move beyond control as an issue and back to an appropriate routine as quickly as possible.

C. Consequences should be reasonable and fair if harm to others is to be avoided and minimized.

D. Always work to de-escalate rather than instigate or inflame any situation. Take only those necessary measures required to ensure safety and welfare to self and to others.

VI. Social Responsibility

A. Never seek only to punish. Find ways to allow consequences and learning opportunities to exist side by side. This will facilitate a transference of learned skills to other settings as well.

B. Always seek to redirect, educate, support, console, understand, guide, and/or rehabilitate in an effort to increase awareness of social responsibility and appropriateness as a treatment or academic goal for the child or young adult.

C. Never replicate or recreate negative social or street standards through misconduct, especially the idea that it is okay to break the rules as long as you do not get caught.
D. Recognize and appreciate the need for an interdisciplinary team approach for the purpose of teaching, guiding, redirecting, supporting, and/or rehabilitating a child or young adult.

Standards

- Establish and post reasonable rules and guidelines of conduct for both staff, children, and young adults which are contextually specific (school, law enforcement agencies and institutions, detention facilities, placement programs, etc.) Make certain through discussion and on going training that all rules are understood and accepted by *all* concerned and at *all* times.
- Always provide and allow for appropriate grievance methods and investigations without any threat of retaliation against children and young adults from staff.
- Never use shame or humiliation privately or publicly as a form of discipline. Always find appropriate and effective measures for correcting and addressing conduct. Be sure to take into account individual differences relative to learning abilities, psychological/mental health issues, level of maturity, and coping skills, always allowing adequate time for recovery and correction.
- Never use deceptive or false and misleading information with children and young adults or when providing verbal or written reports to others relative to incidents of misconduct.
- Always follow rules established which clearly define roles, limits, and boundaries relative to appropriate actions and interaction with children and young adults. Avoid horseplay, cover ups, dual relationships (trying to be their friend or socializing), false representations of roles (intentional or unintentional), favoritism, deception, ineffective efforts to control or maintain control, provoking and instigating. Remember that unless you are related to a child

or young adult you are likely in some position of power and authority over them making a completely causal and open relationship virtually impossible depending on your professional roles and responsibilities.

- If any actions (verbal or behavioral) escalate or otherwise worsen the emotional state or actions of a child or young adult the staff member involved should examine carefully their approaches, personal emotional state, and motivations. Such an increase in the negative behavior or emotional state of the child or young adult usually indicates ineffective, inappropriate, and incorrect actions on the part of the adult staff member.

- Recognize limitations relative to your ability to understand and assist. Call in support from other professionals specifically trained to address the issues. This could include, but is not limited to: social services, mental health professionals, child protective services, and medical professionals. In this day and time working with children and young adults often includes the role of case manager and team member. Never presume to know more than professionals trained in specific disciplines or try to override or undermine proven practices and approaches. Diagnoses and treatment plans should be carefully understood and followed without question except where dire or adverse reactions are evident. Appropriate staff and personnel should be notified immediately. Never humiliate or shame children or young adults based on your knowledge of their academic standing, medications, developmental issues, family or life circumstances, personal issues, and/or diagnoses. Accept and respect all professional limits and boundaries.

- Never seek to meet or serve your own unmet and/or inappropriate needs through any professional associations with children and young adults. Interactions should always remain neutral, non-personal, fair/just, unbiased, and in the best interest of the child or young adult.

- Children and young adults should never be punished or reprimanded based on the history of their parents, family members, or legal guardians. Furthermore, records of other people should never be

reviewed in front of a child or young adult given the reality that some information should never be shared by anyone but the adult relative and only at their discretion.
- Deception, dishonesty and fraud should never be used in any professional role with children or young adults. This includes law enforcement agents who should always recognize and respect the legal rights of minors and young adults. Never take advantage of any lack of knowledge or awareness on the part of children, young adults, or their families. Follow mandated policies and procedures regardless of the situation at hand relative to protecting and assisting children, young adults, and their families.
- Monitoring systems should always be in place, with requirements for constant scrutiny and examination of actions, records, and grievances/complaints related to adult staff regardless of context or setting.
- Senior staff, supervisors, and administrators should never simply assume their respective systems are working. Professional roles related to children and young adults often attract people who are abusive and irresponsible in different ways and considerations, and who may be seeking opportunities based solely in the needs for power, control, and punishment. This is especially true in juvenile justice related contexts. Every prospective employee should be screened for and warned about such practices *before* they are hired.
- Programs, institutions, agencies, and organizations should never exist and thrive solely by preying on those groups of people and individuals who are the least likely and capable of defending themselves and standing up for their rights.
- All policies, services, and procedures should be fully enforced, explained, and offered to all who qualify based on needs and circumstances. Organizational needs should never take priority over the needs of the people for whom they exist to provide necessary services.
- Existing programs and services should be constantly monitored and evaluated for success, effectiveness, appropriateness, efficiency, and usefulness relative to money allocated to service provision. Those

programs found to fall short of established goals should be restructured to provide services which would put available funding to use where it is needed the most. No organization should be allowed to exist solely because of its political power to maintain itself. This often applies to law enforcement divisions, educational programs, long standing institutions and agencies, and government waste.
- Carefully and periodically review and reemphasize the Ethical Principles and Standards with all employees at least on an annual review basis. Require signed acceptance statements relative to all policies and procedures outlined within these guidelines and standards.
- Every organization, agency, institution, and all associated staff should be held fully accountable for its performance and compliance with ethical principles and standards by a neutral regulatory panel or board.

Chapter II

Nature vs. Nurture: Developmental Issues

In almost every undergraduate psychology course there is a discussion of the nature versus nurture debate. Questions usually include the importance of hereditary and genetic factors (nature) as compared to environmental or contextual factors (nurture). The argument is about the degree of influence of how either or both of these considerations play into determining personality characteristics and behaviors throughout lifespan development. Emphasis is always placed on the importance of these factors especially during the early years. The conflict is now always resolved with an understanding of the importance of both sources of input and impact relative to growth and development and to future outcomes either of effectiveness or complication and maladjustment.

I cannot stress enough the importance of the home/family context relative to determining both current and future outcomes. There exists sufficient evidence within all psychological literature and research to indicate a clear interaction between both nature and nurture. There is no accepted way to date of changing basic biological/genetic foundations which determine physical appearance and predispositions to many other aspects of other characteristics relative to personality and temperament. On the other hand is the reality of the many ways in which we *can* control and influence many of the environmental factors we face every day of our lives. There will always be certain things in addition to physical aspects of our being we cannot control as associated with such life circumstances as the parents we have, the time at which we are born, many of the conditions into which we are born, the makeup of our family constellation, etc. However the one thing adults can control is the home/family environment into which children are born and raised. The single most important element is the quality of care and interaction between parents and children.

Further evidence indicates the importance of the first five or six years of every child's life since this period of development includes such rapid and extreme changes both on a physical level and on a psychological/emotional level. One of the most profound cases I have ever had involved a thirteen year old boy named Ricky who had a very serious and obvious jagged scar on his left arm. The scar looked like some type of extreme injury that went untreated for quite some time and covered about a six to eight inch section including the areas just above and below his left elbow. I asked him how this happened and to my amazement he told me he didn't know. This encounter was our first meeting and I was doing an intake evaluation with him to determine his needs and an appropriate treatment plan. Because of the seriousness and prominence of this scar I urged him to go home and ask his maternal grandmother, who was his legal guardian, how this happened. I suspected it somehow involved his mother because of information Ricky supplied indicating he was taken from his mother and adopted by his grandmother when he was six months old.

The next day I called Ricky back into my office at the school site and asked what he had discovered. Immediately he started crying, telling me that after pushing his grandmother for the information she finally told him the whole story. Grandma pulled out a picture of him at six months of age showing him with both arms and both legs in casts. She told him his mother had broken all four of his limbs in some sort of substance induced rage. Apparently this was not discovered for a few days. Grandma wasn't sure how the authorities were notified, but after a temporary period of being in a foster home Ricky was permanently placed in the custody of his maternal grandmother. This boy cried as he told every horrifying detail of his story, identifying the new rage he now felt toward his mother who was actually part of his life at this point. He told me he could now understand why he wasn't able to watch any kind of violence without becoming very panic stricken and overwhelmed. Because of this information he was also able to understand a recurrent dream he had of his mother's hand reaching down to grab him. Just before she grabbed him he always woke up terrified.

The significance of this incident to me is the apparent evidence that even before we have the verbal and intellectual processing skills to encode memories which are easily retrieved and explained, memories can be encoded both physically and emotionally based on the visual and tactile experiences in early infancy. Ricky was able to tell me about these associations without any prompting from me. At the age of thirteen he had already started acting out in some very serious ways, serious enough to get him removed from a public school setting and placed in an alternative school. The single most unfortunate aspect of my interaction with this kid was his removal from this alternative school for defiance only a few days later, so I never had the chance to work with him on any kind of long term basis to help him resolve the extreme emotions which fueled his extreme behaviors. Once he was removed I had only one additional contact with his grandmother. At that time I gave her a referral and encouraged her to get him into therapy with someone qualified to deal with this kind of abuse and trauma. I can only hope she did as I suggested. Since that time I have had no way of following up with this boy to know how things eventually went for him. If no one intervened successfully after my initial contact he very likely got into more trouble as he got older, possibly acting out rage he now understood, but without any reasonable means to resolve. This is one of the unfortunate aspects of many of the systems which are in place to help kids face and cope with the negative aspects of their lives. As kids get moved around from setting to setting there is often no consistent or appropriate follow up with needed services to assist with mental health issues.

Imagine the importance of having completed the appropriate level of training needed just to begin working with a kid as damaged as Ricky was. This is only one example of the need for implementation and enforcement of the Ethical Principles and Standards I presented in Chapter I relative to limits and boundaries associated with the professional ability to work with kids on different issues and from different professional disciplines. It was very hard for me to believe no one had ever told Ricky the truth about what happened. Furthermore, it was difficult to believe he had never asked about the scar before I met him. My basic professional beliefs include the idea of dealing with rather that ignoring the obvious. There was a statement I heard repeatedly in graduate school indicating "if it's in the room you have to deal with it." This means as professionals we must address everything we observe as being significant or even potentially significant. Development of needed skills and approaches takes practice and time. Care must always be taken to "at least do no harm" in any situation involving interactions between people, especially between adults and kids.

The factors which fuel and even create negative emotions and behaviors can be present at any stage of childhood development. The earlier the traumas through any form of abuse and victimization, the stronger the negative reactions are likely to be in the long run. In my professional experiences I have discovered most serious acting out behaviors begin toward the end of elementary school or right after the transition into middle school. The unfortunate reality is the likelihood of previous indications of damage which go unnoticed in school until the child begins to act out by engaging in negative behaviors. Because girls are less likely to act out behaviorally the need for intervention with them often goes unnoticed as long as they are quiet, even if quiet means withdrawn and depressed. Boys generally externalize their negative emotions while girls often internalize them. However, I believe this previous trend is changing as more and more girls refuse to buy into the stereotypes of the well mannered, "sugar and spice" images of the past. In the majority of cases girls still tend to act out less violently than boys, but I believe that factor is also beginning to change. Because I have worked in so many school settings and on several high school and middle school campuses I am noticing an increase in violent and physically aggressive behaviors between girls as well and at times toward boys. Assaults from girls toward boys often are overlooked and unpunished compared to the boys who almost always have to face sometimes severe consequences. The assumption of female to male aggression is that of the male having done something to deserve the abuse. Males are less likely to report abuse from female partners for fear of damage to their concept of masculinity. There is very little doubt in my mind females know this and take advantage of this factor.

Also accepted as a rather well known observation is the reality that when kids are exposed to abuse and victimization in the home/family context they are likely to act out first in their school context. From there their acting out behaviors begin to filter out into the streets, especially since virtually all schools now have zero tolerance policies for things such as violence on school grounds. As soon as negative behaviors are observed, especially if there are recurring incidences, it is critical at that point to not only give consequences, but to also begin some form of intervention and even investigation into other possible contributing factors present in the kid's life outside of the school setting. Such efforts, when accompanied by appropriate referrals to other professionals in other fields outside the school environment, could be effective in discovering complicating and contributing factors for the purpose of avoiding any further escalation in frequency or severity of acting out behaviors.

Let's look for a moment at some of the most common complicating and contributing factors present in the lives of troubled kids. Most of these kids come from very chaotic and conflicted homes where families, if together, are often dealing with a great deal of marital strife and a great deal of financial hardship. When the mix includes substance use and domestic violence then the conditions are more likely to cause extreme trauma to the kids living within this environment. Quite often if there are incidents of domestic violence there are also incidents of abuse toward the kids. Even repeated exposure to domestic violence is enough to cause extreme emotional damage to the children who are generally helpless when it comes to intervening or preventing the violent acts. One of the most destructive factors relative to chaotic and conflicted family situations is the inability to prevent the violence. It is easy to know what will eventually happen, especially if there are patterns and cycles of violence. However, the most uncertain factor is the inability to predict exactly when these things will again erupt. In some cases the incidents are frequent with only short periods of time between them. In other cases kids will often do everything in their power to try and keep peace in the family only to realize that no matter what they do there is no way to prevent or control what eventually becomes an inevitable and unavoidable experience. In these kinds of environments kids often blame themselves for the violence especially when they are unable to control it or even more importantly are unable to protect themselves or their moms, or in more and more cases to protect their dads.

Even more traumatic than the above examples are those settings where there is only a single mom with any number of kids, and the single mom continues to act out and make very bad choices in the relationships she has with men. I had a fifteen year old client once by the name of Randy who would literally stand outside the bedroom door of his mother's room while she was in there having sex with someone who was a virtual stranger. While in the hallway he would be holding a knife in case he had to go into the room and rescue his mom from being hurt. There were numerous occasions when he had to act on his fears and rush in, threaten the guy with the knife until he stopped assaulting the kid's mom and left. The first time Randy found the courage to finally take action was at the age of ten when he decided he was probably big enough physically to protect himself if necessary. He said usually the guys would leave once he entered the room rather than get into a scuffle with a kid. Because of the nature of what he described I had to report his mom to Child Protective Services which meant Randy and his siblings got removed from the home and eventually placed with their maternal grandmother. Rather than see her part in all of this the mom blamed me for destroying her family and refused to allow me to continue working with her kids. In time Randy ended up on probation and in a community school where I was assigned to his case by probation. With time he was able to understand I did what I had to do to help him and his siblings and we made quite a bit of progress in helping him deal with his past. This is just one example of many I could give with similar or equal circumstances.

The result for kids in these kinds of environments is the tendency to internalize their rage – not anger, rage. This is especially true for boys and especially for the oldest boy in the household who usually feels the greatest degree of responsibility to protect his mom and his younger brothers and sisters. I believe in every one of these cases kids develop rage fantasies because of their inability at younger ages to actually do anything to intervene and to actually make a difference. This rage is coupled with an extreme amount of fear which only fuels the rage because of their feelings of helplessness and hopelessness. In these fantasies kids will spend a great deal of time acting out in their heads what they would like to do in reality. Depending on their environment and the awareness of violent acts, or their exposure at young ages to violent movies and video games, these enraged, frightened, helpless, hopeless kids will concoct an almost unbelievable scenario of revenge which includes acts of torture and ultimately ends in the death of the perpetrator of the violence.

This is also true for kids who are direct victims of the violence and other forms of abuse. At times the rage fantasy might even include revenge toward the adult or adults who continually expose the child to violence and abuse. As the child grows up physically the rage continues until the child has their first opportunity to unleash the rage on someone else. At that moment the child will usually experience a strong feeling of relief at finally stopping and controlling their victimization and fear. Also, at this moment this child realizes fear and victimization can be eliminated or at least significantly reduced through violent acts against others which they can actually control. This moment of acting on and acting out their rage reinforces both the rage and the need to act out, often setting the kid up for a future of violence which they then create in order to never feel vulnerable or 'at the mercy of externals' ever again. This is the cycle of violence initiated by the adults in a kid's life which gets perpetuated and carried down to the next generation in some form, even if it isn't exactly the same as the violence to which they were exposed as kids. Rather than domestic violence it may take the form of bullying other kids; open and active defiance of any form of authority which feels the same as the abuse they originally experienced; or even worse in the form of street related crimes and acts of violence played out through gang rivalry and competition set up by law enforcement officials and other agencies. The ineffectiveness and inappropriate actions taken by educators, law enforcement, probation, courts, judges, district attorneys, juvenile hall, and various other placement staff, not to mention the virtually useless concept of state youth facilities, only make the rage of kids stronger. This occurs as kids again experience the abuse from people who should help them rather than offer them the same kinds of abuse, violence and disregard they have experienced as young children within their home/family environment.

It is not uncommon to find the content of rage fantasies to be so much stronger than the violence these kids learn to perpetrate on others. Thank goodness this is generally the case, because the content of rage fantasies generally reflects the degree of rage and fear they experienced during the violent and abusive acts. During milder forms of rage fantasies kids may actually turn the violence on themselves by imagining their own deaths even by suicide, with the hope those who are suppose to love and protect them would perhaps love them and want them once they were no longer alive. The essence of revenge in these kids is based in the act of punishing the adults who caused them harm by creating intense feelings of guilt and regret which would then last for a lifetime. What a horrible waste of energy and creativity bound up in hatred and resentment about which and with which they can do nothing. When adults in positions of power and authority over kids create any form of disrespect or disregard toward kids, at that moment they provoke the rage boiling within these kids just below the surface. It is important to understand anyone who is filled with rage always has some degree of rage available to fuel them into an extreme overreaction to any situation which feels threatening in any way. Adults and children alike who hold onto this kind of rage never go from zero up. They start at whatever level of rage is churning within them and go up from there. Because it is impossible, without some amount of investigation, for any adult to know the stories behind a child's need to act out, extra care should be taken not to provoke any child to anger while trying to address negative behaviors.

I believe virtually every overreaction exhibited by a child during any type of interaction or exchange with an adult is usually the fault of the adult who acts or reacts arrogantly, thoughtlessly, and carelessly. This is equivalent in the child's unconscious experience of actually blaming the child for everything which has ever gone wrong in that child's life. To the child this adult is just like every other adult in his or her life who fails to see there are many circumstances in the kid's life they not only did not create, but also could not stop or prevent. This type of interaction further frustrates the kid who probably doesn't know why she or he just did what they just did, much less how to correct it. The failure to see an overreaction as an indication of serious underlying conditions and factors reflects a very strong disregard for this kid's well being. Emotional overreactions from a child almost always indicate a history of trauma which has likely gone unaddressed or unnoticed throughout the child's life. To further abuse and victimize only worsens the turmoil they feel inside and fuels their need to act out even more in order to protect themselves from a perceived threat. There are some cases when a child, who has been correctly diagnosed with an impulse control disorder such as Attention Deficit Hyperactivity Disorder (ADHD), acts out solely because of an inability or difficulty to control impulsive behaviors with the disorder being the primary cause. However, kids with temperaments which are difficult to deal with are also more likely to have been the victims of abuse as a result of the frustration their behaviors can create for the adults in their lives. Abuse coupled with impulse control problems creates an even more dangerous circumstance relative to rage and rage fantasies.

Perhaps the single most important factor of childhood development, in addition to their level of intelligence, is the level of emotional maturity a child has achieved as compared to their chronological age. Environments or contexts which expose any child to abuse and victimization through acts of violence or exposure to violence will also limit and distort their emotional development. This result is due primarily to the lack of appropriate modeling of emotions by adults, and by the child's lack of opportunities to learn how to deal with and express their emotions in appropriate ways. It is not unusual to encounter a kid who is still amazingly immature at sixteen or seventeen. A significant lack of emotional or psychological maturity limits the success of interventions with kids of any age. Quite often kids under the age of sixteen do not yet possess enough maturity, which includes a certain level of reasoning and understanding, to be able to understand or grasp the idea of what is in their best interest.

In my experience the most effective and long-lasting interventions are based in a kid's ability to recognize certain kinds of behaviors and reactions as acceptable, with negative behaviors and reactions only further complicating their lives. It is only at the moment when a kid can understand this perspective she or he can benefit from attempts to address and correct maladaptive actions and reactions. Because of this it is extremely important for adults to avoid the need to compete with any kid to be the one who is right. Kids, especially adolescents, often don't care what adults think unless they can see how it fits into their realm of possible benefits. This represents the need for adults inside and outside the home/family context to choose their battles carefully based in some sense of the level of risk of unfortunate outcomes and consequences to the kid if they fail to learn from and correct their maladaptive behaviors. I believe for interventions to be effective they must provide not only consequences, but also an opportunity to learn from the mistakes made which led to negative outcomes. Any exercises offering the opportunity to learn will always be more beneficial to the kid and thereby increase the speed with which they are able to see things for themselves relative to their own best interest.

Another factor preventing or impeding appropriate emotional development and maturity is a lack of effective parenting. This is especially true with parents who are overindulgent. These parents often give kids anything and everything they want and rarely try to set limits and boundaries. Parents in lower income brackets will try to make up for the lack of material things by going overboard in other areas; while parents in middle and upper income brackets just simply do too much perhaps to make up for their lack of direct involvement in their children's lives. In either scenario these are kids who also never learn to soothe themselves or calm themselves down because parents are always trying to fix things and overprotect them. I believe it is extremely unfortunate when parents treat their kids like they are little princes and princesses, giving them the impression they are more special than anyone else in the world. Kids who are overindulged and overprotected by their parents are in for a rude awakening when they eventually realize no one else in the world will give them the same kind of preferential treatment.

I had an occasion once at a local ice cream shop to encounter such a kid. I was out with a friend and got up from my seat to get our ice cream. When I returned a little girl about nine or ten years old was sitting in my chair. Her mom was there and was clearly aware her daughter had taken my chair and yet made no effort to make her get up. I politely asked the girl to move so I could sit down and she ignored my request. After my second attempt to get her to move, knowing her mom heard my request I literally told the child "obviously someone has given you the idea you are more special than you really are. Now get out of my seat." Both the little girl and her mom were clearly shocked, but the child got up and moved not only away from me but to the other side of her mom. My friend and I laughed at the looks of surprise mom and daughter displayed. Mom looked away indignantly when I proclaimed to my friend "I hope the little girl and her mom both learned something." This is not my usual means of interacting with kids. However, I was really annoyed because the mother did nothing to make her daughter move as I would have done with my daughter when she was a child. To this day I still get a feeling of satisfaction out of thinking about and telling this story. As you might imagine they were European Americans who were totally oblivious to the realities of life. I felt I had a duty to inform and I did so. You can be sure neither of them ever forgot the experience, even if it was to remember me as some kind of smart ass. At least I tried.

Virtually any kid will try to pull adults into an argument. By doing so kids are able to often shift the focus away from the real issues to something entirely different such as you don't trust me, love me, or care about me. In such interactions it is important for the adult to be more mature than the kid. However, all too often I see or hear adults engage in exchanges with kids in which no other adult would willingly participate. How ignorant and arrogant for adults to think they can treat kids with any less respect and appropriateness than they would be able to treat other adults. Kids truly are too sophisticated in their level of awareness about fairness and mutual respect to ever allow adults to get away with such futile and foolish attempts to intervene and redirect. The reasons adults get away with such things is often due to the back up they receive from colleagues within the same environment, often insisting kids are lying about abuse or inappropriate behavior the kid experiences from the adults, when in fact the kid is telling the truth. This is especially evident in school settings and in agencies associated with so-called law enforcement and juvenile justice. Unfortunately many parents side with the officials who insist they are only trying to do what is in the best interest of their child; or they comply out of fear that to do otherwise would only create more negative outcomes for their child and thereby for their family. Many adults do not want to believe or even entertain the possibility of another adult, especially someone in a position of power and authority, lying to them about their child. This reflects the assumption and hope many people have of adults in professional roles and contexts being trusted to act in an unquestionably respectful, ethical, and professional manner at all times. The assumption is adults in such positions should and do honor the implied and specified ethics of the professional role they have chosen which associates these adults directly with children.

The most shocking reality associated with this issue often occurs behind closed doors within various settings where other adults are not present. Or, the other possibility is the adults who are present are working equally as ineffectively and inappropriately in the same setting or context. Many times I have overheard deans, principals, probation officers, and law enforcement officials interacting one way with kids and in another entirely different manner when parents or adults outside that particular system are present. It is not uncommon for the kid present to be expected to endure unbelievable verbal abuse simply because of the power differential. Whenever such competition exists certainly the adults will 'win', but in reality everyone looses, especially the kid involved. This kind of exchange only further enrages and provokes kids to act out even more aggressively, blocking their ability to see or even care about what might or might not be in their own best interest. Giving in at this point and under these conditions leaves the kid feeling like she or he has lost and the only way out is through compliance. This form of surrender on the kid's behalf feels like they are in effect kissing some adult's ass who can only win because of the power they have over a kid to make their lives a living hell. The fact so many officials back each other up and cover up the injustices only makes this kind of behavior even more reprehensible and abhorrent. I wouldn't respond favorably to such an approach. Why should any kid be expected to do so?

So much of my work with troubled kids includes having to help them learn to deal with adults in their lives that are abusing and disrespecting them on different levels outside their home/family. This goes on in virtually every different context where I work with kids. Because I cannot change the adults causing the damage, I am left to try and get a kid to understand how to deal with these kinds of realities in ways which won't further complicate their lives. If a kid is at least fifteen or sixteen, and depending on their level of emotional and psychological maturity, I can usually accomplish this. When I explain things in terms of the best interest of the kid they are usually able to understand that taking care of themselves relative to certain realities is not the same thing as kissing someone's ass.

As I mentioned in the principles and standards, different fields which involve working with and or supervising kids often attract adults who have a number of unmet needs or even worse inappropriate needs to abuse/victimize, control, humiliate and shame kids. Quite often kids are helpless in defending themselves from such abuse simply because other adults are often reluctant to believe adult staff or professionals would actually commit such acts against kids. I have known of several kids who went to placement facilities only to return more enraged or even more addicted to alcohol and drugs than when they left. So often staff members within different settings are willing to break the rules sometimes out of a need to simply hang out and be accepted by the very groups they are hired to assist and supervise. There are also incidents inside juvenile detention facilities where staff members approach kids with the intention of getting one kid to "take care of" another kid disliked by staff. One kid even told me once he was offered $200.00 and a weapon to take another kid out. Fortunately this kid refused realizing staff would never back him up if he got caught. This was not something I could prove since the kid would not give me a name, telling me he would deny everything if I told anyone about what he had told me. Plus I wasn't willing to put my life on the line in any situation like this.

Less serious offenses on the part of adults involve only the need to provoke anger in a kid. In so many cases I literally see adults who are as emotionally and psychologically immature as kids in their charge. I have even had staff members from different programs with which I collaborated attend my Adolescent Psychology class at a local community college. Back on the job I realized in many cases they had not learned anything from my presentation of these concepts about themselves and their ineffectiveness. People like this are generally so narcissistic they are unable to even entertain the possibility they might need to do some open and honest self assessment to look for areas where improvement is needed. Both adult men and women seek to control and provoke kids almost equally, even if in different ways. I try to get staff members to understand if any kid walks away from them more enraged and out of control than they were before the interaction started, then the adult or adults involved in that situation likely did something inappropriate.

The truly tragic reality is many times these adults actually believe they are doing the right thing and in the right manner. I often wonder how dysfunctional their families are and how damaging their own personal backgrounds probably were as well. It is not uncommon for adults to model what they were exposed to as kids unless they possess the ability to transcend and rise above, and the resiliency needed to bounce back from their own hardship of abuse and victimization. The only good thing which can come out of these kinds of errors is the chance I have to help kids learn how to deal effectively and realistically with these kinds of staff. This gives the kids an opportunity to learn how to avoid such people when they are in settings and circumstances where these kinds of people are present. It also gives them a chance to learn how to keep such people from pulling the kid into the adult's need to provoke and then punish. I can't even begin to understand what kind of satisfaction adults get out of this kind of interaction. I think such approaches clearly reflect specific biases against certain populations of kids deemed to be somehow undeserving of support, respect and consideration.

Some of the most infuriating situations kids have to endure are the cover ups by cohorts and colleagues who support and accept the injustices committed against kids. In most instances these adults know they are wrong and in some cases are actually breaking the law and violating basic human rights. Even law enforcement officials often act like immature adolescents as they compete with these kids to control the streets and bust kids, rather than use appropriate measures to try and assist or intervene in order to effect change and help them avoid entry into the adult criminal systems. Street gangs already enjoy the competition they sense from breaking the law and trying to get away with their offenses. In many instances they are actually mimicking the actions and tactics utilized and exhibited by law enforcement. It is obvious to me law enforcement agencies and staff often prey upon those with the least abilities and means of defending themselves from being targeted. This again reflects the immature thinking of these adults when it comes to trying to be effective in their jobs. So many agencies exist based on the game of money and numbers which equals job security, often creating false situations to justify their efforts to detain and otherwise supervise minors. All of these types of mistreatment and maltreatment clearly exist as complicating factors for kids and their families who are targeted in this manner. I fully believe kids have to be held accountable for their behaviors and misconduct. However, the important distinction between older adult offenders and juvenile and young adult offenders is that kids can still be redirected; whereas for many adults it is often too late because of the more permanent nature of their maladaptive ways of viewing and dealing with life.

This brings me to the issues of money/funding and the need to make sure available grant and foundation funds are used in the most effective, efficient and beneficial ways for nurturing and assisting kids in need of the services being provided. This is why I suggest that no program, institution, agency or organization be allowed to continue solely because of it has the political power and influence needed to maintain itself. This is equally true for educational contexts as it is for other public or private agencies and institutions. The importance of early interventions with the hope of preventing future problems is especially applicable within the educational systems. It seems kids who often need the most assistance are the least likely to get what they need because of the misuse and ineffective use of funding. This is especially true if a child exhibits a serious lack of self control along with learning disabilities or difficulties. I can imagine everyone, including a teacher, who decides to devote their lives to serving kids and meeting the needs of those in their charge entering their respective field with the optimistic goal of making a difference. Reality quickly sets in, even for therapists, as we try to implement theoretical paradigms and techniques or treatment plans we were told in school would be effective in reaching virtually every child. What our professors failed to tell us is there will always be a few kids who don't readily fit into any of the molds, profiles or models we were told to use in order to be effective.

As a result and over a period of time our levels of frustration and confusion begin to build to levels of anger and annoyance relative to the unexpected difficulties we have encountered and yet were not warned about sufficiently. The only way to avoid burn out at this point is to develop the ability and willingness to adapt and adjust as we go along. Learning how to better serve those who need greater attention and assistance is a requirement of educational systems and issues related to special needs. Even then there will always be the challenge of assisting regardless of our personal feelings toward any kid. When it becomes personal each of us needs to recognize our limited willingness or ability to intervene and try to find others who are better trained and/or equipped to work effectively with the child who now only frustrates and angers us. Collaboration, rather than removal of kids and denial of needed services, is essential at this point. Each of us has an obvious ethical and moral obligation to do everything in the best interest of each and every child. This reality must be embraced and honored to the maximum level possible, especially as related to ethical, legislated, and efficient uses of funding.

When it comes to funding relative to educational settings clearly a significant amount of money and effort should be concentrated on efforts to reach kids from the very beginning of preschool. By doing so every child then has a much greater chance of being successful at the higher grades and on into their adult lives. When any child fails to thrive within any context specific efforts need to be made to identify those factors serving as obstacles and barriers. Referrals should then be made to appropriate sources where those deficiencies, disadvantages, and needs can be addressed and remedied or at least contained and improved. This is also one of our unquestionable ethical and moral obligations to do whatever it takes to provide children and their families with any and all assistance necessary for children to learn and achieve. It is under these conditions and circumstances where the concept of team work and interdisciplinary efforts come into play. Money spent appropriately at younger ages, to include work with parents in helping them understand and improve their respective roles and responsibilities, will greatly reduce spending later in a child's development and academic years.

Of tremendous importance, and as part of the nurturing process, is the need to teach children to dream and then give them the confidence and means to achieve those dreams and goals. This was done in earnest when I was a child. I never imagined any other option than going to college or otherwise seeking out some level of advanced job or vocational training. Quite often when I ask a troubled kid what they want or wanted to be when they grow up they look at me as though dreaming about their future is a foreign and unfamiliar concept to them. How tragic to think a kid in middle or late adolescence has never been given an opportunity to think about or dream about their future careers and the kind of life they would like to have as an adult. Clearly this is one area where we as professionals fail to do our jobs as effectively and thoroughly as we should relative to our obligation to nurture kids in our charge.

A serious amount of effort needs to be invested in teaching parents how to parent and nurture effectively and appropriately. I firmly believe parenting roles and responsibilities should be taught in each and every high school in thus country. This is especially true for teen parents who should be required to take classes which would provide them with the most basic skills needed to effectively conduct their own open and honest self evaluations and assessments. The goal would be to give them at least a place to start in being able to make improvements within themselves in order to be effective in providing appropriate guidance for their children. Awareness of their own experience of being nurtured as a child - or the lack thereof - would be essential as part of their process of self assessment and even personal inventory. This, I think, is a major shortcoming of many parenting programs being utilized today. The basic assumption of many parenting classes is people having a rapport of mutual respect and regard between them and their children which just needs to be repaired and improved. In reality many people referred to parenting classes lack the skills to take care of and provide for themselves on many levels, much less be effective in guiding their children. My RFLAGS Model presented in my first book is equivalent to what I call "Parenting 101". It helps adults examine their own issues before they can ever be effective in their roles and responsibilities as parents. How can any individual be good at parenting if their own lives are in conflict and chaos because of their inabilities or difficulties making appropriate choices in their own lives? If they cannot control and direct their own futures and destinies successfully how can they possibly nurture their children effectively?

    The concept of self improvement through honest self assessment is one of the main aspects of my model and theories making them a more effective and powerful learning tool in improving the lives of both adults and kids. The concept of *righting wrongs* proposed in the title of my first book addresses the need for intervention with all adults in the hope of *protecting kids* as an effort to prevent problems in their lives now and into the future. The beauty of my approaches to parenting lies in the reality they can be used equally and as effectively with adults and kids. I love getting kids to identify the roles and responsibilities of adults in any role and watch them as they begin to realize the extreme shortcomings of many of the adults involved in their lives within different contexts and environments. The awareness of these deficits on the part of adults helps kids understand why their lives are so complicated in various areas and aspects. Once they realize what needs to be done, kids can at least take an active role in improving their chances of being successful as adults. This is especially true when compared to the lack of achievement and growth missing in the lives of adults who play vital roles in their lives. Furthermore, this is essential for kids who are in middle to late adolescence as this is their last chance before entering adulthood. The importance of spending considerable amounts of money with this population is critical. Such an investment in this age range will greatly improve their chances of success as adults.

One of our main responsibilities as parents is that of nurturing and raising our children to be independent, high functioning, responsible adults, with the intention of them ultimately and successfully leaving us to start their own adult lives and experiences. This doesn't mean severing ties and connections with them. It simply means we have given them the means to take care of themselves in a world offering many obstacles and challenges. The success of future adults depends deeply on the effectiveness of adults in each and every role which is part of a kid's growing up experience within all settings outside the home/family context. If any one of us fails to maximize our efforts to meet the needs of kids in our charge then we miss an opportunity to provide something of value to that child's development - something you or I, and only you or I could have given them which might have proven useful to them at some important moment, or during a critical process of problem identification, problem solving and decision making. How senseless and easily avoidable it is to miss the chance to create this missed opportunity by simply doing what is right and in the best interest of everyone involved. The art of effective nurturing leads to optimization of the potential of every child's inherited nature.

Chapter III

Abuse and Victimization of Kids

Everything about the writing of this book has now changed. As of June 14, 2004, two weeks prior to this writing, I was permanently banned from the Indio Juvenile Hall facility, and the Dessert Youth Academy placement program. Because I had to file a 'Suspected Child Abuse Report" with Child Protective Services against Mr. Allen, a senior probation officer (SPO) within the institution, my career in Riverside County as I had known it ended. I had been allowed full access to this facility for over eight years by this point, and yet was told I would be arrested on sight for trespassing if I ever tried to step foot back in the facility. This reaction resulted from a demand made by Brian Casier, my supervisor at Riverside County Department of Mental Health, that I owed Candice Collins, the director of Indio Juvenile Hall, a "professional courtesy". I was ordered to tell her about the suspected abuse report. These kinds of reports are generally reported confidentially in order to protect the mandated reporter, but my supervisor insisted that this provision was not applicable in this situation. He had worked very directly with juvenile probation for many years and was always more loyal to them than to the staff at mental health he should have protected. The previous supervisor who, retired the year before and facilitated every aspect of my work with Riverside County Departments of Probation and Mental Health, would never have made this demand.

I walked across the county complex from my office, went into Ms. Collins' office and told her I was going to file the report as a mandated reporter, telling her I had every reason to believe the assault against the kid had probably occurred. She became extremely enraged and yelled at me stating "you have just become a threat to the institution". She further stated "everyone knows that you are pro kids and you always take the side of the kids". Her biggest concern was that "now that you have filed the report, it will go public. This incident has already been investigated and handled internally." This, of course, told me the incident had actually occurred as reported to me by the kid who was horribly assaulted a few weeks earlier in an isolation room within the facility by the SPO. Furthermore she told me: "if you're going to believe everything these kids tell you and report everything you see around here, then we will have nothing but problems with you." She even agreed with my defense that I had no choice but to file the report given the fact I am a mandated reporter, again raising her voice and yelling at me: "then go back to your office and do what you have to do!"

Needless to say I was hurt, astounded, and shocked by both her overreaction and her lack of professionalism. In all of the eight plus years I had served this population of kids, I had never before been put in a position of having to report something this horrific. I immediately went back to my supervisor and told him "she's really pissed". By this time I was really angry with my supervisor. He dropped everything he was doing and went straight to juvenile hall to try and reason with her. This all started about 2:30 PM on a Thursday afternoon. When I left at 6:00.PM my supervisor had not returned from juvenile hall. The main reason for Ms. Collins overreaction was that my office was in the process of reassigning me to juvenile hall full-time in order to shield me from other reassignments related to the budget problems we were experiencing at both the county and state levels in California. I would have worked half-time in the juvenile units doing crisis interventions and medication monitoring with the kids, also serving as liaison between the kids and our psychiatrists. The other half-time position would have been my continuation as staff psychologist for the Desert Youth Academy (DYA) lock-in placement program located within the facility, a job I had volunteered for some eighteen months earlier. Until the day of this experience with the director of Indio Juvenile Hall, I had served as a therapist and assessment specialist for the institution since I started with Riverside County Department of Mental Health in March 1996. This suspected child abuse report was the first I had ever made against juvenile hall staff in over eight years. I worked with all twenty of the placement minors in Desert Youth Academy, and always saw other minors assigned to me on the outs when they were locked up in juvenile hall. Everyone, including the previous and current directors, had _always_ told me how much they appreciated my assistance and presence in the facility, telling me and my supervisors they had the utmost respect for me and my work as a psychologist. I was given a lot of credit for the success of the countywide DYA program through my work with the kids as their psychologist.

It wasn't until the following morning I went into my supervisor's office to find out what had happened between him and the director. To my utter dismay and disbelief the director had refused to budge. She had called in her regional director for the entire Riverside County Department of Probation which oversaw the operations of Indio Juvenile Hall. My supervisor had to call in our regional manager for the department of mental health. Both the director of juvenile hall and the director of probation reportedly said nothing but good things about me to my supervisors. They even told them about me being favorably "pro kids" and "always taking the side of the kids" – with a different twist on that line than when I was in her office. They both fully understood I had no choice but to file the suspected child abuse report, and even understood this was the only time in over eight years I had found it necessary to take such action. Furthermore, they understood that because of the budget problems it was "Dr. Roberts or nothing" and still refused, stating over and over again I was now a "threat to their institution". Even the police officer who came to my office the following week to interview me about the incident I had reported told me he tried to get the director to understand I was only doing my job. He couldn't get her to change her mind either.

The obvious reality which came out of this is that the staff at juvenile hall and staff within the entire department of juvenile probation apparently have much to hide. This condition of cover up and deception had been building since the 9/11 attacks in New York City and Washington DC. Clearly their level of paranoia must be grounded in the perception there is a lot wrong with their system. This is something I have always suspected, being constantly aware of the blatant mistreatment (in the sense of abuses of power and authority) of kids at all levels of probation and incarceration. Some years ago I was investigating, with the help of two reputable probation officers, an apparent injustice against a kid who was being sentenced to the California Youth Authority (state prison for kids). He was being prosecuted for stabbing an adult gang member from Los Angeles as this kid and his older brother and cousin tried to protect themselves from being assaulted by the entire group of five LA gang members. Even the family of the gang members came forward to defend the kid and his brother and cousin. None of this was allowed in court and the kid was sent to CYA for three years without any prior history of arrests or any history of gang involvement. The knife was a tiny pocket knife the kid carried around with him, and the man he stabbed was only superficially injured. The three young men were on their way to a Posada, a very popular Christmas event celebrated within the different Spanish-speaking cultures.

To make this even worse, the kid was told by police if he would cooperate and tell them everything, nothing would happen to him. Instead, and according to a direct account to me about all of this from the kid, he was charged with assault with a deadly weapon and coerced into pleading guilty to a serious felony. The police report I read was a serious exaggeration and misrepresentation of the incident and the truth as reported to me by the kid. Even the two probation officers told me they didn't believe a word of the report and believed the kid was telling the truth. The one probation officer who had recommended CYA was actually told by the supervisor of juvenile probation he *had* to do so and do it without questioning. I spoke with this kid's father by phone, urging him to get a private attorney for his son. He cried as he told me "as a poor man I have to choose which one of my sons I can help. Because my older son is facing prison I feel I have to get an attorney for him. I feel bad having to make such a choice, but this is all I can do." This is a translation from the words he said to me in Spanish. The older son pleaded guilty to less serious charges and got out on probation only, but with an adult record.

This was one of the crisis cases I was called in by juvenile hall staff to work on with the hope of helping this kid, a victim of the juvenile justice system, through this unbelievable ordeal. When Debbie Waddell, the supervisor of Indio Juvenile Probation at that time, found out I was working on this with the probation officers they were apparently seriously reprimanded. I was given a message from their supervisor that if I continued to investigate this case I would be banned from probation. That was nearly five or six years before the June 14, 2004 outrage and nothing has changed since then either with probation or law enforcement and related organizations and agencies. The supervisor in charge of juvenile probation at that time was one of those who openly spoke out against kids, using many of the labels I have mentioned to describe them. She hated the fact I would dare to oppose her and her efforts to get kids off the streets at any and all costs, even if done unjustly and illegally. This supervisor was, of course, white.

There were other incidents over the years I knew about, but wasn't obligated to report because they didn't involve direct physical, emotional, sexual abuse, or neglect. I realize the idea of emotional abuse is questionable, but because these kinds of events are perpetrated upon kids by law enforcement officers, officers of the court, and probation staff there is no way to investigate the situations. This is clearly one of the problems with the so-called juvenile justice system when their power and authority goes unmonitored and uncontrolled. The reality of juvenile records being protected, because the kids are underage minors, only gives law enforcement and related personnel more opportunities to get away with unimaginable injustices against kids and families who are the least likely and least able to defend themselves. Another major problem is the reality in juvenile courts of there being no jury. Kids are, therefore, convicted and sentenced based on reports filed by law enforcement and probation staff only. Even to this day cops openly brag about not writing up any report against a minor they can't make stick, so they generally give outrageous charges forcing the kid to plead down to lesser charges. The minor is given the impression by public defenders that they will lose if they fight the case, and will then get extremely severe consequences. As a result kids generally accept the plea bargain, sometimes pleading guilty to things they didn't even do. This never happens for kids who can afford private attorneys and the court officials and participants all know this.

My removal from the juvenile justice system is a clear reflection of the likely cover-ups taking place regularly behind the "blue curtain" nationwide, including where I now live and work in Mobile, Alabama. My supervisors were even told by the director of juvenile hall the incident I reported to Child Protective Services "had already been investigated and handle internally." In my mind this means it was covered up given the fact the only one removed from the setting was me and not the senior probation officer who allegedly assaulted the kid. Furthermore, the kid for whom I reported the alleged abuse probably had no idea this would be something I would have to report, so I never detected any feelings of revenge on the part of the victim. The kid knew too much information about the incident for me to doubt his honesty and account of the situation. Included in his account were the indications the assault was caught on tape, witnessed by staff to include the person watching the monitors in the control room, and commented on by staff to the kid about 'how messed up it was', further stating 'we now know what this guy is all about'. SPO Waddell was white and the kid was Hispanic.

My account of these matters is not about revenge, because I can and have moved on. I am simply and literally telling this to bring attention to the abuse and victimization of kids within this particular context so-called the 'juvenile justice system'. Even though this was a local event I firmly believe it represents realities for juveniles around the country. Similar acts of abuse and victimization occur within other contexts such as schools, religious institutions, political arenas and ideologies, and social levels and perspectives. All of these are outside the home/family context I talk a lot about in my first book. They don't even include the injustices and other circumstances existing within the communities where kids must deal with all kinds of issues about which they either can do nothing or very little. The irony of me being distinguished from those within all areas connected to juvenile justice by the label of "pro kids" is absolutely absurd! As I recounted this story to one of the field probation officers recently I made this very point with her, further explaining their perception of "always being on the side of the kids" is not accurate as they are trying to imply. The last implied part of that phrase which is deliberately omitted when presented to me and to the staff at mental health is that I am on the kids' side 'against probation'. I told her I firmly believe kids have to be held accountable for what they do. However, with the consequences kids face, they should be given very effective and appropriate opportunities to learn from their actions. They should be supported by everyone involved in their lives at that point to facilitate their chances to redirect their lives and energy. Instead they often receive serious maltreatment and harassment, both of which only make them more enraged, increasing their need to act out without caring about themselves or others because of this form of abuse and victimization from authority figures.

The ultimate irony for probation and law enforcement is they can only keep their jobs relative to juvenile offenders if there are juvenile offenders around. When law enforcement officials do their jobs effectively (even if inappropriately), the number of juvenile offenders drops and these personnel become afraid of losing their jobs which can only be justified through numbers which guarantee funding. The broader issues of funding will be addressed in a later chapter. All too often I have seen kids placed and/or kept on probation or in certain programs just to keep numbers up and justify the existence of the programs and jobs of related staff with no regard for the well being of the kids.

The only way to view abuse and victimization of kids is to understand adults are the perpetrators of the various forms of maltreatment and are the only ones who can prevent such injustices. Furthermore, because many of the people within the general population only want their streets safe no matter what the cost to kids, these injustices are allowed to go unchecked and unmonitored as long as private citizens feel protected. The serious misperceptions of many adults reflect their false sense of safety and security which are easily and laughably violated by the kids. It is extremely important to realize that the more kids are mistreated the more they are going to act out. As their rage increases so does their desire to act out on members of society who are perceived by the kids to have 'everything' compared to the realities of the kids who feel they have nothing. While not completely justifiable, their thinking is an understandable reality.

All too often the messages given to kids and the behaviors modeled for kids from adults within all contexts is that everything is okay as long as we don't get caught. There is no doubt in my mind kids are taught this everyday and in every setting imaginable. This is no less true relative to political, corporate, and religious scandals which are common knowledge and unfortunately rather common occurrences. It seems apparent to me when kids are caught up in any system which only provokes and feeds their rage, they simply get deeper into the system because of their inability and unwillingness to care about themselves or others. They firmly believe there is no reason to care since no one seems to care about them. Within school settings kids who are mistreated and neglected become so frustrated and discouraged they give up, drop out, and otherwise stop trying to better themselves educationally. Kids generally cannot respond to negativity in any other manner given their lack of psychological and emotional maturity. Many adults are no better at problem solving than kids appear to be when the kids are denied opportunities to learn, by people who treat them with disrespect, and who seemingly care nothing about them.

The single most important factor within this text is that the kids who are abused and victimized the most represent the troubled youth identified and addressed in this book as society's underdogs and throwaways. These kids and their families are always the least likely and least able to defend themselves from most injustices. This lack of defense against offensive actions and realities represents different considerations. For many there is the sense of hopelessness and helplessness which may have developed as a result of life circumstances about which people believe they can do nothing. For others there is the fear of going up against authority figures based in the belief things will only get worse if they even try to defend themselves or stand up for their rights. Another reason lies in the lack of knowledge and awareness many people have relative to what their rights really are, and how to go about guaranteeing themselves the consideration and opportunities they deserve and are actually entitled to receive.

One other reality is that some families just don't care enough to get involved in the lives of their kids to even bother protecting and defending them. I see this all too often for kids who come from extremely destructive and chaotic family environments. Sometimes adults within these kinds of family settings are struggling so hard just to survive from day to day they don't have the energy or the time to take on yet another battle. However, for some kids their parents and guardians are so selfishly involved in their own lives they actually don't care about the needs of their kids. These are the families who for me are the most difficult to work with because of my own anger toward parents who bring kids into the world with no desire or intention to give them a good life. These are the kids who often result simply as an outcome of irresponsible sexual behavior on the parts of their parents. In my first book the title deals with the concept of "righting wrongs". Represented by this phrase is nothing more or less than adults doing everything possible to make themselves better people before they even become parents, or at least after their kids are born. This is where the ideas of both intervention and prevention come into play. Parents who at least eventually work on their own issues are generally able to tear down walls between themselves and their kids. They finally establish new relationships rather than repair relationships which never worked well for the kids involved. This is the part about "protecting kids".

This is a good point at which to reintroduce my Roberts FLAGS Model presented in my first book <u>At the Mercy of Externals: Righting Wrongs and Protecting Kids, 2nd Edition</u>. The FLAGS are the negative emotions of <u>F</u>ear, <u>L</u>oneliness, <u>A</u>nger, <u>G</u>uilt, and <u>S</u>hame. My RFLAGS Model graphically depicts how all of us tend to act out anxiety and depression based in these five negative emotions. While these are not the only emotions, I have found and still find them to be the most destructive when these emotions become the motivations and provocations of thoughts and actions. Let me briefly review the cycle which originates in unchecked and often unconscious emotions. Kids who are damaged by histories of sexual, physical, and emotional abuse as active forms of abuse, and neglect as a passive form of abuse, will have tremendous emotional damage and open wounds, with the depth and extent of their wounds being positively correlated to the degree of abuse. The lack of conscious awareness of the negative emotions and open wounds is a direct result of the kid's lack of opportunities in the early and critical years for appropriate and proper emotional development. All too often kids are not allowed to experience emotions and generally are not given opportunities to learn the appropriate expression of emotions. This is especially true inside home/family contexts plagued with tremendous chaos, conflict and instability. On the other hand other kids only see adults who have no control over their emotions, so nothing appropriate is displayed or taught. This means quite often people are reactive as a matter of habit based in observations and experiences within extremely dysfunctional environments. The result is that of having a level of strong emotions present at all times and boiling just below the surface with little or no conscious awareness of, or regard for their presence and potential.

The imagery of a pressurized tank with a gauge on the top is a good metaphor. People with this level of raw unidentified and unaddressed emotions fail to see the needle on the gauge as usually half way to the danger zone most of the time. So for them the needle doesn't go from zero to fifty, it goes from fifty up to the point of the person (tank) exploding. As the emotions build in intensity the level of physical discomfort, annoyance, and frustration build to the point when even kids often say or think to themselves "fuck it, nobody else cares so why should I?" At this point of hopelessness and helplessness the kid or adult will begin to act out their emotion-based anxiety in ways intended to alleviate, escape, release or even resolve anxiety. There are a number of acting-out behaviors from which a person can choose, and the larger the number of inappropriate and ineffective choices made will equate exactly to the degree of complicating factors people experience in their lives. These complicating factors only lead to more distress and the need to act out until the person recognizes the necessity of trying to determine where, why and how these overreactions are generated. For kids the opportunities to seek understanding of their thoughts and behaviors are rarely if ever presented to them. Therefore their need to act out only increases.

When you put these kids into systems where they are exposed to additional abuse and victimization then the patterns are set for them to continue down a destructive path causing harm to themselves and to others. The right interventions at the right time and by the right person or persons can be extremely effective in helping kids redirect their energies through more positive and productive activities and aspirations. To do anything less is in my opinion criminal — as much so as any criminal activity in which a kid might participate. Think about how the systems often set kids up to compete with rather than learn from the very adults there who could actually help them. Instead adults all too often provoke kids and fuel their negative emotions, thereby only increasing their rage and the desire to act out rather than change their thinking and actions.

The very tragic reality is that it wouldn't take much for any adult to learn to be effective when working with troubled youth. All that is required is for adults to develop the willingness to look beyond what kids do and see them for who they are meant to be. This means looking for the piece of heart present within every kid, even the ones who are the hardest to reach. There is always goodness inside of every kid and it is extremely important to look for and nurture that goodness through kindness, non-judgmental acceptance of the kid, and with the awareness that kids who have good lives and stable homes usually don't end up complicating their lives. In too many instances adults look at kids as being bothersome nuisances, an attitude which only brings out the worst in both adult and kid. My experience indicates that by looking beyond what kids do and seeing the potential for good inside of each and every one of them, kids respond by opening up and working with, rather than competing against the adults who are part of their lives. For any kid to trust an adult it must be apparent what the parameters are relative to each and every respective role. People in positions of power and authority must be up front in every situation about what and why they have to report or otherwise act on certain bits of information. As a psychologist the sky is the limit for me in this area because I am only required to report incidents of abuse and neglect, and threats of harm to self and to others. I make this clear from the very instant we meet so there will be no misunderstandings. If a kid knows they can really trust us to tell them the truth they will open up and tell us most everything about which they need to talk.

    The miracle about this approach is kids get to know up front you are there to help them, not to try and bust them. Because so many adults use deception and outright lies to get information from kids, very few kids are willing to even try, much less trust any adults who come into their lives. Kids seem to always view adults as having ulterior motives in every interaction adults set up with kids, especially in professional settings and contexts. One of the ways I gain a kid's trust is to assure her or him I don't trust many adults within certain settings any more than they do. As they hear me confirm their suspicions that adults are often out to trick them, the kid begins to think I must not be "one of them". This approach is clearly the "pro kids" part of me. I spend at least the first ten or fifteen minutes going over issues of confidentiality with them and explain carefully why and how my job is different than the jobs of many people in their lives, especially within school and juvenile justice-related systems. I swear to them in any manner necessary to get them to at least try and believe I am being totally honest with them. In effect I am bashing other adults based in the reality that I know what I am saying is true relative to the tactics often used to set kids up and trick them into trusting long enough for the adult to get the information needed to use against them. Adults are shameless in these kinds of tactics and feel perfectly justified in betraying a kid's trust rather than getting to know a kid in ways which could foster growth and change. Because of my approach kids see me as an ally rather than as the enemy and they begin to open up more and more as they see and accept the fact I am for real.

Because I went into East Los Angeles in September 1992 knowing I knew nothing about the people and their environments, they were able to see my sincere desire to learn *from* them, not just *about* them. This gave me an opportunity to look into their world without any assumptions or prejudices. By very genuinely using this approach I learned a lot about what it is like to live in areas where there are very few positive opportunities and factors, but with an over abundance of negative circumstances and realities. What I found was a very sincere desire on their parts to both teach me about themselves and their environments, and to *then* use what I had learned in school as we worked together to try and make life better for them. I firmly believe they also wanted me to learn as much as I possibly could from them so I could continue to help others in different areas, but with the same kinds of life situations of stress and distress. This to me is where the idea of spiritual psychology comes into the picture.

In my first book you read that I am not a religious person at all. However I do consider myself to be a very spiritual man whose beliefs include: the concept of one Source; innate goodness in everyone; being altruistic and non-judgmental; unconditional acceptance and regard as a form of love; and karma, in the sense of what goes around comes around. The innate goodness is the eternal Soul of each person. Being altruistic means doing something for nothing to help others, which also requires some degree of work and sacrifice on the part of the doer. The concept of karma has to do with the idea that whatever we put into motion – positive or negative – is what comes back to us. I do not believe in the concept of love as spoken about during the hippie era of "free love"; rather in the concept of love as consideration and respect for people as spiritual beings regardless of what we observe about them. This doesn't mean we have to join with them or even like what they do. It simply means we must look beyond what we see, and understand each of us is going through our own personal process which no one can control or redirect except as acts of personal and very individual conscious and unconscious choices and actions. I believe the concepts of being non-judgmental and practicing unconditional acceptance have a lot to do with recognizing the profound uniqueness of each and every person alive.

Even my RFLAGS Model is based in this kind of spiritual psychology, believing in the innate goodness and uniqueness of each individual and also explaining why these characteristics often go unnourished and underdeveloped. The model and related topics seek to explain why we do what we do strictly from a cognitive and behavioral perspective only, with negative emotions being the fuel feeding the distress and stress we try to act out rather than resolve. From a spiritual viewpoint I also feel kids are much less responsible for their actions and reactions as are their adult counterparts. This is not to say kids are not accountable for their actions and reactions; they are just not as responsible for them as kids as they will be as they get older, and after they have worked with me for a while. In other words, there are reasons why kids do what they do which explain rather than excuse what they do. This is a very simple concept and is the one most often misunderstood and misinterpreted.

The standard profile for troubled youth include a number of complicating factors, all of which are listed in my first book. A brief summary of factors includes chaos and conflict within the family which create a great deal of instability. Quite often kids are unsupervised for a number of reasons, leaving them feeling both neglected and free to experiment with many different things. Then there are the families who are so self-absorbed in daily living they have little or no time for family togetherness, resulting in a serious lack of interpersonal and intrapersonal connectedness. Some families so overindulge their kids and the kids come to expect everything about life to be easy and without meaning or merit. In so many troubled families kids experience threatening circumstances through constant open conflict which can include domestic violence and abuse toward the kids, sometimes by both parents. Within single family homes things often get more complicated with single parents struggling just to survive and provide for themselves and their kids. Unfortunately with many single parent homes there is a greater likelihood of strangers being introduced into the mix by parents who date and have live-in significant others or sexual partners. As a result in many situations there is an increase of siblings who share only one parent. The larger the family tends to be the more responsibility falls upon the older kids to take care of the younger siblings, resulting in resentment aimed in many different directions and for many different reasons toward the parent or parents. If the parent living outside of the family is also uninvolved in the family with the kids, there is further resentment and frustration, not to mention constant questioning as to why things are the way they are. All of this is made worse when alcohol and drugs are part if the mix, along with any degree of criminal activity. Parents who are incarcerated bring a sense of shame on the kids who are embarrassed to have parents who are also criminals. This is even worse when the mother is the one or one of the ones incarcerated.

One other problem is when the criminal activity in the home actually helps improve the conditions of the family, sending a very confusing message to the kids who buy into the concept it is okay to break the law as long as you don't get caught. This also adds a huge responsibility for everyone in the family to keep this as a secret about which no one can know. From there a further breakdown of the family results when kids are removed and placed into foster care situations, often made worse when they eventually have to be adopted out to strangers, who in many cases only use foster kids as sources of income. Kids who end up in this kind of circumstance often face extreme abuse and neglect and are often turned back into the system as they get into trouble and begin acting out their rage. This then becomes another abandonment issue about which they can do nothing.

Things continue to deteriorate as kids get into the juvenile justice system where they are all too often only further abused and victimized by people within every aspect of the system, including the court level. Some kids are actually never even picked up from juvenile hall or placement and have to be sent to foster care facilities until they reach the age of eighteen or older, depending on the state. Add to this the elements of hardship, hunger, poverty, homelessness, insecurity, uncertainty, Fear, Loneliness Anger, Guilt and Shame and you have a volatile mixture which constantly fuels negative thoughts and actions. These are behaviors based in negative emotions which lead to anxiety and depression, hopelessness and helplessness, and then to the need to act out that which cannot be controlled. All of this is too unimaginably complicated for adults and kids to understand or even recognize without assistance. All anyone knows in these circumstances and conditions is that life sucks and they feel like shit, believing there is nothing they can do to change things. It's like the trapped lab rat or dog in an old cognitive/behavioral experiment that eventually gives up and lies down in the cage on the electrified grid once any chance to control or escape the unimaginable situation is gone. With all of this, how can kids possibly be held completely responsible for their actions? These are factors and realities many kids live in daily. And, while these realities do not represent excuses for their actions, it is easy to see why kids do what they do given the conditions of their lives.

How can any adult fail to question and consider the needs and circumstances of the lives of troubled youth who are at extreme risk of making seriously bad decisions and choices? One of the best examples of an adult who corrected her perspectives and biases was a woman who worked in juvenile hall as a unit counselor. She had no children of her own and openly despised virtually every minor who got locked up. Eventually she was reassigned to probation as a probation officer with the responsibility of doing investigations into kid's lives, and then using these results to make recommendations to the court. I never liked anything about the way she handled kids in the hall and to my surprise she called me one afternoon in my office at the clinic. She was actually crying as she told me about a kid who really needed some help with serious problems in his life and family. I was so taken aback I found myself wondering what had happened to her, so I asked her to explain the change in her feelings toward kids. She told me she had never imagined what the lives and realities of these kids might include until she was reassigned. By going out into their homes and environments she was forced to look at how complicated their lives actually were.

During the conversation this transformed probation officer expressed deep regret for damage she had likely done to other kids, and made a verbal commitment to me insisting she would try to make up for it in the future. She was later put in charge of a day treatment program run by probation for kids on probation. At the end of about one year she was replaced because other staff felt she was too lenient with kids. However, under her supervision several kids successfully completed the program and received their diplomas. Her immediate replacement and the senior probation officer supervising the program were soon reassigned for the same reasons. The two who were in charge since that time, ran the program as though it was a lock-in program where kids could be simply detained during the day and sent home at night. Kids became extremely frustrated and angry about the lack of support they received, complaining constantly about the lack of regard the probation officers and staff had for the kids and their well being. In so many instances these are the issues I have to help kids deal with in therapy, using the approach of validating their perception of reality and then helping them learn to deal with it without further complicating their own lives and circumstances. What a waste of my time and what a waste of resources which could and should be used more effectively and appropriately. This is one of those programs I referred to which exists only for the sake of staff keeping their jobs and not for the betterment of the kids in their charge – a money and numbers scandal at its best!

Over the years I have seen some very good probation officers leave juvenile probation and move up to adult probation simply because they no longer agreed with the way things are run. There is very little doubt in my mind these conditions are likely representative of conditions for kids around the entire country, especially with the thinking and philosophies under, and remaining since the Bush administration. One of the most outrageous deceptions of the George W. Bush administration was and still is the misuse of money to treat gang kids like terrorists. I knew nothing about this extreme injustice and complete deception to the American public until nearly a year after 9/11.

In October or November 2002 one of our therapists from the children's service department where I lived and worked in California, invited Debbie Waddell, the aforementioned senior probation officer (the very one with whom I clashed on a regular basis due to her obvious hatred for juvenile offenders) to come and make a presentation to our staff during our weekly staff meeting. The SPO brought with her Anthony Villalobos, one of the assistant district attorney's so he could also talk about their work in the field with kids and their families. The program they discussed was called the Youth Accountability Team (YAT) and was an informal probation program. Parents were given the opportunity to access this program when their son or daughter got into trouble for a minor offense. That minor offense was then held over their heads for six months as a threat of prosecution if the kid did anything to violate their informal probation. These were charges that would have never been prosecuted anyway because they were petty things like fighting at school, truancy, runaway, and possession of small amounts of marijuana. During this six month period probation officers and law enforcement could show up at the minor's residence anytime they wanted and search the kid's bedroom and bathroom, and other parts of the house if people naively gave them permission to enter other rooms. If there were no violations during the six months the entire matter, including informal probation, was dropped. The charges initiating the informal probation were kept so they could be added to any new charges which might come up at a later time. The SPO explained that the purpose of the program was to keep kids out of trouble, in school, out of gangs, and away from drugs and alcohol. One additional component was that of providing support to families who were having difficulty managing the behaviors of their kid or kids. So far it sounds like a really good program except for the searches which could be conducted.

However, the SPO Waddell literally leaned forward over the table and exuberantly exclaimed: "but what we're _really_ doing is using this program to get them into the system by fingerprinting and photographing them. We can search their homes anytime we want and work to obtain evidence against them so that when we can get 'em, we can really get 'em!" This is a direct quote. I don't think I will ever forget her words. The exuberance in her voice was shocking as she openly bragged about the outright deception being perpetrated upon unsuspecting families who thought the informal probation program would be there to help them, rather than something which would ultimately be used against them and their kids.

After SPO Waddell's last statement ADA Anthony Villalobos, chimed in saying with equal exuberance: "yeah, and we have more rights than ever before to invade people's privacy. We can do all kinds of surveillance, including wire taps on phones, without even having to get permission from a judge." He explained that all of this became possible after 9/11 and the US Patriot Act when the US Congress made the definition of terrorism so broad that law enforcement agents are able to list street gangs as domestic terrorist groups, and gang members as domestic terrorists. The US Patriot Act also enhanced the power and authority of all levels of law enforcement, AND protected them with a veil of secrecy. Simply enter the terms "US Patriot Act and Domestic Terrorism" into any search engine and you will be astounded at what you will find. Since then I have learned that the Patriot Act further made _any_ criminal code in the United States a potential act of domestic terrorism if such acts posed any threat to life or property. These determinations are made on a case-by-case basis and solely at the discretion of law enforcement.

I have also learned that under the laws of the Homeland Security Act and the US Patriot Act all law enforcement officials have the right to go after anyone simply _suspected_ of domestic terrorist activities. Once _suspected_ of terrorist activity, anyone can be detained as an enemy combatant without any rights related to due process. All of the corruption within the Bush administration trickled down through all levels of law enforcement around this country based on the examples set and sanctioned by the Bush administration and its cronies. Very few people know that large sums of money earmarked for Homeland Security have been deceptively spent by local law enforcement agencies to buy ridiculous equipment in areas where terrorist attacks are the least likely to occur. If the money had been spent as presented to the American public, all of our ports and borders would now be secure! Furthermore, billions of dollars were funneled down to local law enforcement agencies to establish such programs as the Youth Accountability Team, so-called gang prevention task forces, and probation controlled school programs. None of these programs are monitored independently by anyone or any group, which means there is no accountability or independent oversight and scrutiny.

I listened with utter amazement as the SPO Waddell continued and openly talked about "those incorrigibles" referring to all juvenile offenders as being beyond hope or help as indicated by the use of this term to describe them rather than use it as a reference to their behaviors. She used the term repeatedly talking about "those incorrigibles (this)" and "those incorrigibles (that)" until I could no longer sit quietly. The members of our staff who know me really well and understood my feelings about kids and injustice, told me later they were surprised I let it go on for as long as it did.

I literally interrupted SPO Waddell's bravado by stating: "Excuse me! First of all I'm surprised you would say these things in front of me knowing how I feel about the way you think and talk about kids. However, this only confirms for me all over again the apparent hatred you have for kids in the system. Your use of the term incorrigibles to describe kids, rather than refer to their behavior is appalling and offensive to me. Even more appalling and offensive is the fact you would use the YAT program against kids and their families." I then looked at ADA Villalobos and told him: "by the very fact you're sitting here with her I must assume that you feel the same way as she does about kids. I find it hard to believe that you would brag openly and publicly about the fraudulent and deceptive misuse of a program. You trick parents into trusting you and probation without explaining to them that by voluntarily signing their kids into YAT, parents are actually giving you permission to use whatever means necessary to gain information against them and their kids." I then told both of them "you can be sure I will let everyone in the community know of your actions and intentions, and will encourage them not to sign their kids up for your Youth Accountability Team."

Both of these people were stunned at my confrontation, looking like two deer caught in the headlights of a car. ADA Villalobos never said another word, and SPO Waddell quickly started back peddling in an effort to save face. Immediately she began to apologize and tell me very patronizingly and insincerely, "well Dr. Roberts, you're right. I do need to watch what I say about kids. I'll have to be more careful in the future." With that the entire presentation came to a screeching halt and both of them left with their tails tucked between their legs. My supervisor and other staff later congratulated me for speaking out against them and backed me fully. SPO Waddell is the one who threatened to ban me from probation at an earlier time when I was investigating the case I mentioned earlier in this chapter.

I followed through on my promise to warn the community as much as I could. Since that time I have also tried to get this obvious misuse of money appropriated for homeland security revealed to the general public, but so far no one will break the story. However, I have had it confirmed for me consistently by political officials, law enforcement officers, and even a news reporter not only in California, but also here in Mobile, Alabama. One reporter told me the FBI participated in training local law enforcement officials how to treat kids as enemy combatants and use them for combat training by sending agents into areas where the threat of a terrorist attack is virtually nonexistent. I have talked with one TV reporter, a radio talk show host in Fargo, ND, and wrote numerous times to the Democratic National Committee and finally to the John Kerry presidential campaign headquarters, all to no avail. On the streets locally everywhere around this country there are a large number of heavily tinted black SUV's hanging out in lower income neighborhoods. Kids in California would walk up to these vehicles and to vans parked in their neighborhoods and offer those inside a beer, laughing at the fact everyone knew they were there. I have heard numerous stories from kids who are shocked to hear taped telephone conversations from their private residences played for them when they are brought in even if only for questioning. They would be detained for hours in "the white room" at the county sheriff's office in Indio, CA and released without charges and without any written record of their detention.

In my opinion kids are being used by law enforcement for entertainment and harassment purposes only. Given the fact we don't have any active terrorist groups in this country as those existing in other parts of the world (the exception being white supremacy groups and militias), the gangs and other kids are easy targets for such activities. The people being targeted are the young underage street kids and not the heads and older gang members. Probation officers and members of the gang task force show up at the homes of kids any time of the day or night to perform searches, even when the kid whose house is being searched is doing well. Gang task force members are more than willing to speak out to kids about how much federal money they are being paid because the kids are considered to be terrorists. I know of two instances in California when families were simply moving from one location to another, and the cops would show up and dump out everything the family had packed up for the move, making them have to pack everything all over again. Law enforcement officials even here in Alabama have confirmed my information. One former member of Homeland Security was absolutely shocked at the extent of information I had been given by law enforcement officials in California. This is not only a scam against disadvantaged kids, but against the entire American population who knows nothing about these secretive and underhanded misuses of power, authority, trust, and money. As I stated earlier, please go online into any search engine and enter the terms "US Patriot Act" and "domestic terrorism". You will be shocked and outraged by everything you will find. Hopefully you will then take at least some minimal action to help hold public servants accountable for these injustices.

These are other examples of how so much of my time with kids is spent trying to help them cope with these forms of abuse and victimization. I teach them to deal with these realities without giving law enforcement additional opportunities to become more deeply involved in their lives. Because of the way things are being handled kids are immature enough to see this as a challenge and as a form of competition and cops know this.. These tactics make them want only to fight more against the system rather than back down and let the system win. These kinds of abuses and injustices only fuel the rage of the kids as cops act out their own childish fantasies of again playing "cops and robbers". None of this is working in the sense of helping redirect and rehabilitate kids. More and more kids are getting locked up for serious and violent offenses committed out of rage which I believe is strengthened and intensified because of kids being incorrectly labeled and mistreated as terrorists.

With all of this going on no wonder law enforcement officials and personnel don't want caring people like me around to expose their misdeeds and misconduct. There is very little doubt in my mind that recent increases nationwide in violent crime are directly related to the harassment and socioeconomic profiling sanctioned by the federal government and passed down to the state and local communities. Because I am so outspoken about all of this I believe I am probably listed on at least a few government reports as a threat to national security. Keep in mind I did not go looking for any of this information. It was handed to me again and again as a result of the arrogance and ignorance of those given the responsibility to "keep the peace" by "serving and protecting" __all__ of the "American people". First and foremost I am an advocate for those kids and families who are the most vulnerable in our society. This sense of personal obligation results not only from my duties as a psychologist, but also from the deep Spiritual convictions to which I subscribe. I truly hope Karma will play out against those political figures and other groups who have violated our trust and who have violated many of the rights we hold sacred in this country!

Dr. David L. Roberts Ph.D.

I strongly propose and support a nationwide campaign staged by low income, disadvantaged families and their supporters protesting these acts of injustice and deception. Unless people organize at a grassroots level, these kinds of injustices will only continue. In a recent live talk radio interview I did through the University of California, Irvine, I was informed that in California corruption is finally being both expose and prosecuted. I told the attorney conducting the interview that so far this doesn't seem to have "trickled" over into other parts of the country, including places like Mobile, Alabama where the may reportedly wont' even allow city employees to use the word "Gangs publicly. The slogan for this grassroots campaign is:

F.A.T.E. Stops the H.A.T.E.
And
Equalizes the R.A.C.E.

Fairness		Harassing
Accountability	STOPS	Antagonizing
Truth	THE	Terrorizing
Ethics		Exploiting

And Equalizes the

Resilience, Assurance, Competence, and Excellence

With this approach it will be possible to peacefully with unite those being targeted to make a public stand against social injustice through violations of human rights and civil liberties. In my experience these injustices are not even racially motivated in many cases. They are motivated by an apparent loathing toward *all* lower socioeconomic people frequently viewed as low class citizens. This should be a campaign emphasizing inclusion, rather than exclusion, for everyone. Rather than racial profiling, public service agencies, institutions, and organizations at all levels of government are using socioeconomic profiling as a means of sustaining their existence and securing their jobs at the expense of low income, disadvantaged families and kids. All of this is part of the money and numbers games I talk about frequently. The really alarming fact about all of this is that the "veil of secrecy" is so strongly enforced, very few people know about any of these violations of trust and civil liberties. Please help me spread the word and put a stop to all of these injustices!

Chapter IV

Criminality

While I tried to edit the last chapter to reflect changes in my career and perspective in California, this chapter will explain everything which has changed since then. I find the extent of change in my life since the writing of the first three chapters in this book in the summer of 2004, and during the succeeding 18 months, to be almost beyond belief.

As I resume my writing it is now fall 2005 (Revision in 2010 as well). I have relocated permanently and officially back to my home state of Alabama after retiring from my job with Riverside County Department of Mental Health California at the age of 50 and as of February 2005. The changes detailed in chapter three left me with no choice but to leave the state of California given the reality that high risk youth were "no longer a priority" in light of serious budget problems and a lack of "evidence-based treatment" for this population within the mental health system at both the county and state levels. Keep in mind that funding for various law enforcement agencies is now almost limitless relative to changes since 9/11 and based in the misuses of the Homeland Security and US Patriot Acts. I was pulled in from my field work with the kids, even at the school sites, and reassigned to work exclusively in the clinic doing walk-in assessments. The reassignment by my office was in response to a significant loss of staff and a need to prioritize all cases based on more serious needs of intervention rather than any opportunity to provide preventative therapy for virtually any population. Without any sense of superiority I felt anyone with evaluation skills could do the job to which I was reassigned and I immediately began to rethink my professional future. The loss of professional contact with "my kids" was an almost unbearable loss given the fact by this time I had dedicated my entire career to this population of high risk, troubles kids.

I also know that the probation department and law enforcement agencies were able to get back at me for speaking out so openly against them. I have to let go of, and learn from all of that rather than be destroyed by it. I am very proud of the work I did in both Los Angeles and in Riverside County.

During the time I spent in California following the changes in my job I put a great deal of thought into how I should proceed and where I should go. My family ties in Mobile, Alabama were a major deciding factor in my decision to 'go home'. One of the things missing in my previous work with at risk youth was the reality I had nothing else to offer this group of kids but support through my work as a psychologist. There was nothing I could offer them in exchange for their efforts and willingness to redirect their lives. The loss of contact with the kids was a devastating blow to me emotionally, and my anger and grief gave way to a determination to evolve into more than I had already become personally and professionally. I also felt very strongly the need to protect myself from agencies and institutions having the ability to shut me down with no recourse available to me to fight for my right to fulfill my calling in life. I fell very strongly that my work with troubled kids is what I am supposed to do both from a professional and spiritual perspective.

As a result of the changes in my career path I am now in the process of establishing a non-profit youth center which will give high risk kids the opportunity to progress on all levels. The center, under the name of Liberating Youth, Inc., will offer advocacy; counseling/social services focusing on redirection and support; adult education; and on-the-job training. This project will be a freestanding private venture intent on collaborating with other organizations and institutions. This is all going well and will become a reality within the next few years. This book and my first book will both serve as the foundations of what will become a very structured program format allowing me to offer more of what these kids need in order to have a better chance of being successful. One main goal of this project is to provide the "evidence-based treatment" needed to prove that with the right approach, program format, and resources these kids can be redirected toward more positive goals.

My primary focus with this new program will be transitional age kids, ages 16 to 24, and we will seek to address all of the needs of this very vulnerable group of troubled kids. While this chapter is about criminality it is important to point out that not all troubled kids are involved in criminal acts. However, it is very easy for kids in this category to fall into criminal behavior given the right combination of complicating factors and feelings of helplessness and hopelessness described earlier in this book and addressed in detail in my first book. Other groups of troubled kids besides juvenile offenders and gang kids include: gothic kids, devil worshipers, witches who practice black magic, white supremacy groups, some skaters, taggers (graffiti artists), punks, rockers, emos (kids identifying themselves as being emotionally disturbed), homeless/street kids, and substance abusers. Some kids simply want to be identified as non-conformists and nothing more, while some kids seek to organize in order to promote some type of hate-based cause. Of interest to me is the reality that each of these groups generally represents different dynamics psychologically. Some of them are driven to have fun, to stand out in a crowd, to be part of a larger group, or some out of a need to survive as is often the case with homeless kids and runaways. With each of these groups it is extremely important to approach the individual members as human beings first and foremost and then try to understand what their group affiliation represents to them.

Of critical importance is the need to avoid judging them for their appearance or actions. It is also necessary to avoid making their exterior identity a constant focus of interaction or intervention. One of the most interesting cases I ever had was with a kid by the name of Eric. He was referred to me by probation and I was warned he was dangerous because he was a devil worshipper. I chose to ignore this and was able to get to know one of the most intelligent and talented kids I have ever known. I told him up front everyone who knew him was reportedly afraid of him and his religious beliefs, assuring him I was not threatened in anyway by him or his religious practices. Eric thought it was funny that everyone was afraid of him and I simply addressed this factor as something he would have to deal with if he continued with his current practices. There were so many other aspects of his character which were much more interesting to me, so I set out from the start to get to know who Eric was deep down inside. I worked very diligently to know his soul and to identify those things in his life and past which gave him cause to hate.

Dr. David L. Roberts Ph.D.

We met for several times before I directly addressed his religious beliefs. By this time I had been able to determine a very high level of intelligence he possessed, and had the opportunity to read many of his thoughts expressed in some of the most profound poetry I had ever read. His use of words painted a vivid picture of what was truly in his soul — both negative and positive aspects. Eric told me his father was a very conservative fundamentalist Christian who had "forced religion down his (Eric's) throat" for many years. He said he chose to worship the devil to get back at his father. I congratulated him on his choice as having chosen the one thing his dad could never have been comfortable with for himself or for his son. We then talked about Christianity as a religion and I simply pointed out the reality of Eric buying into Christianity by worshipping their devil as the evil opposite of their concept of God. The look on his face was priceless and I knew he was intelligent enough to realize he really wanted no part of any aspect of Christian theology. Within a matter of two or three weeks Eric completely changed his manner of dress from dark to lighter colored clothing, and stopped wearing the skeleton hand necklace he always proudly sported. This was all it took for him to realize the futility of his choice against the purposes it was intended to address. We successfully concluded his therapy over a two year period as I followed him through school during his junior and senior years. His goals were to become a chef so he could support himself through college and into a career as both a writer and an actor.

This is one example of a troubled kid who chose to stand out as different and deviant, and yet never got involved in any criminal activity. He had also been into heavy substance use, but that resolved over time as he realized his own desire to protect his mind and his ability to think clearly and purposefully. The concept of deviant doesn't necessarily equate with the concept of bad or evil. To deviate simply means to fall anywhere outside the range of what is considered to be normal or average. Individuality and its appropriate expression and manifestation are extremely important in my work with kids. I try to help them deviate from the norm without drawing negative attention to themselves beyond anything they might be able to withstand. I also try to help them draw their own lines relative to how far they want to deviate away from average before the expression of their individuality becomes counterproductive. Some kids are simply average.

However I have found a rather large percentage of troubled kids to be way above average on many levels. This represents a much larger percentage than for those kids who would register in any way below average as defined by whatever set of group standards you may choose.

Pro-criminality or pro-criminal thinking are two terms commonly used in current literature and discussions about juvenile offenders. These concepts are defined as a mind set whereby participants in criminal activity see absolutely nothing wrong with their choices. There is a commonly held belief among many criminals that the ends justify the means, with the ends being some gain on the part of the offender without any regard for their victim(s). As I stated in a previous chapter many kids get angry about getting caught, but feel no anger toward themselves for having committed a crime. Criminal acts are much more likely to occur in partnership with other participants from the viewpoint of strength in numbers and the loss of individual identity when part of a duo or group. I believe most of the criminal behavior in which kids engage early on is motivated by peer pressure, getting even, and getting ahead materially or in social/peer position or status. Kids rarely put themselves in the place of their victims as a way of trying to imagine how their targets might feel in response to their criminal victimization.

Jesse, one of my clients, and a group of his friends were arrested for assaulting and robbing a pizza delivery man one evening. I knew all three of the kids involved and had an opportunity to interview each of them separately. Each of these kids was angry about getting caught and as a group were motivated by their perceived need for money to spend on alcohol and marijuana. Having already established a high level of trust with these kids I was able to confront them relative to their misperception and misinterpretation of the situation. Jesse was the one who more readily saw the error of his thinking and was able to admit they wouldn't have gotten arrested if they had not done anything wrong in the first place. He was then able to see that his anger should be toward himself and his own actions and bad choices rather than against the victim who identified the kids and the police who arrested them. He also allowed me to guide him into seeing things through the perspective of the way their victim probably experienced the entire incident. All three of the kids were low income, high risk kids with numerous complicating factors present in their lives and histories. Jesse cried as he imagined the reality of the older man probably working more than one job and simply trying to provide for his wife and children. Jesse was motivated by anger fueled in part by his own abandonment and financial hardship resulting from his dad's exit from his life some years earlier. The other kids were able to see things differently as Jesse confronted them with the same approach I had used with him.

It is important to understand none of this work with Jesse and this group of kids would have been possible if I had screwed up in any way in my efforts to build a rapport of trust and mutual respect with these and all of the kids I have served over the years. My position as a psychologist rarely ever puts me in a position of authority over kids. Over the years professionals in other fields who work with kids often get jealous or even threatened by my ability to join professionally with kids in an exchange which actually results in the achievement of very positive goals. When I have worked in the field at various school sites and juvenile placement programs and facilities, it is obvious to every other adult present the kids I serve appreciate and respect me. Numerous times I have been confronted by staff members from other programs challenging my role and job with these kids, suggesting that trying to be their friend was not the answer. Actually, to some extent, that *is* the answer in a professionally appropriate and responsible relationship between me and the kids. I have told several adults I chose my profession wisely and carefully. I get to nurture and support, rather than lord over kids in positions requiring a great deal more control relative to circumstances and context than my job requires. It has always been very clear to me that those adults who were jealous and accused me of being "pro kids" were likely frustrated I was getting greater positive results from these kids more often than these other professionals were able to achieve. The adults who worked as effectively with kids as I did were never negatively impacted by my professional relationships with my kids. Rather they worked collaboratively with me to further insure the success of the kids we shared in our respective roles.

Those who care within other professions don't seem to last very long unless they learn to reach out to and actually reach those kids they seek to serve. In reality not every kid is easy to reach. This only means it is necessary to try harder and with approaches based on a very personalized and individualized style with each kid. Unfortunately those caring professionals, within systems where kids are being confined and supervised by law enforcement staff, are often forced out. This happens as a result of the overwhelming majority of other male and female staff drawn to these environments and driven by strong agendas to break down and dominate those under their charge. Believe me, there are likely very consistent personality profiles which could be developed to identify and describe those who are the most likely to choose jobs which give them authority over troubled kids. Working with troubled kids as part of most any group setting is often quite challenging. However with the right combination of training in sensitivity, realities and circumstances present in the lives of these kids, and in ethical principals and standards, a great deal of progress could be made from which all involved would benefit.

In recent years it seems that more and more people and politicians are focused on incarcerating and punishing offenders rather than making attempts to rehabilitate as was the focus for many decades. There is nothing to be gained by this thinking or the actions taken to simply house and punish without any significant efforts being made to offer juvenile/youthful offenders and adult offenders the opportunities to redirect their lives and futures. I believe very strongly there is a very big difference between older adult offenders and juvenile/youthful offenders relative to the ease with which kids can be redirected compared to older adult populations. This is also true in general mental health populations as well. The reality with kids is that their personality characteristics are still somewhat fluid rather than fixed and rigid as they are with many adults.

After having worked successfully with literally hundreds of troubled kids since 1992 I am convinced that with the right combination of efforts and support kids will make different choices as long as they see it is in their own best interest to do so. The only lasting changes made by kids are those they make for themselves and not out of any sense of guilt or obligation to other adults in their lives. Criminal activity and pro-criminal thinking can easily become permanent ways of living and dealing with life. The incarceration of kids without opportunities to redirect their lives is in itself criminal. Every effort needs to be made to educate the public and change the focus of juvenile justice more toward addressing every aspect of their lives and personalities beyond their observable behaviors and reactions. Scientific evidence indicates that brain development and maturation continue until approximately age 25. Therefore, both juvenile <u>and</u> young adult offenders need redirection and support services rather than incarceration in many cases. Re-entry programs cannot undo the damage of extended confinement for crimes which do not really require such drastic consequences.

One of the biggest problems at the present time is the mentality of those in charge of these programs and the decisions as to how they will be run and staffed. I have watched over the years in Los Angeles and Riverside Counties in California, and now in Mobile, Alabama, as law enforcement agencies and institutions have fortified the blue curtain to exclude the option and need of collaborating with other agencies and professionals. Every effort should be made to expand their resources and outreach to other systems involved in the lives of these kids. Rather than reach out, most (if not all of these systems) have built walls around themselves and their programs, foolishly believing they know everything there is to know about working with offenders of any age. I firmly believe this is based in a need to guarantee and protect their own existence relative to staff, salaries and benefits. Law enforcement officials – not officers - and related staff within all environments are some of the highest paid workers in the country. They tend to be very territorial and secretive in order to protect themselves from outside scrutiny and accountability. I have said many times it is more often about money and numbers with many agencies and less about effectiveness and desirable outcomes. This is self-preservation in its ugliest and most destructive form.

At this point in our national history I also firmly believe the climate of secrecy, supremacy, domination, and an arrogant disregard for ethics and integrity allow for serious misuses of power. We have seen this clearly within politics, corporations, and religious institutions whose leaders appear to believe themselves to be above the laws and rights of people here and around the world. This is gang mentality at its worst, existing and modeled at all levels of government and business. It is no wonder kids think in the ways they do, believing it is okay to break the laws and violate the rights of others as long as they don't get caught. Even our top political figures try to cover up their misuses of power by trying to put a new spin on their original reasoning and justification which were, in many cases, outright lies as well. Criminality at any level and within any environment or context serves the same purposes and follows the same attempts at illogical justification as is found with kids and adults involved in street crime. Even officials within the so-called justice systems are often corrupt and yet protected by those who hire and supervise them as was the case in the situation I outlined in chapter three. It is time for a change if we ever want to change the thinking of our younger generations who witness these scandals and coverups on a profoundly frequent basis.

I think it is time for every professional in this country to be forced to attend regularly mandated classes and workshops regarding laws and ethics relative to every existing profession and religious institution. We have all lost sight of what is important in this country and in the world as evidenced by the arrogant positions exhibited even within religious organizations in this country and around the world. There is a natural progression in the development of pro-criminal thinking and it is often fueled by rampant greed and arrogance. How can we expect kids to make different choices when they see adult leaders in many settings pursuing their own personal and institutional agendas without any regard for the laws and rights of others? Everything in our culture needs to be reprioritized to match the true meaning and philosophies of democracy and freedom. There can be no positive gains when systems and individuals within our country are, or believe themselves to be above public scrutiny and accountability. There are so many disparities within our society whereby the rich make progress at the expense of the poor and those less able to defend themselves. There is no context in which this is more apparent than in our criminal justice systems, and especially at the juvenile offender level. Systems of checks and balances which are supposedly in place over any organization should be independent of those working within the systems regardless of their nature and purpose. Outside public scrutiny and accountability are essential if we are to avoid corruption and any misuses of power and authority.

The current political climate in this country which is dominated and controlled by special interest groups has given rise to the '*right*-makes-right' philosophy as a way of governing and otherwise running this country. People in the general public are misinformed and often lied to relative to realities existing in the lives of many ordinary and vulnerable people. The US Patriot Act in conjunction with the Homeland Security Act have given more authority to law enforcement agencies without any significant and effective use of independent monitoring. There is too much power in the hands of a relative few under the guise of "antiterrorism", to the point even kids suspected of street-related crimes can be treated as terrorists under the provision of the US Patriot Act. The general public has very little awareness of the level of power and secrecy provided by this legislation which opens the doors for private citizens, who have no involvement in terrorist activity, to be treated as urban terrorists. I saw this happen on an extensive scale in the last few years I worked in California as represented by the example I gave earlier in this book about the senior probation officer and the assistant district attorney. I even heard a law enforcement agent giving a talk to the kids in the lock-in placement program where I worked in juvenile hall openly bragging about the equipment purchased and the outrageous salaries paid to local law enforcement agents and agencies. He thought it was funny he had access to so many resources which could be used to fight street crime, and was using this information to let kids know they were nothing more than terrorists in his eyes if they engaged in any form of criminal activity.

The kids I talked with after this presentation were shocked at the reality of being listed as terrorists and reacted with a "we'll show them" kind of response. This kind of bravado allowed by the US Patriot Act gives law enforcement officials the opportunity to misuse their power. Furthermore, it only increases the determination of kids with a pro-criminality mindset to see this as a challenge. I witnessed an unimaginable level of the abuse of power while in California since 9/11. Kids were picked up and held for hours in secret locations without any written record of this ever occurring. The abuse of power resulted in a ridiculous show of force for even the most minor of offenses. Kids were questioned without adult or legal representation, and were detained without their parents or families having any awareness of their whereabouts. These kids were released without being charged with any crime and were sent back into the streets even more angry than before, and with an increased determination to win the war of terrorism being waged against *them*.

The same tactics were used with adult offenders, but only when they could be ultimately charged with a crime even if they had to be provoked into "resisting arrest" or "assaulting a police officer". As with the kids there was never any record of these adults being detained without probable cause. They had to appear in court to face charges which were often times dismissed or treated as misdemeanor crimes which would never have occurred without harassment from law enforcement officers. Most of these acts were targeted against African American and Hispanic individuals likely due to their vulnerability and limited ability to pay for private legal representation. The fact that juvenile offenders are not judged by a jury gives rise to unbelievable misuses of power and authority since documentation is simply the word of a kid (terrorist) against law enforcement personnel. More care is taken with adult offenders who might have to go to trial before a jury in adult courtrooms. This is accepted, but not discussed, as common practice in the juvenile justice systems. It is a clear mirror image of the tactics being put in place and utilized by our current political administration in this country and around the world.

In Alabama the juvenile courts I have knowledge of commit kids to mental hospitals, run by the Alabama Department of Mental Health and Mental Retardation, when they cannot be legally charged and detained. Such court ordered hospitalizations are referred to as "evaluations" and last anywhere from one to two full weeks. Kids are then released to local state funded mental health clinics in many cases with erroneous diagnoses and on medications clearly not needed. Patient rights are violated and only against low income, disadvantaged families covered by Medicaid. The justification given to families is that juvenile records can be sealed. However, in reality medical records are permanent records and do not fall under this option. Kids are afraid to come forward because they do not want to face public humiliation of having been incorrectly labeled as "mentally ill". I am certain that these hospitalizations wrongly inflate statistics reported by race and socioeconomic status nationwide relative to minorities and mental illness. However, this keeps all of these related and interconnected agencies in business and fully staffed. All of this can be backed up with proof.

Major changes are needed relative to the pro-criminal mindset of our political leaders at all levels of government. The American people need an itemized account of money designated for protection against terrorists and terrorist attacks which were misappropriated and misspent around the country by local law enforcement agencies. The kinds of vehicles and surveillance equipment now owned by many relatively small town law enforcement agencies only feeds the egos of the officers and does not match the needs of these small communities or the needs of the country as a whole. The deception of fear and the cover of secrecy presented repeatedly to the American people has given people in positions of power and authority the opportunities to misuse their power and authority. These injustices trickle down from the federal level all the way to local levels. This has likely resulted in an increase in the numbers of people incarcerated with very little if any effort made to rehabilitate them. It has also likely created criminals and sentences people didn't deserve and wouldn't have received if they had not been harassed by so-called "peace officers". Based on my awareness of things said by law enforcement personnel, the idea is clearly to get as many *potential* criminals into the 'system' as possible so they can be monitored before or until they do something really big. I firmly believe these factors are responsible for our more overcrowded detention centers and prisons, and for recent increases in violent crimes nationwide. Furthermore, I firmly believe this was money MIS-spent which could have been utilized more effectively toward preventing rather than compelling and provoking crime.

With the current political and social climates in our country, the number of complicating factors for troubled youth is only rising. Very little money is being spent in any arena to provide resources needed by low and middle income families. Our educational systems are failing to meet the educational needs of kids of all ages, and represent the same kinds of closed systems as are present within governmental and legal systems. Much of this is fueled by the lack of concern and regard for others espoused by religious extremists within our own country who seek only to promote their non-mainstream agendas of supremacy and self righteousness. Most of the so-labeled "faith-based" programs only seek to further their cause of spreading their views around the country and the globe, lacking any true sense of altruism or respect for other religious or even spiritual points of view. Their goals are to simply increase their membership numbers, rather than do anything just for the good of others, representing a high level of deception as well. People here and abroad are paying a price for this kind of arrogance and elitism.

My hope for the future is to be able to combat these realities through the nonprofit youth center I am working to establish under the name of Liberating Youth, Inc. All of these points will be made through the center to the kids and to the community to help them understand both the obvious and sometimes invisible obstacles they face everyday. With the youth center I will have the opportunity to provide these kids with the skills needed to guard themselves against obstacles which can only be fought by bettering themselves in all aspects of their lives. Knowledge is power and I hope to inspire the kids we will serve to be both aware of and informed about every factor in their lives which could serve to keep them down. The only way at this point to fight the larger corrupt systems is to teach and empower kids and families how to expose them and shut them down. Once kids begin to improve the choices they make and better their chances in life then there will be less need for incarceration and involvement of law enforcement officials. The fight has to be at the community level and not just against the systems and leaders specifically. We have to teach kids to act and be smarter than those who would seek to hold them back. Education is the key to the future for all who fall into the underdog category in life. Kids would laugh when I told them they could actually shut down juvenile hall and juvenile probation if they would simply stop breaking the law and giving these agencies the opportunity to control them and their destinies. While they agreed with me and liked the idea, they couldn't see how this would ever happen. It is my goal to make this belief a reality in the future.

Chapter V

Substance Use and Addiction

Drugs and alcohol are two of the biggest obstacles kids face relative to educational success and lifestyle choices. The two biggest factors which lead to substance use are availability and peer influence more than peer pressure. It's like the old adage of "everybody's doing it." Unfortunately the contexts in which these kids live are full of opportunities for kids to drink and use. In many cases this is true both within the home context and out in the community. When you look at the temptation to drink and use, coupled with the wide variety of complicating factors present in the lives of troubled kids, it is no wonder they begin to experiment with things which will dull the harshness of many of the realities in their lives. I tell kids no one sets up a goal of becoming an alcoholic and/or a drug addict. It just happens, especially when kids and adults fail to pay attention to their increasing use of substances coupled with the emotions and circumstances motivating them to seek different forms of escape.

Kids in this day and time do not seem to be afraid to engage in many different potentially harmful experiences and activities. Early experimentation with drugs and alcohol are often quite common first choices. Not every kid who drinks will use drugs. Nor will every kid who smokes marijuana try harder substances. However, the initial choice to drink or use even tobacco opens the gate to try other things if for no other reason than curiosity. Adolescents in general have a very limited sense of danger given their abilities to convince themselves 'nothing can go wrong for me'. Because kids have very little fear about danger to themselves and their bodies and minds, fear tactics do not serve as a deterrent to risky behaviors. They see others engaging in risky activities and over time come to see such activity as simply part of the norm within their frame of reference. Boredom is one of the biggest contributing factors to ongoing substance use. There is a lot of time taken up by substance use from the efforts to obtain the substance, use it or drink it, and experience the effects induced by the substance. For kids with too much time on their hands it is very easy to fall into this cycle as a way of simply filling time and fighting boredom in many cases.

Then there is the factor of socializing with friends. Unfortunately many adults and kids come to believe substance use makes them more appealing and helps them to make accomplishments and overcome different factors only when they are under the influence of some type of substance. Shyness, social awkwardness, boredom, anxiety, and numerous other intrinsic inhibiting factors simply go away while drunk or high. These realities then become reinforcements in the desire to continue using and drinking. People in general fail to understand that the physiological effects of substance use are nothing more than the bodies reaction to the presence of something not naturally found in the body. The reaction is simply the body's attempt to fight off and contend with the invasion of something foreign and is usually experienced as a state of euphoria. The fact that in most cases the effects are pleasant only reinforces the desire to use and drink again. Because kids have trouble with limits there is a strong tendency to overindulge in many of their activities. Even if the experience ultimately makes them sick, the initial experience of the induced altered state brings them back after a period of recovery.

Addiction is also one of the biggest obstacles in reaching these kids through therapy and other attempts to help or assist them. I do not believe a kid should be expected to be completely clean and sober for someone to try to intervene on their behalf. It is completely futile to work with a kid while they are directly under the influence, but it is an unrealistic expectation that a kid will achieve and maintain sobriety, and then seek out services of assistance. Furthermore, substance use cannot be the only or even the primary focus of every interaction adults have with kids. It is important to accept it as a reality, with the awareness that as a therapist, educator, counselor, or mentor we have no control over their activities outside our offices. It is also important to see it as a byproduct of the FLAGS identified in my first book and in early chapters in this text. If we try to take a position of authority over them, kids will often see this as a challenge to their rights to make whatever choices they want to make. The process will then become more of a competition, rather than an attempted intervention of trying to deal with every aspect of a kid's nature and needs. Unfortunately, the more you tell a kid they can't do something, the more likely they are to do it if for no other reason than proving they can. How many of us as adults make this same mistake out of sheer stubbornness? As I've said before, just because we can do something doesn't mean se should.

Kids fail to see they are actually addicted to something until they are forced to face this reality. One of the best interventions is to find out exactly how many times they drink or use within a given week or month. If their use is daily then challenge them to go for one week without drinking or using. Ask them to pay attention to how hard it is to resist the temptation, and encourage them to be totally honest about their success at their next session with you. This will help make them aware of the existence of a problem which they and only they can address. Accept the fact they and only they can make the decision to address the problem and be patient with them. Help them identify both the positives and negatives related to their substance use. Openly challenge their belief of things being better when they are drunk or stoned, but do not make this a confrontation. Offer everything simply as something for them to think about and give them the option as to how to deal with it in their own way and in their own time. To make sobriety a prerequisite for treatment will cancel out the opportunity to work with them on the complicating factors in their lives which cause them to engage in excessive behaviors in the first place. The use of my Roberts FLAGS Model is the best way to help them literally see how and why they choose to act out rather than deal with their problems.

If you are looking for a rationale as to why they should not drink and use, focus on health issues; not as scare tactics, but as realities they will have to deal with someday. It also a good idea to have them look at others around them and honestly examine the state of their lives. Help them to see that people who are addicted have very limited options in life. Get them to see how all consuming the practices associated with addiction really are. Try to help them see what it is like to be around people who are addicted, and yet be clean and sober themselves. Focus on the realities that people who are addicted generally are not motivated to do anything positive with their lives. Point out the reality of addiction taking away the pleasure of getting high and simply becoming a need to maintain a certain physiological state in order to avoid withdrawal. Also point out the reality of everyone eventually having to make a choice to stop using and/or drinking in order to stay healthy and alive as well. Be careful to deal with the reality of everyone having the right to do whatever they want as along as it is not harmful to others. Point out how foolish it is to do things harmful to themselves even though they can choose to do so. Tell them regular use of alcohol and drugs will eventually even hurt those who care about the user. These approaches give kids the option to see that it truly is in their best interest to control all forms of substance use. Kids will rationalize alcohol, tobacco, and marijuana as not being so-called "hard drugs". Methamphetamines and cocaine-related drugs are even considered by kids to be moderate drugs. Heroin and LSD are the ones which scare them the most, especially when coupled with the idea of shooting up. As a professional you may have to settle for controlled use of marijuana and alcohol as a success, with the hope they possess some degree of control over their use. Like it or not, many people drink and smoke weed. It may take them getting in trouble on a job, at school, or with law enforcement before they realize the true consequences of regular use. If you have laid the groundwork they can build on it in the future as needed.

Always keep in mind successes with troubled kids are often few and far between. Also remember success for this population comes in less obvious forms than with higher functioning individuals who can more easily secure jobs, make plans for the future, achieve moderate to high academic standards, stay out of trouble, and stay clean and sober without much effort. Even one week of avoiding trouble at school or with law enforcement is a huge accomplishment for many of these kids. A month of perfect attendance, fewer problems at home, and an improvement in their overall outlook are tremendous successes. Each success should be acknowledged and reinforced by giving the kid a sense of their ability to control their lives, choices and destinies. It is also important to help them see how each success is in their own best interest and not for the benefit of others. While other people in their lives may benefit from their accomplishments this cannot be, nor should it ever be, the reason presented to them as to why they should want to do better. Never try guilt tripping them into doing something solely for mom or dad. The only person and perception which matters is the kid sitting in front of you along with what she/he thinks and learns about themselves in the process. If you can learn to be proud of relatively minor successes imagine how you will feel when you see a previously troubled kid graduate from high school knowing you were part of the process which helped graduation become a reality.

One particular intervention which is especially helpful for kids is to help them understand how much of the illegal activity in which they engage actually reflects various useful skills. Many kids who use drugs regularly often deal drugs in order to support their habit. Unfortunately a significant degree of criminal activity arises from their need to support and fund their drug use. Kids are generally shocked and amused to realize how many of their illegal actions build and develop useful skills relative to possible future legitimate career choices. Think about how much time and energy goes into establishing a drug dealing business. Kids learn a lot about planning, purchasing, market supply and demand, warehousing, pricing, competition, marketing, and establishing and maintaining a repeat customer base. While this may sound a little absurd, it is all true, and is helpful in getting kids to see the need to redirect their efforts and talents toward more positive and less risky legal ventures. It is not about kids changing with the goal of becoming someone different, it is about helping them use their energy in the right ways and changing their mindsets and frames of reference. The same energy which goes into illegal and risky behaviors is the exact same energy they would use for more beneficial and legal choices. It's about helping them to work differently with who they already are! These insights can actually encourage kids to finish school and even consider going to college to study different areas of business. Give them credit for their ingenuity and at the same time help them see and understand all of the reasons why engaging in any form of illegal business activities is completely wrong and immoral. Help them look at the devastating effects on the lives of those to whom they sell. Also get them to imagine the impact drug use has on the families of those to whom they sell. At the same time it is important to clearly point out the risks of continuing a career based in crime. However, it is really hard to get kids to let go of these pursuits given the fact these activities are very lucrative. However, it is necessary to try and get them to stop before it is too late. Give them an awareness of what even a juvenile criminal record can do to jeopardize their futures.

I cannot stress enough the need to look beyond what a kid does and see them for who they are deep inside and to see them for who they can become. No effective work can be accomplished with a kid unless they have total trust in your word and work. Kids must know you are there for their benefit only and not to serve some conscious or unconscious hidden agenda you may have on the table or in your head. Kids today are too sophisticated for adults to be able to pull something over on them. Troubled kids have usually had so many negative and damaging interactions with other adults before they got to you that you will have to work very hard to establish and maintain trust all along the way. Kids are very perceptive to and sensitive to efforts to manipulate or control them and will react by shutting you out or walking away. Always admit when you are wrong and apologize, and at the same time seek to repair any inadvertent damage which may have been done to the relationship you have worked to establish with your client, student or child. The use of positive psychology approaches allows everyone to emphasize the goodness in each kid and to then identify the obstacles blocking the emergence, growth and development of the goodness present in each child you meet.

Do not ever be hesitant to "join" with a kid in your efforts to assist them. The concept of joining is a family therapy term whereby the caregiver literally forms a bond of interest in and positive regard for their clients. This, of course, must be accomplished within appropriate professional limits and boundaries, and only within the context where assistance is being offered. Never make promises you cannot or may not want to fulfill outside the therapeutic or professional association. Kids will only get hurt and you will become like every other adult in their lives who has let them down. Never cross the line and bring a troubled kid into your personal life on any level. You must seek only to help them find and create what they have with you as a professional outside the professional context and within their own world and contexts. Many caregivers try too hard and cross lines which must never be crossed both for the sake of the kids and for the sake of the service provider. You cannot be everything to everyone, and to try this is both futile and foolish. The goal is to teach and empower rather than foster dependence and the appearance of a relationship which could never exist in reality. You can really be their "friend", but only within that professional context.

The need to look beyond what kids do and see them for who they are and can become is critical when working with high risk, troubled kids. Do not be afraid of fowl language or curse words. Let them speak in any manner which will allow them to express themselves comfortably. Never let them cuss you out, but do not react if words like fuck, shit, piss, bitch, pussy or other such words if this is the way they need to tell you a story or details about their lives. After all, these are the kinds of words many kids use when speaking to their friends. The single most important thing in therapeutic interactions is to have the client talk with you. You can help them at some point to understand when such language is and is not appropriate, but LET THEM TALK! Do not be such a prude. This will set up barriers between you and every troubled kid and can be easily avoided by simply focusing only on what is really important - the need to connect with them and get to know everything about them you need to know and understand in order to help them.

Furthermore, if you are not comfortable working with this population of kids, DON"T! However, if your heart goes out to them and you want to reach them, learn how to do so effectively. Be like a friend to them without crossing professional lines and boundaries. One of the biggest compliments a kid can give you is for them to refer to you as their "homie" or "dog". This level of comfort is a sign they see you as someone who they can trust to care about, help and protect them. At the same time remind them, if and when necessary, you are their therapist, teacher, mentor, etc. You will know when it is time to do this when they invite you to a party or to hang out with them and their friends. Never cross these kinds of lines, but be appreciative of their high regard for you. Have them imagine what it would actually be like for you and for them relative to everyone's ability to have fun at such an event or gathering. They will readily see it wouldn't work. After all, what kid would be comfortable drinking, using, or committing criminal acts in front of a professional whose opinion of them really matters? And what professional would be willing to risk everything just to be their buddy on this level?

A successful professional relationship with any kid can only be established if the kid feels and sees you are real and genuinely care about them. You must be interested in getting to know them on all levels before issues of addiction, criminality, and other critical matters can be dealt with and resolved to their benefit and satisfaction. All interactions must be appropriately informal to the deepest level possible with each individual kid. The limits on confidentiality must be clearly and thoroughly revealed at the onset of the initial contact, even when it comes to information which will or will not be shared with their parents or guardians. Unless an issue or behavior is life threatening, I never reveal such information to other adults under any circumstances. I have told many parents and other adults that I am not there to be their detective. Furthermore, I believe very firmly if a parent doesn't see or even suspect negative behavior, then it is not my obligation to reveal my insights to them except under very specific circumstances. I would never reveal anything, except as mandated by law, unless I have cleared it with the kid and have given them the chance to deal with others on their own first. I make all of this very clear to parents and other adults at the outset of my interactions with kids. At the same time I assure them I will not withhold any information I believe poses a danger to the kid or to adults involved in their lives. I cover all of this in front of the kid and during the initial contact. Most adults readily agree, and appreciate and understand the fact kids generally will not talk to adults close to them, including parents, about every aspect of their lives. Parents and other adults are usually appreciative of the fact their child has someone to talk to who they can trust. Without this arrangement upfront there is little chance of success with the kid. Kids will talk about virtually everything in their lives if they know they can trust the adult with whom they are speaking.

The only time I ever violated this position was with Jose. He was 13 at the time and would come into my office stoned every week. His mother was a very stern and strict woman and was blaming me for the lack of progress with her son. I warned him two weeks in a row that if he came back to my office stoned I would take him out to his mom and show her why nothing was working. He didn't believe me and left me no choice on the third week after my warning. After my intake interview his mom never came into the office with him except for that first session. This is often the case for parents of troubled kids who are simply looking for someone else to "fix" their kid. I never penalize a kid for the lack of parental involvement and never discourage parental participation. Jose's mom would drop him off at the clinic and would wait for him in the car. He would go behind the building and hit is marijuana pipe before he came into the office. By the time I saw him he was as high as a kite and thought this was really funny.

At this third session I told Jose I was taking him out to his mom in the parking lot. At first he didn't believe me until I stood up and told him to come with me. At that point he got really angry, cussing me along the way to the parking lot. All I could do was remind him that I had warned him, but assuring him I was not going to take the blame from his mom for his lack of progress. His mom saw us coming and got out of her car. She wanted to know what was wrong and I told her to look at her son. She didn't see how stoned he was, so I told her what was happening. To his surprise I made him empty out his pockets in front of his mom, exposing his bag of weed, his pipe, and a lighter. He was enraged with me and his mom was enraged with him. I told mom Jose's use of marijuana before our sessions was the reason no progress was being made. She made him get into the car and assured me she would handle this when they got home. I told him I would be here for him if and when he wanted to come back. He yelled some obscenities at me assuring me he would never be back to see me again. While I felt bad about all of this, I clearly knew he left me know choice. Out of my work with hundreds of kids over the years this was the only time I had to resort to such measures and was the only time a kid was angry with me as he or she left my office.

After a year or so had passed I was on one of the units at juvenile hall. As I entered the unit I heard a voice announce to the other kids and staff, "that guy's a rat!" This is the very worst thing a kid could ever saw about me or anyone and I had to address him in front of the other kids. When I identified the kid I was surprised to see it was Jose. I walked over to the table where he was sitting and said, "Hello Jose. Long time no see." He seemed surprised and embarrassed that I would approach him. Virtually every kid on this unit knew me and I couldn't let this go with his accusation of me being a rat. I said to him, "so you think I'm a rat, huh? Why don't you tell these kids and staff I ratted you out to your mommy about coming into my office stoned every week." He was horrified and knew he had really screwed up, then refusing to speak to me. I told him, "I'm still here if you need me." He finally looked up and said, "no way. Fuck you man!" The other kids laughed and I called the kid I needed to see into the office on the unit. The kid who knew me was really pissed off that Jose had disrespected me like he did. He wanted to jump him for me, but I insisted that would not be necessary since I had handled it in a way which didn't allow Jose to get away with what he said. I had to spend a little time with my other client assuring him I am not a rat and had to describe the reasons why I took the actions I did both a year earlier, and on this particular day. He fully understood and agreed to let it go with regards to retaliation towards Jose.

Another year passed and I saw Jose again in juvenile hall. I approached him and simply reminded him "I am still here for you if you ever need to talk." This time he simply said "no", and I gave him one of my business cards in case he changed his mind. One year later Jose was back in juvenile hall. Before I could even run into him he sent word to me through the staff he needed to see me. With this incarceration Jose was facing serious charges and was likely on his way to the California Youth Authority for a number of years. When I met with him the first thing he did was apologize to me for his disrespect. I assured him it really was okay and nothing he had ever done or said had changed the way I feel about working with him. He started crying and gave me the details of everything that had happened in his life since our first meetings some three years earlier. There was nothing I could do but listen to him and try to help him find some hope for the future beyond his impending sentence to CYA.

Jose told me he wanted to explain why he wouldn't talk to me when he had the chance initially. He told me about having been molested by a neighbor in his neighborhood when he was 12. The incident had been reported and the man was arrested and convicted of the molestation, but the incident had been very embarrassing to Jose and he didn't want to talk with anyone about it. Jose had no idea of the impact it had on him psychologically and didn't realize until this moment with me that talking about it with someone he could trust was exactly what he had needed all along. He was amazed at how easy it was to talk with me about this. I simply asked him a couple of yes or no kinds of questions so I would have a general idea of the extent of the abuse. He didn't have to give me details I could easily figure out from his yes or no responses. I felt so bad for him during these moments, but he readily understood his unwillingness and inability to talk with me previously was all his choice and had nothing to do with me or my efforts to connect with him previously. He also was able to see for himself he lacked the maturity three years earlier needed to see and handle things differently before now.

We spent three hours together that afternoon in an office within juvenile hall. This session was one of the saddest and most difficult sessions I have experienced before or since, and yet it was one of the most rewarding experiences of my career. Jose readily agreed if he could have talked with me previously he probably would not be facing several years at CYA. I helped him understand himself in ways he had never seen before with anyone else. We addressed the wounds left by the abuse and gave him ways to understand the incident and the impact on him to give him the relief he needed about his involvement and his future. As we stood up at the end of the session I went around the desk to hug Jose. He took my hand before he moved toward the door and said, "Doc, you'll see I'm going to be somebody someday. Don't be surprised in a few years when I show up at your office and prove that to you." We both had tears in our eyes as he spoke and I assured him I had the utmost respect for him regardless of anything he had done that got him into trouble. I also assured him I would be looking forward to his visit and to his future success.

These are the moments and memories which make it all worthwhile. I never heard from Jose again since that last encounter. There is no way for me to know how his life has turned out, or to know if he is even still alive for that matter. But, I know in my heart Jose connected with me that day like he had probably never connected with anyone else in his life. Because of that opportunity to talk with him and offer him some insight and guidance into some very complicated and difficult issues I know we both benefited tremendously from the experience. Never assume you haven't gotten through to any kid. Who knows, if I had stayed in California Jose may have come to my office looking for me. The one thing I know for sure is neither Jose nor I will ever forget the time we shared just before he left for CYA. Above all else Jose knew I genuinely cared for and about him. This is all it takes for one person to make a difference in the life of a kid.

This is one example of how kids try to cope with complicating factors by using and drinking. The real tragedy in this whole story is that Jose's mom didn't care enough to get more deeply involved in her son's treatment. She should have told me about Jose's history of sexual abuse, even if he had told her not to do so. It is tragic when people are unable or unwilling to see how all of us tend to act out emotion-based anxiety and depression. The lack of opportunities to gain assistance from adults who can be trusted to care and to offer assistance is tragic. When experiences and perceptions get buried rather than dealt with the severity of the experiences and circumstances determines the levels of helplessness and hopelessness which result and lead to acting out behaviors such as substance use and criminal activity. Anyone might develop pro-criminal thinking after experiencing any extreme violation or injustice, especially as a child who cannot defend her/himself adequately anyway. If Jose's mother had recognized and understood the need for Jose to face and deal with his emotions then Jose would likely have been able to make better choices as he grew older. Believe me, it is never too late to offer assistance. But, also believe me when I say it is extremely important not to become another complicating factor in a kid's life by mishandling your interactions with any kid. It will be far better for every kid for us to do nothing than to do anything which makes their lives worse than they already are! Please don't ever let that happen.

Chapter VI

Sexual Issues and Concerns

The adolescent years are often a time of confusion and stress especially relative to sexual issues and concerns. It can be made more complicated with kids trying to figure out whether or not to become sexually active and even worse for kids who are dealing with sexual orientation issues. Kids nowadays are much more open to sexual activity and I think it is absolutely absurd that kids cannot be taught everything there is to know about sex in so-called sexual education classes. So many adults, especially people who are conservative and religious, are overly afraid of dealing with the sexuality of kids both as parents and professionals in various settings. Too many people have their heads buried in the sand when it comes to the realities of sexual temptations kids face even beginning in elementary school. Kids talk to each other and will make up the details if they are not given the full amount of information required for them to make informed decisions relative to remaining abstinent or deciding to become sexually active. Conservatives have way too much power in deciding what is appropriate relative to sexuality and it is time for law makers to put a stop to the fantasy of abstinence being the most likely choice by today's teenagers.

It is always interesting to me to learn how little parents and other adults actually know about what is going on in the private lives of kids. As I described earlier, kids are sneaky and have many ways through the technology of today to engage in all kinds of activities without any awareness on the part of parents and other adults. Kids often have secret codes and language when it comes to discussing private matters, and especially relative to sex. Recently kids were wearing gel bracelets out in public in front of every adult in their lives both at home and out in the communities and schools. It was eventually revealed that the colors of the bracelets represented various sexual acts in which kids either would participate or had already been willing to participate. I learned about this from one of my female clients I was meeting with at a school site. She was very open about the bracelet system and how it worked. The most shocking aspect of it for me was the reality that in some areas a gang-like mentality was forming within some groups of girls which would actually result in open confrontation and violence. I never got the whole picture, but I got enough information to realize how alarming it was. Even very young girls in elementary school and middle school were wearing bracelets indicating they had allowed boys to engage in various levels of touching. Other bracelets indicated participation in oral sex, all the way to vaginal and anal sex as well usually by older girls. Girls who were willing to engage in sexual behaviors were referred to by boys as "girls with benefits". This system spread around the country and went on for months before adults became aware of what was actually going on in the lives of their kids.

With the Internet, cell phones, and other portable devices kids are in almost constant contact with each other both locally and even around the world if they so choose. Chat rooms for kids are quite common, offering a rather rapid means of spreading information to every other kid with access to the same communication possibilities. Web sites and chat rooms can even be used to ruin the reputations of kids or to threaten them with violence if they are unpopular, or are being brutalized by bullies. In my experiences, girls are much more brutal and ruthless than boys could ever hope to be in many different contexts. Because people fail to see the realities of what is happening there is a very strong double standard when it comes to punishing boys much more severely than girls for the same kids of offenses. This is true when it comes to sexual activity as well. Males are always given more serious consequences and penalties for inappropriate or illegal sexual contact than females receive. This was recently very evident in the case of a female school teacher who was sexually involved with a middle school boy. She received no jail time. If it had been a male involved with a female student the outcome likely would have been drastically different. Sexual misconduct is sexual misconduct no matter who commits the acts.

One of the most unfair situations relative to sexual activity between adolescents involves kids who are romantically involved and one (usually the boy) turns 18 and continues to have sex with his now underage girlfriend. I have known of cases where boys were charged with statutory rape for a sexual relationship that had been going on for quite some time before the change in age. There are girls who take advantage of boys sexually as well, and are equally as harassing in some of their interactions as any boy could ever hope to be. However, again the consequences for girls are generally less severe or even non-existent in some cases even when adults in various contexts witness the behaviors. Boys are still viewed as being the villain if they are the offender, and as the "bitch" or wimp if they are the victim. Sexual standards must become equally applicable to both genders given the realities of sexual interactions in general in today's culture.

Safe sex has two different meanings for today's kids. Some practice safe sex with regards to preventing both sexually transmitted diseases and pregnancy. However there are other kids who forget about sexually transmitted diseases and focus only on preventing pregnancy without any consideration of the spreading or contracting of diseases. This is likely the main cause for the increase of sexual experiences which do not involve vaginal intercourse. It is important to teach kids that anyone who is infected with some form of STD is contagious through virtually any form of sexual intimacy. Kissing is still safe unless there is the presence of some form of oral infection. Mutual masturbation is relatively safe unless one or both partners are infected with diseases which can be spread by touch. If one partner has any infectious secretions, sores, or warts then the infections can be spread if partners touch themselves after touching their infected partner, or by being touched by an infected partner if that partner had touched themself first. These kinds of contacts transfer bodily fluids and are potentially risky with the presence of any sort of infection – bacterial, fungal, or viral. The same logic applies with both oral and anal sex as well. While non-vaginal intercourse will eliminate the possibility of pregnancy, there is still the possibility of the transmission of STD's.

This kid of logic on the part of kids requires all aspects of sexual activity be addressed in sexual education classes. Girls are still technically virgins as defined by the act of vaginal intercourse being the means of taking a girl's virginity. This relates to the concept of limited sexual encounters supposedly practiced during the Victorian era as though the only sexual experiences strictly involve vaginal intercourse, in the so-called missionary position, between a man and a woman who have never had any other sexual partners. Very few adults limit their sexual practices to this range of intimacy. If the truth from the past could be known, it is unlikely that very many people throughout time limited their sexual experiences to such a quaint and acceptable act as vaginal sex in the missionary position. With all of the media exposure to and promotion of sex today people are much more likely than ever to experiment sexually than at any other point in the history of the United States. And kids are likely to be even more open to and about sexual experiences than many of their adult counterparts. Based on my awareness of sexual activity from the perspective of the kids I have worked with over the years, even many of the girls who pride themselves in being virginal by abstaining from vaginal intercourse are the very ones who come with other "benefits" as reported by the boys they are often dating. Sexual activity is sexual activity no matter how you look at it. This reality and the realities of the level of sexual activity in which kids of today are engaging require a very thorough education in all aspects of sexuality rather than the watered down and unrealistically limited sex education programs being taught in most settings.

Kids appreciate this kind of openness and honesty when I have shared these considerations with them over the years. I talk to both boys and girls about these factors, admittedly using less vulgar or graphic language with the girls than I might use with the boys. However, the messages are the same. I also try to get girls to understand that in reality a lot of adolescent boys are only after sex. This is especially true with troubled youth who have very little awareness of how appropriate romantic/dating interactions look given the lack of appropriate role models in the contexts where they live and learn. Some of the most significant complicating factors in the lives and histories of troubled kids are directly related to the sexual indiscretions and obvious mishandling of dating and marriage on the part of their parents and parental figures. It is not uncommon for kids to have parents who have kids with multiple sexual partners, even with mothers and fathers acting out sexually at about the same rates. A lot of kids know very little about love and the realities that sex without love can easily confuse even the brightest and most experienced adults. Adults and kids are equally as likely to look for love in all the wrongs places without realizing or identifying their sense of desperately needing and wanting to be loved by someone - anyone. I have told girls in front of boys that some guys are dogs. The girls laugh and the boys ultimately agree given their admission of frequent score keeping of the number of virgins they "bag". I have actually worked with boys who put marks on belt buckles as a public display of their sexual conquests.

It is extremely alarming to me that many kids, and especially girls, believe having a baby will solve many of their problems. It is quite common for girls to want a baby as a way of having someone to love unconditionally who will love them unconditionally in return. Unfortunately many girls believe the only way to keep a boy is by having sex with him, or even worse believing they can get a boy to stay with them if they get pregnant. Some girls have openly lied to boys about being on birth control and have even resorted to poking holes in a condom with a pin in the hopes of getting pregnant as well. None of this ever works out as planned, again emphasizing the need of teaching kids about every aspect of sexuality, including the realties and responsibilities associated with parenting. In my book <u>At the Mercy of Externals: Righting Wrongs and Protecting Kids, 2nd Edition</u>, I have proposed teaching the concepts presented within that text to kids as early as middle school, but certainly by their first year of high school. The focus of my theories emphasizes adult roles and responsibilities and the resulting negative impact on kids when those roles and responsibilities are not met to the fullest extent possible. With the right combination of information, insight, and facts kids will be better prepared to make fully informed decisions about many of the choices they face during their adolescent years.

Sexual orientation and its related diversity are much more openly discussed among kids now than at any other point in our history. It is not uncommon to find boys and girls who openly and comfortably identify themselves as either bisexual or homosexual. Kids are much more accepting of these realties than are many adults, and people in general are much more accepting of sexual diversity among girls than they are with boys or males in general. I clearly believe this represents a double standard perpetuated primarily by heterosexual males in this country. Heterosexual males of all ages are commonly turned on by sexual activity between females, and are absolutely repulsed by even the notion of sexual intimacy between two males. Females together are hot and sexy in the eyes of straight males, and the males who engage in sexual activity with other males are somehow less than masculine if they engage in any form of homosexual activity. Homosexual acts are homosexual acts regardless of whether they occur between male couples or female couples. I think many heterosexual males are afraid of male-to-male sex, possibly having thought about or even experienced it themselves at some point in their lives. The teachings of religious radicals do not help any of this either. I have never met anyone who will tell me that any aspect of their true sexual nature is based in choice. Heterosexuals never even have to think about being straight. However, homosexual individuals have to choose how they are going to deal with their sexual orientation throughout their whole lives, with 'how to deal with it' being the only choice involved. This is a very significant issue for adolescents as many adolescent suicides successfully carried out are thought to be related to issues of homosexuality and the pressures to conform to heterosexual standards and expectations.

I always ask where an adolescent kid falls in the spectrum of sexual orientation which I believe exists as a continuum from completely heterosexual, to varying degrees of bisexuality, to the other end of being completely homosexual. Straight kids readily identify as straight and seem surprised I would even ask. Rarely does any kid admit upfront they are anything other than heterosexual. Even so I still explain the full range of sexual diversity and assure them we can talk about this at any point in the future if they have questions or need information. Steven, one of my previous clients waited for nearly three months to come back to this as an issue for him. It is unlikely he would have ever brought it up at all if I had not laid the groundwork at the outset. Steven was 17 and was able to reveal his homosexual identity to me and we were able to help him come to terms with it during therapy. There was nothing about Steven that met any of the stereotypes, so he was able to hide his identity if he chose to do so. By exploring the issues with him he was able to see this was simply another part, and only a part, of his over all personality. I urge all kids and adults not to let any aspect of their sexuality to be the most obvious and overriding factor expressed outwardly regardless of their orientation. Unfortunately for many people the idea someone is homosexual still cancels out every other aspect of who they are in addition to this one aspect.

I believe the most reliable indicator of true sexual orientation can be found in the content of private masturbation fantasies. During the act of masturbation there is no reason to lie to yourself, or to even be overly afraid to explore experiences perceived to be wrong or forbidden by most. It is not uncommon for many adults to have some rather intense masturbation fantasies which can include rape scenes all the way to bondage and domination, as well as much more deviant scenarios. This is no less true for issues related to sexual orientation. When Steven first brought up his belief he might be homosexual I immediately asked him if he masturbated. He embarrassingly admitted he did. In response to my question about the gender of fantasy sexual partners he readily admitted they were always male and were often times guys he went to school with and who were on his football team. This is a good technique to use for kids who may be simply questioning their sexual orientation. In real life sexual situations it may be necessary to try and fake arousal or create a fantasy stimulus in order to get aroused, but during a masturbation fantasy there is no reason to hide from your real attractions and turnons. No one can physically fake an attraction to anyone they do not find to be attractive or arousing. So in a very few instances when sexual orientation was an issue I have encouraged a kid to try and fantasize in private about sexual activity with a same gender partner. This will not be possible without some predisposition to do so, and is a very good indicator of where any individual falls in the range of possible sexual identities.

Over the years I have only worked with one kid who was HIV positive. Anthony had been infected at birth by his mother and had full blown AIDS by the time we met when he was 13 years old. He had been arrested for burglary and I was asked by probation to see Anthony while he was in juvenile hall. Even though he had an AIDS diagnosis he was being successfully treated with a variety of HIV medications and was in good health. However, the juvenile hall staff members were afraid of him and the idea they and other kids might be infected by him. I had to spend a great deal of time trying to educate the staff, with the help of one of the nurses on staff at the facility, about the spread of HIV and the limited precautions which needed to be taken in order to protect kids and staff with which Anthony had contact. In addition to infection issues I had to make sure everyone was aware of issues of confidentiality and the reality of Anthony being protected under the Americans with Disabilities Act. Unfortunately, by the time I got to Anthony, all adult staff members in the facility were talking about the fact he was infected.

Anthony was isolated from the other kids when we first met and I had to spend time with him addressing his fears of people finding out. I also had to warn him about his need to avoid fighting with other minors in order to avoid any form of blood-to-blood transmission. I was amazed at how uninformed Anthony was about his disease and spent time, again with the nursing staff trying to answer his questions and help him find some hope for the future. Anthony came from a very complicated family background, having been placed with extended family members after his mom and stepdad were arrested and imprisoned for serious drug related charges. Following the arrest and imprisonment of his mom and stepdad Anthony and all of his siblings had been permanently placed in the custody of different family members. Anthony's mom never took care of herself and had been very sick from time to time with AIDS related infections. His stepdad actually died in prison from AIDS related complications while I was working with Anthony.

Ultimately Anthony was released from juvenile hall and returned to an alternative school where I continued to work with him. However, it wasn't long before he got arrested for charges serious enough to get him sentenced to the California Youth Authority. I lost track of him after that and have no idea of his current condition or whereabouts. As far as I know none of the other kids who knew Anthony ever found out about his HIV status, at least not while I was working with him.

The only other case I had involving family members who had HIV/AIDS was that of two brothers whose parents had both died from AIDS related illnesses. The focus of treatment for these two boys centered around significant grief issues complicated by the reality of their parents having died from AIDS. The younger of these two brothers went on to be very successful in life relative to finishing high school and making plans for college as revealed to me the last time I saw him. The older of the two had become a serious drug addict and was involved in a number of serious criminal activities, with the younger brother significantly worried about whether or not his older brother might be either murdered or die from a drug overdose. Both of these boys were adopted by a loving family as prearranged by their father prior to his death. But, the impact on them was so tremendous as to alter their lives forever. Any death of a parent or parents when kids are still growing up is tragic, but because of the stigma associated with AIDS, these kinds of deaths seem to be more complicated. This is especially true given the reluctance of kids to talk with anyone about the realities of how their parents died. These brothers were especially upset with their father who apparently infected the mother as a result of his extramarital affairs. Many females get infected by their male partners without any awareness of their health status and often without any awareness of their infidelity.

When dealing with kids and sexual issues I try to get kids to understand the various ways in which HIV can be spread. They are usually shocked to learn it can spread as a result of physical violence. Any physical altercation involving exposure to open wounds will easily lead to infection if one of those involved in the fight is HIV positive. While this may be rare relative to the likelihood of occurrence it still needs to be explained to any kid who has a tendency to engage in any form of physical violence, and in addition to the practice of unsafe sex.

Another rather interesting form of sexual diversity has to do with fetishes. Jimmy was a 14 year old brought into our clinic by his father and step-mom after they caught him crossdressing. He was mortified and no one on our staff readily volunteered to take the case before I found out about it. I saw it as an opportunity to learn about another interesting aspect of human nature. Of course Jimmy denied having crossdressed to our front office staff, and our therapists expected he would continue to deny it even with them. I knew he was embarrassed about the whole thing, so I saved the crossdressing issue for last during our initial intake interview. However, when the time came in the interview to address his reason for being in my office, I asked Jimmy if he had any kind of sexual fetishes. He didn't know what a fetish was and I had the opportunity to open up the entire discussion by defining the term "fetish" for him.

I told Jimmy a fetish can be understood as any object or objects which lead to or are associated with sexual arousal and pleasure. He denied he had any feelings associated with gender confusion, and even denied he had any homosexual tendencies. His denial of homosexual tendencies continued over the entire time span I worked with Jimmy off and on for nearly two years. Personally and professionally I believe this is another aspect of his personality he will have to, or has already had to face since our termination of therapy some years ago. His father was actually okay with the idea his son might be gay and even agreed with me it was a possibility, but just couldn't understand or accept his crossdressing activities. Jimmy was using underwear and other items of clothing belonging to both his step-mom and step-sister. They were not amused to say the least.

Jimmy and I focused on several other aspects of his life including the divorce of his parents, specific feelings he had toward his biological mom, and the fact he had Attention Deficit Hyperactivity Disorder. He was a good kid and was rather intelligent, but in special education classes because of his hyperactivity and problems paying attention and staying on task. Ultimately, the ADHD related symptoms were addressed and controlled through medication and he was eventually mainstreamed into regular classes. By helping Jimmy understand how much his crossdressing fetish deviated from the norm he was able to see his need to try and redirect his sexual interests toward more acceptable ideas and interests. My biggest concern for him was the fact he probably would have a great deal of trouble finding sexual partners in the future who would share or even be able to tolerate his crossdressing. I was also concerned about the additional embarrassment he would likely face someday if people outside his family found out. At the same time I was willing to go along with his fetish if he had insisted it was really important to him. Fortunately he was able to see how detrimental this could be to him in the long run and was able to compromise with me. Jimmy's most favored objects of women's apparel were high heeled shoes. I was able to help him imagine how attractive they were on women and he seemingly learned to settle for this image without needing to wear the shoes himself. This may all sound a little strange, but it was a very real issue for this kid. It seemed that as we resolved the problems associated with his ADHD symptoms, and helped him gain some much needed insight and resolve relative to his biological mom and his parents divorce, his need to crossdress appeared to diminish.

When we successfully terminated Jimmy's therapy which extended over a two year period he was doing well according to self report and reports from his family and school staff. We worked together on average once every two to four weeks. His father was fully involved in the process, and respected Jimmy's need to work with me privately on most occasions. Jimmy was fully involved in school activities and was a member of the cadet corps at school, participating in regular marching and other drill activities. This was a very interesting case and I made sure Jimmy knew I was available to him if he ever needed to return to therapy. Of course that option changed when I moved out of the area, but two years passed since our last session which was enough time for Jimmy to have graduated from high school. You never know what issues you will be asked to address with clients, so it is extremely important to keep an open mind and learn to be creative with your interventions. Never shame them or cause them to feel any more embarrassment than they may already feel. Also be prepared to support them in any direction they choose as long as they are not making choices specifically harmful to themselves or to others. Be sure to never take on a case you are not qualified to address, or in some cases not comfortable with addressing. An example for me would be trying to work with fully autistic kids, a population I know very little about, a population with very specific and special needs.

Another case involved a kid by the name of Gabriel who had been arrested for voyeurism toward one of his female cousins. He was caught several times at the age of 14 outside her bedroom window watching her undress while he masturbated. Finally his family felt they had no choice but to report him and Gabriel was arrested and charged with voyeurism and indecent exposure. He was convicted and labeled as a sex offender and sentenced to 12 months at a state program within the California Youth Authority for convicted sex offenders. Once he returned from CYA he was assigned to me by probation for therapy and monitoring through the mental health system. Gabriel was kind of quiet and obviously embarrassed about his actions and conviction. He told me he never felt like he fit into the program of sex offenders, but had to comply with their requirements and play the game in order to get out of the system.

During my initial intake Gabriel was able to give me the details which led up to his arrest and conviction. He told me his family had been very supportive even though they were angry, hurt, and embarrassed by the whole experience. He told me he never understood the origins of the compulsion which drove him to spy on his female cousin and invade her privacy. As we went through my normal intake interview he admitted to a history of heavy use of methamphetamines. He had been clean since his confinement and had not gone back to using meth since his release. One of the significant side effects of meth use is increased sexual arousal which is virtually uncontrollable for many users. This is one of the main reasons adults will use meth as an enhancement to their sexual activities. Gabriel readily admitted that every time he spied on his cousin he had been using meth heavily, and only felt this compulsion when he was really strung out. I have worked with several boys and girls who have described their meth related sexual compulsions as being insatiable, generally lasting for hours with a strong need for climax, but often without the ability to reach orgasm. Part of the compulsion is to satisfy themselves by achieving an orgasm which rarely if ever occurs. I worked with one kid years ago in juvenile hall who reported he masturbated frequently until his penis was raw and infected while under the influence of meth.

All of this registered with me as I interviewed Gabriel. When I asked him if anyone in the juvenile system ever asked him about his history of substance dependency he told me they had not. Given all he told me about not feeling like he met the profile of a sex offender, and only engaging in this kind of behavior while under the influence of heavy meth use, it was clear to me meth was the problem and not Gabriel. As soon as I revealed this to him he was shocked at how much it made sense, and readily agreed and started to cry. This was such a relief to him and he clearly knew I was not looking for an opportunity to make excuses for his past behaviors, nor was he looking for anything more than an opportunity to understand how he could have done these kinds of things to his cousin and to the rest of his family.

Ultimately I met with Gabriel's family and with his probation officer. Each one of them agreed with my assessment of the source of Gabriel's compulsion, especially in light of the fact he had no history of problems within any setting prior to his use of meth. Many other family problems were relieved, even in light of the fact both of Gabriel's parents were meth users. Gabriel and his siblings were removed from the home and placed with other relatives while their parents went through mandatory drug treatment. Eventually the family was reunited and efforts were made to improve their deplorable living conditions by giving them adequate housing and constant monitoring by social services. Gabriel was able to keep himself clean and sober and out of trouble, with a primary focus on his need to be there for his siblings in addition to wanting a better future for himself. The tragedy of all of this is the reality of Gabriel having a juvenile record as a sex offender for the rest of his life. Hopefully he had his juvenile records sealed as I urged him to do once he reached the age of 18. Maybe this offense will never come back to haunt him at any point in his future. There is no doubt in my mind that Gabriel was not a sex offender, only a meth addict who experienced this unfortunate side effect which manifested itself as inappropriate sexual behavior.

The last topic I want to address in this chapter is the issue of sexual abuse and its long range impact on kids. If you have read my first book, then you know about my RFLAGS model and the connections between abuse and victimization and lasting emotional damage which lasts into adulthood if not dealt with and resolved to whatever degree possible. The first of two cases I want to share with you is that of a kid by the name of Billy. He was 14 the first time I met him and was living with his dad who was an active alcoholic. Billy was referred to me by probation as were most of my cases at the time. He was living with his dad while his mom spent time in prison for charges of child endangerment resulting from her involvement in and the cover up of Billy's molestation at the hands of mom's most recent live-in boyfriend. By the time I met Billy he had already been in a lot of trouble with law enforcement and was one of the angriest kids I had ever met and worked with by that point in my career.

Billy's history of abuse was known to his father, but as time passed in my work with Billy the full extent of his molestation was revealed. It was very difficult for Billy to even talk about what he had been through, so we spent a great deal of time trying to focus on his criminal activity and on his need to deal with anger and face its sources. I had to work very carefully with Billy to establish and maintain a strong rapport of trust and compassion for him as a person and relative to his history of abuse. It took nearly a year before the full extent of his abuse was revealed to me by him, and after hearing the details I clearly understood why it took so long. His story was the most horrific and upsetting case I had ever heard and it broke my heart to learn how much Billy and his younger sister had suffered through their repeated sexual attacks by this pedophile.

According to accounts from Billy the sexual abuse started with Billy's sister. Once he found out what was happening to her the abuser turned on Billy primarily to gain control over him in the same way he was able to control his sister using threats and other forms of intimidation, clearly intended to instill the utmost level of fear possible in these two kids. The abuse occurred over a period of about four years for both Billy and his sister, and seemed more brutal and violent toward Billy. About one year into my work with Billy I pushed him one additional time to talk about the abuse. At first he was angry, but seemed to trust me enough by this point to believe me when I told him we needed to face his past. In spite of his anger and tears he was able to relate unimaginable details of the worst encounter he had with this man.

Apparently the man had a piece of land with a small house on it somewhere out in the middle of nowhere. Billy was told he and his 'molester' were going away for the weekend. Billy was helpless in his efforts to refuse and had absolutely no support from his mom. The weekend turned into the worst experience of Billy's childhood with the man drugging him repeatedly, tying him face down to a bed, and raping him repeatedly over the course of three days, even at times using various objects with which to sodomize him. Billy was about 11 years old when this happened, and even though he physically survived the brutal attacks, he was almost irreparably damaged emotionally by the experiences. Billy sobbed as he told me the details and I was unable to hold back my tears as I observed his intense emotional pain. He told me when they returned from the trip his mother completely ignored the fact he was physically hurt. At some point soon after this most recent event the abuse was exposed outside the home by Billy's sister. Authorities were called in, but before anything could be done Billy's mom took the kids and helped her boyfriend flee across state lines. They were on the run for months, with mom having full awareness of what had been occurring, and yet still helping this man escape the legal consequences he deserved.

According to Billy the abuse continued for both him and his sister until the man was finally apprehended and arrested. The offender and Billy's mom were taken back to the state where all of this occurred and Billy ultimately ended up in the custody of his dad, with his half sister going to live with another relative. In a letter Billy received from his mom after she and the pedophile were convicted and imprisoned, mom talked about how much she still loved the man who had repeatedly raped her own children, telling Billy of her intentions to get back together with the guy after both had served their time. Needless to say Billy was devastated by his mother's lack of regard for what he and his sister had endured, and he openly hoped she and the boyfriend would not survive their time in prison.

Billy was an emotional wreck after relating all of this information to me. He agreed to let me go and get his dad from the lobby. I wasn't in very good emotional shape either. Billy made me promise I wouldn't tell his dad the details of what he had just shared with me. I agreed and assured Billy I would leave that up to him as to whether or not he ever told anyone about this again. When I approached Billy's dad in the lobby he seemed alarmed I guess by the look on my face. I assured him Billy had just revealed to me the details of his molestation and had asked that I not tell his dad what Billy had said. The dad readily agreed to this telling me he didn't know if could endure knowing what had actually happened without wanting to go after Billy's mom and her boyfriend. Even though dad was an alcoholic he worked and took care of his son. The scene in my office when I returned to Billy with his dad was one of the most touching sites I have ever witnessed. Billy and dad hugged each other tightly and both sobbed uncontrollably. I lost it as I listened to dad tell Billy how sorry he was not to have been there for him and his sister. Dad also told Billy how deeply he loved him, expressing a wish that he could have taken Billy's place in all of this.

I worked with Billy for a total of about two years until he got into more legal trouble. He was gang involved and was facing some very serious charges and was on his way to the California Youth Authority the last time we met. I never heard from Billy or his dad after that and can only imagine that Billy was probably never able to get his life on a different track than the one he had already chosen before I met him. In my heart I believe Billy's anger likely fueled every decision he had made and will likely fuel all future decisions as well. I don't see how this horribly damaged young man could ever recover from the extreme nature and extent of his abuse. He could never resolve his feelings of being less of a man because he had been the "bitch" of a pedophile. At times Billy even questioned his own sexual orientation, confused as to whether his abuse meant that he was now gay. No matter how hard I tried he never seemed to understand that the only thing left over from the abuse for him was the emotional damage he would have to face likely for the rest of his life. This was the only case I ever had where I truly believed there was little or no chance for this kid to ever be stable and productive in life. I think of Billy often and can only offer a prayer for his safety and for his soul.

The second case is that of a 16 year old girl by the name of Laura. This has a much more positive and hopeful outcome compared to the story of Billy. Laura had been arrested for assault resulting from a fight at school with another girl. She ended up on the informal probation program I described in chapter three and I was asked by probation to work with Laura at the alternative school site where she was attending school. Even more significant than her altercation at school was her habit of self mutilation and her rather frequent suicide attempts, none of which her family had ever taken seriously. Laura had been hospitalized three times prior to our initial contact and the family had never followed up with services from the department of mental health as recommended as part of her discharge plans. The day we met she had several obvious cuts on her left forearm which I just happened to see when she moved her arm and her sleeve went up far enough to expose the wounds. I was conducting the interview without any family members present and at the school site where I saw a number of kids referred to me by probation.

While conducting the interview Laura revealed her history of suicide attempts and hospitalizations, which included three attempted overdoses and a number of incidents where she would jump out of a moving car. She looked like she was probably anorexic, but adamantly denied having problems related to an eating disorder. Laura described an extremely chaotic and dysfunctional family environment with parents who argued often, a dad who was emotionally unavailable, and a mom who seemed to be as emotionally unstable as Laura. Based on my experiences with other female clients who exhibit extreme emotional instability I was thinking during the entire interview Laura had likely been sexually molested as well. This is often true for girls who get into the juvenile justice system, with a very significant number of them having experienced varying degrees of sexual abuse and rape. When I asked Laura about this she started crying, and with much assurance from me, told me she had been molested for about four years by a next door neighbor.

Anytime a child or even an adult reveals they have been sexually abused in any way it is important to find out only the extent of the abuse. It is not necessary or important for any therapist to know all of the graphic details which occurred. In most cases it can be especially difficult for the victim to even discuss what happened especially if it is a female client talking with a male therapist. Professionally I believe it is even more difficult for boys in general to talk about any kind of male-to-male sexual abuse given the additional perceived stigma associated with male-to-male sexual contact. This is especially true if a boy was penetrated anally in any manner. The information needed by a therapist can be obtained through a series of simple "yes" or "no" questions, unless the client feels comfortable enough to disclose on their own. As a male therapist who also works with female clients I try to always be in control of any discussion of sexual matters. There is no effort on my part to unnecessarily limit the discussion. However, because of the fear on the part of every male therapist when dealing with female clients, I never want to be accused of any form of sexually inappropriate behavior. I know of male therapists who will not see any female clients behind close doors. I am not quite that paranoid, but realistically I have to be cautious.

The kinds of questions to be asked in order to understand the extent, nature, and frequency of any kind of sexual abuse or assault are as follows:

- Did you know the person who abused you?
- Were they male or female?
- Were they related to you?
- What was the nature of your association with them?
- How many times did the abuse occur?

- How old were you when it first started and when it finally ended?
- Is the abuse still happening?
- Was there ever more than one person involved?
- Have you been threatened in anyway if you tell someone about the abuse?
- Did the abuse involve inappropriate touching?
- Were you expected to reciprocate the acts?
- Did it involve kissing?
- Did it involve any form of masturbation – self, other, or mutual?
- Did it involve performing a sexual act while being observed or recorded?
- Did it involve oral sex?
- Did it involve vaginal penetration?
- Did it involve anal penetration?
- Did it involve penetration with any kinds of objects?
- Did it involve any type of bondage, torture, or shame/humiliation?
- Were you given alcohol or drugged?

It is important before asking any of these questions to remind the client of the limits on confidentiality. If there is any resistance after that to talk about what has happened it is of extreme importance to help the individual understand the importance of revealing the information. This is necessary in order to protect your client and to make sure the abuse doesn't happen to others as well. It is advisable to explain the reporting process and to make sure not to make any guarantees as to how it will be handled by the agency with which you have to file the report. Furthermore, it is good to make the client aware of what will likely happen once the report is filed. In the event the child is in, or may face imminent danger as a result of the report, or there is any possibility the abuse will continue, immediate action must be taken to protect the child. This can generally be handled when talking with the agency accepting the report. Many times I have written the report in front of an adolescent victim and have even called in the information while they were sitting in the room with me. This gives them the assurance I have been totally honest and accurate with them during the session and relative to what I report.

With Laura's case the abuse had occurred over a four year period with a man who lived next door to Laura and her family. Laura was age seven when it began and age 11 when it ended. The wife of this man and Laura's mom were close friends. In spite of Laura's efforts to resist being sent over to this house, her mother regularly sent Laura over to stay with this couple. The abuse only stopped because the old man died. Two years into the abuse Laura told her mom, but her mom not only refused to believe her, she also refused to investigate it further. As a result the abuse continued for two more years. This, coupled with all of the dysfunction within Laura's home/family context, left Laura with little recourse other than to turn her anger inward and toward herself.

Soon after I finished my initial intake Laura's mom showed up at the school that day to take Laura home. She agreed to meet with me and Laura as I requested and I began to question her about much of what Laura had told me. I told her that while there was no need to file a suspected abuse report given the fact the man had died, I did tell mom of my intentions to let Laura's probation officer know what had occurred. In front of me Laura's mom called her a liar. Before this went any further I confronted mom with her lack of concern and regard for her daughter's well being relative to both the abuse and Laura's history of suicide and other self-injurious behaviors. I didn't even give mom a chance to respond before I openly told her she should be ashamed of herself for not taking better care of her daughter. My plans to report all of this to probation would at least help me monitor Laura's safety and would insure mom's compliance with my treatment requirements and recommendations. Mom felt threatened and outraged, but I told her I didn't care, assuring her I would do whatever I could do legally to insure Laura's safety. Laura was relieved and I was able to form a strong professional bond with Laura that day which lasted through nearly three years of treatment.

Out of all the kids I have worked with over the years Laura scared me more than any of the others relative to her suicidal tendencies and emotional instability. For the entire first 18 months of her treatment I worried she would end up dead. Fortunately with the right combination of medications and treatment approaches Laura finished high school and was attending a trade school to learn massage therapy as is used within medical settings. She was one of the most intelligent kids I have ever met, and this was likely the strongest factor in her favor and ability to resolve the issues of her past.

Mom never fully accepted the fact Laura was molested, but Laura learned to resolve this as best she could even without her mother's support. Laura was hospitalized only two more times after I started seeing her and was able to stop self mutilating altogether once she was able to approach this behavior from the viewpoint of an addiction. During all of this Laura's eating disorder also ended and her self esteem went up 100%. She held her head up high and felt a great deal of pride in all she had accomplished and relative to all of the things she was able to face and overcome. My RFLAGS Model was paramount in helping her understand why she did the things she did given her extensive history of abuse and victimization, and her extremely dysfunctional home/family context. Just before I left California Laura was doing well and had fallen in love. Hopefully she will be able to put the past where it belongs – in the past.

As you can see sexual issues and concerns with high risk, troubled kids are quite complicated and numerous. It is very important to always seek out additional training and consultation when faced with a new therapeutic situation you are not qualified to handle. Many adults are given the opportunities to monitor and assist kids in need of support and guidance. However, as I have said many times, many adults with the very best of intentions often do the most harm, especially when they venture into areas where they have little or no training which would allow them to be effective. Arrogance is not a virtue, and each of us should realize the important need of working collaboratively with other professionals within various fields when working with troubled kids. No single person or institution can meet all of the needs of kids within this population.

Chapter VII

Intelligence, Talent and Potential

Complicating factors disrupt and impede virtually every aspect of the lives of high-risk, troubled kids, including their academic needs, and academic successes and achievements. I cannot stress enough the need for everyone involved professionally and personally in the lives of high-risk kids to look beyond what they do - and in some cases beyond their lack of accomplishments — in order to see them for who they are meant to be and can truly become. Take some time to once again thoroughly review the list of complicating factors I included as an appendix in my book <u>At the Mercy of Externals: Righting Wrongs and Protecting Kids, 2nd Edition</u>. There is no point in moving forward in this book without a clear and very conscious awareness of the number of significant external factors which often interfere in the lives of this population of kids. At the same time we need to hold kids accountable for their mistakes and misdeeds, we must also look at those factors which likely motivated their behaviors and lack of progress. This is not a way of excusing their shortcomings; but a way of understanding their existence relative to what now needs to be done in order to help kids correct their mistakes and play catch-up in other areas of their lives.

Probably the biggest single factor relative to how kids view their potential for future success is based in their perception of how "smart" they are and how much academic progress they have achieved. My experience over the years has revealed to me how complicating factors impede success and achievement in a number of areas with these impediments then becoming additional complicating factors. The older a child gets the less likely they are to try and make the gains they need if they are to be successful in life or to develop a positive self image and a sense of hope for their future. It is quite common for kids to equate their lack of academic skills to incompetence and the perception they are not very "smart". Once these beliefs become ingrained in their self image these beliefs become self-fulfilling prophecies. Therefore, the longer we wait to intervene the less likely we will be able to do so successfully.

In my experiences of working with kids within various academic settings I have found there to be a combination of factors impeding academic success. It is not at all uncommon for troubled kids to engage in disruptive behaviors within the school context. Boys tend to act out, while girls tend to internalize. However, as previously stated, I believe in recent years this has begun to even out as girls tend to now become more aggressive and oppositional as they enter adolescence when coupled with a similar set of complicating factors as those experienced by their male counterparts. Because of the differences in how boys and girls still seem to respond to complicating factors early on, girls often get little or no attention, and boys tend to get excessive amounts of negative and punitive attention. Neither scenario works, and I hold teachers and other school personnel accountable for their unwillingness and inability to recognize acting out behaviors and withdrawal behaviors as indications of a deeper level of underlying issues and needs, which in many cases they are not trained to address.

One of the most significant factors hindering the education process for kids today is the reality that schools have become more of an environment for kids to socialize and/or "hook up", than for them to learn. For many kids the importance of socializing now takes precedence over getting an education. Kids are always about ten steps ahead of most adults when it comes to technology and various forms of communication devices. Many people, including parents, are becoming more and more addicted to these devices which facilitate a number of distractions for kids and school personnel. As a result priorities have shifted away from important issues such as education and accountability, to simply engaging in what are generally very trivial dialogues. Nowadays I have to frequently tell parents to turn off their cell phones even during therapy sessions. They are usually offended that I would have this expectation. Clearly parents are frequently modeling a set of priorities which are not in step with reality. Low performing schools tend to also be battle grounds for gangs and other forms of criminal activity and recruiting as parts of social networking.

The suggestion that low performing schools should be shut down is probably unrealistic given the fact that schools are generally set up to serve certain geographical areas of any given city or region. However, it is extremely necessary to hold teachers and school officials responsible for being both ineffective and incompetent relative to the right approaches needed to simply engage kids in the education process. Those school personnel who do not meet even minimal standards relative to the academic outcomes of their students need to be fired. If they then want to return to the educational setting, teachers and other professional staff will need to be retrained, and in many cases re-educated and re-credentialed, before being allowed to take any position within any school district. Teachers' unions and corrupt school systems need to be completely reevaluated and totally revamped relative to the programs being offered and the professionals providing both administrative and classroom services. No educational group should be able to sustain itself based solely on its abuses of power and authority sanctioned by people only interested in protecting their jobs regardless of appropriateness or effectiveness. Too much money is being wasted on poorly trained and uncaring staff.

Most professionals, as previously addressed, who choose to work with kids often enter their fields with an idealistic impression of the unhindered good they will be able to do. Unfortunately this unrealistic view ignores the full range of complicating factors professionals are likely to encounter within the settings of their chosen careers. Many quickly become disillusioned and disheartened, while others label kids as some form of undesirable element and seek to have them removed from the setting. All professionals need to be better prepared before they enter their professions to deal with the full range of human nature which exists, even among children of all ages. I believe a careful screening process and continuous monitoring relative to the effectiveness of every adult professionally involved in the lives of kids is critical. The concept of "No Child Left Behind", or any other school program, will be a joke unless the needs of every child are identified and met within all contexts, and by whatever means are required.

One of the biggest errors made within many academic settings is often the unwillingness on the part of school officials to spend the money needed to evaluate and then offer programs to meet the needs of kids who somehow fall outside the range of the so-called "mainstream" students. Too many kids within the juvenile justice system have serious learning disabilities which were never caught, and if caught were never appropriately addressed. I never use the term "learning disabilities" with kids. Instead, I refer to "learning difficulties" which make it more difficult for some kids to learn compared to other kids who seem to have less trouble moving ahead. In my mind the word "disability" suggests to a child that they have a defect which makes them unable to learn. By simply substituting the word "disability" with "difficulty", kids will be much more likely to put in the extra effort as long as they know they eventually will be able to accomplish the task at hand. Like it or not, some kids really need additional assistance in order to move forward academically. Educational professionals should always be held accountable for any failure to assist a child who has any form of special needs. Much can be accomplished in many cases with one-on-one tutoring which many schools are reluctant to provide. A reduction in much of the bureaucracy of many school districts would free up a great deal of money needed to help the kids succeed. Also a simple enforcement of national, state, and local regulations and mandates would resolve much of the neglect and failure to comply.

One of the most alarming factors relative to a child's academic success is the lack of awareness on the part of parents relative to both student and parental rights within educational settings which are guaranteed and protected by law. Unfortunately, many school districts take advantage of this lack of information and in fact do not want parents to know the full extent of services schools are required to provide. Parents are always amazed and enraged when I inform them of their rights to have their child evaluated when academic progress is not occurring. Many times I have confronted school staff during meetings held to determine student needs. These types of meetings are often referred to as "individualized education plans" (IEP) and are often conducted with the hope of parents not asking too many questions and not being fully aware of state and other mandated guidelines. This is one of the reasons schools look at professionals, such as me, who do not work within academic settings as "outsiders". Many districts will go out of their way to keep people from outside the academic setting from attending IEP meetings. One of the biggest threats school districts face today are the actions of advocacy groups who will intervene on behalf of the child and their parents. In many cases school districts are reluctant to work collaboratively with other agencies such as mental health groups in order to avoid taking responsibility for a child's needs and the risk of exposure for not doing their jobs as required by law. However, school officials will readily demand that parents take to child to a mental health center for medication if the child is considered to be a behavioral problem within the school setting. In Mobile, Alabama some school officials tell parents not to bring their kids back until they are medicated. This is absolutely against the law.

A perfect example of this involved one of my middle school kids who was facing an "opportunity transfer" to another school for disciplinary reasons. I knew enough about this case to know Jimmy was not receiving any of the services he needed. Furthermore, I knew none of the teachers or staff at his school liked him. Jimmy's mother asked that I attend the meeting as Jimmy's psychologist and the school granted permission for me to do so. My hope for being present at the meeting was to help school staff work differently with Jimmy while I continued to work with him and his family on a number of rather serious issues present outside the school setting. However, it became apparent early in the meeting the school staff had made up their minds to simply get rid of this kid.

I listened quietly for a while, trying occasionally to offer some suggestions and to let them know some details of the work I was trying to do with Jimmy and his mom in my office. They were not interested in any of my input and it became apparent they no longer wanted Jimmy around. The man leading the meeting started trying to convince Jimmy and his mom why it would be to "Jimmy's advantage" to change schools and start over in a new setting. Within another school district where I had worked previously I knew this was referred to as an "opportunity transfer" and I called the school staff on their deception, pointing out the reality of the only people benefiting from this transfer were the school staff at Jimmy's current school. In front of the staff I began to inform Jimmy's mom of her rights and of the school's obligation to try several other options which had never even been mentioned. Needless to say, the man directing this meeting was outraged, but had to contain his anger as he agreed with my observations of the situation. The school staff finally agreed to help Jimmy change teachers, and agreed to give Jimmy a behavior contract which would put all of this on Jimmy if he failed to meet their requirements.

This was a very fair agreement and settlement. Jimmy and his mom were elated. During the meeting I stressed the importance of Jimmy not blowing this opportunity to remain at his current school, pointing out I had put my neck on the chopping block for him. In spite of Jimmy's assurance to me, his mom and the school staff, Jimmy only lasted two weeks before he blatantly violated the contract and ended up being transferred as originally planned. My actions during the meeting were actually very professional and reserved, but I still got my point across. I was extremely disappointed in Jimmy's unwillingness to comply with their expectations and was able to make him take responsibility for his own outcome of getting, in effect, kicked out of school. The school staff never confronted me on my methods, but readily rubbed it in my face when Jimmy failed to live up to the agreement. I had the satisfaction of holding them responsible for their obvious deception, and word spread quickly around the district I was an advocate for my clients. A great deal of care was taken over the years to keep me from finding out about other meetings even with other clients. However, I made sure every parent and client who was involved in any form of individualized education plan agreement let me know when meetings were scheduled. While I was not liked by school staff, I was respected and appreciated by my clients and their families. Think of the countless number of times this and other school districts are able to deceive kids and families all around this country. This reinforces my belief in the need for independent monitoring and accountability at all levels within institutions and agencies, especially when it comes to service provision to kids.

Positive Psychology is a recent trend growing in popularity and applicability within the general field of psychology. This approach to dealing with clients of all ages was introduced in 1998 by M. P. Seligman, past president of the American Psychological Association. References to this theory can be found online in an extended abstract entitled "Positive Psychology: An Alternative Vision", by Derrick Klaassen, from Trinity Western University. It is available and can be viewed and/or printed out online at www.meaning.ca/articles/print/positive_psychology.htm. Mr. Klaassen gives a wonderful summary of the concept and suggests ways for it to be applied within the entire field of psychology. The main premise of Positive Psychology is to move away from focusing only on what is wrong with someone (pathology) to focusing on and identifying what is right with them. This approach offers therapists and other professionals an opportunity to look for the good in their clients as I have been doing throughout my career. The theory offers a tremendous opportunity for all people within the so-called "helping professions" to help individuals focus on the issues of optimism and choice, and has the potential to have a profound impact on the re-shaping of society and social standards. It fits into the Existential and Humanistic philosophies of emphasizing the value of the person and the importance of freedom to make choices and the need to accept responsibility for the choices we make.

A very useful and compatible theory within the field of education is that of Multiple Intelligences developed in 1983 by Dr. Howard Gardner, professor of education at Harvard University. A summary of the theory and a short, but useful bibliography are presented by Dr. Thomas Armstrong online at www.thomasarmstrong.com, and is entitled simply "Multiple Intelligences". Dr. Armstrong lists the "eight different potential pathways to learning" which are:

- Words (linguistic intelligence)
- Numbers or Logic (logical-mathematical intelligence)
- Pictures (spatial intelligence)
- Music (musical intelligence)
- Self-reflection (intrapersonal intelligence)
- A physical experience (bodily-kinesthetic intelligence)
- A social experience (interpersonal intelligence), and/or
- An experience in the natural world (naturalistic intelligence)

In another online offering available at www.multi-intell.com/MI_chart.html, you can find a chart-like format describing in detail each of the realms of intelligence mentioned above. This approach to education and the relatively new approach of Positive Psychology go hand-in-hand when dealing with high risk, troubled kids. Our perception of how smart we are is a very important factor in determining our overall perception of self-esteem and self-image. This is no less true for kids of all ages. I would encourage readers to look into both of these theories in order to get a deeper and broader understanding of their relevance to this discussion and to their applicability as compatible approaches to understanding troubled kids. One of the most outstanding premises of the theory of Multiple Intelligences is the concept referred to as "islands of competence". This suggests that each of us is competent within at least one of the areas listed above. It is safe to say many people, including kids, possess some degree of competence in many, if not all of the areas, with everyone having those areas of competence which are dominant. These areas of emphasis represent more the innate potential within everyone, and only serve as a place to start relative to identifying and developing skills within all areas to whatever extent possible respective to each individual. Keep in mind the word "ignorance" means nothing more than to be lacking in knowledge or awareness. It does not indicate an inability to learn – although it often suggests an unwillingness to learn or the lack of opportunities to learn.

As professionals working with troubled kids it is extremely important to figure out all of the good qualities and characteristics which all kids possess. In many cases it is necessary to help kids see how many of their ill chosen negative behaviors and activities represent these islands of competence. One example of this is represented by my previous explanation of the qualities and skills exhibited by criminal activities such as drug dealing and weapons sales. So many kids who are troubled possess almost unimaginable and underdeveloped skills, which fall under the headings of several, if not all of the above categories. It is our job in working with troubled kids to help them see how these skills can be utilized more positively and productively in their lives. This can only be done by educating them about the existence of these skills and the opportunity to understand them and implement them appropriately. This falls under the realm of our roles as teacher and mentor with this population of kids. While it is important to identify and address therapeutic issues, it is equally important to identify areas within a kid which are simply unrecognized and underdeveloped. To fail to do so is to further support the shortcomings kids experience within the academic settings where these kids are often labeled as unreachable and incorrigible. It is our job to foster hope within these kids by helping them see they are not the screw-ups they have been told they are.

In order to educate kids about their levels of intelligence, talent and potential we must help them understand they are indeed capable of much more than they realize. There is no greater joy for me than to watch as a kid discovers who they really are and can become as opposed to their negative self image created internally and based on misinformation from outside – my concept of being at the mercy of externals as addressed in my first book. Depression is thought to be based in negative and pervasive thoughts and patterns of thinking which perpetuate the depression and related helplessness and hopelessness associated with depression. A simple change in perspective can bring about remarkable results in the lives of troubled kids as they change what they believe and know about themselves. It is so important to understand that this change in perspective must be established on a conscious level within the psyche of each kid. In some cases this takes a great deal of time given the limited amount of time we are able to spend interacting face-to-face with our clients. Therefore, it is important to use designated time wisely by first joining with the kid to gain a keen awareness of their potential and their goodness, and then working diligently to help them see this for themselves.

The importance of changing their thought patterns relative to beliefs and what they think they know to be the truth lies in the need to address unconscious, habitual ways of thinking and seeing life and the world around them. Most of these kids lack the presence of positive role models who can model and encourage these ways of thinking, so we have to become in effect surrogate parents in assisting them to understand things differently. This process of thinking begins by identifying and spelling out their erroneous thoughts and beliefs which are automatic. From there it is important to help them understand and create a process of making this new way of thinking an intentional, conscious process which must be established to replace their negativistic thought processes and belief systems about themselves and the world. One of the most exciting parts of working with this population is learning as a professional to think creatively and actively in order to tailor-make a scheme which will work for each individual under your care and supervision. This is likely the greatest challenge to professionals as it requires a great deal of intelligence, talent, inspiration, and potential on our part. However, this is what makes the journey of working with these kids so rewarding and such a wonderfully creative experience for those of us who serve as teachers and mentors in their lives. Rather than simply seeing ourselves as fulfilling some specified professional role in their lives, we need to understand we are joining with them in a joint effort to create something new for them – foundations and tools upon which, and with which they will be able to build their own road to success for the rest of their lives.

The term "success" needs to be addressed as well. It is important to remember that successes with this population will not always be bold, huge steps forward. Therefore, every step forward relative to insight which leads to positive changes internally and then to progress in life externally must be acknowledged and reinforced. Never let these kids down or disappoint them! While it is not possible to be perfect, it is important to work toward perfection relative to our abilities and skill levels when working with this population. When you make an error in evaluation, assessment, or observation immediately acknowledge it and apologize for it. Then give the kid the opportunity to explain why you were wrong from the perspective of the kid. Be adult and strong enough internally to allow this to happen so you will learn from your mistake and then be better able to help this kid and the kids who will follow.

No professional is ever just in the teacher role, especially with this population of kids. Troubled kids have much to share and to teach us as professionals about the realities they face and the issues they are trying to understand and resolve. Understand that most actions and thought processes of troubled kids represent their best efforts to cope with and make sense of their lives and the world. It is very important to understand these perspectives as their truth or reality, even if they are factually incorrect. Before you ever challenge what a kid believes or thinks, it is of the utmost importance to understand their perspective on everything around them. When you know that their perceptions are right, even if they are harsh in content or presentation, you must acknowledge the accuracy and legitimacy of their interpretations of people, events and other realities in their lives. This is true even if kids are saying negative and angry things about adults in their lives whether these adults are their parents, relatives, teachers, probation officers, law enforcement officials, or any other adult within their range of experiences. To do anything less is to insult them and will drastically jeopardize your ability to continue working effectively with them. Do not make the mistake of defending adults whose behaviors and words are indefensible and inexcusable, a huge mistake often made by adults in positions of power and authority. Never expect or accept anything less from a kid than you would from an adult. Also, never talk to a kid in any manner you would not use with an adult. If you do you will be "just like every other adult" in their lives.

When kids reveal to you the presence of negative role models in their lives it is critical to help them learn how to deal effectively and appropriately with these obstacles. At the same time you acknowledge the accuracy of their impressions you must guide them toward accepting the existence of these realities. At this point in the process it is necessary to help kids understand that accepting something as real is not the same concept as liking whatever the negative reality is or represents. If you can get them to accept the existence of any reality it is then possible to help them develop coping skills which will help keep them out of trouble and on track toward making progress in their lives. This is where the concept of 'what is in their own best interest' comes into play. As you can see, even the realities of their lack of academic progress can be addressed from this perspective by helping them understand how it is in their own best interest to try and make up for lost time. Unfortunately the realities in the lives of many of these kids are unchangeable. This is especially true relative to people and circumstances present in their lives which are unlikely to change. However, there are a number of ways they can learn to work around obstacles as long as they know they have support from whatever positive resources are available.

Ignorance on the part of professionals involved in the lives of troubled kids is inexcusable. When this ignorance is coupled with the arrogant belief that we know without question what is best for them, this is truly abhorrent. Therefore it is extremely important to learn all we can before we ever attempt to interact with them. Furthermore, it is extremely important to understand our roles with these kids as both teacher and student. It is only by working consciously and deliberately to continue expanding our knowledge and awareness of the realities and issues these kids face on a daily basis that we can ever hope to even reach them, much less help them. Case conferences and consultation with well trained and knowledgeable professionals should be sought out on an ongoing basis throughout our careers. Always read about new theories and approaches in order to increase your base of knowledge and awareness of changing factors and trends. Attend regular continuing education seminars. More importantly let the kids share with you their knowledge of and awareness of life in the streets so to speak. This kind of information from them is invaluable and will serve you well in joining with them in an effort to see the world and life as they see it. Most of all be sure to follow the inspired and compassionate whisperings of your soul. If this makes no sense to you then you should never work with this population of kids.

As you evaluate the intelligence, talents and potential of each individual client, look for their islands of competence. Much of this insight into their capabilities will be gained through an understanding of their efforts to cope with and interpret those external factors present in their lives. This means looking at the criminal acts they commit as a way of identifying their creativity, ingenuity, resourcefulness, resilience, and the ability to transcend the obstacles and challenges life has presented to them. For example - and in addition to drug dealing and the selling of weapons - look at the artistic skills kids exhibit through graffiti created in the streets. While these acts are illegal they will reveal the level of artistic ability a kid possesses. After assuring them you won't "rat" them out or "snitch" on them, if possible look at their art pieces either in person or by asking them to bring in photos or sketches of their work. Pay attention to the tone and content of the piece and ask them to explain what it means to them. One of the most well thought out forms of graffiti are the murals painted in honor of friends and family members who have died. Through this form of artistic expression it is possible to see the depth of their emotions and their ability to feel pain. Their pieces often represent their own sense of the RFLAGS of Fear, Loneliness, Anger, Guilt, and Shame. It also reveals their sense of pride and bravado, and gives us an opportunity to understand what motivates and excites them.

Never underestimate any aspect of who and what these kids are in the present as all of this information also reveals what and who they are capable of becoming in the future. What an incredible and awesome opportunity to be part of the process which brings their positive potential into reality.

Potential is potential either way; and energy is energy either way as well. The main role of professionals is to simply help them use the same energy which they use negatively in a more positive manner. Our work with them is never about making them "change", because you will find this suggests to these kids that in order to become successful they have to "change" into someone else. This could not be any further from the truth with the reality that you only want them to change how they use their potential and the energy which makes that potential a reality. This kind of challenge they can achieve and likely will be willing to accept it, because they will understand they simply need to change how they work with who they already are, and nothing more. It represents a change in perspective and motivation, and not in a change of person.

JJ was one of the most intelligent, perceptive and insightful kids I have ever met. As with many other kids he was searching for an opportunity to engage in a very deep and intellectual discussion with someone who understood him as he really was. On the surface he was very entrenched in the gang culture and was very committed to its causes. At the level of his soul he was eager to learn and share what he knew with someone who could appreciate his good qualities. We spent many sessions talking about many philosophical issues such as spirituality, human nature, political and social issues, and purpose in life. His eagerness to participate was evident and he enjoyed the opportunity to appropriately show off his ability to think. JJ was wise beyond his years and he was one of those kids I tend to see as an "old soul". By taking the time to get to know JJ on a very deep level he was willing to let me see parts of his nature he had never revealed to anyone else. People knew he was smart, but had no real idea of his depth of wisdom and potential for tremendous personal and spiritual growth and development.

I worked with JJ over a period of three years. He finished high school and was gainfully employed. JJ had dreams of going to college and wanted to eventually become a psychologist "like you Doc". What an honor to have a kid like and respect you enough as a professional that he or she wants to emulate many of the characteristics they see in you both personally and professionally. He was especially interested in the spiritual concepts and perspectives I shared with him. These included the concepts of individuality, uniqueness, karma (which all kids understand as "what goes around comes around"), altruism, God as the energy that is us, an afterlife, unconditional love and expectance, the possible connections between us and others who have died, and the importance of making observations rather than judgments. At the age of 19 JJ became a father, and while the relationship with his girlfriend didn't work out, he fought for and was granted custody of his son because his girlfriend was proven to be an unfit mother.

Things were going well for JJ until two of his closest friends were killed in gang related shootings. Daniel, the second one of these kids who died, was someone I had worked with a few years earlier who had already been shot twice in a previous gang related incident. The last time I saw Daniel before I went to his funeral was in juvenile hall and just after the first time he was shot. He swore that he had learned his lesson and was done with the whole gang scene. Daniel went to the California Youth Authority for two years. When he was released he was working in a construction related career and was doing quite well. I learned at his funeral that after the shooting of the first kid who was a mutual friend of both JJ and Daniel, that Daniel again resumed his gang involvement to retaliate for the death of his friend. Within a matter of weeks Daniel was ambushed by the rival gang as he drove through an intersection apparently on his way to carry out his own act of retaliation. Another kid in the vehicle with Daniel was critically injured, but survived.

All of this was too much for JJ to face and he apparently decided to carry out the acts of retaliation Daniel and the other kid had planned to commit. Ironically, JJ's level of intelligence, coupled with his pro-criminal thinking would be the unfortunate combination of factors which led to his downfall. JJ always believed he was smarter than the law enforcement officials who tried to bring him down over the years. He believed he would never get caught for any crime he committed and had apparently been able to pull this off since early in his adolescence. The deaths of his two friends rekindled his allegiance to the gang culture and JJ was arrested and charged with one count of murder and one count of attempted murder. By this time JJ was 20 years old and entered the adult criminal system for the first time, and unfortunately in a big way. I found all of this out when his picture flashed up on the TV screen of a local news broadcast as the reporter announced his capture and arrest. The announcement was also made that JJ would be facing two consecutive life sentences if convicted.

I was devastated and angry with him all at the same time. Our interactions had decreased over time as JJ started working, but he would occasionally call me or drop by my office fairly often just to check in. Because he was in the adult jail I was not able to have any private contact with him as I could have done if he had been in juvenile hall. About three weeks after his arrest JJ's brother told me JJ wanted me to visit him at the jail. At first I was reluctant to do so, primarily because I didn't know what to say to him. I knew him well enough to know he already knew how I felt about what he reportedly had done, also knowing it was now too late for me to help him.

After a few days of thinking about this I decided to go to the jail with JJ's brother. Because we had to talk on a monitored phone line through a glass panel there was really very little we could discuss. The opportunity to talk openly and freely was gone. The look on JJ's face when he walked through the door into the visiting area was one of being glad to see me. However, his expression changed drastically as he realized the circumstances under which we were meeting. We talked to each other via this monitored phone system, often times with tears in our eyes, for about 15 minutes. He told me of his plans to fight his case as an act of self defense, but I knew the DA was going to really go after JJ as they did with other gang members in an effort to send a message to the streets that no gang violence would be tolerated. JJ talked about his son and the fear he would never be there as the child grew up. Toward the end of the visit JJ apologized for letting me down. I accepted the apology because I knew he was perceptive enough to know the depth of my disappointment. I assured him I would always care about him, and would always regret the choice he had made, even though I understood why he felt he had to make it. I told him I felt really bad for everyone who had died in the process of retaliation between the rival gangs. We focused on their families and on JJ's family who would experience a devastating blow if he was convicted as charged.

The last thing JJ said to me before I left the jail was, "Doc, I found out I can become a psychologist in prison." We put our hands together on our respective sides of the glass and I told him, "There is no doubt in my mind you will find a way someday to do what's right." I have no idea how all of this turned out since I left California soon after this visit. He knew I was leaving and returning to Alabama. Someday I will track him through the system and find out where he is and how he is doing. I knew within myself I had done all I could do to try and save this kid from himself and the streets. In spite of this awareness I grieved the loss of what he could have done if he had made the right choices. Believe it or not, I still have hope for him and still believe in the goodness I know to be present in his soul. I do hold him accountable for screwing up his life as well as the lives of many others involved on either side of the incidents which led up to JJ's actions and arrest.

This example of JJ represents very clearly the reality that no matter how hard we try with this population it is completely impossible to control everything going on internally or externally in their lives. Therefore, it is necessary to never base any interaction on controlling a kid as the approach used by the professional. With law enforcement officials and in certain other contexts control of the situation and circumstances is necessary, but efforts to *only* control the kid set up a very destructive atmosphere of competition. This is represented by what I call the "yes-you-will; you-can't-make-me" kind of interaction which must be avoided at all costs in order to keep the interaction from becoming a pointless power struggle. Sometimes within specific settings "no" is simply no, and "you can't do that and get away with it" must be enforced. But, remember with kids it is important to give them the opportunity to learn from their mistakes and understand why it is critical for them to make the right decisions. In other words help them see what is in their own best interest and why this is so. If you as the authority figure cannot accomplish this goal then collaborate with others who can.

Even though JJ was unable and, to some degree, unwilling to withstand the pressures of certain realities in his life, there have been hundreds of other kids I have worked with over the years who were able to resist. Most of my kids finished high school and very few of them ever entered the adult criminal systems. If they did get into the adult system it was generally limited to the local or county level, and not to the extent of the state or federal levels. In fact many of the kids I served over the years simply disappeared from my points of reference and environments where I would have encountered and interacted with them again. This is what you want; to have kids reach a level where they are able and willing to move forward on their own. After all the goal of every "parent" should be to teach their kids the right ways to live so they will someday successfully leave the nest.

Chapter VIII

Psychological Issues and Concerns

One of the most alarming realities of incarcerating juvenile offenders is that incarceration alone is not a sufficient deterrent to pro-criminal thinking and activity. In fact incarceration often increases pro-criminal thinking and related activities. This reality becomes even more obvious as kids continue to re-offend and are re-incarcerated. The deeper a kids gets into the system the less likely they are to be rehabilitated, with the odds of them becoming adult offenders only increasing. However, when incarceration is coupled with appropriate and effective mental health services and other forms of redirection and support the chances for rehabilitation are greatly increased. The key words in the previous sentence are "appropriate" and "effective" relative to treatment approaches with this population of troubled kids. Not all troubled kids will become juvenile offenders, but it is very accurate to say the vast majority of juvenile offenders are troubled kids. Of course, many law enforcement officials now see this population of kids as job security, especially at the juvenile offender level. These officials now work to maintain the status quo rather than seek out more effective ways of working with this group, such as the theories and approaches I am offering and have used successfully for many years now. Remember, if juveniles stop offending there would be no juvenile justice system in any part of this country. This is one of my goals – shut down juvenile justice nationwide! This kind of thinking makes me a real threat to law enforcement officials, rather than an inspiration for them to assist versus incarcerate.

Generally speaking staff within the various settings of juvenile detention, including juvenile hall facilities, various residential placement programs, and state level juvenile detention centers, are not trained to work effectively with these kids relative to mental health needs. More money is spent on punishing these kids than is spent on trying to intervene in a manner which will increase the likelihood of their success and prevent future offenses. I believe this is true as well within the adult systems. The difference is that kids are much easier to reach than are the adult offenders given the reality of the personalities of kids being much more fluid than those of adults in their mid twenties and older. Therefore, it makes sense that early intervention in the form of appropriate and effective redirection and support efforts would decrease the number of adult offenders.

There are many factors associated with this issue, the biggest of which I believe to be the ignorant arrogance of law enforcement agencies in general who make crime a game between them and the kids they seek to arrest. Unfortunately kids who re-offend begin to see their interactions with law enforcement as a competition, just like the cops and robbers game I played with my friends as a kid. Even more unfortunate is the reality of law enforcement officials being the very ones who set this scenario into motion. A rather alarming number of law enforcement officials see themselves as the only people who can control and stop crime. We need law enforcement officials to be part of a collaborative solution, rather than contributing negatively to the problems which already exist. As I stated previously, no single individual, institution, organization, or agency can be all things to these kids.

Most of the efforts of so-called peace officers are concentrated within the communities which have a high prevalence of low income families. It is common knowledge these areas are prime breeding grounds for crime, not because of the people living there, but because of countless complicating factors which in reality are often beyond their ability to control and influence. The hurricane season of 2005 hit everyone in this country with the horrors associated with the ever expanding divide between the rich and the poor. We were shamefully exposed worldwide relative to the realities of the different classes existing within our own society. The entire world witnessed what should have been experienced by every American as a disgraceful crime against humanity right here in the United States of America. This fact was laid bare by the existence of lower class citizens created and perpetuated by our own society and culture. Like it or not we are a society divided into upper, middle and lower classes and it is time to put an end to this!

Psychological disorders are much more prevalent within low income communities and populations compared to higher income groups and communities. This in no way suggests low income people are somehow innately more impaired than others. Rather this fact represents the significant impact of complicating factors which are much more numerous and prevalent among low income people than among their higher income counterparts. Poverty easily leads to despair as low income people fight simply to survive while facing ever increasing hardships with very few opportunities to pull themselves up and out of their environment. Poverty tends to be multigenerational in many cases as the need to survive outweighs the need to seek out opportunities to get ahead. Realistically low income families often depend on every family member to contribute financially to their existence. All too often low income individuals see government handouts as a quick fix, failing to realize their income will be forever limited and determined by government agencies, institutions and politicians. There is no security in this kind of solution and low income adults need to be aided in ways which will give their children the opportunity to complete their education and move on to bigger and better jobs. This approach utilizes both prevention and intervention as approaches to break the cycles of poverty and despair.

Poverty can easily become a mind set if individuals buy into the notion there is nothing I can do about this. If the right amount of money was spent to intervene with kids and their families, then the money saved over time by reducing the numbers of adult offenders could be used to provide the kinds of ongoing support services needed to fight against poverty. Low income European American families tend to live in less densely populated rural areas of the country, while low income non-European American families tend to live within more densely populated urban and suburban areas. This is likely representative of the disproportionately higher percentage of low income non-European American groups as compared to their European American counterparts. The higher the level of concentration of low income families within any area increases the likelihood of increased crime levels and decreased levels of opportunities to fight against their socioeconomic positions. This fact alone demands attention and demands remedy through intensive efforts to intervene and prevent the complicating factors which perpetuate poverty. As a nation it is imperative that we reprioritize and maximize our efforts to assist people in need. This is the only way to decrease the gap between the haves and the have-nots and to stop the ever increasing divide between these two groups.

One of the most shameful aspects of our political system is the reality of so-called conservatives being much less concerned about the plight of those who are "left behind". The current administration has guaranteed that the lives of low income people everywhere will only get worse as cuts are being made in the very programs needed by low income individuals in order to survive. The irony of all of this is conservatives supposedly represent those who are devoutly religious. However, their need to promote their own biased agendas is more important than following the Biblical teachings they use to promote their own self-serving causes. Because many conservatives have a natural tendency toward punishment and war they fail to recognize everyone's interconnectedness and the need to find non-violent solutions to various situations whenever that is a realistic option. Under the most recent conservative control and reign we have had more money being spent on war and law enforcement than at any other time in our existence. This is true because of legislation such as the Homeland Security Act and the US Patriot Act both of which bring war efforts and law enforcement into some kind of holy, infallible union. There is no doubt in my mind that deception and corruption are more widespread throughout this country than at any other time as well. My beliefs are based in the ever increasing number of scandals and violations of our rights which are being exposed at the political level, coupled with my own experiences of witnessing the unfair and unjust treatment of kids and their families through my work as a psychologist. There is no God in any of this and I find it hard to believe that the misuse of money appropriated for homeland security is not being monitored more closely throughout the country. We are being lied to and the low income people within our nation are paying a particularly high price for governmental arrogance, secrecy and elitism. So far none of this has changed very much even under the Obama administration.

Because of the above mentioned factors and misuses of power the psychosocial issues and concerns, especially as they apply to low income groups, will only become more serious and pervasive. Also, because of the current political climate it is unlikely that any law enforcement group is going to be willing to give up funding for their jobs and so called missions. Of course some of these missions are aimed at our troubled kids with law enforcement officials able to treat them as domestic terrorists at even the slightest hint of criminal involvement. Too much of what drives law enforcement agencies and institutions is self preservation in the form of the old money and numbers game. As long as they can give some proof, even if it is exaggerated and inaccurate at times, that there is a vital need to maintain the status quo they will be able to push the fight to preserve their existence. More and more around this country various professional groups become increasingly territorial. These groups will defend their ways in spite of evidence indicating money could be better spent if reapportioned more appropriately and effectively. Unfortunately, many of our current political leaders support the "strong arm", "iron fisted" approaches to fighting unrest rather than preventing its emergence and existence. Investigations after hurricane Katrina, coupled with other incidents are finally beginning to expose some of the corruption and abuses of power and authority which has existed and increased since 9/11. A lot more still needs to be done to change the current mindset in Washington DC.

A search of the literature relative to psychological disorders among juvenile offenders supports my strongly held belief of many of our juvenile offenders needing opportunities for redirection and support from various agencies and institutions. There is no other way for them to break their cycles of engaging in crime-based acting out behaviors as long as they are driven by emotional and mental instability. While there are numerous articles available one of the articles I found online brings everything into focus. The article is entitled "Psychiatric Disorders in Youth in Juvenile Detention", (L. Teplin, K. Abram, G. McClelland, M. Dulcan, and A. Mericle; Archives of General Psychiatry. 2002; 59: 1133-1143.) Their findings were in line with all of the articles I read and this article was published much more recently than some of the others. Their findings also back up my own stated professional observations based on my work with this population since September 1992. Their diagnostic determinations were based on diagnostic criteria printed in the <u>Diagnostic and Statistical Manual of Mental Disorders, Third Edition, Revised</u> (DSM-III-R).

Dr. David L. Roberts Ph.D.

The research conducted by this team utilized a total sample of 1829 male and female youth, ages 10 to 18 years, and screened within the Cook County Juvenile Temporary Detention Center. Statistical data are broken down into the categories of male, female, African American, Non-Hispanic white, Hispanic, and Other. Included in the sample were 1172 males and 657 females. The numbers broken down by ethnic diversity were 1005 African Americans, 296 Non-Hispanic whites, 524 Hispanics, and 4 "Other". The average age of all participants was 14.9 years. A summary of their findings is as follows and presented as percentages of the total sample:

- 66.3% males and 73.8% females met criteria for at least one diagnosis.
- 60.9% males and 59.7% females met criteria for diagnoses excluding Conduct Disorder which is a common diagnosis for most juvenile offenders.
- 13.0% males and 21.6% females met criteria for Major Depression.
- 12.2% males and 15.8% females met criteria for Dysthymia, a milder form of depression.
- 2.2% males and 1.8% females met criteria for Bipolar I, most recent episode manic.
- 1.0% for both males and females met criteria for Psychotic disorders.
- 21.3% males and 30.8% met criteria for at least one of the Anxiety Disorders.
- 16.6% males and 21.4% females met criteria for ADHD - Attention Deficit/Hyperactivity Disorder.
- 14.5% males and 17.5% females met criteria for Oppositional Defiant Disorder.
- 37.8% males and 40.6% females met criteria for Conduct Disorder.
- 50.7% males and 46.8% females met criteria for one or more substance use disorders, with marijuana and alcohol use being the most prevalent.

A summary of their findings relative to ethnic diversity and gender specific to each of the three categories is as follows and presented as percentages of the total sample. Abbreviations for each category are African American Male/Female (AAM/F), Non-Hispanic White Male/Female (NHWM/F), and Hispanic Male/Female (HM/F).

- 64.6% AAM, 82.0% NHWM, and 70.4% HM met criteria for at least one of the DSM-III-R diagnoses.
- 70.9% AAF, 86.1% NHWF, and 75.9% HF met criteria for at least one of the DSM-III-R diagnoses.
- 18.6% AAM, 13.8% NHWM, and 21.5% HM met criteria for one of the DSM-III-R affective disorder diagnoses – Major Depression, Dysthymia, or Bipolar I.
- 26.2% AAF, 23.4% NHWF, and 28.7% HF met criteria for one of the DSM-III-R affective disorder diagnoses – Major Depression, Dysthymia, of Bipolar I.
- 1.0% AAM, 2.6% NHWM, and 0.7% HM met criteria for a Psychotic disorder.
- 0.9% AAF, 0.0% NHWF, and 2.1% HF met criteria for a Psychotic disorder.
- 20.9% AAM, 14.4% NHWM, and 25.5% HM met criteria for one of the Anxiety disorders.
- 31.2% AAF, 30.0% NHWF, and 32.6% HF met criteria for one of the Anxiety disorders.
- 17.0% AAM, 20.9% NHWM, and 13.7% HM met criteria for Attention Deficit/Hyperactivity Disorder.
- 20.0% AAF, 22.2% NHWF, and 29.3% HF met criteria for Attention Deficit/Hyperactivity Disorder.
- 14.4% AAM, 19.4% NHWM, and 13.6% HM met criteria for Oppositional Defiant Disorder.
- 15.8% AAF, 17.8% NHWF, and 26.2% HF met criteria for Oppositional Defiant Disorder.
- 35.6% AAM, 59.9% NHWM, and 41.7% HM met criteria for Conduct Disorder.
- 34.3% AAF, 58.9% NHWF, and 50.2% HF met criteria for Conduct Disorder.
- 49.1% AAM, 62.6% NHWM, and 55.4% HM met criteria for one or more of the Substance Use Disorders.
- 42.3% AAF, 61.9% NHWF, and 51.7% HF met criteria for one or more of the Substance Use Disorders.

As you can see from this data there is an alarming presence of mental and emotional disorders, coupled with substance use disorders found within this population of troubled kids who become juvenile offenders. The percentages are likely very similar for adult populations, with a general consensus of many adult offenders also having serious unmet mental health needs. Keep in mind the more serious psychiatric disorders do not completely develop until late adolescence and early adulthood. Therefore as kids get older the percentages of late adolescent kids would likely rise if they were followed into the adult systems. Of further importance is the fact of kids not being diagnosed with adult personality disorders. This is due to the accepted reality that the personalities of kids are still fluid and can more easily be redirected with the right combination of interventions and approaches.

Another interesting component of the data revealed by these statistics is that while Non-Hispanic White males and females were the smallest ethnic group within this sample, they had the highest percentages of impairment. First of all, I believe the relatively small number of Non-Hispanic White juveniles simply reflects the disparity relative to ethnic and other cultural differences. In my experiences most European American kids who got arrested rarely were ever locked up to the same extent as their non-white counterparts. In many cases European American families are more likely to be able to afford effective legal representation than are families in the other groups. The other big factor is the greater likelihood of kids from ethnic minority groups being pursued with greater fervor and intensity by law enforcement groups in this country.

My experiences with adolescent populations have taught me it is much more difficult to reach kids under the age of 15. This is due to their lack of maturity, coupled with their lack of ability to reason and think abstractly. From the age of 15 and up it is much easier to reason with kids to help them see what is in their own best interest given the reality they are approaching adulthood. At this point it is easier to help them understand, in spite of the presence of numerous complicating external factors in their lives, that to some extent their own choices and reactions have shaped their lives so far. During this critical period of transition from adolescence to adulthood it is possible to help kids see that their choices will continue to shape their lives into the future. This is accomplished by helping them learn to consciously make the right decisions at this point in life when, consciously or unconsciously, they will be making future decisions anyway. It is important to move these kids away from reactionary motivations toward carefully thought out plans and strategies which will give them hope for the future. Set your expectations high for these kids, but not so high as to make them unrealistic and unattainable.

The chronological years of 17 and 18 are especially significant given the reality of 18 year old kids being recognized as adults under the law – younger than 18 for certain types of violent crimes. This is a time to help them see the importance of putting any criminal past behind them, making sure not to create an adult criminal record which in most cases will follow them for the rest of their lives. This is also the time to help them face any unaddressed or otherwise unresolved needs in their lives, such as mental/emotional health issues, and unmet academic needs. Believe me, this will be the last chance for many kids in this population.

My work with high risk, troubled kids was often done without parental participation or involvement other than establishing eligibility for services and signing consent forms for me to treat their child. When kids were locked up or in residential placement permission for me to see them was granted by the courts. When kids were living within their communities I usually met with them in school settings during school hours, with only a few afternoon appointments at my office. The kids I saw in my office were generally the kids with more serious mental and emotional problems who were also being seen by our psychiatrists for medications. Even when families were present in my office I always met alone with a kid for the greatest part of the time scheduled. Parents were more than welcome to participate, especially if they had information I needed to know about changes in their child's behavior, academic problems, parenting issues, etc. Because parents could see I was getting through to their kids they valued my time alone with their child. They also respected my insistence on confidentiality when it came to the privacy kids need in order to feel comfortable when disclosing. There were very few times I have had to share a kid's personal information revealed to me in sessions with parents or guardians, other than as required by law.

Dr. David L. Roberts Ph.D.

I made it really clear to all parents and guardians I am not here to be your detective. I have always felt if parents are so uninvolved in the lives of their kids as to not know what they are up to, then why should I give them such information. This is especially true with kids who are in the 15 and up age bracket. My ability to join with kids on an appropriate level is always critical to the success of my treatment approaches. Kids always enjoy the opportunity to talk openly with an adult who understands them and the way they see things. This is why it is so important to ignore such things as bad language, clothing style, and other factors which have nothing to do with the work at hand. The last thing troubled kids need is another authority figure telling them how to talk, dress, sit, walk, and act. Working with this population of kids in a very relaxed yet professional manner is one of the most enjoyable parts of my job as a psychologist. Even though the atmosphere is "kick back" as the kids call it, we are constantly working during every aspect of our interactions. My role as an active listener is critical in the process of understanding the kid and their related issues. One of the best ways to accomplish this task is to simply engage them from time to time in a conversation about their friends and routine activities. The more kids talk, and the more they trust me, the more completely I will be able to help them redirect their energies and efforts toward worthwhile goals and activities.

Involvement by family members is especially helpful when trying to get an accurate history on every client. However, it is important to understand the only realities and perceptions which matter are those believed and held by the kid sitting in front of you. While their realities and perceptions may not be accurate, the way they see and interpret everything in their lives is what motivates them either positively or negatively. It is helpful to be able to correct their misinformation when possible, but it is not a necessary factor. You will often find that parents and guardians will only give you their perceptions of the child, and are rarely ever honest about themselves and the part they have played in complicating their kid's life. I never let them get away with this as I always ask the question "What mistakes have you made in life which have complicated your child's life?" I do this in front of their kid and expect them to be honest. If the information is too sensitive, or something I think the kid doesn't need to know, I meet with the parent or guardians alone. Anytime I meet alone with a parent I always assure my client I will not violate their trust, and I NEVER do! After all, the case is under the kid's name and not the name of the parents of guardians. With younger kids involvement by parents or guardians is critical, but with older kids their presence and regular involvement will actually impede the kid's progress in many instances.

Fortunately only a relatively small percentage of kids have serious mental disorders such as Bipolar Disorder or some form of Psychotic Disorder. The more common problems will be different forms of depression, anxiety, behavioral problems, learning difficulties and abuse issues. The most common diagnoses for troubled kids are: Major Depression, Dysthymia, Conduct Disorder, Oppositional Defiant Disorder, specific Learning Disorders, and Polysubstance Dependence (or at least abuse). Diagnoses like Attention Deficit/Hyperactivity Disorder and various Learning Disorders only make all of the aforementioned conditions more complicated to address. I personally believe kids born into any kind of stressful environment with repeated exposure to stressful stimuli will very likely meet criteria for one or more of the possible childhood diagnoses. In many cases children have a genetic predisposition to certain temperaments and coping styles. A stressful environment will only make the manifestation of these genetic predispositions more pronounced. I refer to it as being "pre-wired for sound". The continuing level of stress, along with the numbers of complicating factors, will determine the level of impairment as the child grows older. This relates directly to my Roberts FLAGS Model explained in detail in my first book, <u>At the Mercy of Externals: Righting Wrongs and Protecting Kids, 2nd Edition</u>. It is critical for each of you to both read and understand the concepts in that book in order to gain the utmost benefit from the contents of this current book. This is the reason for combining the two books into one publication as of 2011.

I am not a promoter of medication for anyone unless it is clear they are too impaired by their disorder to function adequately and safely in life. Severe forms of Major Depression, Bipolar Disorder, Psychosis, ADD, and ADHD require medication, as in many cases it is impossible to even work effectively with someone who is extremely impaired by their mental and/or emotional state of mind. Keep in mind mental and emotional disorders are in some cases organic in nature and are very frequently the result of heredity. This can easily be determined by obtaining a thorough family history of other family members who have exhibited the same symptoms. Rather than think of people as having a mental illness I help them understand extreme forms of mental and emotional states are nothing more than brain-based disorders. This helps kids and adults deal with their mental health issues without the stigma of being "mentally ill". It is possible to help people deal more effectively with the concept of a brain disorder which is chronic and needs to be treated as much as any other chronic physical disorder would require. This approach goes along with the current push to reclassify every mental disorder to a medical condition if it is chronic, hereditary, and needs to be treated medically.

The biggest obstacle with disorders needing to be treated with medications is the issue of compliance due to the adverse side effects of many drugs. Therefore it is important to work closely with psychiatrists to find the right balance of medications needed to control symptoms and limit the adverse reactions so often experienced. Recent research indicates medications not only help control symptoms, but help regenerate brain cells and stop further degeneration of brain tissue. Because we still have a lot to learn about the brain it is difficult to help people diagnosed with serious disorders find hope for the future. However, with the current levels of research and advancements increasing frequently, it is possible to help clients understand that all of these conditions will someday be controlled and/or eliminated without having to deal with negative side effects. In spite of the hope for advancements in treatment and in the understanding of brain functioning, compliance remains a major obstacle in working with people who have serious symptomatology. This is equally difficult for both children and adult populations.

(As an aside, I believe the most significant contributing factor to what appears to be an increase in various physical, mental, and emotional disorders is the willful disregard relative to ever increasing sexual promiscuity and indiscriminately risking pregnancy with virtually every sexual encounter. I firmly believe that the more people are acting out due to their own total lack of impulse control, the more likely they are to be carriers of what I call "bad gene soup". This mixed with the "bad gene soup" from their equally as out of control and impulsive sexual partner increases the likelihood of more severe childhood psychological and medical diagnoses of all kinds. I bring this up to every single parent I now see who has several children from different sexual partners - who, along with the kids, are impaired genetically - and they readily agree with my perception. At times I even go as far as to suggest that they not continue having additional children who will likely develop the same or worse kinds of conditions, and they readily agree with me on this point as well.)

For kids who are deeply involved in the juvenile justice system medication compliance is a little easier to maintain when they are incarcerated. Once they are released follow up with mental health services for medication is rare. Even when they are locked up kids have the right to refuse medications and must be informed of this right. All too often I have watched as juvenile justice staff try to force medication compliance with threats of legal consequences if the kid refuses. These individuals get very upset when I refuse to back them on this issue. The most I can do is to try and help kids see how it is in their own best interest to comply, but this does not always work.

For about 18 months I worked with kids in Desert Youth Academy, a lock-in residential placement program housed within the Indio Juvenile Hall Facility in Indio, CA. This is the program run by the Riverside County Department of Probation I mentioned in chapter three. These kids were generally ages 16 to 18 and this was their last opportunity before being sentenced to the California Youth Authority system which was overcrowded, and which is basically state prison for kids. Every kid housed in this program had failed at least two other placement programs and had almost unimaginable criminal records, often times coupled with heavy involvement in gang activity. This was a 20 bed, all male unit and at least 25% to 30% of these kids required medication if there was any hope of successfully completing the program. Because I saw them regularly on the unit, spending extended amounts of time with each of them as needed, I was able to keep them compliant with medications I believed to be necessary as part of their treatment and successful release from DYA. While on medications these kids performed extremely well and I was able to reach them on a level which would have been impossible without medications.

The stability provided by the right combinations and amounts of medication gave me the opportunity to provide insight-based therapy with kids who would have otherwise been unreachable. It was obvious to everyone when they stopped taking their meds as their symptoms would return very quickly, and frequently with a major rebound effect of even more exaggerated symptoms. The changes in their levels of self control were astonishing when their medications wore off. Therefore, it was impossible for the kids not to see the differences for themselves relative to how much they needed medications. A great deal of progress was made by all kids on this unit. Those who needed medication at least left the program with the awareness of their conditions and the stability they gained when they were med compliant. Most of these kids lived in other parts of Riverside County and outside the area where my office was located in the desert. Every effort was made to hook them up with mental health and other support services once they were released, but unfortunately many of those needing medications never followed up with treatment.

One of the most remarkable aspects for me in working with kids in this placement program was the reality that I had never known most of them outside of the facility. Therefore, I knew them only under the kinds of conditions which encouraged right actions and behaviors. They were motivated to be successful since failure in this program meant very serious consequences. So many of these guys were extremely intelligent and possessed amazing skills, talents, and potential. For many of them this was their first time to shine and get a glimpse of the positive things they were capable of doing. The stories of these kids were heartbreaking, with many of them coming to this program after years of being in foster care. These kids had faced more complicating factors collectively as a group than any other kids I had every served. My work with them was the most rewarding part of my career to date and was a tremendous learning experience for me relative to what can be accomplished even with the most trouble kids when the right approaches are used with them. All of the staff associated with this program knew my presence and work with these kids was one of the largest factors contributing to the success of the kids and of the program itself. As you can imagine being banned from this program because of a child abuse report I was required by law to file against senior staff, was devastating to me. Then on top of that to be told this population of kids was no longer a priority with the California Department of Mental Health was infuriating. But, for 18 months I dedicated my life to the kids on this unit and gained insight and wisdom which will be invaluable to me throughout the rest of my career. I have the satisfaction of knowing every kid I worked with was given a glimpse of themselves they had never seen, and I know for a fact they will never forget the amazing experiences we shared.

Because most of the kids in the lock-in placement program were from other parts of the county once they were released I had no further contact with them. However, I always gave them my contact information at the Indio clinic so they could at least reach me by phone if they needed to or wanted to talk with me following their release. In addition to many complicating factors common to all troubled kids, a very high percentage of these kids were also dealing with issues of extreme grief and loss. In many cases these kids had lost one or both of their parents either by death or abandonment, or they had experienced the deaths of a number of their friends and extended family members as a result of gang violence. Many of these kids were chronically sad and angry relative to many external factors which were beyond their abilities to control or influence.

Evan was one of the most remarkable kids from this program. When he was sentenced to this placement program he was already being successfully treated with Lithium for extreme Bipolar I Disorder. Evan was prone more to the manic end of this disorder rather than to the depressive end – with mania and depression being the two opposite poles of this "bipolar" disorder. Evan was extremely intelligent and talented, and at 15 years of age, was one of the younger residents. He was very mature for his age and he had unlimited potential – in either direction. Having never known Evan when he was off his medication it was readily apparent when he stopped taking his meds. His mania was marked by racing thoughts and being hyperverbal, with Evan having very little ability to keep himself on track during a conversation.

The only time during his stay when he refused his meds the change in his ability to interact with me on a rational and calm level was drastic and uncontrollable. At first I couldn't figure out what was happening until I finally asked Evan if he had stopped taking his meds. Initially he denied this, but finally admitted he had started "cheeking" his meds two days earlier. None of the nursing staff or unit staff was aware of this, but everyone could see a tremendous change in his personality. It didn't take long for Evan to realize how critical his medication was and he was enraged by this reality. With a great deal of encouragement on my part he finally agreed it was in his best interest to go back on his medication rather than face removal from the program and re-sentencing to the California Youth Authority. After this incident I had at least four months to work with Evan before he was successfully released from the program. Once released, Evan returned to the eastern part of the county where he was to be monitored by that division of probation for a six month after care monitoring program.

Once out on his own Evan stopped taking the medications he was given at his release. His mom, who according to Evan's account was apparently bipolar herself, convinced Evan he didn't need the medication. Evan never followed up at the mental health center in his area and rather quickly returned to his previous history of self medicating with heavy alcohol use. Within a relatively short period of time Evan resumed his previous use of crystal meth and re-involved himself in his gang culture. He had an almost unimaginable history of extreme physical abuse at the hands of his mother and was again faced with the all of the demons from his past when he returned to his home/family context. I talked with Evan twice by phone and it was obvious he was out of control with his Bipolar I symptoms. There was nothing I could do to make him realize his need to go back on his meds and it was clear he was spiraling out of control in every area of his life. I have no idea what became of Evan since I left California, but my fear is that he is either in more trouble legally and with his substance use, or even worse he could be dead by now. All I can do is hope he remembers how good it felt to be stable mentally and emotionally while he was locked up. If he is still alive I hope someday he will be able to deal realistically with his brain disorder and will learn to take care of himself. He is one of those kids I will never forget.

Evan's story is not at all uncommon. The fact he had very few after care resources available to him once he was released was one of the reasons for his downfall. Evan's case represents many of the overwhelming complicating factors faced by troubled kids on a regular basis, all of which are greatly intensified when there are serious overriding mental and emotional disorders involved. When you add to that the devastating realities many troubled kids face within their communities and family contexts it is no wonder many high risk kids are unable and unwilling to see their own potential for success. None of this will change until the political and social climates in this country change in the direction of a strong desire to reach out collaboratively to those in need, especially those labeled as society's underdogs. I plan to be a very active participant in making these changes in attitude and perspective a reality.

Chapter IX

Be Part of the Solution and Not Just Another Problem

In this day and time I believe our society has become rather adept at renaming realities in ways which are either more politically correct or in some cases in ways which disguise the truth. This is especially true when talking about our different socioeconomic strata. Rather than talk or think about lower, middle and upper classes, we talk about groups described as low income, middle income, upper middle income, and upper income. However, we tend to distinguish the "haves" and the "have-nots" as either high class/high society or low class. These terms conjure up stereotypical images of the characteristics often associated with and attributed to those who are rich and to those who are poor. The rich are generally characterized as being arrogant, greedy, and privileged, while the poor are represented as ignorant, dirty, and worthless. Depending on the context of a conversation the terms high class and low class are often times used as insults against those who seem to think they are better than others, or against those who do not measure up to a certain level of standards arbitrarily set as the norm. Race or ethnicity is not always a part of these kinds of taunts as these labels tend to separate the haves and the have-nots within any cultural or ethnic group. Anyone within any of the socioeconomic levels can be referred to as having negative characteristics associated with either the high or low class stereotypes.

Imagine being born into poverty where poverty has been a multigenerational legacy. Most of the daily efforts are focused on struggling to survive and not much on getting ahead since this seems to be the illusive dream. The chances are you are living in substandard housing located in a "very bad neighborhood". You were probably born to a single mom or into a very conflicted marriage or live-in relationship environment, in which diapers and formula are bought using money needed to provide food and other necessities for all family members. The chances are you will be sustained by programs offering handouts rather than real opportunities to improve quality of life. There are few if any positive role models in your immediate contexts of home/family and community, and you are likely surrounded by substance use, abuse, violence and criminal activity both inside and outside the home/family context. Your days will likely be spent indoors for safety reasons, or you will be allowed to roam freely without supervision depending on the ability of the adults in your life to parent and protect you.

Over time you will likely have several father or mother figures to deal with, most of whom will not like you because *you're not really their child*. If you are the oldest sibling you will likely be given unreasonable responsibilities relative to caring for the adults in your life who cannot take care of themselves or the younger siblings you are likely to have. On the other hand, if you are an only child or the youngest child you will likely be either neglected, or babied to the extent there are no distinctions or boundaries between you and the person or people who baby you to satisfy their own unmet emotional needs. School performance will be dismal and minimal since you will probably have very little self control or ability to focus on schoolwork because of the lack of emotional stability in your life. Much needed quality medical care will likely be unreachable, nutritional needs may be lacking, and the likelihood of developing significant emotional, behavioral, and psychological disorders will be almost inevitable due to the numerous complicating factors present in your life and surroundings. The number of complicating factors within your home/family context correlates directly to the level of Fear, Loneliness, Anger, Guilt and Shame (FLAGS), along with helplessness and hopelessness, you will experience. Any form of abuse and victimization will only make all of these factors worse, and your chances of developing appropriate coping skills and behaviors will be very low. Unless someone within some context teaches you to dream of better things for the future, and provides you with the opportunities and support to make those dreams become realities, your future won't be much better than the life you had as a child.

This chapter is about adult roles and responsibilities covered in depth in my first book, <u>At the Mercy of Externals: Righting Wrongs and</u>

<u>Protecting Kids, 2nd Edition</u>. Again, it is very important to understand the material presented in my previous book to fully understand the important perspective of this chapter. Righting wrongs refers to the need to intervene with older adolescents and adults of all ages, hopefully before they become parents and continue the multigenerational process of abuse and victimization they experienced as children. Protecting kids is the prevention part whereby we work with parents and kids to help them understand how to make better choices by understanding how their past has shaped their lives and often times continues to live in their present. All too often the adults in the lives of kids are a big part of the problem and they need to be taught how to create solutions for themselves and their children or other kids in their charge. Adult roles and responsibilities go way beyond the home/family context and extend out into the other five contexts of community, school, society, politics and religion. This means any adult who has any level of influence and authority over a child as a parent, extended family member, professional, law enforcement, educator, minister/clergy, politician, or any other chosen role must be prepared to right wrongs <u>and</u> protect kids.

As a means of identifying the numerous adult roles and responsibilities take each letter of the alphabet and think of every word beginning with each letter which represents one adult role and responsibility. For instance with the letter "A" you get a list that includes: accept, acknowledge, appreciate, assist, accentuate, acclaim, applaud, accommodate, accompany, accord, activism, admire, admonish, affection, affirm, aid, advocate, ally, alleviate, amend, adjust, adapt, analyze, assess, apologize, appease, articulate, aspire, assert, assure, attend, and avert. If you do this with every letter, using a dictionary as I did, you will be astounded at the number of existing adult roles and responsibilities, even if we ignore them.

Because of the extremely high number of adult roles and responsibilities, I believe very strongly it is necessary to teach these realities to kids before they become sexually active. The content of this book and my first book should be part of a Parenting 101 class which every adult should take before they try to move on to more complicated issues of active parenting. This applies to adults in other roles outside the home/family context as well who need to fully understand what works and what does not work when trying to guide, teach, assist, or otherwise interact with kids of all ages. A thorough understanding of the adult roles and responsibilities, along with a full awareness of the numerous complicating factors all troubled kids face are essential in knowing how to effectively and appropriately interact with kids in our charge.

Another important area of concern relative to teaching these realities is the importance of an explicit, realistic and thorough approach to teaching sexual education classes. I firmly believe if kids understood all that is required in order to be effective in their parenting roles they would be less likely to get pregnant before they have made important accomplishments in their lives. Such accomplishments include: getting an education; preparing for a worthwhile and rewarding career which will allow them to support themselves and a family; and working on undoing any emotional and psychological damage they may have experienced while growing up within the different contexts.

I also believe kids and adults need to understand having a baby should be based in the desire and readiness to become a parent. The most common mistaken assumption of many kids and adults is that a child will solve many of their problems. Very little consideration is given to the welfare and well being of the child relative to complicating factors the child will face if the parent(s) are not ready to assume their parental roles and responsibilities. The decision to engage in sexual activity which puts someone at risk of becoming a parent should be based on fully informed awareness of what causes pregnancy and of everything which will occur once the baby is born. This is especially true if the pregnancy is accidental and the child ends up being unwanted. The best way to prevent excessive use of abortions is to make kids and adults fully aware of the ways to prevent pregnancy beyond the unrealistic notion of an abstinence only approach. An abstinence only model ignores the lack of maturity, awareness and self control of even many adults. All too often lives are complicated and even to some extent ruined with an unplanned pregnancy, especially if the child is unwanted and born into a less than favorable environment which will not benefit the child.

Not every disadvantaged, low income home/family context is dysfunctional. However, the complicating factors kids will face by just being in the low income category will demand that the home/family context be as functional and stable as possible. Let me help you get accustomed to the kind of language associated with kids you need to accept and deal with rather than challenge every time a curse word or vulgar term is spoken. One of the most profound statements ever made to me by a parent was this: "fucked up parents raise fucked up kids." I was so taken aback by this, but all I could do was agree and even laugh at the frankness and conviction with which this statement was uttered. This single mom had a 17 year old son, Vince, referred to me by probation for drug-related charges and gang affiliation. As time progressed it also became apparent that Vince was developing strong symptomatology related to Schizoaffective Disorder which is a combination of psychotic symptoms and extreme emotional/mood instability. His serious addiction to alcohol, marijuana, and crystal meth only made the symptoms of his brain disorders worse.

Vince's mom had in recent years obtained a nursing degree and was working in a hospital. She readily admitted that the early years for Vince and his younger sister had been fraught with extreme substance use and domestic violence within the home/family context. When Vince was about 12 years old his father had been arrested and sentenced to many years in prison. Mom filed for divorce and sought out counseling for herself and was able to get her life on track, just not in time to save her children from the emotional damage done during their early years. There was a significant history of emotional and psychotic disorders from both of the biological parents even though Vince's mom had never developed any of the symptoms herself. Mom's poor choices as an adolescent were the result of the extremely dysfunctional and complicated environment she experienced as a child and recreated for her children. Her mom had the same Schizoaffective Disorder as Vince was beginning to develop in late adolescence.

Vince's situation represents one of the worst sets of complicating factors any family could face. Not only were there many complicating factors which truly put them at the mercy of externals, there was also a multigenerational history of poverty and extreme brain disorders manifested as serious emotional instability and psychotic symptoms. Vince's mom was lucky enough to have the innate qualities of resilience and the ability to transcend the complicating factors from her past. She also never developed any of the symptoms of the disorders for which she carried a genetic predisposition. As her children got older she was also determined to pull herself out of poverty by using her intelligence and insight to get a good education and enter a career where she could help others in need. Vince's mom readily admitted that, while she deeply regretted all of the chaos she helped create in the lives of her kids, there was nothing she could do to change the mistakes of the past. She also had to face the reality Vince had serious mental and emotional disorders which would plague him for the rest of his life, especially if he continued to drink and use, and refuse the medical treatment he so desperately needed. Vince's younger sister had a baby at 15 and never finished high school. Vince's mom was trying earnestly to help her daughter change the direction of her life, both for her daughter's sake and for the sake of her grandchild.

I hope you can see from this example the importance of allowing people to be who they really are when they are sitting in front of you and seeking help for themselves and their family members. If I had been offended by this mom's bold statement of perception and fact, I would have spoiled the entire opportunity for her to express herself and share her insight with me in her own way. Vince's case was not one of my successes given the fact by the time I had the opportunity to work with him he was so entrenched in the gang culture, and his substance addiction was so serious. The complicating factor of extreme emotional and mental disturbance also impeded his ability to face his future with the hope he would someday be stable enough to function effectively in life. I referred Vince to our adult services at age 19 and he was generally non-compliant with the services he needed to stabilize the symptoms related to his brain disorders. There were several times Vince came back to see me for help and guidance. I was able to at least establish a professional relationship with Vince from the beginning which allowed Vince to trust me fully and to know I truly cared about him and the issues he was facing.

The last time I saw Vince's mom she told me Vince had been arrested for drug related charges and now had an adult criminal record. The likelihood of him getting deeper into the adult system was high, with this system being the only way Vince would possibly accept the help he needed for his inability to control many aspects of his existence. I have no idea of Vince's current situation, but I can only imagine he is likely locked up. I can deal with this possibility better than thinking about the possibility he could also be dead.

Sometimes all we can do is try. Even that can be enough to reach someone in a way which will help them in the future, assuming we have made a connection, starting from the point of our initial contact, which will facilitate their ability to remember their experiences with us favorably. I cannot stress enough the importance of dealing with kids and people in general by looking beyond the bad choices they may have made and seeing them for who they were meant to be and can become. When serious mental and emotional problems are present the odds of seeing extreme achievement is reduced, but never eliminated. People with serious mental and emotional disorders must be given hope for future medical advances which will make their symptoms more manageable. We must all hold out hope for eventual cures for these types of chronic brain disorders as we learn more about how the brain functions.

When I think about a family like Vince's I cannot help but wonder where were adults within other contexts who could have and should have tried to intervene and assist this family. Even if efforts were made to assist this family early on in their struggles, they were not successful. Vince's mom told me she wished on many occasions that someone along the way would have tried to help her and her children rather than judge them by the actions of their father and the family histories on both sides. All too often law enforcement officials and even educators will hold a family history against the children of parents with police records, mental disorders, or poor academic performance records. This kind of thinking only guarantees the likelihood of kids following in the footsteps of the parents and other family members that law enforcement officials and educators may have known under less than favorable circumstances. It is wrong to assume the next generation will be exactly like the previous generations. Such an assumption may even explain some of the thinking within this country which has helped to create the classist society we now have. Because Vince's mom was able to get her life on track after her husband's incarceration and their subsequent divorce, this potential had to have been there all along. This example is one where I firmly believe the right interventions early on may have helped stabilize this family before it got to the point of becoming so much more complicated than it already was.

One of the most interesting and challenging cases I ever had involved Gracie and her six children. There were three different fathers involved, none of whom took any responsibility for their roles as fathers in the lives of their kids. This family was known to every social service agency in the area and they were referred to me for family counseling. My work with them covered eight of the last nine years I spent in California. All I can say about Gracie was that she was quite a character. She had a heart of gold, was as immature as any one of her children, and yet very intelligent at the same time. Gracie's criminal history and criminal involvement were rather extensive, and I learned very quickly not to ask too many questions about things which didn't pertain to issues directly related to family dynamics. She was known as a gang mom and a protector of the kids in the streets. The most amazing thing about this woman was the level of trust and respect she gave me in working with her for the benefit of her children.

During the years I was involved professionally with Gracie and her children I was not aware of any active criminal involvement on her part. However, because of my desire not to know more than I needed to know, primarily for my own safety, this was not information I sought. If I had learned or witnessed something I would have had to act on it and I tried very carefully not to put myself in that position. As a psychologist or any other category of therapist working with extremely high risk kids, it is important not to get overly inquisitive in some aspects of people's lives which have included an extensive history of criminal involvement. If you are really good at your job as a therapist with high risk families you will gain a level of trust from people with extreme needs. This will require from time to time that you remind them you are their therapist and not a close personal friend of the family. I had to do this regularly with Gracie.

Gracie's biggest obstacles were her serious health issues which often times made caring for her children very difficult. However, she always managed to get by and never neglected them. I spent a great deal of time occasionally referring her to agencies which would provide her with temporary financial assistance, along with food and clothing. Anytime there was a campaign within my agency to adopt a needy family, I always nominated them, which meant on two occasions Gracie and her kids had the best Christmas holidays they ever had. Gracie was estranged from her immediate family, so there was no assistance available to her from relatives. This was likely her fault given the kind of life I suspect she had lived in the past.

Because Gracie was so respected and protected within the gang culture, she often had assistance from them. By knowing Gracie and her family she helped me gain a tremendous amount of respect from all of the gangs in the area, with her assuring them I was only there to help their children make it in life. Many of my referrals came indirectly from her and I always appreciated her support without feeling obligated to her for it, and she clearly knew this. Her two oldest sons eventually joined a local gang in spite of my efforts to prevent this. Law enforcement officials had their eye on this family constantly to the point of harassing them from time to time. On numerous occasions I defended Gracie's two older boys to law enforcement, especially on occasions when I overheard their derogatory comments made in my presence without any awareness of my professional association with this family. Both of these boys ended up deep in the juvenile justice system, but I never gave up on trying to get through to them at any opportunity I had. This family knew I cared and they were the only people I have ever served when on a very limited number of occasions I spent money on food for them myself when they were truly desperate and couldn't find other assistance in the community.

One of my rather frequent interactions with Gracie and her kids took the form of home visits. I would go into their home and take on somewhat of a father role with the kids by admonishing them for not helping their mother out with simple things like keeping the house and themselves clean. I never felt uncomfortable in their home and always made sure my office staff knew I was going to visit them, always giving an estimated time of return. Sometimes I would admonish Gracie for not doing more than she was doing to take care of herself. The really tragic reality about all of this was that, in spite of my efforts to assist this family, things always seemed to get worse again after a period of relative stabilization. The complicating factors in their lives, along with numerous negative influences immediately available to the kids in their community worked against everything I ever tried to do.

Just before I left California Gracie's health had declined to the point where she was no longer able to care for her four younger children and they were placed in foster care. Because they were placed in foster care due to Gracie's inability to provide the care they needed, Gracie was given the opportunity to visit them when she could and to talk with them by phone. She was devastated and I felt helpless in trying to help at this point, especially since I was basically meeting with her during this time to end our professional association in light of my relocation efforts back to Mobile, Alabama. I believe the younger children may have a better chance in foster care than they would have had with their mom given the realities of her struggles just to take care of herself. I am not sure what she did to push away her extended family members, but no one would even take in her children rather than see them go into foster care. The boys were adjusting well to their new environment and were old enough by this time to understand what was happening to them and why. The oldest of the six boys was there with Gracie and the next oldest was soon to be released from detention. I can only hope her oldest sons were able to pull things together to give their mom the help she so desperately needed at this point in her life.

With this case I had to fight the feeling of having somehow failed this family. I worked very hard to keep the professional limits and boundaries from getting blurred. This is something I learned very quickly when working with this population. There is only so much I can and am willing to do for my clients and to go beyond those realistic limits would be wrong for them and for myself, and in addition to being unethical. My heart breaks at times because of the work I do which results in exposure to almost unimaginable realities many people face on a daily basis. I have never been afraid to try or afraid to learn by admitting I don't always have the answers. Unfortunately, not everyone can be helped to the extent I would like to accomplish. But I have learned over the years to never assume I haven't made a difference by at least trying. There is no way Gracie or any of her six sons will ever forget my interactions with them. Because of this I trust my efforts will someday pay off for these boys and the kids they will likely have someday. At least this is my hope. I turned their case over to another therapist and have not followed up on Gracie since. It was best for me to just live things as they were and wish all of them the best. Sometimes that is all you can do. What a tremendous learning experience this was for me. I value every experience I have ever had both personally and professional, as each has made me a more capable and stronger person and psychologist.

Let me say a little bit more about the risks involved when working with especially high-risk, troubled kids. Professionals within all fields have the legal obligation to report child abuse/neglect, and any threats from someone to hurt or kill themselves or others. While in most situations this is not that difficult or complicated, with kids involved in rather serious criminal activity such reporting can pose a real threat to you personally. Over the years I have learned to clearly and rather frequently repeat the limits on confidentiality. On numerous occasions I have actually stopped a kid from telling me about something harmful they intended to do to others within a criminal context. It is important to learn to watch for this especially if you have been able to establish a very trusting association with your clients. Joining with a kid requires a frequent review of the limits and boundaries of your professional relationship with them. It would actually be unfair for us to unintentionally set them up to disclose information which could get them or us injured or even killed. When this comes up I quickly stop a kid from telling me anything I would have to report. From that point I then tell them I am going to address what I think they may have been alluding to in a way of trying to talk them out of any sort of illegal activity. While this may be a bit controversial I am not willing to put my life on the line to report a possible street crime which will likely occur anyway. Not only would the planned act be carried out, retaliation against the professional and the kid would most definitely be carried out as well. You will need to learn very early in your career to avoid exposure to this kind of risk.

Another interesting factor each of us should be aware of is related to the safety of others outside of the professional relationship you have established with your client or student. If you are really good at joining with troubled kids they are likely to reveal some details of criminal incidents they encounter. On two occasions I was listening to two different clients talk about retaliation from one gang to another. While the details were vague, they gave me enough information to figure out who the intended target(s) were in both cases along with which gang was going to carry out the retaliation. Because I had gained such a high level of respect and trust within all of the gangs in the area of Riverside County known as the Coachella Valley, I decided to take a risk and go to kids in the retaliatory gang I knew could stop this from happening. In both cases the kids giving me the very limited details were the intended victims. Understand this was my own personal choice and I am not suggesting you follow my exact example, but I had to do something to try and save the lives of my clients. Believe me my supervisor nearly had a heart attack after I told him what I had done in both of these cases. He was surprised to find he actually agreed with this being the only way to likely resolve this situation without putting my own life in very real danger and still save the lives of the intended targets.

After giving all of this a great deal of thought over no more that a 48 hour period I went to the kids in the rival gangs who I knew I could talk with openly. These kids were also my clients and knew me well and respected the work I did to try and help them. I approached the rival gang kids with the same vagueness relative to details I had been given. I assured them no one had ratted them out, reminding my clients in the rival gang of how I work with them and of the level of trust they also had with me. I stressed how important the life of each of my kids is to me and essentially pleaded with them not to kill one of my kids. Remember, I stopped the conversation with the intended victims before they put me in a position of having to report anything to authorities. Even though I pieced things together, I had no specific names of shooters and no specific dates or timeframes. In both cases the kids I approached and pleaded with to spare the lives of my kids honored my request and no one on either side got hurt or killed. Because of the way I handled these situations on both sides no one ever knew specifically who I thought the intended victims were, but readily admitted they knew what I was referring to. Furthermore, I never told the intended victims what I had done because I didn't want any of this discussed on the streets, even for the sake of the kids I approached and made my appeals to save the lives of my other kids.

Let me assure you this was the only way to handle this situation without jeopardizing my own life and the lives of the intended victims. If I had obtained enough information to put me in a position of being obligated to report these incidents to the authorities, the number of deaths likely would have included my own. If I had allowed this to continue to the point of having no choice but to report, then the deaths of the intended victims would have been assured. My own conscience would not have allowed me to do nothing, even though I would have been in no danger if I had simply left things alone. However, there is no doubt in my mind my actions saved the lives of the intended victims and gave me more credibility within the gang culture than I had prior to my interventions. Two of the kids I approached in one rival gang told me "Doc, you've got balls, and we've got your back."

Even though all of this goes against everything which is considered to be usual and customary, the decisions I made in both of these situations were the most realistic and ethical actions to take under the circumstances. I could not have lived with myself if I had allowed the concerns about my own safety to lead to the deaths of two kids I could have saved. My decisions in both instances were very well thought out and were calculated risks I was willing to take. In my early years of training I could never have foreseen these kinds of double bind situations down the road. My boss never asked me to promise him I would not do this again. I was very happy he understood why I did what I did in these situations, and I didn't tell my supervisor any of this until after the second intervention. As far as I know my supervisor never told anyone else in the organization I had made these choices and had taken these actions. The only reason I told him then was to request that he look for me if I ever failed to show up for work without reporting in to indicate I would be absent. He agreed. Several times during Law and Ethics workshops I shared enough of the details of my stories to let others know in many cases things are not as black and white as we want them to be. Each time the instructors of these workshops agreed that, while my actions were unconventional, they were the best choices to have made given the realities of the situations.

When working with troubled kids in general I believe it is necessary to be somewhat unconventional in our approaches toward them. I would never advocate or support anything illegal or unethical, but I am willing to meet them at their level of understanding and reality if that is what it takes to reach them. Like I said I am not offended by language as long as it is not being used toward me. The manner of dress and appearance of kids in general is not a big deal when my main goal is to get to know them for who they are in order to more clearly figure out how that relates to who they are meant to become. At the same time, I try to help kids understand what is necessary and appropriate dress and language within specific contexts and environments, especially relative to the workplace and appearances in courts before judges.

I hope to establish the same levels of trust and respect with the kids and the communities in the area where I now live and work in Mobile, Alabama. However, the black gangs in Mobile are much more dangerous and ruthless that the Hispanic gangs I served in California. I never felt really nervous about my work with gang kids until I moved back to Mobile. Now I am much more cautious and to some extent less directly involved. This reality may be the result of the fact gangs have become much more violent on a national level in recent years then they were when I still live in California. I attribute much of the rise in youth violence to the extreme abuses of power and authority sanctioned under the US Patriot since 9/11. However, my goals still include the desire to teach others in this area and even around this country to understand kids the way I do. Kids where I live now do not generally refer to themselves as gang members. Rather they refer to their territories as "hoods", and to themselves as thugs. Regardless of the terminology used this is still the mentality associated with gang involvement visible in virtually every large city in this country. No matter what terms are used to describe or designate their perspectives, these are still kids who deserve the opportunity to look at things differently and realistically. Therefore, it is still of the utmost importance for adults in all professions associated with working to assist troubled kids to always see these kids first and foremost as kids!

It is extremely important not to use labels which define their existences as though their existences accurately reveal identities of the kids involved. Existences for troubled kids only reflect the realities the kids within these existences must deal with and face. These are kids who do bad things, but are not bad kids. These are kids who face hopeless odds, but are not hopeless kids or lost causes. These are kids who have problems, but are not problem kids. The labels we use to describe and categorize kids always reflect our own biases and ignorance. The only way to become knowledgeable is to admit we do not understand, and then seek to understand rather than judge and label. And the only way to understand is to look beyond what kids do and see them for who they are really meant to be. To do anything less is to be just another problem rather than part of the solution.

Chapter X

Interview Techniques and First impressions

This chapter is about your very first contact with a new client or student. While most of the content within this chapter will focus on an initial interview within a clinical setting, professionals within other settings and contexts could adapt this model to their specific purposes. In reality therapists and social workers within clinical settings are not viewed, and should not be viewed by anyone as authority figures. Therefore, we likely have more freedom to be relaxed with kids than other professionals can risk. First of all the depth of information needed during a clinical interview is much more intensive than would even be appropriate in a less formal and less focused context such as a school. However, the need for the interviewer to be real and genuine is essential if any progress is to be made relative to getting to really know who the individual is beyond such external factors as their behaviors and appearance. The content of this chapter is focused on working with troubled, high-risk kids <u>only</u>, and will attempt to help you understand what I mean by the level of comfort and rapport needed to work effectively with this population. In other words allow them to be themselves with cuss words, slang and graphic details of their real life situations, as long as they are simply trying to open up and communicate with you as needed. You will know the difference between kids trying to comfortably communicate as compared to deliberately trying to shock and/or offend you. Their desire to shock or offend will likely occur if we mishandle of our initial approach and our attempts to connect and begin to join with these kids in a professional manner. The outcome of our initial contact with any high-risk kid depends solely on our level of training, compassion, knowledge, and caring; and based solely in our abilities to convey all of this immediately.

Dr. David L. Roberts Ph.D.

In most settings the single most important factor to know relative to what a new client is thinking about you or expecting from you as the adult is that this experience will not be favorable. The chances are you will be viewed as just another "asshole" in a long line of previous "assholes" who have tried through stereotypical fear tactics and deception to impose unwanted controls on the kid simply for the sake of control. In a clinical setting there will likely be the additional stigma that you as the therapist will think the kid is "mental". The kid will likely be resistant to interacting and will even be suspicious and apprehensive about what may be about to happen. The most critical step at this point is to handle this with the knowledge and desire that this interaction is going to benefit this kid in ways he or she could never even imagine. This can only be accomplished if you as the adult in this situation are very passionate and sincere about your work with this population, and if you have the ability to put the kid at ease rather quickly. Any missteps at this point will jeopardize all future interactions.

As I have stated before kids today are too sophisticated to be fooled by any adults who are nothing more than arrogant, ignorant, insincere, control freaks. Kids may comply with demands, but only out of a sense that a power struggle would be pointless, representing a form of surrender rather than a willingness to learn and grow from the interaction. Let's face it, most adults can 'win' in any professional situation if winning is the only goal. Competition between adults and kids is a lose/lose exchange. Even if the adult wins what have they really won – nothing more than the defeat of the kid they were supposedly trying to reach. The old "I'll show you who's boss" routine doesn't work with today's adolescents. Keep in mind that many kids are not mature enough to resist the stubborn stance of "you can't make me." Kids will often times deliberately fail to succeed if they feel like succeeding is equivalent to kissing the ass of some adult. This is the reason that helping a kid understand what is in their own best interest is the best and only approach which works, especially with troubled kids. The only way an adult can know what is in a kid's best interest is to first of all succeed in joining with the kid and being able and willing to try and see the world through the eyes of each individual kid. Nothing short of this attempt at building a strong positive rapport and a high level of trust will facilitate an alliance with the kids who often need the most assistance and guidance. Each kid must see that you are real and can deal with them and the very real complicating factors they face on a daily basis. It is imperative that they see your compassion and earnest desire to understand before you can assist. None of this can be faked without the adult looking like a insincere fool in the eyes of any kid.

As you enter the waiting area where your client will likely be sitting with family members, always approach the kid first by extending your hand to them and introducing yourself by name. A simple "you must be (kids name). I'm Dr. Roberts and it is a pleasure to meet you." The parent(s) will be a little taken aback in some instances that you did not acknowledge them first, but ignore this. After all the case you are about to open will be in the name of the kid and not in the name of his parent(s) or guardian(s). In reality most of the experiences involving kids and adults, adults generally acknowledge each other before they acknowledge the kid who actually will be their main focus. After the initial introduction I always tell the adults present that I will be working alone with their daughter or son for the first session, assuring them I will give them a little time if possible or at least bring them in initially at their next appointment. I handle the first contact with virtually every kid this way unless they are under the age of six. Adolescents will be able to hang in with you for the entire first session, whereas younger kids will only be able to take so much before you will need to get the adults to join the session. This is the only way to put kids at ease and give them the freedom to openly express themselves and tell you why they think they are in your office. If you inform the adults that this is your standard and consistent approach with every client they will usually understand. I handle this quickly enough that they don't have the opportunity to object before the kid is already in my office and they are left sitting in the waiting area.

For the kid to trust you fully they must be present at every meeting with adults unless it is clearly in their best interest not to be there. Even then it is important to make them fully aware of the nature of such a meeting both before and after the meeting occurs. There has _never_ been a time that I didn't end my initial intake interview with the kid having a completely different and more positive demeanor. This is so obvious to the family members or guardians that in some cases they are actually speechless. I bring the adults in with the kid after I have completed my extensive interview and explain to them how I work with my clients. If necessary I also ask for clarification on some historical details relative to family and medical issues. Of utmost importance is for adults to understand and accept that I am not there to be their detective and that I expect them to respect the privacy of what I discuss with their daughter or son. I remind them that kids in most cases are not generally completely honest with those who are responsible for their well being. I explain that the only way for me to work successfully with their child is for them to trust me and my work so the kid will have at least one person in their life with which they can discuss anything. Furthermore, I tell the adults that I will make sure their kid knows about every contact I have with them between sessions so the kid will know I am not going to side with the adults against the kid at any time. The only information provided to me by adults which I withhold from my client is information which would be in some way damaging to the kid. The best examples would be: the child being the result of a rape, or of a parent's very personal history of abuse and victimization.

My primary caseload includes transitional age, troubled kids, ages 15 and up. Kids from other age groups are welcomed, but I find this group of troubled kids to be the most reachable. This really depends on how out of control their lives are relative to problematic behaviors and other types of bad choices. Kids under the age of 15 are less mature cognitively than older adolescents and are more prone to give into peer influence and follow their impulses to fit in and prove something to others. From the age of 15 and up kids are better able to see that they are growing up whether they want to or not. This gives me a greater chance of helping them understand their need to make better choices based in what is in their own best interest given the reality they are fast approaching adulthood. Most kids will understand that the kinds of accomplishments they need to make during their teenage years are much more difficult to achieve as they take on adult roles and responsibilities. Furthermore, this age group generally represents those adolescents every other program has failed to reach; so, for them this may be their last chance to redirect their lives through guidance from at lest one caring adult. It is, therefore, critical that professionals at all levels not screw up this opportunity by approaching these kids inappropriately and ineffectively. Plus, kids in this age group talk about wanting to leave home by the time they are 18. This gives me the opportunity to help kids set goals which would make this option manageable if that actually becomes their choice at 18. Parents are able to see that using this as a goal will only help insure their kid's progress prior to reaching that age. Most kids do not actually choose to leave home at 18 once that day arrives. However, knowing the option will be a viable plan if they make the right preparations will help them see why certain changes are in their best interest.

In many cases after the first session parents are able to see significant changes in the way their daughter or son is behaving and thinking, and they welcome the opportunity for me to work alone with their child as much as possible. Family members are always welcomed in my office, but the majority of my time and focus must be on my client. Children under the age of 12 or 13 are more likely to be dealing primarily with family issues needing to be resolved. However, by the time a kid reaches the age of 15 or higher, the focus must be on them and their future. In reality if interventions are not started before they reach 15 then the chance of impacting the family dynamics are unlikely anyway. At this point, especially with troubled kids, the focus must be on helping them identify and cope with whatever realities they have experienced in the past so than can move forward in spite of these potential obstacles. Many of the adults in the lives of troubled kids are not interested in making changes for themselves, but expect someone to fix their child for them. Fixing a child is not the issue. Redirecting and supporting a child and the way they use their energy, abilities, and thought processes are the goals. Sometimes with troubled kids this is less likely to occur if the family members are directly involved in their treatment. So do not penalize a kid by refusing to work with them if the family does not want to be involved. In many cases this actually works out more favorably for your client. Always follow the laws of your state regarding parental consent. However, a signature is all you need and participation of adults should not be required as the only way you will agree to work with the kid!

Keep in mind that in many instances by the time a kid reaches your office for therapy they have attended any number of meetings regarding their behaviors and/or lack of progress academically. In these kinds of meetings the kid is usually in the room with several adults who sit around and talk about the kid as though he or she was not even present. In order to get my clients to understand and trust that I will never disregard their worth or input I purposefully exclude the adults in their lives from our initial session. This simple change in the process of getting to know a kid through their own eyes is much more valuable than having a room full of adults who often only express their biases against the kid. In reality you will find that adults have a tendency to play the victim role and exaggerate or outright lie about their issues and concerns of a kid. Parents and teachers are really bad about this and I always confront people regarding the parts they play in making things worse rather than finding effective solutions for the kid. Two powerful questions directed at adults are: "what have *you* done to further complicate the life of this kid?"; and "what have you done for this kid that has *helped* rather than made things worse?" I firmly believe in holding adults accountable for the damage they have done regardless of whether or not it was done intentionally.

Let me actually take you through one of the most interesting interviews I have ever conducted. This particular intake session truly represents everything I have shared with you so far in this chapter. I will explain the information I am trying to obtain on a section-by-section basis and will then actually set up a narrative of the interaction. Please bear with me as I think you will find this informative and interesting. Many of the details, including the kid's name, will be changed, but everything else I share will accurately represent the tone of the entire session which lasted about two hours. Generally at least 90 minutes is needed.

The Interview

I enter the waiting area, looking around for the kid I believe most likely to be my new client. It is rather easy since, at this point in my career, I am the only therapist in the building who works with the truly high risk, troubled kids. I spot my target and walk up to him with my hand out and say, "You must be David Ortiz." He remained seated and shook my hand as I told him, "I'm Dr. Roberts and I'm going to be your therapist." I looked to the woman sitting to David's left and asked her if she was with David. As I shook her hand and again said "I'm Dr. Roberts and I'm going to see your son alone for the first session as I do with all of my kids", she introduced herself as his mother. "When we are done I'll bring him out to you and then you can come into my office with him if we have enough time. If not I'll be glad to meet with you at the beginning of his next appointment with me." With that David got up and I walked with him back to my office.

As we approached the lobby door I explained that I would have to use my key. I told David, "Don't worry. You can get out. You just can't get in without someone opening the door for you." Once through the door I explained, "This is a children's service unit so you'll have to ignore all of the pictures (obviously for younger kids) on the wall. My office is just down this hallway and is the second door on your left." As we enter my office I tell David, "Please sit in the chair by my desk for this session only. I have to do a lot of writing and it's just easier if I can ask questions and write down information without having to turn around all the time. The next time you come you can sit wherever you like."

David sat in the chair I had indicated and immediately slouched down with his right leg crossed over his left at his knee, his right elbow and right knee resting on the edge of my desk, his ass nearly hanging off the front edge of the chair, and his head back against the wall. David was wearing a blue bandana on his head, and was dressed in hardcore California street-style gang attire, which at that time mimicked the way prisoners dress inside the penitentiaries – khaki pants and shirt, with the shirt buttoned only at the very top; very baggy pants, with a "wife beater" style undershirt exposed by his open top shirt. His boxers were visible through his undershirt and his pants were worn very low beneath his waist. Last, but not least, David was wearing the signature Nikes and black framed sunglasses with very dark lenses associated with the standard gang uniform of the time. His body language clearly expressed a "fuck you" kind of attitude, with his posture in the chair telling me he was bored and was not going to be part of this exchange. I ignored all of this and proceeded with my introduction as to the manner in which I work with all kids.

"David, the most important thing I want you to know is that everything in this room is confidential and I can assure you I will never betray that unless you tell me you are being abused, or have the intentions to hurt or kill yourself or someone else. When you are in this room I don't care how you talk – shit, fuck, damn, piss, or hell are all okay as long as you're not using those words against me. Believe me I will never give you a reason to do that. The only thing that matters to me in here is that you talk to me in any manner that makes you feel comfortable. I will never lie to you about anything and my only goal today is to treat you differently than you have ever been treated by any other adult so I can simply get to know you better. Do you have any questions so far?"

"Nope", he replied with a slight and curious smile on his face.

"Then let's get started. Today I need to ask you a lot of questions and I will be writing down a shortened version of what you tell me. I have no secrets and nothing to hide here, and I'm not here to trick or deceive you in anyway. If at anytime you want to know what I'm writing down I will show it to you and let you read it, or I'll read it for you. If I ask you a question about something you have done in the past, let me know if this is or is not on any of your records at school or with the courts. If it is not known to anyone else then I will not write it down. Even though it has never happened to one of my clients, your records from this office could be subpoenaed, especially if you go out of here and blow up a McDonald's or shoot kids in a playground or school yard. Then people are going to want to see what I missed and will look in my records to try and find it. Because this could happen I will never write down anything that could cause you more problems that you have caused for yourself by that point. The *last* thing I want to do is to create more problems for you. Anything you tell me that is not known to others will be written down in a way which will only remind me that you appear to have an extensive history of criminal activity and refused to give me the details. I will never bullshit you about anything! Do you have any questions about any of this?"

"Nope", He says and then asks, "Fuck dog, are you for real?"

I laughed and said, "Yep!"

With this I knew I had gotten through to him. I had not acknowledged any of David's mannerisms or the way he was dressed. I had treated him with respect and like a human being, rather than like the thug he wanted me to see. The kid within him came out rather quickly by me being real with him and by assuring David that I was there to get to know him, to help him as much as possible, and to defend and protect him if that became necessary, and if it would be appropriate for me to do so. He also knew that I was not there to judge or misjudge him, or to mistreat or deceive him in any way. This kind of approach is the only approach that works and works consistently with troubled kids.

As I sit shuffling my papers, trying to get organized and ready to begin my intake interview, I told David, "I have only one request."

"What's that?" he asked.

I replied, "I need you to take off your sunglasses."

Obviously offended, David asked, "What for? Do you think I'm fucking stoned or something?"

"No", I responded, "I just want to be able to look into your eyes while we are talking."

With that David smiled, almost trying not to laugh, and sat up in his chair. He took off his sunglasses, folded them carefully, and placed them on my desk. In the process he had uncrossed his legs and his entire demeanor changed. I had never witnessed such an immediate and complete transformation in my entire life, and couldn't help but laugh and ask, "Who the fuck are you now?"

David asked, "What the fuck are you laughing at?"

"Not at you," I assured him. "You're just not the same kid now who walked into my office 15 minutes ago. You know, those glasses are going to get you killed someday."

With that clarification David started laughing. He could clearly see how the simple act of removing his sunglasses had allowed him to literally remove that hardcore exterior image he felt he needed to portray in order to protect himself from me and my attempts to invade his privacy. I asked him, "Are you ready to get this interview over with?"

David laughed and said, "It's okay, Doc."

"I know your name is David Ortiz and that you are 15 years old. Are you still in school?"

"Yep," he replied, adding, "but I get into a lot of trouble at school and they don't want me there."

"What grade are you in and what school do you attend?" I asked.

"I'm in the ninth grade and attend (XYZ) High School."

"Did you fail a grade?"

"Yep, I got held back in the third grade because I was having a lot of trouble with reading."

"Are you in special ed?" I asked.

"Yep, and I hate school!" he added.

Do you feel like you're getting the help you need in school, or do you feel like they go out of their way to harass you?"

"They fuck with me all the time" David replied. "Every time I turn around they're searching me for drugs or weapons, or I'm being sent to the office for something I didn't even do!"

"Do you dress like this at school?" I asked while surveying his attire.

"Yep.", he answered.

"Then you understand you are just asking for trouble aren't you?"

"Yeah, but it isn't fair", he reasoned.

"Fair or not, it's a reality that isn't going to change. I'm not suggesting you do anything to change the way you dress for school. I'm just asking you to be aware that you will always be treated with disrespect as long as they see you kind of flipping them off by the way you dress. When we meet I'll never tell you what you have to do. I'll just try to give you some things to think about so you can decide what behaviors and choices are in your best interest. Let's move on. Tell me what gang you're in."

"Why do you want to know that?" he asked.

"Well it's rather obvious that you're in a gang. Does probation have a record on your suspected gang involvement which includes the name of your gang?"

"Yeah."

"Then just tell me which gang so I'll know as well. Because they already have it on record I'll write it down in my notes so I won't need to ask you again in the future. Like I said earlier, if there is no record anywhere of any part of your life you want kept secret, just tell me and I *will not* write down what you say. Remember, too, I'll show you my records today or at any point in the future if you want to check to see if I have lied to you about anything."

"No, I believe you Doc. My gang is Eastside Desert Locos," he announced proudly while throwing up his gang sign. (This gang did not exist.)

ProKids, Inc.; The Message and The Movement

From there I asked several questions about his history of gang involvement, including when he got jumped in. He gave me the details of how bad the initiation was, announcing with pride that, "Those fuckers didn't even knock me down once!"

"What do they call you in the gang?" I asked.

"What the fuck you wanna know that for?" he asked defensively.

"Just to see if you trust me. I promise I'll never write it down or tell it to anyone else. Plus it will give me a chance to see if I have ever heard of you from other kids."

With that explanation he proudly told me, "They call me Little Bro."

"I have heard of you from some of the other kids I work with. Do you know Little Peeps, and Cyclone?"

"They're in my gang. How do you know them?"

"They were referred to me from probation just like you were. Ask them about me and they'll tell you I'm for real", I explained.

I use this approach frequently with this population *only*. The longer I work within any certain area, the more kids I get to meet. This is happening in Mobile with the kids I am seeing here as well. Eventually all of the kids on the streets either will have met me or at least will know about me by word-of-mouth. I never give out personal information of the other kids and always assure the kid in front of me at the time that I won't do that to him either. I am not concerned about the confidentiality of this as much as I am concerned with trying to put these kids at ease relative to the work I do with them and their friends. In reality all of the kids will likely see me at some point with other kids either in a school setting or when they get locked up. I never do this with other populations of kids.

"Without going into any details just tell me if you have any history of criminal activity related to violence and weapons. Also let me know if there is a record of any of these actions." I continued.

"Yeah Doc, I have been charged with assault with a deadly weapon, and there are other things I have done that I don't want to tell you about now", he answered.

"Do you have any other charges such as burglary or anything related to drugs and alcohol?"

"Yeah, I got arrested for a beer run and once for possession of marijuana."

Rather than dwell on the gang issues and criminal activity I decided to move on for now. These are factors I will continuously monitor throughout the entire time I will work with this kid and other kids. It is important to at least get a glimpse of what their criminal history may include, without appearing to be too nosey at this point. Don't over go overboard during the first interview. The level of rapport and trust needed to explore these kinds of issues in more detail will develop more fully over time. It is always important not to write down details of activities which could cause problems for a kid later on if any kid's records are requested by his parents or, are ever subpoenaed for court.

"Tell me what kinds of drugs you have tried, and give me the list of drugs you use regularly. It will be okay to write this information down since you would have to get caught using any substances for you to be charged with a crime. But if you don't want me to write down anything other than what is known by your family or by probation I won't do that. Just tell me."

"Fuck Doc, I've tried a lot of things, but the only ones people know about are alcohol and marijuana. I drink a lot on weekends and smoke weed every day. I sometimes use meth and have tried cocaine, but you can't write those down. I am afraid of hard drugs because I see what they do to people around me."

"I don't mean to offend you by asking, but are you being honest with me? The only reason I'm asking is so I can understand how important drugs are as a part of your life. I'm not here to judge you or to even try to control you. You can clearly do whatever you want to do, but it is my job to at least warn you about the dangers and health risks of these kinds of choices."

"That's cool doc, but I am being honest."

"I appreciate that and I believe you David."

"Do you ever hear things or see things that other people don't see?"

"What do you think I'm fucking mental or something?"

"No David, I just have to ask. You'd be surprised to know that sometimes the answer to that question is 'yes'. It's just part of what I need to know about you. I don't think you're mental and I'm glad that doesn't happen to you. If it did we would need to deal with it though."

"Do you ever get really depressed about things in your life?"

"Sometimes I get down about my friends who have been killed, but when I drink and smoke weed it goes away. I never think about killing myself."

"Drinking and smoking weed are not going to make your feelings go away permanently. Hopefully you will let me work with you on the deaths of your friends so I can help you learn how to deal with their deaths in ways that will help you and maybe even protect you."

"We'll see Doc."

"Did you at anytime in the past think about killing yourself?"

"I used to before my father got arrested."

"Tell me a little about that."

"He always drank a lot and would beat up my mom. I tried to stop him and then he would beat up on me. My mom always tried to protect me, but things only got worse."

"What was your dad charged with?"

"Selling drugs. He's going to be locked up for a long time. I haven't seen him since I was 10. I'm glad the son of a bitch is gone!"

"It sounds like you still have a lot of anger toward him. Do you use that anger on the streets?"

"Sometimes. I really hate it when guys beat up on bitches, so I always kick their asses when I see this happen! I would never hit a girl."

"But you call them bitches. We need to work on the way you see females in your life."

"Whatever, Doc."

By this point in the interview you can see that I have accomplished a number of things with David and have gained his trust and respect. These two components will always be very fragile with this population so you must work consistently to never let your clients down. As you can see I know a lot about David's home/family context and about his experiences within his community and school contexts as well. David has willingly shared a great deal of information with me about his criminal history and his use of various substances. The single most important accomplishment occurred when David removed his sunglasses and was able to clearly see the two very distinct sides of his personality. None of this would have been possible if I had approached David any differently than the way I did. In later years of running into him as he got older the two things he remembered most were the realization associated with the sunglasses, and the fact I treated him differently than any other adult previously involved in his life. David will carry these experiences with him for the rest of his life.

During this first part of the interview I now have an idea of David's emotional state and know that he doesn't appear to have any desire to commit suicide, and has no psychotic symptoms. I can tell from his ability to express himself that he is rather intelligent, a characteristic that I suspect very few people ever recognize in him. The only way other people would be able to see David as I was able to see him would be by using the exact same kind of approach I used. Because most adults would have focused exclusively on David's obvious outward appearance and behaviors David would not be able to let down his guard and allow people to see his soul. By using this approach with kids I am able to get a very clear picture of their intelligence, talents and potential. I am also able to see who they really are and who they are meant to become, even if these potentialities never fully take hold. By the time I finished working with David even at the end of our first session, David had a different perception of himself than he had likely ever had. With my awareness of his potential and his intellect I asked the next question intended to challenge his self perception and at the same time introduce another perspective.

"Tell me David, how smart are you?"
"Not very. I can't do math and I still have trouble reading."
"David, I didn't ask you about your school performance, I asked you about how smart you are."
"What's the difference?", he asked.

"Your lack of progress in school clearly has nothing to do with your level of intelligence. You have been actively involved in every part of this interview so far and have clearly understood everything I asked. You also showed me that you put a lot of thought into figuring out things in your life, like the way your dad's drinking and violence affected your life."

"I never thought about it that way. I always thought that because I am in special ed that I must be kinda dumb.", he said, expressing both surprise and relief by the tone of his voice.

"David, I would imagine that you are probably lucky to be alive, Right?"

"Yeah."

"This tells me that you obviously have the ability to make plans and carry them out in ways that have allowed you to survive many things in your life, right?"

"Yeah!"

"I would also imagine that you have probably participated in activities that required you to do a lot of planning related to business deals you have made, right?"

"Yeah. How the fuck do you know that Doc?"

"I've been working with kids who have lives and problems similar to yours since 1992. I even worked and trained in East LA and upper South Central LA before I moved to the desert. In LA I worked with kids from 18th Street, White Fence, Sangra, Playboys, Avenues, Lomas, Hazard, Red Door, Red Dragon, and Asian Boys. The only difference between you and them is that you live outside of LA.", I explained.

"Whoa, Doc. I didn't know you have worked with all of those gangs." he said sounding impressed.

I continued, "All kids involved in street crimes generally have good planning skills and a great deal of business experience. I'm sure you know about marketing and advertising, getting and keeping new customers, competing for sales, setting competitive prices, buying and selling, warehousing and storing, and profits, right?"

"Yeah, Doc, I do!" he said laughing in disbelief.

"Then you have valuable skills you could someday use in ways that won't get you killed or locked up, huh?"

"Yeah Doc, but you make a lot more money my way than by being legit."

"Yeah David, but making money illegally always comes with a price doesn't it?"

"Yeah Doc, it does."

"Then all I want you to do is to at least think about what I have said and to be aware that you are much smarter than you have ever been able to see before today."

Kids will always be amazed when you tell them how useful their skills are even though they were obtained from illegal activities in which they are involved in the streets. It is very important to not let them think you are validating their activities as valuable. Rather, that you are simply pointing out how they can turn the negative misuse of the skills and energy into positive endeavors if they would choose to do so in the future. This rather simple reality puts a different twist on their self perspective relative to their levels of intelligence, talents, and potential. It gives them a chance to also understand that not all of their time has been wasted, even though they put everything on the line every time they engage in illegal activities. Revealing other possible results of their activities will also give them some sense of hope relative to their potential to become someone other than who they have become so far. This approach also gives them the opportunity to understand that you are not asking them to change into someone new. You are just asking them to work differently with who they already are, relative to the true nature of their soul and their potential for good in the future. Always work with kids in this population with the notion of "what goes around comes around". This is their slogan for the concept of Karma which is found within all spiritual teachings. By pointing this concept out as Karma you can also give them a glimpse at how they already use basic spiritual concepts in their lives. Of course with troubled kids this phrase is more related to the idea that "if you kick my ass I'm going to kick yours." They can be given the opportunity to understand that this concept has far greater application, including the fact that when you put good things out there good things will come back to you as well.

The rest of the interview revealed that David had an older half brother and two younger sisters. It is important to ask kids to tell you who lives with them in their home. Always start by listing the adults living in the home/family context and find out their ages and the specific relationships they represent, such as parents, mom/boyfriend, dad/girlfriend, step parents. Always ask if adults are married, divorced or never married. Don't be shocked or even react if a kid tells you they have a homosexual mom or dad who has a same-sex partner living in the home. You will need to ask how the dynamics of all of these relationships impact the kid sitting in front of you. Also ask if the parental relationships work or if they are conflicted and involve a lot of arguing or even domestic violence which can go both ways between partners. Don't forget to ask if mom beats up her partner. This is more common than you might imagine. Be sure to discuss the details of any immediate family members who have died.

When asking for the list of siblings, always get the ages of each sibling and get their last names. Different last names will give you an indication of how many different fathers are involved and how many half siblings there are. Always ask about relationships between siblings and get a clear indication of who is responsible for the care of siblings – older siblings, or the parent(s) or guardian(s). Ask about siblings who live away from your client's home/family context. Find out if they have simply grown up and left home or if the parents have children with other parents besides the biological parents of your client. Always get names and ages. Believe me this is all important in getting a clear picture of your client's family constellation, which may at times involve distant galaxies as well. Getting this kind of detailed information will give you clues about other questions to ask. Write all of it down. If it is really complicated show the diagram to your client and point out how the family dynamics really complicate their life in ways that are beyond their control. Kids must be allowed to see the numbers of complicating factors present in their lives. This will give them the chance to see and understand that their problems are more about where they have come from and what they have been through, and much less about who they really are and are meant to become. <u>At the Mercy of Externals; Righting Wrongs and Protecting Kids, 2nd Edition</u>, was a title chosen very carefully for my first book relative to the realities of kids within this population of high risk, troubled kids.

After exploring all of the family members and respective relationships you only need to find out more about your client's medical history, including what they know about their mom's pregnancy and delivery. It is important to learn if mom drank or used during her pregnancy and if there were any complications. Obviously some of this will need to be clarified with the mom if that is possible. Included in this category is the family history of illnesses and hospitalizations to include mental and emotional disorders as well. You may have to be creative in obtaining this information by asking questions such as: "was any member of your family ever thought of as being strange or weird?" This will get some interesting responses.

The last topics to be explored will be specific educational needs and goals, including the kid's take on whether or not they think they will finish high school. This must be explored in detail, with attempts made to encourage educational pursuits in light of the realities associated with failure to make even minimal academic achievements. From there it is important to focus on future plans and goals. One of the biggest problems created by educators today is the lack of efforts they put into helping kids imagine what they want to be when they grow up. You will find that many of the troubled kids you will work with have never even thought about this. Their biggest concern is with simply growing up. They have very little awareness of trying to imagine anything beyond that accomplishment. It will be part of your work with your clients to teach them how to dream and to help them understand the importance of doing so. If a kid suggests something that is highly unlikely given what you know about them or about the odds of anyone achieving that goal, then help them explore some alternatives just in case.

I had the opportunity to work with David for about six months. During that time we made a lot of progress in helping David understand differently many aspects of his life. Unfortunately David didn't finish school. But the last I heard he was alive and I know he never got re-incarcerated within the juvenile justice system. I saw him at his house when he was 19 and it was obvious that he was still deeply involved in his gang activity. He told me he seldom ever used drugs anymore, but still drank on weekends and smoked weed occasionally. He looked really healthy and we laughed about the incident with his sunglasses. I have no way of knowing what has become of David, but I do have the satisfaction of knowing that I made a positive impression on him and on his way of thinking. At least that is something, and hopefully something he will pass down to his children someday.

List of Critical Interview/Assessment Items for Troubled Kids

- Identifying information
- School attended and current grade or grade completed
- Diagnoses
- Referral source(s)
- Current medications and dosages
- Presenting problems
- Assessment for harm to self or other to include suicide, homicide, and all forms of self-injurious behaviors
- Assessment for any form of abuse
- Mental status exam
- List of all family members and people living in the home. Always include ages, first and last names, relationship to child, living or deceased, and marital status. This section should also include lists of parents living outside the home, stepparents/significant others, half and step siblings, and any other relatives or non-family residents living in the home.
- Assessment of family relationship dynamics between all involved
- Child/family history of physical, medical, mental, and/or emotional problems and hospitalizations
- Academic history and related issues
- Social interactions of child
- History of criminal activity of child and parents/others
- History of substance abuse by child and parents/others

- Most traumatic life experience
- Most traumatic event witnessed
- Most offensive act committed
- Sexual activity (if age appropriate)
- Sexual orientation (if age appropriate)
- Knowledge of STD's and pregnancy prevention (if age appropriate)
- Personal changes and improvements client would like to make
- Fears and nightmares
- Sources of anger
- First childhood memory
- Immediate and long-term goals

Chapter XI

Focus and Funding Needs

For anyone to work effectively with troubled kids it is necessary to be both earnestly interested in working *with* them and genuinely interested *in* them. This must be the focus of every interaction. It is also important to put aside all professional pretense and superiority and truly enjoy the time you spend with each kid, every time you meet. Dress somewhat casually and learn to speak and understand their language. Be familiar with their music and their fads and trends. If a kid uses a phrase with which you are unfamiliar, ask them to explain what it means. There is a big difference between being "cool" and making the mistake of trying to be one of them. At all times you must be the cool, caring adult who is actively seeking to serve every kid to the fullest extent possible relative to your professional role with them. Be the authority figure only when the situation and circumstances demand this stance. Otherwise be professionally relaxed and casual in your efforts to reach out to kids who are starving for positive and supportive adult interactions.

The example of David in the previous chapter was a good example of what is required to reach even the most reluctant of participants. If I had approached David any differently than I did he would never have opened up to me, nor would he have continued working with me. This level of willingness to participate must be established during the first interview if you are to be able to proceed with therapy, counseling, teaching, or mentoring relative to troubled kids. Your effectiveness depends on your ability as an adult to carry the lead in conversation with kids in general. Kids who are not in the "troubled" or "high risk" categories are usually more polite and will tolerate your interactions even if they are perceived as disingenuous. Troubled kids feel absolutely no obligation to tolerate anything given the realities that their lives have been about nothing less than compromise after compromise within every context in order to survive. Never expect a troubled kid to settle for less than they deserve or need. After all, why should they? If, as a professional, you are motivated by any other drive than that of serving and meeting needs, then you should find another professional role involving populations other than troubled kids. It's that simple!

The focus of treatment and other forms of interaction is different when dealing with troubled kids as compared to kids who fall into other categories. Non-troubled kids who present for treatment or some form of assistance are more likely to be dealing exclusively with learning disorders and other types of disorders which are strictly physiologically based. These types of disorders would include Attention Deficit Hyperactivity Disorder, Attention Deficit Disorder, Post Traumatic Stress Disorder, situation specific depression and anxiety, developmental disorders, and symptoms suggesting early onset of more severe mood and/or psychotic disorders. While troubled kids may be dealing with some of these diagnostic categories, they will also have a collection of serious complicating factors coexisting in and dominating their lives as well. They will present with referrals from various agencies and institutions for more extreme behavioral problems which match symptomatology of Conduct Disorder and Oppositional Defiant Disorder as primary diagnoses. Secondary disorders will likely include emotional and mental disorders with the overriding emphasis on the behavioral problems represented by the primary diagnoses of Conduct Disorder and Oppositional Defiant Disorder. Accompanying secondary disorders which are most common for troubled kids include ADHD, Learning Disorders, Major Depression, and Polysubstance Abuse. Even though there may be indications of developing personality disorders, such diagnoses are never made for kids given the fluidity of their emerging personality traits as compared to those of adults.

After my initial interview with David we met on a regular basis and he willingly kept his appointments because he looked forward to our time together. If nothing else David was initially curious about me and the difference he perceived with me compared to other adults in his life. As I got to know him better it became much easier for me to identify and define who he was meant to be and to nurture that potential in a way that my perceptions could become his perceptions. My insights were of no use to him until they became his insights tailored according to his own need and ability to understand and apply them. And only those insights which were appropriate and accurate were useful to him. Many of the good qualities I saw in David were difficult for him to believe until he began to try them out in different areas of his life. The fact alone that David didn't get any deeper into the juvenile justice system is proof that something clicked within him. He may not have finished high school, but I got his attention as evidenced by his own successful redirection of at least some of his energy. David was proud to know me and openly talked with his friends about me, many of whom I knew professionally as well. What an amazing and humbling impact to have on a kid considered by most to be worthless and unreachable. Failure to accomplish this level of trust and regard with any troubled kid is almost as abusive as anything else that has gone wrong in their lives. The ability to simply keep a kid engaged is a sign of success even if they are reluctant initially to open up. This is why it is critical that adults be able to take the lead in guiding the interactions toward the goal of getting to know the kid. It is the only way to have any kid know how it feels for someone to truly take an interest in them and care about them and their realities.

Depending on how complicated a troubled kid's life is the therapy, outreach and support could cover a period of several years. It is not uncommon for troubled kids to get locked up, sent off to placement, or even be on the run for extended periods of time. However, they will eventually resurface and it is important to always look for them and reach out to them on an on going basis. They will never tell you to "fuck off" unless you do something which shatters their impression that you truly care about them. NEVER LET THIS HAPPEN! You may have to accept their desire to terminate their association with you, but make sure this happens on a positive note and with an open ended return and availability policy such as: "Unless something unforeseen happens in my life, I will always be here for you when you need me!" They will never forget this promise and will look for you when the time is right. If you have treated them with the respect they deserve and have successfully demonstrated your ability to care about them, they will eagerly come back to you knowing that you will never see them as a failure. Meet them wherever they are in life and start from there in helping get them back on track or to guide them in an entirely different direction. Your ability to care must never wane, no matter what they do or have done. A certain level of occasional disappointment is appropriate, at the same time knowing they understand your level of frustration with and unspoken disapproval of certain activities and choices. Their connection to you indicated by their return to you reflects their appreciation for the differences between you and them relative to life choices they have made or are making. They don't expect you to bless their misdeeds, but they do expect consistency in your ability to guide and assist them when they are sincerely seeking assistance.

As I mentioned earlier in this text, don't make every meeting a counseling or therapy session – at least not obviously so. Each encounter with a kid should always constitute some form of therapy or counseling since you should always be looking for insight into the kid's experiences and perceptions. However, this can easily be accomplished by simply engaging them in a conversation about the events since the last session or by showing an interest in the time they spend with their friends. Don't be judgmental of their accounts of how they party or pass time with their friends. Use these accounts as opportunities to warn them of danger and to give them some reality checks relative to any misperceptions they may exhibit. Do not be overbearing with these observations either, always remaining conscious of your inability to control the choices they make. Remember that the most you can hope for is an opportunity to offer them some insights into their actions and choices which will give them the desire to change relative to what is in their own best interest. Never deceive yourself about your ability to set limits for them. However, it is appropriate to let them know how much you worry about their safety and to tell them how much you would be impacted by their incarceration, death or serious injury. It is also appropriate to remind them that death can be both literal and figurative – physical death, and death by incarceration for life. By admitting your limitations relative to impacting their lives and choices you keep the responsibility squarely on them. By letting them know how much you care you give them something to think about that will at some point be useful in helping them make better choices. This is especially true when they get locked up and have a lot of time to think.

Keep in mind too that the kids you work with have the ability to help their friends make needed changes in their lives as well. All you need to do is to help them recognize these opportunities and see how helping their friends can be accomplished without making your kids look like "pussies" or "bitches". One of the hardest things kids have to face on the streets is the death of a friend or a family member. By getting them to understand that there will be moments when they can save lives by simply being the one who keeps a level head they will be able to step up and do what's right. When the time is right a simple statement made to their friends could help diffuse a situation which is potentially dangerous and/or life threatening. Such a statement made out in the streets by the kid you serve could be, "Wait a minute. Let's think about this before we do something stupid given the fact we are all fucked up." This is especially helpful in a situation where everyone involved is drinking and/or using, which is often the case. It is easy to get your kid to become aware of how alcohol and drugs cloud everyone's ability to think things through before acting impulsively. There is no doubt in my mind that by sharing these kinds of skills and insights with my kids over the years, countless lives have been saved as a result. In many instances your kid can and will become the catalyst for change on the streets and in other contexts with her or his friends.

If all of us handle things right with the kids in our charge we can have a tremendously far reaching impact on kids within an entire geographical area. This alone is one of the reasons for the importance of seeing every interaction with each kid as being extremely significant, and possibly your last relative to circumstances beyond your control. With this perspective it is possible to increase our efforts to be more appropriate and effective in our contacts with troubled kids. You will be astounded to learn how quickly the word will spread that Mr., Mrs., Miss, Officer, or Dr. so-and-so is really cool and can be trusted if you need someone to talk with about your problems. Think about how quickly the word spreads about anyone who is experienced by kids as being an asshole or a bitch. Either way these labels stick in the minds of kids. The same is true for each of us as adults who hear and think certain things about the adults or kids within our range of experiences. Remember that negative reputations are difficult to change.

If a kid tells you someone in their life is an asshole or a bitch and you know this to be an accurate observation, acknowledge it as appropriately as you can. Then take care to help the kid deal with this reality in a way that will serve their own best interest without giving the so-called asshole or bitch any further opportunities to complicate the kid's life. This has happened many times in my career since in many cases I have known most of the authority figures directly involved in a kid's life and experiences. Many times I have told a kid that "I agree with you. However I am going to trust that you will not tell others that I said so as this could create serious problems for me professionally. Now, what can you do to keep this person from causing you more problems given the reality that they will probably always be the asshole or bitch you think they are?"

Even when I do not know first hand that their observation is accurate, I accept it as their reality and encourage them to prove the adult wrong by doing what is in the kid's own best interest. Clearly at times the behaviors of kids can make it difficult for others to like them, but adults within all contexts should make every effort to always separate what a kid does from who they really are. If adults could be more objective in their interactions with troubled kids, they would be able to see serious mistakes they make which only incite and escalate a kid to anger and obnoxious behaviors. By challenging kids not to give adults the opportunity to be right about kids being lost causes, kids can get a lot of satisfaction out of making changes which will prove the adults to be wrong. Sometimes this scenario involves kids' perspectives of and interactions with family members as well.

While this approach must be handled in a professional manner, failure to acknowledge the kid's perspective will only make you "just like every other fucking asshole/bitch in my life." This will defeat your purpose of working supportively with your kid and will also jeopardize your ongoing professional relationship with her or him. Sometimes kids are just trying to be manipulative, but in a majority of cases with troubled kids their perceptions are very accurate. Keep in mind that most of the authority figures involved in their lives do not like them anyway. Therefore it is easy to assume that a kid's interpretation of their experiences is likely accurate. Many adults are often guilty of siding with adults no matter what the truth is. Be sure to resist this temptation and do not allow yourself to be pulled into an agreement when you know the truth contradicts what any adult is saying about a kid. This is part of the arrogance I am referring to relative to adults who have authority over kids. Adults very frequently gang up on troubled kids because in many cases the adults have done things they know to be in direct violation of the kid's rights and needs. This is especially true within the contexts of law enforcement and educational settings. Like it or not everyone knows that it is quite common for adults to cover for other adults if the general consensus is that of not liking a kid and not wanting them around. Believe me, troubled kids are especially sensitive to and aware of this kind of reality in their range of experiences within many, if not all of their environments. Like I said in a previous chapter, be part of the solution and not just another problem.

Matthew Stevens was 17 when he was referred to me from probation for mandatory counseling. He was in the 11th grade and was always getting into trouble at school. The principal at Matt's high school was 'finally' able to get him charged with assault and placed on permanent probation. Needless to say Matt was pissed about this. While Matt was viewed as a troublemaker he was well liked by many school personnel. Matt is a prime example of the importance of making the kid your focus of treatment and or interaction, rather than siding with the adults in her or his life. This is especially true with kids who are older and more mature as was the case with Matt.

Matt initially came on to our clinic with his mother to be registered for services. As was the case with many of my new referrals, I was not there at that time of day to meet Matt or his mother. The front office staff scheduled Matt for my next available intake slot on the following Tuesday. Most of the time a kid is accompanied to the office by his parent or guardian. However, Matt was alone, having taken the bus in order to keep his first mandated appointment with me. Even though he was a little apprehensive about the experience of meeting with a psychologist, he told me he was glad that his mom was not present; explaining that she always embarrassed him and made him mad. He told me his mom was mad at him for getting into trouble and didn't have time to be part of his treatment at a "mental clinic". I went through my usual routine and put Matt at ease very quickly. He was so glad to have someone to talk with who respected him and he opened up to me very willingly.

Very early in the interview it became obvious that Matt was extremely intelligent and that he had no clue of the extent of his intellect. He was very articulate and insightful relative to numerous complicating factors dominating his past and his present. All Matt knew for certain was that he was really pissed off about the way his life had been and the way it seemed to be going relative to his family. When we got to the family profile part of the interview he told me that his mom was married to a man of a different ethnicity than hers. His biological father had died a few years before our meeting, but had not been part of Matt's life until just before his dad died. Matt found out from his father that Matt's mother had kept them apart because Matt's father knew things about her past she didn't want Matt to know. Matt's mom told Matt about his dad and his whereabouts only because Matt's dad had contacted her to tell her he was dying from cancer and wanted to see his son. She apparently agreed in spite of her reluctance for Matt to have contact with his dad and Matt got to spend a relatively short amount of time with his dad before his dad died. During all of this Matt learned that the man he always thought was his dad was in fact only one of mom's many boyfriends from the past.

Matt learned that his dad's cancer was associated with his history of heavy drug and alcohol use. While Matt had some idea about his mother's own history of drug addiction, he never knew that he had been born addicted to heroine. His dad told Matt that he was eight weeks premature and was not expected to survive, at least not without serious brain damage. To everyone's amazement Matt not only survived, but he beat the odds and had only minimal deficits relative to his cognitive functioning. Matt knew he had some problems with memory and comprehension, but had learned over the years to compensate for these deficits rather than let them impede his progress. However, Matt had no idea that all of this was related to his mother's addiction to heroine, a secret she had wanted to keep from him.

Obviously Matt confronted his mother with all he had learned. She reacted with a sense of righteous indignation, expressing her regret that she had told him about his real dad. Her regret was for herself and the fact that the truth came out about her past and the impact it had on Matt's health and well being early in his life. Apparently the physical complications Matt had when he was born had given mom reason to stop using heroine, even though she continued to drink and use other substances until Matt was 15. Matt's mom was extremely abusive to him over the years and he deeply resented her for this. Learning the truth about her past and about his dad only deepened his resentment toward her for all she had put him through. The only thing that made this bearable was the fact that as mom cleaned up when Matt was 15 and she tried to make all of this right with him. However, the damage had been done. In spite of mom's efforts to set things right she continued to live a very complicated lifestyle which had a very negative impact on Matt even at the time when I met him.

It is important to keep in mind that troubled kids usually have parents who were or are more troubled than the kids. Furthermore, it is not uncommon to work with kids who are more intelligent and insightful than their adult counterparts. Sometimes this is related to the extensive history of substance addiction for the adult which has negatively affected their ability to reason and function. Because of this it would be wrong to refuse to work with any kid because their parent(s) do not want to be involved in their treatment or other attempts to intervene on behalf of the kid. In reality all you really need from a parent or guardian is their signature giving you permission to work with their kid. As I stated previously, even when troubled parent(s) are involved, their involvement often creates a toxic environment in which very little progress, if any, can be made as long as they are part of the therapeutic process. This would have been the case with Matt and his mom. This is why it is so important that the main focus of treatment or other forms of intervention always be on the kid. Others should be involved if and only if it is in the best interest of the kid, and then only if the kid agrees to their involvement when you are dealing with a kid who is 15 years of age and older. Make sure that you as the professional are always in control of the process being implemented on behalf of any kid, regardless of their age. Do not be afraid to stand up against other adults if it is in the best interest of the kid. Believe me, some of my most successful interventions have resulted from my willingness to set very clear limits with adults by confronting them on their self-serving overindulgence and deception. The mom of one of my clients told me she respected me because I was not afraid of her, telling me she would remove herself from the process since it was clearly in her son's best interest that she do so.

Keep in mind that adults are not usually motivated to make changes. The more impaired they are the more likely they are to have serious personality disorders. These disorders become permanent and ineffective ways of trying to cope with life. For older adolescents in these situations the only solution is to work with them separately from the negative adult influences in their lives. By this point in a kid's life, it is generally too late to help the family repair itself. The longer a family stays broken the more likely it will become irreparably damaged. In this case the only thing to do is to try and literally save kids from these circumstances. This is the only way to keep them from repeating the mistakes of the parents by helping them identify and understand what the mistakes were and will continue to be. Part of my hope with the kids I see is that even if they cannot make the changes for themselves, they will at least protect their own children from harm when they become parents.

As I continued my interview with Matt he reluctantly revealed that he and his family were living in one of the local motels (referred to as "roach motels") occupied by people who had no other place to live. Matt was really embarrassed by this and no one in his life knew about this reality. He managed to keep it away from all of his friends even though they had been living in the motel for several months. The real insult about their current living situation was that Matt's mom and stepdad lost their last two apartments because of their recently acquired gambling addictions. No matter how much Matt begged them to stop gambling and save up the money they needed to get a new place, they continued to waste their money at the local casinos. The marriage between Matt's mom and his stepdad was really conflicted primarily because both of them had so many complicating factors present in their separate lives and personalities. Apparently because of their financial problems Matt's mom had started drinking again. Things were really bad for Matt and it became apparent to me why he was getting into trouble outside the home/family context. The thing that really surprised me that was he was not getting into more serious trouble than he actually was.

During this first session I was able to give Matt a glimpse into his unrecognized and unrealized potential. I helped him understand the two most amazing characteristics he possessed – resiliency (the ability to bounce back), and the ability to transcend or rise above the complicating factors present in his life. In this first session he was able to realize the level of his intelligence in spite of the fact his mother had always told him how stupid he was. Matt was able to see that he had the ability to continue beating the odds as long as he nurtured and maintained the desire to do so. He was also able to see that the problems he had in life were about where he came from and what he had been through, and had nothing to do with anything inherently wrong with him. I was able to help him make observations about his family which gave him insight into many realities present in his life which were beyond his control to either influence or change. This included the reality that his mom would likely never change to the point of being stable and likable. He was able to see that all he needed to do was find and hold onto hope for the future as a way of surviving until he was old enough to leave his mom. Thank God he was 17 and not even just a few years younger. At least at this age I could help him see that everyday is one day closer to him being able to become independent as long as he prepared for that to happen by at least finishing high school.

I worked with Matt for about 18 months. By that time he had turned 18 and had his high school diploma. He faithfully and willingly took the bus every two weeks in order to keep his appointments with me. Each visit was filled with new insights and awakenings, coupled with the continual reinforcement of Matt's belief in himself and in his ability to succeed. After a few sessions I scheduled his appointments so he was my last client for the day. With that I offered to take him back to the motel where he lived rather than have him walking or taking the bus after each session. At first he was reluctant for me to see where and how he was living. After assuring him that his living conditions were a reflection on his parents and not on him he agreed. It took a few times of taking him to the motel before he agreed to let me meet his mom.

Keep in mind that parents of troubled kids who are troubled themselves often want to play the victim role. Matt's mom was no exception to this rule. She came out of the motel room rather than have me see the real conditions under which they were living. Matt stood beside me as I listened to his mom tell me how complicated her life was and how much trouble Matt had caused her especially in recent years. I had warned him about this and he had agreed to let me handle it for him, assuring him that I would if it became necessary.

After listening to this bullshit for several minutes, I simply told Matt's mom that I knew the truth about her and her past, and also knew the reasons why they were living in a motel. I told her she should be ashamed of herself for not realizing what an amazing son she has, telling her how sad it was that a relative stranger saw more in Matt then she did. With Matt standing right beside me I told her she should be grateful that her son had recovered from his addiction to heroine, which he acquired during her pregnancy, without having any serious residual effects as a result. I told her that I was offended that she would treat Matt with the level of disrespect and disregard she obviously displayed for him, with the assumption I would not see through her efforts. Furthermore I assured mom I was not buying any of this, and gave her a very vivid description of who I believed her son to be.

After a while mom started crying, telling me that she was sorry for the way she had talked to me about Matt. She told me that I was right about him and that she owed him more credit and respect than she was giving him. I assured her that I knew Matt was not perfect, but that he was a lot better off than he should be given all she had put him through. I told her I was not there to judge her, but that I would never allow her or any other parent to get away with attempts at such deception. None of this was done in a threatening manner and mom knew that I was simply right about what I had told her. She knew that I had not bought into her lies like other adults had always done in the past at the expense of her son. She acknowledged that since I had been working with Matt everything in his life had improved drastically. I told her that Matt was doing that for himself first and foremost and not for her, even though there were benefits for her in the changes Matt was making. Before I left I told Matt's mom that she was welcome to come to my office anytime she wanted to do so, but only if she was there to support and offer something positive to the work I was doing with him. I gave her my direct office phone number and urged her to call anytime she felt there was something significant I needed to know about Matt and any negative choices he might be making. She agreed and thanked me before she went back into the motel room.

Matt was astounded that his mom had allowed me to address her like I did, telling me she usually went off on anyone who challenged or crossed her. I pointed out that I did not once approach her in a manner that would have given her cause to feel the need to defend herself. He agreed that by stating my awareness of the truth so boldly I let her know that I was not going to buy into her one-sided, self-serving tales of woe. Matt also told me that no one had ever defended him as I had done with his mom or with anyone else for that matter. He clearly appreciated the fact that I not only believed what he had told me, but that I cared enough about him to stand up for him. There is no way Matt will ever forget the experiences we had together professionally. As he neared the end of his senior year I was able to write a grant request to the local police department and was given enough money to buy a complete computer system for Matt. He was shocked and very grateful, assuring me that he would make good use of the computer when he started college in the fall at the local community college. Matt's mom was grateful for the support and assistance I was able to offer her son. When I terminated my sessions with Matt he and his mom and stepdad were still living in the same ratty, rundown roach motel where they were living when Matt and I first met. The difference now was that Matt had a diploma, had reached the age of 18, had a job, and was making specific plans for the future which would take him out of that situation permanently.

Treatment goals for kid such as Matt are really quite simple. The three most common goals I make for each of my troubled kids are these:

1. (My client) will not engage in any activities or behaviors which could result in any form of disciplinary action within the school setting and will work to maintain a GPA equal to her or his intellectual capabilities.
2. (My client) will not engage in any activities or behaviors which could result in such negative consequences such as arrest, confinement, retaliation, addiction, injury to self or others, or death.

3. (My client) will make future plans and goals to include getting a diploma or GED, securing a job, seeking out advanced job training and/or educational opportunities, and focusing on career possibilities which can be easily and readily verbalize.

As you can see these are very simple and straightforward goals which address virtually everything that could go wrong in a kid's life between sessions. They also address the need for forward thinking relative to a future which will come even if they are not prepared to face it. Each of these goals is specific and measurable, and can be easily monitored during the course of treatment which must include assistance and support to facilitate the achievement of these goals. I have taken many kids to visit job training programs such as Job Corps. On a number of occasions I have taken kids to register for school at a local college or trade school, and have helped them fill out the necessary forms to apply for financial aid. Frequently I talk with my kids about the need for establishing and maintaining a high credit rating, explaining the outcomes and obstacles they will face if they fail to do so. I have explained why the rewards received through criminal activity are more risky than they are worth. With every kid I explain the importance of having a strong work ethic along with the awareness that no one owes anyone anything. Furthermore, I work with each kid to get them to understand the limitations and demeaning effects of hand outs and so-called easy money. As often as possible I have met collaboratively with kids and their teachers, social workers, and/or probation officers in an effort to garner additional support from others and to make sure everyone involved in my client's life is on the same page.

Collaboration is much harder to accomplish now that it was when I first started working with this population. Law enforcement agencies and educational institutions have become much more closed to outside collaboration in recent years. I believe much of this is based in their need to protect themselves from scrutiny relative to the realities of the lack of assistance and support kids are now receiving within these contexts. There is no doubt in my mind that there are many ethical and legal violations occurring within these institutions. As a result the civil rights of many kids are being violated on a regular basis. The survival tactics of isolationism and territoriality relative to job security and the money and numbers games played by many institutions and organizations have become more important than the greater good and welfare of those they are meant to serve. There is no survival of the fittest. Rather, there is the survival of those with the greatest political power and influence needed to maintain themselves and guarantee their existence without any regard to effectiveness and appropriate use of funding. Ignorance quite often feeds arrogance, and arrogance feeds contempt and complacency. There is no room in the lives of society's underdogs for such thinking, or for these kinds of pissing contests.

All of my experiences over the years since 1992 with this population have given me a great deal of insight into the needs of these kids regardless of their geographical locations. Furthermore, my observations relative to the decline in services for this population cannot be denied either. The current political and social climates focus on punishment and incarceration rather than on any form of effective rehabilitation efforts toward redirecting lives and destinies. I know all of this because of my opportunities to look behind the scenes and look into the minds and closed societies within the agencies and institutions which are the biggest perpetrators of these injustices. All too often I have heard law enforcement officers literally state that the only way to deal with troubled kids is to get them off the streets. Some of these officers do not care if the kids are locked up or dead since either stated reality accomplishes their goal of getting troublemakers off 'their' streets. This is especially true between officers and kids when law enforcement officials have set up the competitive atmosphere of "we'll show you who's boss". This perspective explains the many occasions when I have had full awareness of the exaggerated and intentionally erroneous police reports which get these kids deep into the systems. And this observation is backed up by my awareness of statements made directly to me by cops and probation officers stating they will never waste their time writing up charges they cannot "make stick". The problem is that I cannot prove any of this because it all involves juveniles and juvenile records which are protected from outside scrutiny. I know for a fact that the proof of many of these kinds of injustices has been destroyed or altered to protect officials from disciplinary action or prosecution. Everyone behind the "blue curtain" knows that what I am saying is true, including those involved in prosecuting the cases.

Dr. David L. Roberts Ph.D.

The other biggest culprit is the educational system in this country. Here again, as I have stated previously, kids are denied access to much needed services. In many cases efforts are made behind the scenes to block awareness of both student and parental rights, and the existence of such services and laws. As with law enforcement agencies I know all of this first hand as well. However I have no way to prove any of this given the fact student records are protected and officials have ways of covering for each other rather than have any of this exposed. Just this week in Mobile, Alabama a local news station investigated and exposed the outrageous expenditures of school board members relative to travel expenses. The trips were reportedly for training seminars and conferences. However, the expenses included very expensive meals and hotel accommodations for these school officials. There is no doubt in my mind that a significant percentage of the administrative overhead in virtually any school district could be cut drastically. This would free up more funding for student services rather than wasting it on bureaucratic overkill. Talk about entitlement programs! While teachers deserve to be paid well for their services, they must earn their level of pay based on academic results and progress of their students. Teachers unions and contracts have greatly hurt the public school systems and give teachers undeserved protection from accountability.

All of this said, I still have no concrete ideas of how to combat all of the injustices on my own other than by speaking out as I am doing here and as I do within the communities. I learned the hard way in California that I could not fight the corrupt systems directly. Instead I had to educate the public relative to their rights and to their need to stand up against injustices. The lack of means relative to defending themselves legally has to account for the fact that so-called minorities are so over represented within every existing criminal system. However, the problem with many low income families is that they do not have either the know-how or the means to take a stand needed to protect and guarantee their rights. People within the African American communities are much more likely to speak up and out about injustices. On the other hand many Hispanic American families are often afraid to do so because of their cultural beliefs and customs of not challenging authority figures. Furthermore, people in general who are considered to be lower class citizens are afraid of retaliation from authority figures, especially law enforcement, if they do take a stand. The only way I can see is for large numbers of people to join forces and begin to demand the quality of services they deserve. There is a great deal of truth in the strength-in-numbers philosophy. This seems to be the only force big institutions and organizations understand and regard.

The emphases of funding provided to serve and assist low income, high risk, troubled kids need to be focused on providing the most appropriate and efficient services possible. These services must include educational programs which inform and empower low income families about their rights in all arenas. Determination of what these services and programs would include must be decided initially by examining the ineffectiveness and inappropriateness of existing programs. It would be important to look at what works and keep those components, while taking care to eliminate ineffective programs which exist only because of their ability to sustain themselves because of political issues and connections. The key to the success of any programs and the appropriate use of funding depends on the concept of collaboration. No one entity can possibly meet every need for kids within this population and it is foolishly arrogant for them to even try to justify their isolated existence. Programs for this population must be comprehensive and contributors must be patient relative to measurable outcomes.

There is no doubt in my mind that the right use of funding will prove in the long run to be very cost effective relative to reducing the numbers of adult offenders and the numbers of recipients of public assistance. So much money is being mismanaged and misspent that it wouldn't take very much for people to weed out the useful from the ridiculous. During the transition period toward the reductions in the need for large prison systems and outrageous law enforcement efforts, professionals could be retrained to put their skills to work preventing problems rather than only punishing offenders. For many this would take away opportunities to satisfy their childish need to play cops and robbers. I am not sure how easy it would be to get people with these kinds of personalities and approaches to populations in need to let go of their control issues and need for competition. These egotistical needs would have to be replaced with such altruistic notions as being of service to others without any secondary gains to service providers being the goals. Based on those I know working within the systems which are the most useless, I am not even sure if such a transformation is possible with many of these individuals. After all, they have been given unchecked power and authority, all protected by a veil of secrecy under Homeland Security and the US Patriot Act. There is no doubt in my mind that the recent rise in violent crimes is the responsibility of those who have been federally sanctioned with the opportunity to abuse their power and authority. The competition set up in the streets between themselves and groups, including kids they now treat like terrorists is culminating in what will likely become a national backlash against law enforcement by those they target with their unchecked abuses of power and authority. Even if or when conditions improve, we as a society need to learn from the injustices being perpetrated at this point in history.

Successful programs will need to be very comprehensive in and of themselves. Each program and program professionals will need to have a strong commitment both to this population and to the time it will take to serve these kids and facilitate their success. Evaluation of outcome results will need to extend out as much as three to five years beyond program completion in order to adequately prove program effectiveness. Every program must be scrutinized and monitored relative to responsibility and accountability on all levels. There is no doubt that efforts to assist and redirect the lives of troubled kids are time consuming and expensive. However, nothing is more time consuming and expensive that the current means and efforts being implemented and enforced which have proven to be useless relative to desirable positive changes and outcomes. As I stated earlier, the hurricane season of 2005 exposed to the world the scam being perpetuated within this country relative to the inhumane treatment of low income groups. Even though the storms revealed the injustices and inequalities present in the South, there is no doubt that these same conditions exist throughout the entire country.

While there are no quick fixes or easy solutions I am doing my part to at least start with what I know. As of August 25, 2005 I have incorporated a nonprofit youth center under the name of Liberating Youth, Inc. We had our first board meeting on September 19, 2005 and filed our application that same week with IRS for 501(c)3 status. Liberating Youth, Inc. (LYI) is a comprehensive program with a structured format, all of which has been copyrighted as of July 2005. I will be both the executive director and the clinical director, and we will carefully evaluate outcome results once the program is implemented. Our 501(c) 3 status was granted in August 2006. While waiting for this process to mature, and while waiting to secure start-up funding, I have set up my own private practice under the corporate name of ProKids, Inc., using law enforcements' criticism of my work with the kids in California as the banner under which I will practice and franchise the LYI model. All of this will be carefully studied and documented as we progress. When the time is right I will make every effort I can to publish, publicize, and franchise the LYI concept around the country. All work under the name of ProKids, Inc. will roll over into LYI once we having funding to get the LYI project started. In the meantime we will be applying for local, state and federal funding to make LYI in Alabama a reality as the first of many LYI locations to come. Watch for us under the internet heading of LIBERATINGYOUTHINC.org in the very near future.

In California I frequently told the kids with whom I worked that my goal was to someday completely shut down the juvenile justice systems as we know them today around the country. The kids would laugh, but would agree that if they would stop getting into trouble there would be no juvenile court, juvenile hall, juvenile placement facilities, or juvenile probation. While this is somewhat of a lofty goal, it is not a bad goal to have. With the LYI concept and the ProKids, Inc. format I plan to work toward the realization of some form of this goal before I die. Talk about a collaborative effort! However, rather than underestimate me, wish me luck and join me in my efforts. One such approach I referred to earlier is my F.A.T.E. Stops the H.A.T.E. and equalizes the R.A.C.E. campaign. If every likeminded individual and organization would join forces with me in this effort we could literally change and improve the futures of millions of low income, disadvantaged kids. This will only happen when people in this country begin to altruistically focus on concepts related to pure, non-religious Spirituality, rather than dogma and doctrine associated with present day forms of organized religion emphasizing money and numbers. Please help me help those in need!

Chapter XII

Psyche-Soul-ology

Recently I was having a conversation with a friend of mine. He asked me about the work I do with troubled kids, and specifically how I conceptualize my work and why it is so important to me. Personally I love this kind of question because it opens up what I consider to be a philosophical discussion regarding my own personal philosophies which motivate and inspire me. Our discussion culminated in the title of this chapter, a phrase which seemed to capture all of my philosophies under one heading – Psyche-Soul-ology. Initially we both laughed about it, but after some *'philosophical'* consideration we both agreed that my new term seemed to sum up everything I believe and practice relative to high risk, troubled kids. It is also the Spiritual Philosophy through which I live every moment of my life. Let me explain.

According to <u>The American Century Dictionary</u>, 1995, the word psyche is defined as "the soul, spirit, or mind." However, every derivative of the word psychology refers basically to all things mental or of the mind. The above referenced dictionary defines soul as "the spiritual part of a person, also regarded as immortal." And, finally, the suffix "-ology" refers to a discipline, or a branch of study, or a field of knowledge relative to various subjects and interests. What was initially something amusing to my friend and me suddenly seemed to embody a more accurate label for the profession I claim given the fact that I refer to myself as a spiritual psychologist.

To me there is no way to separate or ignore the connection between the mind (psyche) and the heart (soul) within the field of psychology. No one has yet figured out where the soul resides within the human body – assuming there is such a thing as a soul. However, many people seem to refer to issues related to the heart as being almost synonymous with the concept of soul. My tendency is to associate the soul with the heart, and the mind as being the connection between that part of us which is human and that part of us which is spirit(ual). This stems from my belief that we are spiritual beings having a human experience, rather than human beings searching for a spiritual experience. I have heard a quote (origins unknown to me) suggesting "the longest 18 inches in the world is the distance between the heart and the mind." It seems that all too often people tend to be more grounded in one at the exclusion of the other. Many clients in therapy are considered to be "stuck in their heads" suggesting they try to rationalize and over analyze everything within their realm of realities. However, the mind is associated with thinking and reason, while the heart is associated with emotions. In reality there is no way to deny the connection between the two since the two different entities drastically interact with each other, quite often over-interacting. The process of interaction between the heart and the mind can either be conscious or unconscious relative to our overt awareness of the connection between the two. But, there is no denying that emotions drive thoughts and thoughts drive emotions. The key is to develop the art of allowing them to work in unison and in harmony with each other. After all both are more compatible than competitive if we would only allow them to be.

This is no less true with high risk, troubled kids. Consider all of the complicating factors I listed in my first book, <u>At the Mercy of Externals: Righting Wrongs and Protecting Kids, 2nd Edition</u>. (If you haven't read my first book you cannot get the maximum benefit offered by this current book!) Complicating factors generate both thoughts and ideas about realities present in kids' lives. Because they are *complicating* factors they also generate emotions – emotions which in many cases are quite strong. My RFLAGS Model – explained fully in my first book - graphically depicts how intense negative emotions result from abuse and victimization, even if the abuse and victimization result from environmental or situational factors. As we know many environmental factors represent the "external" factors to which I refer and are quite often beyond the ability of individuals, especially kids, to control or even influence. The RFLAGS Model further depicts how people of all ages are usually cut off from and thereby unaware of these intense negative emotions which emerge as depression and anxiety. These emotional states which we experience physically then lead to hopelessness and helplessness. From there the emotionally-based states of mind or belief systems then lead to various acting out behaviors which unfortunately become counterproductive attempts to cope with damaging external factors. These failed attempts to cope — which are the origins of adult personality disorders - create a vicious cycle of maladaptive behaviors and only increase the emotions because of the futility of these actions. This scenario coupled with the difficulty of making connections between the emotions and the past get lived out in the present and perpetuated into the future. These conditions continue until the issues are identified and the emotions are faced and resolved to whatever extent possible. The goal is to leave the past, and the emotions it generated behind, thereby learning to break the destructive cycle of acting out. This redirecting of energy allows the individual to learn and utilize effective coping skills which will lead to productive, rather than destructive, outcomes.

The above outlined process is basically a process of recovery from the past which unites psyche (mind) and soul (emotions or heart) in a symphony of harmony rather than discord. My approach of attempting to redirect an individual's use of their energy allows them to write a new "score" which they can then "conduct" and "orchestrate" toward more favorable and controllable outcomes. This takes them to an internal reality that everything we need in order to survive and thrive can only be found within ourselves — within our psyche and within our soul as they merge into a force of one which works for, rather than against each individual. Therefore, my strongest belief is summed up by my statement that "The Energy which *is* Us is God *in* us." My statement is based in another of my very strong beliefs that there is no heaven or hell, no good or evil, only the misuse or right use of our Energy which is God.

When I work with high risk, troubled kids I do not ask them to change into someone else. I simply ask them to work differently with who they already are by redirecting their use of the Energy which defines them and their potential. In order to do this every professional must be able to look beyond everything negative manifested externally — manner of dress, language, criminal activity, substance use, defiance, anger/rage, etc. — and see the Soul or higher Self within every child we meet, even into their early adulthood. This can only be done if we learn to make observations rather than judgments about what we see. At the same time we must be able and willing to look beyond what we see on the outside and look for the goodness which is present within the Soul of every child. The best last chance we have is to reach out especially to those kids who have reached or are approaching late adolescence and early adulthood. Recent scientific evidence relative to brain development suggests that adolescence continues into the mid 20's for each individual. Think back to how much you thought you knew at 20 compared to all you learned even by 25 and beyond, and tell me this observation is not accurate.

I also firmly believe that present day religions have failed miserably in their responsibility of helping us find God within our core nature. Religious people across the board all believe that God is somewhere "out there", whether in or at church, temple, synagogue, or mosque; or on the other side of this life in whatever manner that gets depicted. Unfortunately the so-called other side is usually described as a place of paradise which can only be attained by the strict adherence to specific religious rituals and practices – and nowadays, as in the past, even acts of violence as sanctioned by religious extremists.

Religious followers are generally taught that many things within our worldly existence are grounded in evil and in some concept of the devil or Satan. The confession printed in the liturgical text of one of the many Christian sects requires that penitents "bewail and bemoan their manifold sins and wickedness." We are cautioned to be ever watchful and on guard from the likelihood of assault from all sides and within every context except our places of worship. No one within today's organized religions is taught to find refuge within by simply acknowledging the God who already lives within us and who seeks not to be worshipped, but to be celebrated and honored through our lives. The only way to honor God is through the right use of the Energy within Us which is God in us. As a practicing "Psyche-Soul-ologist" I believe it is my spiritual responsibility to introduce society's underdogs to the Divine which already exists within them. I can do this without introducing them to counterproductive religious dogma which represents rigid and authoritarian beliefs. This increases the likelihood they will be able to stop being "at the mercy of externals" by realizing that everything they need is already at their disposal internally.

Since I have now returned to the 'deep south' and am living again in "LA" (Lower Alabama) I find myself being somewhat apprehensive and reluctant to share my spiritual beliefs even within the context of this book. Because this text is written primarily for professionals working with kids within in various fields of study and contexts, I almost feel that I have to go with the dominant thinking of the region if this book is to be accepted at all. Because of the so-believed "blasphemous" nature of my beliefs, many people within this region and other extremely conservative regions of the country would reject this book outright after reading this, the last chapter in the book. That is how narrow minded religious conservatives are when it comes to "defending their faith".

It took me many years to even begin to think as I do now, given my strict religious upbringing within a very conservative Christian religion. My need to look beyond what I had been taught grew out of numerous experiences in my life where religion either failed me or directly opposed an area of enlightenment I chose to pursue. Just reading <u>The Celestine Prophecy</u> series, published in the late 1990's by James Redfield, or using <u>The Book of Runes,</u> by Ralph Blum as sources of guidance took a great deal of courage on my part. I know first hand how damaging extreme religious dogma can be as applied to the teaching of spiritual concepts which should be user friendly and adaptable with time and according to individual needs. Over time I have learned to appreciate many sources of inspiration beyond traditional religious texts. I no longer seek out writings which only support a set of beliefs I was told were the embodiment of Truth.

The most helpful realization I ever gained was the reality that any beliefs related to anything "spiritual" or to God are all "faith-based". This clearly means that *nothing* we believe about God can be proven. Therefore it is impossible and foolish to state with certainty that any spiritual beliefs are "THE TRUTH". Faith-based beliefs truly mean that the believers or espousers of such beliefs believe in something they *cannot* prove, but choose to believe in anyway. While there is nothing inherently wrong with this reality there is a great deal of room within this way of thinking for abuse and victimization. This is especially true when people are taught to believe in something by making them afraid to believe in anything else.

One of my next projects will be to study more about the psychology connected to religious beliefs and institutions. With everything going on in the world today it becomes more obvious all the time that the Christians, Jews and Muslims are all fighting to gain the top position. They treat this as some cause worth dying for without realizing they could all be wrong! I will not believe that any form of God is truly backing their unholy causes. Nor will I ever believe that strict adherence to their externally imposed and outwardly exercised rituals of prayers, fasting, rites of worship, confession, and penance make them any better or more deserving of God than "the others". The concept of evil is a powerful tool relative to instilling fear in the "hearts" (souls) of the faithful. I recently heard in a documentary about religions that the Hebrew word for Satan simply refers to the one who opposes God. It seems to me to be absolutely absurd for people to engage in this battle between good and evil, when both of these concepts are based in nothing more than faith. To be completely honest, as I gained more awareness of alternatives to the beliefs I was taught as a child I became enraged with the fear tactics used against me to insure my adherence to what I was taught. Well, believe me, I am no longer afraid, but seem to become only more outraged with all I see relative to the constant misuse by political and religious figures of the Energy which is God. None of this would bother me so much if not for the potential destruction of the world and humanity literally connected to this way of thinking and believing.

All of that having been said, let me now tell you how this ties into the work I do with high risk, troubled kids. Over the years I have had many opportunities to work with troubled kids who were incarcerated within in various juvenile justice contexts. Because of this I know all about the so-called "ministries of outreach" provided within these settings by religious groups. Kids within these settings will usually attend these services only because they offer the kids some diversion from their otherwise monotonous and boring daily routines. However, after the true nature of these presentations becomes obvious to the kids they will choose not to attend future meetings. Only a very few of the kids buy into what they are being told and then only for a short period of time.

Keep in mind that many of these kids already feel like they are worthless lost causes. These religious groups then come in and tell them they are indeed worthless lost causes because the Devil lives in them and dominates their lives. They are told that the only way to "save" themselves is to renounce Satan as the devil and the evils of sin by acknowledging their shameful nature. They are then told they must confess their sins and ask for forgiveness before they can invite Jesus into their hearts, and he will then save them from eternal damnation. The presentations are often made by those who state, "We were just like you before we found Jesus". The kids look at these people and see them as no better off than they were before their "conversion" into a "new person". In reality all these people have done is trade in one lifestyle of dependence on external factors for another lifestyle of dependence on a different set of external factors. Only this time the kids see their new existence as being far less appealing than what they reportedly left behind. After all, the last thing these kids want is to take on beliefs which require a strict and continuing adherence to rituals and other "acts of faith" as a means of guaranteeing their salvation and protection from eternal damnation. It is interesting to me that different religious sects differ in their view and interpretation of the permanence of salvation, with some believing literally in a "once-saved-always-saved" approach.

The thing that gets to me the worst about all of this is the fact that none of this focuses on the concept of the God within or the innate goodness within each of us. While I believe there are some who are inexplicably flawed toward the deviant side of violence and self destruction, I believe these to be very few in number. I also believe these people have very serious brain disorders which rob them of access to the inherent goodness present in each of us. I am talking here about people like serial killers and serial sex offenders who seemingly have no conscience or self control. Even here, though, I look at this as their inability to "act right" due to abnormal brain functioning which blocks their right use of their energy, rather than as a manifestation of pure evil as some would say. Think about the countless numbers of people throughout history who were killed in some rather gruesome and inhumane ways because they were thought to be either possessed, or witches and warlocks.

I am not here to take anything away from people. Nor do I believe that religion in and of itself is always bad. However, I do believe that my way of looking at God and the world makes more sense. If nothing else it is certainly less threatening relative to the possible annihilation of the world. It requires nothing more or less than simply celebrating and honoring the God within us through right living which includes altruistic service to others. This is drastically opposed to the historical need and competition between organized religions to be right relative to the claim that their God is the only "true God", and their founders were the only "true Prophets" or "Sons of God". No one has the right to force their religious beliefs upon anyone else. The only thing which matters should be that everyone finds some path to God through which they can base their faith as being the right path for them. Add to that whatever you need in order to make it meaningful, but remain fully mindful that no one knows the "truth" about anything related to God and spirituality.

Troubled kids respond very well to the fact that any belief in God is an act of faith and is by nature then unprovable. Most kids believe religious people to be nothing more than hypocrites anyway. Many times the most dysfunctional people in their lives are also very religious, allowing kids to see how foolish religion can be when it is misused and misunderstood. Kids are very open to the idea that nothing more is needed than to see God as an integral part of who we already are. It is very easy to get them to imagine the path God might want them to follow compared to the path they are beginning to choose. They are relieved to learn that they do not have to change into someone else in order to change the way they use their energy and skills. And, kids are really interested in Spiritual alternatives to religion which are much more interesting than traditional religious approaches.

Many kids are fascinated by fantasy and mysticism. They are intrigued by the idea of reincarnation as a possibility and are very interested in psychic phenomena. One of the most amazing experiences to give a kid is the use of guided imagery through hypnosis which I am trained to do. They like the idea of out-of-body experiences and the possibility that we stay connected spiritually to those who have died. They are also intrigued by the concept of meditation which leads to an altered state of consciousness. These are things I can talk about with them openly and knowledgeably because of my interest in these spiritual approaches as well. Initially I sometimes have to help a kid get around their fear of looking outside of biblical teachings for other spiritual experiences and other pathways to God.

This is true mainly for kids who have a background in traditional religious teachings. Once I get them over that hurdle the sky is the limit in terms of what they can discover for themselves relative to limitless faith in the infinite possibilities of the Energy in Us which is God in us.

As I stated earlier I am not trying to take anything away from anyone. However, I feel that all of what I have learned and revised especially within the last 18 plus years, and actually starting in 1983, has only enhanced my belief in the existence of a Higher Being. I discarded everything I was taught to be the "Truth" as a child as I faced my own sets of traumatic life experiences and found that nothing I had been taught was useful because it made no sense to me. There is no doubt in my mind that my spiritual life is now based in celebrating and honoring God by being true to my concept of the God within, to my concept of myself as being called according to His purpose, and to my concept of actively living my life in the here and now in service to others. It took a lot of courage to make these changes because I firmly believed I risked the so-called "wrath of God and eternal damnation" for turning my back on what I had been taught. But there is no doubt in my mind that I am stronger on all levels because of my willingness to make these changes. My spiritual experiences since these changes have served to reinforce my faith-based belief that I am on my *own* right path.

I share with kids the prayer I quoted in my first book, from Ralph Blum's The Book of Runes, which states that with all that I am "I will to will THY WILL". In other words from the core of my being I want to want what You want, or I desire to desire what You desire. This statement is uttered not only as a prayer, but as an ongoing commitment to seek out and actively live out each individual's role in the overall Plan of God. Recently I realized that the more spiritually mature version of this prayer is simply "I will Thy Will". Rather than simply wanting or desiring to do so, this is an active statement of commitment to the Will of the Divine, based in the belief this is really all that matters if there truly is a God in charge of all which exists. This is in opposition to the religious perspective of living to die with the only things worth looking forward to being found on the other side, and then only if you say all the right things, practice all the right rituals, and believe only what you have been told to be the truth. The tragedy of religion is that religious leaders teach blind acceptance of what they espouse, equating doubt with sin. Doubt in a religious connotation includes any thinking or pondering which is contrary to what is being taught from the pulpit as the "Truth". This is nothing short of brainwashing with fear tactics being used to insure compliance with interpretations of religious doctrine and dogma. Believe me when I say that I know what I am talking about given the fact this is the way I was raised!

Individual uniqueness is a central theme to what I believe. When I tell a kid they are so unique that there are things in this life which they and only they can do, they are amazed at this perspective. By helping them see that because there is one and only one of them, they begin to understand their importance in a sense of some overall possible Plan which is bigger than each of us. They can understand that even if I could completely clone them physically, their clone could never be exactly like the person they already are. I explain that their clone would literally have to experience all of the exact same things in life they had experienced in order to be exactly like them. Kids understand this would be a phenomenological impossibility and can appreciate the likelihood that what I am saying is probably the truth. Individual uniqueness is the place to start with every troubled kid you meet. This is what gets their attention and ignites their willingness to consider other ways of looking at and experiencing life into their future which they will create either consciously and deliberately, or unconsciously and passively.

I wholeheartedly believe each of us possesses a very strong intuitive, psychic side to our overall nature and personal capabilities. However, very few people are taught to recognize this skill and nurture it into a conscious life tool which will guide us through every phase of our existence. It in interesting to me that many people openly admit they believe in psychic phenomenon, with many stating they have experienced something which they can only explain as being supernatural. There is a strong interest in the ability to connect with those who have died as evidenced by a large volume of literature and several television shows and movies which present these phenomena as realities. Many people also believe in near death experiences which transform lives for the better in most cases. People are interested in the prospect of miracles and the connection between the mind and the body when it comes to healing. To me all of these misunderstood and under utilized phenomena are very real parts of the Energy in Us which is God in us. If God is all knowing and possesses all of these kinds of powers, why would we be any less capable if we are truly created in the image of and by God?

This is no less true for troubled kids. All of this serves as a way to get their attention relative to looking differently at themselves and at life in general. This kind of thinking and questioning opens up infinite possibilities for kids who have very little, if any hope for their future. Since no one knows what the "Truth" really is anyway, why not at least give kids the opportunity to consider these possibilities along with other possibilities to which they have likely been exposed. Believe me, these kinds of subjects will open up some rather incredible discussions with kids who are open to such considerations. Not all kids are, and it is very important to acknowledge and respect the beliefs of every individual unless those beliefs are harmful to them in some way. However, a vast majority of troubled kids are desperately seeking knowledge and possibilities which will serve them better than the realities they have been exposed to so far in their lives.

My exposure to hypnosis started with my own therapist who worked with me for about five years in Los Angeles. At first I was very skeptical about allowing him to "put me under", but I finally agreed to at least experience the process of relaxing in preparation for hypnosis. This was all it took for me to be hooked on the entire experience. He only used hypnosis with me five times and each time was focused on a specific issue. In addition to the office sessions which he recorded for me, I practiced the experience of hypnosis at home using his tapes. Within no time I was able to induce my own hypnotic state without the guidance of a tape or a hypnotherapist. What an incredible skill to have! I have learned to use it as I meditate and pray, especially at times when I need to work through things in my life which are confusing or even baffling to me at the time. Hypnosis simply takes you inward and away from distractions so you can work on the things stuck in your subconscious mind.

After using the skill for my own enhancement, I eventually took a weeklong class with a well known hypnotherapist while I was still in California. From these experiences I would use hypnosis in my classes at the local community college as just an interesting experience for psychology students who wanted to either participate or simply observe. I also used hypnosis very selectively over the years with some of my troubled kids I served as their psychologist – or Psyche-Soul-ologist. I would strongly encourage everyone to take a class in hypnosis, if for no other reason than to dispel the myths associated with the art as it is portrayed for entertainment and amusement purposes. No one will do anything under hypnosis they would not be willing to do under other circumstances. I believe that hypnosis can easily be misused in ways which could traumatize people, especially if it was used as a means to put people in touch with traumatic experiences they have had. I also believe it is useless in the recovery of suppressed memories given the fact that people in general are very suggestible. However, I do believe it is very useful with troubled kids only as a way of getting them to literally look at themselves in the imaginary mirror to see who they are becoming compared to who they are meant to be. This is the only way I have ever used hypnosis with anyone outside of my own meditation experiences.

While this is not a book about hypnosis, I do want to clarify how I use this with kids. After I explain to them that hypnosis has nothing to do with mind control or humiliation, and is only a state of deep relaxation, they are usually interested in at least trying the relaxation exercise. Hypnosis is actually used very frequently in various settings under the guise of "guided imagery". No one should use a guided imagery technique without the awareness that you have no way of knowing or controlling how your individual group members will experience even something related to grief recovery. Any form of hypnosis has the power to unleash strong and often unpleasant emotions; therefore, the use of hypnosis must be carefully implemented for a very specific purpose. Never take on any more than you are trained to handle. This is my reason for only using hypnosis with troubled kids as a means of getting them to see themselves differently. I would never try to get into their emotions, have them relive traumatic, or otherwise abusive experiences, or take them back into their past. Even in my classes I only used the imagery to help students see themselves as successful now and on into their future as they graduate, pursue additional education goals, and explore career options. I never do anything I think could traumatize anyone.

Because many troubled kids drink and at the very least smoke marijuana, I find it easy to get them to relax by having them think of hypnosis as the ultimate natural high. This also gets them to be aware that there are other ways, besides substance use, to help them feel good about themselves and their lives. This approach even works really well with hardcore gang members. Once I have a kid in the altered state of consciousness as achieved through the deepest level of relaxation possible, I take them into a room which they create in their minds. They can put anything in this room which makes them feel safe and comfortable. The only specific request I make is that the room include a large full-length mirror which is either attached to a wall or is supported by a frame and sits on the floor as with a dressing mirror.

After giving them some time to acclimate themselves to the room they have created in their mind, I ask them to stand in front of the mirror they have also created. While in front of the mirror I have them visualize themselves wearing the clothing and displaying the personae they literally wear out in the streets with their friends. After some time and some additional requests, I have them visualize their twin standing beside them to their left. This twin is to be dressed in the style and with the personae as the kid I have come to know and respect. I get them to spend a great deal of time carefully observing the stark difference between the two figures reflected in the mirror. My constant comment is that these twins represent different sides of the same person and are not two different people. They get this.

At some point I suggest they merge the two figures into one person, with the image of the kid as I know them superimposed over the kid I have never really known. This gives them the opportunity to see that their true nature can become their dominant nature if they would allow that process to begin. As they look at the kid I know superimposed over the kid on the streets I ask them to watch as the kid from the streets begins to fade, leaving only the kid I know as the unified self. I tell them that both sides of their nature still exist and that it is up to them as to which one dominates their choices for the future. I have them imagine the loss of the kid I know if they fail to make this transition as they learn to use their energy differently in more productive ways. I then have them imagine the kinds of positive things in life which would make them feel like they were successful in leaving the negatives parts of their past behind. I have them imagine things like graduating from high school, possibly pursing job training or education beyond high school, and then successfully selecting and starting a career. I also have them imagine how their lives will likely turn out if they continue making the wrong choices.

This is a very powerful experience for each kid. I have them look at the clock before we start and when I bring them back into full consciousness. Generally I keep them under for about 40 to 45 minutes. They are always amazed at the fact time has passed without their awareness of it doing so. I can get them to see that the negative images they imagined will be the way life is for them if they do not learn to take control over their destiny and make the decisions which will give them the future they deserve. After a little passes time for them to re-acclimate themselves to their surroundings I have them describe to me the details of what they literally created in their minds. This experience of recalling the details helps to make it stick and always gives me the chance to know what their mind did with my suggestions. This is fun for them and at the same time offers them insights it would be hard for them to attain just by talking about these issues. There is no way they will ever forget the experience. It is very important to watch every aspect of their body as they experience the hypnotic state. This is the only way to make sure they are experiencing everything as you desire it to be for them and is the only way to know how deep they go into the subconscious state. The kids find it hard to believe how incredible the experience was for them. They find it even harder to believe they were able to let it happen so successfully.

Another amazing experience is helping kids talk about friends and other loved ones who have died. The next step is to help them understand their grief experience as an adjustment to the fact these relationships changed, but did not end. This eliminates the pressure they may feel to forget and move on as though there is no lasting connection, at least not until after they have also died. One of the most significant factors in my own spiritual growth and development has been my work with a psychic who is also my strongest and most reliable spiritual advisor. I met her in January 1994 and have continued having regular readings at least two or three times a year. The most remarkable thing she did for me was to make me aware of my connections to several very special people in my life who have died. There is no doubt she was able to connect with them as evidenced by information revealed to her which could have only come from the individuals who made their presence known. It was within these moments that I learned my relationships with these souls did not end. Our relationships simply changed into something even more meaningful than what I had known on earth with them given the added dimension of a sense of eternal connection. I was given the assurance that we do continue beyond this existence. These experiences also gave me the assurance that there is a life after this one and also let me know it is not like anything I had been taught through any religious institution or frame of reference. Through the guidance of my spiritual advisor I learned that my intuitions relative to many things in life were my own spiritual abilities. She taught me to embrace these skills as the spiritual gifts they are.

My psychic, who wishes to remain anonymous, taught me that I have psychic abilities as well, something traditional religions disapprove of and denounce as heresy. She also stated that each of us has the skill, but very few ever work to consciously develop it due primarily to religious opposition and media portrayal of such skills as spooky. I already knew that I had a strong ability to "read" the kids with whom I worked. Quite often I have shocked them with questions regarding very specific issues about which no one else knew any details. Early in my career I just dismissed these readings as lucky guesses, but they clearly made an impact on my kids. Over time I nurtured these skills and eventually began to have the experiences as a medium with the kids I serve. This seems to happen only with kids who are open to the discussion of such possibilities. Only those kids who were comfortable talking about and learning about what is referred to in recent decades as "New Age Spirituality" were able to bring these kinds of encounters into the session. I never did anything to cause this. Nor is it something I can conjure up or do on demand. It always happens naturally as I discuss issues of death and grief with kids, and with other more informal acquaintances who have also experienced losses of friends and family members. Furthermore, there is no way for me to predict when or if these incidents will occur.

There is nothing magical about this. It just happens and is a very humbling experience for me. However, I believe it happens because I opened myself up to the desire to experience as much as I could relative to psychic and other spiritual phenomena. I pray openly for the abilities to heal, to see, to prophesy, to know, and to convey, all as what I consider to be the building blocks of deeper wisdom. How ridiculous for some people to think that I have opened myself up to the devil relative to things which are so sacred in nature. My awareness of the presence of another soul begins as a feeling of tension or tightness seated deeply in my chest. I have learned with time to pay very close attention to this when I am working with a kid. It feels like an intense level of energy and it seems that the souls somehow think themselves into my head. I do not see them as much as I see pictures of them and receive messages from them which seem like shared thoughts sent to me from them. Even if a kid is not open to such experiences, it will still happen occasionally. When it does I will find an indirect way to use the information I am being given to question the kid and help them deal with whatever comes up. It makes sense to me that anyone who works as a therapist would, or at least should have a very strong intuitive nature. I believe that intuition and psychic abilities are one in the same and should be pursued and developed as very useful clinical skills. I do not support anything bordering on witchcraft, black magic, voodoo or Ouija board/séance types of activities. While I do not believe in evil I do believe in the existence of negative energy which we cannot explain and do not need or want to encounter.

Each of these kinds of experiences has always been helpful to the kids with whom I have had the experiences. The detailed information revealed to me is undeniable by the kid. Every kid is absolutely astounded, intrigued, and transformed by the experience, including hardcore gang members who are at first alarmed that I can see and know such things about them and their past. My psychic tells people that I am "the only psychic for the gangsters". I tread very carefully into this with kids who are suspicious of people in general. If I sense any kind of resistance I back off, but still find some way to address some degree of what is happening within me. As a result I have never had a kid regret the experience. Because of the somewhat controversial nature of the experience I have to ask kids to not discuss what happened with other people who might not understand or appreciate what we shared. There is nothing unethical or immoral about what I do with any kid, but some people would accuse me of exposing kids to things which are evil in nature. This could not be any further from the truth. If this happens with a kid who knows other kids who have the same experiences with me I will ask permission from the kid to tell the others. If the other kids feel comfortable doing so, they can then discuss every aspect of what happened. I find this only reinforces the reality of what happened, even though this reality is ironically mystical in nature.

There is no doubt in my mind that the so-called "gifts of the spirit" listed in biblical texts are nothing less than the same psychic phenomena I am addressing here. Think about people who go into trancelike states who are said to be "filled with the spirit". Taken out of context they would be thought by many to be either psychotic or possessed. The same is true for people who possess the gifts of healing and prophecy. There are even biblical accounts of people who encounter the souls of people who have died. If God truly lives within us, and if the Energy which is Us is God in us, then it would make sense that we have more skills available to us than we allow ourselves to explore. The ability to develop these skills on our own reduce our dependency on religious institutions which do little more than foster dependency in order to keep their money and numbers factors strong. Organized religion is one of the biggest money and numbers games around.

With all of this said, I now close out the writings of this text, feeling and believing that everything expressed herein is Divinely Inspired. It is my hope that all who read this text will learn to utilize the approaches put forth in this and my first book. By doing so we can truly begin to help low income, disadvantaged, troubled kids successfully redirect the use of their Energy which is God within them. There is truly nothing magical about any of this. However, I believe very strongly that it is impossible for anyone to inspire others, especially kids, if we are not truly inspired spiritually. Therefore I urge each reader to think outside the traditional boxes, looking deeply within your own soul to find who you are truly meant to be. Failure to do so will completely undermine your efforts to successfully reach out to those within our society who are the most vulnerable. Please do not make the mistake of being one of those with the best of intentions who does the most harm. Learn to see and experience the world of troubled kids through their eyes and by understanding their realities. Only then can you be both compassionate and passionate in your work and dealings with this group of kids. Openly practice the concepts and approaches associated with Psyche-Soul-ology for yourself and for those you serve. Read the Oath toward the end of Chapter 6 in <u>At the Mercy of Externals: Righting Wrongs and Protecting Kids, 2nd Edition</u>, and truly take it to heart relative to all roles you play in the lives of kids. Be good to yourself and to the kids under your charge. And, may The Source be with you!

ProKids, Inc.; The Message and The Movement

K.I.T. CADETS:

KIDS IN TOUCH AGAINST VIOLENCE

Revised Program Manual - 2011

Developed and Implemented in 1992 – 1994 by:
David L. Roberts, Ph.D.
Predoctoral and Post Doctoral Intern 1992-1994
Now a Licensed Clinical Psychologist

In conjunction with the:

California School of Professional Psychology
Children, Youth, and Family Services Consortium
Tara Pir, Ph.D., Internship Supervisor
&
Murchison Street Elementary School in East Los Angeles, CA
Murchison Street Family Center
Robert Bilovski, Principal
Arturo Valdez, Center Coordinator

Presented by Dr. Roberts in July 1994 at
The International Congress of Applied Psychology
Madrid, Spain

Copyright June 2011
Do not duplicate in any form or use without the expressed
written permission of the author.

Dr. David L. Roberts Ph.D.

Abstract

School-based mental health offers an opportunity to develop programs which address the needs of families victimized by violence. One such program is the K.I.T. Cadets Program which is implemented in two phases.

Phase I targets fifth and sixth grade students identified as high risk for future involvement in potentially violent activities. Children are taught in groups of no more than 15-21 participants to think differently about violence, highlighting their opportunities to influence the thinking of others. Groups are offered for six weeks, with a pizza party offered at the end of the program for those kids who missed no more than one class. Students are then publicly graduated, with parents/guardians present, as "K.I.T. Cadets", and commissioned as "Ambassadors of Peace".

Phase II targets all other fifth and sixth grade students, using a two-day classroom presentation format. In both phases children are taught to identify violence experienced in their homes, communities, and schools, in addition to the larger scale violence portrayed through the media and various electronic devices. Subjective experiences of the students provide the course material. Feelings associated with violence are identified, and alternatives and solutions are generated.

In this revised program guide the K.I.T. Cadets Program will be described, including target populations and criteria for participation. Program implementation will also be addressed, to include the training of facilitators/instructors.

Table of contents

Introduction	503
The K.I.T. Cadets Program:	511
Guidelines and Program Format	511
Criteria and Referral Process	511
Phase I Program Format	513
Week I	514
Week II	517
Week III	521
Week IV	526
Week V	528
Week VI	531
Graduation/Recognition Activities And Preparation for Next Group	532
Phase II Program Format	534
Initial Presentation	535
Follow-up Presentation	537
Program Summary	540
References	541
Exhibits I-IX	542

Introduction

The K.I.T. Cadets Program was developed originally in East Los Angeles, based on the specific needs of children living in areas where high levels of crime and violence are commonplace. Because of these factors, this program is not necessarily designed to meet the needs of other communities where crime and violence are not so prevalent. However, this program is easily adaptable to any areas where children and their families live in constant fear, and is also adaptable to serve the needs of any ethnic or cultural mix which might exist. This approach is simple, and very effective.

Beginning in 1992 through 1994, Murchison Street Elementary School, located in East Los Angeles, CA, was involved in the Healthy Start Program, S.B. 620 Health Start Grant sponsored by the State of California. The Murchison Street Family Center was one of the first school-based clinics established in California to meet the many needs of various communities and their residents by offering non-traditional services through the school site itself. Described as a coordinated services center, the Family Center was designed to serve as liaison between families and children, and different outside agencies to meet the psychological, medical, and social service needs of all people within the community served by this elementary school. By providing case management and coordination of all types of services, the Family Center also facilitated the successful provision of services from the various outside agencies involved. This approach to prevention and intervention was very successful in meeting these needs and fostering a community environment intended to facilitate school success.

The main goal of the Children, Youth, and Family Services Consortium of the California School of Professional Psychology (now under Alliant International University) was to provide both pre-and postdoctoral interns and practicum students for school-based mental health service provision. These service providers, of which I was one, addressed the mental health needs of the children and their families through individual and family therapy, and through various support groups designed to meet the needs of both the students and parents. Mental health services were provided in conjunction with other interns from the Los Angeles County Department of Mental Health and the University of Southern California.

Murchison Street Elementary School was, and still is, part of a community unique in several aspects. The population was predominantly Hispanic/Latino and the community was located in the Hazard Park/Boyle Heights area of East Los Angeles. Because the community is bordered on the north and east sides by industrial areas, on the west by Hazard Park and the Los Angeles County, University of Southern California (LACUSC) Medical complex, and on the south by Interstate 10, it was a community completely closed off from the rest of the city. For the residents to access any type of community services it was necessary to go beyond these boundaries, even for something as simple as a trip to the market for food.

Within this community is the Ramona Gardens Federal Housing Project, an area known to be extremely unsafe due to the high level of gang activity and related crime and violence. The residents within this area live well below the poverty level, with many families often existing solely on different forms of public assistance. Also, many of the adult residents at that time were undocumented and, therefore, were afraid of exposure and possible deportation. There were, and probably still are, only a few African American families living in this area, along with a very small number of European American and Asian American families as well. However, these smaller groups probably comprise less than one or two percent of the total population of this community. This area was made famous by a movie entitled "American Me" released in the early 1990's. The movie gave the entire history of the Hazard Gang and their territory within and around this housing project and Murchison Street Elementary School.

Perhaps the biggest single factor relative to crime and violence, in addition to the socioeconomic status of the people within the community, was the existence of the Hazard Gang. This particular gang is still one of the oldest and best established gangs in all of Los Angeles. The gang members were a very dominant, powerful and visible part of the community even when I was there. Virtually all of the crime and violence was due to the fighting within the Hazard Gang, and between the Hazard Gang and other groups who frequently invaded their territory in an attempt to settle some type of vendetta, or through competition to dominate and control.

The problem of violence within this community was on such a large scale that there were generally multiple major violent incidents occurring within any given week. These incidents included the full range of: drive-by shootings; shoot outs between gang members, either within the Hazard Gang, or between Hazard and other outside gangs; theft; vandalism; sexual assault; domestic violence; child abuse and neglect; prostitution; illegal substances and weapons trade; and various hate crimes, to include bombings of different apartments targeting families representing other ethnic groups viewed by the majority as outsiders, and therefore, unwanted and unwelcomed.

There is no possible way to understand the conditions and complicating factors existing within these types of areas all around this country unless we go into them with the intention of learning and understanding. It literally takes a willingness to work within these areas to even grasp the kinds of problems and needs of people living within such communities. Keep in mind that each respective community nationwide has its own set of specific complicating factors, needs and issues. The only programs which are going to be effective in meeting these needs are those programs created by people who either live in these areas, or who have been involved on the same level I was - and continue to be - with the families enduring these deplorable living conditions and other harsh realities. Those professionals who remain detached from these environments can only pretend to know the needs and realities which exist. Successful program development must come from within such communities, and cannot be approached from the narrow perspective and viewpoint that any prepackaged program format can be the answer for all, and applicable to everyone and to all situations and circumstances. Programs must be designed and/or adapted to the specific population(s) they are intended to serve.

The beauty and sheer genius of school-based/community-based approaches relative to prevention and intervention is that they provide exposure and scope which can lead to such understanding. These programs only work when school systems are willing to work collaboratively with agencies and individual professionals trained specifically to understand and meet the needs of specific groups of kids and families. All factors particular to any given group must be taken into account. These factors include: socioeconomic conditions; ethnic/cultural mix; components of violence and crime unique to certain areas; and the specific needs of certain groups of people relative to issues of legal status and acculturation. If professionals and politicians are not willing to become involved at this level then it will _not_ be possible to provide the necessary services specific to the needs of any given community.

There are no easy answers or "quick fixes". Nor is it possible for any single group, agency, institution, or organization to be all things to all people. This speaks specifically to law enforcement, large federal and state funded and sanctioned programs, and public educational systems. Professionals and politicians alike must be committed to looking at long range benefits when assessing the cost effectiveness of any program. The programs developed through the Healthy Start grants during the 1990's in California were among the best approaches to date. They addressed not only the concerns of society at large, but also the needs of the people often seen as undesirable, low class members of society – groups I refer to as "society's underdogs". Even though very few people are willing to identify the American social system as classist and elitist, it is time to face the fact that it is. It is also time to face the reality that we are a blended society, with the need to abandon the thinking that any one group is better than another in any regard.

Furthermore, the world is changing to such an extent that many of the borders and boundaries which existed just a few years or decades ago are being erased through the ever increasing changes brought about through technological advances and mass communication. Until the world adapts to these changes and abandons the ideas of any group having the right to dominate others, we will continue having the same problems existing today with the probability of these problems only intensifying. We must be committed as a society to providing equal opportunities, and guaranteeing and protecting the human rights and civil liberties of all. We must accept the concept that the survival of our civilizations depends on the combined efforts of a world community united rather than divided.

The K.I.T. Cadets Program outlined in the following pages was developed based on the perceptions and observations made and gained by the present author. This program description represents the combined experiences of working for two years (1992-1994) within the setting I have described. It grew out of the needs of the children and their school relative to curbing the violence not only in their community, but also in their homes, and on their school campus. Though simple in concept, this program has proven to be extremely effective as determined by reports from various school administrators, teachers, and support staff. These school personnel indicated an overall reduction on campus of acting-out behaviors of children identified as high risk for involvement in various forms of violence including bullying.

The simplicity of this program format is found in the fact that it utilizes the concerns and needs of children as the course content. What better source than this? The K.I.T. Cadets Program utilizes aspects of anger management, cognitive/behavioral theory, developmental theory, psychodynamic theory, and family systems theory. It includes general systems theory as it also applies to the community and the world in which these children and their families must live.

Anger management is addressed through cognitive/behavioral theory, to include problem identification/resolution and decision-making skills, by encouraging children to generate alternatives to current acting out behaviors. According to Piaget (Gleitman, 1986; Gormly and Brodzinsky, 1989), eleven and twelve year old children are developmentally capable of both concrete and abstract thinking. This allows them the opportunity to understand cause and effect, and is a good time chronologically to teach that for every choice there is a consequence or outcome.

Erikson (Gleitman, 1988; Gormly and Brodzinsky, 1989) took cognitive/behavioral, developmental theory further by including psychosocial crises or conflicts associated with each stage of development. Because the K.I.T. Cadets Program is intended to serve fifth and sixth grade kids (specifically identified kids in Phase I, and all others in Phase II), Erikson's fourth and fifth stages of his developmental model are especially applicable. These stages are "competence versus inferiority", and "identity versus identity confusion" respectively. At these stages children are mastering social skills, and defining and further establishing a sense of self. It is possible through the K.I.T. Cadets Program to even address deficits relative to trust, autonomy, and initiative outlined in Erikson's earlier stages of development. Prevention and intervention techniques such as those incorporated into the K.I.T. Cadets Program are needed at both the elementary school and middle school levels to catch these children during their significant stages of development and social/educational transitions.

Psychodynamic theory is also an essential part of this program. Malan (1979) addresses the development of defense mechanisms for the avoidance of mental and emotional pain and conflict, and to control impulses considered unacceptable. The researcher discusses behaviors which represent the acting out of anxiety created by hidden or repressed feelings. This is a major concept approached through the K.I.T. Cadets Program, as it is designed to bring out these repressed feelings as part of the prevention and intervention concept.

Because the K.I.T. Cadets Program takes into consideration the environmental factors of school, families, community, socioeconomic elements, and political/governmental components, general systems theory applies to this program. Goldenberg and Goldenberg (1985) present the connection and use of general systems theory to family systems theory as proposed by various theorists and researchers. The basic concept is that an entity, or a whole, is indeed greater than the sum of its interconnected parts.

School children are primarily affected and impacted by six different systems or contexts within which abuse and victimization can occur. These systems operate within larger systems and include: family, community, school, society, politics, and religion. It is within all of these systems that children are potentially victimized and stigmatized by violence, prejudice, and hardship. Obvious attempts were being made in the 1960's, 70's and 80's to address the interaction of these various systems relative to violent behavior (Apter and Goldstein, 1986). It was only in the 1990's that the importance of school-based mental health and other nontraditional services were being emphasized as a necessary component of collaboration and intersystem relationships.

The program descriptions for Phases I and II of the K.I.T. Cadets Program to follow will focus on the referral process; definition of and identification of the population of students served; and the actual course format and content. Also included at the end of this program description will be examples of the various referral and consent forms, as well as letters to the parents, and certificates of award and appreciation given to the students upon completion of the program.

Again, remember that the K.I.T. Cadets Program is designed to meet the needs of elementary and middle school kids who live in areas where criminal and violent activity are prevalent and commonplace. This program is easily adaptable to serve any ethnic or cultural mix given the existence of other factors previously discussed. Program effectiveness and success are based on the level of understanding and clinical training of the program facilitator(s). It is very necessary to be familiar with the nature and reality of the circumstances under which children within violent areas live, and within the specific area(s) served by the program. All facilitators must have the ability to draw out repressed feelings in children, even when the children insist that known violence has no impact on them or their lives.

Keep in mind this is not an "anti-gang" program. It is an "anti-violence" program intended to give children exposure to alternatives to violence. Basically, K.I.T. Cadets are graduated as "Ambassadors of Peace" and are given the hope that they can make a difference even on a small scale. Self esteem and helplessness/hopelessness are addressed by teaching children that they deserve better than what they have had so far in life. Improvement is also facilitated by teaching them they are important, and can therefore, make a difference not only within their subjective world, but also in the world existing often beyond their scope of awareness. Prevention and intervention with the target population can give children the tools they need to withstand the negative pressures and peer influence associated with pre-adolescence, and later in the upper grade levels.

Children are often relieved to gain the awareness that the darkness within the world as they know it can be improved one step at a time. They are also relieved to learn that they do not of necessity have to be part of the violence which impacts and often destroys not only their hope, but their lives. Some of the fear is at least reduced as they are empowered with the knowledge and the tools which will help them make a difference by allowing them to make different choices. They also learn that hope comes only through education, understanding, and appreciation of individual differences, coupled with the determination to succeed. Use of this program can give hope to those children who so often have lost their ability to dream.

The K.I.T. Cadets Program is all about choices and trying to ensure that kids are making the right choices needed to secure their success as they enter adulthood. While kids oftentimes cannot control or influence the decisions made by adults in their lives, kids can learn from the mistakes of others. Clearly, as children enter adolescence, their futures are increasingly determined, consciously or unconsciously, intentionally or unintentionally, by the choices they then begin to make. It is the conscious intent of this program to educate kids relative to this very significant reality. No concept can be anymore important than this when it comes to helping shape the lives of the kids we seek to serve!

The K.I.T. Cadet Program:
Guidelines and Program Format

Criteria and Referral Process

The K.I.T. Cadets Program is designed to meet the needs of elementary and middle school children impacted and traumatized very directly by violence in their lives and/or families; and of children at risk for involvement in violence as indicated by various acting out behaviors including bullying. These acting out behaviors are defined as poor impulse control, violent outbursts, and physical assault/confrontation toward other children and/or adults. These children are often removed from classroom settings and play areas because of their inability or unwillingness to more appropriately deal with their anger and anxiety. They are also frequently sent to the school office for disciplinary action, often resulting in on-campus and off-campus suspension, transfer to alternative schools, or outright expulsion from school.

The K.I.T. Cadets Program is divided into Phases I and II. Phase I is composed of groups of fifth and sixth grade students who meet in a group format for six weeks. Groups are didactic and experiential in nature, with full involvement encouraged relative to active listening, discussion, and participation in the activities planned. Groups are limited to no more than 45 minutes. Because many of the children in any group generally have problems with impulse control, it is important to limit the groups to no more than 15 to 21. It is also best to have at least one other person viewed by students as an authority figure who can dole out disciplinary action if necessary as a way of limiting any acting out behaviors during the group sessions. In addition to a program assistant, this third person can also take an active role during the sessions as long as they are following the program guidelines specifically and acting as an authority figure only if and as needed for behavior management. The actual format of these groups in Phase I will be outlined in more detail in the sections to follow.

Phase II consists of classroom presentations to all fifth and sixth grade students on a weekly, classroom by classroom basis in as many elementary schools as allowed by school districts. This format includes an initial Monday presentation and a Thursday follow up in the same week. Both presentations should last at least 45 minutes as in the group setting. Presentations consist of basic discussions of what violence is and the feelings associated with violence. More detail will be given about this phase as well in the sections to follow.

Candidates for the K.I.T. Cadets Program are identified from different sources and through different opportunities to observe exhibited behaviors. Many referrals are received from teachers (Exhibit I) who work with the child in the classroom, and therapists/counselors who see the child in individual sessions from within or outside of the school. The program in California, where K.I.T. Cadets originated, featured "The Family Center" and staff met every Monday morning for case management and review. The assistant principal who received the referral forms, the interns, and often the school psychologist on site participated in these weekly meetings.

The purpose of this consultation and collaborative effort was to review the referrals from teachers and other sources and determine the best approach to meeting the needs of the child and their family. At this time the child may be referred to a variety of services available, usually including individual and family therapy, to identify and clarify the specific needs and sources of conflict. Sometimes the needs could be addressed relatively easily, but often required a combination of approaches and ongoing case management. Children who met the criteria described above were referred to the next available group in the K.I.T. Cadets Program.

Other equally effective means of identifying appropriate program participants included classroom observation, playground/lunch area observation, and regular checks to see who is sitting in the principal's office. Because my training has also included working for two years at an alternative education site for middle school age children at risk for gang involvement, ultimate expulsion, and likely school drop out, I have additional clues which elementary school staff may not recognize as warning signs. The most prominent warnings signs are type of clothing worn, style of haircut, mannerisms emulating gang affiliation, attitudes of toughness/intimidation and control, and wearing specific colored items to include shoes, bracelets, and bandanas. Many times some of these types of indicators are not displayed by children in the classroom. They generally know better. Also, children are more likely to act out in the play areas and lunch areas because these environments are much less structured and supervision is often minimal.

One other possible means of referral is to solicit referrals directly from teachers and other school personnel just prior to the formation of a new group (Exhibit II). The teachers are told the kinds of behaviors to look for, and are asked to submit the names of students who meet the criteria so they can be included in the next group. *<u>Keep in mind that these groups are not intended to be a dumping ground for kids who are simply disruptive in class. Make sure referrals met the criteria specified for participation.</u>*

Phase I Program Format

Remember this phase is intended for fifth and sixth grade students only, and consists of six forty-five minute weekly sessions. Referrals for subsequent groups should be sought at least by the fifth week of the current group. This is important since it takes time to obtain the referrals and permission from parents needed for student participation in the program. Remember to limit the group to no more than 15 to 21 students. Also be sure to have one co-facilitator to work with you who is viewed as an authority figure by the kids around the school. Additional assistance can be obtained through follow up with K.I.T. Cadets from previous groups who might still be having trouble with anger management and impulse control who would benefit from a "refresher course" so to speak. Their duties can include taking attendance, giving out name tags each week, and assisting with planned art projects, to include being responsible for giving out and retrieving all art supplies, especially markers and scissors. The added attention for returnees gives them a boost. However, watch to make sure their participation doesn't go to their heads by occasionally reminding them of their limited role and responsibilities.

Before any child can participate in the K.I.T. Cadets Program, specific written permission *<u>must</u>* be obtained from the parents (Exhibit III). The examples of consent forms included are both in English and Spanish, as many of the parents at the Murchison Street Elementary School site in East LA were Spanish-speaking only. Occasionally parents may call with questions and concerns. These concerns are often based in fears of danger that involvement in such a program may pose a threat of retaliation against their child. Generally, once the program format is discussed with the parent or guardian, their fears are eliminated and permission is granted without further hesitation.

Weekly reminder notices (Exhibit IV) are sent out to the teachers to inform them of the students in their classroom accepted in the program, and subsequently to insure that students are present in group each week. Teachers are generally very willing to send the students each week, and will inform you of their absence from school, or of any other conflict which might exist in any particular week. If a participant misses more than one week they are to be dropped until the next group. A review of the missed week must be conducted to help the student catch up and understand the full curriculum in order to appropriately receive a certificate of completion.

Week I

With consent forms in hand and students before you, certain issues need to be addressed and the program needs to be explained. The best arrangement for the room is to have three tables set up in a U shape, open toward the chalk board or marker board. This allows for full mobility and access to each student as the needs arise for issues of behavior management and clarification, and occasionally to comfort a child who has revealed something particularly difficult or painful. Keep in mind that I ran these groups over a two year period in East Los Angeles and basically encountered every possible scenario imaginable relative to topics related to violence and bullying. Be sure that you and your staff are comfortable in your own skin with whatever may come up and remember to refer for anything which seems to be more than you can handle in a group setting. Always have at least one licensed therapist available who is sensitive to the issues and needs of these kids who will also be able to intervene as needed.

As you open up the discussion be prepared for anything from first had accounts of having witnessed killings, rape, physical assault, child abuse, domestic violence, and suicide within their family of origin, to various other forms of crime. You will hear very intense stories which will likely have a greater impact on you initially than will be observed in the students. These factors are the reasons why issues of confidentiality and respect must be addressed and explained at the beginning and throughout the process.

In the first meeting the main goal is to get the students to identify the types of violence highlighted in the media and even in video games. It is important to list all examples of violence and bullying given by the students so they can see the list in its entirety upon completion. It is also important to take their examples seriously, but at the same time helping them to distinguish some examples which may be given as not necessarily representing violence. For instance, if a child gives an example of someone speeding down a street or highway, ask them for clarification to see how this fits into their definition of and understanding of violence. Point out that if the person speeding is being chased by the police, then this is part of violence because of the potential for a violent outcome relative to those people breaking the law and to innocent victims who might get injured.

Try not to be shocked by the level of awareness kids have relative to acts of violence and things associated with violence. The list will undoubtedly include weapons, alcohol, drugs, sexual misconduct, stealing, vandalism, various acts of violence, bullying, and gang involvement. Be sure to include issues of harassment and discrimination as opportunities for violence. Once the students have run out of examples ask them to identify places where they might see or experience violence. If necessary suggest that violence occurs on the streets, on television, in music, in movies, in their homes, on their playgrounds, within their communities, and at school. Make these suggestions one at a time, giving them time to respond by generating examples from these contexts which they do not readily associate with violence. Make sure to include active forms of sexual, physical, and emotional abuse, and the passive form of neglect as acts of violence. It is during this time you may begin to get examples which are personal and difficult for a student to talk about. Be very sensitive to this and carefully guide the discussion away from becoming too heavy emotionally for any particular student. Remember these groups are *not* intended to be therapy groups. They are educational and experiential only. <u>Make certain that no one laughs at a response from another student, and remind them continually about **confidentiality and respect**.</u>

Once the list is completed it is time to ask for specific examples of how violence has impacted each student personally. Encourage everyone to participate unless it is obvious they are not comfortable doing so. With any kid who is hesitant it would be a good idea to talk with them after the group to see if there are any particular problems they may be withholding or trying to hide. If this is your first time to facilitate the K.I.T. Cadet Program you may find these stories to be alarming. Do not be afraid to express openly, but appropriately, your concern and empathy about how difficult the lives of these children must be. This lets them know the violence they take for granted as being a part of their everyday lives in not normal. Also, an expression of how you are feeling emotionally lets them know of your ability to take care of them during this process. If any story is not shared in a clear, concise manner, always ask for clarification to insure that everyone has heard the details accurately. Even if a story is not completely factual, the telling of their stories will clearly reflect the realities with which they live internally.

As the children run out of stories, ask them to consider how violence presents itself on their playgrounds, especially at school and within their communities. Ask the students by show of hands how many of them have ever been in a physical fight. At this point those who do not identify themselves honestly will likely be "outed" by the other students. This must be controlled, but can be used to help the students know it is safe to share honestly within the group setting. This part of the discussion helps to establish the fact that violence begins on a relatively small scale and can build into so much more. It also gives the students the awareness that by changing some of their behaviors they can begin to eliminate at least some of the violence for which they might be responsible. This empowers them and eases their sense of helplessness and hopelessness.

These are two approaches to talking about violence by generating lists and listening to personal experiences which will easily fill the first forty-five minute meeting. The children generally love to talk about violence, especially their own personal accounts of how violence has impacted them and their families. Be sure to wrap up the first meeting by again addressing the need for confidentiality and respect. Tell the students how important it is for them to attend all six meetings, stressing the policy that more than one absence will mean they will need to repeat the program in the future. The idea of the pizza party on the seventh week is usually a great incentive for them to stay involved.

Before dismissing them tell them a little of what to expect for the next meeting and give them a general overview of the remaining weeks. Ask for any questions and comments, then dismiss them by reminding them they can stop at least some of the violence at school, at home, and in their communities by simply staying out of it as much as possible. Make sure they understand you do not expect them to intervene in any acts of violence or bullying, letting them know it is okay to report such events to authorities and other adults. Let them know that anyone who needs to talk with staff after this and any future meeting can stay after the others are dismissed. For any student(s) who stays behind after the meeting try to determine what the issues are and what you as a professional need to do to possibly refer them and their family for additional assistance. Be sure to contact parents and professionals about any concerns which may arise, and be prepared to report any suspected acts of abuse or neglect which may be revealed and as required by law.

Week II

After having identified violence as being more than the types of violence portrayed and emphasized in the media, the second week is intended to focus on the feelings/emotions children experience relative to violence. It is important to understand that the only way many children can deal with the emotional overload they experience is to deny that emotions exist. Furthermore, it is important to understand that many families do not know how to teach their children it is okay to have feelings and to talk about these feelings with people you trust – trust being the key word.

After reviewing the content of the first week's meeting, and as you begin to introduce the topic of feelings for the second week, you will find that some or all of the kids are at a loss about feelings associated with violence. They will likely not be able to identify these feelings at a personal, conscious level. If this is the case then ask them to imagine how others might feel if they witness a violent act such as a shooting or a stabbing. It may even be necessary to give them an example such as someone feeling "frightened". Many of the children initially may deny they are ever afraid of anything, and will give the impression that violence is not a problem for them personally. Remember the only way many of these kids survive emotionally is to deny the feelings they actually experience. Understand this type of denial and inability to identify and talk about their feelings is what puts them more and more at risk for ever increasing opportunities to act out their anxiety and emotion-based anger.

As the children begin to identify feelings following whatever degree of prompting is necessary, list them on the board or other available medium. Continue asking for more and more suggestions, even making a few of your own, until you feel the list is complete. Make sure that the list includes emotions related to the RFLAGS model – Fear, Loneliness, Anger Guilt and Shame as the core of emotions which need to be identified and worked through. This model is very useful in conceptualizing the issues associated with this population of kids and is found in my book At the Mercy of Externals: Righting Wrongs and Protecting Kids, 2nd Edition (included as part of this volume) which all facilitators should read. A companion to this book, as a helpful tool relative to the application of my theories, is Psyche-Soul-ology: An Inspirational Approach to Appreciating and Understanding Troubled Kids, also included within this volume. It is at this point where you want to introduce the RFLAGS Model to help kids understand the combination of emotions which lie at the heart of acting out behaviors even in the lives of adults. The RFLAGS Model ties all of this into every violent act known to these kids including bullying.

At this point list these five main feelings on the board under the heading of "Negative Emotions/Feelings", writing one under the other in the order of the word "FLAGS". Emphasize that, while these five feelings are not the only emotions we experience, they are generally the most difficult ones for anyone to identify and deal with effectively. Draw a horizontal line to the right of the first heading and write the words "Anxiety/Depression". Ask the students what other words they use to describe this state of anxiety/depression which "feels bad", and list these words under this column.

After this list has been exhausted draw another horizontal line from the words "Anxiety/Depression" and write the words "Helplessness/Hopelessness". A little further to the right put the words "Acting-Out Behaviors".

Explain that the emotion-based state of anxiety/depression often builds to a point where people, including kids, give up and then start acting out the emotions they are ignoring. Ask them to make a list of all the acting out behaviors they can identify, helping them with a few suggestions of your own to facilitate the process.

The main point of the diagram and discussion is to help the students understand that many activities are initiated in order to avoid the experience of "feeling bad". Take a little time to generate alternatives to acting out which would help them deal with their emotions differently than ignoring them and acting them out. Such suggestions should include talking about their feeling with friends, families, teachers, or therapists and counselors. Help them learn to choose their friends and activities carefully as a means of avoiding people and situations which can be potentially harmful to themselves and to others.

Personal experience suggests it is important to stress that the K.I.T. Cadets Program is not an anti-gang program; but, rather an anti-violence and anti-crime program. This can be explained by sharing the positive kinds of "gangs" which all of us participate in such as various religious groups, social groups, common interest groups, etc. Explain that a "gang" is simply a group of people who find some benefit in being together, resulting from common interests and the need for association. Point out the dangers and realities associated with gangs based in criminal activity and violence.

Emphasize that the "gangs" most often recognized today do not share interests which are legal or safe, with no focus on the common good for society at large. Stress that your concern for each student in the room is the fact that if they make the wrong choices relative to friends, associates, and activities, they then expose themselves to the likelihood of making mistakes which will greatly limit their futures and their options. Emphasize your concern that some of their choices can even get them seriously and permanently injured, and/or killed, or incarcerated. This is a harsh reality which they already know, but often fail to even see as a possibility for them personally.

At this point ask the students if they have bad dreams during the night. Then ask them to tell about the content of their dreams. Listen for common themes which will emerge of being chased, getting captured, hurt or killed, and watching these things happen to themselves, and others, especially family members. Ask them if they ever have the experience of trying to scream, but being unable to do so. Ask them if they ever dream about being chased by the devil, or by characters from the scary movies, video games, and television programs most of them will tell you they watch or play. As more children begin to share others, reluctant to do so at first, will likely begin to tell of their experiences as well. Again, stress the importance of confidentiality and respect.

At this point ask the students to identify the common themes they heard in the details of dreams shared within the group. Then explain that their dreams often represent and reflect the things going on in their everyday lives. Ask them to make a list of the feelings they experience during and from their dreams. When this list is completed show them how the list of feelings they identified as being associated with violence are the same kinds of feelings they experience in their nightmares. Tell them this indicates they are experiencing these feelings in their dreams because they have trouble identifying them in their waking existence and environment.

This meeting is usually very powerful in helping students understand they really do experience feelings and emotions relative to the violence with which they live. Tell them it is normal and healthy to have these feelings, but that it is not healthy to ignore what they are feeling. Bring this out through the pattern of feelings linked to anxiety and depression and also linked to the acting out behaviors listed previously on the board. Tell them the way to deal with these emotions effectively is to identify them and talk to others about them as they occur. If these options are not possible for them at home, then make sure there are referral sources for these kids with professionals who can facilitate this opportunity.

End this session by explaining to the students that they can avoid many of these problems by being careful not to make choices which will put them more at risk for experiencing violence. Tell them that by simply trying to avoid fights with other children and siblings they can eliminate some of the stress they feel and actually create for themselves. Help them clearly understand how the cycle of ever increasing violence and retaliation works even at their level of simply fighting with their peers. No one fights fair anymore. Most people fight with "backup" against another person to insure their victory. If the children are afraid of being perceived as weak then point out what a cowardly choice it is to have a fight unequally balanced by the numbers of people pitted against each other. Tell them that fighting then becomes a never ending cycle of retaliation and fear of that retaliation.

Also help them identify the actions or issues which usually initiate the original fight. Most often the children will reveal that the fight starts because of a look referred to as "mad dogging", or from some insult by one person to another regarding a family member, usually a parent. Ask if these things are really worth fighting about and possibly being permanently injured or even dying for, pointing out how insignificant these acts and insults are compared to the scale of violence which will likely result. Teach them it is better to walk away and avoid a fight rather than get drawn into another kid's anxiety and need to act out. Teach them to think about probable consequences and let this be the main focus of the last four remaining groups. This gives them a sense of having some control over their safety and involvement in violence. This is the main goal of the K.I.T. Cadets Program, and is also the message they can take back to their friends, families and, communities. This is the idea of confronting the violence on a small scale which can have ever increasing effects on a larger scale. K.I.T. Cadets can make a difference!

At the end of every meeting be sure to check on the well being of all participants before they leave. Again, make appropriate referrals as and if needed for whatever issues or reactions may arise.

Week III

Week III is the time to incorporate the art work and skits. You will find that activities are necessary to both hold their interest and to further emphasize the goals of the program. Also, use the remaining weeks to address any concepts not fully understood during the first two weeks. Be sure to always review and summarize the content of the previous meetings. You will find it very beneficial to reinforce these topics and issues again, so do not feel that the kids need to understand everything all at once. This expectation may exceed their ability to understand or your ability to teach these concepts based on your initial lack of training and experience with this program format and related issues. It is important to recognize your own limitations relative to perception and awareness of what constitutes the reality of this population. Even with experience the most you can hope for with some of the children is to be able to plant a seed which will grow and serve them at some point in the future. Do not assume too quickly they are not benefiting from the program or that you are not effective in your efforts.

The art supplies needed include ten pairs of scissors, two sets of colored markers, two bottles of white glue, two large pieces of poster board for each of the next three consecutive weeks, and news magazines depicting scenes of violence and representing the causes and issues associated with violence. Pictures related to violence can also be obtained through the Internet from various web sites. This will provide enough materials and supplies for the two groups designated to do the artwork each of the next three weeks.

Each of the next four remaining weeks will have a specific theme for the artwork and discussion time. The theme for Week III will be to identify scenes of violence. Spend the first few minutes of Week III explaining how the last four weeks of the program will work. Remind them again about the pizza party Week VII for those who successfully complete the first six weeks. Tell the children the group will be divided into three permanent groups of five for each of the remaining weeks. These groups will be rotated each week so all students will have the opportunity to participate in both the skits and the artwork. The idea of skits will likely evoke some anxiety, but assure the students they will be assisted by one of the adults facilitating the group.

After explaining the approach for the remaining weeks, begin the discussion for Week III. The theme will be to identify contexts for and scenes of violence by asking the students to again talk briefly about any violence or bullying they have personally witnessed in the media or in their personal lives. These are the same scenes they described in the first meeting. This will get them focused on what constitutes different forms of violence. Contexts related to issues of violence include: home/family, school, community, societies (nationally and internationally), politics, and religion. These should be listed and discussed using examples from the children's experiences and awarenesses to explain violence within each setting. Society, politics and religion will likely need some explanation for the students to see their connection to violence and the potential for violence nationally and internationally. Limit this time to no more than fifteen minutes, including the explanation of the focus and intent for the remaining weeks.

As this discussion ends, divide the large group into smaller groups by assigning the students numbers of one, two and three as they count off around the table. Do not give them the opportunity to choose their own group as this will likely result in mass confusion and hurt feelings. Also, be sure to divide the girls evenly through the three groups. Groups one and two will be involved in the artwork for the first week, and group three will be the first group to participate in the skits.

This is also a time when the students selected from previous groups will be especially helpful in facilitating the artwork experience. Students who need a "refresher course" as described previously should be limited to probably no more than two per subsequent groups. Give them the responsibility as K.I.T. Cadets (they have already graduated) for setting up the supplies on two tables in another part of the room for the artwork. Remind the returnees that they have been selected to set an example for the newest group of students, insisting that they take their role very seriously as Ambassadors of Peace. Also give them the responsibility for helping the other students understand the kinds of pictures to be cut out and/or selected for each week and used in the collages they will be creating. At the end of the twenty minutes allotted for the artwork, also ask the helpers to make sure all art supplies are accounted for before the session ends. No student should be allowed to leave the room until all supplies are turned in, especially the markers and the scissors. During the artwork time the helpers can be responsible for gluing the appropriate pictures on the poster board for each group. The markers can be used to write words or phrases relative to violence under the pictures selected. Be sure to explain that these posters will be displayed publicly with the names of the students displayed under each poster. This will encourage them to take pride in their work and to take it seriously. It is important for you as a facilitator to oversee all of these activities to insure proper completion and control of the process. This is the suggested approach to the artwork activities for each of the last four weeks.

Dr. David L. Roberts Ph.D.

Make sure the students understand that they are looking for pictures related to the topic presented each week. Tell them they will be given an opportunity during Week VI to look over their projects and make any corrections or additions they feel might be needed before the posters go on display. Explain that a collage is intended to tell a story through the pictures they select and include in each final poster.

Because the helpers are peers of the students involved in each group, they will not be able to provide the full guidance needed. It is interesting to note that some of the helpers may try to become authority figures in their roles as helpers. This attempt will not work, so help them keep their own control issues in check by not giving them more responsibility than they can handle appropriately. Failing to implement these precautions seriously will likely result in damage to the self esteem of the 'helpers' who are also serving 'returnees'. Before they are ever utilized in any group meet with them separately and fully explain their role and limitations of that role. Helpers are not necessary for the group doing the skit each week.

The theme of the skit each week should reflect the overall theme of that week's activities. Because these children live in such harsh environments there are basically no issues they would not be able to deal with relative to the subject content of the skits. They will either have personal experiences relative to each topic, or will at the very least be extremely familiar with any topic chosen. So, do not be afraid to tackle the difficult issues these kids face on a rather frequent basis. This includes the topic of death and dying, as well as topics related to sexual misconduct. If public or private schools prohibit discussion of such topics, then the K.I.T. Cadets Programs should always be offered outside the purview of such institutions.

The suggested theme for the first week's skit is that of the death of a friend as a result of something like a drive-by shooting or a retaliatory attack by gang members or rivals in other settings such as schools and neighborhoods. This could also include an unjust act committed by law enforcement agents. Though this is a gruesome topic, it is one with which all of the children can identify because of the prevalence of such occurrences within their communities and frames of reference. Dealing appropriately with this theme will help the students get in touch with the feelings and emotions already present in each of these children. Remember, this program is intended to identify and address the extreme nature of the subjective world of the students referred to the K.I.T. Cadets Program you are sponsoring and facilitating.

With five children in each group it is suggested that each child be assigned a topic for a one minute dramatization. Children can be paired off in order to have this dramatization presented as though they were telling a friend about what has occurred. Ask the first child to tell one of the other children the details of how the friend was killed. This will require very little input from you as they will already have access to such details.

Ask a second child to join and talk about the reaction of the family who suffered the loss. Because this also involves the emotional reaction of the family, some input from the facilitator will likely be necessary, even to the point of identifying feelings the family might experience under such circumstances. This can be done more easily if there is a child in the group who may have experienced the event in reality.

The third child should be asked to relate the details of attending the funeral and burial. Again, some assistance may or may not be necessary with details and specifics. Make sure no one mentions the names of any real individuals who may have experienced this kind of event in their lives. You may again be surprised to learn that one child in the group has actually had this experience in reality and can easily fill this role. They will likely do this without hesitation given the fact it will be presented as a dramatization rather than as a real and personal experience.

Feelings of anger and fear relative to the death of the friend should be presented by the fourth child. The anger would likely include anger related to the loss itself and the injustice associated with the loss. The fear would be based in the reality that this could happen again in the future to another friend or to a member of their own family.

Finally, the fifth child, to whom all of this information has been related, should be asked to talk about their feelings of sadness, and discuss with the others how they could memorialize their friend. In many areas this includes getting permission to paint a mural to commemorate the loss. It could also include a commitment from this group to do what they can to stop the violence and try to teach others how they can help as well, and as part of their role once they become K.I.T. Cadets. This last part can instill a sense of hope that things will change in the future. It also emphasizes the importance of support needed in dealing with these kinds of tragedies which are prevalent in the subjective world of low income, disadvantaged kids and their families.

This skit is prepared and rehearsed during the twenty minutes the other groups are working on the art projects. Watch your time and make sure there is ten minutes left out of the forty-five allotted to present the skit. Be sure there is also a little time at the end to tie all of this together, and to normalize the reactions which students may have relative to the subject content.

As always pay attention to any child who may be traumatized by any of this, and ask them to stay after the group leaves in order to talk about what they are feeling. <u>**Keep in mind that the K.I.T. Cadet Program format will not and cannot create emotions.**</u> However, it can bring to the surface existing emotions which need to be identified and dealt with rather than suppressed. Talking with any child privately will give you the opportunity to assess the degree of emotional upset and possibly discover the source. Always be prepared to make appropriate referrals to address the specific needs which may arise. <u>**Understand that whatever is triggered within any of the students was there before the presentation, so do not feel guilty or blame the course content.**</u> Be glad that this program can serve as such a vehicle to bring out these emotions which may otherwise go undetected and unresolved in these children.

Week IV

The theme for Week IV is that of identifying things associated with violence. Remember to briefly review material covered in previous weeks. This theme utilizes the ideas generated in week one where the students were asked to identify those elements of violence such as weapons and various acts associated with violence. Spend the first fifteen minutes getting the students to recall the elements identified the first week. After doing this break them up into their groups again, with groups two and three given the task of working on the respective collage for the week, and group one given the task of preparing the skit. Follow the same approach outlined in Week III, emphasizing the theme relative to both the artwork and the skit.

In working with the kids who are to prepare the skit, explain that they are going to dramatize the effects of peer pressure, including forms of bullying, as used to entice others into participating in activities often associated with violence. This week will require that the students participate in more than one of the one minute presentations.

The first topic will involve one student trying to sell a gun to a student. Think of any possible persuasive tactics which might be used including suggestions of needing a gun for protection, a gun representing power, being a coward for not buying it, and the enticement that "everyone has a gun and it will give you respect".

In the second skit have two students trying to convince another to join a gang or some other group associated with violence. Use such examples as gangs being necessary for back up and protection, for loyalty and friendship, for partying and popularity, and for power and respect.

The topics of the other three skits are: peer pressure to smoke a joint (marijuana); getting one or more kids to ditch school; and trying to get a kid to steal something from a store or from another student. Use the same approach for each of these segments as with the first two segments outlined above. The five topics for these skits deal with things which could occur in the schools and communities of these students. As with the skit from the previous week they will likely have very little difficulty coming up with their own lines of persuasion. It is probable that very little prompting will be necessary from the facilitator, as the children usually will have been approached in this manner in the past, or may have approached others as well.

Again allow a ten minute time period for the presentation of the skits and the discussion of the subject matter. Because this week is not so intense compared to the topic from the previous week there may not be any significant emotional reaction from any of the students. However, be alert to any problems which might arise and address these in the same manner outlined previously. Be sure to always praise the students for their efforts and participation is all aspects of the weekly meetings.

Keep in mind that the K.I.T. Cadets Program is never to be used to gain information which could be held against a kid in any manner. Therefore, be careful not to ask too many personal questions as to how they know some of what they know. This tactic simply is not a focus of this program.

In order to protect integrity and respect of and for this program, no one outside of this program is to have access to anything shared within the context of this program. This program is intended only to increase awareness and change perspectives so that the participants can redirect their thinking and their lives, and is never to be presented as punishment or appear to be judgmental against any participant. Program facilitators are never to become detectives for any outside agency or group! If this ever happens the program will be temporarily shut down and staff will be dealt with accordingly for a breach of confidentiality and lack of professionalism. New facilitators will be brought in and trained according to the strict guidelines provided by the structure and intent of this program format. This is a very serious matter.

Week V

Week five focuses on racism, prejudice, and bigotry, to include **all** of the "isms" associated with diversity. Because much of the violence is motivated and fueled by prejudice against any type of human difference it is important to include this topic as a primary focus during one of the six weeks when the kids meet. As before, allow fifteen minutes for this discussion at the beginning of the meeting.

Begin by asking the children to define racism, prejudice, and bigotry. Because homophobia is such a big part of what motivates kids to fight, do not eliminate it as a part of the discussion. Asking them to define these terms will give you an idea of their level of understanding of the topic. Usually at least one child will be able to define one or all of the terms. Once this happens then other students will be able to identify with the subject matter and will begin to offer input into the discussion. Ask them to list all types of prejudice and discrimination they can identify. A good approach is to also ask them to give the names often used which reflect racial prejudice. Generally a child will not give an example of a name used against their respective ethnicity. However, it is important to help them identify these names as well, especially if the group is predominantly composed of one particular ethnic group. Stress to them that they are not to add any previously unknown terms to their vocabulary outside of the group setting.

After the students have listed all of the things associated with this topic, focus on other types of discrimination to include sexism, religious intolerance, age, physical or mental disabilities, and heterosexism. Basically address every possible aspect of diversity which could be used to hurt another person including all forms of harassment. As you can, be sure to include historical examples of prejudice such as the Holocaust, the Civil Rights Movement, women's groups, political issues related to immigration, socioeconomic status, and issues such as gender abuse related to male dominated cultures. If possible also give a brief account of some way you have personally experienced discrimination.

After completing this part of the discussion, use the lists generated and the examples given to bring all of this down to a more personal level for the kids. Ask them to think about how prejudice fuels and motivates the violence in their homes, communities, playgrounds, and school yards. It is good to ask them to imagine times when they could be, or have been targets of prejudice. Ask them to examine their own use of prejudice toward members of the opposite gender, toward other ethnic groups, or toward any groups perceived to be different from themselves. Be sure to include bullying as part of this discussion as well. Also include examples of hate groups existing in this country and in other parts of the world. Be sure to explain that prejudice is a way for one group to try and dominate another group through intimidation – a power struggle suggesting that one group is better than the other. Also get them to see how gang involvement is connected to prejudice and territorial issues.

Because of the importance of this topic it is okay to take a little extra time for discussion if necessary. However, be sure to leave enough time for the preparation and presentation of this week's skit. Remember that the sixth week does not include a skit presentation and is intended as a time to finish up the artwork and to summarize all of the discussions from the previous weeks. It is not necessary to finish all of the artwork for this week since there will be an opportunity to do so in the last meeting.

Skit presentations for this week will be made by group two, with groups one and three working on the art activity. As before, the skits are to be one minute in length, and for this week are to focus on issues of discrimination against women, African Americans, Asian Americans, European Americans, and Latin Americans. If the ethnic mix is different in your groups then choose other groups as appropriate. Be sure to always include attitudes toward women. Issues of heterosexism may not be appropriate for a skit, but it is appropriate to address this during the discussion time because of the student's tendency to use such words as "gay", "fag", and "queer" as part of their efforts to antagonize and incite other kids.

If you think the kids can handle it, it is good to select a child who represents the specific target of prejudice to be dramatized. It is obviously important to emphasize that the students are only acting, making sure to debrief them after the presentation is finished. Make sure all participants are fully in agreement with their respective roles. The debriefing should take place after each segment of the skit presentations in any given week if it is necessary and appropriate to do so. Remind the students that these skits are intended to only increase their understanding of the topics and are not to be carried out any further following the meetings. Constantly remind participants that the program goal is to graduate them as "Ambassadors of Peace".

The reason for selecting a female to represent discrimination against women, and an African American student to represent discrimination against African Americans is painfully simple. This approach allows the other students to see how hurtful and offensive these discriminatory situations really are as experienced by the targets of the discrimination. The best approach is to pair two students against each other in each of these situations. If necessary, borrow a few students from the other groups to serve as stand-ins during the actual skit presentations. If a child is too sensitive or objects in any way to this kind of verbal assault, then you or other adults present can be called in to play the target of such abuse. A very careful evaluation of the group is necessary before this weeks meeting even begins.

At the end of the skits, be sure to emphasize again that this was only a dramatization, and the point of the presentation was to reveal the cruelty of prejudice and discrimination. Tell the students that human differences are to be respected, appreciated, and understood rather than being used as a means of hurting, dominating, or offending others. Ask the students about how serious these issues are relative to hatred and violence. Also point out to them that very few people, if any, actually represent ethnic purity, explaining that we are all a mixture of different ethnicities and cultural influences. Point out that at any time the balance of a situation could change, so that one group who may have majority status in one setting could be "out numbered" in another setting. Again, watch for any signs of distress experienced by the students which may need to be assessed further after the meeting has ended.

Week VI

As stated earlier, Week VI is the time to finish all of the artwork and tie up all loose ends of the previous weeks. Allow at least fifteen minutes to summarize the program material and reinforce the objective of teaching the group members ways to protect themselves and others from violence and bullying. Be sure to use this time to focus on alternatives to violence which are realistic to the world in which the kids live. Before the children come into the room, have all of the collages laid out on the tables, grouped according to subject matter. Because these collages will look similar in content it is necessary each week to label each collage on the back relative to subject matter and to the kids who participated in its creation.

After the group members enter the room, ask them to spend some time looking at the artwork, instructing them to see if anything needs to be added. This may be a time to select a few more pictures, or to have them use the markers to write words or phrases as captions under the pictures selected. Supervise this activity very carefully and remind them that their collages will be on display, along with their names, identifying them as K.I.T. Cadets, Ambassadors of Peace.

Having allowed a sufficient amount of time for the review of the artwork, ask the students to take their seats in order to begin the discussion of things learned from this program. During the discussion ask the students to recall and summarize the topics discussed. This summarization of the program content should be a very active, rapid fire discussion, challenging the students to recall as much as possible. Really focus at this point on anger management, conflict resolution, decision-making skills, sensitivity to the feelings of others, and impulse control. Make sure they understand that they have the power to save their own lives and futures and the lives and futures of their friends and family members as well. Be sure to listen for any topics which need clarification, or need to be addressed again in a manner relative to the level of understanding displayed by the students. Listen carefully to make sure the students have been able to apply what they have learned on a very personal and subjective level. Ask each student to tell how the program has changed their lives and the way they see things compared to before they participated in the program.

After the six week program has ended for each group, the artwork should be displayed for a time in a very prominent place where other kids will be able to see it and learn about the K.I.T. Cadets Program and its graduates. This is to encourage other students to view the work, think about violence and its harsh realities, and to familiarize themselves with the program. Having the names of the graduates listed serves the purpose of reinforcing the responsibility they have to share what they have learned as K.I.T. Cadets and as the Ambassadors of Peace they were commissioned to be.

Have all of these materials ready so that the students can be involved at the end of the meeting in hanging their artwork and posting the list of names if at all possible. The best approach is to divide the collages into three groups of two posters each (one for each theme and the groups spanning the three weeks of artwork), and have two bulletin boards selected which can be easily and quickly decorated by the students. Make sure that each group of collages is labeled to accurately reflect the theme of each weekly presentation and focus. All of this serves to give the students a sense of pride in the program and in the work they have accomplished.

Graduation/Recognition Activities & Preparation for the Next Group

Be sure to have the permission slips (Exhibit VI) ready to distribute to the students explaining to the parents that there will be a pizza party the following week for the K.I.T. Cadets. This party is best if held after school on whatever day is best relative to scheduling. The party serves as further reinforcement and reward for their hard work and participation in the program and _only_ K.I.T. Cadets can attend. All that is needed is pizza and sodas for the kids. They really look forward to this closing event.

If your school or agency holds any kind of general assembly during the week then use this time to present the certificates of award and appreciation (Exhibits VII and VIII). This type of graduation is another important reinforcement of the goals and mission of the program. To present the awards in front of the entire student body also helps to increase awareness of the K.I.T. Cadets Program. Take a few minutes to explain the program to the entire audience, specifically pointing out the responsibility the K.I.T. Cadets have to the rest of the school and their community. In a lighthearted manner tell the students to watch these K.I.T. Cadets and remind them of their responsibilities as Ambassadors of Peace if they are seen fighting or participating in any kind of bullying, altercation, or name calling. This helps the K.I.T. Cadets think twice before they act impulsively. Remember, this is one of the main reasons these kids were selected or referred for participation in the program.

Encourage parents to attend the graduation either by sending an invitation to them through their kids or by sending a letter home announcing the time and date. The letter is probably your best option. Murchison Street Elementary School, where this program was originally developed, held a weekly assembly on Monday mornings from 8:00 A.M. to 8:15 A.M. as a general way of getting the week started. The staff also used this as an opportunity to make announcements of special events, or to address concerns that administrative staff may have. This was a tremendous time to have the graduation of the kids in front of the entire school population. If your school or agency does not have such an event, then seek out an appropriate alternative as this part of the program is extremely important to the overall process and program format.

If the aforementioned options are not possible relative to the graduation and pizza party components as separate events, then these can be included as the closing aspect of Week VI. The last meeting needs to include only the kids, and should follow the full format as explained in the section describing the activities, goals, and focus of Week VI. However, at the end of the last meeting parents can be invited to be present for the graduation only. The graduation would then be followed by the pizza party only for the kids as their exclusive reward for successfully completing the entire six week K.I.T. Cadets Program.

You have just completed Phase I of the program for this group of students. At the same time you should have already started soliciting referrals from all sources such as teachers, school counselors, principals, assistant principals, or by direct observation of students in settings such as playgrounds and lunch areas. It takes time to obtain the referrals and permission from the parents allowing participation in the next K.I.T. Cadets Program. Observation can be done on an ongoing basis during the year, making sure to keep a list of the children identified. If you do not have access to areas for observation then come up with other systems of referral for each group relative to your specific situation and opportunities. Remember to also seek referrals during any type of case review meetings which may be scheduled within any setting dealing with high risk kids. **_Remember to always stress that this program is not intended to be a behavior modification group for kids identified with Attention Deficit Hyperactivity Disorder._** The only referrals are for kids prone to acts of violence unrelated to poor impulse control associated with ADHD symptomatology. Do not have any more or less than 15 to 21 kids in each group. If there are waiting lists then it is possible to run separate groups of fifteen simultaneously to accommodate demand.

Phase II Program Format

Phase II is simply a repeat of the first and second week meetings of the Phase I group activities. This phase utilizes the same didactic approach as in Phase I, but consists of a classroom presentation format targeting all third and fourth grade classes. These presentations should also be limited to no longer than forty-five minutes. The first step in planning is to identify all of the classes and respective teachers. Then set up a weekly schedule to include an initial Monday presentation and a Thursday follow up within the same week.

Once the schedule has been completed, taking into account school activities and holidays which might conflict with scheduling, distribute a memo to the teachers explaining the program and presenting the proposed schedule (Exhibit IX). Ask for feedback from the teachers to confirm the availability of classroom time and to identify any additional scheduling conflicts which might arise. Also, be prepared for last minute changes which may develop relative to the needs of the teachers. Make attempts to combine classes if possible or reschedule for another time.

You will find that the teachers are generally very receptive to the opportunity for their students to address issues of violence. All of this should be done early in the school year. One further observation is that children seem to be less interested in learning toward the end of the school year when they are getting tired of school and looking forward to their time off. This also appears to be true for K.I.T. Cadets Program groups as well.

Initial Classroom Presentation

As with the K.I.T. Cadets Program groups it is best to have someone co-facilitate the classroom presentation with you. Be sure that teachers stay with the classes rather than see this as an opportunity to take forty-five minutes off as some will be apt to do. The teachers need to understand the presentations as well in order to work it into other classroom activities if possible and reinforce the concepts. Like the old saying goes that "two heads are better than one", two facilitators can help generate more ideas and encourage more participation. The teacher can help with this process as well and also serve as the authority figure in the room in order to control any behavioral problems likely to come up if no authority figure is present. You might want to alternate weekly the responsibility of being the main presenter. Rely on your partner to offer input on topics being missed, and to watch for students who want to participate, but may be overlooked. Be really aware of any tendency to call on boys more the girls. Have fun with all of this!

Dr. David L. Roberts Ph.D.

Begin the presentation by asking the students if they are aware of the K.I.T. Cadets Program. After allowing for their input, give a full explanation of the program, including an explanation of the differences between Phases I and II. As in the K.I.T. Cadets Program groups remember to emphasize the importance of respect for each other and the need for confidentiality relative to the presentations and the participants. Make sure the students fully understand these concepts before proceeding. Ask for a show of hands as a form of commitment to these requirements.

Once this is accomplished ask the students to begin thinking about how violence affects them personally. Ask if there are any students in the room who fight. Be prepared for other students to identify those who do and are unwilling to admit their guilt. This is a good way to get started. Then ask them to define violence by giving examples of what violence is. Because these students are younger than the K.I.T. Cadets Program groups, it may be necessary to give them more assistance in generating ideas than is necessary for the older kids. Usually, after only a little prompting, the children are able to generate many examples which should all be listed on the board in the classroom.

As in Phase I, Week I, the focus is on understanding and identifying what violence is, and then getting the students to talk about their personal experiences with violence in their school, homes, and communities. You may be surprised at some of the stories told relative to the shocking content. It is important to be prepared for anything. One interesting factor about the classroom presentations is that teachers usually have the opportunity to better understand the lives of the kids they teach. In many cases it increases their ability and willingness to empathize with the kids and often makes them more understanding relative to the needs and realities these kids face. Teachers always appreciate the willingness of presenters to offer this opportunity to them and their students. Your efforts will be acknowledged.

Again, be sure to watch and listen for any distress which may result in any of the children. If it appears to be getting too heavy and too personal, take a few minutes to address the emotional reactions of the children. Do not pretend that the emotions are not present and fail to address them. Make a real effort to normalize emotional reactions and help the students identify and understand what they are feeling. You must create an atmosphere of safety because of the potentially devastating effect that telling and listening to these stories could have on the children.

The most potentially devastating stories will deal with things happening privately and personally within families. Deaths of family members, spousal abuse, and any form of child abuse are the toughest subjects to deal with. If a child begins to tell a story of this nature, especially about incidents of family violence and abuse, do not react in any way which may cause the child to feel that they have done something wrong by sharing this information. Simply address this context as you would other less horrific examples, but intervene and limit the discussion for the sake of the privacy of the child and the respective family. Tell the child you would like to talk with them privately about really personal matters after the presentation ends. Be sure to talk to the teacher and then to the child at the end of the presentation to determine what needs to be done relative to reporting, referrals, and assistance to both the child and their family.

End the first presentation by summarizing what has been learned, and by explaining that the follow up presentation will be held on Thursday of the same week. Tell them at that time they will be asked to talk about the feelings and emotions they have relative to violence. Explain also that they will be taught some alternatives to violence which they can use for themselves, and which can be shared with others, even with family members. Remind them that you and their teacher will be available to them should they need to talk about anything privately. Explain that learning to talk about their experiences and feelings is a very important part of what you are trying to teach them.

Follow-up Classroom Presentation

As you begin the follow-up presentation ask the students to recall the discussion from Monday. If necessary remind them of the things which were discussed. Tell them that today they are going to be asked to talk about their feelings/emotions associated with violence. This discussion will require more prompting on your part as the children will not likely be able to easily identify their emotions. Be sure to list all feelings or emotions on the board as they are identified. As with the K.I.T. Cadets Program groups it may be necessary to generalize the discussion to how others might react to violence. This approach is usually easier for the students relative to getting them to open up without having to be too personal in what they share. In reality many kids pay more attention to how others feel than they do to their own emotions. Part of the goal of this program is to teach them to identify and resolve their own emotions before they become the permanent unconscious fuel for their acting out behaviors.

The one emotion which many of the students are likely to deny is fear. While some students will readily admit they are afraid, others will say they are never afraid. To admit fear in their minds reveals vulnerability and weakness to their peers, which in reality could open them up to threats, ridicule, and harassment in the form of bullying. This is where the use of dreams serves as a handy means of identifying feelings of which the students may be unaware. As with the K.I.T. Cadets Program groups most of the students will be able to share the details of their nightmares. As some of the children begin to share, others will find it easier to participate as well. Be sure to list very carefully all of the emotions represented in their dreams. List them on the board, asking the students to identify common themes of running away, being chased, getting hurt or killed, and witnessing various aspects of violent acts toward themselves and others. Write this list on the side of the board opposite the list of emotions generated earlier.

If there seems to be a short supply of dreams, ask the students if they ever have dreams about being chased by the devil or by characters depicted in the violent TV shows, video games, and horror movies they watch or play. Make sure no single student dominates any aspect of the presentations. Some of the students will be reluctant to share out of a fear of being embarrassed or laughed at relative to dream content and emotions which may be revealed. Remember to always stress the importance of respect and confidentiality at the beginning of and during the presentations. If necessary and appropriate do not be afraid to share a personal nightmare you may have had as a child. This will show the students that you are as human as they are and will help them be willing to open up more as a result. Sometimes I tell them about monsters living under my bed when I was a child, and being chased by the devil who was riding in a long antique limousine. They will laugh appropriately and likely begin to share their stories more comfortably. Be sure to limit the sharing of your own personal experiences since the intent is only to get them to open up and share their own personal experiences and stories.

Once the list of dream content has been completed compare the list of details and emotions associated with the dreams to the list of feelings associated with violence. As the students talk about their dreams always ask them how their dreams make them feel once they wake up. Keep everything in this presentation focused on feelings and emotions, emphasizing the fact that these are all normal reactions to violence and to other things that frighten them. The comparison between the lists helps the students make the connections between the objective emotions and their own subjective experiences. Introduce The FLAGS Model into this week's presentation to help them see how negative emotions are tied to acting out behaviors as presented during the second meeting of the actual K.I.T. Cadets Program.

Be sure to allow at least ten minutes to assist the students in generating realistic alternatives to violence as dictated by the contexts and environments in which they live. Emphasize the roles they can play in helping to stop violence, and in protecting themselves from violence as well. Be sure to leave them with a sense of hope for the future. Encourage them to talk with their families about what they have learned. Also teach them to talk to people they know they can trust about what they think and feel. Ask them to talk to their families about specific ways to handle situations involving violence in their neighborhoods. This kind of planning and communication helps these younger students have a greater sense of control and power over their lives and the fear they face on a routine basis.

Remind the students again that you and their teacher are available to help them in any way possible. Commend them on their participation and thank them for their attention. The children will appreciate the time you have taken to talk with them. They truly need the opportunity to receive this kind of attention and validation.

Dr. David L. Roberts Ph.D.

Program Summary

This concludes the program guidelines needed to successfully utilize this approach relative to dealing with violence. The main reason this program works is that it utilizes the real life, subjective experiences of all of the children involved both in Phase I and Phase II. The program is also easily adaptable to any ethnic or cultural mixture of the students and the school, and can be presented in any language necessary to meet the needs of the students involved.

In other words, The K.I.T. Cadets Program is culturally sensitive and takes into account the factors impacting the children living in areas where intense violence, poverty, and serious criminal activity are commonplace. The program considers the issues of family environment, school environment, and community environment. In addition it takes into account the socioeconomic factors present as well.

Again this program is not intended to address issues of violence in all schools or areas. Communities not directly affected by violence on such a large scale may find it difficult to relate to the issues presented. However, when used with the populations it was designed to serve such as inner city schools, this approach appears to be very effective in meeting the needs of these communities. All school staff and staff associated with the Murchison Street Elementary School and Family Center talked openly about how the K.I.T. Cadets Program drastically improved conditions on their school campus. Parents were extremely pleased with the results as well. The program was so effective that I was nominated and invited to present the concept at the International Congress of Applied Psychology, in Madrid, Spain, in July 1994. The professor listed on the title page who supervised my internship nominated me to the congressional committee.

The nine exhibits included after the "References" section have been intentionally left blank for the purpose of professionals having the opportunity to create your own forms based on the needs and issues relative to your circumstances and parameters. They are included so you will realize the importance of creating whatever forms will be required according to the specific guidelines and expectations dictated by your program environment. I truly wish you the best in your efforts to both implement and utilize the K.I.T. Cadets program within your respective communities.

References

Apter, S. J., & Goldstein, A. P. (Eds.). (1986) Youth violence: Programs & prospects. New York: Pergamon Press.

Gleitman, H. (1986). Psychology (2nd ed.). New York: W. W. Norton & Company.

Goldstein, I., & Goldstein, H. (1985) Family therapy: An overview (2nd ed.). California: Brooks/Cole Publishing Company.

Gormly, A. V., & Brodzinsky, D. M. (1989). Lifespan human development (4th ed.). New York: Holt, Rinehart & Winston, Inc.

Malan, D. H. (1979) Individual psychotherapy and the science of psychodynamics. London: Butterworths.

Dr. David L. Roberts Ph.D.

Exhibit I
Referral Form

ProKids, Inc.; The Message and The Movement

Exhibit II
Letter to Teachers

Exhibit III
Permission Letter to Parents
In English and Spanish

Exhibit IV
Notification to Teachers

Dr. David L. Roberts Ph.D.

Exhibit V
Reminder Notice to Teachers

Exhibit VI
Permission Letter to Parents for
The K.I.T. Cadet Pizza Party

Dr. David L. Roberts Ph.D.

Exhibit VII
Certificate of Award

ProKids, Inc.; The Message and The Movement

Exhibit VIII
Certificate of Appreciation

Dr. David L. Roberts Ph.D.

Exhibit IX
Phase II Notification to Teachers

ProKids, Inc.; The Message and The Movement

The Roberts Grief and Loss Analysis Scale (RGLAS):
Redefining Depression and Anxiety Associated
With Non-traditional Loss

Master of Science Thesis
1989
Georgia College and State University
Department of Psychology
The Roberts Grief and Loss Analysis Scale:
Item Selection and Analysis

Doctor of Philosophy Dissertation
1993
California School of Professional
Psychology – Los Angeles, CA
Department of Clinical Psychology
(Now under Alliant International University)
The Roberts Grief and Loss Analysis Scale:
A Reliability and Validity Study

Copyright January 2011

Introduction

The Roberts Grief and Loss Analysis Scale (RGLAS): Redefining Depression and Anxiety Associated with Non-traditional Loss, is a compilation of both my master's thesis and my doctoral dissertation. Within these pages you will find a written account of all of my research efforts and findings to date. The RGLAS - originally referred to as "The Grief Analysis Scale" - has been recognized within both of my graduate programs in psychology as a significant step toward understanding depression and anxiety associated with non-traditional forms of loss. While the RGLAS has been studied through both item selection and analysis, and relative to a reliability and validity, it has not been implemented in its current form. It is my hope that someone will be inspired not only to use the RGLAS in its current form, but to also conduct additional research in order to move the RGLAS into professional usage. The next step would be to conduct research with transitional aged kids relative to both reliability and validity with this population as well. So far the RGLAS has proven to be a valid and reliable indicator of levels of grief and sadness in adults and associated with dysfunctional family environments and other complicating factors.

The RGLAS in intended to be used in conjunction with the approaches and theories delineated within this current book, ProKids, Inc.: The Message and the Movement - A Guide for Parents and Professionals. I have every confidence that the RGLAS will be useful as an assessment instrument utilized by licensed and trained professionals as a means of identifying both the severity and presence of unresolved grief. Grief and loss associated with non-traditional losses outside the realm of death and dying issues are not readily identified, diagnosed, and treated in therapy. During the defense of my dissertation in 1993 my dissertation chair stated that he believed "Dr. Roberts has redefined depression and anxiety". The committee was so intrigued and impressed by my dissertation results that they literally took over the discussion of the content. After a rather lengthy and enthusiastic discussion they apologized to me for their discourse, and congratulated me on my work as being both scholarly and of merit relative to my development of an instrument that would add credibility to my Roberts FLAGS Model (RFLAGS) and related theories.

It is with great pleasure that I offer the aforementioned data to you, the reader, as an opportunity to join with me in my efforts to complete this final stage of research, with an opportunity to coauthor and participate in the ultimate publication of the RGLAS. Proposal submissions of your research ideas should be forwarded to me for approval, with the understanding that only a few persons or groups will be chosen to conduct the final research. My contact information can be obtained through www.DavidLRobertsPhD.org; or through www.ProKidsInc.org as well. Research must be conducted at the Ph.D. level and only through a graduate clinical psychology program fully accredited within the state where the research is conducted, and through the American Psychological Association. Both of these requirements must be documented and the research must be completed as a dissertation project through a clinical psychology format. I look forward to hearing from anyone and everyone who is interested in accepting this challenge.

Key words: Psychology, Grief, Loss, Depression, and Anxiety.

THE ROBERTS GRIEF AND LOSS ANALYSIS SCALE: ITEM SELECTION AND ANALYSIS

By

DAVID LOUIS ROBERTS
A Thesis submitted to the Graduate Faculty,
Department of Psychology,
Of Georgia College and State University in
Partial Fulfillment of the Requirements for the Degree
Master of Science

Milledgeville, Georgia
1989

Table of Contents

Introduction	559
Summary of Grief Processes	562
Clinical Application of Grief Processes	565
Grief as a Diagnostic Category	571
Summary	574
Method	577
Subjects	577
Materials	579
Procedure	580
Results	585
Discussion	587
References	591
Appendix A	597
Appendix B	605
Appendix C	617

INTRODUCTION

A review of the literature concerning grief suggests that similarities exist between grief processes regardless of the type of loss experienced. However, there appear to be few studies which will demonstrate a relationship between various types of loss and a generalized sequential process of grief remediation as viewed from a purely mental health perspective. Most research regarding grief remediation is done on as individual case study basis, is rather stimulus specific (i.e. death or divorce), and is viewed from a physiological perspective. Included therein are psychological factors, but the primary concern is the resulting impairment of physical health relative to unresolved grief.

Based upon research found in the literature the probability of the psychological factors leading to physical problems seems to indicate that unresolved grief should be diagnosed before psychological problems take on a more serious physical property. The detection of unresolved grief as manifested by psychological impairment would then become a preventive approach in therapy for people seeking professional help (primarily inpatient services) for either affective or anxiety-based disorders which may be directly linked to unresolved grief. At the point where grief can be diagnosed, affective (depression) or anxiety-based disorders may become symptoms and complicated bereavement of unresolved grief then would become the disorder.

Therefore, the primary assertion in the present study is that a process of resolution exists which is applicable and needed in all grief situations relative to the intensity of the grief or the type of loss and that failure to complete such a process results in grief. Furthermore, observation by the present author suggests that in an inpatient psychiatric setting the need exists for detecting unresolved grief as evidenced by impairment of current functioning indicated by psychiatric diagnoses of either affective or anxiety-based disorders. This is not to say, however, that grief is always an issue or root factor in these diagnoses; but, rather, that in some cases unresolved grief may deserve its own diagnostic category and treatment approaches. Much of this will be borne out by the presentation of the discoveries made in the literature search, looking first at the proposed processes of grief, comparing them for similarities, and then looking at research specific to loss issues and some of the respective considerations.

The purpose of the present study is to begin the process necessary to formulate a diagnostic instrument to be used in testing that would indicate unresolved grief as a possible diagnosis and treatment consideration. Since loss is such a significant part of human existence, it follows that its impact quite often can lead to potentially devastating results if grief processes are not resolved to some satisfactory completion. Based on both the personal observations of the present author and the search of the literature, it is believed that the importance of loss and associated grief issues must be acknowledged as significant aspects of mental health.

The present author attempted to discover the existence of an instrument that was designed to effectively measure generalized, rather than specific unresolved grief. To date no such discovery has been made. All of the research literature reviewed thus far represented and proposed grief processes that were similar in nature, but were situation-specific, related to a particular loss, and studied in that light (Templar, 1970). The methods of study included self-rating scales developed for a particular setting, and the use of published anxiety or depression scales. Primary examples included: the "Texas Revised Inventory of Grief" developed by Faschingbauer, DeVaul, and Zisook (1978); The Grief Experience Inventory" developed by Sanders, Mauger, and Strong (1985) (Sanders, 1980); and "The Health Questionnaire" used in the Harvard Bereavement Study (Parkes & Weiss, 1983).

These three examples were intended to measure grief reactions specific to death. The development of a test to detect unresolved grief should attempt to generalize grief as a process of recovery from loss, with the severity of grief relative to the significance of the loss, regardless of the loss experienced. Such a generalization could extend and unify the study of grief in the diagnosis of various psychological disorders which could be attributed to or associated with a significant loss or a series of significant losses. Again, the assumption being made is that psychological disorders can be, in some cases, the symptoms of unresolved grief. Because it is beyond the scope of the present study, no attempt is made to relate grief to physiological disorders, although it is acknowledged that such disorders can also be the result of unresolved grief. Only when such disorders are diagnosed as psychophysiological are they relevant to the present study.

In order to understand the nature of this study it is necessary to explain and define the terminology used. Of primary importance are the definitions of loss, grief, unresolved grief, the specific behavioral domains, and the population to be sampled for study. Loss occurs when an individual, with or without choice, relinquishes, abandons, or otherwise forfeits an object, person, concept, or identity held as important, meaningful and significant, and is then faced with accepting the resulting void and choosing alternative views, goals or conditions necessary to compensate for the emptiness which remains or changes which occur. Loss is then defined as an individually resultant void for which compensation must be sought. Grief is defined as any emotional process necessary in accepting the loss, compensating for the void, and adapting to new conditions and/or situations. Unresolved grief is defined as the failure to successfully complete the grief process. The behavioral domain then becomes unresolved grief as manifested by evidence of impaired current functioning exhibited primarily by either affective of anxiety-based disorders. The population chosen for study in the research process of the proposed instrument consisted of a general population sample of 114 participants for the purpose of item analysis. Ultimately, the test will be designed to detect unresolved grief in the population defined as psychiatric patients in an inpatient psychiatric facility. The inclusion of either affective or anxiety-based diagnoses will be supported by the literature review. Expansion to other target populations will also be considered outside of inpatient programs.

In the sections following, a review will be presented of the grief processes proposed by the different researchers in their studies. An attempt will be made in this presentation to identify similarities between the proposed processes and to relate these similarities to the present study for the purpose of establishing criteria needed in the selection of test items which would be representative of the behavioral domain. Such a review will attempt to identify a set of common steps which will further support the need for the development of a test which will indicate failure to complete as appropriate process necessary in the resolution of grief.

Summary of Grief Processes

Oelrich (1974) describes stages of a mourning process and then proposes different emotional responses within the process, studying patients diagnosed with a fatal illness. Comparisons are then made between the processes of facing death and of relatives accepting the death once it has occurred. The first step in the grief and mourning process involves the response of shock and disbelief. As the second stage develops, awareness and anger associated with the awareness become evident. The author seemed to be presenting two additional stages, though they were not as clearly identified. In the third stage, as the individual deals with the loss and the resulting void, a process of idealization of the lost person or object takes place. All negative aspects are pushed out of consciousness and only positive and desirable features are remembered. The fourth stage marks the resolution of grief, the complete process taking a year of more. The emotional responses associated with this process are anxiety, grief, depression, anger and hostility, and shame and guilt. Contrary to the present author, Oelrich includes grief as one of the emotional responses rather than as a descriptive term for the entire resolution process.

Raphael (1980) proposes a model of grief counseling. In the adult model of bereavement the author presents a framework of grieving that included five phases with the emotional response identified as a part of each phase. Phase one is labeled shock and included the emotional response of numbness and disbelief. In phase two the individual becomes aware of the reality of the loss and experiences the pain of absence or separation. The related emotional responses in phase two are anger, yearning, pining, and longing. The third phase is marked by an intense preoccupation with the lost person or object (the object is not necessarily concrete). As the individual continues this preoccupation, which is repeatedly not reinforced, the fourth stage of a gradual acceptance of the loss emerges. The fifth and final stage occurs once the individual is able to give up the relationship which existed. It is interesting to note that no mention is made of depression, though it could be concluded that reference is made by use of such terms as yearning, pining, and longing.

Corazzini (1980) developed a theory of loss which is also referred to as a time of grief. A brief description is given of the "bereft self" representing a temporary state that governs and possibly controls the behavior of the grieving individual. This temporary state includes all of the experiences of the individual during the time of grief. The "bereft self" develops in three phases. The first phase is labeled simply loss. The elements of depression and despair mark the beginning of the second phase known as consolidation. Depression and despair develop as a response to the reality of the loss and are part of attempts to disengage from the lost person or object in order to meet the demands of the future and develop a sense of respect for the past. During this phase the individual deals with sadness emotional catharsis and readjustment toward the final phase of the reintegration which marks the resolution of the state of the "bereft self". The second phase of consolidation is considered the most important because without its successful completion resolution is not possible. Corazzini acknowledges delayed grief and describes it as a "shallow grief response". This corresponds to the term "unresolved grief" used by the present author and represents a failure to complete a necessary grief process. It is further acknowledged that grief can be both inhibited and abortive, either of which still characterizes unresolved grief.

Tatelbaum (1980) identifies three stages in a mourning process. The first phase of shock and numbness is of a short duration, lasting a few hours to several weeks. The second phase, which is the longest, is marked by suffering and a profound sense of disorganization. The final stage is reorganization. Not only is the second stage the longest, it is also the most intense. The emotional responses of the second state are suffering, hysteria, bitterness, anger, self-pity, and guilt. Functioning is impaired because of the oftentimes overwhelming emotions and changes that must be faced. Of primary significance is the emotional state of depression which is characterized by various physiological symptoms: withdrawal, apathy, lack of concentration, and low self esteem. Suicide is most likely in this stage.

Preoccupation with both the past and the future is common as are attempts to idealize the lost person of focus. The stage of reorganization marks the resolution of the emotional, physical, and psychological aspects of the second stage. At this point normal functioning resumes as the individual begins to re-emerge from the grief. As with other grief processes reviewed, there is no set time for the completion of grief as grief responses are very much individualized.

In the research presented by Modell-Hirsch (1979), a model is proposed for the bereaved widow. The model consists of four periods: initiation, disorganization, reorganization, and restoration. The period of initiation is marked by such emotional responses as shock, numbness, helplessness, vulnerability, and insecurity. During the period of disorganization the individual experiences everything as changed and new. Grief is strongest during this period but is complicated by the demands of daily living. As the period of reorganization begins the individual continues to deal with the reality of the loss and the demands for new patterns of living. This is a period of increased awareness and the ability to cope effectively. The individual must deal with both the feelings and events. There are swings back and forth between regression and progression, with the latter beginning to gain more solid ground. The final period of restoration occurs after the successful completion of the grief process. It is evidenced by an end to all forms of mourning behavior and represents more the result of successful grief than a step or period of the grief process.

Stroebe and Stroebe (1987) first introduce the cycle of uncomplicated grief and follow this with an entire book dealing with complicated, unresolved grief. At this point only the normal grief cycle will be reviewed. This cycle consists of four phases: numbness, yearning and protest, despair, recovery and restitution. The phase of numbness is characterized by shock and disbelief. The bereaved person attempts to continue life as before the loss occurred. Such futile attempts lead to anger, anguish, restlessness, tension, and apprehension. During the yearning and protest phase awareness develops as the individual seeks the lost person. This is often a time of extreme emotional and physical distress. Anger toward the deceased is prevalent, as is anger which becomes directed toward others. As the searching continues the third phase of despair develops as the reality and the irreversibility of the loss is recognized. Life looks hopeless and apathy and depression set in. Withdrawal is typical at this point. As these associated feelings lessen in frequency, the individual then begins the fourth phase of recovery and restitution. This phase is marked by an acceptance of both the loss and the resulting changes, and by attempts to regain independence and a sense of purpose in life. Though grief does not end forever, it does become a considerably less significant part of the individual's life.

Perhaps the best known supporter of grief research is Elizabeth Kubler-Ross. Kubler-Ross (1969) proposes the five stages of grief: denial, anger, bargaining, depression, and acceptance. Some distinct similarities between these stages and the processes, periods, and phases of previously cited researchers are evident. The only Kubler-Ross stage which needs to be addressed is perhaps that of bargaining. The other four stages are rather self explanatory. Bargaining is the attempt to delay acceptance of the loss as evidenced by searching for the lost person or object, idealizing the lost person or object, and statements such as "what if..." and "if only...". As these efforts prove futile because of a lack of reinforcement, the grief process continues on through depression and acceptance as reality becomes more clearly perceived.

Clinical Application of Grief Processes

Attempts have been made to apply grief remediation to various loss situations (Bugen, 1977, 1979; Berstein, 1977; Bradley, 1983; and Schoenberg, 1980). Again, much of this research has been conducted relative to a narrow scope of losses. Even so, a review of some of the literature available reveals the serious psychological (and oftentimes physiological) consequences associated with unresolved grief. Researchers have addressed such issues as death, terminal illness, and divorce, as well as a number of other separation issues and significant life changes which result in loss. A study of the research in these areas further substantiates the significant impact of loss associated with human existence and mental health.

Much research has been conducted with regard to terminally ill patients and their familial and social support systems. In four later works by Kubler-Ross (1978, 1981, 1982, and 1983) specific case studies are presented dealing with the application of the sequential steps of grief remediation in assisting the terminally ill as they face impending death. Attempts are also made to assist family members and friends of terminally ill patients by making available various workshops and group sessions, indicating that they too must deal with a grief process which is similar to that of the terminally ill individual.

Anticipatory mourning associated with terminal illness is addressed by Geyman (1983) and Lebow (1976). Geyman reports that new approaches are being developed and attitudes are changing concerning the death and dying process and the associated elements of necessary grief work. The purpose of the study by Geyman was to summarize changing societal trends related to death and dying; to review the impact on the family of the death and dying of a family member; and to present a comprehensive, practical approach to the care of both the dying patient and the family. The approach consists of two primary elements identified by the author. These elements are a pre-death phase and post-death follow up for the surviving family members. Geyman also addresses the symptoms and behavior present in unresolved grief which could be used as a guide or indicator of individual resolution. The thesis presented by Lebow is that, if acted upon properly, the period of impending death can provide an opportunity for both the family and the patient to deal with critical adaptational issues in a mutually beneficial manner. Anticipatory mourning, as presented by Lebow, includes elements of cognitive, affective, cultural, and social reactions to expected death. Adaptational tasks include remaining both involved with and separate from the patient, adapting to role changes, bearing the effect of grief, coming to terms with the impending loss, and saying good-bye.

Other studies deal with post-death grief and bereavement counseling. In a major study by Lindemann (1944), grief reactions of those bereaved after death had occurred are studied. The grief work associated with this situation consists of elimination of a sense of bondage to the deceased, readjustment to the environment from which the deceased was absent, and the formation of new relationships.

Corazzini (1980), in addition to proposing the three phases of grief presented earlier, also proposes an approach to the theory and practice of loss therapy. The necessary counseling skills presented for the effective treatment of bereaved clients are: remaining open to the loss, being empathic, encouraging reminiscing, and being insistent on the loss. The tasks indicated for the bereaved include: perceiving the openness of the counselor, expressing one's feelings, reminiscing, and acknowledging the loss. All of these elements in the therapeutic setting are necessary for the bereaved to progress through the three proposed phases of grief work. One very interesting point about Corazzini is the proposed application of this approach to all situations of loss, though the research focused primarily on the specific loss issues of death. Corazzini suggests that a universal, generalized application would be possible by adjusting the approach to the need and situation relative to the loss experience of the individual. This is the first discovery found in the literature by the present author of a generalized approach to the relationship between grief and loss regardless of the form of loss.

Raphael (1980) suggests another approach to bereavement counseling. This author addresses the significance of loss-related life crises, with particular emphasis on major bereavement. A model of bereavement is proposed for both children and adults, identifying responses both particular and similar in each group. However, for the purpose of the present study only those responses identified as adult reactions were considered because responses are reported as being different between children and adults. Special attention is paid to bereavement patterns of adults which are either pathological or high risk. These patterns result from incomplete or inappropriate grief responses and are manifested by such outward signs as: delayed, absent, or distorted grief; extreme anger and/or guilt; antisocial behavior; depressive illness and/or suicidal tendencies; and psychosomatic symptomatology and increased susceptibility to illness. The identification of these bereavement patterns is especially important and relevant to the present study.

All of these elements are also reported by Geyman (1983) and are comparable to those listed as symptoms. According to comparisons between Raphael and Corazzini and their respective approaches to bereavement counseling, striking similarities are discovered. Corazzini's approaches were presented earlier. Those introduced by Raphael include: the offering of basic human comfort and support; encouraging the expression of grief; promoting the mourning process relative to the person, their loss and the prospective relationship between the two; and offering bereavement counseling as a facilitating process. Raphael addresses not only the specific loss of death, but also other losses which are coincidental with death. Both Raphael and Corazzini advocate a more generalized application of grief processes. The other losses addressed by Raphael are relative to the longer-term adjustment processes associated with bereavement. Loss is further acknowledged by Raphael as perhaps the greatest of all human pains.

Jasnow (1985) presents a rather philosophical approach suggesting that grief results from either a literal or symbolic loss of connection to a perceived life-supporting system. In this article comparisons are made between grief and depression, questioning the possibility of grief as its own psychiatric entity. The point is made that grief results from or is precipitated by a specific loss experience and becomes complicated grief after the passage of a reasonable amount of time sufficient for resolution. The author suggests that at this point grief constitutes a psychiatric condition which is different from depression which is oftentimes not precipitated by a specific loss. Death is associated with the threat of loss of continuity and the human need to deny death. Therefore, the author proposes a convergence between religion, art, and psychotherapy necessary for therapists to effectively deal with asking the right questions, rather than providing the answers to their patients.

The loss issues presented by Jasnow are simultaneously abstract and concrete, literal and symbolic, further substantiating the generalizability of loss and grief experiences proposed by the present author. Kamm (1985), unlike Jasnow, does not address complicated grief, but focuses on therapeutic interventions which would result in a successful resolution of grief, much the same as an obstetrician works with a patient toward the successful completion of pregnancy. Both Kamm and Jasnow address the importance of therapeutic intervention in dealing with grieving individuals, not seeing either condition as illness, but both as an opportunity to experience all aspects of a normal life.

Smith (1985) continues the generalized approach to loss and grief concentrating on aspects such as the nature of loss, and the difference between grief and depression. The author presents a three-dimensional schema of loss which includes: the sudden or gradual occurrence of loss;

type of loss, presented as person, animal, object, or idea; and the intensity or significance relative to the loss. The intensity or significance of loss is truly personalized to the individual who experiences the loss. Loss could be as abstract or varied as to include a dent on one's car or the loss of an important ideal or dream. Failure to complete the natural process of grieving a significant loss could create unfinished business or unresolved grief issues. The author proposes two dynamics employed by an individual in the avoidance of grief. These are fear of pain and the social script to be strong.

The unfinished business that could result from the failure to grieve does not go away, but could remain by avoidance or be maintained by an extreme, prolonged grief process. Smith proposes that the avoidance of unfinished business could be a covert stimulus of overt depression, and that prolonged grief is possibly continued because of secondary gains obtained by the grieving individual. The author then presents a number of Gestalt therapy approaches to deal with these situations in order to abate grief which has become a pathological state or condition. It is interesting to note at this point that Stern (1985) presents three case studies dealing with grief therapy involving one patient stuck in grief, another obsessed with anticipatory loss of an irrational nature, and the third case of a therapist's own grief issues associated with the suicide of a patient. A review of these three cases reveals specific incidences in which unresolved grief or unfinished business is present. It is interesting to note in the third case the therapist's own struggle in resolving personal grief issues.

As examples of the generalized, universal approach now being pursued by various researchers, including the present author, three specific studies were discovered dealing with what have been, until now, non-traditional associations between grief processes and loss. Brink (1985) addresses issues related to the elderly. These include, in addition to widowhood, chronic physical disability and the associated loss issues relative to retirement. According to Brink, depression is generally the characteristic response to these issues among the elderly. A depression scale developed by Brink is used to determine the depressive state of elderly clients in an attempt to devise a therapy approach suitable for each individual patient. Flexibility in approach to treatment is the key in therapeutic intervention.

In another study, Breen (1985) addresses the loss issues relative to adult children of alcoholics, proposing that their emotional loss of parents often preceded their physical loss. The traditional sequence of steps in a grief process presented by Kubler-Ross (1969) is used as a model for viewing repressed grieving the author suggests is present for adult children of alcoholics. Breen suggests that children raised in an environment with alcoholic parents are forced to repress their normal emotional development, thereby repressing the grief relative to the situation. It is suggested further by Breen that a blockage of emotion as witnessed in a client may be indicative of loss experiences associated with alcoholic parents and that such repression should be explored during therapy in that context.

The third study, conducted by Hays (1985), presents loss issues and grief responses attributed to the adult survivor of childhood incest. The therapeutic approaches necessary in dealing with issues of incest are quite complicated and dependent on a number of factors such as coping styles of the individual and the point of development at which the incest occurred. The grief processes consist of two stages. Stage one is a denial-based coping style referred to as closing off, and stage two is a working-through process of opening up. Both stages combined represent the traditional stages of grief presented by Kubler-Ross (1969). The research presented by Hays includes specific case studies as examples of the proposed stages.

Of special pertinence to the present study is a book by O'Connor (1984) which deals with the traditional grief considerations (primarily of death) and the related processes and loss issues. It also extends the perspective to a more universal, generalized concept of association between grief and loss. Particularly interesting are the chapters dealing with individual coping styles relative to various life crises and the handling of loss from such perspectives as personality, type of loss, intensity of loss, and previous loss experiences. O'Connor addresses the significance of loss and its position relative to the self. This corresponds closely to other studies of life events which result in significant changes and/or loss, particularly represented in studies by Holmes and Rahe (1967); Holmes and Masuda (1984); Jenkins, Hurst, and Rose (1982); Kobasa (1979); and Patrick, Hart and Holmes (1982).

Grief as a Diagnostic Category

As stated previously, there may be instances when unresolved grief warrants its own diagnostic category. This suggestion is substantiated by several studies. Jasnow (1985) addresses complicated grief as a diagnostic category. Jansen (1985) also presents the same premise by comparing the concepts of normal versus pathological grief. First exploring a variety of both traditional and non-traditional loss issues, Jansen then proceeds with the comparison of the two grief responses. The proposed distinguishing factor is the overwhelming and intolerable nature of the grief experience, resulting primarily from dependency issues in relation to the lost object or person which can lead to pathological grief. The author further explores pathological grief as an underlying issue which is oftentimes contrary to the client's presenting problem(s). Such issues as self-esteem, attachment, and autonomy must be addressed in therapy once pathological grief is diagnosed.

Jacobsen (1986) presents a case study of pathological grief which began 25 years prior to diagnosis and was exacerbated by multiple intermittent losses. In order to identify pathological grief the author stresses the need for thorough evaluation of an individual's history of significant losses. In the case presented the pathological grief is evidenced in the individual by depression, through dreams, guilt feelings, and social withdrawal. Apparently previous hospitalizations failed to reveal or uncover the substantial loss/grief issues which were present. Jacobsen suggests that oftentimes patients find it difficult to talk about losses and are therefore reluctant to do so. It is also suggested that the patient failed to associate emotional problems with the history of losses. Presenting problems include depression and alcohol abuse, as well as a number of problematic personality characteristics revealed through personality testing. Jacobsen suggests further that there may be a correlation between various personality characteristics and a predisposition for pathological grief reactions, and states that more research is needed to determine such indicators.

In another comparison of normal to pathological grief Hartz (1986) clearly states a proposed need for a diagnostic category of complicated bereavement. Hartz indicates that one of the major distinguishing features is the length of bereavement, suggesting that intense grief lasting longer than one year may be classified as pathological. Since grief symptoms are basically the same as symptoms of depression, Hartz suggests that the time factor alone may be significant enough to diagnose complicated bereavement as reported in an earlier reference to Jasnow (1958), depression precipitated by loss constitutes a psychiatric condition. Perhaps both the factors of time and a precipitating element of loss should be considered along with the history of significant losses proposed my Jacobsen (1986). Hartz recommends additional research which would be necessary in clearly identifying diagnostic criteria for a valid diagnosis of complicated bereavement. It is also suggested that in the absence of an independent diagnostic category, such a diagnosis should at least be coupled with diagnoses of various mood disorders. It must be determined whether or not the mood disorder would exist without the precipitating loss/grief issue. By at least making unresolved grief a part of the diagnosis when implicated, then treatment procedures could perhaps be made more effective and inclusive.

In the introduction to a book presenting research articles from 16 different sources dealing with separation/individuation issues, loss issues and treatment approaches, Bloom-Feshbach and Associates (1987) address the same issues in an in depth preliminary overview of the chapters which follow. Loss and separation are elements of human existence which begin in infancy and continue throughout the entire life span. The editors suggest that failure to successfully grieve losses in later life is a direct result of impaired development of a sense of individuation, object constancy and representation as experienced in very early childhood separation at crucial developmental stages. The inspiration found by the present author in the introduction offered by Bloom-Feshbach et al. (1987) was the shared premises and conjectures as evidenced by the existing research. Presented were the dynamics of separation responses which included the elements of anger, denial, anxiety, depression, sadness, conflict, and inappropriate or destructive attachments which indicate a predisposition toward unresolved grief. As a result of these elements people perpetuate irrational fears, behavior, attitudes, and self-concepts which could turn grief reactions into pathological reactions.

The inability to mourn is equated with the inability to experience life. One primary purpose of the research material compiled by the editors is to propose and even initiate an understanding between the clinical and developmental areas of psychology. The introduction clearly presents opportunities for viewing attachment theories and separation issues from both developmental and clinical viewpoints. Another important element to the present study is the editors' universal, generalized consideration of loss, including both the traditional and non-traditional, the obvious and not so obvious, as represented by the varied research perspective presented within these chapters. The merging of these two areas of psychology asserts their complimentary natures and substantiates their approaches and applications in diagnosing and treating unresolved grief. It is not suggested, however, that inappropriate early developmental issues cannot be overcome and corrected to at least some extent. But, imagine the implication for individuals for whom no corrections are made. The resulting vulnerability to loss would be devastating, the cycle of loss and grief becoming for some too burdensome. When abnormal development occurs in this regard, imagine too this fact coupled with environmental stressors which simply exacerbate an already unfavorable predisposition. It is suggested that mastery of grief and loss issues leads to strength and positive growth of the self.

Stroebe and Stroebe (1987) are referred to earlier in the presentations of various concepts of stages of grief. Consider now their proposals of both depression models and stress models presented as possible means of distinguishing normal from pathological grief. Their comprehensive research considers the health outcomes of bereavement and as such includes within the health perspective the element of mental health as part of the overall health picture. Though this is beyond the purposes of this study, a consideration of these two models is helpful. The depression model is important in understanding the emotional symptoms of grief. Grief is viewed from the viewpoints of psychoanalytic theory, attachment theory, cognitive/behavioral theory, and a learned helplessness model. The learned helplessness model equates helplessness and hopelessness as essential elements in depressive symptoms of grief which could lead to pathology. The stress model on the other hand views grief and bereavement as stressful life events which can affect not only mental health, but also physical health.

Of central importance to the stress model are the elements of control. Oftentimes depression is dependent on the duration and impact of stress.

The primary emphasis of both models concentrates on coping styles of grieving individuals. Neither model could adequately account for either abortive or delayed grief reactions which also constitute unresolved grief. Strobe and Strobe lean toward the stress models of grief, indicating that the stressful nature of grief is the precipitating factor in both physical and mental pathologies. A primary justification for the inclusion of anxiety-based disorders as a diagnostic consideration in the psychiatric population is found within this research. Other authors make the same distinctions between depression and anxiety (Parkes and Weiss, 1983; Bugen, 1977 and 1979; Bloom-Feshbach et al., 1987). The evidence found in the literature clearly indicates both diagnostic categories as possible indicators of symptoms of unresolved grief. Furthermore, as observed by the present author, patients in two psychiatric hospitals have these diagnoses when assigned to grief therapy as part of their treatment. However, assignment seems to be rather arbitrary and unsubstantiated.

Summary

All of the articles reviewed above are acknowledging processes, using such terminology as bereavement, stages, and phases of grief (some pre-death and some post-death; and some loss-specific and some loss-general). Again, the intent of the present study is to generalize loss-specific applications of grief work to loss-general processes for a much broader application in detecting unresolved grief. The conjecture is that grief is a recovery process necessary in coping with any form of loss, with intensity of grief relative to the intensity and significance of the loss. Other studies, as reviewed previously, further support this inference by proposing models to deal with actual situations of theory, research, and practice. Direct observation by the present author within psychiatric settings serves as impetus for this study. It seems useful to attempt to provide therapists with an instrument that would allow them to assess and understand a patient's perception of, and association between grief and loss. Furthermore, if unresolved grief is found to be present, it would be beneficial to identify the point in unresolved grief at which a patient is currently trying to function. The intention would be to identify a problem which exists at the time when intervention is sought.

Once successfully developed, the Roberts Grief and Loss Analysis Scale (RGLAS) will serve as a diagnostic instrument to be used in conjunction with grief or bereavement counseling when pathological grief responses are detected. All experiences of the present author within a psychiatric setting indicate that losses oftentimes may be the bases to which many psychological disorders can be traced when unresolved grief is a factor. Identifying and dealing with any form of unresolved grief would be a valuable approach to treatment within all therapeutic settings, perhaps building or establishing a better understanding of loss situations which could lead to such disorders, and replacing diagnostic attempts which have previously been based upon expert guesswork with a more reliable and valid method.

It should be noticed that the present study is based somewhat on a pilot study (Roberts, 1986) conducted by the present author. The pilot study consisted of the development of a testing instrument to study similarities in grief processes associated with various forms of loss. In the earlier study participants were asked to provide a list of adjectives related to loss and grief. From that list of personal observations of the present author, along with a review of the grief literature, the original Grief Analysis Scale was complied and administered. The participants were studying a grief film series (UMCOM, year unknown). The instrument used in the previous study (see Appendix A) was revised and this revision is the instrument upon which the present study was conducted. The pilot study revealed no significant differences between two groups who had studied grief and two groups who had not studied grief. Though not completely conclusive, the findings in the pilot study indicated as association between grief and loss situations which will serve as another basis to attempt the development of a suitable instrument. The results indicate that people made an association between grief and loss regardless of the type of loss.

If grief is indeed an emotional response to any loss situation, then the present study should help in substantiating this conjecture. This will be accomplished by the ultimate development of a test to detect possible symptoms of unresolved grief within psychiatric populations. Ultimately, when the test is proven to be both reliable and valid, then unresolved grief would be indicated by significantly lower scores in the psychiatric populations when compared to the general population. Though this is the long-range goal, the present study is concerned only with the initial steps of item construction and item analysis to yield the first form of the RGLAS. Much additional research will be needed before the long-range goal will be met.

Method

Subjects

The participants from the general population used for the purpose of test administration and item analysis numbered 114. These individuals were members of intact groups including two undergraduate psychology classes, one undergraduate sociology class, one business group, one group of military wives, and one group of employees from a private psychiatric hospital. Random selection of participants was not used because of the limited availability of groups willing to be tested. Even though three of the groups consisted of college students, the deliberate attempt was made to seek out other adult groups as well. It was believed that the more diverse the sample from the general population was, the more it would resemble the target population for which the Roberts Grief and Loss Analysis Scale is intended. Personal observation indicates that people in psychiatric settings tend to be beyond typical college age.

Of the 114 participants 91 were female, 21 were male, and two were undesignated simply because they failed to mark either male or female on the data sheet. Age categories included: 35 participants age 18-25; 31, age 26-35; 7, age 36-45; 14, age 46-55; 3, age 56-65; 2, age 65 or older; and again 2 were undesignated. Other demographic information gathered included marital status and educational levels. Marital status information included: 61 participants married; 33 single; 9 were divorced; 5 with significant others; 4 with significant other or spouse deceased; and 2 were undesignated. Information provided from educational level completed included: 2 participants with less than 12 years; 12 with high school diplomas; 64 with less than four-year degrees, but more than 12 years; 26 beyond the undergraduate level; and 2 were undesignated. Even though this demographic data collected has not been used as part of the analysis of the proposed instrument, it is interesting to note the composition of the sample used in the research which clearly added diversity to the mix of subjects. Ethnicity was not taken into consideration.

Following the procedures of item construction, item analysis, and compiling the first form of the RGLAS, the target population for which the test is intended was sampled for testing. The sample for the target population consisted of patients at a private psychiatric hospital with diagnoses of either affective or anxiety-based disorders. The identification and definition of this group was addressed in the introduction of this paper. At the time of this writing only 14 subjects from this population were tested. Demographic information was obtained from this group as well. Of the 14, 13 were female and 1 was male. Age categories included: 2 participants, age 18-25; 3, age 26-35; 6, age 36-45; 2, age 46-55; and 1, age 56-65. Eight of the 14 participants were married; 2 were single; 2 were divorced; 1 indicated a significant other; and 1 indicated their spouse or significant other as deceased. Education levels included: 3 participants with less than 12 years; 2 with high school diplomas; 6 with some college; and 2 with schooling beyond the undergraduate level. The participants in this group were all made available through a large private psychiatric hospital in the middle Georgia area. All individuals were admitted to an inpatient treatment program on a general adult unit of the hospital. Only those patients admitted by psychiatrists and given diagnoses of either affective or anxiety-based disorders were included. The purpose of obtaining access to this group will be described in the procedure section of this paper. Flaws and problems in dealing with this group will be addressed in the discussion section.

Testing for the general population sample was conducted over a seven month period, including both the locating and testing of the groups mentioned earlier. The psychiatric patients were gathered and tested over approximately a three month period. All participants were treated in accordance with the "Ethical Principles of Psychologists" (American Psychological Association, 1981). Prior to gathering data, all research was cleared through respective ethics and review committees at both Georgia College and State University, and the hospital where testing was conducted on the psychiatric patients.

Materials

The Roberts Grief and Loss Analysis Scale as presented to the sample of the general population consisted of 200 items formulated and selected by the present author on the basis of their potential relevance to unresolved grief. Of primary importance were the issues pertaining to separation/individuation (Bloom-Feshbach et al., 1987), helplessness/hopelessness (Strobe & Strobe, 1987), significant loss experiences (O'Connor, 1984; Holmes & Rahe, 1967), social factors (Parkes & Weiss, 1983), dependency/independency (Parkes & Weiss, 1983), and various sexual considerations such as incest (Hays, 1985). While specific references have been made to researchers above, it should be noted that these issues chosen for item selection were addressed to some extent by the other researchers previously mentioned. It is believed that the items constructed represent the elements of the behavioral domain identified as unresolved grief and should indicate its presence in an individual.

Originally 200 items constructed for this project were to serve as an item pool from which items would be chosen for analysis. It later proved more economical to include all 200 items at once for the purpose of item analysis, thereby eliminating any items which might not adequately discriminate within the behavioral domain of unresolved grief. Once the items were formulated a true/false method of response was chosen whereby participants would either agree or disagree with the statement. This would indicate the relevance of each statement to their current feelings and level of functioning. Because of the nature of the statements, the lower the score, the higher the indication of unresolved grief would be.

The original form of the Roberts Grief and Loss Analysis Scale (Appendix B) included a title page, an instruction page, a demographic sheet, and the body of the test. Each participant was provided with a copy of the instrument, two copies of the consent form, an answer sheet, and a pencil. All demographic information and responses to the 200 statements were marked on the answer sheet which was designed to be scanned by computer. The consent forms were standard in nature and format, explaining the purpose of the study, confidentiality concerns, voluntary participation, and identifying the researcher and affiliated school. One copy was turned in to the researcher, and one copy was retained by the participant for their records.

Once the data was collected on the 114 participants from the general population, item analysis was completed using an index of discrimination on extreme upper and lower groups. This process yielded a revised edition of the original 200 items, reduced to 100 items (Appendix C). The 100 items remaining then became the instrument presented to the psychiatric patients in hopes of achieving a contrasted group comparison between the general and psychiatric data collected. In addition to revising the body of the test, the consent form also had to be modified to meet requirements of the hospital administrative staff. The only change was for the purpose of obtaining access to patient medical records. This was done to determine suitability for testing by checking admitting diagnoses assigned by admitting physicians. No additional confidential patient information was reviewed or verified in any manner. The problems of this procedure will be addressed later.

If the patient agreed to participate they were given a copy of the consent form and the other copy was returned to the present author. All other testing materials remained the same as those used by the general sample. The format for the consent form was basically the same as before. No changes were made in the title page, demographic data which was requested, or instructions for the Roberts Grief and Loss Analysis Scale. The revised edition of the RGLAS is included as Appendix C of this paper. Again, demographic information was collected and patients were asked to provide this information and mark responses to the test items on the same type of answer sheet used by the general population sample. Pencils were provided to this group as well.

Procedure

The 200 item instrument, as outlined in the materials section (Appendix B), was given to the participants in a standardized form by the present author. Remember that randomicity was not employed in obtaining participants due to the limited number available. Groups used for testing were obtained through various contacts in the middle Georgia area, including college faculty and business professionals. The materials, as outlined previously, were distributed prior to the arrival of participants in order to better use the time available. Once all participants were in the room the consent form was reviewed, making certain that all aspects of the research were fully understood. After answering any questions, the participants were asked to sign both copies and keep one for their records, passing the other copy forward for collection by the researcher. Confidentiality was further protected in this manner by having signed consent forms collected separately from the unsigned answer sheets and test materials. Participants were then asked to review the demographic information requested, and instructions were given as to the proper way to indicate the responses on the answer sheets. The instruction page was addressed next, giving participants an opportunity to read it thoroughly and ask any questions. Care was taken to make certain that the participants understood how to use the answer sheet.

Verbal exchange between researcher and participants consisted of an initial personal introduction, a review of the consent form, and explanation regarding the demographic information, and addressing any questions about the printed instructions. Participants were asked not to talk during the testing and were told not to write their names on any testing materials. A central location was designated within the testing room, providing a place for the test materials to be turned in once testing was completed. Answer sheets were all passed to one individual who was instructed to shuffle them thoroughly, further facilitating anonymity. All of the participants were asked to remain seated until everyone had finished the test. They were also asked not to take any of the testing materials from the room. After all test materials were collected the present author made a brief presentation giving more details about the nature of the study, not giving any new information, just expanding on information already provided. Also presented were plans for further research toward the development of the Roberts Grief and Loss Analysis Scale, including specifics about the psychiatric population targeted and the behavioral domain of unresolved grief. Any questions regarding testing, grief, or the present research were also addressed. Actual time required to take the test averaged about 40 minutes.

After all of the above data was collected the answer sheets were checked to make certain all answers were clearly marked and that answer sheets were ready for computer scanning. Code numbers were assigned beginning with 001 through 114 for the purpose of identifying individual scores and other pertinent data. Both Anastasi (1988) and Aiken (1971) were sources chosen to determine proper analysis approaches. Using the data complied by the computer, item analysis was done using extreme groups defined as the upper and lower 25% of all scores. An index of discrimination table was constructed and the difference was computed for each of the 200 items based on the extreme groups. Because a high score indicated little unresolved grief, this group of the 25% of the sample with the highest scores became the low grief group, and the group of the 25% lowest scores became the high grief group.

According to Anastasi the index of discrimination is a very acceptable measure of item discrimination when compared with other measures. An item would yield the maximum discrimination between those with low total test scores (indicating low unresolved grief) if all of those with low test scores marked the item one way. This would give a discrimination index of 100, the highest possible value for the discrimination index. If there is no difference in how those with low scores marked the item and how those with high scores marked the item, the discrimination index would be zero. By eliminating items with a low discrimination index, the scale becomes a more homogeneous measure, because the items retained are those which measure something similar to the other items. Anastasi recommends that an index of discrimination of no lower that 50 serve as the cutoff point for retaining the item.

In order to increase reliability and to have the opportunity to analyze more of the original items, the desired number of retained items was set at 100. Sample size was too small at this point to warrant discarding a substantial number of items. A difference, or index of discrimination greater than or equal to 50, yielded 41 items. By dropping to a difference of 40 an additional 51 items were retained. The remaining 8 items, to give the total of 100, was achieved by using an index of discrimination no lower that 35. These 100 items were retained in the same form as when included as part of the original pool of 200 items. The item analysis provided the first form of the RGLAS (Appendix C) which was then used to test the psychiatric patients. In both forms of the test items were randomly reversed in order to avoid a response set of answering all items either true or false.

The process of obtaining permission from the hospital where the psychiatric patients were to be tested was rather difficult. Never in the past had the hospital allowed such research to be conducted, so no specific policy regarding internal review procedures existed. The present research served as a prototype to establish in internal review board and policies regarding future research consideration at the hospital. Permission to treat the patients was finally granted after dealing with four administrative personnel and with the psychiatrists who admitted patients to the adult unit. Because of requirements by the hospital consent had to be granted by the patients at the time of their admission. This was the only possible way for the present author to have access to medical records to determine patient admitting diagnoses only, and only for the purpose of verifying suitability for testing. The consent form used with the general sample had to be revised to include the statement granting access to medical records. The physicians were provided with complete sets of testing materials accompanied by a cover letter explaining the nature of the study. They were asked to either approve or disapprove the study for access to their patients by signing the cover letter and returning the complete packet to the researcher. Only one of the seven doctors refused to cooperate, even failing to return the packet.

Once this process was completed and the entire project was again cleared through the Institutional Review Board at Georgia College and State University, testing began as consent forms were collected. The physicians asked that no research testing be conducted until all psychological assessment had been completed. This meant a delay of at least 48 hours from the time of admission. In order to keep standardization comparable with the general population sample, testing of psychiatric patients was done in groups of two or more. Since the consent form was signed at the time of admission, the form was explained again by the researcher to make certain that participants understood the study and still wished to participate. The affective (depression) and anxiety-based disorders are milder in form than some others, so patients were coherent and capable of understanding the consent form and the nature of the testing.

The testing materials were the same as used with the general sample with regards to demographic information requested, instruction page, title page, and answer sheets. The only changes were in the consent form and the fact that this version of the RGLAS was 100 items shorter than before the item analysis and selection. Patients were taken to a room on the adult unit which was rather secluded and free from distraction. After the consent form was explained again the participants were shown how to complete the demographic information. They were then asked to read the instructions and begin the test if there were no further questions. As in the previous phase of the research no names appeared any place on the answer sheets or test materials. Answer sheets were turned in to the researcher by one participant and, as others were collected over time, they were all shuffled together to further facilitate the assurance of confidentiality and anonymity. No results or any information regarding the test or participation in the research became part of the patient's medical records in any form. Actual time required to take the revised 100 item form of the RGLAS averaged about 25 to 30 minutes.

An additional measure of internal consistency and as an indicator of reliability, a split-half procedure was employed by comparing odd versus even numbered items. The 100 items, retained from the item analysis on data obtained from the 114 participants from the general population, were the items checked for reliability. The Pearson Product-Moment Correlation Coefficient was the statistical approach used for comparison of the split-half forms of the test. A Spearman-Brown formula was then used to indicate a reliability coefficient that might result from doubling the length of the test. An internal consistency approach to the reliability of the scale was used because it was the present author's intent in constructing the items to find items which were all measures of the homogeneous behaviors domain of unresolved grief.

Results

Testing of the 114 participants from a sample of the general population resulted in scores ranging from 83 to 193. Remember, the lower score is likely to represent or indicate some degree of unresolved grief (see procedure section). The scores in the high grief group ranged form 83 to 135. In the low grief group scores ranged from 175 to 193. There were 29 participants who scored in the upper group and 29 who scored in the lower group. The mid-range scores from 136 to 174 included 56 participants. Item analysis using these extreme upper and lower groups to establish an index of discrimination table listing differences for each item eliminated 100 of the 200 items. As mentioned earlier an index of discrimination greater than or equal to 50 yielded on 41 items. A difference of 40 yielded as additional 51 items. To retain the desired 100 items an additional eight items emerged when the acceptable difference was lowered to 35. The 100 items retained became the first form of the RGLAS which was then administered to the psychiatric patients. No analysis had been done on data gathered from the psychiatric patients because of the inadequate sample size (see discussion section).

The results from the Pearson Product-Moment Correlation analysis yielded the following data. Scores in the split-half procedure were based on an N of 114. The mean for the odd numbered items was 84.91, with a mean for the even number items of 83.54. The split-half yielded a correlation coefficient of 0.9367. According to Anastasi (1988), desirable reliability coefficients fall in the .80s of .90s. Using the Spearman-Brown formula to determine the effect of doubling the length of the test, a coefficient of 0.9673 was obtained. Both coefficients are statistically significant beyond the $p \leq .01$ level.

Discussion

It is difficult to interpret the results of the present research. The group of 114 participants from the general population sample could be expanded in the future. A larger sample might result in the retention of the 200 items. One erroneous assumption on the part of the present author was that the scores in the general population sample would tend to be very high and narrow in range. A range of scores form 83 to 193 seems to indicate a higher degree of unresolved grief in the general population than was expected, assuming unresolved grief in the behavioral domain measured by the proposed instrument. Careful consideration of these results adds to them some degree of logic, since people generally experience many losses in their lives. Possibly unresolved grief affects an individual's level of current functioning. Perhaps a combination of poor functioning as evidenced by psychiatric hospitalization or some type of outpatient therapy and unresolved grief are necessary to consider unresolved grief as problematic.

The present study has provided a first form of an instrument called the Roberts Grief and Loss Analysis Scale (RGLAS). Results thus far indicate internal consistency as evidenced by high reliability in split-half procedures. Correlation results were statistically significant beyond the $p \leq .01$ level. Because of the processes involved in item construction the instrument appears to have content validity as well. Care was taken to construct items based on both personal observations and a thorough search of the literature. It is believed that the items retained as a result of analysis are homogeneous and represent the behavioral domain of unresolved grief. Consideration was given to research literature proposing both situation-specific approaches to grief and situation-general approaches. Much of the current research agrees with the generalizability of grief beyond the traditional scope of issues related to death and dying. These indications from the literature became a part of the item construction process. Research conducted in the pilot study by the present author (Roberts, 1986) indicated no statistically significant difference in a participant's ability to generalize grief to various loss situations. The results from the pilot study served as a further reference for item construction, providing encouragement that an instrument to detect unresolved grief, regardless of the form of the loss, is needed.

In what should have been the second phase of the present study, many problems were encountered in trying to test the psychiatric patients. It was hoped that a substantial number of patients would have been available for testing in order to expand the present study into a contrasted-groups comparison for the purpose of establishing an indication of validity. Because the hospital required consent at the time of admission, it was not possible to obtain consent personally or control the manner in which the research opportunity was presented. There were a number of different people involved in the admissions process. Even though they were instructed as to the nature of the study, the consent form became part of an admissions packet composed of 10 to 15 other forms used by the hospital. This made a burdensome admissions process even more complicated by giving both patient and admissions personnel another form with which to contend.

The attempt to include the psychiatric sample was further complicated by the emotional state of patients at the time of admission. Anyone being admitted to a psychiatric hospital for inpatient treatment of affective or anxiety-based disorders is generally quite distraught. They are generally too preoccupied with the admissions process, and even with fears of hospitalization, to be willing to consent to participation in a grief study. If consent could have been obtained within 48 hours of the admission, as originally intended, and obtained by the present author, more participants would likely have been available for testing. Out of approximately 45 to 50 admissions suitable for testing during the three months of research, only 14 agreed to participate. It is difficult to pinpoint the exact problems which led to the result; but it is safe to guess, however, that a big problem was the lack of control by the present author over the process because of hospital requirements.

Some consideration has been give to future research possibilities. Additional data may be obtained from the general population sample using the full 200 items originally constructed. To date, not enough participants have been gathered, or data collected to permanently discard the 100 items eliminated by item analysis. If the 200 items were used the same procedures presented within this paper would be employed again. The items would be reviewed and, if necessary, revised to either change or replace existing items which indicate little or no discrimination as revealed by current procedures and results.

Regardless of whether of not the present form of 100 items is used or additional data is sought on the original 200 items, the next phase of research would be to seek validity of the proposed instrument. The first effort would attempt to indicate concurrent or diagnostic criterion-related validity. The Roberts Grief and Loss Analysis Scale is not designed to be predictive in nature. Rather, it is designed to reveal the possibility of a condition or level of functioning which may already exist in some or many individuals. If, after testing, the scores of psychiatric patients are significantly different from the scores of the general sample, it can be said that the instrument has criterion-related validity. If the scores are not significantly different for the two samples, an additional item analysis using the index of determination between the psychiatric and the general sample could be done, to find and use in a revised form those items which most clearly differentiate between the two samples.

Construct-related validity will also be sought in future study. One such consideration outlined by Anastasi (1988) is the analysis of construct validity through convergent and/or discriminant correlations. One possible instrument for analysis of construct-related validity might be the MMPI, chosen for the correlations between scores on the RGLAS and the MMPI depression scale, the masculinity-femininity scale, and/or the social introversion scale. Scores from the psychiatric sample may show significant convergent correlations with these MMPI scales and may reflect low or discriminant correlations with other scales such as hypochondriasis and schizophrenia scales.

In future studies, testing may be extended to an additional population sample for the purpose of establishing norms, reliability, and validity. All testing will be conducted within clinical settings and may be expanded to include self-identified gay males and lesbians in addition to the psychiatric sample already identified. Losses possibly associated with a homosexual population may include loss of family; losses associated with negative social stigma; and perceived loss of self-worth. These loss issues and others should be identified and substantiated through a search of the literature. Testing of both groups and a comparison of data with the general population sample should indicate whether or not the test discriminates between these groups ad the general population sample. Norms, reliability, and validity then would be sought on both groups in hopes of developing a test which could detect unresolved grief in both populations for the consideration of clinical intervention toward the resolution of grief issues. Additional search of the literature is also needed to substantiate the inclusion of the second group, although it is believed that the inclusion is appropriate and will be borne out in the literature and future research. No suggestion is being made that homosexuality represents any type of psychiatric condition. Participants in a homosexual sample would be sought through counseling settings using individuals seeking intervention to enhance coping skills. Such intervention would probably include grief resolution, making the RGLAS a viable consideration with this group as well.

The results obtained thus far with the RGLAS indicate the possibility or potential for a reasonably substantial instrument. In light of this, future research may proceed as proposed using the revised form of the RGLAS resulting from the present study. Some attempt may be made to include the additional population proposed, and efforts will be made to improve upon some of the existing procedures.

References

Aiken, Jr., L. R. (1971). <u>Psychological and educational testing</u>. Boston: Allyn and Bacon

American Psychological Association, (1981). Ethical principles of psychologists (revised). <u>American Psychologist, 36,</u> 633-638.

Anastasi, A. (1988). <u>Psychological testing</u> (6th Ed.). New York: Macmillan.

Berstein, J. E. (1977). <u>Loss and how to cope with it</u>. New York: Seabury.

Bloom0Feshbach, J., Bloom-Feshbach, S. & Associates (Ed.s). (1987). <u>The psychology of separation and loss</u>. San Francisco/London: Jossey-Bass.

Bradley, L. J. (1983). Developmental assessment. <u>Counseling and Human Development, 15,</u> 1-16.

Breen, J. (1985). Children of alcoholics: The subterranean grieving process. <u>Psychotherapy Patient, 2,</u> 85-94.

Brink, T. L. (1985). The grieving patient in later life. <u>Psychotherapy Patient. 2,</u> 117-127.

Bugen, L. A. (1977). Human grief: A model for prediction and intervention. <u>American Journal of Orthopsychiatry, 47,</u> 196-206.

Bugen, L. A. (1979). <u>Death and dying: Theory/research/practice</u>. Dubuque, IA; Wm. C. Brown.

Corazzini, J. G. (1980). The theory and practice of loss therapy. In B. M. Schoenberg, Bereavement counseling — A multidisciplinary handbook (pp. 71-85). Westport, CT: Greenwood.

Faschingbauer, T., DeVaul, R., & Zisook, S. (1978). Texas revised inventory of grief. Houston: Honeycomb.

Geyman, J. O. (1983). Death and dying of a family member. Journal of Family Practice, 17, 125-134.

Hartz, G. W. (1986). Adult grief and its interface with mood disorder: Proposal of a new diagnosis of complicated bereavement. Comprehensive Psychiatry, 27, 60-64.

Hays, K. F. (1985). Electra in Mourning: Grief work and the adult incest survivor. Psychotherapy Patient, 2, 45-58.

Holmes, T. W., & Masuda, M. (1974). Life change and illness susceptibility. In B. S. Dohrenwend & B. P. Dohrenwend (Eds.), Stressful life events: Their nature and effects. New Your: Wiley.

Holmes, T. H., & Rahe, R. H. (1967). The social readjustment rating scale. Journal of Psychosomatic Research, 11, 213-218.

Jacobsen, R. H. (1986). Unresolved grief of 25 years duration exacerbated by multiple subsequent losses. Journal of Nervous and Mental Disorders, 174, 624-627.

Jansen, M. A. (1985). Psychotherapy and grieving: A clinical approach. Psychotherapy Patient, 2, 15-25.

Jasnow, A. (1985). Grief and the loss of connection. Psychotherapy Patient, 2, 27-33.

Jenkins, C. D., Hurst, M. W., & Rose, R. M. (1979). Life changes: Do people really remember? Archives of General Psychiatry, 36, 379-384.

Kamm, J. A. (1985). Grief and therapy: Two processes in interaction. Psychotherapy Patient, 2, 59-64.

Kobasa, S. C. (1979). Stressful life events, personality and health: An inquiry into hardiness. Journal of Personality and Social Psychology, 37, (1), 1-11.

Kubler-Ross, E. (1969). On death and dying. New York: Macmillan.

Kubler-Ross, E. (1978). To live until we say good-bye. Englewood Cliffs, N.J.: Prentice Hall.

Kubler-Ross, E. (1981). Living with death and dying. New York: Macmillan.

Kubler-Ross, E. (1882). Working it through. New York: Macmillan.

Kubler-Ross, E. (1983). On children and death. New Your: Macmillan.

Lebow, G. H. (1976). Facilitating adaptation is anticipatory mourning. Social Casework, 7, 458-465.

Lindemann, E. (1944). Symptomatology and management of acute grief. American Journal of Psychiatry, 101, 141-148.

Modell-Hirsch, S. (1979). Some effects of unexpected, unwilled dissolution of marriage caused by the adult male's death. In I. Gerber, A. Weiner, A Kutscher, D. Battin, A. Arkin, & I. Goldberg (Eds.), Perspectives on bereavement (pp. 131-139). New York: Arno Press.

O'Connor, N. (1984). Letting go with love: the grieving process. Apache Junction, AR: La Mariposa Press.

Oelrich, M. (1974). The patient with a fatal illness. <u>American Journal of Occupational Therapy</u>, <u>28</u>. 429-432.

Parkes, C. M. & Weiss, R. S. (1983). <u>Recovery from bereavement</u>. New York: Basic Books.

Patrick, J., Hart, C. A., & Holmes, T. H. (1982). Recent life events and illness onset. In S. day (Ed.). <u>Life Stress</u>, 109-120.

Raphael, B. (1980), A psychiatric model of bereavement counseling. In B. M. Schoenberg, <u>Bereavement counseling: A multidisciplinary handbook</u> (pp. 147-172). Westport, CT: Greenwood.

Roberts, D. (1986). <u>Testing for similarities in grief processes associated with various forms of loss</u>. Unpublished manuscript.

Sanders, C. M. (1980). A comparison of adult bereavement in the death of a spouse, child, and parent. <u>Omega</u>, <u>10</u>, 303-322.

Sanders, C. M., Mauger, P. A., & Strong, Jr., P. N. (1985). <u>The grief experiences inventory</u>. Palo Alto, CA: Consulting Psychologist Press.

Schoenberg, B. M. (1980). <u>Bereavement counseling: A multidisciplinary handbook</u>. Westbrook, CT: Greenwood.

Smith, E. W. L. (1985). A gestalt therapist's perspective on grief. <u>Psychotherapy Patient</u>, <u>2</u>, 65-78.

Stern, E. M. (1985). Three instances of the emergence of grief. <u>Psychotherapy Patient</u>, <u>2</u>, 3-14.

Stroebe, W. & Stroebe, M. (1987). <u>Bereavement and health</u>. New York: Can bridge University Press.

Tatelbaum, J. (1980). _The courage to grieve_. New York: Lippincott and Crowell.

Templer, D. I. (1970). The construction and validation of a death anxiety scale. _The Journal of General Psychology, 82_, 165-177.

UMCON (United Methodist Communication) (year unknown). _Growing through grief: Personal healing_. (Film). Nashville, TN: UMCOM.

Appendix A

The Roberts Grief and Loss Analysis Scale

Dr. David L. Roberts Ph.D.

The Roberts Grief and Loss Analysis Scale

An instrument to test for similarities in grief processes associated with various forms of loss.

Developed by:
David Louis Roberts
1986

ProKids, Inc.; The Message and The Movement

Consent Form

I, _____, agree to participate in the research entitled "Testing for Similarities in Grief Processes Associated with Various Forms of Loss", which is being conducted by David L. Roberts. I understand that this participation is voluntary. I can withdraw my consent at any time, and have the results of my participation returned to me, removed from the experimental records, or destroyed.

The following points have been explained to me:

1. The reason for this project is to develop a test which can detect similarities in grief processes associated with various forms of loss.
2. The method for gathering information will be the distribution of a test which has been prepared utilizing weighted scale statements and word associations.
3. The investigator will answer any further questions about the test and procedures at any time during the administration of the same.
4. All results will be kept completely anonymous and confidential and will not be released in any individually identifiable form without my prior written consent as required by law and ethics.

_____   _____
Signature of Researcher   Signature of Participant

_____
Date

Please sign both copies. Keep one and return the other to the investigator/researcher.

Dr. David L. Roberts Ph.D.

Research at Georgia College and State University which involves human participants is carried out under the oversight of the Institutional Review Board. Questions or problems regarding these activities should be addressed to:

Dr. Marjorie G. Prentice, Dean of the Graduate School/Associate Vice President for Academic Administration, 207 Parks Hall, (912) 453-5163.

Part I

<u>Instructions</u>: Rate each statement from 1 (strongly disagree) to 5 (strongly agree) by circling the number which best represents you opinion.

1. Loss initiates a grief process.   1 2 3 4 5
2. The greater the loss the more intense the grief.   1 2 3 4 5
3. A grief process consists of a series of steps.   1 2 3 4 5
4. Different types and intensities of loss exist.   1 2 3 4 5
5. Grief is an emotion related strictly to death.   1 2 3 4 5
6. Grief is a recovery process.   1 2 3 4 5
7. Grief is more that a period of sadness.   1 2 3 4 5
8. Grief is the most intense emotional reaction to loss.   1 2 3 4 5
9. Lesser emotional reactions than grief occur.   1 2 3 4 5
10. Grief is the expression of true feelings.   1 2 3 4 5

Dr. David L. Roberts Ph.D.

Part II

Instructions: Give a short answer to complete each of the following sentences.

1. Grief is

2. Loss is

3. Death is

4. Recovery is

5. Process is

6. Intensity is

7. Emotion is

8. Feeling is

9. Sadness is

10. Acceptance is

Part III

<u>Instructions</u>: Circle any words below which describe elements associated with loss. Mark your answers as quickly as possible and make no changes in you responses

Acceptance	Escape	Sorrow
Alone	Expectance	Suffer
Anger	Fearful	Threatened
Bewilderment	Furious	Uncertain
Bitterness	Gratitude	Unsettled
Blame	Guilty	Unstable
Blank	Helplessness	Vulnerable
Broken	Hopelessness	Worry
Burden	Hurt	
Challenge	Indecisive	
Change	Insecurity	
Control	Isolation	
Concern	Pain	
Confused	Pity	
Defenseless	Pressure	
Denial	Regret	
Depression	Relief	
Disappointment	Resentment	
Disbelief	Sadness	
Distress	Selfish	
Empty	Shock	

Dr. David L. Roberts Ph.D.

Please furnish the demographic information requested below. It is not mandatory, but will be beneficial in studying the results of this test.

    Sex - M or F
    Age
    Marital Status
    Occupation
    Educational level completed
    Most recent loss experienced: Death Divorce Shattered Dream Unreachable Goal Other (please specify) - _____

Appendix B

The Roberts Grief and Loss Analysis Scale

Dr. David L. Roberts Ph.D.

The Roberts Grief and Loss Analysis Scale

A generalized approach in the development of an instrument to detect unresolved grief which may be associated with various types of loss.

Developed by
David L. Roberts

ProKids, Inc.; The Message and The Movement

Consent Form

I, _____, agree to participate in the present study which is an attempt to develop the Roberts Grief and Loss Analysis Scale (RGLAS), an instrument to be used for the detection of unresolved grief issues associated with various forms of loss. The present study is being conducted by David Louis Roberts, a student at Georgia College and State University. I understand that this participation is voluntary. I can withdraw my consent at any time and have the results of my participation returned to me, removed from the experimental records, or destroyed.

I understand the following points:
1. The purpose of this study is to develop a test which can detect unresolved grief associated with various types of loss. THE TEST IN ITS PRESENT FORM IS PURELY EXPERIMENTAL and poses no known stress, discomfort, and risk. However, if a participant experiences any harm, a referral can be made for further assessment.
2. The method for gathering information will be the distribution of a test which asks for individual responses of either true or false to statements relative to loss or grief. Responses are neither right nor wrong and no attempts are being made to deceive participants.
3. The investigator will answer any further questions about the test and procedure at any time during the administration of the same.
4. I understand that all results will be kept completely anonymous and confidential and will not be released in any individually identifiable form without my prior consent as required by both law and ethics.

_____   _____

Signature of Investigator   Signature of Participant

_____

Date

Dr. David L. Roberts Ph.D.

Please sign both copies and keep one for you records. The other will be kept by the investigator.

Research at Georgia College and State University which involves human participants is carried out under the oversight of the Institutional Review Board. Questions or problems regarding these activities should be addressed to: Dr. Marjorie G. Prentice, Dean of the Graduate School/Associate Vice President for Academic Administration, 207 Parks Hall, (912) 452-5163.

Demographic Information

Please furnish the demographic information requested below. It is not mandatory, but will be beneficial in studying the results of the test. Mark your responses on the answer sheet in the upper left hand corner of side one. The lines are not numbered, but you are to use the first four (4) lines starting from the top down. Ask the test administrator to explain if you have any questions.

1. Sex: 0 - Male
   1 – Female
2. Age: 0 – 18-25
   1 – 26-35
   2 – 36-45
   3 – 46-55
   5 – 56-65
   6 – 65 or older
3. Marital status: 0 – Married
   1 – Single
   2 – Divorced
   3 – Significant other
   4 – Spouse or significant other deceased
4. Educational level completed: 0 – less than 12 years
   1 – 12 years
   2 – less than 16 years
   3 – 16 years
   4 – more than 16 years

Dr. David L. Roberts Ph.D.

Instructions

Loss events include a number of different experiences and are usually a significant part of everyone's life. For most people loss experiences begin in childhood with the death of a pet, school friends moving away, divorce of parents, or death of grandparents. During adolescence teenagers experience a loss of childhood as they mature toward adulthood. Loss continues to be experienced through adulthood often taking on new forms related to goals, career, finances, relationships, marriage, parenting, and aging. Some less obvious loss experiences may include bullying, sexual abuse, physical abuse, neglect, incest, alcoholic parent(s), rape, or even homosexual orientation.

You will not be asked to list or otherwise reveal your personal loss experiences. You are asked, however, to consider some of the non-traditional loss issues listed above as you respond to the following statements. Please indicate your response by marking the letter A or B that best represents you feelings and perceptions. For example, by marking A you are indicating that you agree with the statement and it is a true expression of your present feelings. If you mark a B you are indicating that you disagree with the statement and it is a false expression of your present feelings.

$$A = \text{True} \quad \text{and} \quad B = \text{False}$$

An answer sheet is provided for your responses. Please DO NOT MARK ON THE TEST ITSELF. Mark each response clearly and be sure to thoroughly erase any mark should you decide to change your response.

Sample Statements:	True	False
1. I try to hide my feelings.	A	B
2. I am afraid of my true feelings.	A	B

As you take the test, remember that there are no right or wrong answers or responses. It is important that you respond to EVERY statement. Consider each statement carefully and then mark your response based on your FIRST reaction. Mark your answers as quickly as possible. Begin with number 1, Part I on the answer sheet. *__Do not list your name anywhere on the test or answer sheet.__*

The Roberts Grief and Loss Analysis Scale

1. I have experienced many losses in my life.
2. I am afraid more losses will happen.
3. I blame myself for my losses.
4. I handled my losses better in the past than I do now.
5. I should be able to control my losses, but I can't.
6. I have always handled losses well.
7. I have no control over events in my life.
8. I often worry what will happen next.
9. I have very few fears.
10. I find it difficult to leave my home.
11. I often feel alone.
12. Most people don't seem to care about me.
13. Sometimes I think life isn't worth living.
14. I often feel anxious and don't know the reasons.
15. I don't have any goals or dreams.
16. Nothing works out for me.
17. I have usually had someone to talk to who understands me.
18. People are too concerned about their own problems to care about mine.
19. I sometimes cry for no apparent reason.
20. I often feel angry.
21. I wonder if life would be different if I had made different choices.
22. I use alcohol more now that in the past.
23. I use drugs now more than in the past.
24. I need to drink or use drugs to help me deal with my losses.
25. I don't have many friends.
26. My family does not understand me.
27. I feel like I have no purpose in life.
28. I believe that if I don't face a loss then it didn't happen.
29. I am really good at kidding myself.
30. I have never been able to face unpleasant events.
31. I am not a weak person.
32. I need someone to take care of me.

33. I lose everything that means something to me.
34. I have to face my problems alone.
35. I don't know how to be strong.
36. My life is constantly being interrupted by loss.
37. Each time my life is interrupted by loss I find it more difficult to get back on track.
38. My life has been filled with very little sadness.
39. My experiences with loss began early in my life.
40. I often wish I could start my life over again.
41. Sometimes I feel so overpowered by loss I consider suicide.
42. Sometimes I feel so down I just go to bed.
43. I am afraid if I face a loss I will be overpowered by grief.
44. My parents were very unstable people.
45. I was not very close to my parents when I was a child.
46. As a child my family life was filled with conflict.
47. My family does not support me.
48. I get satisfaction from caring for other people.
49. I have many social ties.
50. I don't trust other people to help me with my problems.
51. I worry about being alone.
52. My life feels very complicated.
53. I often awaken from a dream feeling frightened.
54. I often awaken from a dream feeling anxious.
55. I often awaken from a dream crying.
56. I often awaken from a dream feeling sad.
57. I have trouble remembering my dreams.
58. I worry about what the future holds.
59. I have hope for the future.
60. I don't know how to make the future better than my past.
61. I often feel overwhelmed.
62. Life is bigger than I am.
63. I try to take control of my life, but I don't know how.
64. Society does not approve of me.
65. I often feel ashamed of things I have done.
66. I often feel ashamed of things others have done to me.

67. I have many secrets.
68. Sometimes I must keep things to myself.
69. I seldom feel guilty.
70. Sometimes I feel guilty and don't know why.
71. I feel responsible for my losses.
72. If people knew some of my secrets I would experience more losses.
73. If I risk being myself I will experience more losses.
74. I feel like life is fair.
75. I don't speak out for myself.
76. I feel preoccupied with the losses I have experienced.
77. I can't stop thinking about the losses I have experienced.
78. I don't know what I have done to deserve so much conflict in my life.
79. I feel I am being punished for things I have done wrong.
80. God must be punishing me for something.
81. I don't like myself very much.
82. I am unworthy of being loved.
83. I have no trouble with intimacy.
84. I tend to be a very private person.
85. I often avoid contact with others.
86. I wish I could be different.
87. I wish I could be more independent.
88. I have trouble believing in myself.
89. Other people seem to be better than I am.
90. I find it hard to make friends.
91. I don't want to get to know people because I may lose them.
92. New ideas frighten me.
93. I don't have any goals in life.
94. My biggest goal is to get through this day.
95. I don't have dreams or plans for my future.
96. I don't seem able to look beyond today.
97. Everything feels good for me now.
98. I must be a failure since nothing works out for me.
99. People think I am stronger than I really am.

100. I don't seem to be able to organize my life.
101. I don't seem to be able to control my thoughts.
102. I don't' seem to be able to think positively.
103. Most of my thoughts are positive.
104. My thoughts frighten me.
105. I often feel angry because my childhood was so complicated.
106. I often feel sadness because my childhood was not happy.
107. I try to blame others for my losses.
108. I try to blame circumstances for my losses.
109. I wish my future looked brighter.
110. The finality of loss is hard to accept.
111. I like being responsible for my actions.
112. I don't like being responsible for my own decisions.
113. I don't like being responsible for my choices.
114. I would rather be dependent than independent.
115. Independence frightens me.
116. I feel nervous about making decisions.
117. I feel nervous about making plans.
118. I don't believe in a supreme being.
119. If God is so good then I shouldn't keep hurting like this.
120. I try to find things to keep me busy so I don't' have to think about my losses.
121. I don't have time to grieve.
122. I am afraid if I start crying I won't be able to stop.
123. People who cry are in control.
124. Emotional people are weak.
125. If I let me emotions show I will be weak.
126. If I let me emotions show I will be out of control.
127. I must be in control of my emotions at all times.
128. When I was a child I was punished for crying.
129. My childhood was filled with turmoil.
130. I worry too much about problems I cannot change.
131. I didn't have much of a childhood because I grew up too fast.
132. As a child I was taught to hide my feelings.
133. I have always been a person who takes care of others.

134. I seldom consider my own problems.
135. I hide my feelings so I can be strong for others.
136. I am afraid to feel.
137. I am not afraid to hurt.
138. I am afraid to reach out to others for help.
139. When I look at my past I see nothing but pain.
140. My past is filled with many unpleasant memories.
141. My parents never seemed to care for me.
142. My parents never seemed to approve of me.
143. My parents often seemed ashamed of me.
144. My parents often said negative, hurtful things to me.
145. As a child I never had a positive adult influence.
146. I used to wish that bad things would happen to other people.
147. Sometimes bad things happened because I had bad thoughts.
148. I wish I could control my emotions like others control their emotions.
149. I am not a failure.
150. People seem to depend on me.
151. People don't ask for more than I can give.
152. I try to do whatever someone asks of me.
153. Life demands too much of me.
154. As a child I lost my innocence at an early age.
155. I find that I often over/under eat.
156. I find that I sleep too much/little.
157. I cannot find new things or people that are meaningful to me.
158. I am afraid to try again.
159. When I consider my losses I feel bitter about things I have lost.
160. I don't want to seek new social ties.
161. I no longer enjoy activities that I liked in the past.
162. I no longer enjoy people that I like In the past.
163. I am more withdrawn now than in the past.
164. I fear that I am too much withdrawn from life.
165. People seem to avoid my company.
166. I have no trouble adjusting to change.
167. I often grieve over changes that have occurred.

168. I am tired of struggling with life.
169. I wish I was more of a survivor.
170. I find reality to be too painful.
171. I don't like myself when I cry.
172. I sometimes ease my emotional pain by causing myself physical pain.
173. Sometimes I feel that people won't let me grieve.
174. Grief is an emotional reaction only related to death.
175. I should not grieve losses other than death.
176. People don't seem to understand the pain I feel inside.
177. I do not find it difficult to accept my losses.
178. My life is filled with regrets.
179. I don't have any confidence in myself.
180. I find it difficult to cope with life events.
181. I deserve a better life, but I don't know how to make it happen.
182. I feel trapped and cannot identify by what.
183. It is too late for me to make changes now.
184. I am afraid to look closely at myself.
185. I am afraid to look closely at my feelings.
186. I blame others for my problems.
187. All of my dreams have been shattered.
188. I like who I am inside.
189. My moods change often.
190. I don't trust people.
191. As a child I was taught to keep my problems to myself.
192. As a child I was taught that if you ignore your problems they will go away.
193. There are parts of my life that I cannot accept.
194. Grieving does not change anything.
195. I sometimes feel that life is too complicated.
196. I have hurt so much that I feel numb to emotional pain.
197. I know I need to be active, but I don't have the energy to get involved.
198. I cannot survive any more losses.
199. Nothing in life is too painful to face.
200. Life becomes less painful as I get older.

Appendix C

The Roberts Grief and Loss Analysis Scale

Dr. David L. Roberts Ph.D.

The Roberts Grief and Loss Analysis Scale

A generalized approach to the development of an instrument to detect unresolved grief that may be associated with various types of loss.

Consent Form

I, _____, agree to participate in the present study which is an attempt to develop the Roberts Grief and Loss Analysis Scale (RGLAS), an instrument to be used for the detection of unresolved grief issues associated with various forms of loss. The present study is being conducted by David Louis Roberts, a student at Georgia College and State University. I understand that this participation is voluntary. I can withdraw my consent at any time and have the results of my participation returned to me, removed from the experimental records, or destroyed.

I understand the following points:
1. The purpose of this study is to develop a test which can detect unresolved grief associated with various types of loss. THE TEST IN ITS PRESENT FORM IS PURELY EXPERIMENTAL and poses no known stress, discomfort, and risk. However, if a participant experiences any harm, a referral can be made for further assessment.
2. The method for gathering information will be the distribution of a test which asks for individual responses of either true or false to statements relative to loss or grief. Responses are neither right nor wrong and no attempts are being made to deceive participants.
3. The investigator will answer any further questions about the test and procedure at any time during the administration of the same.
4. I understand that all results will be kept completely anonymous and confidential and will not be released in any individually identifiable form without my prior consent as required by both law and ethics.

_____   _____
Signature of Investigator   Signature of Participant

_____
Date

Dr. David L. Roberts Ph.D.

Please sign both copies and keep one for you records. The other will be kept by the investigator.

Research at Georgia College and State University which involves human participants is carried out under the oversight of the Institutional Review Board. Questions or problems regarding these activities should be addressed to: Dr. Marjorie G. Prentice, Dean of the Graduate School/Associate Vice President for Academic Administration, 207 Parks Hall, (912) 452-5163.

Demographic Information

Please furnish the demographic information requested below. It is not mandatory, but will be beneficial in studying the results of the test. Mark your responses on the answer sheet in the upper left hand corner of side one. The lines are not numbered, but you are to use the first four (4) lines starting from the top down. Ask the test administrator to explain if you have any questions.

1. Sex: 0 - Male
              1 – Female
2. Age: 0 – 18-25
              1 – 26-35
              2 – 36-45
              3 – 46-55
              5 – 56-65
              6 – 65 or older
3. Marital status: 0 – Married
                           1 – Single
                           2 – Divorced
                           3 – Significant other
                           4 – Spouse or significant other deceased
4. Educational level completed: 0 – less than 12 years
                                        1 – 12 years
                                        2 – less than 16 years
                                        3 – 16 years
                                        4 – more than 16 years

Dr. David L. Roberts Ph.D.

Instructions

Loss events include a number of different experiences and are usually a significant part of everyone's life. For most people loss experiences begin in childhood with the death of a pet, school friends moving away, divorce of parents, or death of grandparents. During adolescence teenagers experience a loss of childhood as they mature toward adulthood. Loss continues to be experienced through adulthood often taking on new forms related to goals, career, finances, relationships, marriage, parenting, and aging. Some less obvious loss experiences may include bullying, sexual abuse, physical abuse, neglect, incest, alcoholic parent(s), rape, or even homosexual orientation.

You will not be asked to list or otherwise reveal your personal loss experiences. You are asked, however, to consider some of the non-traditional loss issues above as you respond to the following statements. Please indicate your response by marking the letter A or B that best represents you feelings and perceptions. For example, by marking A you are indicating that you agree with the statement and it is a true expression of your present feelings. If you mark a B you are indicating that you disagree with the statement and it is a false expression of your present feelings.

$$A = \text{True} \quad \text{and} \quad B = \text{False}$$

An answer sheet is provided for your responses. Please DO NOT MARK ON THE TEST ITSELF. Mark each response clearly and be sure to thoroughly erase any mark should you decide to change your response.

Sample Statements:	True	False
1. I try to hide my feelings.	A	B
2. I am afraid of my true feelings.	A	B

As you take the test, remember that there are no right or wrong answers or responses. It is important that you respond to EVERY statement. Consider each statement carefully and then mark your response based on your FIRST reaction. Mark your answers as quickly as possible. Begin with number 1, Part I on the answer sheet. ***Do not list your name anywhere on the test or answer sheet.***

The Roberts Grief and Loss Analysis Scale

1. I often worry what will happen to me.
2. I am afraid more losses will happen.
3. I have very few fears.
4. I often feel alone.
5. I often feel anxious and don't know the reasons.
6. People are too concerned about their own problems to care about mine.
7. I often feel angry.
8. I don't have many friends.
9. My family does not understand me.
10. I am really good at kidding myself.
11. I have to face my problems alone.
12. My life is constantly being interrupted by loss.
13. Each time my life is interrupted by loss I find it more difficult to get back on track.
14. My life has been filled with very little sadness.
15. I often wish I could start my life over again.
16. Sometimes I feel so down I just go to bed.
17. I have many social ties.
18. I don't trust other people to help me with my problems.
19. I worry about being alone.
20. My life feels very complicated.
21. I often awaken from a dream feeling frightened.
22. I often awaken from a dream feeling anxious.
23. I often awaken from a dream feeling sad.
24. I worry about what the future holds.
25. I often feel overwhelmed.
26. Life is bigger than I am.
27. I try to take control of my life, but I don't know how.
28. I often feel ashamed of things I have done.
29. I often feel ashamed of things others have done to me.
30. I have many secrets.
31. I seldom feel guilty.

32. Sometimes I feel guilty and don't know why.
33. If people knew some of my secrets I would experience more losses.
34. I feel like life is fair.
35. I don't speak out for myself.
36. I feel preoccupied with the losses I have experienced.
37. I can't stop thinking about the losses I have experienced.
38. I don't know what I have done to deserve so much conflict in my life.
39. I feel I am being punished for things I have done wrong.
40. I have no trouble with intimacy.
41. I tend to be a very private person.
42. I often avoid contact with others.
43. I wish I could be different.
44. I wish I could be more independent.
45. I have trouble believing in myself.
46. Other people seem to be better than I am.
47. I find it harder now to make friends.
48. Everything feels good for me now.
49. People think I am stronger that I really am.
50. I don't seem to be able to organize my life.
51. I don't seem to be able to control my thoughts.
52. I don't seem to be able to think positively.
53. Most of my thoughts are positive.
54. My thoughts frighten me.
55. I often feel angry because my childhood was so complicated.
56. I often feel sadness because my childhood was not happy.
57. I try to blame circumstances for my losses.
58. I wish my future looked brighter.
59. The finality of loss is hard to accept.
60. I feel nervous about making decisions.
61. I feel nervous about making plans.
62. I try to find things to keep me busy so I don't have to think about my losses.
63. If I let my emotions show I will be out of control.
64. I must be in control of my emotions at all times.
65. My childhood was filled with turmoil.

66. I worry too much about problems I cannot change.
67. I didn't have much of a childhood because I grew up too fast.
68. I hide my feelings so I can be strong for others.
69. I am afraid to feel.
70. I am not afraid to hurt.
71. I am afraid to reach out to others for help.
72. My past is filled with many unpleasant memories.
73. My parents often said negative, hurtful things to me.
74. I used to wish that bad things would happen to people.
75. I wish I could control my emotions like others control their emotions.
76. People ask for more than I can give.
77. I find that I over or under eat.
78. I find that I often sleep too much or too little.
79. I am afraid to try again.
80. When I consider my losses I feel bitter about things I have lost.
81. I am more withdrawn now than in the past.
82. I have no difficulty adjusting to change.
83. I often grieve over changes that have occurred.
84. I am tired of struggling with life.
85. I wish I was more of a survivor.
86. Sometimes I feel that people won't let me grieve.
87. People don't seem to understand the pain I feel inside.
88. I do not find it difficult to accept my losses.
89. My life is filled with regrets.
90. I don't have any confidence in myself.
91. I find it difficult to deal with life events.
92. I deserve a better life but I don't know how to make it happen.
93. I am afraid to look closely at myself.
94. I am afraid to look closely at my feelings.
95. My moods change often.
96. I don't trust people.
97. There are parts of my life that I cannot accept.
98. I sometimes feel that life is too complicated.
99. I have hurt so much I feel numb to emotional pain.
100. I know I need to be more active but I don't have the energy to get involved.

Dr. David L. Roberts Ph.D.

California School of Professional Psychology
(Now under Alliant International University)
Los Angeles Campus

The Roberts Grief and Loss Analysis Scale (RGLAS):
A Reliability and Validity Study

A dissertation submitted in partial satisfaction
of the requirements for the degree of
Doctor of Philosophy in Clinical Psychology

By

David Louis Roberts

1993

ProKids, Inc.; The Message and The Movement

Copyright by
David Louis Roberts
1993

Dr. David L. Roberts Ph.D.

California School of Professional Psychology
Los Angeles Campus

The dissertation of David Louis Roberts, directed and approved by the candidate's Committee, has been accepted by the Faculty of the California School of Professional Psychology in partial fulfillment of the requirements for the degree of

DOCTOR OF PHILOSOPHY

<u>May 4, 1993</u>

Dissertation Committee:
David P. Fox, Ph.D., Chairperson
Sam Chan, Ph.D.
Joan Murray, Ph.D.

1993

Dedication

This dissertation is dedicated, in part, to Melissa Dawn Roberts Everette, my loving daughter. She has been, and still is my inspiration for much that I do. The love we share serves as a basis from which we can both continue to grow and change.

As I have watched Melissa struggle with the challenges of her life I have come to understand many of my own struggles. For her and for myself I have struggled to right the wrongs we have both endured. Melissa is a source of joy and encouragement. Many times she has helped me to find meaning in life and reason to continue my journey. To her and for her I am eternally grateful.

I also dedicate this dissertation to the loving memory of Adan Lopez, my spouse, my friend, and now my guardian angel. Our love helped me understand and improve my Self, and gave me the safety to resolve many of the losses and injustices from my past. Adan's life and courage in the face of AIDS taught me to value life's struggles and to face my fears. His childlike faith mirrored the beauty of his soul and challenged the very depths of my being. His death taught me to identify the important things in life, and revealed to me the peaceful beauty of the dying experience shared by people deeply in love. No greater experience is possible than two people sharing quality of life and death with dignity. It is in death that life has meaning and the soul defines and discovers its value.

The love we have at the end of life is all that anyone takes with them. It is this same love that will always keep Adan alive in my heart and mind: the same love that will someday bring us back together again. Thank you Adan for allowing me to share your love, your life, and your death. Your heart took you to God; our love helped us find peace; and my life is richer for it all.

Dr. David L. Roberts Ph.D.

The Ghost of Yesterday

The rose you gave me lies alone on
my bedside table,
And the candle I lit reflects it's soft
shade of pink.

The white chiffon curtains are blowing
quietly in the gentle breeze,
and my champagne glass, once half full,
has fallen over.
There is nothing more to celebrate.

Forever has come and gone;
and, although it was here much quicker
for you than for me,
I can hear the clock ring twice.

My tears turned into streams and the
streams have run to the river.
The flow of the river almost put
out my candle.

Although I have asked God to take the pain
out of my heart,
I still hurt,
and I miss you.

Melissa Dawn Roberts Everette

Yesterday

Last night I dreamed of a delicate body,
dressed in white chiffon,
standing alone on the mountain top.
I was in a valley below and I called to her.

As she turned to see the voice that called out,
I noticed her elegant poise, her graceful steps,
accompanied with a perfect smile.

She seemed to be without fault,
and her way of facing the world
was fearless, brave, courageous.

With a sudden slap from reality,
this wonder became faceless,
yearning for the appearance she once had.

Because I thought that I could not live up to the body,
the mind she thought we shared,
I turned to leave.

By some force, unexplained to me,
I could not turn away.
She kept calling to me
in a slight whisper that only I could hear, but I could not answer.

To my amazement, this wonder floated down the mountain
to meet me half way.
I made the decision to follow her call,
and we traveled to the top together.

Dr. David L. Roberts Ph.D.

After we sat quietly for a while,
I knew it was time to go.
Although she warned me of fear, I left.

When I got back to my valley,
I found my body shriveled, cold, and lifeless on the ground.

I looked to the top of the mountain in confusion.
With the same grace and beauty, she turned.

I saw my face on her,
my lifeless body, and then I woke up.

Melissa Dawn Roberts Everette

A Prayer for People with AIDS

May God give you strength.
May He help you find that in His love.

May God give you happiness.
May He help you find it when you need it most.

May God give you wisdom.
Let Him guide you in a safe direction.

May God give you hope.
Let Him help you find that in tomorrow.

May God help you to understand.
May you find answers in His light.

May God give you the courage to know you are no alone,
even when you loneliness is felt the deepest.

May God give you love.
He will hold you closest in your times of need.

Melissa Dawn Roberts Everette

Table of contents

Dedication		629
List of Appendices		637
Acknowledgements		639
Abstract of the Dissertation		641
Chapter I	INTRODUCTION	643
	Statement of the Problem	644
	Definition of Terms	646
Chapter II	REVIEW OF THE LITERATURE	649
	Grief Reactions	649
	The Differences Between Depression and Grief	650
	Etiology of Unresolved Grief	652
	Summary	654
Chapter III	METHODS	657
	Subjects	657
	Design	660
	Instrumentation	661
	Roberts Grief and Loss Analysis Scale	661
	Beck Depression Inventory	663
	Center for Epidemiological Studies – Depression Scale	663
	Procedures	663
Chapter IV	RESULTS	667
Chapter V	DISCUSSION	671
	Assumptions and Limitations	673
	Recommendations for Future Research	674
References		679
Appendices		685

LIST OF APPENDICES

Appendix

 A. Roberts Grief and Loss Analysis Scale – Original 200 Item Scale - Thesis

 B. Roberts Grief and Loss Analysis Scale – 100 Item Scale – Thesis

 C. Letter to Dr. Aaron Beck

 D. Letter to the National Institute of Mental Health Center for Epidemiologic Studies

 E. Letter to Clinicians

ACKNOWLEDGEMENTS

I would like to give special thanks to David Fox, Ph.D., Sam Chan, Ph.D., and Joan Murray, Ph.D., for their guidance, support, and encouragement during this difficult process. You were the best dissertation committee that anyone could hope to have and I am grateful for your time and effort.

Also, I want to thank all of the mental health professionals who willingly provided access to the patients in my clinical sample.

Special thanks go to the many friends from both my recent and distant pasts who believed in me and support me through many of my life struggles, in addition to my graduate training. Chief among these is Tom Freese, my support and strength through the especially difficult experience of Adan's illness and death. Only tom knows the full range of realities that were part of the ordeal. Tom was my "best man" for the Holy Union Ceremony that united Adan and me eternally. Tom was also the only one by my side at the moment of Adan's death. Together we shared two of the most important events I have ever experienced. I love you Tom and I am grateful that you are part of my life.

Other special friends include: Charles Johnson, my friend since first grade; Susan Chapman; David Gray; George Nash; Denver Piccard; Javier Gonzales; Armand Cruz; Daniel Rugamas; Harold Stram; Janet West; Gary Smith; and my library "Mom" Tobeylynn Birch. Each of you holds a special place in my heart and mind. Thank all of you for your contributions to the Self I have become.

Heartfelt thanks are also offered to the many administrators, faculty, and students at CSPP-LA who comforted me through and after Adan's illness and death. Also, I offer thanks to my support systems outside of CSPP-LA.

Finally, I want to acknowledge the friends I have lost to AIDS. It is my prayer that this dreadful epidemic will end soon. Until then we must all as mental health professionals and humanitarians do everything to foster hope, comfort, and loving acceptance to those infected with, and affected by this horrible disease.

ABSTRACT OF THE DISSERTATION

The Roberts Grief and Loss Analysis Scale (RGLAS):
A Reliability and Validity Study

by

David Louis Roberts
Doctor of Philosophy in Clinical Psychology
California School of Professional Psychology – Los Angeles
(Now under Alliant International University)
1993
David Fox, Ph.D., Chairperson

The purpose of the present study was to seek indications of reliability and validity on the Roberts Grief and Loss Analysis Scale (RGLAS). The present research is Study II in the process of test development. Study I (Roberts, 1989), completed as a Master of Science thesis, involved item selection and analysis.

For the purpose of attempting to establish reliability, a comparison was made between test/retest scores on the RGLAS using a nonclinical group and a clinical population sample. Further analysis on the clinical sample consisted of comparisons between the RGLAS and both the Beck Depression Inventory (BDI), and the Center for Epidemiological Studies – Depression Scale (CES-D). One additional comparison was sought between the BDI and the CES-D to determine the degree of relationship between the two depression scales.

Significant correlations were found between the nonclinical test/retest subjects. Analysis also revealed a significant difference between sample means of the nonclinical/clinical comparison. Significant correlations were also found between the RGLAS and the two depression scales. Also, the correlation between the BID and the CES-D was significant as well.

One of the main premises of this study was that there is a difference between clinical depression and unresolved grief. The belief of the present author is that depression is always part of grief, but that grief is not always part of depression. Because of the significant correlations between the RGLAS and the two depression scales, an additional attempt was made to test the strength of the difference between dependent r's. This data analysis procedure yielded a significant difference between the r values in the comparisons on the RGLAS to the depression scales, when compared to the r value between the depression scales alone. These results leave the door open for future research to include factor analysis.

Chapter I

INTRODUCTION

Because loss is such a significant part of human existence it follows that its impact can lead to potentially distressing psychological effects. It is believed by the present author that the importance of loss and associated grief issues must be acknowledged as significant aspects of mental health. This is especially true in attempting to generalize loss beyond more traditional associations with death and dying.

In the original study, Study I (Roberts, 1989) (included within the document), a review of the literature concerning grief suggested that similarities exist between grief processes regardless of the type of loss experienced. However, there appeared to be few studies which demonstrated a relationship between various types of loss and a generalized sequential process of grief remediation as viewed from a purely mental health perspective. Most research regarding grief was done on an individual case study basis, was rather stimulus or source specific (i.e. death or dying), and was often viewed from a physiological perspective. No attempt was made to connect unresolved grief with issues related to deficits in psychological/ emotional development during childhood, deficits which could be experienced as loss. Such losses could result from: inadequate parental nurturing; sexual, physical, or emotional abuse; neglect; poor object relations; a home environment of substance abuse and dependence; problems associated with socioeconomic status; issues related to ethnicity; parental figures who are psychologically impaired; developmental issues related to sexual orientation; and/or other tragic events experienced during childhood. Any of these environments are referred to in current literature as a dysfunctional background relative to psychological development. The detection of unresolved grief - as indicated by client self report, clinical evaluation, and the eventual use of the Roberts Grief and Loss Analysis Scale (RGLAS) - could indicate depression as a symptom of complicated grief manifested by psychological impairment and impairment in current functioning during adulthood relative to developmental deficits. Further development of the RGLAS for use in this type of evaluation process will be the goal of the present study (Study II).

In Study I the RGLAS (Appendix A) was constructed and it has been revised to be used in the present study. Items were selected by the present author based upon a review of the literature, and upon personal experience and observations. Item analysis yielded the present instrument (Appendix B) which consists of 100 items.

The present study will look at issues of test-retest reliability, predictive validity, and discriminant validity using RGLAS scores from clinical and non-clinical comparison groups. Identifying and dealing with any form of unresolved grief would be a valuable approach to treatment within therapeutic settings. Perhaps the RGLAS will serve to build and establish a better understanding of the impact of deficits in emotional/psychological development upon current adult functioning. Hopefully the RGLAS will replace diagnostic attempts currently based upon subjective experience with a more reliable and objective method of assessment and diagnosis of unresolved grief or complicate bereavement.

Statement of the Problem

The present study is designed to serve as Study II in a series of attempts toward the development, utilization and professional circulation of the Roberts Grief and Loss Analysis Scale (RGLAS). As stated earlier Study I consisted of item selection and analysis, resulting in the present form of the RGLAS to be used in this study (Appendix B). In the present study an effort will be made to establish indications of test-retest reliability, predictive validity, and discriminant validity.

It is the belief of the present author that grief is a normal part of everyone's life at various points in time. As the ideas regarding the RGLAS and the items themselves have evolved the RGLAS appears to be grounded more and more in losses associated with deficits in emotional/psychological development and manifested as complicated bereavement. It is likely that the RGLAS is also a measure of depression, as depression is generally acknowledged as one aspect of a grief process. However, grief involves emotional elements other than just depression, and the RGLAS is designed to serve as an indication of unresolved grief in adulthood – and possibly in transitional aged adolescents. Because the test items are selected based on loss issues relative to deficits in emotional/psychological development it is hoped that the RGLAS will reveal unresolved grief resulting from childhood issues, multiple losses, and inadequate emotional development. These issues are generally encountered in therapy and must be dealt with via facilitation of some grief process if resolution is to be achieved and psychological growth and reparation are to begin or successfully continue.

If used in clinical settings the RGLAS should serve as an indication of such unresolved grief and, therefore, could also be a measure of the degree of dysfunctional background present in the client. Theories of psychotherapy and clinical observations of troubled individuals and clients suggest that denial, anger, anxiety, depression, fear, and sadness are often rooted deep in a client's past. Even though experienced consciously as new relative to present situations, it is likely that these emotional elements may represent cumulative unresolved grief connected to poor or stunted emotional development in childhood. As will be shown this possibly indicates that cumulative unresolved grief from the past may lead to complicated bereavement in the present and manifested by psychological impairment and impairment in current adult functioning.

When used in clinical settings as part of an assessment process the RGLAS should indicate the presence of complicated bereavement regardless of the nature of the loss or losses. It is acknowledged that depression and anxiety are part of grief. Because of this reality, when the RGLAS is used in conjunction with measures of depression and anxiety there may be some degree of correlation between the RGLAS and other instruments such as the Beck Depression Inventory (BDI) (Beck, Ward, Mendelson, Mock, & Erbaugh, 1961) and the Center for Epidemiological Studies – Depression Scale (CES-D) (Radloff, 1977). However, if complicated bereavement is the overriding factor, then the score on the RGLAS should serve as an indication of this possibility. The RGLAS is designed so that the lower a person scores on the RGLAS, the higher the indication should be of complicated bereavement resulting from unresolved grief.

If a client is given an initial diagnosis of depression and/or anxiety, and scores high on the depression/anxiety inventories, and high on the RGLAS, then this correlation should serve as an indication of the accuracy of the initial diagnosis. If scores are high on the RGLAS and low on the depression scales then there is an indication of both low unresolved grief and low depression. However, if the scores are lower on the RGLAS and higher on the depression/anxiety inventories, then complicated bereavement may be present along with symptoms of depression/anxiety also present. If scores are low on all three scales, then there is an indication that there is not a significant degree of depression/anxiety; but, possibly a high degree of unresolved grief. With this result exploration should be made of childhood experiences of loss related to dysfunctional backgrounds.

As it is a generally accepted practice that no assessment instrument or procedure should be used in isolation, the RGLAS should work well with indicators of depression and anxiety in either confirming or ruling out, as a clinical issue, complicated bereavement which results from unresolved grief. The RGLAS is not designed to be used with psychological disorders any more serious or severe than depression and/or anxiety. However, the RGLAS could be used in future research to study the interaction between biological and environmental factors influencing personality development and the later development of more serious pathology.

Definition of Terms

In order to clarify the nature of this study it is necessary to define the terminology used as it was defined in Study I (Roberts, 1989). Of primary importance are the definitions of loss, grief, unresolved grief, depression, anxiety, and dysfunctional backgrounds. These terms are defined operationally relative to the nature of the present study. An assumption, also, is that the intent is the generalization of loss from traditional associations with death and dying to less common associations with various types of non-traditional loss.

Loss occurs when an individual, with or without choice, relinquishes, abandons, is denied, or otherwise forfeits an object, person, concept, or identity held as important, meaningful, and significant. That individual is then faced with having to accept any resultant psychological state sometimes experienced as a void. They must then choose alternative views, goals, or conditions necessary to compensate for the emptiness which remains or changes that occur. Loss is then defined as an individually significant resultant sense of void for which compensation must be sought. Grief is defined as any emotional process associated with accepting the loss, compensating for the void, and adapting to new conditions and/or situations.

The behavioral domain targeted by the RGLAS then becomes unresolved grief, interchangeable with complicated bereavement, defined as and manifested by evidence of impaired current functioning relative to dysfunctional background and often masked as depression and/or anxiety. The RGLAS is designed to detect unresolved grief in clinical settings for patients seeking outpatient psychotherapy, and in some instances of psychiatric hospitalization.

Depression is addressed only as part of the grief process and is defined simply as one of the stages of grief. Normal grief is synonymous with transitory symptoms of depression. However, complicated bereavement or unresolved grief involves more severe depressive symptoms which may then serve as symptoms of more pathological forms of grief. As indicated in the literature review to follow, this manifestation of depression has a possible etiological basis associated with losses experienced in conjunction with dysfunctional backgrounds. This could result in developmental deficits regarding attachment along with deficits in emotional development.

Anxiety is also recognized as a part of the grief reaction and is defined as fear related to the loss that has occurred. It is the conjecture of the present author that depression is always part of the grief process: but that grief is not always part of depression. It is further suggested that anxiety is also part of depression; but that depression is not always part of anxiety. Therefore, only depression relative to grief, and anxiety relative to depression are factors in the present study.

The final concept of dysfunctional background is defined as any environmental interference during childhood which impedes proper emotional and psychological development, and resulting in deficits in such development. This interference is directly related to problems of inadequate parenting and other environmental factors (as listed previously) regardless of the nature of such inadequacies. It is proposed that such interference results in impaired adult functioning, and would possibly indicate substantial looses in childhood. The degree of dysfunctional backgrounds would then be directly correlated to the degree of adult dysfunction, especially with regard to resolution of grief as a reaction to any significant loss. The conjecture is that in unresolved grief there is likely a complicated reaction resulting directly from previous unresolved grief relative to multiple childhood losses encountered within dysfunctional families. The personality deficits and defects would likely make adult grief problematic until such prior issues could be identified, faced, grieved, and resolved.

Chapter II

REVIEW OF THE LITERATURE

The review of the literature in Study I (Roberts, 1989) was focused on various grief processes and the attempt to expand conceptualization of loss and grief beyond the traditional associations with death and dying. That study consisted of item selection and item analysis in the initial development of The Roberts Grief and Loss Analysis Scale (RGLAS). Item analysis yielded the present 100 item form of the RGLAS upon which reliability and validity studies were conducted in Study II, the research proposed here.

The present review of the literature is intended to explore the differences between grief and depression. Also there is the need to look at some of the etiological factors which could lead to complicated bereavement or unresolved grief. Most of the grief literature presents research that studies only issues related to death and dying. It is the intent of the present research to emphasize the universality of grief as a reaction to loss, with the extent of grief relative to the significance of the loss. This literature review will look first at grief reactions and the distinction between grief and depression will be explored. Finally, the etiological factors that could result in unresolved grief will be presented. To date the present author has found no study which attempts to identify loss and grief as measurable entities resulting from dysfunctional backgrounds. Once successfully developed, the RGLAS will serve as such a measure that will be useful within many clinical settings.

Grief Reactions

Different researchers and authors present various categories of grief. Originally grief was divided into two categories. Freud (1857) wrote about mourning as opposed to the more pathological state of melancholia. Jansen

(1985) continued this dichotomous conceptualization identifying normal versus pathological grief. Furthermore, Jansen viewed grief in clinical settings as a process relative to multiple, non-traditionally associated kinds of loss situations. Pathological grief is identified by the magnitude of sadness and fear, terms used by Jansen apparently in place of depression and anxiety. These elements which are part of normal grief are said to be overwhelming and intolerable in pathological grief.

Others begin to expand the various types of pathological grief into categories, still using the dichotomy of normal versus pathological grief. The concepts are basically the same, though the terminology is different. Delayed, inhibited, or chronic grief is identified by Marris (1975) as categories of pathological grief. The terms delayed and inhibited are rather self explanatory. However, the term chronic grief is important because of the element of time or duration. This is also identified as an indication of abnormal grief by Demi and Miles (1987), Marris further suggests that inhibited grief is usually permanent and is especially relevant to childhood grief experiences.

Parkes and Weiss (1983) identified three "syndromes" of pathological grief reactions. These are the syndromes of unexpected grief, ambivalent grief, and chronic grief. Their concept of chronic grief is the same as that proposed by Marris. The other two categories delineate reactions correlated to sudden losses and to the nature of the relationship between the lost object and the bereaved. Parkes (1985) discusses the psychiatric disorders which are manifested in pathological grief, identifying these as further evidence of unresolved grief. These are essentially the same concepts as those presented by Marris (1975).

The premise of the present author is that while the grief reaction may be relative to the circumstances of a specific loss, the pathological state of unresolved grief is directly linked to unresolved grief experienced from dysfunctional backgrounds. Duration of grief and the manifestation of various abnormal behaviors are indicators of complicated bereavement.

The Differences Between Depression and Grief

It is difficult to distinguish between the emotional states of grief and depression. A stated earlier by the present author, depression appears to always be part of grief, but there is no evidence that grief is always part of depression. Belitsky and Jacobs (1986) address the issues of depression versus grief. They acknowledge that grief includes depressive symptomatology. Duration and intensity of symptoms seem indicative of complicated bereavement. Belitsky and Jacobs propose that the somatic symptoms are most prevalent in the early stages of bereavement. In later stages it is proposed that the psychological symptoms of depression appear. The persistence of these symptoms is suggested as an indication of complicated bereavement. Psychological symptoms include depressed mood, hopelessness, restlessness, helplessness, worthlessness, and suicidal ideation. It is further suggested by these authors that depression associated with grief is agitated depression, not retarded or anergic depression. Furthermore, anxiety is included as another component of grief. This anxiety is said to derive from the anxiety associated with separation from the lost object. Some initial transitory emotional distress is recognized as part of a healthy healing process. However, in unresolved grief the emotional distress continues and heightens, interfering with normal functioning and continuing beyond the expected duration of uncomplicated bereavement or normal grief.

In a related article by Smith (1985) depression is distinguished from grief by the presence of a decrease in self-esteem, such that the person grieving feels like a bad person because of the loss experienced. It is further suggested that grieving may feed an underlying depressive tendency and develops into a full blown depressive episode clearly tied to the grief of the lost object. A person with a history of depression then is likely to experience complicated bereavement because of unresolved grief issues already present. Grief is presented by Smith as a healing process without which unfinished business is said to last forever. Smith also addresses losses which are much more abstract than the obvious loss of a person to death. Losses such as termination of a job, loss of goals or dreams, divorce, illness, robbery, and loss of childhood dreams are presented as examples of less commonly associated loss experiences. This suggests a direct connection to the present study, even indicating etiological factors beginning with childhood looses which often go unresolved because the ability to grieve is halted or not supported or even recognized.

Beck (1967) defines depression by a list of five attributes. The first attribute is the emotional manifestation of a specific change in mood, accompanied by feelings of sadness, loneliness, and apathy. Second are cognitive manifestations of low self esteem associated with self blame and self reproach. The third attribute is the motivational manifestation of withdrawal, wishes to hide or escape, and suicidal ideation. Vegetative and physical manifestations are fourth and include changes in sleeping and eating habits, fatigue, and loss of sexual desire. Finally, there is a change in previous levels of activity with marked retardation or agitation.

These symptoms or attributes of depression are recognized by other writers as part of a normal grief process (Lehman, 1983; Zisook, Schuster, & Schuckit, 1985; Zisook & DeVaul, 1983; Sinaikin, 1985; Raphael, 1980; Lindemann, 1944; Clayton, 1987). However, each of these writers indicates that unresolved grief results in an increase in depressive symptoms, especially along the lines of agitated depression with various acting-out tendencies. Anger, guilt and fear are also part of this complicated bereavement. Curtis (1982) connects fear, guilt and anger to emotional elements of acting-out behavior, stating that these can lead to the formation of symptoms and decompensation. These are related to the same elements of complicated bereavement of which the manifestations of extreme anxiety and depression could be viewed as symptoms, not as separate and unrelated entities.

Fox (1987) addresses depression, anxiety, and stress as adaptations to suffering. It is suggested that in suffering the person feels controlled from outside the self with a sense that something is being done to the individual. There would appear to be a strong element of suffering for the person experiencing complicated bereavement exacerbated by previous unresolved grief issues. Some purpose in the resolution of grief could simply be the healing of childhood wounds "suffered" within dysfunctional environments.

Etiology of Unresolved Grief

One major work dealing with loss and grief is that of Weenolsen (1988). This work is important to the present research because it presents five levels of loss which are directly supportive of the premises of the present author. These five levels are: primary, secondary, holistic, self-conceptual, and metaphorical. The presentation of these five levels attempts to explain why loss affects people so deeply.

Significance of any loss is very individualized, with the degree of connection to the lost object correlated with the sense of loss which results. The five levels indicate that a loss can have a very significant impact on an individual at all points of their being, affecting not only the physical person, but also the emotional, psychological, and spiritual being as well. The primary and secondary levels deal with the more obvious effects of the loss. It is more difficult to deal with the metaphorical, holistic, and self conceptual levels because they are more abstract and therefore not always so obvious. The author suggests that unless loss is dealt with at all levels of the psyche, then transcendence of loss is not achieved and some remnants of the unresolved levels are likely to be problematic at a later time.

Weenolsen uses many case studies in support of the theory proposed. In this approach a great deal of attention is given to the etiological factors during all stages of development, from childhood through adulthood, which inhibit the ability to transcend loss. It is suggested that loss, especially significant loss, becomes a permanent part of the self. Because of this factor unresolved grief appears to be synonymous with the concept of an absence of transcendence, with the author presenting grief as that process by which loss is transcended. To be completed transcendence must occur at all levels of loss. Personality defects resulting from environmental factors (dysfunctional background) account for the inability to adapt to and transcend loss which can lead to pathology. Weenolsen is careful to address both biological and environmental factors in the etiology of adult pathology. A great deal of emphasis is placed upon life history.

All of this relates directly to the present study in support of the generalization of loss beyond traditional associations of death and dying. It also supports the premise that complicated bereavement represents "old grief", "old fear", and "old anger" remaining from previous losses which have not been resolved. The etiological components are addressed by other authors as well.

Pedder (1972) presents the object relations viewpoint of good-enough mothering allowing for internalization of a good-enough object which will facilitate healthy adult mourning. Anxiety disorders manifesting in bereaved persons are said to be tied to both past personal history and family history (Jacobs, Hansen, Kasl, Ostfeld, Beckman, & Kim, 1990). In another article, Striker (1983) addressed the psychodynamic etiology of depression relative to loss and grief as a reactivation of earlier feelings of loss experienced in childhood. The research by Zisook and Lyons (1990) suggests a causal relationship between unresolved grief and depression relative to both individual and familial histories of depression. Pollock (1988) writes about associations between adult abandonment, loss, and vulnerability as the etiological results from childhood abandonment.

Other authors address these same factors in complicated bereavement, delineating specific deficits in emotional and psychological development in childhood (Cerney, 1989; Belitsky & Jacobs, 1986; Jacobson, 1984; Alarcon, 1984; Volken, 1983: Bowlby, 1982). Bowlby (1988) recognizes that childhood bereavement is not always handled by adults in such a way as to allow the child to resolve loss experiences. Worden (1991) addresses historical factors of past losses and separations as well as early parenting relative to complicated grief reactions. Middleton-Moz and Dwinell (1986) present both the common losses experienced by children of dysfunctional families and the grief process required in adulthood to resolve these losses. Major emphasis is placed on adult experiencing of the affectivity of repressed memories, learning to tolerate the affective reality, and then accepting the irretrievable losses from childhood.

Summary

This review of the literature has presented current examples of research and theories delineating grief reactions, comparisons of grief and depression, and etiological factors present in unresolved grief or complicated bereavement. The literature is generally specific to the issues of death and dying, although some writers are making generalizations of grief as a process involved in any type of loss experience. Again, no literature has been discovered by the present author proposing an instrument which could serve as an indication of unresolved grief relative to etiological factors associated with dysfunctional backgrounds. When successfully developed, the Roberts

Grief and Loss Analysis Scale (RGLAS) will serve as such an instrument. As more research is conducted with the RGLAS, its usefulness within clinical settings will be substantiated. It is important to note that the RGLAS is not intended to be used only with people who are in an obvious state of mourning. It will prove useful with any person presenting with complaints of depression and anxiety, especially with issues related to attachment and abandonment. Because the RGLAS may also be an indicator of dysfunctional background, unresolved grief may still be the problem, with the other manifestations serving simply as symptoms of complicated bereavement.

Chapter III

METHODS

Subjects

Fifty subjects were recruited on a voluntary basis in each of the non-clinical and clinical groups used in this study (N=100). Subjects in the nonclinical group were selected from various college and/or business setting, as determined by availability. Subject pools with persons in the 20-55 age range were targeted. Subjects in the clinical group were recruited from psychiatrists, psychologists, and other mental health professionals either known personally by the present author, or by referrals from other mental health professionals. Other sources for clinical subjects included various clinic settings which ran support groups for clients diagnosed with depression disorder. In these settings group members being treated for bipolar disorder were identified by the group leaders and their data was excluded from the analysis. These approaches for the purpose of recruiting subjects were made either by mail (Appendix E) or through personal contact.

Differences in recruitment approaches between clinical and non-clinical subjects were determined by availability and by varying degrees of difficulty in obtaining subjects in each group. Subjects in clinical settings generally were not accessible in large numbers. Use of the subjects in grief support groups was ruled out due to possible contamination of data, even though such groups would have been available. It could be assumed that people in such groups likely would be experiencing intense grief reactions which may be normal given the duration of grief relative to recency of loss. This possibly would have invalidated and biased results and would not be useful to the present study. The intent in this study was to identify unresolved grief masked as depression and/or anxiety, not to study persons already identified as grieving a specific loss or losses. Given the intent of the RGLAS such persons in grief groups should score considerably lower depending on the recency of their loss. Furthermore, because factor analysis was not performed in the present study, it would have been unnecessary at this time to recruit individuals from the general population using selection criteria other than to control for such factors as age and resultant life cycle issues relative to age.

The other concern at this time regarding demographic information was ethnicity. It was assumed that if an individual is working in a predominantly American-based, English-speaking professional organization, then they have acculturated to a point of understanding the nature of the items in the RGLAS. The same assumption was made of those individuals attending classes in an American college or university program not to include local community colleges. Demographic information pulled for indication of acculturation as revealed by principal language spoken and fluency in English. Only test data from those fluent is English was used in analysis procedures.

It appeared, therefore, that these approaches to recruiting subjects were best suited to the present study. Individual selection of subjects from mental health professionals seemed to be the only way of controlling for subject selection and participation in the clinical group with regards to diagnostic criteria. Originally subjects were expected to be tested within the first three to five weeks from their initial session for therapy and/or assessment. However, because of reluctance on the part of therapists to include new patients in research, criteria for participation were extended to include patients who were in on-going psychotherapy, with original diagnoses of depression and/or anxiety. Therapists indicated that a greater number of patients would be approachable as subjects by extending these particular criteria. Only two sets of data were collected in the first three months of data collection attempts. All other data was collected within the next six weeks after this change in criteria was made.

In the clinical group only those prospective participants with diagnoses of either affective and/or anxiety-based disorders were sought. Evidence of these disorders was based both on the client's presenting problem and initial assessment by a therapist. Such assessment by a therapist consisted of expert opinion based on initial interviews, and/or diagnostic measures typically used by each specific therapist or clinic. These screening measures were intended to eliminate those clients with more serious disorders. As indicated previously in the literature review depression and anxiety appear to be associated with grief. However, complicated grief is likely to include some manifestation of agitated depression, as evidenced by some form of acting-out behaviors. Any more severe impairment simply was not suitable for inclusion in the present study.

Subjects in both groups were limited to the age range of 20 to 55 years. This age range was believed to be representative of the general are range of persons seeking outpatient counseling services. The median age of subject's was expected to be between 30 and 35. The greatest number or adult clients in clinical settings presenting with depression and/or anxiety were thought to fall within this age range. This possibly reflects life cycle issues closely related to families of origin and dysfunction. Age was thought likely to be the only significant factor involved. It was not believed by the present author that other issues such as gender differences were relevant at this time. However, such demographic information was collected for possible future analysis. A summary of this information follows below.

In the non-clinical group there were 16 males and 34 females. There were only two in the group in the age range of 20 to 24. Sixteen subjects were between the ages of 25 to 30. Seventeen subjects were between the ages of 31 to 40. Ten subjects were between the ages of 41 to 50. In the 51 to 55 age range there were three subjects. Obviously, the highest concentration of subjects was in the range of 25 to 40.

Also in the non-clinical group there were 30 who were married, and 12 who were single. Five subjects were divorced; two lived with a significant other; and one whose significant other or spouse was deceased. With regard to level of education 24 had more that 16 years of schooling, 15 had at least 16 years of schooling, six had less than 16 years, and five had no schooling beyond high school.

Also included in the non-clinical sample were four African Americans, one Asian American, 16 Caucasian Americans, 15 Jewish Americans, ten Hispanic Americans, and four identified simply as "other". All participants were at least fluent in English if it was not their primary language.

The clinical sample consisted of 18 males and 32 females. Three were in the age range of 20 to 25. Twelve were between the ages of 26 to 30. In the 31 to 40 age range there was a total of 20 subjects. Those in the 41 to 50 age range totaled 12. Three were in the range of 51 to 55. In this group 22 were married; 15 were single; six were divorced; and seven lived with a significant other.

With regard to the level of education in the clinical sample: ten had more that 16 years of education; ten had completed 16 years of education; 17 had completed some education beyond high school; seven had completed high school; and six had less than 12 years of schooling. Also in this group three were African American, one was Asian American, 29 were Caucasian American, eight were Jewish American, eight were Hispanic American, and two indicated "other". As in the non-clinical sample all of these subjects were at least fluent in English, even if it was not their primary language. The main difference from a demographic perspective between the non-clinical and clinical groups is in years of education. The groups appear to be more closely matched in other categories.

Design

The purpose of this study was to establish test-retest reliability within the non-clinical sample, and predictive validity between non-clinical and clinical population samples on the Roberts Grief and Loss Analysis Scale (RGLAS) (Appendix B). The RGLAS was given to the clinical group and then compared to the Beck Depression Inventory (BDI) (Beck, et al., 1961) and the Center for Epidemiological Studies – Depression Scale (CES-D) (Radloff, 1977) for the purpose of establishing discriminant validity. Both instruments were described in the literature as being valid for patients in establishing a diagnosis of depression (Stehouwer, 1985; Sweetland & Keyser, 1986). The CES-D was also described as a valid indicator of anxiety (Sweetland & Keyser, 1986). The comparisons were for the purpose of determining degree of correlation between these two scales and the RGLAS.

Further substantiation of the RGLAS was sought by comparing correlations between the BDI and the CES-D, and then comparing the RGLAS to these correlations. There is no indication in the literature that correlations have ever been sought between the BDI and the CES-D. Such comparison between the BDI and the CES-D further indicated the reliability of these instruments in measuring the construct of depression. This was simply an additional attempt to substantiate their relevance and usefulness in the present study.

The hypothesis is that the RGLAS measures unresolved grief of which depression is a part; the other two scales are not designed to measure unresolved grief. It is proposed by the present author that depression is always a part of grief, but that grief is not always a part of depression. If the RGLAS actually measures unresolved grief then, even though the RGLAS may correlate to either the BID or CES-D, such correlation should not be so high as to preclude a distinction between the RGLAS and the depression/anxiety scales. Establishing test-retest reliability of the RGLAS should serve as an indication of stability across time. Comparison between the RGLAS results from the general and clinical samples should sufficiently demonstrate predictive validity for the RGLAS. Discriminant validity should be indicated by the comparisons between the RGLAS and the depression inventories.

Instrumentation

Roberts Grief and Loss Analysis Scale

The RGLAS, developed and revised by the present author, was the instrument upon which discriminant validity, predictive validity, and test-retest reliability were sought in the present study. Item construction of the original 200 items (Appendix A) was based on both a review of the literature, and personal experience and observations of the present author. The present scale consists of 100 items (Appendix B) that have been designed to detect unresolved grief in clinical populations presenting with diagnoses of either affective and/or anxiety-based disorders.

The RGLAS is a self-report paper and pencil test, with responses to the items as true or false. The 200 items were extracted from the original 200 item instrument by the means of an index of discrimination procedure as outlined by Anastasi (1988). Comparisons for discrimination were made between the group of people scoring highest on the RGLAS (indicating low unresolved grief), and the group scoring lowest (indicating high unresolved grief). This comparison indicated whether or not people in these extreme groups marked an item in the same manner relative to others in their group, with groups determined by RGLAS scores. The groups represented the upper and lower 25% of the total sample (N=114).

If everyone in each group marked an item the same, the index of discrimination would be 100 when the groups were compared. If there is no difference in responses between the groups then the discrimination index would be zero. A difference, or index of discrimination greater than or equal to 50, yielded 41 items. By dropping to a difference of 40 an additional 51 items were retained. The remaining eight items to give the desired total of 100, resulted from an index of discrimination no lower than 35. For the present study the wording in items 70 and 99 (Appendix B) was altered slightly for clarification of meaning. This resulted from questions raised by various expert sources in an attempt to eliminate any confusion between the experience of emotional pain, as opposed to physical pain. These are the only changes made in items selected and analyzed in Study I.

For an additional measure of internal consistency and as an indicator of reliability, a split-half procedure was employed for the 100 items in the present form of the RGLAS. The Pearson Product-Moment Correlation Coefficient was 0.94. A Spearman-Brown formula was used to indicate a reliability coefficient that might result from doubling the length of the test. This yielded a correlation of 0.97. Both coefficients were significant beyond the $p \leq .01$ level. Data analysis was conducted using data collected from 114 subjects, with the scale yielding only one overall score for each subject.

All responses to test items on the RGLAS are either "0" for true or "1" for false. Because of this scoring procedure, scores range from 0 to 100, with a lower score indicating a higher possibility of the presence of unresolved grief. The following items are reversed as a built-in lie scale and are reflected in the overall test score: 3, 4, 17, 31, 34, 40, 48, 53, 70, 82, and 88. The items were also reversed in the original 200 items analyzed in Study I.

Beck Depression Inventory

According to Stehouwer (1985), the BDI has a significant correlation coefficient for both test-retest reliability and concurrent validity. The BDI is also recognized by Stehouwer as having face validity and content validity. This test is a self-report, paper and pencil test. Studies to analyze the BDI for internal consistency demonstrate a correlation coefficient of 0.86 for the test items. For the purpose of reliability, a Spearman-Brown yielded a coefficient of 0.93. Reliability between a patient's clinical state as assessed by psychiatric hospital staff observation of inpatient clinical subjects, and BDI scores was above 0.90. Concurrent validity with the BDI and the MMPI-D Scale is listed as 0.75. Data analysis between test items and total BDI scores demonstrated positive correlations which were significant at the .001 level. According to Anastasi (1988), desirable coefficients fall in the 0.80s and 0.90s, but 0.75 is an acceptable indicator. The BID yields only one score, with a range of 0-63. Within that range is a further breakdown of scores ranging from normal functioning to a state of severe depression. Permission for reproduction and use of the BDI was sought and granted directly from Dr. Aaron T. Beck (Appendix C).

Center for Epidemiological Studies – Depression Scale

The CES-D as studied by Orme, Reis, & Herz (1986) is reported to measure both anxiety and depression, with some discrimination validity between these factors. Apparently, it also measures state and trait anxiety, as well as self esteem. The CES-D is also a paper and pencil, self report test. Roberts & Vernon (1983) report that the CES-D should only be used as a screening devise for depression; but, suggests that, as such, it is acceptable. Permission for reproduction of and use of the CES-D was sought and granted directly form the National Institute of Mental Health (Appendix D).

Procedures

When working with the non-clinical group the RGLAS was administered to participants on a voluntary basis in a group setting of two or more.

Subjects were asked to sign a consent form which explained the nature of the research, assuring each of their anonymity and confidentiality. Consent forms were collected before testing began. Only the last four digits of a subject's social security number were used to identify the data collected from test results and demographic information. Subjects' names were not associated with test data collected in any phase of research or analysis. No explanation of the test was given prior to testing as to the intent or purpose of the present research. Such information possibly would have biased subjects' responses to test items.

Subjects were told to read the test instructions carefully and then proceed with completing the answer sheets provided. Each subject was asked to put the last four digits of their social security numbers at the top of the answer sheet. This was necessary to match participants at the time of retest. The time required to take the RGLAS was about 30 to 40 minutes at both test and retest sittings. The retest session was followed by a brief presentation about the research study and the ultimate purpose and usage of the RGLAS. At the time of retest the procedure remained exactly the same as the first test session. These sessions were spaced two weeks apart. This group was the only group involved in test-retest procedures.

Subjects in the non-clinical group currently involved in psychotherapy were eliminated from participation. This was indicated as part of the demographic information collected from each subject. Subjects involved in outpatient psychotherapy were not suitable for inclusion in the sample as there would have been no way to control for extraneous variables such as psychotherapy outcome between test-retest sessions.

Those subjects in the clinical group were approached a little differently. The RGLAS is suitable for either group or individual testing. The clients approached by the mental health professionals solicited for assistance in data collection were recruited on an individual and voluntary basis to participate in the present research. Such participation was sought following determination by the therapist regarding suitability for participation as previously outlined. Only those clients deemed as suitable participants by the mental health professionals were approached. As previously stated diagnostic criteria consisted of client self report of depression and/or anxiety, accompanied by an intake assessment and diagnosis to avoid clients who were more severely impaired. Such assessment and diagnosis was conducted by the clinicians providing research participants.

Because of the nature of the data collection with the clinical population sample it was not possible to test subjects in groups as with the non-clinical sample. Clients were generally not accessible in groups in outpatient settings. Attempts to test clients in groups of two or more would have complicated data collection beyond reasonable expectations and time constraints. Participants were tested individually, with every effort made to provide an interference-free, confortable testing environment. Clients were given the same consent form as provided to the non-clinical group with the addition of allowances for the two additional inventories. With this group the last four digits of their social security numbers were also used to identify their responses to the RGLAS, the BDI, and the CES-D. Total testing time for all three scales lasted from one hour to an hour and fifteen minutes.

No results were made known to either group, although the overall results of the present study would have been shared with the therapists who agreed to assist me with my research. To date no such requests have been made. All scoring of the RGLAS, BDI, and the CES-D was done by the present author. Because the test is experimental in nature at this point, test results would have been potentially damaging to participants before reliability and validity analyses have been completed. If the testing had caused undue distress to participants in the non-clinical group, then referrals would have been made for possible therapeutic intervention. To date no such requests have been made.

Those in the clinical group already had a therapist to assist in dealing with issues that may have surfaced. Precautions were taken so that these clients did not feel coerced into participation since the request came from the therapist. This could only be guaranteed by the therapist involved. Care was taken by the present author to stress the importance of this point to those therapists offering assistance in data collection. Emphasis was placed on voluntary participation, stressing that such participation would not impinge upon the therapeutic alliance. Participation in research should have in no way affected the ability of a client to begin or continue therapy with the clinician.

Chapter IV

RESULTS

The main objective of the present study was to attempt to establish test-retest reliability, predictive validity, and discriminant validity. The data analysis procedures employed were outlined by Anastasi (1988). Data analysis with the nonclinical group consisted of test-retest reliability, and correlations between RGLAS scores for the clinical and non-clinical groups. The Pearson Product-Moment Correlation Coefficient was employed to determine the correlation between nonclinical subjects' scores in the test-retest procedure using the RGLAS only.

The scores for the non-clinical group, first testing session, ranged form 23 to 98, with a mean of 71.28. The range of scores for the second testing session was from 30 to 95, with a mean or 73.50. The Pearson Product – Moment Correlation Coefficient for the analysis of the test-retest reliability yielded a correlation coefficient of $r = .88$, $p \leq .001$.

Clinical and non-clinical group data were analyzed using $\underline{t}$-tests to determine predictive validity of the RGLAS. This comparison revealed a significant difference between the two samples as an indication of the test's ability to identify a specific clinical population. Therefore, the clinical population, as a result of the data analysis, should consist primarily of those clients presenting with depression and/or anxiety as a symptom of unresolved grief as indicated by the RGLAS score and comparisons to BDI and CES-D scores.

For the purpose of comparing the difference between groups a $\underline{t}$-test was used on the non-clinical/clinical comparison, using the data from the first test session of the non-clinical subjects as the non-clinical sample. Again, the mean for the non-clinical group was 71.28, with a mean for the clinical group of 40.25. Scores for the clinical group ranged for 03 to 78.

The analysis yielded a t value of 1.99, $p \leq .05$, with 98 degrees of freedom for a two-tailed test.

Data analysis with the clinical group assessed discriminant validity to establish degree of correlation between the RGLAS and the BDI and CES-D scores. Ideally correlations between the RGAS and the other two scales should be relatively low, although results indicated some significant correlation between the RGLAS scores and scores on the BDI and CES-D. Because anxiety and depression are part of grief such results were expected. However, because there are other factors involved in unresolved grief, any difference should serve as an indication of unresolved grief as an overriding consideration. Again, the Pearson Product-Moment Correlation Coefficient was employed to determine degree of correlation for this group as well.

Comparison between the clinical RGLAS subjects and the BID, using the Pearson Product-Moment Correlation Coefficient, yielded a correlation coefficient of $r = -.68$, $p \leq .001$. The mean of the scores on the BDI was 17.48 on a range of possible scores of 0 to 63. The actual range of scores on the BDI for this group was 01 to 46. Again, the scores on the RGLAS for the clinical sample ranged from 3 to 78, with a mean of 40.24, with a possible range of 0 to 100.

The Pearson Product-Moment Correlation Coefficient calculated for the comparison of the RGLAS scores to the CES-D scores yielded a correlation coefficient of $r = -.69$, $p \leq .001$. The scores on the CES-D ranged from 7 to 44, with a possible range of 0 to 60. The mean on the CES-D was 24.94, compared to a mean of 40.24 in the RGLAS.

One further analysis procedure was conducted to determine a reliability coefficient for scores between the BDI and the CES-D. This procedure also utilized the Pearson Product-Moment Correlation Coefficient for the purpose of comparing the two depression scales, and then making further comparisons between these scale and the RGLAS.

Comparison of the BDI to the CES-D yielded a Pearson Product-Moment Correlation Coefficient of $r - .86$, $p \leq .001$. Again, the mean for the BDI was 17.48, and the mean for the CES-D was 24.94.

Because of the likelihood of a significant correlation between the RGLAS and the two depression scales, an additional procedure was employed. This analysis was for the purpose of establishing the significance of the difference between the dependent r's. This comparison tested the strength of the relationship between the RGLAS and the BDI, and also between the RGLAS and the CES-D, all compered to the strength of the relationship between the two depression scales.

Calculations to determine the significance of the difference between dependent r's yielded a t value of 3.13, $p \leq .005$ on a comparison of the relationship between the RGLAS and the BID to the relationship of the RGLA and the CES-D and the relationship between the CES-D, yielded a t value of 2.94, $p \leq .005$.

Chapter V

Discussion

The results of the present study were as predicted, even regarding the correlations between the RGLAS and the BID and CES-D depression scales. Data analysis revealed a significant correlation on the RGLAS with regards to test/retest reliability. Also, as predicted, data analysis revealed a significant difference between scores on the RGLAS for the non-clinical and clinical groups. These results allowed for a rejection of the null hypothesis in both cases. The RGLAS appears to have reliability across time, <u>and</u> predictive validity between non-clinical and clinical samples.

While it was hoped that correlation analysis would reveal a non-significant correlation between the RGLAS and the BDI and CES-D depression scales, again the results were as predicted. It can still be assumed that depression is part of grief, but that grief is not always part of depression. Because, even though the correlations were significant, the analysis to test the strength of the relationship between the RGLAS and the depression scales indicated that the RGLAS is still possibly measuring something in addition to depression. When the relationship between the RGLAS and the depression scales was compared to the relationship between the depression scales themselves, the difference was found to be significant. It is within this difference that there seems to be some credibility to the possibility that the RGLAS is designed to measure unresolved grief relative to dysfunctional backgrounds. Hopefully future research will serve to further substantiate this premise.

The significant correlations seemed to be indicative of the lack of depression present with low unresolved grief. Twenty-one of the subjects had score combinations that allow for this profile. Also, the presence of unresolved grief with depression was found in the profiles of 19 subjects.

Remember that the scores of the RGLAS are reversed so that the lower the score, there is a higher degree of unresolved grief thought to be present. Participants with an indication of low unresolved grief and low levels of depression had high scores on the RGLAS and low scores on the depression scales. Those with a higher degree of suspected unresolved grief combined with depression were found in the profiles of 19 subjects. No subjects had high scores on all three instruments. Only four had the combination of low scores with all three scales. Ideally, this last combination would have been the desirable outcome to establish a clear distinction between the RGLAS and the BDI and CES-D depression scales.

It is important to point out that no one in either of the population samples questioned the face validity of the RGLAS as a measure of unresolved grief. Also, none of the mental health professionals who provided subjects challenged this premise either. The only concerns raised had to do with the scoring of zero for true and one for false. Two of the subjects in the non-clinical sample said that this made the instrument difficult to understand. Even though this concern was expressed by some, others seemed to have little or no trouble in responding to the statements. This statement is based on the indications of the response patterns observed by the present author as the tests were hand scored. Most subjects appeared to respond to the statements in a consistent manner.

Because of the apparent confusion regarding the use and interpretation of scores on the RGLAS, in the future the responses will be reversed. This means that a response of "true" to an item will be scored as a "1", rather than a "0" as in the form of the RGLAS used in the present study and in the previous study. The result of this change will be to simplify the scoring and interpretation of scores, making them comparable to scoring procedures used on other assessment instruments. Hopefully, this change will make the RGLAS more user friendly for both patients (subjects) and mental health professionals using the RGLAS. Also, results will likely be easier to understand when they are reported in either written or oral presentations of test data.

Even though there were significant correlations between the RGLAS and the depression scales, there appears to be a significant difference in the relationships when the correlations are compared to the correlation between the depression scales alone. These results leave the door open for future research and analysis on the RGLAS in the hopes of someday making the RGLAS available for professional circulation and application. The high degree of correlation between the BDI and the CES-D leave little doubt regarding the appropriateness of their use in the present study for the purpose or comparison to the RGLAS. This correlation between the depression scales further substantiated their use in clinical setting as appropriate measures of depression.

Assumptions and Limitations

The present research sought to challenge current theories of depression. It was suggested by the present author that in many individuals presenting in clinical setting with affective and/or anxiety-based disorders, these emotional states may be symptoms masking a more serious pathology of unresolved grief. This unresolved grief may manifest itself in the form of current depression, anxiety, anger, fear, or guilt. If this premise is accurate, then these feelings and emotional states represent "old feelings", and "old emotional states" remaining from losses that could be associated with any significant source of trauma or dysfunction experienced in childhood. Individuals may proceed through adulthood with relatively few problems until some current loss triggers all other aspects of accumulated unresolved grief, then resulting in complicated bereavement and experienced by the patient as crisis. Once childhood losses are dealt with in therapy, depression and/or anxiety are often relieved, and the person takes on new awarenesses and insights allowing them to deal more effectively with losses which may be part of either the present or their future.

The implication is that depression and/or anxiety may not result directly from current losses; but, rather from previous losses which remain unresolved. People under these conditions who are experiencing all of the characteristics of depression and/or anxiety may indeed be experiencing the residue of childhood losses which remain unresolved and likely unacknowledged, being lost somewhere in the person's unconscious mind. For persons who experienced healthy, nurturing family environments in childhood, this type of intense emotional reactivity to loss is not likely to occur. Their depression is not necessarily a symptom of grief, but may be present for them only because depression is recognized as being part of a grief recovery process. For those individuals from dysfunctional backgrounds, depression is likely to be agitated, with some form of acting-out behaviors present, and manifested as a symptom of complicated bereavement.

The RGLAS revealed a high correlation to the BDI and CES-D, all as measures of depression. However, because the RGLAS is designed to pull for other elements such as anger, fear, guilt, and shame, it can still be argued that the RGLAS is measuring more that depression. Future research using factor analysis to establish subscales within the RGLAS should support this contention. People from dysfunctional and non-dysfunctional backgrounds will experience losses differently. Each group can be expected to be depressed and anxious as part of a normal grief process or reaction. However, those individuals with unresolved grief from childhood will be depressed beyond normal time frames generally associated with healthy grief reactions.

Also, for many people in the group experiencing unresolved grief, current losses may not even be recognized giving the impression of being depressed for no apparent reason, or without a specific identifiable source of origin. These are the individuals who should benefit the most from the RGLAS, because the RGLAS should reveal their depression and/or anxiety as symptoms of a much more complicated syndrome - namely unresolved grief – with an etiology rooted in childhood losses suffered within a dysfunctional environment. It is further proposed that the degree of unresolved grief and impairment in current functioning and emotional states will be directly related to the degree of dysfunction in childhood.

Recommendations for Future Research

Because of the very favorable results of this study and the previous study (Roberts, 1989), there are several recommendations for future research. As mentioned previously the next step will be to conduct a study involving factor analysis. Since the RGLAS appears to be measuring a construct in addition to depression and/or anxiety, factor analysis should help to more clearly define the realm of emotional elements which are likely part of unresolved grief. Some of the possible subscales will likely include anger, fear, guilt, shame, and social isolation or loneliness. Comparisons will be made between the subscale scores and the overall score on the RGLAS for each individual. Data from the clinical sample in the present study will be combined with data collected from future clinical subjects for the purpose of such analysis.

Future research will likely use various demographic elements such as age, gender, ethnicity, socioeconomic status, and level of education as some of the probable factors. One of the limitations of the present research was the inability to control for and account for the length of time a subject has been in therapy. This type of control will be needed in order to establish an indication of the effect on overall test scores of the length of time a subject has been in therapy. Comparisons could then be made to determine the significance of time as a factor in predicting therapeutic outcomes and possible correlations between this factor and scores on the RGLAS. Such information would be gathered as part of the demographic information requested.

Because of recent changes in the field of psychotherapy with regard to short-term therapy now being required by many managed care organizations, the RGLAS may prove to be a useful tool in identifying major areas of focus needed for the patient. Once the RGLAS proves to be a valid measure of unresolved grief relative to dysfunctional backgrounds, then this instrument will help to compensate for the constraints and limitations of short-term psychotherapy.

Those already working as mental health professionals are aware that in many cases a significant amount of time in therapy is often necessary before a patient can begin to associate current emotions with emotions experienced in childhood. It takes time for both therapists and patients to get through the many defenses which block such insights and awarenesses. Perhaps the RGLAS could speed up this process by providing an objective measure of the degree of dysfunction which may be present for any given individual.

Failing to address the etiological factors which interfere with optimal adult functioning is similar to putting a small bandage on a serious wound that cannot heal properly. Such an approach leaves the patient with no opportunity to resolve the losses and related grief issues from the past, wounds which must be healed before proper emotional development can be approached and attained. To do less than heal the wound is to do a great disservice to those in therapy.

Furthermore, unless these issues are resolved it is likely that they will continue to impede desired levels of adult functioning. As patients find themselves facing future crises these outmoded coping skills are likely to resurface, requiring again that the wound either be treated properly and healed, or simply bandaged again in the hope it will just go away. Hopefully professionals in the fields which regulate health care will recognize the benefit to both the patient and the other parties involved in healing the wounds.

It is also proposed that the RGLAS be used as an assessment instrument with other specific populations. For instance, if translated into Spanish and other languages the RGLAS may be useful in dealing with losses associated with issues of acculturation. It could be used with specific groups who are dealing with, or who have dealt with, experiences of multiple losses. Two good examples are: those presently dealing with losses associated with HIV/AIDS; and survivors of ethnic cleansing witnessed in the holocaust of the Jews and presently with groups in other parts of the world.

It is also believed by the present author that future research should address the needs of people in this country who are involved in gangs and in the more recent groups identified as tagging crews. If their emotional needs could be identified and worked with, then perhaps some efforts could be made to provide people in these groups with alternative ways of thinking and functioning. Recent experience by the present author with the aforementioned groups indicates that there is a tremendous need to develop ways of assessing the needs of these individuals in an effort to address the needs and attempt to find some solutions. Furthermore, it is important to recognize the emotional and psychological needs present in members of these and other subcultures, many of whom are adolescents. Hopefully the RGLAS can be a part of the endeavor as well.

It is the hope of the present author that others will take up some of these ideas proposed for further research. As a diagnostic tool the RGLAS appears to have a number of potential uses within a variety of settings, and with a variety of different target populations. Its use with other diagnostic instruments and procedures seems to be a valid consideration given the results obtained in the two studies completed to date as part of the process associated with test development. Future research, including factor analysis and the attempt to establish norms on specific population, should further substantiate the Roberts Grief and Loss Analysis Scale as a significant and relevant diagnostic tool.

References

Alarcon, R.D. (1984). Single case study: Personality disorder as a pathogenic factor in bereavement. <u>The Journal of Nervous and Mental Disease</u>, <u>172</u>(1), 45-47.

Anastasi, A. (1988). <u>Psychological Testing</u>, (6th ed.). New York: Macmillan.

Beck, A. T. (1967). <u>Depression</u>. Philadelphia: University of Pennsylvania Press.

Beck, A, T., Ward, C. H., Mendelson, M., Mock, J., & Erbaugh, J. (1961). An inventory for measuring depression. <u>Archives of General Psychiatry</u>, <u>4</u>, 561-571.

Belitsky, R., & Jacobs, S. (1986). Bereavement, attachment theory, and mental disorders. <u>Psychiatric Annals</u>, <u>16</u>(5), 276-280.

Bowlby, J. (1988). <u>A secure base</u>. New York: Basic Books.

Bowlby, J. (1983). Attachment and loss: Retrospect and prospect. <u>Annual Progress in Child Psychiatry and Child Development</u>, 29-47.

Cerney, M. S. (1988). "If only..." Remorse in grief therapy. <u>Psychotherapy Patient</u>, <u>5</u>(1,2), 235-248.

Clayton, P. J. (1987). Preventing depression: The symptom, the syndrome, or the disorder? In R. F. Munoz (ED.), <u>Depression Prevention</u> (pp. 31043). New York: Hemisphere Publishing Corporation.

Curtis, J. M. (1982). Emotional elements of mental illness: Psychological concomitants of stress. Psychological Reports, 50, 1207-1213.

Demi, A. S., & Mile, M. S. (1987). Parameters of normal grief: A Delphi Study. Journal of Psychology and Judaism, 11(2), 91-102.

Fox, D. (1987). Suffering and atonement as a Psycho-Judaic construct. Journal of Psychology and Judaism, 11(2), 91-102.

Freud, S. Mourning and melancholia (1917). In Standard edition of the complete psychological works of Sigmund Freud (Vol. 14). London: Hogarth Press, 1957.

Hartz, G. W. (1986). Adult grief and its interface with mood disorder: Proposal of a new diagnosis of complicated bereavement. Comprehensive Psychiatry, 27(1), 60-64.

Jacobs, S., Hansen, F., Kasl, S., Ostfeld, A., Beckman, L., & Kim, K. (1990). Anxiety disorders during acute bereavement: Risk and risk factors. Journal of Clinical Psychiatry, 51(7), 269-274.

Jacobson, R. H. (1986). Single case study: Unresolved grief of 25 year duration exacerbated by multiple subsequent losses. The Journal of Nervous and Mental Disease, 174(10), 624-627.

Jansen, M.A. (1985). Psychotherapy and grieving: A clinical approach. Psychotherapy Patient, 2, 15-25.

Lehman, H. E. (1983). The clinicians view of anxiety and depression. Journal of Clinical Psychiatry, 44(8), 3-7.

Lieberman, P. B., & Jacobs, S. C. (1987). Bereavement and its complications in medical patients: A guide for consultation-liaison psychiatrists. International Journal of Psychiatry in Medicine, 17(1), 23-39.

Lindemann, E. (1944). Symptomatology and management of acute grief. <u>American Journal of Psychiatry, 101</u>, 141-148.

Marris, P. (1975), <u>Loss and change</u>. Garden City, NY: Doubleday.

Middleton-Moz, J., Dwinell, L. (1986). <u>After the tears</u>. Deerfield Beach, FL: Health Communications, Inc.

Orme, J., Reis, J., & Herz, E. J., (1986). Factorial and discriminant validity of the Center for Epidemiological Studies Depression (CES-D) Scale. <u>Journal of Clinical Psychology, 42</u>(1), 28-33.

Parkes, C. M. (1985). Bereavement. <u>British Journal of Psychiatry, 146</u>, 11-17.

Parkes, C. M., & Weiss, R. S., (1983). <u>Recovery from bereavement</u>. New York: Basic Books.

Pedder, J. R. (1982). Failure to mourn, and melancholia. <u>British Journal of Psychiatry, 141</u>, 329-337.

Pfeifer, D. (1982) A new perspective on agitated grief reaction. <u>Journal of Contemporary Psychotherapy, 13</u>(1), 61-69.

Radloff, L. S. (1977). The CES-D scale: A self-report depression scale for research in the general population. <u>Applied Psychological Measurement, 1,</u> 385-401.

Raphael, B. (1980). A psychiatric model for bereavement counseling. In B. M. Schoenberg, <u>Bereavement counseling: A multidisciplinary handbook</u> (pp. 147-172). Westport, CT: Greenwood.

Roberts, D. L. (1989). <u>The Roberts Grief and Loss Analysis Scale: Item selection and analysis</u>. Unpublished manuscript.

Roberts, R. E., & Vernon, S. W. (1983). The Center for Epidemiological Studies Depression Scale: Its use in a community sample. <u>American Journal of Psychiatry.</u> <u>120</u>(1), 41.46.

Sinaikin, P. M. (1985). A clinically relevant guide to the differential diagnosis of depression. <u>The Journal of Nervous and Mental Disease,</u> <u>173</u>(4), 199-211.

Smith, E. W. L. (1985). A gestalt therapist's perspective on grief. <u>Psychotherapy Patient,</u> <u>2</u>(1), 65-78.

Stehouwer, R. S. (1985). Beck Depression Inventory. In D. J. Keyser & R. C. Sweetland (Eds.), <u>Test Critiques, Volume II</u> (pp.83-87). Kansas City: Test Corporation of America.

Stricker, G. (1983). Some issues in the psychodynamic treatment of the depressed patient. <u>Professional Psychology Research and Practice,</u> <u>14</u>(2), 209-217.

Sweetland, R. C., & Keyser, D. J. (Eds.). (1986). <u>Tests.</u> Kansas City: Test Corporation of America.

Volken, V. D. (1984-85). Complicated mourning. <u>Annual of Psychoanalysis,</u> <u>12-13</u>, 323-348.

Weenolsen, P. (1988. <u>Transcendence of loss over the life span.</u> New York: Hemisphere Publishing Corporation.

Worden, J. W. (1981. <u>Grief counseling and grief therapy.</u> New York: Springer Publishing Company.

Zisook, S., & DeVaul, R. A. (1983). Grief, unresolved grief, and depression. <u>Psychosomatics,</u> <u>24</u>(3), 247-256.

Zisook, S., and Lyons, L. (1990). Bereavement and unresolved grief in psychiatric outpatients. *Omega, 20*(4), 307-322.

Zisook, S., Shuchter, S., & Schuckit, M. (1985). Factors in the persistence of unresolved grief among psychiatric outpatients. *Psychosomatics, 26*(6), 497-503.

Appendices

1. Appendix A – <u>see Appendix B in the thesis document</u> – Roberts Grief and Loss Analysis Scale – full 200 item instrument.

2. Appendix B – <u>see Appendix C in the thesis document</u> – Roberts Grief and Loss Analysis Scale – full 100 item instrument developed as part of the thesis, and used as the instrument of focus in this dissertation.

3. Appendices C, D, and E referenced within the dissertation have not been included. All correspondence and statements of fact and agreement will need to be constructed relative to guidelines and parameters established under future research efforts. I can be reached through www.prokids.org and www.davidlrobertsphd.org by those interested in conducting additional research on the RGLAS.

www.ingramcontent.com/pod-product-compliance
Lightning Source LLC
Chambersburg PA
CBHW071055230426
43666CB00009B/1713